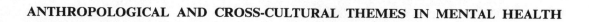

ANTHROPOLOGICAL AND CROSS-CULTURAL THEMES IN MENTAL HEALTH

UNIVERSITY OF MISSOURI STUDIES LXV

ANTHROPOLOGICAL AND CROSS-CULTURAL THEMES IN MENTAL HEALTH

An Annotated Bibliography, 1925–1974

Armando R. Favazza and Mary Oman

University of Missouri Press

Columbia & London, 1977

The authors wish to express their thanks to
Drs. James M. A. Weiss and David Davis for
their support of our project, to Drs. Barbara
Favazza and Arthur J. Robins for their expert
editing assistance, and to Michael Reagan for
his advice in selecting articles for review.

Library of Congress Cataloging in Publication Data

Favazza, Armando R
    Anthropological and cross-cultural themes in
mental health.

    (University of Missouri studies; v. 65)
    Includes indexes.
    1. Psychiatry, Transcultural—Bibliography.
2. Ethnopsychology—Bibliography. I. Oman,
Mary, 1948–   joint author. II. Title.
III. Series: University of Missouri—Columbia.
University of Missouri studies; v. 65.
RC455.4.E8F38   016.3628′4   76–48620
ISBN 0–8262–0215–2

Contents

Foreword

by Victor Barnouw
Professor, Department of Anthropology
University of Wisconsin—Milwaukee

This is an appropriate time for the appearance of this annotated bibliography, a time when many people are trying to make some synthesis or integration of the disparate findings of anthropology and psychiatry. Dissatisfaction with the traditional Freudian synthesis has led to many attempts at revision. Although neobehaviorism is well entrenched in academic psychology, its relevance to other social sciences often seems ambiguous. And how shall we assimilate findings about ESP and related phenomena reported by laboratories of parapsychology whose scientific credentials are now receiving increased recognition? Within each field—anthropology, psychology, and psychiatry—there are conflicting schools and strong differences of opinion about many issues. Moreover, during the past hundred years, there has been an avalanche of publications promoting these different viewpoints, an almost unassimilable mass of books and articles. More than forty years ago Otto Rank complained, "There is already too much truth in the world—an overproduction which apparently cannot be consumed" (Taft: 1958, p. 175). Nevertheless, efforts to synthesize and to better understand the mass of information about human behavior will necessarily continue. One very helpful guide to such efforts is this annotated bibliography.

In the next few pages I will briefly review the history of American anthropology so we can gain some perspective on how we have come to our present situation and what that situation may promise for the future.

The Pioneer Period, ca. 1880–1940

The early years of American anthropology were devoted to studies of North American Indian cultures. The relatively few investigators of these tribes had a sense of urgency about their work, for they could often see the old ways of life disintegrating before their eyes. Some of this pioneer work had a government incentive. Founded in 1879, the Bureau of American Ethnology in Washington published a remarkable series of annual reports, including, for example, those on the Zuni by Frank Hamilton Cushing (1857–1900) and Matilda Coxe Stevenson (1850–1930).

The emphasis of this early work was ethnographic, descriptive rather than theoretical. Franz Boas (1858–1942), leading teacher of the first generation of professional American anthropologists, also gave priority to fieldwork and ethnographic documentation, for he regarded the systematizations of the nineteenth-century cultural evolutionists and diffusionists as premature. What first needed to be done, he argued, was to amass an adequate body of ethnographic information about the non-Western cultures of the world. Boas himself did fieldwork among the Central Eskimo (1883–1884) and the Indians of the Northwest Coast, notably the Kwakiutl (1885–1942, off and on). Among his impressive group of students at Columbia University, Alfred L. Kroeber (1876–1960) did field work among the Arapaho and tribes of California; Robert H.

Lowie (1883–1957) worked among the Crow; Paul Radin (1883–1959) studied the Winnebago; and Elsie Clews Parsons (1875–1941), Ruth L. Bunzel (1898–   ), and Ruth Benedict (1887–1948) worked among the Zuni and other tribes.

In surveying the history of American anthropology in 1960, Ruth Bunzel suggested that much of the sense of urgency about recording North American Indian cultures had waned by 1920. This was partly because many of these cultures had broken up by that time. There were no more camp circles of tipis and no more buffalo hunts. Besides, much of the ethnographic recording had been done (Mead and Bunzel: 1960, p. 574). However, in the more conservative and marginal areas of North America valuable fieldwork continued to be conducted. In the 1930s A. Irving Hallowell and Ruth Landes were both studying Canadian Ojibwa groups, Morris Opler was doing fieldwork among the Apache, and Clyde Kluckhohn, Gladys Reichard, Alexander Leighton, and Dorothea Leighton carried on research among the Navaho. Meanwhile some students of Franz Boas and Ruth Benedict turned to the study of South American Indian tribes. To mention only a few, Jules Henry worked among the Kaingang and Pilagá, Irving Goldman among the Cubeo, and Charles Wagley among the Tapirapé. Moreover, some American anthropologists went beyond the conveniently accessible American Indian field to more distant regions. In the 1920s Margaret Mead, for example, worked first in Samoa and later among Melanesian tribes; W. Lloyd Warner spent three years (1926–1929) among the Murngin of northeastern Arnhem Land in Australia; and Hortense Powdermaker worked in a Melanesian society in the island of Lesu in the southwest Pacific (1929–1930).

All of the studies mentioned so far were of "primitive" tribal societies of the sort traditionally studied by anthropologists. But in the 1930s there began to be investigations of peasant societies, particularly by anthropologists trained at the University of Chicago. In 1930 Robert Redfield published *Tepoztlán: A Mexican Village: A Study of Folk Life,* and in 1939 there appeared both John F. Embree's *Suye Mura: A Japanese Village* and Hsiao-t'ung Fei's *Peasant Life in China: A Field Study of Country Life in the Yangtze Valley.*

The peasant community studies of Redfield, Embree, and Fei showed the influence of the school of functionalism associated with Bronislaw Malinowski (1884–1942) and A. R. Radcliffe-Brown (1881–1955). Radcliffe-Brown, who taught at the University of Chicago from 1931 to 1937, advocated sociological analysis of the network of social relations in a particular society, rather than an overall cultural inventory. Malinowski and Radcliffe-Brown were both interested in the synchronic study of a society, comparable to the physiological analysis of an organism, and they were not concerned with the problems of historical reconstruction that had preoccupied many earlier researchers. Malinowski set out to learn how the Trobriand Islanders of Melanesia, among whom he did fieldwork in 1915–1918, lived in their environmental setting, how they extracted food from it and distributed it among themselves, how they handled social conflicts and promoted social cohesion and cooperation.

Malinowski believed that the culture of a society is instrumental in satisfying the biological and psychological needs of its members. This applied to magic and religion as well as to economic and political institutions. Indeed, Malinowski emphasized the integration and interrelationship of all aspects of culture and social organization.

In contrast to Malinowski, Radcliffe-Brown, a social anthropologist, was not concerned about how culture satisfies human needs. For him the function of an institution is the contribution it makes to structural continuity in the society. Thus Radcliffe-Brown never became involved, as did Malinowski, in the issues of psychoanalytic theory.

Culture and Personality

Malinowski was one of the first anthropologists to make use of Freudian theory in fieldwork. In *Sex and Repression in Savage Society* (1927) he inquired whether an Oedipus complex would be apt to develop in a matrilineal society like that of the Trobriand Islands, where the roles of husband and father are very different from those of the Western world. Malinowski suggested that there is a different kind of complex in the Trobriand Islands, involving a man's wish to marry his sister and to do away with his maternal uncle rather than his father. Malinowski recommended that we are "not to assume the universal existence of the Oedipus complex, but studying every type of civilization, to establish the special complex which pertains to it" (Malinowski: 1953, p. 82).

Malinowski's treatment of this theme was inconsistent, since he accepted an orthodox Freudian suggestion that among the Trobrianders hatred was deflected from the father to the mother's brother, thereby conceding the Freudian premise. He was also criticized by Freudians for lacking competence in psychoanalytic matters. However, Malinowski did show that different societies may have variations in the structuring of the family romance due to differences in forms of family organization and patterns of child rearing.

This insight also appears in the early works of Margaret Mead and Ruth Benedict, two students of Franz Boas. By 1930 Boas was advocating the study of the individual under the stress of his particular culture.

In keeping with this interest, anthropologists began to collect life histories from American Indian informants at around this time. Paul Radin's *Crashing Thunder: The Autobiography of an American Indian* appeared in 1926. Among later outstanding documents of this sort were Walter Dyk, *Son of Old Man Hat: A Navaho Autobiography* (1938); Clellan S. Ford, *Smoke From Their Fires: The Life of a Kwakiutl Chief* (1941); and Leo W. Simmons, *Sun Chief: The Autobiography of a Hopi Indian* (1942). The treatment of these life history documents was usually ethnographic rather than analytic; the Indian told his story and the anthropologist wrote it down.

Margaret Mead's work, from the start, was more analytic, and her fieldwork was problem centered. In Mead's first book, *Coming of Age in Samoa* (1928) she asked the question, "Are the disturbances which vex our adolescents due to the nature of adolescence itself or to the civilization?" (Mead: 1939, p. 11). This was a nature-versus-nurture problem involving the relative importance of physiological or sociocultural conditions. Mead found that adolescence in Samoa was not accompanied by emotional conflict or rebellion and that the source of adolescent tension in the Western world must therefore be sought in its cultural institutions. Mead's next two works, *Growing Up in New Guinea* (1930) and *Sex and Temperament in Three Primitive Societies* (1935) were similarly problem centered, with findings related to issues facing present-day Americans. These works, then, were not camera-eye ethnographies of the traditional sort, covering all aspects of native life from house building to magical rites. Instead, some particular aspects of life were singled out for examination, with comparisons and contrasts made with life in the United States.

Ruth Benedict's *Patterns of Culture* (1934) applied a configurationist approach to the study of cultures. Cultures were seen as wholes, often heading in different directions, for in each society there is a tendency toward cultural integration. In Pueblo culture, for example, Apollonian values are emphasized; the mild-mannered, self-controlled, and dependable man is the ideal. But most other North American Indian cultures, Benedict claimed, are Dionysian, valuing the experience of unusual psychic states, achieved by fasting, drug taking, or alcohol. Benedict emphasized that human nature is very plastic. Persons born into an Apollonian society are likely to become Apollonian, accepting the prevailing world view of the society, just as they learn to speak its language. The same is true of persons born into a Dionysian society, like the Kwakiutl of the Northwest Coast. Both Benedict and Mead, however, wrote about "deviants" who had difficulty in accepting the traditional ways of the society. Benedict's *Patterns of Culture* was not at all Freudian. She did not focus much on early childhood experiences, and there is hardly any mention of individuals.

A more clinical, psychoanalytic approach was developed by the Linton-Kardiner school. Beginning in 1937, seminars were held at Columbia by Ralph Linton, an anthropologist, and Abram Kardiner, a psychoanalyst of modified Freudian persuasion. Kardiner coined the term *basic personality structure,* referring to aspects of personality common to all members of a particular society, stemming from the early experiences they had shared. This school's work may be seen as a continuation and elaboration of Malinowski's approach in *Sex and Repression.* Like Margaret Mead's work, it resulted in a new focus (for anthropologists) on childhood and child-rearing practices in different societies. The outstanding research study to emerge from this school was Cora Du Bois, *The People of Alor: A Social-Psychological Study of an East Indian Island* (1944). In addition to an ethnography, this work involved the recording of eight biographies, the administration of the Rorschach (ink blot) test, a word-association test, Porteus maze test, and a collection of children's drawings. A noteworthy innovation in this study was the use of "blind" analyses. The Rorschach tests were submitted to a Rorschach specialist, the drawings were given to a drawing analyst, and the life histories were interpreted by Abram Kardiner. The Rorschach and drawing analysts made generalizations about Alorese personality traits only on the basis of the materials they were given. Nevertheless, there proved to be a good deal of correspondence in their independent analyses.

A similar work was *Truk: Man in Paradise* by Thomas Gladwin and Seymour B. Sarason (1953), which also made use of life-history material and projective techniques. In this case a modified Thematic Apperception Test, drawn to reflect local conditions, was given as well as the Rorschach test. Both were analyzed "blind" by Seymour Sarason, a psychologist.

The approaches followed in the Alor and Truk studies seemed well designed, and the use of blind analysis appeared able to check subjective, impressionistic judgments on the part of the ethnographer. It seemed as though an excellent formula had been worked out for field studies in culture and personality. Nevertheless, these methods were not much applied in subsequent work, largely due to criticisms of projective tests, particularly the Rorschach, made by some psychologists (Zubin: 1954; Mischel: 1968, p. 120). Moreover, there were also criticisms of the field of culture and personality in general, especially of national character studies that had been made during or shortly after World War II (Orlansky: 1949; Lindesmith and Strauss: 1950).

During the 1950s, then, there was some disillusionment with culture and personality. Anthropology graduate students turned to other kinds of research, such as the neoevolutionism of Julian H. Steward and Leslie A. White. Some students were attracted to human ecology, in which Andrew P. Vayda and Roy A. Rappaport were pioneers. There were also linguists and cultural anthropologists who did research in the field of cognitive anthropology, with the attempt to understand how the world is structured linguistically for the speakers of different languages (Tyler, ed: 1969).

However, some research in the field of culture and personality continued, often with greater attention being given than formerly to methodology and sampling. Questionnaires replaced projective techniques in some studies. The Six Cultures Project of the 1950s carried out by John and Beatrice Whiting and their colleagues had aims similar to those of the Linton-Kardiner studies and also focused on the childhood years, but they did not make use of projective tests, except incidentally. In each of the six cultures studied, special attention was given to 24 mothers, who had children between the ages of three and ten and who were interviewed on a standard schedule. Behavioral observation and interviews were the main methods used. This has been one of the most ambitious large-scale culture-and-personality projects (Whiting, ed: 1963; Minturn and Lambert: 1964; Whiting and Whiting: 1974).

Among other recent large-scale projects are the Cornell-Aro psychiatric study of the Yoruba, compared with Stirling County in Canada (Leighton et al: 1963), the psychological study of a Mexican village (Fromm and Maccoby: 1970), and a comparative study of four East African tribes to learn what psychological differences there are between pastoralists and farmers (Edgerton: 1971). Each of these studies made use of standardized questionnaires. Fromm and Maccoby, however, also used the Rorschach and Thematic Apperception tests, and Edgerton used the Rorschach test. Among these studies, Fromm and Maccoby kept closest to the Linton-Kardiner kind of approach in the intensive study of a particular community, with the use of projective techniques. The other studies involved cross-cultural comparisons with an effort to apply standardized instruments, such as questionnaires, to the members of different groups.

Some researchers have given sentence completion tests. Joel Aronoff, for example, used this method to compare and contrast cane cutters and fishermen in the West Indies (Aronoff: 1967).

In this selective, retrospective review of culture-and-personality studies, I have touched on some highlights of field research. Reference should also be made to another kind of investigation: the use of the Human Relations Area Files (HRAF). The HRAF is a filing system containing ethnological data about a few hundred societies. Researchers who use these files usually try to establish statistical correlations between certain institutions, concerning which some causal relationship has been hypothesized. Many such studies are listed in this annotated bibliography.

The Present Situation in Anthropology

After World War II anthropology rapidly grew in popularity as an academic discipline. Between 1960 and 1975 the number of anthropology M.A.'s produced each year doubled every five years, and the number of Ph.D.'s produced each year doubled every six years (D'Andrade et al: 1975). However, while this academic boom was under way, fieldwork opportunities were shrinking. It is much harder nowadays for a graduate student to go out and do field research. In the 1950s and 1960s, for example, it was easy enough to do research in India, but for a few years after January 1972 virtually no American scholars received visa clearance for research purposes. This was due to the political situation, especially India's resentment of the United States' "tilt" toward Pakistan during the Bangladesh crisis. Village studies by anthropologists were regarded with particular disfavor by the Indian government, since American anthropologists were now often suspected of being spies. Similar political considerations kept American anthropologists out of the Philippines. Of course, they could not work on the Chinese mainland under Communist rule, although anthropologists have done research in Taiwan and Hong Kong in recent years. Most of Southeast Asia is also closed to anthropologists today, and the situation has also become difficult in much of Africa and Latin America. Even in the United States there is a new militancy on many Indian reservations that makes it difficult for anthropologists to get an entrée where they were formerly welcome. Although the world has become smaller through international air service and quick communications, there are now many more hurdles with passports and visas than formerly. Ralph Linton wrote about how easily he traveled about the world some years ago. "Prior to World War I it was possible to travel almost anywhere on earth with no better credentials than a checkbook" (Linton: 1949, p. 6). But that is not the case today.

During the pioneer period of American anthropology, it was appropriate to emphasize field-work and descriptive ethnography, while tribal cultures could still be studied. New ethnographic data will always be of value, but our main need at present is for more understanding and analysis, and our current dilemma should be seen as an opportunity. We must try to extract some general principles from the mass of ethnographic data accumulated so far. That is why, as mentioned earlier, this annotated bibliography comes at an opportune time. Both anthropologists and psychiatrists must develop more theoretical coherence in their disciplines. That is, of course, no simple task. This annotated bibliography, at any rate, can be a most helpful guide to the literature now available, letting us know where to look and what we may expect to find in the array of references that follows.

Literature Cited

Aronoff J: Psychological Needs and Cultural Systems: A Case Study. Princeton, D. Van Nostrand Co., 1967.

D'Andrade RG, et al: Academic opportunity in anthropology, 1974–90. Am Anthropologist 77: 753, 1975.

Edgerton RB: The Individual in Cultural Adaptation: A Study of Four East African Peoples. Berkeley: University of California Press, 1971.

Fromm E, Maccoby M: Social Character in a Mexican Village: A Sociopsychoanalytic Study. Englewood Cliffs, NJ, Prentice-Hall, 1970.

Leighton A, et al: Psychiatric Disorder Among the Yoruba: A Report from the Cornell-Aro Mental Health Research Project in the Western Region, Nigeria. Ithaca, NY, Cornell University Press, 1963.

Lindesmith AR, Strauss AA: A critique of culture-personality writings. Am Sociological Rev 15:587–600, 1950.

Linton R (ed): Most of the World: The Peoples of Africa, Latin America, and the East Today. New York, Columbia University Press, 1949.

Malinowski B: Sex and Repression in Savage Society. London, Routledge and Kegan Paul, 1953.

Mead M: Coming of Age in Samoa, in from the South Seas: Studies of Adolescence and Sex in Primitive Societies. New York, William Morrow, 1939.

Mead M, Bunzel RL (eds): The Golden Age of American Anthropology. New York, George Braziller, 1960.

Minturn L, Lambert W: Mothers of Six Cultures: Antecedents of Child Rearing. New York, John Wiley & Sons, 1964.

Mischel W: Personality and Assessment. New York, John Wiley & Sons, 1968.

Orlansky H: Infant care and personality. Psychol Bull 46: 1–48, 1949.

Taft J: Otto Rank. New York, Julian Press, 1958.

Tyler SA (ed): Cognitive Anthropology. New York, Holt, Rinehart, and Winston, 1969.

Whiting BB (ed): Six Cultures: Studies of Child Rearing. New York, John Wiley & Sons, 1963.

Whiting BB, Whiting JWM: Children of Six Cultures: A Psycho-Cultural Analysis. Cambridge, Mass, Harvard University Press, 1974.

Zubin J: Failures of the Rorschach Technique. J Proj Tech 18: 303–315, 1954.

Foreword

Eugene B. Brody, M.D.
  Professor of Psychiatry and Human Behavior. Formerly Chairman,
  Department of Psychiatry and Director, Institute of Psychiatry and
  Human Behavior, University of Maryland School of Medicine, Baltimore.

Comparative studies of behavior in relation to culture abound in the literature of psychology and psychiatry. They refer to publicly acceptable and personally comfortable as well as socially deviant and subjectively distressing ways of thinking, feeling, and acting. Most authors take as given the idea that these reflect not only individual biography—unique developmental and adult experience—but also a mode of participating in a current social process. This process involves the learning, transmission, and sharing of rules for behavior. But normative behavior is an abstraction, and people rarely conform to all of the rules all of the time. Failure to conform may be passive, reflecting lack of information, motivation, energy or resources. Or it may be active, and labeled "nonconformity." When it is extreme, or when it violates profoundly held ideals and values, it is sometimes taken by ordinary citizens as well as mental health professionals as a sign of "sickness" or at least of impaired "mental health." But even the violation of culturally central belief systems may not be sufficient to permit the unequivocal identification of behavior as mentally unhealthy. Within cultures there are a variety of statuses, which have a variety of expected behavior patterns or roles attached to them. Persons occupying certain statuses are permitted behavior and gratifications not accessible to persons in other statuses. And within overall culture areas, there are differences in prestige and power, ethnicity, rural or urban residence, occupation, education, and the like. These provide matrices or functional contexts within which different behavior patterns stand out as different and troublesome, or may be submerged and invisible against a nondemanding or congruent background. This tremendous variety makes the understanding of nonconforming behavior a major focus for the integration of theory and data from many fields. These include the social, biological, and psychological sciences and the psychoanalytic and psychotherapeutic study of people seeking help for their personal discomfort, or sent by an uncomfortable society for a type of behavior change called "therapeutic."

The biology of behavior ranges from the genetics of mental illness to the neurochemical mechanisms necessary for adapting and coping. The social background of behavior ranges from the ways in which human groups are organized and relate to each other to their socially transmitted ways of thinking, feeling, and acting. These reduce the range of decisions necessary for individuals and make up the skeleton of what has been called culture. Studies of social role in particular attempt some linkage between the idea of culture and that of social organization. Role behavior incongruent with such personal statuses as gender or age is sometimes considered indicative of illness.

The study of culture provides most of the themes regarded as anthropological in the mental health literature. But anthropologists, in contrast to mental health specialists, look for regularities in nonconformity. Ethnographers have been concerned not only with cultural mandates, but with patterns of accommodating to them and the transmission of possible rules for nonconforming as well as heeding them. Thus ideas of informal as well as formal organization emerge and covert as well as overt cultural patterns. The possibilities for rule-breaking not regarded as sickness become infinite as behavioral contexts vary, private as well as public behavior is considered, and both are expanded to include acts regarded as mistaken or symptomatic as well as intentional and responsible. The field of psychological anthropology (or anthropological psychology) is then expanded to include individuals' experiencing at all levels of consciousness and of rationality.

The most significant reports bearing on individual experiencing, conflict resolution, and symptomatic behavior stem from psychoanalysis and its later derivatives in the form of psychodynamics and intensive psychotherapy. Their central concern is with behavioral determinants outside the focus of awareness whether defined as preconscious or unconscious. The former are accessible to introspection, although with effort or the interpretive help of a specialist. The latter are inferred on the basis of ambiguous, inconsistent, or repetitive maladaptive behavior or from dreams and other images emerging in states of sleep or altered consciousness. These are made coherent in the process of recall for purposes of reporting or review, and this last process of filtering and organization according to the restraints of culture, time, space and logic is, itself, a subject of study.

"The unconscious" may be viewed as a repository of forgotten or repressed memories, or of experiences never converted into the symbols of speech and hence not so identifiable. Repression can maintain gaps in comprehension leading to failure to learn from experience and to culturally inappropriate behavior. Or "unconscious" may simply be regarded as a metaphor for determinants of repetitive behavior experienced by the actor as inconsistent, maladaptive, upsetting or simply not "making sense." Psychoanalytic interpretation, with the analysand's collaboration, attempts a construction of the latter's unconscious inner world and private frame of reference. Knowledge of the inner frame illuminates hitherto ambiguous or inconsistent behavior and reveals it as coherent within that frame. Similarly, anthropological interpretation, based on the examination of contextual detail and participant-observation in an informant's (and in many informants') daily life (or lives) can reveal logic, purpose, and coherence in previously not understood behavior. Anthropological interpretation has sometimes been enriched by the investigator's knowledge of the psychoanalytic concept of transference. Within the confines of a prolonged relationship an informant's transference may produce behavior more consistent with idiosyncratic past personal history than with cross-sectional rules for living.

One approach to understanding the boundaries of public and private meaning, and that not fully in the focus of awareness, has been to do ethnography in circumstances and contexts universal to all human beings. The subjective meaning of behavior is determined in part by the culturally determined symbolic and interactional features of the context in which it emerges. Most universal contexts are inherent in the life cycle—from being born through reproducing to becoming sick and dying. As a context is regularly encountered in every culture, behavior arising within it may be regarded in part as a particular expression of common human aims or tendencies. But human beings are characterized by conflict between incompatible aims and tendencies. As individual biographies vary, the meaning of the behavior in question also requires its understanding as the possible resolution of unconscious or experienced conflict. The behavioral resolution of such conflict may be taken as an attempt at personal integration with the multiple functions of solving a problem and arriving at individually necessary meanings. As it defends against the expression of inadmissible or personally troublesome needs and in so doing constricts or inhibits a person's life, or gratifies other aims which also become troublesome, it may be called symptomatic. If growing up in a culture produces similar conflicts dealt with similarly by many persons, their conflict resolutions may constitute a group pattern. Or pre-existing group patterns may be used in the service of individual defensive needs permitting the gratification of particular aims without their conscious confrontation. Myth, ritual, patterns of child rearing and of adult behavior as they are constrained by the social control system may represent, among other factors, the collective expression of conflict resolution.

The task of unraveling the individual and collective, the private and public, the psychodynamic and sociocultural roots of behavior is immense. This book is designed to provide one of the necessary steps in accomplishing that task. It will help the student and investigator identify the authors whose work is devoted to this problem, and the ways in which anthropological themes fit, clash, and compromise with those of mental health.

References

Brody EB: Symptomatic behavior: ego-defensive, adaptive, and sociocultural aspects, in American Handbook of Psychiatry, vol. 3. Edited by Arieti S and Brody EB. New York, Basic Books, 1974.

Brody EB, Newman LF: Experience, Symbol, and Meaning: Toward a Psychoanalytically Informed Ethnography. In press.

Klein GS: Psychoanalytic Theory: An Exploration of Essentials. New York, International University Press, 1976.

Introduction

Anthropology and psychiatry are both magnificently rich disciplines. This richness can be conceptually overwhelming, however, because it gives rise to difficulty in attempting to define the limits of the two disciplines. Anthropology and psychiatry are, like most scientific fields, experiencing an information explosion. The sustained growth of social and community psychiatry, for example, has pushed the boundaries of psychiatric concern into such diverse areas as economics, politics, and community organization and development. The increased diversity of research interests within the scope of anthropology is only partly reflected by the fields of applied and medical anthropology, psychological anthropology, primate ethology, human biology, and the approaches of ecological anthropology and the "new" scientific archaeology.

Psychiatry and anthropology interface in innumerable ways. Historically there have been great collaborative efforts, such as those of Sapir and Sullivan, Parsons and Lindemann, Ruesch and Bateson, Kardiner and DuBois, Erikson and Kroeber, Redlich and Caudill, Leighton and Kluckhohn, Henry and Levy, and the Mid-Town Manhattan and Stirling County studies. Interdisciplinary work is difficult at best, however, and the enormous data base of the disciplines almost precludes any one individual's becoming totally proficient in both.

Our interest in the psychiatric-anthropological interface developed with the realization that many of the broad areas of concern for psychiatrists paralleled those of anthropologists. We believe that the development of an interface discipline should be based on knowledge of the literary themes common to the two disciplines. We read Galdston's (1971) book on the psychiatric-anthropological interface but found our interest whetted rather than satisfied. As we gathered a broader base of information, we focused on three themes and eventually published lengthy articles dealing with the psychiatric-anthropological interface in relation to the Oedipus complex, national character, and feral man (Favazza: 1975; also see annotations 3484, 3485). To examine the psychiatric-anthropological interface in greater detail, a search for literature was initiated in the mental health journals. It became obvious that there was a considerable number of articles that would be of interest to anthropologists and psychiatrists alike. The research potential offered by the compilation of these materials was clear, and preparation of a meaningful, general bibliography was initiated.

We utilized the NIMH computer bibliographic service and received a printout of articles dealing with psychiatry and anthropology. Even though the bibliography we received extended over several years, we were amazed that fewer than 75 articles appeared. The problem, of course, is that the wide variety of anthropological topics is extremely difficult to code. Certainly article titles alone can be misleading.

We then turned to Driver's comprehensive reference guide, *The Sociology and Anthropology of Mental Illness* (Driver: 1972). This work lists 5,910 titles of relevant articles and books published between 1956 and 1968. The author obtained the titles by searching seven major bibliographic sources *(Cumulated Index Medicus, Cumulative Book Index, Current List of Medical Literature, Dissertation Abstracts, Index to American Doctoral Dissertations, International Index: A Guide to Literature in the Social Sciences and Humanities, and Sociological Abstracts)*.

Driver's work did not completely suit our needs. The type of material he included clearly differed from ours. The following are examples of articles included in Driver's work that are not relevant to our approach:

"The hyperactive child syndrome"
"Non-medical leaves from a mental hospital"
"Philosophies, not laws, determine admission practices"
"A study of the psychiatric interview"
"Child psychotherapy and its affective principles"
"Psychiatric considerations in acne vulgaris"
"Psychodynamic approach to psychoneurosis"
"The experience of solitude in the schizophrenic patient"
"Children of schizophrenic mothers"
"Time extended marathon groups"

Using major bibliographic sources, Driver compiled titles from a staggeringly large number of publications; our approach was to examine a more limited number of especially important journals. There is some overlap between many of Driver's references and ours for the same time periods reviewed. A spot check, however, shows articles that we have included that are not found in Driver's text. A few examples of such articles are the following:

Fried M: Effects of social change on mental health. Am J Orthopsychiatry 34:3–28, 1964.
Firth R: Suicide and risk-taking in Tikopia society. Psychiatry 24:1–17, 1961.
Green HB: Socialization values in the Negro and East Indian subculture of Trinidad. J Soc Psychol 64:1–20, 1964.
Metraux R: The dispersion of significance in a changing culture: Montserrat, B.W.I. Int J Soc Psychiatry 6:225–229, 1960.
Preble E: Social and cultural factors related to narcotic use among Puerto Ricans in New York City. Int J Addict 1:30–41, 1966.
Yap PM: The possession syndrome: a comparison of Hong Kong and French findings. J Ment Science 106:114–137, 1960.

It would thus appear that, although the titles of Driver's work and ours are similar, the books differ because of different approaches in retrieving material and in conceptualizing the content. The books, we believe, complement each other. Driver's book is more inclusive and covers the years 1956–1968, while our book is more exclusive, more anthropologically and cross-culturally oriented, and covers the years 1925–1974.

Our idea received a boost at the American Psychiatric Association meeting held at Anaheim, California, in May 1975. The senior author (A.F.) moderated a panel on "Anthropology and Psychiatry." The panelists included psychiatrists E. Mansell Pattison, Joseph Westermeyer, Ronald Wintrob, and Edward Foulks. Despite the 7 A.M. time and the competition with 20 other concurrent panels, we were delightfully surprised that about 70 interested psychiatrists and other mental health professionals attended the panel discussion. Strong support was voiced for the bibliographic effort which we had been working on for several months. It was generally felt that our project would be of great value in developing the field of "Anthropological psychiatry." Without much support it is doubtful that we would have been able to carry through with our massive undertaking.

Sources

We chose 1925 as the starting date for our bibliography because we felt that the perspective of half a century would prove useful. In the early 1920s intellectual exchange between psychiatrists and anthropologists became quite intense following Bronislaw Malinowski's work in the

Trobriands and his subsequent thesis of the nonexistence of the Oedipus complex in that society. Interest in the universality of the Oedipus complex has persisted as a continuing controversy up to the present.

We then turned to the *Index Medicus* and *Psychological Abstracts* in order to select most of the journals for review. The names of these 68 journals, as well as the total number of articles with anthropological and cross-cultural themes, are listed in Table 1. We believe we have included most of the significant mental health journals published in English. It was beyond our expertise to include foreign language journals. Obviously we have not reviewed *every* mental health journal printed in English. There was a limit to our energy and perseverance. We also did not include *Transcultural Psychiatric Research Review,* although we do call our readers' attention to it. This interesting journal frequently publishes reviews of books and articles from other pertinent journals. In general, we have not included book reviews among our annotations.

Identifying articles

Our most difficult task in compiling the bibliography was identifying articles that would have anthropological relevance. Anthropology, as the study of biological and cultural man, has an almost limitless topic orientation. The panhuman, comparative, and diachronic perspective of the discipline, as well as its synchronic focus, is reflected in anthropology's interest in and interaction with many other disciplines, such as sociology, history, psychology, psychiatry, ecology, ethnology, economics, and geology, to name a few.

We selected those journal articles we think contribute to broad central themes, as well as current directions, in anthropology. These are themes most anthropologists would identify and accept as anthropological in subject matter. Examples include articles encompassing certain key concepts: cultural system, tribe, native, ethnology, primate, aggression, race; and articles with topical-area emphasis on non-Western cultures and groups. Anthropology's recently increased concern with complex society is reflected in articles on subcultures in industrial society, peasant society, and urban life. Only a minority of the articles have a methodological and theoretical orientation that is anthropological. Our bibliography thus is more a reflection of material that could be a valuable research tool than a compilation of anthropological orientations per se.

Many of the articles are clearly anthropologically oriented. Examples include:

Abernethy V: Dominance and sexual behavior: a hypothesis. Am J Psychiatry 131:813–816, 1974.

Henry J: Anthropology and psychosomatics. Psychosom Med 11:216–222, 1949.

Seligman CG: Temperament, conflict and psychosis in a stone-age population. Br J Med Psychol 9: 187–202, 1929.

Turnbull CM: Some observations regarding the experience and behavior of the BaMbuti pygmies. Am J Psychol 74:304–308, 1961.

These are articles, however, which some critics might not uniformly identify as possessing an anthropological theme. We have used our best judgment and in borderline cases have carefully reviewed the bibliography of an article. If clear-cut anthropological sources were incorporated, we tended to include the articles in our list. The differentiation between anthropological and sociological themes was often very subtle, and we decided upon a liberal policy of inclusion. In general, this policy makes the bibliography a more helpful document.

Many of the cross-cultural articles are not anthropologically oriented. These articles, however, provide data that are especially amenable to cultural and social research and may contribute to

Table 1.
Journals Selected for Review and Total Number of Articles
with Anthropological Themes, 1925-1974*

Acta Psychiatrica Scandinavica (1926) 22
  (*Acta Psychiatrica et Neurologica*)

American Imago (1943) 52

American Journal of Orthopsychiatry (1930) . .130

American Journal of Psychiatry (1925) 189

American Journal of Psychoanalysis (1941) 4

American Journal of Psychology (1925) 13

American Journal of Psychotherapy (1947) 50

Archives of General Psychiatry (1925) 35
  (*Archives Neurology Psychiatry*)

Behavioral Science (1956) 12

Behavior Research and Therapy (1963) 0

British Journal of Medical Psychology (1925) . .41

British Journal of Psychiatry (1925) 88
  (*Journal of Mental Science*)

British Journal of Psychology (1925) 91

*British Journal of Social and Clinical
  Psychology* (1962) 48

Bulletin of the Menninger Clinic (1936) 20

*Canadian Psychiatric Association
  Journal* (1956) 36

Child Development (1930) 101

Community Mental Health Journal (1965) 7

Comprehensive Psychiatry (1960) 19

Contemporary Psychoanalysis (1964) 9

Diseases of the Nervous System (1940) 12

Family Coordinator (1952) 19
  (*Family Life Coordinator*)

Family Process (1962) 15

Hospital and Community Psychiatry (1959) 8
  (*Mental Hospitals*)

International Journal of Addictions (1966) 15

International Journal of Psychiatry (1965) 23

International Journal of Psycho-analysis (1925) 50

*International Journal of Psychoanalytic
  Psychotherapy* (1972) 3

International Journal of Psychology (1966) . . .133

*International Journal of Social
  Psychiatry* (1955) 146

Journal of Abnormal Psychology (1965) 2

*Journal of Abnormal and Social
  Psychology* (1925) 163

*Journal of the American Academy of
  Child Psychiatry* (1962) .7

*Journal of the American Academy of
  Psychoanalysis* (1973) 2

*Journal of the American Psychoanalytic
  Association* (1953) 15

*Journal of Child Psychology, Psychiatry
  and Allied Disciplines* (1960) 14

Journal of Clinical Psychology (1945) 24

*Journal of Consulting and Clinical
  Psychology* (1937) 27
  (*Journal of Consulting Psychology*)

Journal of Cross-Cultural Psychology (1970) . .183

*Journal of the History of Behavioral
  Sciences* (1965) 13

Journal of Marriage and the Family (1938) . . .223

Journal of Nervous and Mental Disease (1925) .72

Journal of Operational Psychiatry (1970) 5

Journal of Personality Assessment (1936) 44
  (*Journal of Projective Techniques,
  Rorschach Research Exchange*)

*Journal of Personality and
  Social Psychology* (1965) 43

Journal of Psychiatric Research (1961) 9

Journal of Psychology (1935) 115

Journal of Psychosomatic Research (1956) 13

Journal of Social Psychology (1925) 554

Marriage and Family Living (1959) 72

Psyche (1925) 13

Psychiatry (1938) 187

Psychiatric Quarterly (1932) 31

Psychoanalytic Quarterly (1932) 35

Psychoanalytic Review (1925) 29

Psychoanalytic Study of the Child (1945) 11

Psychoanalytic Study of Society (1960) 21

Psychological Bulletin (1925) 21

Psychological Medicine (1939) 4

*Psychological Monographs:
  General and Applied* (1925) 19

Psychological Reports (1955) 75

Psychosomatic Medicine (1939) 34

Psychosomatics (1960) 9

Psychotherapy and Psychosomatics (1952) 17

*Psychotherapy Theory Research
  and Practice* (1964) 3

*Quarterly Journal of Studies
  on Alcohol* (1940) 46

Social Psychiatry (1966) 27

Social Science and Medicine (1967) 50

*Year in parentheses indicates year we began our review of the particular journal.

the renewed interest in nomothetic-idiographic synthesis in anthropology. The cross-cultural material provides contemporary quantitative data on cultural change and cultural pluralism that add to the information contained within the Human Relations Area Files. Although some of the articles contain controversial positions on specific topics, the quantitative analyses presented therein provide a base for statistical reanalysis by the researcher. Two limitations may be noted with respect to many of these cross-cultural studies. First, a holistic focus on "culture" in the anthropological sense is not a characteristic of these articles which, for the most part, consider cultural influences as an aside to the investigation. Secondly, only a few of the articles represent a synthesis of the material.

Table 2. Numbers of Articles in Mental Health Journals According to Fields of General Anthropology

	Cultural	Physical	Linguistics	Archaeology
1925-1930	42	14	0	1
1931-1935	60	16	7	0
1936-1940	109	32	8	1
1941-1945	145	22	11	0
1946-1950	196	15	6	3
1951-1955	209	22	20	0
1956-1960	329	36	18	0
1961-1965	421	45	28	1
1966-1970	837	48	41	4
1971-1974	821	47	41	0

As an aid to readers we have organized the data in different ways. At the most general level, anthropology may be considered an amalgam of four fields: cultural anthropology, physical anthropology, anthropological linguistics, and archaeology. Each article has been categorized according to its relevance to these four fields. Table 2 shows these general categories as reflected over time. The reader should be aware that some articles may deal with more than one topic. In such instances, we have listed such articles under more than one heading. We have followed this policy in all the tables.

Cultural areas

A large number of the articles surveyed deal with specific populations and with geographically delimitable culture areas. Table 3 lists the number of articles for each culture area over time. Heading the list by a wide margin are articles dealing with Asia (555), followed by American subcultures (418), Africa (317), Europe (309), Native America (250), Mideast (209), Latin and

South America (191), and Oceania and Australia (154). Articles are cross-referenced between specific nations and specific groups of people. In the following categorical breakdowns, therefore, the number of articles, as noted in parentheses, may differ from the total number for each major category.

Included in the "Asia" category are eight general articles as well as articles dealing with the following areas and peoples:

Afghanistan (5)
Ainu (4)
Arakan (2)
Atayal (1)
Batak (2)
Borneo (1)
Burgher (1)
Burma (8)
Canton (1)
Ceylon Tamil (1)
Chamorro (1)
China (22)
Chinese (48)
Communist China (7)
Hong Kong (28)
Iban (1)

India (191)
Indonesia (8)
Japan (105)
Japanese (33)
Korea, North (11)
Korea, South (2)
Laos (6)
Malaysia (14)
Meo (1)
Mongols (1)
Moslem (19)
Murut (1)
Nuristani (1)
Okinawa (5)
Pakistan (19)
Pakistan, East (3)

Pakistan, West (1)
Philippines (27)
Saipan (1)
Sarawak (4)
Semang (1)
Senoi (1)
Singapore (4)
Sri Lanka (6)
Sumatra (3)
Tagalog (1)
Taiwan (16)
Thailand (21)
Tibet (1)
Tungus (1)
Vietnam (2)

We have separate headings for China and Chinese, Japan and Japanese, because some articles do not clearly indicate the location of the study population, although it would appear that many of the articles dealing with Chinese and Japanese populations do refer to studies done in China and Japan. It is interesting to note that despite recent Western involvement in Vietnam only two articles dealing with Vietnam were recorded. The reader should refer to the Subject Index for the specific articles dealing with each group.

Included in the *American Subcultures* category are articles on the following:

Amish (2)
Appalachia (2)
Chinese-American (20)
Doukhobor (1)
Danish-American (1)
Filipino-American (6)
French-American (1)
French-Canadian (11)
German-American (3)
Greek-American (1)
Haole (1)
Hutterite (12)
Hawaiian (28)

Hawaiian-Filipino (1)
Hawaiian-Japanese (1)
Hungarian-American (2)
Irish-American (4)
Italian-American (20)
Italian-Canadian (1)
Issei (3)
Japanese-American (54)
Jewish-American (15)
Korean-American (2)
Mexican-American (43)
Mennonite (2)
Negro (202)

Nissei (2)
Norwegian-American (3)
Okinawan-American (1)
Oriental-American (3)
Polish-American (2)
Portuguese-American (1)
Puerto Rican-American (9)
Russian-American (1)
Samoan-American (3)
Scandinavian-American (1)
Slovak-American (1)
Swedish-American (2)
Swiss-American (1)

In the Subject Index we have listed articles on Negroes by specific themes. The largest number of articles deal with Negro cognition, family, identity, intelligence, mental disorder, and personality. As might be expected, many of the articles on American subcultures deal with the problems of immigration and acculturation.

Included in the Africa category are 42 general articles as well as articles dealing with the following areas and peoples:

Table 3. Numbers of Articles in Mental Health Journals According to Cultural Populations and Culture Areas

	Asia	American Sub-cultures	Africa	Europe	Native America	Mideast	Latin & South America	Oceania & Australia
1925-1930	5	5	1	3	6	0	1	3
1931-1935	11	11	8	3	5	1	0	2
1936-1940	10	13	5	6	24	1	2	3
1941-1945	9	22	2	19	17	0	5	10
1946-1950	16	28	4	26	16	2	7	7
1951-1955	19	44	8	17	20	18	8	5
1956-1960	52	35	37	32	13	35	24	16
1961-1965	71	51	34	31	30	23	33	14
1966-1970	167	104	110	101	51	56	49	41
1971-1974	195	105	108	71	68	72	62	53
Total	555	418	317	309	250	208	191	154

Agni (1)
Afrikaaners (5)
Akan (2)
Amhara (1)
Ashanti (3)
Bacongo (1)
Bakitara (1)
Bambuti (2)
Bantu (12)
Banyankole (2)
Bashi (1)
Bassa (1)
Belgian Congo (2)
Bena Bena (2)
Bushmen (1)
Chagga (1)
Congo (2)
Dogon (3)
East Africa (13)
Egypt (11)
Egypt (ancient) (2)
Ethiopia (15)
Ewe (2)
Fan (1)
Fang (1)
French Guinea (1)

Ga (1)
Gabonese (1)
Ganda (5)
Ghana (23)
Gold Coast (1)
Gusii (7)
Hausa (2)
Hutu (1)
Ibibio (1)
Ibo (2)
Ibusa (1)
Kafa (1)
Kamba (2)
Kasangati (1)
Katangese (1)
Kenya (23)
Kikuyu (1)
Kipsigi (5)
Kpelle (4)
Lesu (1)
Liberia (9)
Logoli (9)
Logos (1)
Luo (2)
Lusaka (1)
Malawi (1)

Mano (2)
Mashona (1)
Mauritius (2)
Morocco (1)
Ngoni (1)
Nigeria (27)
Nsenga (1)
Nupe (1)
Nyanja (1)
Nyasaland (1)
Onitshas (1)
Rhodesia (7)
Rwanda (1)
Serer (1)
Senegal (3)
Sierra Leone (3)
Soli (1)
Somali (1)
Sousou (1)
South Africa (28)
Sudan (4)
Swazi (1)
Tanzania (10)
Temne (6)
Tiv (2)
Togoland (2)

Tunesia (1)
Uganda (22)
Ugandan Asians (2)
Wabena (1)

Wapogoro (1)
Wolof (1)
Xhosa (3)
Yao (1)

Yoruba (15)
Zambia (21)
Zulu (6)

Among the topics included in these articles are race relations, tribal identity, cultural change associated with modernity, cognition, and personality development. Very few of the articles provide detailed ethnographic data. Reference is made several times to Carothers's book *The African Mind in Health and Disease, A Study in Ethno-psychiatry* (Carothers: 1953). This book even in its most recent edition, has been relatively controversial because of its stereotypes of Africans (Carothers: 1972). Since Carothers's work is quoted frequently in transcultural psychiatry, we urge the interested reader to see Lumsden's letter "On Transcultural Psychiatry, Africans, and Academic Racism" (Lumsden: 1976). In contrast to Carothers's anecdotal comments are the generally excellent clinical studies by Dr. T. Lambo on the Yoruba of Nigeria (see Author Index).

Included in the Europe category are 10 general articles as well as articles dealing with the following areas and peoples:

Austria (3)
Balkans (1)
Belgium (6)
Bulgaria (1)
Croatia (2)
Czechoslovakia (4)
Denmark (15)
Dinaric Alps (1)
Finland (10)
France (23)
Germany (72)
Great Britain (85)

Greece (30)
Hungary (5)
Ireland (14)
Italy (24)
Komi Republic (1)
Kvaen (1)
Lapp (2)
Netherlands (9)
Norway (14)
Poland (4)
Scandinavia (1)
Scotland (19)

Sicily (1)
Slovenian (1)
Sweden (20)
Switzerland (8)
United Soviet
   Socialist Republic (14)
Wales (2)
Yugoslavia (9)
Zadruga (2)
Zyrians (1)

Quite a few European-focused articles were the result of interest in the national-character concept that was so popular during and immediately following World War II. As might be predicted, one's enemies could best be described as possessing a flawed national character. German culture, for example, was seen by some as having a paranoid trend and as fostering paranoid individuals. In fact, in 1944 a plan to transform German culture was proposed by an emminent group of American psychiatrists, psychologists, anthropologists, and other behavioral scientists (see annotation 462).

The range of topics is broad in this category. Several articles deal with a comparison between a population in Scotland and Ghana. Material from the Scandinavian countries often deals with social class issues. London, the center of the British Empire, is the setting for a group of articles on the problems of immigrants, especially those from the West Indies and South Asia.

The "Native American" category includes articles on the following North and South American native groups:

Aleut (3)
Andean Indians (1)
Apache (24)
Athabaskan (2)
Blackfoot (2)
Bororo (1)
Camba (1)

Canadian Indians (4)
Carrier (1)
Cheyenne (1)
Chilicotin (1)
Chippewa (4)
Coast Salish (2)
Coconuco (1)

Cree (4)
Cree, Misstassini (1)
Dakota Indians (3)
Digueno (2)
Eskimo (27)
Forest Potawatomi (1)
Guatemalan Indians (2)

Hopi (15)	Pauite (1)	Seminole (1)
Indian-Metis (1)	Papago (7)	Sioux (9)
Iroquois (1)	Pawnee (1)	Tarahumara (1)
Kaska (1)	Peruvian Indians (1)	Teton Dakota (1)
Mapuches (1)	Pilaga (5)	Toltec (1)
Maya (11)	Pima (1)	Tsimshian (1)
Menomini (3)	Plateau Indians (1)	Ute (1)
Mohave (10)	Plains Indians (5)	Wintu (1)
Navaho (37)	Pomo (2)	Yakima (1)
Nez Perce (2)	Quekchi (1)	Yuma (1)
North American Indians (42)	Quiche (1)	Yurok (5)
North Pacific Coast Indians (5)	Salteaux (7)	Zuni (10)
Osage (1)	Saskatchewan Indians (2)	Zia (2)

In this category the Mohave Indians are unusually well covered due to the work of psychoanalyst-anthropologist George Devereux. Erik Erikson, another psychoanalyst-anthropologist, produced material on the Yurok and the Sioux, while Boyer has contributed studies on the Apaches. The systematic study of North American Indians has a tradition that goes back to Franz Boas, the mentor of Ruth Benedict. Her book, *Patterns of Culture,* stimulated much general interest in the Indians of the Southwest. Collaborative psychiatric-anthropological work in this area rapidly occurred. In 1941 the U.S. Office of Indian Affairs joined with the Committee on Human Development of the University of Chicago to establish the Indian Education Research Project (also referred to as the Indian Personality and Administration Project). The project studied the development of children among the Hopi, Sioux, Navaho, Papago, Zia, and Zuni. In 1944 two psychiatrists, Alexander and Dorothea Leighton, published a practical guide for Indian Service workers, *The Navaho Door: An Introduction to Navaho Life.* In 1946 Clyde Kluckhohn, the anthropologist, and Dorothea Leighton published *The Navaho,* and in 1947 they published a companion volume entitled *Children of the People.* In 1949 the Leightons published *Gregorio, the Hand Trembler: A Psychological Personality Study of a Navaho Indian* as part of the Ramah project. The Ramah project was a brainchild of Kluckhohn who, under the influence of Sapir and John Dollard, planned in 1936 a long-term study of the socialization of Navaho children. The Ramah Navaho were chosen for the study because of their geographical isolation from other groups and the relative lateness of their contact with the Indian Service. *Gregorio* was the first of the Peabody Museum (Harvard) Reports on the project, and the authors specifically acknowledge the guidance and encouragement received from the psychiatrist, Adolf Meyer, and the anthropologist, Ralph Linton.

Indians of the Arctic and sub-Arctic regions were a central focus of many of the North American "Culture and Personality" articles. The work on acculturation by Hallowell and by Honigmann is well known in this area. In fact, Hallowell's *Culture and Experience* (1955) and Honigmann's *Culture and Personality* (1954) are still widely read. Many of the current articles about North American Indians deal with the serious problems of suicide and alcoholism which are frequently found in a reservation population. Joseph Westermeyer, a psychiatrist-anthropologist, has written excellent papers in this regard (see Author Index). Edward Foulks, a psychiatrist-anthropologist, published a stimulating monograph in 1972 entitled "The Arctic Hysterias of the North Alaskan Eskimo." The rich tradition of systematic study of North American Indians does not, unfortunately, extend to Indians of South America.

The "Mideast" category includes 10 general articles as well as articles on the following areas and peoples:

Arab (39)	Iraq (5)	Moslem (19)
Arab-Gulf States (1)	Israel (81)	Palestinian (3)
Armenia (3)	Jew:Iranian (1)	Saudi Arabia (3)
Bedouin (3)	Jew:Iraqui (3)	Shirazi (1)
French-Arab (1)	Jew:Yemenite (1)	Turkey (19)
Iran (15)	Lebanon (23)	

A great many of the Mideast articles stem from Israel, and the majority deal with that interesting experiment in communal living, the kibbutz. Most of the studies of children reared in a kibbutz fail to demonstrate a significant rise in psychopathology. The Israeli-Arab wars of the 1970s have focused much public attention on the area, and several of the recent articles attempt to interpret aspects of the conflict in psychological and behavioral terms.

The next category, "Latin and South America," includes nine general articles as well as articles on the following areas and groups:

Argentina (9)	Cuba (5)	Mocheros (1)
Bahamas (3)	Dominican Republic (1)	Monteserrat (4)
Barbados (1)	Grand Cayman (1)	Netherlands West Indies (9)
Black Carib (1)	Grenada (1)	Peru (15)
Bolivia (2)	Guatemala (8)	Puerto Rico (37)
Brazil (31)	Guyana (1)	St. Thomas (1)
British Honduras (1)	Haiti (8)	Tobago (2)
British Guiana (2)	Jamaica (9)	Trinidad (9)
British West Indies (7)	Ladino (4)	Uruguay (1)
Caribbean (4)	Menjala (1)	Yucatan (6)
Chile (6)	Meso America (1)	Zapotec (1)
Colombia (6)	Mestizo (6)	Zinacanteco (3)
Costa Rica (2)	Mexico (44)	

The dramatic increase in articles dealing with Latin and South America occurred during the late 1950s, a period in which the Cuban revolution made headlines and in which the Puerto Rican emigration to New York City was blossoming. Articles on the "Puerto Rican Syndrome" and on the Puerto Rican personality reflect an interest in understanding better the backgrounds of this great new wave of immigrants.

Books by the anthropologist, Oscar Lewis, focused attention on Latin Americans, on peasant society, and on the "culture of poverty." *Life in a Mexican Village* was published in 1951, *The Children of Sanchez* in 1961, and *La Vida* in 1966. Readers particularly interested in Mexican-American and Puerto Rican subgroups should see, in addition to our bibliography, *Latino Mental Health: Bibliography and Abstracts* (Padilla and Aranda: 1974). As Mexican migrant workers in the United States organized politically, more interest in Mexico was demonstrated by psychiatrists and psychologists.

Also included in this area are articles dealing with voodoo, a phenomenon that has long attracted widespread attention. Ari Kiev's articles on voodoo are major contributions to the field of transcultural psychiatry.

Brazil is the scene for many fascinating articles, such as that on a group of Japanese-Brazilians, the Kachigumi, who had a collective delusion that Japan was victorious in World War II (see annotation 2617). Eugene Brody has done excellent cross-cultural work on Brazil, much of which can be found in his book *The Lost Ones: Social Forces and Mental Illness in Rio de Janeiro* (Brody: 1973, also see Author Index).

Our last category includes 24 general articles dealing with "Australia" and four on "Oceania" as well as articles on the following areas and peoples:

Alorese (1)	New Britain (1)	Ponape (1)
Arapesh (1)	New Guinea (11)	Pukapuka Atoll (1)
Bali (5)	New Ireland (1)	Samoa (7)
Dobu (1)	New Zealand (16)	Tahiti (1)
Ifaluk (3)	Fijian (10)	Tikopia (1)
Maori (8)	Fore (1)	Tolai (1)
Marquesas (1)	Guam (3)	Tonga (1)
Melanesia (1)	Gururumba (1)	Trobriands (3)
Mundugamor (1)	Papua (7)	
Normanby Island (2)	Polynesia (3)	

This category also includes 31 articles on Australian aborigines in general as well as articles on the following aboriginal groups:

Aranda (2)	Hooker Creek (1)	Warburton Ranges (1)
Arnhemland (5)	Kimberly (1)	Western Desert (1)
Arunta (2)	Lardil (1)	Yolngu (2)
Bamyili (1)	Walbiri (3)	Yowera (1)

Oceania and Australia have long been favorite haunts of anthropologists, and the published ethnographic material is immense. In our bibliography a large group of early articles on this area was written by that most interesting and controversial psychoanalyst-anthropologist, Geza Roheim. As Harris (1968: 428) notes:

> Roheim had the virtue of clarity and frankness, always stipulating that the fundamental causal sequence rises from infant experience to adult practice. Everything else is superficial. It is the Oedipus complex which lies at the root of all psychologically significant sociocultural happenings, and from Roheim's perspective anyone who denies this is suffering from a repressed Oedipus complex of his own and should at once rush off to be analyzed. Contrary to popular impression, in the argument between Roheim and Malinowski over the effect of the Trobriand matrilineal organization on the Oedipal situation, it is Roheim who holds the trump card. By Malinowski's own admission, the Trobriand child is brought up largely under the influence of the usual nuclear pairs. Mother's brother enters the picture only when the child is seven or eight years old, an age by which the Oedipal constellation is firmly entrenched.

Continued psychiatric concern in this area is reflected by *The Tahitians* by Robert Levy, a psychiatrist-anthropologist (Levy: 1973). This work successfully deals with the private and public worlds of the Society Islanders. John Cawte, a psychiatrist, has written *Medicine is the Law: Studies in Psychiatric Anthropology of Australian Tribal Societies* (Cawte: 1974). Our bibliography contains a number of articles dealing with Australian aborigines, with a special interest in acculturation and suburethral incision rites. Eric Berne, the founder of Transactional Analysis, is represented by a series of early articles on the epidemiology of mental illness in various Pacific islands. It is interesting to note that Berne doubted any cultural etiology of mental disorder, because he figured the differences between individuals in any culture to be greater than the differences between cultures (see annotation 1145).

Specific themes

Another way of appreciating the diverse, anthropologically thematic mental health literature is to examine an overview of specific themes. We divided the themes into 24 areas. Although topics are indexed separately, we have combined certain related topics in Table 4. Articles that deal with more than one theme are listed for each theme.

The most heterogeneous category is *General Culture, Psychiatry, and Personality.* This category includes articles that do not fit into specific themes, as well as articles that clearly can be identified as "culture and personality." Samples of articles in this category include "Bereavement in a Samoan Community" (2733); "Locus of Control and Creativity in Black and White Children" (2475); "Leaving the Kibbutz: An Identity Conflict" (2999); and "A Psychoanalytic Approach to Kabuki: A Study in Personality and Culture" (1368).

"Child-rearing" and "Socialization" articles were quite rare until the mid-1950s. Although the concept of childhood psychological development has been a central concern of dynamic psychiatry since the turn of the century, the usual focus was on intrapsychic development of the child. It was not until the forceful growth of the community mental health movement that widespread interest developed in the socialization process and in child-rearing practices. Typical articles in this category include "Child Rearing and Child Care Among the Sino-Thai Population of Bangkok" (3588); "Socialization Practices of Parents, Teachers and Peers in Israel" (3470); "Infancy in a Cultural Context" (3385); and "The Observation of Anglo-, Mexican-, and Chinese-American Mothers Rearing Their Young Sons" (3372).

The themes of "Ritual," "Religion," and "Mythology" have never been central to mental health professionals. Mythology has intrigued primarily psychoanalysts who have attempted to explore the psychic unity of Man, relating myths to an understanding of parallel psychological conflicts and themes in diverse cultures. The enmity between professionals in the fields of mental health and religion was stimulated by Freud's contention that religion was "nothing but" a projection of psychological needs. Freud, for example, postulated that a belief in God the Father really was a projection of man's need for a loving biological father. The religious indictment against "coveting thy neighbor's wife" conflicted with the mental health tenet that desires or fantasies were not pathological, although acting out these fantasies might well be harmful. Reconciliation between professionals in religion and mental health has been slow but steady. Religion has been identified as an integrative factor in community life; as *Action for Mental Health* demonstrated, many people turn first to ministers for help with a mental health problem (Joint Commission: 1961). Articles dealing with the relationship between mental health and religion, however, still seem to stir up intense emotions. The topic of abortion, for example, is intimately linked with religious convictions by many, but in the mental health literature the topic is dealt with in terms of public health and medicine rather than morality. Typical articles in this category include "Subincision Among Western Desert Aborigines" (2398); "The Case of a Japanese Sect in Hawaii" (2622); "The Social Desirability Responses of Children of Four Religious-Cultural Groups" (2342); and "Mythic Symbols in Two Pre-Columbian Myths" (2466).

The category "Folklore and Dreams" has contributed the fewest number of articles to our bibliography. Although dream analysis is used extensively in psychodynamic psychotherapy, most modern work in the area has focused on the psychophysiology of the dream process. An interesting recent discovery is that the Senoi, a Malaysian group, regularly integrate group dream analysis into their everyday life. It is doubtful, however, that the Senoi experience has much relevance to clinical practice in other cultures. Typical articles in this category include "History and Psychodynamics of Attitudes to Handicapped Children in European Folklore" (2201); "Survival Strategies in Ethiopian Folktales" (2827); "Sex Differences in Dreams in Uganda" (2888); and "Changes in Mastery Style with Age: A Study of Navaho Dreams" (2826).

"Native Medicine and Psychotherapy" is a category in which almost all the contributions are

Table 4. Numbers of Articles in Mental Health Journals According to Year and Subject

	1925-1930	1931-1935	1936-1940	1941-1945	1946-1950	1951-1955	1956-1960	1961-1965	1966-1970	1971-1974	Total
General Culture, Psychiatry, and Personality	11	20	42	47	50	60	53	77	98	102	560
Child Rearing and Socialization	0	0	3	6	10	12	28	27	21	41	148
Ritual, Religion, Mythology	5	8	4	7	11	9	10	24	19	11	108
Folklore, Dreams	1	0	3	2	6	6	4	6	5	10	43
Native Medicine & Psychotherapy	1	1	0	1	4	1	3	13	24	30	78
Psychotherapy: General	0	0	1	1	8	9	17	18	39	31	124
Acculturation & Immigration	2	3	4	6	6	8	20	21	37	37	144
Aggression	0	0	4	3	11	2	4	16	11	32	83
Testing Performance and Technique	2	5	12	16	11	19	46	46	125	122	404
Cross-Cultural Research	2	2	4	2	3	4	41	57	198	166	479
Mental Illness, Health, & Culture	3	5	14	7	15	22	48	54	110	97	375
Incest, Freudian Concepts, & Oedipus Complex	2	3	5	2	1	8	10	11	3	9	54
Sexuality Sex Roles & Behavior	3	4	5	12	10	4	10	10	34	24	116
Values, Role, Attitude	0	1	1	11	14	27	47	42	79	104	325
Drug and Alcohol Use	0	1	1	6	8	11	11	10	24	29	101
Race & Racism	5	10	11	14	9	3	7	4	13	11	87
Constitution and Physical Types	5	4	8	6	9	8	2	6	3	3	54
Nonhuman Primates	1	2	7	5	1	0	7	23	19	19	84
Ethology	3	3	9	4	2	4	14	5	12	12	68
General Physical Anthropology	5	7	7	6	3	10	13	10	15	13	89
Social Class, Economy, Politics	4	2	2	2	4	3	12	8	25	10	72
Family, Kinship, and Marriage	0	0	2	11	8	23	18	50	122	88	322
Language & Communication	0	7	8	12	8	20	18	28	45	37	183

quite recent. Interest in this category may be an outgrowth of the community mental health movement's emphasis on indigenous therapists. The term *indigenous therapists,* in this sense, refers to consumers—usually members of American subcultural groups—of mental health services who, because of their unique cultural identity and personal talents, can offer mental health services to clients whom "middle-class white therapists" presumably could not treat effectively. Most articles in this category deal with shamans, witch doctors, and native healers. Typical articles are "An Indian Healer's Preventive Medicine Procedure" (3544); "Witchdoctors Succeed Where Doctors Fail: Psychotherapy Among Coast Salish Indians" (3514); "The Art of a Native Therapist" (2925); and "Shaman and Incubus" (2003).

The category "Psychotherapy: General" deals primarily with articles that point out the influence of culture on the practice of psychotherapy. These articles, too, are increasing in number probably as an outgrowth of the community mental health movement's attention to providing services that are meaningfully integrated into the individual's total culture. Typical articles in this category include "Psychiatric Consultation to a Filipino Community in Hawaii" (3632); "The Significance of Sociocultural Variables in the Psychiatric Treatment of Black Outpatients" (3553); and "Developing a Community Mental Health Clinic on an Indian Reservation" (3265). This category also includes articles on the therapy of institutions, such as mental hospitals. This term refers to the treatment in institutions as a whole rather than to the treatment of institutionalized patients. Articles of this sort include "The Mental Hospital as an Institution" (3180); "Goffman's Model of Mental Illness" (2898), and "Hospital Culture as Collective Defense" (2678).

The category "Acculturation and Immigration" provided 144 references. The mental health of immigrant populations is still problematic. Zwingmann and Pfister-Ammende's recent book is an excellent summary of research in this field (Zwingmann and Pfister-Ammende: 1973). Malzberg's works on immigrants are classics (see Author Index). Other recent work includes "Children of West Indian Immigrants: Rates of Behavioral Deviance and of Psychiatric Disorder" (3587); and "Migration and Health: Adaptation Experiences of Iranian Migrants to the City of Teheran" (3602). The concept of acculturation has not been commonly used by mental health professionals. The recent upsurge of articles on the topic parallels increasing recognition of the concept and its relevance to mental health. Articles on acculturation include "The Impact of Culture Change on Mistassini Cree Youth" (3462); and "Acculturation and Changing Need Patterns in Japanese-American and Caucasian-American College Students" (3459).

The category of "Aggression" provided only 83 references, a small number in light of the importance of the concept. The aggressive drive is a core concept in psychoanalytic theory, but the paucity of articles on the topic reflects that it is a difficult one to study. World War II provoked a jump in the number of articles. Then, from 1951 to 1960, only six articles appeared. With Western involvement in Korea and Viet Nam, interest in aggression was apparently revived. Typical articles include "Societal Restrictiveness and the Presence of Outlets for the Release of Aggression" (3630); "Aggressiveness and Testosterone Levels in Man" (3557); "Frustration and Self-Aggression in Social Isolate Rhesus Monkeys" (3495); and "Assassination in Laos" (3398). Although aggression is not a popular theme, the articles demonstrate the varied approaches being utilized in its study.

"Testing Performance and Technique" is a category that includes articles dealing with a host of psychological instruments. The range of instruments literally goes from A to Z, from Adjectival Adjustment Checklist Index to Zung's Self-Rating Depression Scale. Although different instruments are needed to measure different things, the very large number of instruments probably indicates some inherent weakness in the field. Certainly, in comparison to many biological measurements the majority of psychological instruments lacks precision. For a complete listing of all the instruments used, the reader should turn to "Testing Techniques" in the Subject Index. Examples of articles in this category include "The WISC and the Mescalero Apache" (3589); "The Use of the Eysenck Personality Index with a Student Population in Uganda" (3505); "Human Figure Drawings as Indicators of Value Development Among Thai Children" (3491); and "Cross-Cultural Use of the Porteus Maze" (3463). Many of the references to testing techniques also contain indications of the performance of the group under study and consider the question of the cross-cultural applicability of various measures.

The category "Cross-Cultural Research" provided 479 references, almost all of which have been published since 1956. In fact, from 1925 to 1955, only 17 cross-cultural research articles were published. *The Journal of Cross-Cultural Psychology* was founded in 1970, and interest in cross-cultural studies is growing. Typical articles in this category include "A Cross-Cultural Study of the Affective Meanings of Color" (3162); "Differences Between National Suicide Rates" (3168); and "The Development of Short-Term and Incidental Memory: A Cross Cultural Study" (3617). The reader interested in recent work on cross-cultural research and cross-cultural perspectives in learning should see the books by Brislin et al. (1973, 1975).

"Culture, Mental Illness, and Mental Health" is a category particularly significant to the clinician. Some clinical departments of psychiatry already have professional anthropologists on their staffs, and the practice may increase. A good description of the application of anthropological insights to clinical practice is found in the series of articles recently published by the Department of Psychiatry at the University of Miami (Psychiatric Annals: 1975). Miami, of course, is a city with a large Spanish-speaking population. Ari Kiev, head of the Cornell University Program in Social Psychiatry, has written and edited several of the major texts in this area. Among his recent books are *Magic, Faith and Healing* (1964); *Curanderismo: Mexican-American Folk Psychiatry* (1968); and *Transcultural Psychiatry* (1972). The Subject Index of our bibliography lists 375 articles in this category. A representative sample includes "Culture and Mental Illness: A Social Labeling Perspective" (3616); "Transcultural Aspects of Puerto Rican Mental Illness in New York" (3583); "Suicide and Culture in Fairbanks: A Comparison of Three Cultural Groups in a Small City of Interior Alaska" (3566); "Psychosocial Study of Stammering in Egyptian Children" (3565); and "Differences Between Mental Disorders of French Canadians and British Canadians" (3563). Also included in this category are articles on culture-bound syndromes (see Subject Index), examples of which are "On the Epidemicity of Grenade-Amok" (3400); "El Susto: A Descriptive Analysis" (3228); and "Koro in a French Canadian" (3041). This last article is interesting because the koro syndrome is usually found in Asia, and its presence in Western culture raises questions about the conceptualization of culture-bound syndromes.

We have grouped together articles on "Incest," "Freudian Concepts," and the "Oedipus Complex" into one category. While Freudian concepts permeate articles in many categories, they are often central to the theme of incest and the Oedipus complex. In actual numbers this category, along with "Folklore and Dreams," is fairly small and reflects a slight but continued interest in the themes. Representative articles include "The Individual, Incest and Exogamy" (3593); "Oedipus-Interruptus: A Psychiatric-Anthropological Interface" (3485); and "Levi-Strauss and Freud: Their Structural Approach to Myths" (3184).

Although the sex drive is a central concern in psychoanalytic theory, a new interest in the themes of "Sexuality, Sex Roles, and Sex Behavior" has been stimulated by modern "liberation" movements, especially those related to women and to homosexuals. Representative articles in this category include "Male Pregnancy Symptoms and Cross-Sex Identity" (3327); "Accommodations to Purdah: The Female Perspective" (3567); "Female Personality Patterns in Two Cultures" (3226); and "Homosexuality in the Philippines and the United States: The Handwriting on the Wall" (2475).

"Values, Roles, and Attitudes" forms a large category containing 325 articles. Interest in these themes reflects a central tenet of community psychiatry; namely that local community input will have a marked influence on the success of a mental health program. Most articles consider attitudes not as broad theoretical concepts, but rather as specific measures of cultural differences and personality configurations. Studies on attitudes often incorporate implicit applications toward understanding the phenomenon of modernization. The majority of these articles deal with social attitudes as well as attitudes about ethnic identity, nationality, child rearing, and sex.

Typical articles include "U.S. and British Self-Disclosure, Anxiety, Empathy and Attitudes to Psychotherapy" (3609); "Effect of Ecology and Subjective Culture on Individual Traditional-Modern Attitude Change, Achievement Motivation, and Potential for Economic Self-Development in Japanese and Eskimo Societies" (3201); "The Effects of Differential Exposure to Modernization in the Value Orientations of Palestinians" (3603); and "A Cross-Cultural Comparison of Adolescent Perceptions of Parental Roles" (3053).

Although there are numerous articles on "Drug and Alcohol Use" in the mental health literature, we were able to identify only 101 that contained an anthropological theme. Because drug and alcohol abuse are so difficult to treat adequately, it would seem potentially profitable for mental health researchers to explore anthropological insights. Two classical articles in this field are Horton's "The Function of Alcohol in Primitive Societies: A Cross-Cultural Study" (391) and Bales's "Cultural Differences in Rates of Alcoholism" (469). The marked increase in articles in the past decade reflects the spread of the drug abuse epidemic into white, middle-class populations, as well as increased governmental support for studies related to alcoholism in ethnic groups. Representative articles include "Psychosocial Aspects of Drinking Among Coast Salish Indians" (3515); "Alcohol Sensitivity and Ethnic Background" (3482); "Peyote in the Treatment of Alcoholism Among American Indians" (3421); "Sociological and Economic Aspects of Drug Dependence in India" (2954); "The Social Structure of a Heroin Copping Community" (2813); and "Use of Alcohol and Opium by the Meo of Laos" (2916). The last article, by Joseph Westermeyer, is an example of the integrative functions of alcohol and drug abuse.

Articles on "Race and Racism" contributed only 87 references to our study, and the number of articles published over time has been relatively constant since 1925. The slight increase since 1966 probably reflects the general heightening of public concern about racism. The paucity of articles may be related to the often expressed sentiment that racism's presence is self-evident; therefore, the need is more for corrective action than for further study. Representative articles include "Skin Shade and Need for Achievement in a Multiracial Society: Jamaica, West Indies" (3383); "Conservatism, Racial Intolerance and Attitude Toward Racial Assimilation Among Whites and American Indians" (3422); "Racial Differences in Rate of Depression" (3281); and "Interracial Perception Among Black, White and Mexican-American High School Students" (3266). For the interested reader an additional bibliographic source on racism has been published by the National Institute of Mental Health (NIMH: 1972).

"Constitution and Physical Types" is a small category of only 54 articles. The number of articles has been decreasing and probably will continue to do so. The work of Sheldon and Kretchmer on body types met with initial enthusiasm but in clinical practice proved to be unsatisfactory for either diagnosis or prognosis. Recent articles include "The Differential Stereotyping of Similar Physiques" (3573); "The Development of Body-Build Stereotypes in Males" (3047); and "Body Build of Paranoid and Non-Paranoid Schizophrenic Males" (2883). It is of interest to note that the latter article reports negative results, while the former articles deal with psychological reactions related to body build rather than with the inherent mental health implications of body build per se.

The study of human beings has always been the central focus of mental health professionals who, in general, have lacked the interest, expertise, and facilities to work with "Non-Human Primates." Nevertheless, interest in this area is increasing due in great part to work done by researchers at the University of Wisconsin and Stanford University. Representative articles include "Depression in Infant Monkeys: Psychological Correlates" (3581); and "Primate Social Isolation" (3555); and the "Dynamics of Interpersonal Spacing in Monkeys and Man" (3423).

The category "Ethology" has contributed a sustained but low number of articles since 1925. The field has never been clearly defined and few universities, for example, have separate departments of ethology. Ethologists may work out of various departments such as biology, anthropology, psychology, and psychiatry. The field achieved widespread public recognition through interest in the writings of Konrad Lorenz. Formal scientific recognition was expressed by the recent granting of the Nobel Prize to several ethologists. Recent articles in this category include "Human Territoriality" (3478); "Dominance and Sexual Behavior" (3418); "Evaluative Bias in Interspecies Comparison" (3401); and "An Application of Ethology to Aspects of Human Behavior" (3358).

"General Physical Anthropology" has received little consideration and interest in mental health journals. This category contains a wide variety of themes and includes such recent articles as "Information Detection Through Differential Galvanic Skin Responses in Bedouins of the Israeli Desert" (3278); "Physiological Effects of Social Environments" (3527); and "The Influence of Heat Upon Intellectual Test Performance and Cardiac Activity of Three Goups in the Negev Desert" (3596).

"Social Class, Economy, and Politics" is a wide-ranging category and includes articles with a sociological theme. Economy and politics have been peripheral concerns of mental health professionals. The study of economics is so complex that few mental health professions have ventured into it. Brenner's book, *Mental Illness and the Economy,* appears to be a major contribution to the field, but it is extremely difficult to understand unless one is an economist well versed in statistics (Brenner: 1973). Typical articles in this category include "Subjective Culture and Economic Development" (3384); "The Black Family and Social Class" (3625); "A Social Class Dependent Factor in Questionnaire Research" (3312); and "Personal Values and Political Affiliation Within Italy" (2522).

The category "Family, Kinship, and Marriage" demonstrates a rapid increase in articles over the past decade. The large numbers of articles appearing in this category in recent years are partly a reflection of an increased interest in the family and family therapy, but may also be an artifact of our inclusion of specialist journals in our survey. The specialty journals included in our study began publishing in 1938 (*Journal of Marriage and the Family*), 1952 (*Family Coordinator*), and 1962 (*Family Process*). Although these are journals with which some mental health professionals are familiar, there are many more journals in this field. A fair number of articles in this category are of an anecdotal nature, but more scientific studies are appearing with regularity and should continue to do so. Typical articles include "Birth Order in Child Psychiatric Referrals and Kibbutz Family Structure" (3569); "A Note on the Authoritarian German Family" (3532); "Urban Kinship Ties in South India" (3580); and "Type of Marriage and Residential Choices in an African City" (3604). A helpful bibliography on marriage and the family was published by Aldous and Hill in 1967.

The "Language and Communication" category provides 183 references and shows a steady increase over time. Deficiencies in communication have been a focus of various theories about the etiology of some mental disorders. As a research tool the Semantic Differential (38 references) has made a modest impact on mental health studies and may be useful in evaluation of therapy. Representative articles in this category include "A Note on Sex Differences on the Semantic Differential" (3558); "Proxemic Behavior of Primary School Children as a Function of Their Socioeconomic Class and Subculture" (3592); "The Effect of Cross-Cultural Communication on Small Group Behavior in Thailand" (3320); and "The Family and Bilingual Socialization: A Sociolinguistic Study of a Sample of Chinese Children in the United States" (3535).

Our last category, "Cognition," has contributed 173 articles, of which 120 were published within the last decade. This increase reflects a growing interest in cognitive processes by mental health professionals whose primary emphasis has usually been on affective processes. In child development studies the concepts of Piaget have gained acceptance and are seen as complementary to those of Freud. Representative articles in this broad category include "Three Dimensions of Intellectual Functioning in Australian Aboriginal and Disadvantaged European Children" (3607); "Comparing Dimensional Categorization in Natural and Artificial Concepts: A Developmental Study Among the Zinacantecos of Mexico" (3499); and "Achievement Values, Cognitive Style and Social Class" (3239).

The Annotations

Because of the wide variance in the themes, approaches, and quality of the articles we have identified, the task of providing meaningful annotations was quite problematic. We attempted neither to interpret the content of articles nor to judge their validity or value. This task belongs to the interested reader. The number of articles is so large that we thought it wise to keep our annotations brief. We have generally stressed the major conclusions of articles rather than the methodology used to arrive at these conclusions. In lengthy and complex articles we chose to annotate the major themes rather than to be all inclusive. We have, whenever possible, used phrases and words in our annotations that appear in the original articles, thus better presenting to the reader the tone of the articles and of the period in which they were written. This approach at times results in somewhat strange sentences. In Pfeister's article, "Instinctive Psychoanalysis Among the Navahos," for example, our annotation includes the following sentence: "The primitive unconscious hears the for-help-calling voice of the unconscious of suffering persons, and instinctively derives psychotherapeutic practices." We could have rewritten this sentence, but as it stands it gives the reader a clear flavor of the article. The articles are not uniform, and we feel that a uniform annotative style would actually put the reader at a disadvantage. Perhaps we have sacrificed some editorial clarity in order to make the annotations more meaningful.

The annotations are listed chronologically, and alphabetically by senior author within each year. In the final editing of the manuscript we decided not to include 10 articles, necessitating an occasional skip in the numbering. The total number of actual annotations is 3624.

Comments

Research done in a library lacks the glamour of fieldwork, the excitement of clinical work, and the status of laboratory work. For well over a year each of us spent several hours, almost daily, in the stacks of the medical and general libraries of the University of Missouri—Columbia. We also utilized the libraries of the University of Nebraska and Washington University in St. Louis. To the staff of these libraries we express our thanks for their cooperation, patience, and encouragement.

In examining thousands of volumes of journals one's mind is exposed to an almost overwhelming barrage of stimuli. The mental discipline and physical endurance necessary to complete our task was far greater than we had anticipated. Unfortunately, we could discover no shortcuts.

One very positive aspect of our work was the opportunity to become aware of the historical development of psychiatry and psychology. Archaeologists make a fuss about context; as bibliographers we experienced a certain exhilaration in chancing upon famous articles in their original "setting." Although the words are exactly the same when an article is reprinted in a modern anthology, the truly interested reader should go back to the original volume to examine an article in the context of other articles, editorial comments, and advertisements that surround it.

During long hours in dusty carrels one develops an appreciation for lighter moments. In one article on body types, for example, the author was comparing groups of patients graphically. His concluding statement was, "In every curve the females were identical." In another article the author compared college students with "more mature American Legion types." The influence of the times was apparent in the national character articles which were stimulated by World War II. The Chinese were portrayed as kindly, gracious, cheerful, rational, calm, secure, and deeply considerate of others, while our enemies, the Japanese, were described as fanatical, arrogant, sadomasochistic, suspicious, pedantic, and obsessed with pathological obscenity and anal sexuality. In a somewhat confusing article on the inner experience of culture, the author exhorts the mental health worker "to think about what he thinks about in order that he may think about what the patient thinks about." Then there is perhaps our favorite article, which is a critique of a study on simian intelligence. The author notes, "In view of the lack of any adequate control of extraneous cues and the failure of other investigators to obtain remotely similar results, the achievements of the monkey of Liege must be classed with the horses of Elberfeld, and the dog of Mannheim" (see annotation 276). A close rival as favorite is the one entitled "Hamburger Hoarding: A Case of Symbolic Cannibalism Resembling Whitico Psychosis" (see annotation 1823).

Some articles make a point briskly and stimulate the reader. In an article on animal communication, for example, the author notes that the transmission of information involves all animals, from slime molds to man (see annotation 1962). Other articles tend to ramble. In one article, for example, on mythology, the author writes that the sun is a foil onto which ancient man projected many anxiety coping methods, thus processing the sun as if it were a gastro-intestinal or a vaginal continent (see annotation 1562).

Some authors are resolute, even though they are wrong. Thus, the famous Scandinavian psychiatrist Langfeldt noted: "The diagnosis and differentiation of constitutional types enables one to understand the personality itself, as well as the pathological reactions, without any deeper analysis being necessary" (see annotation 789). Other authors, such as Geza Roheim, pack so much fascinating information into an article that it is difficult to untangle the webs they weave. Ernest Becker is an author who, although sometimes vague, can penetrate the reader to the quick. He notes, for example, that "by allowing mental deviants to live, modern society is threatened by the transparency of the culturally fabricated meanings from which humans draw sustenance."

This book then, is a compilation of sustenance-giving, transparent, culturally fabricated meanings as perceived by authors in mental health journals. In these pages you can learn about schizophrenia and Sarawak, about singing societies in San Francisco, about the relationship between barley and wedding rings, about monkeys and Magdalenian art, about New York City and Pukapuka Atoll. For the psychiatrist and the psychologist, discovery of the diversity of anthropological and cross-cultural material already published in the mental health literature may come as somewhat of a surprise. The anthropologist unfamiliar with the vast mental health literature may be equally surprised at the abundance of material published on topics of concern.

Anthropologists will benefit by familiarizing themselves with the diverse cross-cultural subject matter and approaches of specific articles that form a major contribution to the mental health literature. Psychiatrists will benefit from the realization that anthropological themes are not only a significant part of psychiatry's history, but also a potentially significant part of psychiatry's future.

The clinician may find the bibliography helpful in understanding patients from diverse cultural backgrounds, e.g., with exchange students or patients from subcultures.

As Zilboorg noted in 1943 (see annotation 404), "Sociology and anthropology are increasingly intertwined with psychiatry." Thirty-three years later we can note that, while sociology and psychiatry have come together—largely because of the community mental health movement—anthropology and psychiatry are still not closely allied. Hopefully this book will be a step forward in bringing the two disciplines together.

References

Aldous J, Hill R: International Bibliography of Research in Marriage and the Family, 1900, 1974. Minneapolis, University of Minnesota Press, 1967.

Brenner H: Mental Illness and the Economy. Cambridge, Mass, Harvard University Press, 1973.

Brislin RW, Lonner WJ, Thorndike RM: Cross-Cultural Research Methods. New York, John Wiley and Sons, 1973.

Brislin RW, Bochner S, Lonner WJ (eds): Cross-Cultural Perspectives in Learning. New York, Halsted Press, 1975.

Brody EB: The Lost Ones: Social Forces and Mental Illness in Rio de Janeiro. New York, International Universities Press, 1973.

Carothers JC: The African Mind in Health and Disease, A Study in Ethno-Psychiatry. WHO Monograph Series, Geneva, 1953.

Carothers JC: The Mind of Man in Africa. London, Stacey Press, 1972.

Cawte J: Medicine is the Law: Studies in Psychiatric Anthropology of Australian Tribal Societies. University Press of Hawaii, 1974.

Driver E: The Sociology and Anthropology of Mental Illness. University of Massachusetts Press, 1972.

Favazza A: Feral and isolated children, in Mental Health in Children, Vol. I. Edited by S. Sankar. New York, PJD Publications, 1975.

Galdston I (ed): The Interface Between Psychiatry and Anthropology. New York, Brunner/Mazel, 1971.

Harris M: The Rise of Anthropological Theory. New York, Crowell, 1968.

Joint Commission on Mental Illness and Health: Action for Mental Health. New York, Basic Books, 1961.

Levy R: The Tahitians. Chicago, University of Chicago Press, 1973.

Lumsden DP: On "transcultural psychiatry," Africans, and academic racism. American Anthropologist 78(1): 101–104, 1976.

NIMH: Bibliography on Racism. DHEW Publication No. (HSM) 73–9012, Washington, D.C., 1972.

Padilla A, Aranda P: Latino Mental Health: Bibliography and Abstracts. DHEW Publication No. (HSM) 73–9144, Washington, D.C., 1974.

Psychiatric Annals 5(8), August 1975.

Zwingmann CA, Pfister-Ammende M: Uprooting and After. New York, Springer-Verlag, 1973.

Abbreviations of Journals

Acta Psychiatr Scand—*Acta Psychiatra Scandinavica*
Acta Psychiatr Neurol—*Acta Psychiatra et Neurologica*
Am Imago—*American Imago*
Am J Orthopsychiatry—*American Journal of Orthopsychiatry*
Am J Psychiatry—*American Journal of Psychiatry*
Am J Psychoanal—*American Journal of Psychoanalysis*
Am J Psychol—*American Journal of Psychology*
Am J Psychother—*American Journal of Psychotherapy*
Arch Gen Psychiatry—*Archives of General Psychiatry*
Arch Neuro Psychiatry—*Archives of Neurological Psychiatry*
Behav Sci—*Behavioral Science*
Br J Med Psychol—*British Journal of Medical Psychology*
Br J Psychiatry—*British Journal of Psychiatry*
Br J Psychol—*British Journal of Psychology*
Br J Soc Clin Psychol—*British Journal of Social & Clinical Psychology*
Bull Menninger Clin—*Bulletin of the Menninger Clinic*
Can Psychiatr Assoc J—*Canadian Psychiatric Association Journal*
Child Dev—*Child Development*
Community Ment Health J—*Community Mental Health Journal*
Compr Psychiatry—*Comprehensive Psychiatry*
Dis Nerv Syst—*Diseases of the Nervous System*
Fam Life Coordinator—*Family Life Coordinator*
Fam Process—*Family Process*
Hosp Community Psychiatry—*Hospital & Community Psychiatry*
Int J Addict—*International Journal of the Addictions*
Int J Psychiatr—*International Journal of Psychiatry*
Int J Psychoanal—*International Journal of Psycho-analysis*
Int J Psychoanal Psychother—*International Journal of Psychoanalytic Psychotherapy*
Int J Psychol—*International Journal of Psychology*
Int J Soc Psychiatry—*International Journal of Social Psychiatry*
J Abnorm Soc Psychol—*Journal of Abnormal and Social Psychology*
J Am Acad Child Psychiatry—*Journal of American Academy of Child Psychiatry*
J Am Psychoanal Assoc—*Journal of the American Psychoanalytic Association*
J Child Psychol Psychiatry—*Journal of Child Psychology & Psychiatry & Allied Disciplines*
J Clin Psychol—*Journal of Clinical Psychology*
J Consult Clin Psychol—*Journal of Consulting and Clinical Psychology*
J Cross-Cultural Psychol—*Journal of Cross-Cultural Psychology*
J Hist Behav Sciences—*Journal of the History of Behavioral Sciences*
J Marriage Fam—*Journal of Marriage and the Family*
J Ment Science—*Journal of Mental Science*
J Nerv Ment Dis—*Journal of Nervous Mental Disease*
J Pers Assess—*Journal of Personality Assessment*
J Pers Soc Psychol—*Journal of Personality & Social Psychology*
J Proj Techniques—*Journal of Projective Techniques*
J Psychiatr Res—*Journal of Psychiatric Research*

J Psychol—*Journal of Psychology*
J Psychosom Res—*Journal of Psychosomatic Research*
J Soc Psychol—*Journal of Social Psychology*
Marriage Fam Living—*Marriage and Family Living*
Psyche—*Psyche*
Psychiatry—*Psychiatry*
Psychiatr Q—*Psychiatric Quarterly*
Psychoanal Q—*Psychoanalytical Quarterly*
Psychoanal Rev—*Psychoanalytic Review*
Psychoanal Study Child—*Psychoanalytic Study of the Child*
Psychoanal Study Society—*Psychoanalytic Study of Society*
Psychol Bull—*Psychological Bulletin*
Psychol Monographs—*Psychological Monographs: General and Applied*
Psychol Rep—*Psychological Reports*
Psychometrika—*Psychometrika*
Psychosom Med—*Psychosomatic Medicine*
Psychosomatics—*Psychosomatics*
Psychother Psychosom—*Psychotherapy and Psychosomatics*
Psychol Med—*Psychological Medicine*
Q J Stud Alcohol—*Quarterly Journal of Studies on Alcohol*
Rorschach Res Exch—*Rorschach Research Exchange*
Soc Sci Med—*Social Science and Medicine*
Soc Psychiatry—*Social Psychiatry*

ANNOTATIONS

1925

1. Allport FH: The psychological bases of social science. Psychol Bull 22:561–574.

Though frought with disputes and misunderstandings, the liaison between psychology and anthropology seems interesting and full of promise.

2. Berkely-Hill O: Hindu-Muslim unity. Int J Psychoanal 6:282–287.

Disunity derives from Hindu hatred, which is a response both to Muslim violation of the Hindu mother-land, and to Muslim ceremonial cow killing, which violates the cow totem and totemic worship.

3. Garth TR: A review of racial psychology. Psychol Bull 22:343–364.

Studies seem to indicate the mental superiority of the white race. Investigators recognize, however, that experimental results are crude and must be considered tentative.

4. Jones E: Mother-right and the sexual ignorance of savages. Int J Psychoanal 6:109–130.

Malinowski's Trobriand data shows that there is a relationship between mother-right and ignorance of paternal procreation. Freud's concept of the Oedipus complex is reaffirmed by the mother-right system, and the avunculate, which is a deflected defense.

5. White WA: Primitive mentality and the racial unconscious. Am J Psychiatry 81:663–671.

The field of awareness, the foreconscious, the personal unconscious, intrauterine, and psychoanalytic and the racial unconscious are inextricably interwoven. Psychological phenomena may be explained on the basis of any of these levels; however, for complete explanations the archaic contributions of the racial unconscious are significant.

1926

6. Adams GS, Kanner L: General paralysis among the North American Indians. Am J Psychiatry 83:125–133.

The rarity of general paralysis among American Indians belies the theory of the New World as the origin of syphilis. If after a long period of time the spirochete loses the power of producing general paralysis in one race, it might lose its effect with time on another race.

7. Landis C: National differences in conversation. J Abnorm Soc Psychol 21:354–357.

A comparison of conversations between males in England and those in the United States indicates the same direction of interests. Englishmen direct their conversations to female interests when conversing with women, while American females' conversations with men are male-interest oriented. Conversations in London have greater variety than in the United States.

8. Mukherjee KC: Sex in Tantras. J Abnorm Soc Psychol 21:65–74.

Sex in the Tantras may be psychodynamically interpreted.

9. Roheim G: The scapegoat. Psychoanal Rev 13:235–236.

Certain ideas in the Sedna-sopa of the Eskimos are connected with the concept of the scapegoat and the remission of sins.

10. Stratton GM: Emotion and the incidence of disease. J Abnorm Soc Psychol 21:19–23.

The connection between anger and fear is clearer with disease in general, rather than with a particular disease. Disease may lower constitutional resistance and the threshold of anger response.

11. Wertheimer FI, Hesketh FE: Observations and remarks on the physical constitution of female psychiatric patients. Am J Psychiatry 83:499–506.

The recognition of female body types is more complicated than of the male. Better techniques are necessary before anthropometic techniques can be applied to the problem of correlation with nosological types.

1927

12. Cheney CO: The psychology of mythology. Psychiatr Q 1:198–209.

Myth or mythology in general is the product of the longings, cravings, and wishes of mankind existing under varying conditions and is analogous to the longings, cravings, or wishes of children, to dreams of adults, and to delusional ideas of persons with mental disorder.

13. Clark LP: A critical discussion of the constitutional anomalies of epileptics. Psychiatr Q 1:26–43.

There is no constant physical substrate for the epileptic constitution, and anthropological data as yet offer no line of demarcation.

14. Davies M, Hughes AG: An investigation into the comparative intelligence and attainment of Jewish and non-Jewish school children. Br J Psychol 18:134–146.

Jewish boys in London are superior in general intelligence and attainment in English and arithmetic to non-Jewish elementary school children.

15. Farr C: Body structure, personality and reaction types. Am J Psychiatry 84:231–244.

The association of personality trends with certain physical characteristics may be an accident of inheritance, may have a linkage with internal secretions, or may exemplify behavior conditioned after birth by a well-developed or ill-nourished body.

16. Johnson GD: Double meaning in the popular Negro blues. J Abnorm Soc Psychol 22:12–20.

Double meaning in Negro blues is of an overt sexual nature, due to the fact that blues generally deal with male-female relationships.

17. Klineberg O: Racial differences in speed and accuracy. J Abnorm Soc Psychol 22:273–277.

Use of speed as an indicator of excellence is unfair in cultures where speed is unimportant. The superior performance of Yakima Indian children suggests that previous findings of poor performance may be the result of inadequate control for language and education.

18. Malinowski B: Prenuptial intercourse between sexes in the Trobriand Islands, S.W. Melanesia. Psychoanal Rev 14:20–36.

The capricious intercourse of tender years becomes systematized in adolescence into more or less stable intrigues, which later on develop into lasting liaisons. The *bukumatula,* the bachelors' and unmarried girls' house, is an important institution connected with sexual life.

19. Perkins AE: Psychoses of the American Indians admitted to Gowanda State Hospital. Psychiatr Q 1:335–343.

Among hospitalized American Indians there is a striking preponderance of manic-depressive psychoses, few alcoholic psychoses in spite of intemperance, and a lack of dementia praecox. Auditory and visual hallucinations in the benign psychoses are prominent. Despite modern educational efforts, Indians readily revert to conditions insufferable to an educated person.

20. Tilney F: The brain of prehistoric man. Arch Neurol Psychiatry 17:723–769.

Traced through all their intermediate steps upward, the prefrontal and frontal regions of the brain manifest the most conspicuous development. Probably the brain of modern man represents some intermediate stage in the ultimate development of the master organ of life.

21. Willey MW, Herskovits MJ: Psychology and culture. Psychol Bull 24:253–283.

A valid understanding of the development and significance of culture in the life of human beings stands largely on a conception of the interplay between the psyche of the individual in a culture and the culture of which he is a part.

22. Yerkes RM: A program of anthropoid research. Am J Psychol 39:181–199.

A program of anthropoid research should include work in the field or natural habitat, in the breeding and observation station, and in special laboratories.

1928

23. Armstrong WE: Social constructiveness. Br J Psychol 18:396–399.

The only cultural changes that may be termed constructive are the result of individual responses, not a trend of development.

24. Bartlett FC: Social constructiveness. Br J Psychol 18:388–391.

Various social factors operate within a group to modify or elaborate imported customs and evolve new forms. Constructiveness proceeds through a general trend of development that may not be fully realized by group members.

25. Bunker H, Meyers S: An anthropometric study of general paralysis. Am J Psychiatry 84:1015–1073.

Constitutional differences as detected by anthropological measurement account for differences in individual susceptibility and the racial peculiarities of neurosyphilis.

26. Darlington HS: The secret of the birth of iron. Int J Psychoanal 9:71–95.

The iron-working activities, taboos, and rituals of the Bakitara of East Africa are laden with sexual symbolism, which is carried over into the spiritual realm.

27. Gibbs CE: Value of constitution study in mental defect and disease. Psychiatr Q 2:49–58.

Anthropometry may become helpful to the psychiatrist if, instead of classifying end results, it leads to a new focus on processes that result in psychical makeup and physical deficits. The study of brain development is a paramount need.

28. Hadden AC: Social constructiveness. Br J Psychol 18:400–404.

Social adaptation is latent in the majority of individuals in a group, but there is no reason to assume a group consciousness or group mind.

29. Hocart AM: A theory of the smile. Psyche 8: 89–91.

Man's smile has been retained as an index of his mind.

30. Kanner L: The tooth as a folkloristic symbol. Psychoanal Rev 15:37–52.

In folklore the tooth is a sexual symbol, standing for both phallus and semen. The incest motive and bisexual fantasies again and again recur in the annals of dental folklore.

31. Lehman HC, Witty PA: Some compensatory mechanisms of the Negro. J Abnorm Soc Psychol 23:28–37.

Frequency of Negro children's participation in boxing play illustrates compensatory behavior and striving for mastery.

32. Lima M: Race differences in intelligence in Minnesota. J Abnorm Soc Psychol 23:68–71.

Various showings of intelligence for many immigrant nationalities cannot be accounted for by environment and language handicaps.

33. MacCurdy JT: Social constructiveness. Br J Psychol 18:392–395.

Whether there is evidence for group consciousness in group behavior may be a question for anthropologists to answer.

34. Pollock HM: Running amuck. Psychiatr Q 2: 102–103.

Van Loon suggests that the Malayan is unusually prone to emotionalism and suggestibility which, when combined with infections peculiar to the island, may result in a drama called running amuck. The psychoses of Oriental countries should not be compared with those of the Occident.

35. Roheim G: The gods of primitive man and the religion of the Andamanesian pygmies. Psychoanal Rev 15:105–106.

Australian primitives are hysterically-genitally oriented, while the pygmies are rather pregenital and like the neurotic of the compulsion type.

36. Sapir E: Observations on the sex problem in America. Am J Psychiatry 85:519–534.

In comparing American sexual attitudes and practices with those of primitive and other cultures, sexual problems can be examined from a cultural, as well as an individual, viewpoint.

37. Seligman CG: The unconscious in relation to anthropology. Br J Psychol 18:373–387.

The unconscious may be studied by way of dreams, neuroses and abnormal conditions, and myth, legend, and ritual. Primitive people are generally extrovert. Type dreams indicate the independent origin of similar beliefs and customs. Castration fear of neurotics, circumcision ritual, and tooth extraction in Africa and Australia are the results of the same unconscious motivations. The primitive's exaggerated fear of incest is equivalent to the incestuous fears of European psychoneurotics.

38. Vetter GB: The incest taboo. J Abnorm Soc Psychol 23:232–260.

Incest taboos derive from the interactions of common human behavior, the erotic conditioning of the child, and not from some awareness of its genetic implications.

1929

39. Beckham AS: Is the Negro happy? J Abnorm Soc Psychol 24:186–190.

The Negro complex, an emotional sublimation that escapes from reality, permits the Negro to simulate happiness and thus endure his social and economic slavery.

40. Crow WB: Heredity and memory. Psyche 9: 53–60.

Instincts and wishes may be seen as the tendency of the organism to pass from one state of development to another.

41. McCartney JL: Epilepsy among the Chinese with the analysis of a case. Psychoanal Rev 16: 12–27.

Following psychotherapy an upper-class Chinese woman ceased experiencing epileptiform seizures.

42. Potter G: Freudian concepts among early American Indians. Int J Psychoanal 10:100–101.

The concept of the unconscious as the cause of illness is incorporated into the American Indian theory of disease, as shown in the communications of early missionary observers.

1930

43. Briffault R: Instinct, heredity, and social tradition. J Soc Psychol 1:191–226.

Human social values are related to social conditions and are opposed to presocial and nonsocial instincts. Social-instinct values derive from maternal instinct. Values derived from social instincts appear antagonistic to presocial animal instincts.

44. Calverton VF: Modern anthropology and the theory of cultural compulsives. Psyche 10:43–62.

Pure objectivity in the social sciences is impossible due to the doctrine of cultural compulsives as exemplified in the doctrine of the success of evolution and the prevailing of monogamy over other forms of marriage.

45. Clements F: Notes on the construction of mental tests for American Indians. J Soc Psychol 1: 542–548.

Individual, rather than group, tests consisting of familiar verbal and performance elements are most suitable for the Zuni, and probably all American Indians. Children living on the reservation are preferred subjects compared to children at boarding schools.

46. Dhunjibhoy JE: A brief résumé of the types of insanity commonly met with in India, with a full description of "Indian hemp insanity" peculiar to the country. J Ment Science 76: 254–264.

Hindus in Bengal, Bihar, and Orissa offer bhang to guests on festive occasions. In India, hemp drugs taken over a prolonged period produce a special form of mental disorder.

47. Furukawa T: A study of temperament and blood-groups. J Soc Psychol 1:494–509.

There appears to be a correlation between blood type and temperament. This observation has potential value for the fields of education, psychology, medicine, and eugenics. Suicides in Prussia have the Gr.A. blood type.

48. Garth TR: A review of race psychology. Psychol Bull 27:329–356.

The hypothesis of racial difference is not yet established, and many psychologists seem ready to work on the hypothesis of racial equality.

49. Lamb EO: Racial differences in bi-manual dexterity of Latin and American children. Child Dev 1:204–231.

Mexican children develop early skill in manipulation greater than that of the average American children.

50. Lehman HC, Witty PA: Racial differences: the dogma of superiority. J Soc Psychol 1:394–418.

There are greater individual differences within races than between races. Generalizations of inferior intelligence for a racial group are premature.

51. MacCurdy JT: The biological significance of blushing and shame. Br J Psychol 21:174–182.

Shame represents an instinctive seeking for cover in the dangerous or sexual situation by primitive man. Shame in connection with other activities results from the functioning of symbolism.

52. Malzberg B: Mental disease and "the melting pot." J Nerv Ment Dis 72:379–395.

When corrected for sex and age, the natives of native parentage have the lowest rate of first admissions to mental hospitals, the foreign-born the highest. The differing rates have often been attributed to heredity, but differences in environmental or cultural origin seem more important.

53. Schmindeberg M: The role of psychotic mechanisms in cultural development. Int J Psychoanal 11:387–418.

Primitive man's resemblance to psychotics may be examined in terms of concepts of illness, demon possession, healing through the medicine men, and magic. Lack of cultural development is a consequence of ambivalence, excessive anxieties, and psychotic mechanisms.

54. Schroeder T: Witchcraft and the erotic life. J Nerv Ment Dis 72:640–651.

The trial of Father Grandier in 1634 in France reveals that his witchcraft consisted in the fact that nuns and other deprived women had erotic fantasies, in which Father Grandier officiated as would their physical lover, if they could ever have tolerated a physical lover. Having first been infected with ecclesiastical erotophobia, these women were compelled to defend themselves strenuously against the possible imputation that their fantasmal eroticisms were the product of their own organic need.

55. Sharpe E: Certain aspects of sublimation and delusion. Int J Psychoanal 11:12–23.

Paleolithic cave art and other artistic expressions are early examples of sublimation and the delusion of omnipotence.

56. Winch WH: Christian and Jewish children in East-End elementary schools. Br J Psychol 20:261–273.

In the East-End, Jewish children are intellectually superior to Christian children, mostly due to superiority of social class.

57. Young K: Sex differences in certain immigrant groups. J Soc Psychol 1:227–247.

Sex differences in the performance of Portuguese, Italian, and Spanish-American youths on the Army Alpha and Beta are variable, though in all groups the girls surpass the boys on the Alpha.

1931

58. Boehm F: The history of the Oedipus complex. Int J Psychoanal 12:431–451.

Brief consideration of Greek, Egyptian, and American Indian creation myths, and socialization customs of primitive versus contemporary society, shows that the typical Oedipus complex is universal.

59. Garth TR, Ikeda K, Langdon RM: The color preferences of Japanese children. J Soc Psychol 2: 397–402.

Japanese children do not discriminate preference for color as clearly as do other racial groups. The color white is a common point of origin for all races.

60. Kappers CUA: The brain in prehistoric and recent races. Acta Psychiatr Neurol 6:505–528.

Knowledge of the brain of prehistoric races is restricted to the study of endocranial casts. Registered differences do not imply an evaluation of the brain of various races, a subject in which great mistakes have been made as a result of racial prejudice or a priori viewpoints.

61. Lang HB: A note on maternal behavior in two female virgin dogs. Psychiatr Q 5:649–651.

A female virgin dog with masculine activities and tendencies shows a protective attitude toward toys perceived as puppies, while a more feminine behaving dog not only protects substituted young, but is uneasy away from them and becomes irritable when mammary tension is not relieved by nursing.

62. Luh CW, Wu TM: A comparative study of the intelligence of Chinese children on the Pinter Performance and the Binet tests. J Soc Psychol 2: 402–408.

Chinese-American children have the same degree of performance intelligence as American children, insofar as the Pinter norms apply to the American group.

63. Robson GM: Social factors in mental retardation. Br J Psychol 22:118–135.

The difficulties of backward or retarded children are based upon a social defect—relative inability to interpret others' behavior and share in their experience.

64. Rumyaneck J: The comparative psychology of Jews and non-Jews: survey of the literature. Br J Psychol 21:404–426.

The intellectual superiority or psychological uniqueness of the Jew is as yet unsubstantiated, despite claims of observed innate differences.

65. Sumner FC, Sumner FH: Mental health of white and Negro college students. J Abnorm Soc Psychol 26:28–36.

The correlation coefficient between symptom frequency of the Negro college student and House's Normals is 0.75, while that between Negroes and House's Psychoneurotics is 0.47.

66. Todd WT: Differential skeletal maturation in relation to sex, race, variability and disease. Child Dev 2:49–65.

The skeleton follows a developmental pattern which is not obscured by sex modifications. Local living conditions affect the child's physical status but are reflected more in measurements of height and weight than in skeletal differentiation.

1932

67. Banister H: Sentiment and social organization. Br J Psychol 22:242–249.

The foundation of group behavior lies in capacity for organization, or the sentiment-formulation tendency that is innate in man and many other animals.

68. Becker H, Braner DK: Some aspects of taboo and totemism. J Soc Psychol 3:337–353.

An alternate hypothesis to Freud's theories and anthropological criticisms is that neurotic or psychotic individuals of shamanistic rank imposed upon themselves and others taboos that became culturally integrated. Other neurotics later added totem belief, followed by group extension of totem and taboo, and finally rites of sacrifice to the Father-totem.

69. Brown F: A socio-psychological analysis of race prejudice. J Abnorm Soc Psychol 27:364–374.

Racial prejudice arises in the conflicts and dynamics of dominant and subordinate habitats. Movement of the subordinate group into the dominant realm initiates defense mechanisms by the dominant group.

70. Campbell KJ: The relation of the type of physique to the types of mental diseases. J Abnorm Soc Psychol 27:147–151.

Height and weight curves in four of six comparisons for manics and praecox patients are essentially the same, although the male manics average 10 pounds heavier than the male praecox. In every curve the females were identical.

71. Daly CD: Pre-human psychic evolution: a hypothetical theory of the psychological evolution of our species in pre-glacial, glacial, and early postglacial epochs. Br J Med Psychol 12:273–286.

The absence of profuse bleeding in the human female is the result of the suppression of conjugation at the time of the prehuman or early females' period in "heat." The psychic origins of this as well as other physiologic characteristics can be traced as far as the preglacial epoch.

72. Darlington HS: Garden magic. Psychoanal Rev 19:168–181.

Myths related to gardens in many cultures can be interpreted sexually. Mother Earth generally is supposed to be fertilized by the lightning that strikes into her.

73. Glover E: Common problems in psycho-analysis and anthropology: drug ritual and addiction. Br J Med Psychol 12:109–131.

Primitive drug rituals contain an abundance of phallic symbolism and the processes of introjection and projection operate precisely as they do in early infancy. An analytical anthropologist should complete a successful psychoanalysis, have a thorough appreciation of symbolism, dream interpretations, play technique in child analysis, and training in systematic observation of the psychoses.

74. Harvey O: The scientific study of human sexual behavior. J Soc Psychol 3:161–188.

Evaluation of the synthetic, anthropological, laboratory, and child-study procedures of direct observations and the various procedures of personal report show that personal report procedures are most productive.

75. Hollingsworth LS, Madden R: How one race judges another for physical attractiveness. J Soc Psychol 3:463–469.

Judgments of physical attractiveness by Chinese and Caucasian adolescents are very similar.

76. Josey CC, Miller CH: Race, sex, and class differences in ability to endure pain. J Soc Psychol 3:374–376.

Differences between northern and southern Europeans, American Indians, Jews, and Negroes in ability to endure pain are noted by doctors.

77. Odegaard O: Emigration and insanity. Acta Psychiatr Neurol, Suppl. 4, 1–206.

The overwhelming majority of the insane immigrants from Norway are senile and arteriosclerotic or schizophrenic. The old belief in emigration to America as the best treatment for peculiar, troublesome, unmanageable, and maladjusted youngsters is a fallacy.

78. Oliver RAC: The musical talent of natives of East Africa. Br J Psychol 22:333–343.

Africans are superior to American adolescents in the sense of intensity, time, and rhythm; and inferior in sense of pitch, consonance, and memory for tones on the Seashore Measures of Musical Talent.

79. Pfister O: Instinctive psychoanalysis among the Navahos. J Nerv Ment Dis 76:234–254.

The Navahos, like other primitive peoples, possess a deep understanding of hidden meanings. The primitive unconscious hears the for-help-calling voice of the unconscious of suffering persons and instinctively derives psychotherapeutic practices.

80. Pitner R: The influence of language background on intelligence tests. J Soc Psychol 3:235–240.

Verbal intelligence tests must consider the language background of the subjects. Individuals from bilingual environments may not indicate their maximum intelligence on verbal tests.

81. Pratt KC: A note on the relation of activity to sex and race in young infants. J Soc Psychol 3:118–120.

Sex and race are negligible factors in general body activity of the newborn.

82. Richards IA: Human nature: an early Chinese argument. Psyche 12:62–77.

The dialogue between Mencius and Koa Tzu allows a comparison between Chinese and Western philosophical methods and concepts of the mind.

83. Roheim G: Animism and religion. Psychoanal Q 1:59–112.

Man's gods age with him, and the youthful spirits of the Australian desert are replaced by a greybeard, Jahve, or the conventional representation of the Christian God replaces the images of Ares and Apollo.

84. Roheim G: Psychoanalysis of primitive cultural types. Int J Psychoanal 13:2–224.

The psychoanalytic ethnography of the Central Australians, the Papuans, and the national character of the Somali may be examined in terms of the unconscious content of myth, ritual, sexual customs, and dreams.

85. Sapir E: Cultural anthropology and psychiatry. J Abnorm Soc Psychol 27:229–242.

Though cultural anthropology and psychiatry have distinct problems, they can cooperate in highly significant ways. Cultural anthropology is valuable because it constantly rediscovers the normal. The study of other cultures furthers an understanding of the development of ideas and symbols and their relevance for the problem of personality. Cultures vary in the psychological emphasis placed on the elements and implications of manifest culture.

86. Seligman BZ: The incest barrier: its role in social organization. Br J Psychol 22:250–276.

The family, the first human group, was consolidated by the incest barrier, which has a survival value. The incest barrier is sanctioned by the omnipotence of parents and is expressed by rites of ancestor worship. Rules of incest become extended with the elaboration of clan and kinship. All marriage prohibitions are extensions of two primary incest prohibitions and generally reflect people's fear of incest.

87. Suttie ID: Religion: racial character and mental and social health. Br J Med Psychol 12:289–314.

The oscillation between the extremes of matriarchy and patriarchy is an important factor in the evolution and conflicts of cultures. It is absurd to develop separate medical, religious, educational, and social-ethnological psychologies because we deal with the same human mind in its cutural setting.

1933

88. Eder MD: The Jewish phylacteries and other Jewish ritual observances. Int J Psychoanal 14:341–375.

Jewish opinion regarding the nature and use of the fringed garment, prayer shawl, and door scroll plays a role in the unconscious life. Various psychoanalytic theories may be considered in terms of these data.

89. Gardner DA: The community of ideas in Negroes. J Soc Psychol 4:253–256.

Two white groups in Port Arthur differ as much in all respects as do the white and Negro groups.

90. Garth TR: The intelligence and achievement of mixed-blood Indians. J Soc Psychol 4:134–137.

Educational factors are stronger determinants of intelligence scores than purity of race, which has little impact.

91. Hocart AM: Evidence in human history. Psyche 13:80–93.

The understanding of human evolution is hampered by popular misconceptions of the concept of evidence. Direct and circumstantial evidence, or inference, are the foundations of science.

92. Katz D, Braly KW: Racial stereotypes of one hundred college students. J Abnorm Soc Psychol 28:280–290.

Consistency of stereotypy has little relation to prejudice.

93. Luh CW, Sailer RC: The self-estimation of Chinese students. J Soc Psychol 4:245–249.

Chinese students in Nanking show the same tendency to overestimation of self as found among American subjects.

94. McConnell UH: The symbol in legend. Psyche 13:94–137.

Studies of the symbol in legend, religion, and dreams point out the significance of symbolism, and symbol clusters, to an understanding of human cultures.

95. Rosenthal SP: Racial differences in the mental diseases. J Abnorm Soc Psychol 28:301–340.

Generalizations concerning racial differences and mental disease do not stand up to careful statistical examination.

96. Thouless RH: A racial difference in perception. J Soc Psychol 4:330–339.

There is a racial difference in perception between East Indian and British students, which is probably an explanation of difference in Western and Oriental art.

97. Vernon PE: The American vs. the German methods of approach to the study of temperament and personality. Br J Psychol 24:156–177.

The results obtained by the two schools appear to be loaded in a direction to confirm the theories of the schools. The American psychometric approach, most useful for its practical aspects, does not appeal to the German-type psychology.

98. Wile IS: Hand preference in primitive man. Am J Orthopsychiatry 3:95–112.

Stone age man was ambidextrous; a gradual tendency toward right-handedness finally resulted in physiologic domination. Left-handedness was suppressed under the demand for adaptation to changing principles of social organization, preservation, and advancement.

99. Yerkes RM: Genetic aspects of grooming, a socially important primate behavior pattern. J Soc Psychol 4:3–25.

Primate studies suggest that grooming represents a genetically important pattern of primate social response from which useful forms of social service have evolved.

1934

100. Beckham AS: A study of race attitudes in Negro children of adolescent age. J Abnorm Soc Psychol 29:18–29.

The effects of, and responses to, race prejudice and humiliation differ for delinquent and nondelinquent Negro youths.

101. Cooper JM: Mental disease situations in certain cultures—a new field for research. J Abnorm Soc Psychol 29:10–17.

Various culturally related syndromes (wihtiko, amok, and piblokto for example), illustrate the influence of cultural patterns on mental patterns. The etiology of mental illness, however, is mostly the same for primitives and civilized peoples.

102. Faris REL: Some observations on the incidence of schizophrenia in primitive societies. J Abnorm Soc Psychol 29:30–31.

The hypothesis that schizophrenia cannot occur in primitive societies, due to the nature of the social life, is partly confirmed by a field trip to the Belgian Congo and by various ethnographies.

103. Garth TR, Johnson HD: The intelligence and achievement of Mexican children in the United States. J Abnorm Soc Psychol 29:222–252.

The influence of achievement upon intelligence score is greater than that of grade placement.

104. Goldschmidt T: The menstrual taboo and woman's psychology. J Abnorm Soc Psychol 29:218–221.

There is some indication that traditional superstitions and taboos have a strong effect upon menstruating women.

105. Hallowell AI: Culture and mental disorder. J Abnorm Soc Psychol 29:1–10.

As with wihtiko psychosis among the Berens River Saulteaux, there are cultural factors that determine the particular form of mental states and operate as contributory etiological influences.

106. Henry GW: Psychogenic and constitutional factors in homosexuality: their relation to personality disorders. Psychiatr Q 8:243–264.

The homosexual patient tends to have a dysplastic constitution and an arrested sexual development and physiological level of integration. The intrusion of adult sexuality in childhood may be an important factor in a perverse psychosexual development.

107. Henry GW, Galbraith HM: Constitutional factors in homosexuality. Am J Psychiatry 13: 1249–1270.

Homosexual patients show constitutional deviations from the general average that are considerably greater than those of the heterosexually adjusted. The psychosexual histories of the two groups are conspicuously different.

108. Hocart AM: The role of consciousness in evolution. Psyche 14:160–164.

Just as consciousness plays a role in individual development, so it may in racial and cultural evolution, and therefore cannot be disregarded by the scientist.

109. Jenkins LB: Mental conflicts of Eurasian adolescents. J Soc Psychol 5:402–408.

The mixed-descent Eurasian has an "inferior" ego and an impoverished self, is an unadjusted closed personality, and experiences severe mental conflicts. Adjustment depends upon identification with his own group in order to construct a good self-image.

110. Levy-Suhl M: The early infantile sexuality of man as compared with the sexual maturity of other mammals. Int J Psychoanal 15:59–65.

Paleontological evidence indicates that sexual maturity in preglacial precursors of man was achieved at four to five years. Contemporary first onset of sexuality at five years represents phylogenetic recapitulation. The beginning of human sexuality affirmed by Freud is consistent with sexual maturity of larger mammals.

111. Manuel HT: Physical measurements of Mexican children in American schools. Child Dev 5: 237–251.

Compared with American children of the Baldwin-Wood tables, the subjects are about two inches shorter and four to seven pounds lighter. Whether the reason for these differences is race, socioeconomic status, or some other factor is not clear.

112. Middlemore M: The treatment of bewitchment in a Puritan community. Int J Psychoanal 15:41–58.

The 1692 Salem witchcraft epidemic gives clues to various therapeutic psychological mechanisms, including expulsion and replacement rituals, ceremonies of patient identification with a supernatural power, and curing rites of undoing bewitchment.

113. Patrick JR, Sims VM: Personality differences between Negro and white college students, North and South. J Abnorm Soc Psychol 29:181–201.

The white male tends to be more introverted than the Negro male, otherwise college students' performance on personality tests are very similar.

114. Roheim G: Primitive high gods. Psychoanal Q 3:3–113.

It is because our infancy lasts longer than that of other animals that we need the supernatural beings. Demons originate because the parents are not as evil as they appear to the child in the light of the primal scene, and benevolent spirits originate because the parents are not as good as sublimation would have them.

115. Roheim G: The evolution of culture. Int J Psychoanal 15:387–418.

The psychology of primitive man shows that group differences are apparent in the superego, rather than the id. The ontogenetic theory explains human culture in general as well as cultural variability. Fantasy systems are attempts to deal with infantile anxieties, and the complicated mechanisms for dealing with anxiety give rise to civilization.

116. Sapir E: The emergence of the concept of personality in a study of culture. J Soc Psychol 5: 408–415.

The cultural anthropologist cannot afford to ignore the individual in studies of personality and culture, especially in the area of child development.

117. Wolfe DL: The role of generalization in language. Br J Psychol 24:434–444.

The linguistic process of sound symbolism, word meaning, and analogic change are examples of the fundamental psychological process of generalization.

118. Yerkes RM: Suggestibility in chimpanzees. J Soc Psychol 5:271–282.

Extra-species suggestibility in chimpanzees varies with age, sexual stage, and subject-experimenter relationship. Suggestibility illustrates the phenomenon of social facilitation.

1935

119. Beveridge WM: Racial differences in phenomenal regression. Br J Psychol 26:59–62.

The West African has a higher index of phenomenal regression than the European, as measured by a test of tendency to maintain constancy of shape.

120. Boehm F: Anthropophagy: its forms and motives. Int J Psychoanal 16:9–21.

Primitive cannibalism may be compared to analytical findings on the oral stage. The principal motives of incorporation and destruction correspond to the primary oral stage (sucking) and the oral-sadistic stage, respectively, while the form is religious.

121. Chou SK, Chen HP: General versus specific color preferences of Chinese students. J Soc Psychol 6:290–314.

Color preference is a function of the colored object. There is a high correlation between general and specific color preferences. Association, tradition and language influence Chinese color preferences for white and blue.

122. Clegg JL: The association of physique and mental condition. J Ment Science 81:297–316.

There are small but significant differences in body proportions among normal, schizophrenic, and manic-depressive males.

123. Culwick AT, Culwick GM: Religious and economic sanctions in a Bantu tribe. Br J Psychol 26:183–190.

The sanctions that the Wabena believe govern their lives are not equivalent to the sanctions that actually do so. All natural phenomena, and economic behavior, are interpreted in terms of the supernatural.

124. Diserens CM, Wood TW: The concept of economic security among primitive peoples. J Soc Psychol 6:357–368.

Economic, political, and religious institutions were devised from primitive man's rationality and his fundamental need for security. Primitive communal economic behavior also represents striving for security and solidarity.

125. Empson W: The need for "translation" theory in linguistics. Psyche 15:188–198.

Leonard Bloomfield's book *Language* may occasionally lead some linguists astray in its refutation of mentalist theory.

126. Foley JP: Judgment of facial expression of emotion in the chimpanzee. J Soc Psychol 6:31–67.

Common lack of ability by humans to judge chimpanzees' emotions illustrates the need for further studies of primate behavior, especially as the behavior is influenced by cultural stimulation.

127. Katz D, Braly KW: Racial prejudice and racial stereotypes. J Abnorm Soc Psychol 30:175–198.

Ranking of ethnic groups by college students shows that racial prejudice is a generalized set of highly consistent stereotypes.

128. Lindgren EJ: Field work in social psychology. Br J Psychol 26:174–182.

The author's experience in Eastern Asia, among the Mongols and Tungus, demonstrates the need for training in fieldwork and the importance of anthropological and psychological backgrounds for the worker.

129. Malzberg B: Mental disease among foreign-born whites, with special reference to natives of Russia and Poland. Am J Psychiatry 92:627–640.

Natives of Russia and Poland who immigrated to New York State have lower rates of mental disease than the other leading foreign-born groups. Invidious comparisons of immigrant populations from a biological point of view are unjustified.

130. Malzberg B: Race and mental disease in New York State. Psychiatr Q 9:538–569.

Italians have lower rates of mental disease than all foreign-born whites, while the highest rates are found among the Irish and the Scandanavians. Racial theories should not be based only upon statistical differences; one should also consider cultural and environmental factors.

131. Mekeel HS: Clinic and culture. J Abnorm Soc Psychol 30:292–300.

The study of process and personality dynamics from the cultural point of view is most useful. Anthropologists should undergo analysis in order to better understand themselves and their research in other cultures.

132. Murray RSE: The differential aspect of semantic component in relation to psychiatry. J Nerv Ment Dis 82:525–531.

All semantic reaction should be evaluated according to the modern principles of the exact sciences. All ideas fundamentally based on erroneous semantic reaction and therefore productive of discord and disease should be rejected.

133. Nissen HW, Machover S, Kinder EF: A study of performance tests given to a group of native African Negro children. Br J Psychol 25:308–355.

Civilization-oriented performance tests are limited. Performance tests must consider cultural and environmental backgrounds of the subjects in order to be appropriately utilized.

134. Oldfield RC: Towards a functional theory of word-meaning. Psyche 15:129–137.

The meaning of words is derived from (sentence) context and is therefore structural and not functional.

135. Piotrowski Z: Racial differences in linear perspective. J Soc Psychol 6:479–484.

The differences in phenomenal regression between Indian and British students is an effect, rather than a cause, of Oriental-Western art differences.

136. Prasad J: The psychology of rumour: a study relating to the great Indian earthquake of 1934. Br J Psychol 26:1–15.

Rumor is a group response to situations affecting the whole group. Responses and solutions are dominated by emotional and imaginative factors. The determinants of rumor include the emotional nature of the situation and the group mentality of the individuals, as well as social tendencies toward comradeship and suggestion.

137. Purcell VWWS: The language problem in China. Psyche 15:88–107.

Chinese language, which derives from and gives rise to Chinese culture and thought, may undergo change with the impact of Western scientific thought.

138. Tongue ED: The contact of races in Uganda. Br J Psychol 25:356–364.

A thorough understanding of African sociology and native psychology is a requisite to development of African countries, as can be seen in an examination of the problems of law, administration, missions, education, and social-economic life in Uganda.

139. Unwin JD, Flugel JC, Money-Kyrle R: A discussion: sexual regulations and cultural behaviour. Br J Med Psychol 15–16:153–163.

Unwin's findings—that societies premitting prenuptial freedom are in a zoistic condition and behave zoistically, while societies that inflict an ir-

regular or occasional continence are in a manistic condition and behave manistically, and those societies that insist on complete prenuptial continence are in a deistic condition and behave deistically—deserve close scrutiny and further corroboration.

140. Young AM: The changing language of Japan. Psyche 15:198–204.

As Japan takes more interest in the West, its language is in the process of adopting and compiling new foreign words and concepts.

1936

141. Allport G, Odbert HS: Trait names: a psycholexical study. Psychol Monographs 47:1–171.

Psychological terms referring to personality traits may be lexically grouped. Trait names are essentially blanket terms covering one trait in an individual and similar traits in other people.

142. Baker A: Recent trends in the Nordic doctrine. J Psychol 2:151–160.

The Nordic doctrine, though a political success, is a scientific failure.

143. Carey TF: An anthropometric measuring board. Child Dev 7:57–59.

A special board can be cheaply constructed for taking various anthropometric measures.

144. Childers AT: Some notes on sex mores among Negro children. Am J Orthopsychiatry 6:442–448.

Sex mores among Negro children of the higher social level approximate those of white people. Sex customs of Negro children of the lower social level, however, are markedly different than those of whites.

145. Chou SK: Some comments on color preference of Chinese students. J Soc Psychol 7:119–121.

Color preferences are unstable and future research is required.

146. Doob L: Variability and culture. Psychol Monographs 47:375–380.

Individual variability contains the ingredients for culture change. Psychologists must recognize the significance of culture to their methodology.

147. Fritz MF: Diet and racial temperament. J Soc Psychol 7: 320–335.

Degree of activity is largely a function of inheritance rather than diet. Caution is necessary when attributing racial or national aggressiveness to dietary backgrounds, which are partly influenced by custom.

148. Garth TR, Elson TH, Morton MM: The administration of nonlanguage intelligence tests to Mexicans. J Abnorm Soc Psychol 31:53–58.

Mexican-American children are practically equal to American whites in intelligence and performance on nonverbal tests. Verbal tests, which show inferior performance, are probably unfair to Mexican children.

149. Hallowell AI: Psychic stresses and culture patterns. Am J Psychiatry 92:1291–1310.

Anthropologists, if aided by psychiatrists sensitive to the implications of culture, might well collect data on individual behavior in societies with culture patterns different from our own. Such data could have significant psychiatric implications.

150. Hunt WA: Studies of the startle pattern: bodily pattern. J Psychol 2:207–214.

The startle response to gunshot consists of a variety of involuntary bodily motions. The startle pattern is facilitated by simultaneous light and shock stimuli and instructions to react.

151. Hunt WA, Clarke F, Hunt EB: Studies of the startle pattern: infants. J Psychol 2:339–352.

Infant startle responses show that the Moro reflex is present at earliest stages but disappears around the age of four months, when the typical adult pattern appears.

152. Hunt WA, Landis C: Studies of the startle pattern: introduction. J Psychol 2:201–206.

Four types of emotional response are (1) an affective response, (2) an emotional response, (3) social responses, and (4) specific responses. Startle is the simplest initiating element in many varieties of emotion and is therefore of primary importance in the analysis of behavior.

153. Jekels L: The psychology of the festival of Christmas. Int J Psychoanal 17:57–72.

Christmas is related to early rites that served certain emotional needs. The superego-ego reaction plays a role in the development of certain Christian concepts.

154. Jones E: Psycho-analysis and the instincts. Br J Psychol 26:273–288.

The purely psychological part of Freud's instinct theory is assured, but premature biologizing of psychology is to be avoided.

155. Kerr M: Temperamental differences in twins. Br J Psychol 27:51–60.

Identical twins more often belong to the same psychological type than do fraternal twins. The difference is not great except between identical twins and unrelated pairs. The differences measured by the tests are not solely genetic but arise from the interaction of temperaments of individuals of similar genetic constitutions.

156. Korzybski A: Neuro-semantic and neuro-linguistic mechanisms of extensionalization. Am J Psychiatry 93:29–38.

The white man has never been studied on the white level. Animal, primitive, or infantile reactions have been read into the white man. General semantics, through the method of extensionalization, attempts to discern what standards of evaluation belong to the white man's level and correspond to the functioning of his nervous system.

157. Landis C, Hunt WA: Studies of the startle pattern: facial pattern. J Psychol 2:215–220.

Regular facial pattern in the startle response consists of eye closing, head movement, and movement of neck and jaw muscles. The extent of the pattern varies with individuals and with habituation.

158. Malzberg B: A statistical study of mental diseases among natives of foreign white parentage in New York State. Psychiatr Q 10:127–142.

The general picture, according to which natives of foreign stock have lower rates of mental disease than their parents but higher rates than natives of native parentage, is consistent with an environmental explanation of the prevalence of mental disease and indicates that with the passing of years, each generation is adjusting itself to conditions of life in the United States.

159. Meyers MR, Cushing HM: Types and incidence of behavior problems in relation to cultural background. Am J Orthopsychiatry 6:110–116.

Italian children have a high incidence of overt, aggressive behavior; Jewish children evidence feeding problems and seclusiveness; and American children show excessive nervous habits. These different behavior trends indicate a greater need for cultural understanding among teachers and social workers.

160. Opler ME: An interpretation of ambivalence of two American Indian tribes. J Soc Psychol 7: 82–116.

Apache ambivalence about mourning for the dead and affection for the living is the result of unconscious resentment of relatives because of the cultural settings of actual competition and conflict.

161. Razran GHS: Salivating and thinking in different languages. J Psychol 1:145–152.

The investigator measured the amount of saliva secreted when he thought of saliva in various languages. The largest amount was secreted for the Russian word, his childhood language.

162. Shelley HM, Watson WH: An investigation concerning mental disorder in the Nyasaland natives: with special reference to primary aetiological and other contributing factors. J Ment Science 82: 702–730.

A higher incidence of mental disorder exists in members of the Yao, Nyanja, and Ngoni tribes than among other Nyasaland natives. These three tribes have had more intimate contact with European civilization than those evidencing a lesser incidence of disorders. The native inmates of Central Lunatic Asylum do not show any marked variation from the normal in weight and height and cranial index.

163. Shen E: Differences between Chinese and American reactions to the Bernreuter Personality Inventory. J Soc Psychol 7:471–474.

Chinese students have high regard for modesty. Sex differences between the groups are insignificant.

164. Shen NC: A note on the color preference of Chinese students. J Soc Psychol 7:68–81.

Boys' preferences of color words are for darker colors generally, while lighter colors are preferred for specific and general objects.

165. Steggerda M, Densen P: Height, weight, and age tables for homogeneous groups: with particular reference to Navaho Indians and Dutch whites. Child Dev 7:115–120.

Navahos and Dutch whites are generally lighter in weight than American children of the same height.

166. Strecker HP: The body-length-leg ratio in the general population and in mental hospital patients and its possible significance in suicide. J Ment Science 82:38–42.

The ratio is higher in melancholics than in patients with less suicidal forms of mental illness.

167. Tofflemier G, Luomala K: Dreams and dream interpretation of the Digueno Indians of Southern California. Psychoanal Q 5:195–225.

Dreams and their interpretations are a vital part of Digueno culture. Dreams reveal to the dream doctor the patient's conflicts and desires, which are usually of a sexual nature.

168. Tyler C: The teaching of English in China. Psyche 16:178–187.

The study of English in China's secondary schools is necessary before China can take its place in the modern world.

169. Witty PA, Jenkins MD: Intra-race testing and Negro intelligence. J Psychol 1:179–193.

Intelligence-test performance is unrelated to amount of white ancestry for Negroes. Factors other than heredity contribute to average test scores.

170. Zilboorg G: Suicide among civilized and primitive races. Am J Psychiatry 92:1345–1369.

The idealization of the act of suicide among primitive races is a reassertion of one's own immortality. The solution of the psychological and biological nature of suicide will be found in the study of ethnological material.

1937

171. Beaglehole E: Emotional release in a Polynesian community. J Abnorm Soc Psychol 32:319–328.

The folktales and behavior of the inhabitants of Pukapuka Atoll suggest extraverted, repressed aggressive tendencies that are satisfied by sudden violence.

172. Braatoy T: Is it probable that the sociological situation is a factor in schizophrenia? Acta Psychiatr Neurol 12:109–138.

Denmark has a low frequency of schizophrenia while Norway has a much greater prevalence. The great fluctuations in two of the chief occupational branches in Norway—fishing and forestry—and the consequent uncertain standard of living may contribute to an explanation of these differences. The urbanization factor must be borne in mind before entering into genetic theories in explanation of an increasing frequency of schizophrenia.

173. Campbell DG: General semantics: implication of linguistic revision for theoretical and clinical neuro-psychiatry. Am J Psychiatry 93:789–807.

Linguistic factors are important determinants of personality structure, and cognizance of them is essential to any general theory of values upon which the rational treatment of personality deviation depends.

174. Chou SK, Mi CY: Relative neurotic tendency of Chinese and American students. J Soc Psychol 8:155–184.

A higher neurotic score for Chinese students in China than for American students may be due to lack of mental health services rather than actual racial differences.

175. DuBois C: Some psychological objectives and techniques in ethnography. J Soc Psychol 8:285–300.

Some considerations that must be taken into account in the appreciation of psychology to the field of anthropology include personality of the field worker, contacts with informants, linguistic factors, interviewing techniques, and number of informants.

176. Eagleson OW: Comparative studies of white and Negro subjects in learning to discriminate visual magnitude. J Psychol 4:167–198.

Negroes learn faster than whites, since their increments of gain are greater. Constant errors in discrimination of visual magnitude in both groups tend toward the right.

177. Garth TR, Smith OD: The performance of full-blood Indians on language and non-language intelligence tests. J Abnorm Soc Psychol 32:376–381.

Better performance by Indians on nonlanguage performance tests suggests that verbal tests are unfair assessments of intelligence.

178. Hunt WA, Landis C, Jacobsen CF: Studies on the startle pattern: apes and monkeys. J Psychol 3:339–344.

The startle response of infrahuman primates generally resembles the pattern for man and resembles more specific aspects of the pattern for infants.

179. Hunter M: Responses of comparable white and Negro adults to the Rorschach test. J Psychol 3:173–182.

The white group is more introversive, while the Negro group is more extraversive.

180. Kohler W: Psychological remarks on some questions of anthropology. Am J Psychol 50:271–288.

Anthropology is full of disputed questions. Psychology can be of great help to anthropology, especially in relation to questions of perception, religion, power, causation, and magic.

181. Landis C, Hunt WA: Studies of the startle pattern: temporal relations. J Psychol 3:487–490.

The startle pattern is exceptionally rapid. It is completed in 0.3 to 1.5 seconds depending upon intensity.

182. Landis C, Hunt WA, Page JD: Studies of the startle pattern: abnormals. J Psychol 4:199–206.

Patients with dementia praecox, especially catatonics, have more pronounced startle responses than normals or other abnormals.

183. Locke NM, Goldstein H: The relation of birth order, age of mother, and size of family to intelligence. J Psychol 3:89–96.

A negative relationship between intelligence and age of mother, and intelligence and size of family, is found. A possible prenatal influence is postulated, since heredity and postnatal environment do not wholly account for obtained results.

184. Marshall EL: The objectivity of anthropometric measurements taken on eight and nine year old white males. Child Dev 8:249–256.

Not all measurements should be taken at each examination period of a seriatim measurement program.

185. Nadel SF: A field experiment in racial psychology. Br J Psychol 28:195–211.

In a narrative experiment the Yoruba stress logical and rational elements, while the Nupe are concerned with situational elements and time and space arrangements. In the picture experiment the Yoruba are meaning oriented, and the Nupe are enumerative. Actually, there are three different psychological "types" distributed in different proportions among the groups, the third being basically emotional Nupe.

186. Oeser OA: Methods and assumptions of field work in social psychology. Br J Psychol 27:343–363.

A team of specialists with various backgrounds may examine social problems through the method of functional penetrations. The total cultural setting must be considered.

187. Pai T, Sung SM, Hsu EH: The application of Thurston's Personality Schedule to Chinese subjects. J Soc Psychol 8: 47–72.

A high proportion of similarity is found in the most diagnostic items between Americans and Chinese patients in Peiping, pointing to the usefulness of the scale. However, the scales cannot be diagnostically applied to psychotics.

188. Palmer CE, Kawakami, Reed LJ: Anthropometic studies of individual growth: age, weight and rate of growth in weight, elementary school children. Child Dev 18:47–61.

Standard deviations of distributions of annual increments are strongly correlated with both attained weight and growth in weight.

189. Shen NC: The color preferences of 1368 Chinese students, with special reference to the most preferred color. J Soc Psychol 8:185–204.

Color preference based upon actual colors, rather than words, shows an unusually high consistency of preference for white, probably due to language factors.

190. Spence KW: Experimental studies of learning and the higher mental processes in infra-human primates. Psychol Bull 34:806–850.

No systematic investigation of the retention of various types of learned habits has been made in primates.

191. Westbrook CH, Hsien-Swei Y: Emotional stability of Chinese adolescents as measured by the Woodworth-Cady-Matthews questionnaire. J Soc Psychol 8:401–410.

Further experimentation with translations will indicate whether questions reflecting emotional instability are weakened by translation to another language.

1938

192. Abrahamsen D: The function of language and its development in early childhood: partly supported by an examination of the function of language in a child thirteen months of age. Acta Psychiatr Neurol 13:649–658.

Imitations of sounds and sound combinations of an articulated character occur before the linguistic understanding of the same sounds manifests itself. This is a hint as to the importance of sound imita-

tion as a preparatory foundation for the formation of language itself. A child may possess linguistic understanding of articulated and unarticulated sounds, however, without being able to imitate them.

193. Alexander F: Section on culture and personality. Am J Orthopsychiatry 8:31–50.

Developments in psychology require a more explicit recognition of sociological facts in the study of individuals, and, on the part of sociology, a more definite recognition of psychological mechanisms, especially of unconscious emotional reactions to economic and cultural situations.

194. Alexander F: Section meeting on culture and personality. Am J Orthopsychiatry 8:587–626.

Formulating the study of culture and personality in specific and concrete terms avoids unsound generalizations and meaningless abstractions.

195. Anastasi A, Foley JP: A study of animal drawings by Indian children of the North Pacific coast. J Soc Psychol 9:363–374.

Pronounced differences in subject matter, organization, color, and specific detail exhibited across age and sex groups reflect specific cultural and experiential factors rather than developmental levels.

196. Beaglehole E: A note on cultural compensation. J Abnorm Soc Psychol 33:121–123.

Each society emphasizes one segment of human behavior and must offer cultural compensations for satisfaction of usual behavior patterns or for satisfaction of drives that have no overt expression. Balinese temper illustrates how cultural compensation offers a cultural escape.

197. Benedict R: Continuities and discontinuities in cultural conditioning. Psychiatry 1:161–167.

Our adult activity demands traits that are interdicted in children, and far from redoubling efforts to help children bridge the gap to adulthood, adults in our society put all the blame on the child when he fails to manifest new behavior spontaneously or does so in a belligerent manner.

198. Bice HV: A note on a racial factor in responses in word association. J Soc Psychol 9:107–110.

Negroes do not respond with color words as frequently as whites.

199. Bonaparte M: Some paleobiological and biopsychical reflections. Int J Psychoanal 19:214–220.

Castration and perforation complexes derive from primitive biological reactions of fear to one's own substance. Fear of injury must be overcome before oral, anal, and urethral eroticism expresses individual satisfaction. Anxiety over penetration is greater in humans because of the developed brain and threat to ego.

200. Davis K: Mental hygiene and the class structure. Psychiatry 1:55–65.

The state of mentality is intimately related to the vertical structure of our open-class ethic, and the mental hygienist often neglects these vital social factors. Through practicing mental hygiene, one can conveniently praise and condemn under the aegis of the medico-authoritarian mantle, because the valuational system is disguised as rational advice based on science (by means of the psychologistic position).

201. Fernberger SW, Speck FG: Two Sioux shields and their psychological interpretation. J Abnorm Soc Psychol 33:168–178.

The Sioux web shield required the wearer's complete faith in its magical protection. Attachment of the same magical symbolism to the hide shield indicates the psychological significance of magic to the Sioux.

202. Frost I: Home-sickness and immigrant psychoses: Austrian and German domestic servants the basis of study. J Ment Science 84:801–847.

Conflict between family ties and herd or group feelings, combined with loneliness and exhaustion, comprise the principal etiological factors producing psychoses among immigrants. Psychological mechanisms of immigrants suffering from mental disorders center strikingly around those identifications characteristic of group formations. Mystical rites, prayers, ecstasies, and fears associated with the devil are striking features.

203. Greene JE: Comparative studies of certain mental disorders among whites and Negroes in Georgia during the decade 1923–1932. Psychol Monographs 50:130–154.

In Georgia, Negroes are more likely to have mental disorders, especially syphilitic disorders and dementia praecox.

204. Hallowell AI: Fear and anxiety and cultural and individual variables in primitive society. J Soc Psychol 9:25–47.

While the conflicts and manifest symptoms of individuals may vary from culture to culture, neurotics are etiologically comparable in terms of common dynamic processes.

205. Hallowell AI: Shabwan: a dissocial Indian girl. Am J Orthopsychiatry 8:329–340.

A Saulteau (Ojibwa) Canadian adolescent girl was judged insane by the tribe, although she was not truly psychotic. Diagnostic and remedial measures were determined by culturally molded premises.

206. Heilbronner P: Some remarks on the treatment of the sexes in Paleolithc art. Int J Psychoanal 19:439–447.

The shift from concern in the Aurignacian with realistic female forms to the Magdalenian emphasis on unrealistic female forms, and increased presence of male forms, also reflects shifts from the concrete and tangible to the abstract and visual, and from frontal display to profile display. Special significance given to particular sexual representations reveals the origination of the unconscious and later the conscious level of the mind.

207. Jones E: A psycho-analytic note on Paleolithic art. Int J Psychoanal 19:448–450.

Heilbronner's work on Paleolithic art provides another example of the resemblance between primitive mentality in phylogenesis and ontogenesis. The Aurignacian-Magdalenian change may be related to the development of conscious and aggressive motives associated with the harder life of man.

208. Kingsley HL, Carbone M: Attitudes of Italian-Americans toward race prejudice. J Abnorm Soc Psychol 33:532–537.

Anger, resentment, and hate are the most common forms of emotional reaction to racial discrimination. Perceived discrimination is the same for Italians and Italian-Americans.

209. Klineberg O: Emotional expression in Chinese literature. J Abnorm Soc Psychol 33:517–520.

Emotional expression follows culturally specific forms in Chinese literature, though there are some similarities with expression of emotions in the West.

210. Kraines SH: Indices of body build, their relation to personality. J Nerv Ment Dis 88:309–315.

If there exists a correlation between the physique and psychosis, there must be some common factor to both. Such a common factor might express itself during the formative years in the physique. Fluctuations in the activity of this common factor, which will bring on the disease more readily, will not show themselves in the relatively static morphology, though they may be shown in the more plastic physiology.

211. Landes R: The abnormal among the Ojibwa Indians. J Abnorm Soc Psychol 33:14–33.

All Ojibwa neuroses and psychoses fall under one category, windigo, and derive from Ojibwa culturally inculcated male ethos.

212. leRiche H: Growth in South African white boys' institutions. Child Dev 9:379–386.

Compared with American and German data these boys are inferior in weight and height.

213. Linton R: Culture, society, and the individual. J Abnorm Soc Psychol 33:425–436.

The closer and more continuous the individual relations, the greater the influence of noncultural factors relative to social and cultural ones.

214. Opler ME: Further comparative anthropological data bearing on the solution of a psychological problem. J Soc Psychol 9:477–483.

Supportive data, obtained from the Mescalero, Chiricahua, Jicarilla, and Lipa Apache, for the hypothesis that fear of the dead reflects unconscious real resentments, indicate that comparative in-depth anthropological work can be addressed to psychological problems.

215. Opler ME: Personality and culture: a methodological suggestion for the study of their interrelations. Psychiatry 1:217–220.

Rather than relying on a small group or only one representative of a culture for an understanding of its literature, history, and contemporary functioning, scientists must learn to rely upon individual and intimate personal narratives from as large a group as possible, cutting across sex, age, status, and function lines.

216. Roheim G: The nescience of the Aranda. Br J Med Psychol 17:343–360.

The repression of the father as the agency of procreation by the Aranda of Australia serves to separate the realm of sin and pleasure from the "eternal ones of the demon" who have the prerogative maternity. The repression, however, does not operate so strongly that the natives would believe that a tribe consisting only of women would have a prolific birthrate.

217. Sapir E: Why cultural anthropology needs the psychiatrist. Psychiatry 1:7–12.

The social scientist interested in effective consistencies, tendencies, and values must not dodge the task of studying the effects produced by individuals of varying temperaments and backgrounds on each other.

218. Sheback BJ: A note on racial difference in perseveration. J Psychol 5:271–280.

Correlations obtained for Jews and non-Jews indicate that perseveration does not possess functional unity and is specific to the single test. Jews show greater degree of perseveration in some tests but not in others, suggesting that the phenomenon is not racially determined.

219. Smith ME: A comparison of the neurotic tendencies of students of different racial ancestry in Hawaii. J Soc Psychol 9:395–418.

Korean and part-Hawaiians show highest average scores, followed by the Chinese and Portuguese, and finally Japanese and other Caucasians.

220. Telford CW: Comparative studies of full and mixed blood North Dakota Indians. Psychol Monographs 50:116–129.

The hypothesis that mixed-blood Indians perform better on informational tests, principally as a consequence of their cultural background and familiarity with English, in comparison with full-blood Indians is confirmed by the data. The full-blood group is superior on nonlinguistic performance tests. Both groups are equal on the Peterson Rational Learning Test.

221. Wagner PS: A comparative study of Negro and white admissions to the psychiatric pavilion of the Cincinnati General Hospital. Am J Psychiatry 95:166–183.

Mental illness in both white and black individuals is culturally determined. Psychoses among Negroes do not differ from psychoses among white men in terms of etiology, diagnosis, manifestations, or prophylaxis.

222. Weigert-Vowinkel E: The cult and mythology of the Magna Mater from the standpoint of psychoanalysis. Psychiatry 1:347–378.

The complicated theme of the Great Mother, as evidenced in the Phrygian-Roman cult, Cybele and Attis myths, and prehistoric evidence, may be interpreted in psychoanalytic terms.

223. Zubin J: Socio-biological types and methods for their isolation. Psychiatry 1:237–247.

A group can be divided into subgroups of like-structured or like-patterned individuals and the factors that make them alike can be determined. Such division has application in sociology, vital statistics, institutional statistics, and economics as well as psychology.

1939

224. Barahal HS: Constitutional factors in psychotic male homosexuals. Psychiatr Q 13:391–400.

The mere existence of a certain constitutional makeup along with homosexual tendencies does not necessarily imply a causal relationship. It may be, however, that in occasional cases the presence of some of the physical characteristics of the opposite sex may create conflicts predisposing to the maldirection of the libido.

225. Benedict R: Sex in primitive society. Am J Orthopsychiatry 9:570–573.

The etiology of sex perversions is intelligible culturally but unintelligible from a strictly physiological or psychological viewpoint. In all cultures where sex offense is rare, the adult is provided with a respected role in his society.

226. Beveridge WM: Some racial differences in perception. Br J Psychol 30:57–64.

African students show less phenomenal regression for brightness, but more for whiteness, and therefore show more discrimination than British students. Africans are less affected by visual clues than Europeans, though there are large individual differences in amount of mental compromise.

227. Devereux G: The social and cultural implications of incest among the Mohave Indians. Psychoanal Q 8:510–533.

For the Mohave the incest taboo is directed against the antisocial, noncooperative aspects of incest. Incest among the Mohave interferes with socialization and is therefore socially dangerous.

228. Erikson EH: Observations on Sioux education. J Psychol 7:101–156.

Educational difficulties on the Pine Ridge Reservation in South Dakota can be viewed in terms of the trauma of culture change, child-rearing practices, and cultural defensiveness. Sioux dependence upon whites has created an attitude somewhat comparable to compensation neurosis. Differences between Sioux and white child rearing lead to cultural difficulties.

229. Fairbairn WRD: Is aggression an irreducible factor? Br J Med Psychol 18:163–170.

Human aggression can be modified in two ways: (1) by regulation of the channels along which it is distributed and (2) by mitigation of the frustrations that provoke it. The latter method seems most appropriate to the present stage of human culture.

230. Frank LK: Cultural coercion and individual distortion. Psychiatry 2:11–27.

Individual initiative and independent striving are channeled by the retentive acquisitive mode of behavior into property getting and control, necessitating defeat and exploitation of others whenever possible. Modification of early child-rearing practices in the home and nursery may minimize the personality distortions that now prevent social order.

231. Garth TR, Foote J: The community of ideas of Japanese. J Soc Psychol 10:179–186.

More similarities than differences between Japanese and whites are revealed by the study of ideas. Japanese boys and girls are less similar than white and Japanese girls.

232. Greene JE, DuPree JL: Sex differences in certain mental disorders among whites and Negroes in Georgia during the decade 1923–1932. J Psychol 7:201–210.

Among Negroes, consistently higher percentages of female patients are considered recovered when discharged.

233. Hallowell AI: Sin, sex and sickness in Saulteaux belief. Br J Med Psychol 18:191–197.

The Saulteaux' theory of disease acts as a deterrant to the habitual practice, possible spread, and culturally phrased approval of certain sexual practices. It creates a nice balance between the somewhat variable manifestations of the sexual urges of individuals and the ideal norm of sexual behavior, traditionally imposed by culturally determined values.

234. Horowitz RE: Racial aspects of self-identification in nursery school children. J Psychol 7:91–100.

The development of group identification for Negro and white children proceeds from identification of body and identification in terms of similarities and differences. Group identification is an intrinsic aspect of ego development.

235. Karlan SC: A comparative study of psychoses among Negroes and whites in the New York State prisons. Psychiatr Q 13:160–164.

Negroes have no racial predisposition to mental disease. High incidence of mental disease among them is probably due to cultural, social, and economic causes. Due to the inherent constitutional instability of the criminal group, the incidence of psychoses among prison inmates is five to ten times as high as that of the general population.

236. LaBarre W: The psychopathology of drinking songs: a study of the content of the "normal" unconscious. Psychiatry 2:203–212.

The presence of repressed polymorphous infantile perversities in the "normal" American male are indicated upon analysis of songs sung by both college-age men and the more mature American Legion type. This is clear evidence that the Freudian theory of the genesis of the unconscious through repression is applicable to "normal" as well as to neurotic or psychotic individuals.

237. Lasswell HD: Person, personality, group, culture. Psychiatry 2:533–561.

The science of interpersonal relations contains terms relating to person, personality, group, and culture. The meanings of these terms must be made explicit so that professionals can communicate better and verify their findings.

238. Levy DM: Sibling rivalry studies in children of primitive groups. Am J Orthopsychiatry 9:205–214.

In Guatemala and Argentina, the essential dynamics of jealousy, hostility, regression, self-punishment, and guilt are displayed by children during play. Quekchi Indian children differ from the other two groups in sibling rivalry experiments due to differences in their culture.

239. McCulloch TL: The role of clasping activity in adaptive behavior of the infant chimpanzee: delayed response. J Psychol 7:283–292.

In tests of delayed response, an object eliciting clasping is successfully used as a lure. Delays of up to one hour are obtained for a chimpanzee infant.

240. McCulloch TL: The role of clasping activity in adaptive behavior of the infant chimpanzee: the

mechanism of reinforcement. J Psychol 7:305–316.

Clasping is a reinforcing agent that inhibits response to disturbing stimuli and is facilitated by situations that increase excitement.

241. McCulloch TL: The role of clasping activity in adaptive behavior of the infant chimpanzee: visual discrimination. J Psychol 7:293–304.

Clasping of objects serves to reduce degree of disturbance in discrimination tasks. Excitement must be induced in order to obtain satisfactory performance.

242. Maresh MM, Derning J: The growth of the long bones in 80 infants: roentgenograms versus anthropometry. Child Dev 10:91–106.

The anthropometric method of measurement contains inherent errors, while measurements from roentgenograms are suitable for detailed analysis.

243. Menninger K: An anthropological note on the theory of prenatal instinctual conflict. Int J Psychoanal 20:439–442.

The death instinct-life instinct theory may be extended to apply to the infant *in utero*. Concepts of neutralization of self-destructive impulses and externalization of instinctual energy parallel Mohave Indian concepts of the prenatal life of the potential shaman.

244. Paskind HA, Brown M: Constitutional differences between deteriorated and non-deteriorated patients with epilepsy. Am J Psychiatry 95:901–921.

Constitutional differences as reflected in body size and proportions are present between groups of deteriorated and nondeteriorated patients with epilepsy.

245. Peatman JG: Race and culture. Am J Orthopsychiatry 9:428–433.

Franz Boas's approach to the problems of race and culture has healthier social implications than those that lend themselves to racial hatred and violence.

246. Pillsbury WB: Body form and introversion-extroversion. J Abnorm Soc Psychol 34:400–401.

Data from 274 students do not show a relationship between body form as measured by Pignet Index, and introversion-extroversion, as measured by the Guilford questionnaire.

247. Roheim G: The covenant of Abraham. Int J Psychoanal 20:452–459.

Examination of the underlying unifying element of human sacrifice customs shows that infantile mankind continues the repetition of the mother-child situation with the pattern of separation followed by union.

248. Roheim G: Racial differences in the neurosis and psychosis. Psychiatry 2:375–390.

Primitive tribes with primitive culture are more inclined to neuroses and psychoses than civilized mankind. Racial differences in the neuroses and psychoses, when extremely pronounced, probably became manifest in the relations between the id, the ego, and the superego, and therefore, in the type or degree of culture evolved by human groups. It is not mere chance that the Bushmen did not invent civilization.

249. Rowland H: Friendship patterns in the state mental hospital. Psychiatry 2:363–373.

The mental hospital is a social system with a definite structure and many complex social processes and itself should become the object of further specific analysis. Study of friendship patterns among patients and staff is an example of a sociological approach.

250. Steggerda M, Macomber E: Mental and social characteristics of Maya and Navaho Indians as evidenced by a psychological rating scale. J Soc Psychol 10:51–59.

The Navaho and Maya are similar in social inclination, group orientation, cooperation, imaginativeness, thriftiness, and superstitiousness. The Navaho are less clean, more fearful of death and disease, more cruel, less honest, more nomadic, more inventive, and less intelligent than the Maya.

251. Stephen K: Aggression in early childhood. Br J Med Psychol 18:178–190.

Aggression may be changed from a valuable to a dangerous impulse as a result of too severe anxiety in early life. The solution of the problem of aggression lies in supporting and strengthening of the ego in early life.

252. Vigotsky LS: Thought and speech. Psychiatry 2:29–54.

The bond between thought and word is a living process: thought is brought forth in words. A word, deprived of thought, is a dead word. The connection between thought and word originated in the course of development and develops itself. The meaningful word is the microcosm of human consciousness.

253. Wegrocki HJ: A critique of cultural and statistical concepts of abnormality. J Abnorm Soc Psychol 34:166–178.

It is the function, not the mechanism, that determines abnormality, and therefore institutionalized "abnormal" traits in cultures are not "abnormal" entities. Adherence to a statistical-relative concept of abnormality leads to the unwarranted conclusion that abnormality standards differ and are culturally determined.

254. Whitmer HL: Some parallels between dynamic psychiatry and cultural anthropology. Am J Orthopsychiatry 9:95–101.

Although sociology-anthropology and psychiatry can never be wholly united, data for these fields derive from observation of human behavior and the disciplines overlap. Culture follows some principles basic to dynamic psychiatry.

255. Wolters AW: Aggression. Br J Med Psychol 18:171–177.

Aggression is a perversion of a fundamental biological pattern. The self-exhausting nature of emotion, more than the psychoanalytic approach of Fairbairn, offers some hope from fear-induced aggression.

256. Wright HW: The psychology of social culture. Am J Psychol 52:210–226.

Some of the values men jointly realize in producing works of social culture are objective and universal.

1940

257. Aginsky BW: The socio-psychological significance of death among the Pomo Indians. Am Imago 1:1–11.

The Pomo of Northern California have no concept of suicide. Every death is, instead, considered to be the result of supernatural or individual retaliation, precipitated by a form of psychological death.

258. Allen FH: Homosexuality in relation to the problem of human difference. Am J Orthopsychiatry 10:129–135.

Acceptance of self as a unique individual provides the only natural basis for social or group relationship. Homosexuality is a differentiating phenomenon in which the individual attempts to deny the problem of difference. This individual reaction to growth parallels the cultural phenomenon of nationalism.

259. Balken ER, Masserman JH: The language of phantasy. J Psychol 10:75–86.

Criteria that reflect the underlying psychodynamics of conversion hysteria, anxiety state, and obsessive-compulsive neurosis can be extracted from the language of psychoneurotic fantasies.

260. Beaglehole E: Cultural complexity and psychological problems. Psychiatry 3:329–339.

Degree of cultural complexity need not correspond to degree of psychological complexity. Primitive societies may be quite complex.

261. Beaglehole E: Notes on the theory of interpersonal relations. Psychiatry 3:511–526.

H. S. Sullivan's theory of interpersonal relations has wide implications for all who are concerned in any way with the puzzles of human nature.

262. Brown F: A note on the stability and maturity of Jewish and non-Jewish boys. J Soc Psychol 12:171–176.

Differences between Jewish and non-Jewish boys are insignificant for neuroticism, though Jewish boys rate higher in maturity. The greater incidence of functional psychoses in the Jewish population may represent a reaction to the discrepancy between individual thrust and a low social ceiling.

263. Carmichael DM: Some examples of constructive thinking amongst Greenlanders. Br J Psychol 30:295–315.

Constructive thinking among Eskimo Greenlanders is highly conventionalized. It may be inferred that the mental processes involved are psychologically identical for civilized Europeans and primitive people, in contrast to Levy-Bruhl's hypothesis.

264. Chief EH: An assimilation study of Indian girls. J Soc Psychol 11:19–30.

Comparison of assimilation, IQ, and age of a group of public school and Indian school girls indicates significant difference in assimilation score, differentiation between full and mixed-blood girls, and high intelligence related to greater assimilation.

265. Cohen JI: Physical types and their relations to psychotic types. J Ment Science 86:602–623.

The physique of female adults can be regarded as the resultant of two independent modes of variation, one determining differences in size or bulk, and the other determining differences in proportion or type. A relation exists between schizophrenia and manic-depression, on the one hand, and differences in physical proportion or type, on the other.

266. Davidoff E, Goodstone GL, Reifenstein EC: Habitus and personality in mental disease associated with organic disease. Psychiatr Q 14:809–817.

Ninety-one percent of patients with organic illness at a psychiatric hospital had significantly malintegrated prepsychotic personalities, as opposed to 38 percent of patients at a general hospital. Thirty-four percent of the organically ill psychopaths had a dysplastic habitus.

267. Dennis W: Does culture appreciably affect patterns of infant behavior? J Soc Psychol 12:305–317.

The general behavioral patterns of first-year infants in Hopi and Navaho culture are the same as that for white infants, despite differing child care customs.

268. Dennis W, Russel RW: Piaget's questions applied to Zuni children. Child Dev 11:181–187.

The concepts of the Zuni child do not differ from those of French and American children.

269. Foley JP: A further note on the "baboon boy" of South Africa. J Psychol 10:323–326.

Conflicting lines of evidence over the case of Lucas, the baboon boy, render psychological interpretation extremely difficult. The present evidence seems to discount the occurrence of a feral period in the boy's life.

270. Folsom JK: Old age as a sociological problem. Am J Orthopsychiatry 10:30–42.

The aged are influenced by many cultural, economic, political, and personal factors. These factors can be influenced by social action in a manner that would make possible a fuller and more enjoyable, if not longer, old age for many citizens.

271. Frank LK: Freedom for the personality. Psychiatry 3:341–349.

Culture and social life are historical creations of man himself. Human freedom is freedom from the personality distortion and the destructive affects that make overt action and speech an ironic tragedy.

272. Frank LK: Freud's influence on western thinking and culture. Am J Orthopsychiatry 10: 880–882.

Freud's studies have invalidated the concept of man as a rational, volitional, autonomous individual whose conduct is governed by reason.

273. Hallowell AI: Aggression in Saulteaux society. Psychiatry 3:395–407.

The outwardly mild and placid traits of character the Saulteau Indians exhibit and the patience and self-restraint they exercise in overt personal relations are a social facade that often masks the hostile feelings of the individual.

274. Henry J, Henry Z: Speech disturbances in Pilaga Indian children. Am J Orthopsychiatry 10: 362–369.

Pilaga Indians with serious personality disturbances also have a greater proportion of speech disturbances. The severest speech disturbances occur almost exclusively in females. The culture is very antifeminine.

275. Landes R: A cult matriarchate and male homosexuality. J Abnorm Soc Psychol 35:386–397.

Passive homosexuals among a Negro community in Bahia, Brazil, have become priest-leaders in the formally female-dominated priesthood of the *candomble* cult.

276. Lashley KS: Studies of simian intelligence from the University of Liege. Psychol Bull 37:237–248.

In view of the lack of any adequate control of extraneous cues and the failure of other investigators to obtain remotely similar results, the achievements of the monkey of Liege must be classed with the horses of Elberfeld and the dog of Mannheim.

277. Maslow AH: Dominance-quality and social behavior in infrahuman primates. J Soc Psychol 11:313–324.

Different qualities of dominance behavior may be demonstrated for the three main families of infrahuman primates. These differences are correlated with different kinds of social behavior and organization for the Old and New World monkeys.

278. Montagu A: Problems and methods relating to the study of race. Psychiatry 3:493–506.

In our society *race* is not merely a word one utters, but it is an event one experiences. Race, a temporary genetic stage in a process, is a social and not a biological problem.

279. Ogburn WF: Economic bases of family life. Marriage Fam Living 2:24–28.

Variations in types of economic functions have led to variations in type of family organization, from the hunting family, consanguineal family, the great family as found in China, to the modern city family.

280. Pickford RW: Social psychology and some problems of artistic culture. Br J Psychol 30:197–210.

Artistic culture must be considered in light of individual psychology and social group. Sublimation and the superego are important for the psychology of paintings. The social group supports its members through periods of social and personal difficulty.

281. Rado S: A critical examination of the concept of bisexuality. Psychosom Med 2:459–467.

Biologically there is no such thing as bisexuality in man. Masculine and feminine manifestations are not the direct expression of a constitutional component of the opposite sex. The basic problem in genital psychopathology is to determine the factors that cause the individual to apply aberrant forms of stimulation to his standard genital equipment.

282. Roheim G: The dragon and the hero. Am Imago 1:40–69.

The process of transformation of the earliest forms of dragon myths into more complex narratives of the Beowulf type may be psychodynamically analyzed.

283. Roheim G: The dragon and the hero. Am Imago 1:61–94.

The psychodynamic evolution of the Perseus-Gorgon folktale demonstrates mankind's projection of anxieties and desires onto nature.

284. Roheim G: Freud and cultural anthropology. Psychoanal Q 9:246–255.

Anthropology has always admitted that human behavior and culture must ultimately be explained by psychology, but before Freud there was no psychology that could meet these demands.

285. Roheim G: Society and the individual. Psychoanal Q 9:526–545.

The theories of Kardiner are faulty and he deviates from Freudian concepts.

286. Slight D: Psychological and cultural factors in marriage. Marriage Fam Living 2:103–104.

The psychological and cultural factors of marriage cannot be ignored in family research.

287. Wilbur GB: Comments (on the socio-psychological significance of death among the Pomo Indians by B. W. Aginsky). Am Imago 1:12–18.

Investigations of parallels between Western paranoid delusions, childhood psychic development, and the Pomo ideology of death and psychodynamic structure require further consideration.

288. Young K: The impact of Freudian psychology on sociology. Am J Orthopsychiatry 10:869–876.

Freudian psychology has furnished sociology with conceptual tools for the analysis and interpretation of social data and has introduced new techniques of research. The question of individual adjustment to the material and social-cultural world can only be solved by cooperation among sociologists, cultural anthropologists, and psychiatrists.

289. Zingg R M: Feral man and extreme cases of isolation. Am J Psychol 53:487–517.

Feral man lacks culture, the corpus of most patterns of human behavior.

1941

290. Adinarayan SP: A research in colour prejudice. Br J Psychol 31:217–229.

A relationship between conservative attitudes and color prejudice seems to exist. French students' color prejudice is greater than British students' but less than British nonstudents. There are differences in attitudes with respect to colored groups; East Indians elicit the least prejudice.

291. Baum MP, Vickers VS: Anthropometric and orthopedic examinations: a technique for use with children. Child Dev 12:339–345.

The technique of taking body measurements implies a consistent and well-thought-out plan of procedure, cooperative and trained personnel, and appreciation that the examination must be made to offer something to the child besides a period of restriction.

292. Bayton JA: The racial stereotypes of Negro college students. J Abnorm Soc Psychol 36:97–102.

Negro college students' stereotypes are very similar in some respects to those held by white students. Negro students assign characteristics, such as intelligence, to themselves that differ from those assigned to the "typical" Negro by whites. Stereotype formation is strongly influenced by propaganda.

293. Bean KL: Negro responses to certain intelligence test items. J Psychol 12:191–198.

The factors of environmental influence, vocabulary limitations, inability to follow instructions, and difficulty with abstraction and moral judgment may produce an unfair picture of Negro intelligence test performance.

294. Blanco IM: A psycho-analytic comment on English manners. Psychiatry 4:189–199.

It is possible to detect in the English, taken as a nation, the cultivation of oral sucking impulses and the inhibition of aggression of a more direct and brutal type, from biting onwards. Given certain circumstances, these repressions are lifted and the superego is able to tolerate the exercise of the corresponding functions.

295. Bruce M: Animism vs. evolution of the concept "alive." J Psychol 12:81–90.

Data gathered from Negro and white children confirm Piaget's findings of four stages of development of the concept of "alive." The theory of the evolution of concepts is more appropriate than the term *animism.*

296. Burrow T: Neurosis and war: a problem in human behavior. J Psychol 12:235–250.

War is similar to organic dysfunctioning. Man's behavior becomes disorganized so that he is a victim of social neurosis and unable to distinguish right from wrong.

297. Casey RP: Transient cults. Psychiatry 4:525–534.

Both exotic and secular cults rationalize without integrating and so exclude too much of the human nature to which they attempt to minister. The exotic cults permit an easy expression of deep but asocial needs. The religions of secularism leave too little play for primitive impulses.

298. Cohen JI: Physique, size and proportions. Br J Med Psychol 18:323-337.

The conventional indexes of somatotometry offer little hope of revealing true "racial" or constitutional type differences as defined by a tendency towards excessive linear or circumferential development and are masked by general processes regulating size. This influence has to be controlled before "type" differences will become evident.

299. Crawford MP: The cooperative solving by chimpanzees of problems requiring serial responses to color cues. J Soc Psychol 13:259–280.

The directive aspects of solicitation behavior by chimpanzees are significant for a phylogeny of language behavior. Direct orientation by body manipulation may be transitional to pointing behavior as communication.

300. Davidoff E, Reifenstein EC, Goodstone GL: Personality and habitus in organic disease. Psychiatr Q 15:544–553.

An unfavorable reaction to hospitalization on a medical ward depends largely upon previous personality integration, and to some extent upon the severity of the illness, social and economic factors, and the habitus.

301. Doob LW: War reactions of a rural Canadian community. J Abnorm Soc Psychol 36:200–223.

During a period of participant-observation in a Canadian community, the author observed that attitudes toward the war, and toward the efforts of Canada and England, varied as a function of society, culture, perception, and personality differences.

302. Eliasberg W: The challenge of social neuroses. J Nerv Ment Dis 94:676–687.

Our industrial society, which is based on the relentless increase of efficiency, results in resentment, voluntary inhibition, explosions, and hatreds which poison our democracy. Cures for these social neuroses must be found if our democracy is to survive.

303. Elliott HE: Comparison of nonpsychotic women with schizophrenics with respect to body type, signs of autonomic imbalance and menstrual history. Psychiatr Q 15:17–22.

The soma does not function as efficiently, nor in as well balanced a manner, in schizophrenic women compared with normals. There is a greater number of symptoms such as autonomic imblance and aperiodomenorrhea. Kretschmer's concept of a correlation between physique and type of mental disorder is affirmed.

304. Frank LK: Social order and psychiatry. Am J Orthopsychiatry 11:620–627.

Psychiatry can help achieve a social order dedicated to human values by critically examining our cultural traditions in terms of what they mean for the individual and the group, the raising and educating of children, and the institutions that reinforce our cultural patterns.

305. Fries ME: National and international difficulties: a suggested national program for alleviation. Am J Orthopsychiatry 11:562–573.

A national program in child-rearing education would offer immediate insight to the present generation about how the unconscious shapes opinion of national affairs and would assure the integrated development of the next generation so that it will be better adjusted and able to cope with postwar problems.

306. Green AW: The "cult of personality" and sexual relations. Psychiatry 4:343–348.

The cult of personality in courtship and marriage, as revealed in a study of second-generation Poles living in New England, demands its price: a psychic defenselessness against real or putative attacks on the ego by the beloved, a quivering sensitivity which, without moralizing, might be posited as a luxury the poor can ill afford.

307. Hallowell AI: The Rorschach test as a tool for investigating cultural variables and individual differences in the study of personality in primitive societies. Rorsch Res Exch 5:31–34.

The possibility of influence of cultural variables upon mode, quality, content, and originality of apperception must be considered. The Berens River Saulteaux should provide some interesting data upon the use of this technique in primitive society.

308. Held OC: A comparative study of the performance of Jewish and gentile college students on the American Council Psychological Examination. J Soc Psychol 13:407–412.

The only difference in performance between Jewish and gentile students is the lower performance of gentile boys on the linguistic portion of the exam.

309. Humphrey ND: American race and caste. Psychiatry 4:159–160.

The term *race* should be discarded entirely in the cultural reference, and the more appropriate term *caste* employed in its stead. The term *race* should be retained in its biologic context as a taxonomic category for the delineation of types of mankind.

310. Inman WS: The couvade in modern England. Br J Med Psychol 19:37–55.

Masculine efforts at reproduction go back to biblical times. Styes and cysts are attempts, albeit unconscious ones, by modern English men to imitate the woman in her sexual life.

311. Israeli N: Population trends and the family. Psychiatry 4:349-359.

Regardless of a more rapid family turnover, increase in divorces and abortions, a smaller family population may adopt more integrated family life patterns. Whether such integration can offset any increased disintegrativeness is a major problem.

312. Kisker GW: The physico-social basis of mental disorder. J Nerv Ment Dis 93:731-735.

Much of our modern social pathology, both local and international, is a neurotic group expression, the roots of which are imbedded in the social and cultural configurations that have been handed down to us from generation to generation.

313. Korzybski A: General semantics, psychiatry, psychotherapy and prevention. Am J Psychiatry 98:203-214.

Knowledge of general semantics can make psychotherapy more effective and briefer and can also be applied to preventive efforts on a world-wide basis.

314. Leighton AH, Leighton DC: Elements of psychotherapy in Navaho religion. Psychiatry 4:515-523.

Navaho religion offers powerful suggestive psychotherapy that can certainly aid states of anxiousness and render the physically ailing person better able to bear his illness.

315. Maugham WS: The family in England in wartime. Marriage Fam Living 3:4-10.

There is no evidence that the war is undermining the English family. On the contrary the family has been brought closer together in the face of hardship.

316. Meltzer H: The development of children's nationality preferences, concepts, and attitudes. J Psychol 11:343-358.

Grade differences, affective tone and intensity, and stereotypy in national attitudes of young boys and girls may be examined.

317. Meltzer H: Hostility and tolerance in children's nationality and race attitudes. Am J Orthopsychiatry 11:662-675.

Important elements in the development of children's nationality and race attitudes are maternal and paternal rejection, frustration, feelings of belongingness, economic security, human warmth and aliveness, feeling as well as intellectual understanding, and the teacher's concept of democracy.

318. Merton RD: Intermarriage and the social structure: fact and theory. Psychiatry 4:361-374.

Most cross-caste sex relations will be clandestine and illicit. Within a racial-caste structure, the noninstitutionalized statistical pattern of the few intermarriages that do occur will be largely hypogamous.

319. Montagu A: Race, caste and scientific method. Psychiatry 4:337-338.

The term *race* should be discarded entirely in the cultural reference and the more appropriate term *caste* employed in its stead. The term *race* should be replaced by the term *ethnic group* in the biologic or ecologic context and should not be used in any human context whatsoever.

320. Montagu MFA: Nescience, science and psycho-analysis. Br J Med Psychol 18.383-404.

Adult aborigines believe that immigration of spirit children from a source independent of the bodies of a particular man and woman is the cause of conception and childbirth. Such adult knowledge is really an extension and clarification of childhood notions in relation to procreation and is not due to suppression or obfuscation as Roheim suggests.

321. Newman SS: Personal symbolism in language patterns. Psychiatry 4:177-184.

Language behavior may indicate tendencies that are congruent but not identical with those manifested in other types of behavior. An individual's use of language is symptomatic of his functioning and his adjustments as a person in a cultural setting.

322. Pickford RW: Aspects of the psychology of games and sports. Br J Psychol 31:279-293.

Games lead to constructive use of aggressive impulses for the individual in that these impulses are sublimated in the form of constructive territorial combat for the group. Individual anxieties about aggression are satisfied by the concept of fair play. Group games are democratic in essence.

323. Roheim G: Myth and folk-tale. Am Imago 2:266-279.

Data from Australian aboriginal culture clearly demonstrate the distinguishing features of myth as opposed to folktale.

324. Roheim G: Play analysis with Normanby Island children. Am J Orthopsychiatry 11:524-529.

In the matrilineal society of the Normanby Island an Oedipus complex is evident. The strong tendency toward infantilization is a denial of sexuality and aggression. The *mwanejo ukahari* game is a denial of incestuous desires that starts at the infantile level and ends with an attack on the genitals.

325. Roheim G: The psychoanalytic interpretation of culture. Int J Psychoanal 22:147–169.

The ontogenetic theory of culture is preferred to the idea of the collective unconscious. Human culture and human adjustments are conditioned by the prolonged infantile situation. Man conquers nature through the synthetic function of the ego.

326. Shalloo JP: Some cultural factors in the etiology of alcoholism. Q J Stud Alcohol 2:464–478.

The alcoholic is the end product of a complex process of social and cultural conditioning. Understanding of this process requires an analysis of the cultural and social situation as defined by the person.

327. Shirley M, Poyntz L: Development and cultural patterning in children's protests. Child Dev 12:347–350.

The hierarchy of childish protests may be culturally imposed. The child's progress is toward more socially approved expression of his protests.

328. Spoerl DT: A note on the Anastasi-Foley cultural interpretation of children's drawings. J Soc Psychol 13:187–192.

The Anastasi-Foley conclusion that drawings reflect cultural and experiential factors rather than developmental factors is invalid since the subjects' mental age is unknown, sex difference of realistic drawings are similar to those found for 4 to 8 year olds in our culture, and the representation of trajectory is a common phenomenon.

329. Sumner FC, Lee JA: Some resemblances between friends of like sex and between friends of unlike sex among a group of Negro college students. J Psychol 12:199–202.

Male Negro students choose friends with similar interest-attitudes and skin color. Male-female couples are fairly similar in socioeconomic status, skin color, and chronological age.

330. Thompson C: The role of women in this culture. Psychiatry 4:1–8.

Neurotic drives often find expression in the present-day activities of women, but this is no reason for dismissing as neurotic the whole social and economic revolution of woman along her particular path among world-wide changes.

331. Warden CJ, Galt WE: Instrumentation in cebus and rhesus monkeys on a multiple platform task. J Psychol 11:3–22.

The cebus adjusts to multiple-platform tasks more readily than the rhesus and shows effortless progression from stage to stage. Cebus seem to have a better comprehension of the tool-using function of the rake than the rhesus.

332. Wilke WH, Snyder JF: Attitudes toward American dialects. J Soc Psychol 14:349–362.

There are large individual and group differences in attitudes toward American and foreign dialects. Error in regional identification is considerable.

333. Yerkes RM: Conjugal contracts among chimpanzees. J Abnorm Soc Psychol 36:175–199.

Dominance between mates is influenced more by individuality than by masculinity or femininity. Sexual status and relations also affect expression of dominance.

1942

334. Bean KL: Negro responses to verbal and nonverbal test materials. J Psychol 13:343–354.

Though there has been found a small reliable difference in favor of the accuracy of nonlanguage intelligence tests, it is too early to generalize about the type most fair to Negroes.

335. Brickner RM: The German cultural paranoid trend. Am J Orthopsychiatry 12:111–132.

Values congenial to paranoid individuals have been emphasized in German culture for at least several generations. German group paranoia will change only if German culture itself changes.

336. Caballero NC: Municipal day nurseries in Havana. Marriage Fam Living 4:13.

Day nurseries in Cuba must still improve their educational system.

337. Casey RP: Oedipus motivation in religious thought and fantasy. Psychiatry 5:219–228.

Guilt and anxiety underlie many biblical themes.

338. Cook PH: The application of the Rorschach test to a Samoan group. Rorschach Res Exch 6:51–60.

The Rorschach test requires qualification and modification before it can be interpreted for other very different cultures.

339. Cullis WC: Impact of war upon British home life. Marriage Fam Living 4:10–11.

The incorporation of women into the war effort has brought some disruption to their home life, but the women will be better able to share in the making of a new world when the war is over.

340. Curran FJ: Aggressive traits in children. Dis Nerv Syst 3:114–117.

Aggression is found in all infants and children. If appropriate outlets for aggressive impulses are found when the child is very young and continued through adolescence, when aggression is more frequently expressed in speech than in action, the drive can be channeled into socially acceptable forms.

341. deLourdes Sa Pereira M: The woman in the Brazilian family. Marriage Fam Living 4:60–62.

Brazilian women are slowly winning their freedom and becoming more involved in the professions. They have the same political rights as American women, though their differing temperament marks a different expression of these rights.

342. Demerath NJ: Schizophrenia among primitives. Am J Psychiatry 98:703 707.

The reported rarity of schizophrenia is not based on adequate data. Wherever schizophrenia has been reported, the society in question has been in a process of acculturation; therefore, a hypothesis involving the concepts of culture conflict, marginality, and culture shock is tenable.

343. Eliasberg W: German philosophy and German psychological warfare. J Psychol 14:197–216.

The conflict between idealism and realism is relevant to German psychology and psychological warfare. German political propaganda at home can be idealistic; while foreign propaganda must be realistic. The absence of such a discrepancy is an indication of the strength of democracy.

344. Erikson EH: Hitler's imagery and German youth. Psychiatry 5:475–493.

Europe's conscious and unconscious imagery is based on family structure as well as political background. The fascistic-adolescent movements owe their existence to senile systems that neither learn nor die. Hitler is merely a manipulator of these unconscious images.

345. Finch G: Chimpanzee frustration responses. Psychosom Med 4:233–251.

Age is a very important factor in determining both frustration-response incidence and expression in chimpanzees. In frustrating situations involving delay, frustration increases with increased delay. Frustration response increases with increased expectancy, the difficulty of the problem, and with increased motivation. Frustrating situations are summative in their effects.

346. Ginsberg M: National character. Br J Psychol 32:183–205.

The study of national character is to be approached through investigating the collective life of nations, their traditions, and public policy, not through the individual. The objective is to examine how these form congruent systems. National character, though ultimately linked to the genetic stock, is always dynamic.

347. Hallowell AI: Acculturation processes and personality changes as indicated by the Rorschach technique. Rorschach Res Exch 6:42–50.

The least acculturated Berens River Saulteau group is introversive, while the more acculturated group is extratensive and has a faster response time.

348. Harms E: The nervous Jew: a study in social-psychiatry Dis Nerv Syst 3:47–52.

The expression "Jewish nervousness" has no basis in objective fact, as an unusually low percentage of Jews have mental diseases. However, next to the Irish the Jews rank highest in immigration insanity. As a result of immigration, Jews are quite frequently forced into situations where they are met by unethical and unkind social behavior, and therefore their reactions to this behavior should not be attributed to bad mental health on the part of the Jews involved.

349. Heagney M: The family in Australia in war time. Marriage Fam Living 4:12.

Government social services have been maintained during the war in order to preserve the standard of living of the Australian family.

350. Henry J, Henry Z: Symmetrical and reciprocal hostility of sibling rivalry. Am J Orthropsychiatry 12:256–261.

Western culture emphasizes the hostility of the older sibling to the younger one. Study of Pilaga Indian families reveals that all siblings express rivalry for the mother and that overt hostility is reciprocal among siblings.

351. Kallman FJ, Barrera SE: The heredoconstitutional mechanisms of predisposition and resistance to schizophrenia. Am J Psychiatry 98:544–550.

Susceptibility to a schizophrenic process depends upon a specific, single-factorial, autosomal, and probably recessive predisposition that is modifiable in its expression by the effect of mesodermal defense mechanisms.

352. Karpman B: Psychiatry and culture. J Ner Ment Dis 96:17–48.

Psychiatry has made great contributions to science (such as mathematics, biology, sociology, and criminology), art, and literature. When society has learned to respect individual rights, it will build a better and happier social order.

353. Lerner E: Pathological Nazi stereotypes found in recent German technical journals. J Psychol 13:179–192.

Abstracts of German psychological articles show excessively dependent overvaluation of the strength of others, excessive identification, and racial stereotypy.

354. Levy DM: Psychosomatic studies of some aspects of maternal behavior. Psychosom Med 4:223–227.

Maternal behavior is a characteristic feature of the personality in childhood as well as in later life. Distinctly nonmaternal mothers exhibit such behavior also in childhood. A high and significant positive correlation is found between maternal behavior and duration of menstrual flow.

355. Lo CF: Moral judgments of Chinese students. J Abnorm Soc Psychol 37:264–269.

Rankings of vices and ideals by Chinese students, when compared with American student rankings, demonstrate that both groups are critical of sex irregularity, stealing, and cheating. Honesty is viewed as the most important ideal, followed by obedience, thrift, and reverence.

356. Mandujano G: Program for rural Chile. Marriage Fam Living 4:59.

A rural information service can be developed in any country to extend practical knowledge to families.

357. Marmor J: The role of instinct in human behavior. Psychiatry 5:509–516.

Sociobiological unity is the correct way of viewing human behavior. Because of significant social and biological variances there is no such entity as a fixed, immutable, universal human nature.

358. Mead M: Anthropological data on the problem of instinct. Psychosom Med 4:396–397.

We may expect to identify in human beings an original nature that has very definite form or structure, and possibly systematic individual differences that may be referred to constitutional type within that original nature. We must, however, make investigations without particularization in regard to that original nature.

359. Mendoza A: The rural family in Argentina. Marriage Fam Living 4:14.

The rural population suffers from many of the difficulties encountered in developing agrarian countries.

360. Montagu MFA: The creative power of ethnic mixture. Psychiatry 5:523–536.

Social conventions, race pride, and race prejudice—not biological inferiority—cause problems for the half-caste.

361. Nissen HW: Ambivalent cues in discriminative behavior in chimpanzees. J Psychol 14:3–34.

Four of five chimpanzees master a problem in visual discrimination when the stimuli are ambivalent. The maximum number of cues to which an organism can respond in discriminatory tasks is an axis of discriminative behavior that may permit quantitative individual-species differentiation.

362. Parsons T: Propaganda and social control. Psychiatry 5:551–572.

Institutions are vehicles of social control and should be considered along with psychological techniques when studying propaganda.

363. Prince SH: The Canadian family in wartime. Marriage Fam Living 4:25–28.

The war effort is having an effect on family stability, income, morale, health, housing, and adolescent development. Canada is marshaling many services in defense of the family.

364. Roheim G: The origin and function of culture. Psychoanal Rev 29:131–184.

In every primitive tribe the medicine man is in the center of society. Freud was correct in making the analogy between the dynamics and structure of primitive cultures and modern individual neuroses.

365. Roheim G: Transition rites. Psychoanal Q 11:331–374.

Transition rites among Australian tribes have both a latent content, which may be interpreted like a dream, and a manifest content.

366. Roher JH: The test intelligence of Osage Indians. J Soc Psychol 16:99–105.

There is no correlation between degree of Osage Indian blood and intelligence as measured by the Goodenough Test or the Otis Test of Mental Ability. There is no significant difference in intelligence quotient between an average Osage child and an average white child. The general inferior intelligence test performance by American Indians is due to cultural rather than racial factors.

367. Schactel A, Henry J, Henry Z: Rorschach analysis of Pilaga Indian children. Am J Orthopsychiatry 12:679–712.

Pilaga children see in the Rorschach plates an immediate picture of their objective world. Their mental approach is D-Dr, and they do not see movement nor give shading responses. These findings are explainable in light of their unique culture.

368. Shuey AM: A comparison of Negro and White college students by means of the American Council Psychological Examination. J Psychol 14:35–52.

When using controls to account for previous education, significant differences in favor of white students on three subtests are obtained, but not on completion and opposite subtests.

369. Shuey AM: Differences in performance of Jewish and non-Jewish students on the American Council Psychological Examination. J Soc Psychol 15:221–244.

Findings that Jewish college students are superior to non-Jewish students on intelligence tests are not supported when the groups are equal in all other factors.

370. Thompson C: Cultural pressures in the psychology of woman. Psychiatry 5:331–339.

Characteristics and inferiority feelings that Freud considered to be specifically female and biologically determined can be explained as developments arising in and growing out of Western woman's historic situation of underprivilege, restriction of development, insincere attitude toward the sexual nature, and social and economic dependency.

371. Tomasic D: Personality development in the Zadruga society. Psychiatry 5:229–261.

A remarkable feature in the drama of the rise and fall of Yugoslavia was the role of the peasant movement that originated in the Zadruga regions of Croatia. The changing culture and structure of the Croatian village affected the personality of the Croatian peasant and helped to form the peasant movement.

372. Underhill R: Child training in an Indian tribe. Marriage Fam Living 4:80–81.

Papago child rearing emphasizes responsibility to the group.

373. Zilboorg G: Psychology and culture. Psychoanal Q 11:1–16.

Culture has a fundamental, irreconcilable conflict with true scientific psychology and will always tend to abolish it.

1943

374. Angyal AF: The new "cultural movement" in Japan. J Psychol 16:115–124.

Japanese cultural aims as reflected in the journal *Cultural Nippon* include belief in superiority based upon presence of an absolute ruler of divine source, altruistic desire to unite the world, religious cooperation with the state, and superiority of race. The propaganda will fail because it is not keyed to a favorable foreign reaction.

375. Bacon SD: Sociology and the problems of alcohol: foundations for a sociologic study of drinking behavior. Q J Stud Alcohol 4:402–445.

The sociologic study of drinking behavior must be concerned with function, charter, way of activity, material apparatus, place and time, functionaries, participants, rules, sanctions, and sanctioning agents. Techniques include documentary and field study, participant observation, casework studies and life histories, and use of questionnaires.

376. Balken ER: Psychological researches in schizophrenic language and thought. J Psychol 16:153–176.

Common approaches to investigating schizophrenia involve assumptions of cognitive dysfunctioning, a parallel between language and thought, the relationship to primitive thought, and use of tests for normals. An empirically based reformulation and reorientation of psychological methodologies is necessary.

377. Balken ER: The delineation of schizophrenic language and thought in a test of imagination. J Psychol 16:239–272.

Fantasies elicited by Murray's TAT show a lack of relation to life events of the patient, orientation to the present, unawareness of self in relation to outer world or inner experience, and almost complete fusion of subject and object in various productions. Schizophrenic experience may thus be seen as relived "lived" experience.

378. Brennan M: Urban lower-class Negro girls. Psychiatry 6:307–324.

The adjustment of a member of a minority group is always conditioned by the interplay of the normal strivings of the person and the psychological strength of the barriers to the "forbidden areas."

379. Brickner RM, Lyons LV: A neuropsychiatric view of German culture. J Nerv Ment Dis 98:281–293.

Paranoid characteristics form a dominant trait in German culture of which the Nazis are merely a current expression. Immediate and long-term treatment goals for Germany include the restructuring of German culture, education, institutions, and home life.

380. Bromberg W, Tranter CL: Peyote intoxication: some psychological aspects of the peyote rite. J Nerv Ment Dis 97:518–527.

Indians have central emotional constellations that invest Father Peyote with omnipotent force and allow the projection of feelings to inanimate objects or institutions.

381. Brown W: The psychology of modern Germany. Br J Psychol 34:43–59.

After the defeat of 1918, modern Germany underwent regression to militarism and intensification of nationalism. The mutual interaction between the German group mind and Hitler led to hysterical and paranoid tendencies. The postwar treatment of Germany must consider these psychopathological facts.

382. Campbell AA: St. Thomas Negroes—a study of personality and culture. Psychol Monographs 55:1–90.

Patterns of thought and action that exemplify the behavior of St. Thomas Negroes may be studied in light of cultural background. Emphasis on individualistic values is related to insecure social relationships during childhood. The adult is typically insecure, suspicious, and egocentric.

383. Dennis W: Animism and related tendencies in Hopi children. J Abnorm Soc Psychol 38:21–36.

Hopi subjects are more animistic, attribute consciousness to inanimate objects, and have more belief in moral realism than do white American subjects. Animistic concepts, however, are of the same types for both groups. Children's earliest ideas are the same in all societies. Margaret Mead's contradictory evidence is inconclusive since Piaget's method was not employed.

384. Eliot TD: The possibilities of cultural hygiene. Psychiatry 6:83–88.

Blame and hate, naive "death-wishes," may be seen as repressions or fixations on an immature level, when their subjective-projective nature and self-defeating effects are observed, even in war. It may be possible to prevent a whirlwind of international revenge by restraining and treating international criminals as modern criminologists would treat the criminals of the streets.

385. Elwin V: The vagina dentata legend. Br J Med Psychol 19:439–453.

The discovery of the vagina dentata dream and legend establishes parallel psychological development among people as diverse as the Baiga of India, the Chilcotin of northwest America, and the Ainu of Siberia.

386. Farnsworth PR: Attempts to distinguish Chinese from Japanese college students through observations of face-photographs. J Psychol 16:99–106.

The ability of West Coast students to distinguish between Chinese and Japanese college students in photographs is slightly better than chance. Caucasian and Malaysian appearance are incorrectly associated with Chinese ancestry. Stereotypes held on the West Coast differ from those in the Midwest.

387. Fromm E: Sex and character. Psychiatry 6:21–31.

The sexual difference colors the personality of the average man and woman. This coloring may be compared to the key or the mode in which a melody is written—not to the melody itself. Furthermore, it refers only to average men and women, respectively, and varies in every person. These "natural" differences are blended with differences brought about by the specific culture in which people live.

388. Galt WE: The male-female dichotomy in human behavior: a phylobiological evaluation. Psychiatry 6:1–14.

The pattern of man's sex life as a total reaction has been falsely restricted to one or another localized point of excitation. The maladaptation of the centrally motivated sex-response of social man has entailed a spurious dichotomy in the natural unity and coordination between male and female reactions.

389. Goldfarb W: Infant rearing and problem behavior. Am J Orthopsychiatry 13:249–265.

Foster home children show less problem behavior than institution children and are more amenable to case work and therapeutic help when such problems are evidenced.

390. Herschberger R: Sexual differences and character trends. Psychiatry 6:301–305.

Woman, in Fromm's account, is a calculating, hyperconceptual, and extremely sophisticated person. Man, the generous-hearted Adam, is like a strong impulsive animal with a desire to overpower, but haunted by one basic fear: that of failing to have and maintain an erection until all concerned are satisfied. It is easy to show that woman's pettiness is not in the least determined by her natural sexual role but instead is the outcome of cultural forces.

391. Horton D: The functions of alcohol in primitive societies: a cross-cultural study. Q J Stud Alcohol 4:199–320.

The drinking of alcohol tends to be accompanied by release of sexual and aggressive impulses. The strength of the drinking response in any society tends to vary directly with the level of anxiety in a society. The strength of drinking response tends to vary inversely with the strength of the counteranxiety elicited by painful experiences during and after drinking.

392. Janis IL: Meaning and the study of symbolic behavior. Psychiatry 6:425–439.

Semantical content analysis will play a major role as a valid research technique in the future development of the science of communication.

393. Kant F: Integration of constitution and environment in psychiatry and psychotherapy. Dis Nerv Syst 4:261–268.

In his attempt to adequately adjust a patient, the psychotherapist should take into consideration the patient's innate potentialities. He must penetrate beyond the unconscious motives and analyze individually the dynamic structure by integrating constitutional and environmental aspects in the study of personality.

394. Lewin K: Cultural reconstruction. J Abnorm Soc Psychol 38:166–173.

Answers to problems of cultural change can be supplied only by experimental cultural anthropology, but cultural anthropology is still in a descriptive stage. Instilling democracy and initiating cultural reconstruction in Europe must be approached realistically through groups working with leaders and youth.

395. Marks ES: Skin color judgment of Negro college students. J Abnorm Soc Psychol 38:370–376.

Individual raters tend to judge others' skin color with reference to one's own color. This may reflect a tendency to seek a position of neutral emotional content or averageness.

396. Matte I: Observations of the English in war time. J Nerv Ment Dis 97:447–463.

During the London air raids, Englishmen dealt with anxiety by integration in the community, activity, projection, humor, and a belief in actual or imaginary protection.

397. Mead M: Problems of a war time society: the modification of pre-war patterns. Am J Orthopsychiatry 13:596–599.

The adolescent's belief in continuity and orientation toward the future is necessary to counter upsetting effects on the family and individual personality which began during the war years and are likely to continue.

398. Montagu A: Bloody: the natural history of a word. Psychiatry 6:175–190.

Originating at the end of the sixteenth century in the perfectly harmless and proper *blutig*, bloody became naturalized in England as an intensive. It was in polite usage until the middle of the eighteenth century when it began to fall from grace and did not begin the climb back to acceptability until after World War I. A phonetic examination of the word suggests that it is eminently suited for the purpose which it has and will continue to serve.

399. Montagu A: Man's biological outlook. Psychiatry 6:359–360.

Gerrit Miller, in *Man's Biological Outlook*, presents the idea that man is far advanced in the period of "phylogeronty," or racial old age. The truth is that man is the youngest of all the mammalian forms and morphologically the most promising. If man can find a consciously reasoned direction for the life of each person in relation to all others within his society and the commonwealth of nations, he can control the severe threat to man's survival.

400. Montagu A: The myth of blood. Psychiatry 6:15–19.

Blood is a word that, from the beginning of recorded history, has possessed a high emotional content. What modern science has revealed about blood renders all such words as royal blood, half-blood, full-blood, blood-relationship, utterly meaningless in point of fact, and dangerously meaningful in the superstitious social sense.

401. Schreier F: German aggressiveness—its reasons and types. J Abnorm Soc Psychol 38:211–224.

German aggressiveness is manifest in various types: direct, sadistic, inhibited, the ex-soldier, the cynic, the despairing defensive, insecure, fanatic, antiprogressive, and success-oriented aggressors. Causal factors vary with the different types. Reeducation of the German people must take these elements into account.

402. Spoerl DT: Bilinguality and emotional adjustment. J Abnorm Soc Psychol 38:37–57.

Emotional disturbances among bilingual students are related to intrafamily conflicts, extreme social values, identity conflicts, and social frustration. The culture conflict experienced by immigrant groups is complicated by the bilingual environment.

403. Stratton GM, Henry FM: Emotion in Chinese, Japanese, and whites: racial and national differences and likeness in physiological reactions to an emotional stimulus. Am J Psychol 56:161–180.

Emotional differences between Caucasians and Mongoloids are due in part to natural neuropsychic contrasts. Emotional likeness between the two, and also between Chinese and Japanese, is explained by natural constitution conjoined with features in their psychic and physical environment, from childhood.

404. Zilboorg G: Psychiatry as a social science. Am J Psychiatry 99:585–588.

Sociology and anthropology are increasingly intertwined with psychiatry.

1944

405. Beaglehole E: Character structure: its role in the analysis of interpersonal relations. Psychiatry 7:143–162.

The study of national character and therefore of character structure is basic not only to any efficient and effective organization of wartime propaganda but also to a consideration of the most satisfactory appeals and drives around which a lasting peace may be built.

406. Blackman N, Klebanoff SG: The role of rural socio-cultural factors in the functional psychoses. Psychiatr Q 18:301–315.

The overwhelming majority of patients who migrate from an urban to a rural environment are schizophrenics, while the majority of manic-depressives migrate from a rural to an urban environment. Isolation and the burden of gossip are better tolerated by schizophrenics.

407. Chotlos JW: Studies in language behavior: a statistical and comparative analysis of individual written language samples. Psychol Monographs 56:77–111.

Higher intelligence and chronological age are related to more highly differentiated language structure and the use of more nouns and adjectives than lower intelligence and earlier age. Different principles may apply to extensional and intensional words in a sample.

408. Dai B: Divided loyalty in war: a study of cooperation with the enemy. Psychiatry 7:327–340.

From study of a Chinese man who cooperated with the Japanese puppet regime it appears that a person's way of managing his hostile impulses toward people he considers stronger, his pattern of meeting a situation involving personal danger, the degree of his narcissism and receptivity, and the extent of his acculturation or identification with group values may affect his loyalty in war.

409. Eggan D: Hopi marriage and family relations. Marriage Fam Living 6:1–26.

The Hopi stress a form of convenience-partnership with romantic results that are emotionally similar to American style, though in differing proportions.

410. Eissler KR: Balinese character: a critical comment. Psychiatry 7:139–144.

Balinese character is formed in a preoedipal society and may be understood in psychoanalytic terms.

411. Fairbanks H: Studies in language behavior: the quantitative differentiation of samples of spoken languages. Psychol Monographs 56:16–40.

Analysis of schizophrenic and normal student language samples demonstrates that schizophrenics use fewer nouns, conjunctions, adjectives, and prepositions, but more pronouns, verbs, and interjections. The minimal resemblance between schizophrenic and children's language samples does not support the view of schizophrenia as regression to childhood.

412. Havighurst RJ, Hilkevitch RR: The intelligence of Indian children as measured by a performance scale. J Abnorm Soc Psychol 39:419–433.

American Indian children (Hopi, Zuni, Sioux, Navaho, Papago, and Zia) do as well as white children on a performance test of intelligence. Differences may be found within tribes and between groups. The Hopi child is generally above the white norm, while the rest are at white norms of performance.

413. Johnson W: Studies in language behavior: a program of research. Psychol Monographs 56:1–15.

Various measures of language behavior are potentially capable of specifying individual and group differences and correlating these with personality and environmental variables. Various measures include frequency assessments, indices, tests of vocabulary depth, and consciousness of semantic abstraction.

414. Klineberg O: A science of national character. J Soc Psycho 19:147–162.

Problems in the methodology of national character include comparability, causality, and inadequacy. The problem can be approached through analysis of cultural products, vital statistics, and comparative experimentation.

415. Klopfer B: Is inclination to mental disease within a population group a "racial" factor? A statistical study of the frequency of five major mental diseases among Italian, Irish and German immigrants and their descendants in the states of New York and Massachusetts. Psychiatr Q 18:240–272.

The differences between the whole life situation of foreign-born and native-born inhabitants of the United States, and the assimilative powers of the

common new environment, are much more important factors for the frequency of mental disease than is membership in a certain nationality group.

416. Layard J: Primitive kinship as mirrored in the psychological structure of modern man. Br J Med Psychol 20:118–134.

Within the context of Jungian psychology it can be shown that psychological ramifications in modern man reflect patterns of behavior among primitive peoples.

417. Livesay TM: The relation of economic status to intelligence and to the racial derivation of high school seniors in Hawaii. Am J Psychol 57:77–82.

The decided racial differences in economic status correspond to the chronological arrival of the racial groups in Hawaii.

418. Mann MB: Studies in language behavior: the quantitative differentiation of samples of written languages. Psychol Monographs 56:41–74.

Biographies written by schizophrenics and normals show normal language structure to be more highly differentiated than abnormal structure. Type-token ratios are higher in written than oral samples for both groups.

419. Masserman JH: Experimental neuroses and group aggression. Am J Orthopsychiatry 14:636–643.

Small groups of cats placed in a competitive feeding situation establish hierarchies of dominance and submission. Experimentally induced motivational conflicts or displacement from group dominance can result in overt aggression. When dominance is restored the neurotic conflicts are resolved, or hierarchic subservience is accepted. These observations may be relevant to the study of human interrelationships.

420. Masserman JH: Language, behavior, and dynamic psychiatry. Int J Psychoanal 25:1–8.

The communicative aspects of signals, signs, symbols, words, and language are significant considerations in psychoanalysis, as shown by the language of the patient, his dreams, and interpretations. Symbols are related to changing behavioral responses.

421. Masserman JH, Siever PW: Dominance, neurosis, and aggression: an experimental study. Psychosom Med 6:7–16.

Aggressiveness in a goal-competitive situation

appears in animals that have once had dominant access to the goal and then have been subjected to social displacement, or a motivational conflict that inhibits their goal-directed behavior. Aggressiveness diminishes or disappears when the group dominance of an animal is established by the relief of its neurosis, or when given drugs that temporarily disorganize neurotic apperceptions and associations.

422. Meisenhelder E: Social control of American good-will exchange students in China. J Soc Psychol 19:301–310.

The "guest concept" of personal position and language difficulties handicap the exchange student.

423. Mekeel S: Concerning race prejudice. Am J Orthopsychiatry 14:699–705.

Racial prejudice results from insecurity, serves as an outlet for anxiety and aggression, and provides a scapegoat or sacrifice. The provision of other socially sanctioned methods of releasing anxiety and aggression would help to alleviate the power and problem of racial prejudice.

424. Montagu A: Animal and human inheritance. Psychiatry 7:253–256.

While speech may be credited with having created a progressively more complex environment, those who were born into such environments, provided they had the ordinary normal potentialities of a human being, were already preadapted to such an environment. Selection for mental characteristics probably never operated within the human species.

425. Montagu A: Origins of the American Negro. Psychiatry 7:163–174.

Negroes shipped to America came predominantly from the West Coast of Africa. Future researches may show that a far larger number originally came from the Congo, although shipped from the West Coast. The mixed origins of the many Negroes who were shipped first to Europe, Mexico, or the West Indies complicates the picture. The American Negro population of today is a composite of African, white, and Indian elements.

426. Montagu A: The physical anthropology of the American Negro. Psychiatry 7:31–44.

The American Negro represents an amalgam into which has entered the genes of African Negroes, whites of all nations and social classes, and American Indians. As far as his physical characteristics are concerned, the American Negro represents the successful blending of these three principal elements into a unique biological type.

427. Nichols LA: Neuroses in native African troops. J Ment Science 90:862–874.

The African natives, secure, peaceful, and safe, living under a simple system with strong family and tribal ties, are sent into the army where intensive training, discipline, and routine increase and heighten their already great suggestibility and proneness to hysteria. Their lack of education leads to dramatic and gross expression of symptoms.

428. Stainbrook E, Siegel PS: A comparative group Rorschach study of southern Negro and white high school and college students. J Psychol 17:107–116.

Negro secondary students show less fluidity in association, more emotional stability, less impulsiveness, and less anxiety than white students. Negro college students show more associative rigidity, lower personality resources, greater immaturity, and less emotional instability.

429. Wolberg LR: Phallic elements in primitive, ancient and modern thinking. Psychiatr Q 18:278–297.

The formation of phallic symbols is inherited culturally via the phylogenetic tendency to proceed through stages of personality cognitive development. The genital organ may become a chief means of expressing attitudes and feelings and finds expression in a highly disguised and innocuous manner, such as in art forms and literary creations.

430. Zilboorg G: Masculine and feminine. Psychiatry 7:257–260.

World War I challenged the traditional view of femininity. Psychoanalytic thought expresses the perennial struggle between two forces—the free woman, the free, unenslaved mother, and the man who envies her and wishes to deprive her of her primordial right.

1945

431. Anderson HH: Studies in dominative and socially integrative behavior. Am J Orthopsychiatry 15:133–139.

A way must be found whereby a schoolroom of children can grow and develop as socially participating individuals. To foster such growth a propitious environment must be developed. Domination attacks the spontaneity of others and reduces problem-solving and integrative behavior.

432. Banay RS: Cultural influences in alcoholism. J Nerv Ment Dis 102:265–275.

Social factors play a great part in the genesis of alcohol addiction. Drink has become a universal function and panacea, a medium of merry making, and a solvent of sorrow. Such ideas, through art, literature, and folklore, have a deep effect on the collective consciousness of the race.

433. Bull N: Toward a clarification of the concept of emotion. Psychosom Med 7:210–214.

Feeling is dependent on a delay occurring after the assumption of a preliminary motor attitude. It is actually *the feeling of a motor attitude* and indicates a holding-up of final adequate activity. This sequence explains the seemingly divergent points of view of Darwin, James, and Dewey and offers a concrete basis for the study of conflicting motor attitudes and resulting psychosomatic symptoms.

434. Bullen AK: A cross-cultural approach to the problem of stuttering. Child Dev 16:1–88.

Stuttering is rare among New Guinea and Australian tribes, the Navaho, and the Eskimo. Stuttering has developed in white schools and in culture conflict situations.

435. Cattell RB: The cultural functions of social stratification: I: Regarding the genetic bases of society. J Soc Psychol 21:3–23.

The genetic consequences of social stratification include a general dysgenic trend, differing gene frequencies for different social classes, and culturgenic functions that increase the valuable genetic endowment of the population.

436. Cattell RB: The cultural functions of social stratification: II: Regarding individual and group dynamics. J Soc Psychol 21:25–55.

Elements that contribute to the total dynamics of society are class differences in psychological traits, class interactions, effects of class mobility on individuals and groups, the relationship between stratification, mental health, and culture change.

437. Coomaraswamy AK: "Spiritual paternity" and the "puppet-complex": a study in anthropological methodology. Psychiatry 8:287–297.

The anthropologist is rather too much inclined to consider the peculiarities of "primitive" peoples in isolation, neglecting the possibility that these peculiarities may represent provincial or peripheral survivals of theories held by some of the more sophisticated communities from which the primitive peoples may have declined. The Pacific doctrine of spiritual conception, for example, is an isolated phenomenon.

438. Eagleson OW, Bell ES: The values of Negro women college students. J Soc Psychol 22:149–154.

The culturally determined ranked order of values for Negro women are religious, social, political, theoretical, economic, and aesthetic values. There is general agreement of interests between Negro girls and white girls.

439. Erikson EH: Childhood and tradition in two American Indian tribes. Psychoanal Study Child 1:319–350.

The Sioux and Yurok tribes stand in opposition in almost all the basic configurations of existence. Many tribal customs can be understood from a psychoanalytic viewpoint. The mechanical child training recently developed in Western civilization may harbor an unconscious magic attempt to master machines by becoming more like them, comparable to the Sioux' identification with the buffalo, and the Yurok's with the river and the salmon.

440. Frenkel-Brunswik E, Sanford RN: Some personality factors in anti-Semitism. J Psychol 20:271–292.

Anti-Semitic college women have a restricted narrow personality with complete surrender to the superego, producing a lack of individuation and tendency to stereotypy. In order to achieve harmony with society, basic impulses are repressed, finding expression only in projection and moral indignation. General outgroupist attitudes may function to keep the personality integrated.

441. Frankenthal K: The role of sex in modern society. Psychiatry 8:19–25.

The extended use of birth control and the economic independence of women spell doom for the patriarchal family. The newly developing society will be curative for the particular form of neuroses in women that can figuratively be called the penis-envy neurosis.

442. Hallowell AI: 'Popular' responses and cultural differences: an analysis based on frequencies in a group of American Indian subjects. Rorsch Res Exch 9:153–168.

Frequencies of responses given by 151 Saulteau adults and children suggest that there are three categories of popular responses: (1) universal, (2) common to different cultural groups, and (3) unique popular characteristic of a single cultural group.

443. Honigmann JJ, Honigmann I: Drinking in an Indian-White community. Q J Stud Alcohol 5:575–619.

Athapaskan Indians drink alcohol to reduce anxiety. Drinking by white trappers is usually heavier than Indian drinking.

444. Humphrey ND: American race relations and the caste system. Psychiatry 8:379–381.

The caste system is useful for an understanding of American Negro-white relations. As a scientific concept it emphasizes and denotes the essential sociocultural bases of the system, while "race" conveys biological connotations that function to confuse the nature of the problem.

445. Humphrey ND: The stereotype and the social types of Mexican-American youths. J Soc Psychol 22:69–78.

Consideration of the adjustments and roles of Mexican youths in Detroit from traditional, immigrant, and migrant backgrounds illustrates a number of personalities that diverge from the popular stereotype.

446. Kuhlen RG: The interests and attitudes of Japanese, Chinese, and white adolescents: a study in culture and personality. J Soc Psychol 21:121–133.

Maturity scores indicate that Orientals tend to be immature on matters of disapprovals and worries but equivalent to whites on interests and admirations. The Oriental tendency to check "worries" on attitude tests may indicate emotional stress associated with the acculturation process.

447. LaBarre W: Some observations on character structure in the Orient: the Japanese. Psychiatry 8:319–342.

The Japanese are characterized by fanaticism, arrogance, "touchiness," perfectionism, conformity to rule, sadomasochistic behavior, suspiciousness, pedantry and a love of scatological obscenity, and anal sexuality. Americans owe it to the Japanese to modify the Japanese social system with great drasticness, sureness of purpose, and thoroughness.

448. Lee AM: Public opinion in relation to culture. Psychiatry 8:49–61.

The traditional American viewpoint has placed primary emphasis upon communication from the rank-and-file to the leaders. As American society becomes increasingly complex, with a tendency towards more rigid societal forms, this type of communication needs constant attention to be preserved.

449. Lewin B: Comments on Gregory Bateson and Margaret Mead: Balinese character, a photographic analysis. Psychoanal Study Child 1:379–387.

Balinese character furnishes data that intercalate nicely with analytic theory and experience. The photographs transmit an immediate sense of Balinese life.

450. Meerloo AM: A study of treason. Br J Psychol 35:27–33.

Though it is difficult to be objective with respect to Nazi propaganda and persuasion, psychologically a traitor is a person who feels the need to break away from the environment and uses violence to accomplish this.

451. Moloney JC: Psychiatric observations in Okinawa Shima. Psychiatry 8:391–399.

The low incidence of psychoses among Okinawans, despite the misery of World War II, proves that a person can be made psychologically strong enough to absorb almost any degree of psychic trauma without consequent disorganization of his ego.

452. Montagu A: Anthropology and genetics. Psychiatry 8:155–157.

There exists no evidence to confirm that the observed "psychological" diferences between groups of mankind have an inherent basis.

453. Montagu A: On the phrase "ethnic group" in anthropology. Psychiatry 8:27–33.

The advantages of the phrase *ethnic group* are (1) it emphasizes the fact that one is dealing with a distinguishable group, (2) it recognizes the fact that it is a group that has been subject to the action of cultural influences, and (3) it eliminates all obfuscating emotional implications.

454. Montagu A: The physical characters of African and other non-American Negroids. Psychiatry 8:279–285.

The term *Negro* refers to the colored populations of Africa, and the African descendants of some of these populations now living in the Americas and the West Indies. Non-American Negroids may be subdivided into a fairly large number of Negroid ethnic groups. In general, Negroids may be classed as African and Oceanic.

455. Montagu MFA: The acquisition of sexual knowledge in children. Am J Orthopsychiatry 15: 290–300.

Psychoanalytic theories are based upon the reconstruction of early childhood made from the responses of the adult patient. Although the acquisition of sexual knowledge may sometimes follow along the lines indicated by psychoanalytic theory, it does not always do so.

456. Montagu MFA: Intelligence of northern Negroes and southern whites in the first world war. Am J Psychol 58:161–180.

There are no significant inherent psychical differences between Negroes and whites. Differences in performance on tests are best explained by differences in socioeconomic history.

457. Morgan JJB: Attitudes of students toward the Japanese. J Soc Psychol 21:219–228.

Students show a tendency to reject the statement that the Japanese cannot assimilate American culture or that Japanese eyes are inferior. They tend to show distortion and avoid direct judgement of Japanese trustworthiness and cruelty.

458. Myers CS: The comparative study of instincts. Br J Psychol 36:1–9.

Comparative research includes consideration of phylogenetic and ontogenetic problems, mutations, and Lamarckism, relations of instincts among different zoological levels, inherited tendencies, and the role of intelligence.

459. Onishi K, Smith ME: Comparison of attitudes toward Japanese language schools expressed by young Americans of Japanese ancestry in 1937 and 1942. J Soc Psychol 21:209–218.

Students of Japanese ancestry were decidedly less in favor of Japanese-language schools in 1942.

460. Rees L, Eysenck HJ: A factorial study of some morphological and psychological aspects of human constitution. J Ment Science 91:8–21.

Body-type, as determined by an index derived from intercorrelations of body-measurements, may be correlated with psychiatric traits.

461. Roheim G: Aphrodite, or the woman with a penis. Psychoanal Q 14:350–390.

Aphrodite is not only the woman with the phallus but also is the woman who is derived from the male orgasm. She is not only the Lady of the Mandrake, but also the Lady of the Apple.

462. Roundtable: Germany after the war. Am J Orthopsychiatry 15:381–441.

Nazism is the result of cultural patterns and a "German personality." These cultural patterns need to be changed so that a new German personality, without the defects of the past, can emerge. To accomplish this the Allies must stress the guilt of all Germans and change the family life patterns peculiar to Germany.

463. Sumner FC, Clark KB: Some factors influencing a group of Negroes in their estimation of the intelligence and personality-wholesomeness of Negro subjects. J Psychol 19:75–78.

The skin color of Negro judges and subjects has a negative or null influence on estimates of intelligence or wholesomeness.

464. Thorner I: German words, German personality and Protestantism. Psychiatry 8:403–417.

The family-shaped German personality expresses its power orientation in the language it has created. The institutionalization of affectional responses in the family pattern would constitute a really radical German revolution.

465. Tomasic D: Personality development of the Dinaric warriors. Psychiatry 8:449–493.

Under the impact of external influences the organization of Dinaric tribes has gradually disintegrated and is preserved today only in the regions that have remained largely unaffected by social agents. However, the state organization that developed from this ancient system has retained some of the basic traits of the culture from which it sprang, such as the concentration of power, personal rule, and reliance on violence and deceit.

466. Witty P: New evidence on the learning ability of the Negro. J Abnorm Soc Psychol 40:401–404.

Learning effectiveness of Negroes in the Special Training Unit of the Army is equal to that of whites.

467. Woolf M: Prohibitions against the simultaneous consumption of milk and flesh in Orthodox Jewish law. Int J Psychoanal 26:169–177.

The prohibitions during Jewish Passover probably reflect the magical and animistic mentality, and archaic fantasies, of the period in which the ritual developed.

1946

468. Abenheimer KM: A note on the couvade in modern England (and Scotland). Br J Med Psychol 20:376–377.

The equation of eye and egg is a near one. Dreams about the displacement of eyes can be interpreted as a symbolical birth act.

469. Bales RF: Cultural differences in rates of alcoholism. Q J Stud Alcohol 6:480–499.

Rates of alcoholism are influenced by (1) the degree to which the culture operates to bring about acute needs for adjustment in its members, (2) the sort of attitudes toward drinking that the culture produces in its members, (3) the degree to which the culture provides suitable substitute means of satisfaction.

470. Barnett JH: Christmas in American culture. Psychiatry 9: 51–65.

The Christmas celebration in the U.S. is a complex cultural and psychological phenomenon that is intimately related to other aspects of American life and culture. The festival may directly express sincere religious sentiments, folk gaiety, and humanitarianism or may employ social rituals to expiate guilt and reduce hostility and antagonism.

471. Fodor A: The origin of the Mosaic prohibition against cooking the suckling in its mother's milk. Int J Psychoanal 27:140–149.

The Mosaic prohibition and the Jewish Passover ritual originate from two primitive motives: the early patrilineal-matrilineal struggle and the conflict between nomadic and agricultural lifeways.

472. Harris A, Watson G: Are Jewish or gentile children more clannish? J Soc Psychol 24:71–76.

Gentiles make more ingroup choices for friends than do Jewish children.

473. Havighurst RJ: Child development in relation to community social structure. Child Dev 17:85–89.

At the University of Chicago sociologists, anthropologists, educators, and psychologists have been working on collaborative, interdisciplinary studies that stress the factors of culture and community social structure in child development.

474. Havighurst RJ, Gunther MK, Pratt IE: Environment and the Draw-A-Man test: the performance of Indian children. J Abnorm Soc Psychol 41:50–63.

Indian children (Hopi, Zuni, Sioux, Navaho, Papago, and Zia) are superior to whites on the Draw-A-Man test. Environment seems to affect performance, and boys perform better than girls. The validity of the Draw-A-Man test as a measure of intelligence has not yet been established.

475. Humphrey ND: On assimilation and acculturation. Psychiatry 6:343–345.

The changing structure of the family is indicative both of the process of assimilation and of acculturation. Although both processes may be illustrated through reference to the same object, it does not follow that both processes change in the same way, at the same rate, or in parallel directions. Mexicans in Detroit have assimilated a great deal of American culture, but Americans have incorporated few elements of Mexican culture.

476. Inman WS: Styes, barley and wedding rings. Br J Med Psychol 20:331–338.

Folklore concerning the association of eye disease with barley and wedding rings is more than just a historical curiosity. An understanding of the barley legend, as well as the legendary place of wedding rings in treatment of eye diseases, can help in the clinical evaluation and treatment of patients.

477. Kohen M: The Venus of Willendorf. Am Imago 3:49–60.

The motif of the covered head as it appears in the paleolithic statuette is explained as an expression of the artist's anxiety over modeling a nude statue of his mother and his need to restrain fears of incest and castration.

478. LaBarre W: Primitive psychotherapy in native American cultures: peyotism and confession. J abnorm Soc Psychol 42:294–309.

Confession, as an aboriginal psychotherapeutic technique, and the significance of peyote cult group ritual explain the survival of this primitive psychotherapy and its contemporary reemergence in Plains religion.

479. LaBarre W: Some observations on character structure in the Orient: the Chinese. Part One. Psychiatry 9:215–237.

The agricultural economy of the Chinese has fostered a familial organization of society that has shaped not only religion and the state but has also influenced the distinctive Chinese temperament and personality, or national "ethos." Chinese culture has developed interpersonal relationships to the level of an exquisite and superb art.

480. LaBarre W: Some observations on character structure in the Orient: the Chinese. Part Two. Psychiatry 9:375–395.

The Chinese temperament is placid, kindly, gracious, and responsive; unpolitical, unaggressive, unfanatic, and unobsessive; cheerful, poised, fatalistic, and enduring; rational, secure, calm, and deeply considerate of others. The low tension of Chinese life is the essence of its charm. The healthy ego and the satisfied id, rather than the overgrown masterhood of the superego, are Chinese specialization.

481. Lund FH, Berg WC: Identifiability of nationality characteristics. J Soc Psychol 24:77–84.

The ability to identify nationality on the basis of physical appearance increases with age.

482. McGranahan DV: A comparison of social attitudes among American and German youth. J Abnorm Soc Psychol 41:245–257.

German youths favor obedience, admire power, view crime as a disloyalty to the state rather than a personal problem, and emphasize patriotism. Girls in both Germany and the U.S. tend to reflect the typical national pattern while boys deviate from it.

483. McGranahan DV, Janowitz M: Studies of German youth. J Abnorm Soc Psychol 41:3–14.

German youths express prodemocratic sentiments, yet they still exhibit some elements of totalitarianism.

484. Mead M: Cultural aspects of women's vocational problems in Post World War II. J Consult Clin Psychol 10:23–28.

American culture does not generally expect the woman to work outside the home; the current emergence of women in the work force is irregular and partly due to manpower shortage. Vocational choices and activities after the war are dependent upon the economic framework and cultural factors. Alteration of sex role stereotypes is a prerequisite for employment of women in a productive society.

485. Moloney J: On Oriental stoicism. Am J Psychiatry 103:60–64.

Oriental stoicism is a derivative of acculturation.

Okinawan Orientals neither repress nor suppress emotions and are free from psychosomatic disease.

486. Montagu A: Anti-feminism and race prejudice. Psychiatry 9:69–71.

Antifeminism of the nineteenth century and racial prejudice of the twentieth century show many parallels. To remove impediments to social progress, women had to fight. Minority groups have much to learn from the suffragettes.

487. Montagu A: Racism and social action. Psychiatry 9:143–150.

The theoretical attack on racism has now progressed to a second phase in which the theoretical knowledge is utilized in social action and education policies that will prevent racism by supporting and building a society in which racism cannot flourish.

488. Schneirla TC: Problems in a biopsychology of social organization. J Abnorm Soc Psychol 41:385–402.

Trophallaxis and cooperativeness underlie all intragroup approach reactions on all social levels. Dominance theory is inadequate since it emphasizes factors that reduce group intensity.

489. Schnier J: Dragon Lady. Am Imago 4:78–98.

Dragon lady fantasies throughout the world arise from the child's projection of oral aggressive wishes onto the mother and subsequent fear of the dragon lady as a symbol of mother.

490. Seltzer CC: Body disproportions and dominant personality traits. Psychosom Med 8:75–97.

Individuals possessing certain constitutional disproportions have a greater frequency of those dominant personality traits indicating lesser stability, lesser integration, greater sensitivity and complexity of the personality, and lesser capacity for making easy social adjustments. There may be a genetic element in the determination of personality and behavior.

491. Stearns AW: Integration of medical science and sociology. J Nerv Ment Dis 103:612–625.

Physicians have cared for the sick, but no group cares for the poor or bad. In the future, professional groups should form with special interest in crime and poverty.

492. Wilbur GB: The reciprocal relationship of man and his ideological milieu. Am Imago 3:3–48.

Consideration of the primal scene in ancient

Egypt and the development of Egyptian religion shows that the Egyptians produced an intellectual structure that illustrates the psychological development of the individual.

493. Winthrop H: Semantic factors in the measurement of personality integration. J Soc Psychol 24: 149–176.

Semantic blockage largely accounts for attitude inconsistency. Chance plays a larger role in personality integration than self-conscious semantic jurisdiction over attitude formation and retention.

494. Zipf GK: Cultural-chronological strata in speech. J Abnorm Soc Psychol 41:351–355.

There is a general positive correlation between age of a word in a lexicon and frequency of its occurrence.

1947

495. Baumgarten-Tramer F: Democracy and character. Br J Psychol 38:20–22.

A nation can regress to a former phase of development, as in the case of Germany. Democracy is only possible for nations with well developed social feelings and high degree of character.

496. Chadhury AKR: Pakistan—a psychological analysis. J Abnorm Soc Psychol 42:462–465.

The problem of lack of identification between Muslims and Hindus cannot be solved by the creation of religious states or migration. Dissolution of British imperialism, education, separation of religion and state, or the unification of India under communism/socialism are possible solutions to the problem.

497. Devereux G: Mohave orality: an analysis of nursing and weaning customs. Psychoanal Q 16:-519–546.

The Mohave Indians' direct awareness of the trauma of weaning, and the only slightly distorted manifestations of their orality, show unusual direct insight into what are obscure psychological mechanisms to most peoples in whom such id strivings are automatically repressed.

498. Frank JD: Adjustment problems of selected Negro soldiers. J Nerv Ment Dis 105:647–660.

Similarities between Negro and white troops in response to stress are much greater than differences.

Emotional reactions among Negro soldiers are influenced by aspects of racial discrimination.

499. Geddes WR: The colour sense of Fijian natives. Br J Psychol 37:30–36.

Ishihara cards show varying percentages of red-green color blindness among Fijians, East Indians, and New Zealanders. The incidence of color blindness is due to an ethnic, rather than nutritional or racial, factor. Fijian color terminology places an emphasis on intensity and saturation and is not inferior to the European terminology.

500. Goldstein MS: Infants of Mexican descent: physical status of neonates. Child Dev 18:3–10.

Mexican neonates born in the U.S. are significantly heavier in body weight than those born in Mexico. In body weight and length Mexican neonates compare favorably with newborns of other ethnic stock of a similar economic level.

501. Gulick A: The problem of right and wrong in Japan and some of its political consequences. J Soc Psychol 26:3–20.

Various temperamental traits and historical events have shaped the ethical pattern of Japan. Japan's amenability to the idealistic appeal and responsiveness to effective leadership indicate a favorable prognosis for reeducation.

502. Hebb DO: Spontaneous neurosis in chimpanzees: theoretical relations with clinical and experimental phenomena. Psychosom Med 9:3–16.

Fear or mental depression is directly related to a disruption of functional organization. Experience alone can cause psychopathology. Constitutional factors alone can also do so, but in most instances both factors operate together. "Experimental neurosis" in chimpanzees is intimately related to the clinical condition in man.

503. Hellersberg EF: Social and cultural aspects in guidance work and psychotherapy. Am J Orthopsychiatry 17:647–651.

Divergent types of adolescence are produced by divergent cultural conditions in the surrounding adult world. The cure of mentally and emotionally disturbed persons can only be complete if psychotherapy takes the cultural aspect into consideration.

504. Honigmann JJ: Cultural dynamics of sex: a study in culture and personality. Psychiatry 10: 37–47.

Emotional isolation, self-assertion, and passivity

may be regarded as serving the safety needs of the Kaska Indian. Sexual behaviors and attitudes are directed by the basic motivations that the human being acquires in the process of being socialized.

505. Hunt WA: Negro-white differences in intelligence in World War II: a note of caution. J Abnorm Soc Psychol 42:254–255.

Negro standards of intelligence for military admission were more lenient than for white recruits, hence any comparison of military performance between these two groups is biased.

506. Hunt WA: The relative incidence of psychoneurosis among Negroes. J Consult Psychol 11:-133–136.

The relatively less frequent occurrence of psychoneurosis among Negro mental disorders is a cultural phenomenon. Cultural level may influence the form of expression of psychological conflict.

507. Kaufman SH: Prejudice as a sociopsychiatric responsibility. Am J Psychiatry 104:44–47.

Fear of difference in people and lack of understanding of others contribute to prejudice.

508. Kecskemeti P, Leites N: Some psychological hypotheses on Nazi Germany. J Soc Psychol 26:-141–184.

A distinctive type of character structure in the Nazi variant of German culture approximates the "compulsive character" of psychoanalytic theory.

509. Lundin RW: Toward a cultural theory of consonance. J Psychol 23:45–50.

Consonance is not an absolute entity dependent upon the natural properties of the stimulus object. The human organism builds up behavior equipment that is largely culturally determined. Consonance is influenced by general cultural backgrounds.

510. MacCrone ID: Reaction to domination in a color-caste society: a preliminary study of the race attitudes of a dominated group. J Soc Psychol 26: 69–98.

South Africans, unlike other caste groups, do not display an attitude of submission to European domination. This attitudinal position can be seen as a result of awareness of previous independence and a feeling of cultural distinctness.

511. Mead M: Age patterning in personality development. Am J Orthopsychiatry 17:231–240.

When a child who has been dispossessed by the birth of a sibling has the opportunity, upon the birth of a third sibling, to help dispossess the child that replaced him in the lap, the development of a series of integration favorable to symbolic elaboration of experience begins. This suggests one aspect of child-rearing practices that may be utilized to change the trend of a society.

512. Mead M: The concept of culture and the psychosomatic approach. Psychiatry 10:57–76.

Certain types of psychosomatic modification, carrying within them definite possibilities of a pathology that becomes in time structural and irreversible, are associated with our whole way of life.

513. Mead M: The implications of culture change for personality development. Am J Orthopsychiatry 17:633–646.

The individual in a changing culture must not only adapt to a range of situations, but also to a range that involves polarizations, i.e., the modern American must be able to be sedentary as well as migratory.

514. Molina MF: Study of a psychopathic personality in Guatemala. Psychiatry 10:31–36.

An anthropological, sociological, criminological, and psychiatric evaluation of murderer and sex offender leads to the recommendation of capital punishment.

515. Murdock GP: Family universals. Marriage Fam Living 9:39.

An intensive study of family and kinship in many societies has shown that the nuclear family, the father as family member, and incest taboos are universal. Extramarital sex is common in most societies.

516. Parsons T: Certain primary sources and patterns of aggression in the social structure of the Western world: the problem of aggression. Psychiatry 10:167–181.

The "jungle philosophy" tends to be projected onto the relations of nation states at precisely the point where, under the technological and organizational situation of the modern world, it can do the most harm. Certain characteristics of the kinship and occupational systems in the Western world are the basis of this aggressive philosophy.

517. Portenier LG: Abilities and interests of Japanese-American high school seniors. J Soc Psychol 25:53–62.

As a result of prejudice against them, many Japanese-Americans are isolated and prevented from mastering the English language or continuing their education.

518. Rapaport D: Technological growth and the psychology of man. Psychiatry 10:253–259.

A society with stable ideals as a substantial basis for education will be able to absorb and utilize in the furtherance of human happiness even the most rapid technological progress.

519. Seago DW: Stereotypes: before Pearl Harbor and after. J Psychol 23:55–64.

Stereotyped attitudes show considerable stability despite changes in world events or the role of the group.

520. Senter D: Witches and psychiatrists. Psychiatry 10:49–56.

The present clash of Anglo- and Spanish-American culture in the process of acculturation is shaking the foundations of the old native system in New Mexico. New methods in medicine are accepted slowly. Some of the native *albolarios,* however, have become keenly aware of the efficiency of modern hospitals and pharmacies.

521. Sereno R: Cryptomelanism: a study of color relations and personal insecurity in Puerto Rico. Psychiatry 10:261–269.

Cryptomelanism is not caused by the physical or biological consequences of intercourse between Negroes and non-negroes but by the attitude of a culture or of a group toward race differences. Collective neurotic patterns relating to cryptomelanism are pathological reactions to pathological attitudes.

522. Sikkema M: Observations on Japanese early child training. Psychiatry 10:423–432.

The cultural role of Issei parents in Hawaii is quite different than that familiar to Western culture in that parents set few limits, tend to "spoil" young children, and discipline is shifted to the school at an early age. "Strictness" in child training seems characteristic, however of Nisei parents, indicating they may be adopting Western customs of child toilet training. Further study should be done on the indicated absence of eneuresis among Japanese children in Hawaii.

523. Taylor S: Remembering: some effects on language and other factors. Br J Psychol 38:7–19.

Lapse of time, degree of education, social status, language used, nature of material, and social attitudes all influence degree of recall of meaningful prose for Indian college students.

1948

524. Abel TM: The Rorschach test in the study of culture. Rorsch Res Exch, J Proj Techniques, 12:79–93.

A summary of the advantages and problems in the employment of the Rorschach test in many culture areas points out future research needs.

525. Alexander L: Sociopsychologic structure of the SS. Arch Neurol Psychiatry 59:622–634.

The SS was a criminal organization not only because its members actually committed crimes but also because the essential mode of its thinking and its group behavior were those of all criminal organizations. Social and cultural factors in Germany resulted in the ego part of the personality being insufficiently developed or being crushed by educational, social, or other forces.

526. Alexander L: War crimes their social-psychological aspects. Am J Psychiatry 105:170–177.

Group sanction of aggression in Nazi Germany is explained by destructive thinking, widespread fear, restriction of individual rights, and censorship.

527. Arsenian J, Arsenian JM: Tough and easy cultures: a conceptual analysis. Psychiatry 11:377–385.

The easy cultures are not necessarily the "best," but they are the least tension-producing-and-sustaining. Very tough cultures, however, must be expected to be pathogenic.

528. Avhandling A: A psychiatric and sociologic study of a series of Swedish naval conscripts. Acta Psychiatr Neurol, Supp 48:1–201.

Seamen, as compared to nonseamen of the same social class, have a slightly lower percentage of individuals with the worst test results on intelligence tests. There are more psychopaths among the seamen than among the nonseamen. Cases of severe psychopathy ought to be exempted from military training. The special conditions prevailing in the navy with respect to training do not provide the explanation of the many desertions. The relative incidence of desertions is not higher among the men doing service at sea than among those serving on land.

529. Bateman JF, Dunham HW: The state mental hospital as a specialized community experience. Am J Psychiatry 105:445–448.

Therapy is frustrated by a dual cultural system that develops in a mental hospital and that may facilitate or impede recovery.

530. Baumgarten-Tramer F: German psychologists and recent events. J Abnorm Soc Psychol 43: 452–465.

German psychologists failed to maintain their scientific independence under political pressure, and thus prostituted their science.

531. Bellak L, Holt RR: Somatotypes in relation to dementia praecox. Am J Psychiatry 104:713–724.

Mental patients who die of causes other than exhaustive diseases tend to be long, lean, and wiry. Bodily build is not the result of mental illness.

532. Brody EB: Psychiatric problems of the German occupation. Am J Psychiatry 105:286–291.

The artificial pattern of World War II occupation life encourages the development of latent neurotic potentialities.

533. Carothers JC: A study of mental derangement in Africans, and an attempt to explain its peculiarities, more especially in relation to the African attitude to life. Psychiatry 11:47–86.

The African's inherited tendencies to mental disease are probably not very different from the Europeans. The culture of the Africans of Kenya seems well suited to man's mental needs and rarely permits situations that might cause mental breakdown. However, the civilization of the modern European type to which both Europeans and North American Negroes are subjected does not seem as conducive to mental health.

534. Carter LF: The identification of "racial" membership. J Abnorm Soc Psychol 43:279–286.

Jewish and non-Jewish (Mediterranean and European) faces are frequently misclassified, raising some doubts as to the generality of Allport and Kramer's study.

535. Cox HL: The place of mythology in the study of culture. Am Imago 5:83–94.

Through mythology man projects his conflicts, desires, and values thus permitting an identification of his problems and allowing for solutions. Mythology is a cultural Rorschach with culturally structured elements and psychic stresses.

536. Devereux G: The function of alcohol in Mohave society. Q J Stud Alcohol 9:207–251.

The absence of a high level of anxiety and the preservation of certain basic cultural attitudes probably explains why the intoxicated Mohave is not aggressively antisocial, and why Mohave society has fairly withstood the ravages of alcoholism.

537. Devereux G: Mohave Indian obstetrics. Am Imago 5:95–139.

Psychoanalytic interpretations of Mohave belief and practice concerning childbirth reveal that Western interpretations of childbirth also shed light on Mohave psychodymanics, though further work is required in the area of primitive obstetrics.

538. Gillin J: Magical fright. Psychiatry 11:387–400.

"Magical fright" is a seemingly widespread syndrome current among folk peoples in various parts of Latin America. Depression, withdrawal from normal social activity and responsibility, and signs of temporary collapse of the ego organization are commonly observed symptoms of *espanto* or *susto*. Because of the large numbers of people's recognizing the validity of espanto, modern medicine must learn to deal effectively with the results of "magical fright."

539. Grygier T: Psychiatric observations in the Arctic. Br J Psychol 39:84–96.

Observations in a psychiatric ward in the Komi Republic, USSR, suggest that there are some differences between national groups in mental and personality tests and symptoms. There is a striking frequency of epilepsy in Zyrian populations. The cultural background must be part of the clinical picture.

540. Hart HH: Sublimation and aggression. Psychiatr Q 390–412.

The problem of sublimation and aggression, even on a group level, is by no means insoluble when instinctual gratification and frustration are properly balanced. In Western culture we are far from attaining this balance.

541. Hartley EL, Krugman D: Note on children's social role perception. J Psychol 26:399–406.

Differential rates in the development of perception of the parent role and the worker role are displayed by children.

542. Hartley EL, Rosenbaum M, Schwartz S: Children's use of ethnic forms of reference: an exploratory study of children's conceptualizations of multiple ethnic group membership. J Psychol 26:367–386.

Ethnic frames of reference among Jewish, Catholic, and Protestant children develop with age, are situation specific, and differ from those of adults.

543. Hartley EL, Rosenbaum M, Schwartz S: Children's perception of ethnic group membership. J Psychol 26:387–398.

Permanent and momentary ethnic roles are recognized by American and Jewish children, in aggressive and abusive situations.

544. Henry J: Common problems of research in anthropology and psychiatry. Am J Orthopsychiatry 18:698–703.

Anthropologists and psychiatrists can explore common problems by studying the same mental case utilizing techniques appropriate to each discipline and by the formulation of hypotheses in regard to the essential core of specific syndrome types, which may then be studied cross-culturally.

545. Hobbs AH, Lambert RD: An evaluation of sexual behavior in the human male. Am J Psychiatry 104:758–764.

Faulty methods and overgeneralizations cloud the conclusions drawn by Kinsey et al.

546. Jarachow S: Totem feast in modern dress. Am Imago 5:65–69.

The annual convention banquet in modern society is derived from the primitive totem feast in terms of content and symbolism.

547. Jenkins MD, Randall CM: Differential characteristics of superior and unselected Negro college students. J Soc Psychol 27:187–202.

Psychometric intelligence and scholastic achievement fluctuate with respect to environmental background. Consideration of within group variability is important.

548. Kaldegg A: Responses of German and English secondary school boys to a projection test. Br J Psychol 39:30–53.

German boys' responses to Raven's Controlled projection test show high degree of seriousness, pronounced identification, conventionalism, rigidity, dislike of cowards, tendency to view severe punishment as appropriate to any offense, and tendency to believe obviously untrue stories.

549. Kecskemeti P, Leites N: Some psychological hypotheses on Nazi Germany. J Soc Psychol 27:91–118.

Compulsive tendencies in German culture may be examined in terms of the Zusammenbach syndrome, the ascetic syndrome, hardness versus softness, destructiveness, aggression, and guilt.

550. Kecskemeti P, Leites N: Some psychological hypotheses on Nazi Germany. J Soc Psychol 27:141–164.

The characteristics of rational-irrational shifts, generalizing attitudes, withdrawal, submersion, polarization between omnipotence and impotence, and self-contempt reflect some compulsive tendencies in Germany.

551. Kecskemeti P, Leites N: Some psychological hypotheses on Nazi Germany. J Soc Psychol 27:241–270.

Compulsive tendencies in Germany may be illuminated in terms of characteristic protection, depression, orderliness, methodicalness, isolation, possessiveness, doubt, and dogmatism.

552. Kubie LS: Instincts and homeostasis. Psychosom Med 10:15–30.

It is impossible to make any absolute distinction between instinct and drive. In higher animals instinctual patterns are triggered by warning mechanisms rather than by tissue hungers, therefore, on the psychologic level, instinctual aims and objects are also built around the warning mechanism. This agrees with Freud's position.

553. Lantz H: Rorschach testing in pre-literate cultures. Am J Orthopsychiatry 18:287–291.

The experiences of those using the Rorschach test for cross-cultural personality investigation, and the fact that the test was developed to describe the dynamic intellectual-emotional configuration among persons in Western society, limit its value in preliterate societies.

554. Lobb J: Family life in Brazil. Marriage Fam Living 10:8–10.

Various factors serve to maintain the dual pattern of legitimate and illegitimate families in Brazil. Brazil needs to implement programs of social planning that are family oriented.

555. Meredith HV: Body size in infancy and childhood: a comparative study of data from Okinawa, France, South Africa, and North America. Child Dev 19:179–195.

Analysis of stature and weight periodically from birth to 10 years permits construction of a factual source table on racial differences. Throughout childhood, Okinawans are the shortest of the 13 ethno-socioeconomic groups studied.

556. Miller NE, Bugelski R: Minor studies of aggression: the influence of frustration imposed by the in-group on attitudes expressed toward out-groups. J Psychol 25:437–442.

A decreased number of desirable traits is assigned to Japanese and Mexicans following a frustrating experience. Aggression aroused against the experimenters was extended to the foreigners.

557. Montagu MFA: Sex order of birth and personality. Am J Orthopsychiatry 18:351–353.

The relation of the sex order of birth of siblings within a family is significant in that its affects the personality development of each of the children.

558. Mudd EH: The family in the Soviet Union. Marriage Fam Living 10:7.

Russia's concern with the family unit as an integral part of the state is reflected in programs of health care, women's activities, and education.

559. Myers HS, Yochelson L: Color denial in the Negro: a preliminary report. Psychiatry 11:39–46.

An expression of the need for increased self-esteem and security among American Negroes may be the desire for whiteness. Psychosis often includes elements that reflect a need to solve the problem of color and the difficulties in living associated with being Negro.

560. Oesterreicher W: Sadomasochistic obsessions in an Indonesian. Am J Psychother 2:64–81.

A Batak (Sumatra) male schoolteacher receives psychotherapy for an anxiety neurosis. Because cultural forces that repress are not strong, unconscious psychological mechanisms are easily accessible and dream symbolism easily interpretable. His sadomasochistic fantasies are linked to his culture.

561. Osborne EG: Problems of the Chinese family. Marriage Fam Living 10:8.

The picture of family life in China is not clear due to the variability of social customs and the impact of the West. The devastating influence of poverty can be ameliorated by economic development.

562. Roheim G: The song of the sirens. Psychiatr Q 22:18–44.

The irresistible and sexual lure of the water spirit may be explained on the basis of Ferenczi's thalassal regression theory. The uterine or maternal significance of the water may be derived from the milk-water symbolism.

563. Roheim G: The thread of life. Psychoanal Q 17: 471–486.

The relationship in rites and myths between the severed threads on the umbilical cord are but a preconscious substitute for ever-threatening castration anxiety.

564. Rokeach M: Generalized mental rigidity as a factor in ethnocentrism. J Abnorm Soc Psychol 43: 259–278.

The rigidity of an ethnocentric person's concrete solutions to social problems is not an isolated personality phenomenon but an aspect of general rigidity applied to nonsocial solutions as well.

565. Ruesch J, Jacobsen A, Loeb MB: Acculturation and illness. Psychol Monographs 62:1–40.

A rating scale based upon culture distance from American core culture is designed to assess effects of acculturation stress, along with measures of personality and social environment. Acculturation is facilitated by good motivation, age, intelligence, and frequency of contacts.

566. Saenger G, Shulman HM: Some factors determining intercultural behavior and attitudes of members of different ethnic groups in mixed neighborhoods. J Psychol 25:365–380.

In order to improve interethnic group relations in mixed areas, more recreation centers for the less privileged, and a program of cultural education are necessary.

567. Sato K, Nakano F: Nationality preferences of Japanese students after World War II. J Soc Psychol 28:165–166.

Japanese students show a strong preference for Western nations rather than Asian nations.

568. Sereno R: Obeah: magic and social structure in the Lesser Antilles. Psychiatry 11:15–31.

Obeah is a very peculiar species of magic. It is the black man's answer to the white man's intolerance. It is a form of social control as illegal as discrimination.

569. Spindler GD: American character as revealed by the military: descriptions and origins. Psychiatry 11:275–281.

The American military offers a unique subgroup for the study of the American national character because of the range of classes and regional backgrounds that is encompasses. Egocentric values related to the frontier life come in conflict with the demands of an industrialized, urbanized society.

570. Sumner FC: Neurotic tendency and socio-economic status of Negro college women. J Soc Psychol 28:291–292.

The differences in socioeconomic status between most and least neurotic Negro college women are not significant.

571. Taylor WS: Basic personality in Orthodox Hindu culture patterns. J Abnorm Soc Psychol 43: 3–12.

Orthodox Hinduism is a highly developed culture system directly affecting personality structure through emphasis on discipline, conformity, responsibility, and dependence that are sanctioned by religious postulates.

572. Terman LM: Kinsey's "Sexual behavior in the human male": some comments and criticisms. Psychol Bull 45:443–459.

Kinsey's work contains recklessly worded and slanted evaluations, the slanting being often in the direction of implied preference for uninhibited sexual activity.

573. von Domarus E: Anthropology and psychotherapy. Am J Psychother 2:603–614.

Polyandrous societies show ways of solving Oedipus and related complexes that are totally different from our own ways and thereby bring out in high relief our own familial difficulties. The mode of social life determines whether in a given society psychoneurotic and psychosomatic diseases are prevented or not. Changes in sociomental attitudes are necessary if psychotherapy is to succeed in generating such an emotional life in an individual that thinking, willing, and acting can become completely adjusted to the increasingly difficult requirements of a changing society.

1949

574. Abel TM, Hsu FLK: Some aspects of personality of Chinese as revealed by the Rorschach test. Rorsch Res Exchange J Proj Techniques 13:285–301.

Tests of China-born and American-born subjects reveal a status personality for the former, and anxiety over the changing social situation for the latter.

575. Altus WD: The American Mexican: the survival of a culture. J Soc Psychol 29:211–220.

The persistence of the Spanish-language and Mexican culture among army trainees may be explained by continued association with other members of the culture who retain diet, religion, language, and hostility from the majority population. All serve to set persons of Mexican ancestry apart from the mainstream.

576. Barber RG, Wright H: Psychological ecology and the problem of psychosocial development. Child Dev 20:131–143.

Through methods of sampling and recording the psychological habitat, psychological ecology can make important contributions to an understanding of psychosocial development.

577. Barnouw V: The phantasy world of a Chippewa woman. Psychiatry 12:67–76.

The autobiography of Julia Badger reveals her to be a woman living a fantasy world. While the Chippewa still stand in awe of dreams and visions, her neighbors are not favorably impressed by the abundant productivity of her inner world.

578. Benedict R: Child rearing in certain European countries. Am J Orthopsychiatry 19:342–350.

Swaddling practices conform to the values of cultural groups. Swaddling is tightest and kept up the longest in Great Russia, where its isolation is related to the kind of personal inviolability maintained in Russian adulthood. In Poland swaddling is conceived as a first step in the long process of "hardening" a child. Among the Jews swaddling is the baby's first experience of the warmth of life in his own home.

579. Bowman CC: Social factors opposed to the extension of heterosexuality. Am J Psychiatry 106: 441–447.

A social and historical analysis of heterosexual relationships in American society suggests a continuation of present trends in sexual morality toward fewer restrictions.

580. Brown WT: A consideration of human ecology. Dis Nerv Syst 10:239–242.

An individual's environment is composed of both the Induced Environment, which results from his directed, purposeful activity, and the Inevitable Environment, which is composed of such things as the location of one's birth, storms, social upheavals, and epidemics. More time should be directed toward the basic, fundamental, physical phenomena associated with human ecology.

581. Cattell RB: The dimensions of culture patterns by factorization of national character. J Abnorm Soc Psychol 44:443–469.

Factor analysis of variables for 70 nations provides ten factors with sociological or psychological meaning that are essentially demographic, economic, historical, and aspects of group psychodynamics.

582. Clark EL: Motivation of Jewish students. J Soc Psychol 29:113–118.

Jewish students are more motivated to achieve scholastically than non-Jewish students.

583. Devereux G: Magic substances and narcotics of the Mohave Indians. Br J Med Psychol 22:110–116.

Study of Digueno and Mohave Indian cultures reveals that charms are the psychological equivalents of datura, and vice versa. Magic substances, drugs, and alcohol satisfy a constellation of interrelated psychological needs, most of which are rooted in the oral-sadistic stage and are intimately interwoven with death wishes and with the conscious denial of these wishes.

584. Devereux G: The social structure of the hospital as a factor in total therapy. Am J Orthopsychiatry 10:492–500.

Social therapy extends man's right to be himself to the mental patient and can best be achieved through the joint effort of anthropologists and psychiatrists. Social anthropologists can help in the diagnosis, therapy, setting of therapeutic objectives, and in establishing the ethics of social therapy.

585. Escalona S: A commentary upon some recent changes in child rearing practices. Child Dev 20: 157–162.

While cultural emphasis on the psychological implications of child-rearing practices is desirable, increasing awareness of the less rational elements of our behavior is important.

586. Evans WN: The cultural significance of the changed attitude toward work in Great Britain. Bull Menninger Clin 13:1–8.

The present class struggle in Britain is reflected in the semantics of the "left" and the "right." The breakdown of the intellectual tradition that we regard as distinctively European is due to the rapid influx of women into industry, changing conceptions of education, and a changing moral climate. Once a cultural ideal, the gentleman of leisure is now stigmatized as a "spiv" or a "drone."

587. Freud A: Aggression in relation to emotional development: normal and pathological. Psychoanal Study Child 3:37–42.

Aggression, destruction, and their expressions and development are as much in the center of interest for dynamic psychology now as the development of the sexual function was at the beginning of the century. A review of the contributions made by Freudian psychoanalysis to the subject is relevant.

588. Freud A: Notes on aggression. Bull Menninger Clin 13: 143–151.

Aggression may be seen as a quality of pregenital sex manifestations, as a function of the ego (the frustration theory), and as an expression of the destructive instinct. Destructiveness, delinquency, and criminality in children are caused by a stunting of libidinal development and are not open to direct educational influences.

589. Fried EG, Lissance MF: The dilemmas of German youth. J Abnorm Soc Psychol 44:50–60.

German youths today are principally concerned with personal, social, and economic security. The Nazi ideology is still felt, though democratic structures may be underlying.

590. Gillin J: Marriage among the Mocheros. Marriage Fam Living 11:70–71.

Premarital and extramarital sex is common among the mestizo Mocheros of Peru.

591. Hanks LM, Jr: The quest for individual autonomy in Burmese personality: with particular reference to the Arakan. Psychiatry 12:285–300.

The Burman's striving for power is an aspect of his attempt to free himself from restraint. The Burman's real goal is personal autonomy in order to recapture the joyousness of unrestrained human contact.

592. Hanson DA: Aggression in nature and society. Br J Med Psychol 22:151–155.

Although human society depends to a great extent on language and culture, the actions of individuals composing a society nevertheless often are determined by immediate physical and physiological events.

593. Harding DW: Aggression in nature and society. Br J Med Psychol 22:161–165.

To the extent that we are social beings, aggression against others is bound to set up conflict within us. We need to make sure that the purpose for which we violate our social sentiments is important enough to allow us to tolerate the consequent regret.

594. Hartmann H, Kris E, Loewenstein RM: Notes on the theory of aggression. Psychoanal Study Child 3–4:36.

In the same way as libidinal cathexis follow in many instances the pathway established by physiological processes, so aggressive cathexis follows the pathways of certain phases of physiological maturation and also of the stages of libidinal development.

595. Henry J: Anthropology and psychosomatics. Psychosom Med 11:216–222.

The Pilaga Indians reveal a number of psychically related somatic disorders particularly in the areas of speech, hearing, and muscle function. However, they are free from certain expected disorders, which points to the importance of more precise definitions of etiologic factors, and the study of cultural totalities.

596. Himes JS, Holden MH: Growth of tradition in a Southern Negro family. J Soc Psychol 30:137–148.

The processes of cultural assimilation may be examined through the experiences of four generations of a North Carolina Negro family. Integration into the community, property acquisition, and consolidation of behavior patterns are part of the family growth cycle.

597. Hsu FLK: Suppression versus repression: a limited psychological interpretation of four cultures. Psychiatry 12:223–242.

Suppression is the more important mechanism of socialization of the individual in Japan and China, while repression is more important in American and German cultures. Family differences do not explain the origin of loyalty to the wider state of Germany and Japan, or the lack of such loyalty in America and China.

598. Kluckhohn C, Rosenzweig JC: Two Navaho children over a five-year period. Am J Orthopsychiatry 10:266–278.

By utilizing a variety of projective techniques, different testers and interpreters may obtain remarkably consistent personality assessments of two Navaho children.

599. Kramer BM: Dimensions of prejudice. J Psychol 27:389–452.

The dimensional approach to the complex phenomenon of prejudice has many clear advantages, both practically and theoretically.

600. Levinson DJ: An approach to the theory and measurement of ethnocentric ideology. J Soc Psychol 28:19–40.

Ethnocentrism is a stable ideological system of opinions, attitudes, and values concerning ingroups and outgroups. Its generality, contradictions, and content (stereotypy, etc.) point to deeper personality trends that help organize individual social views.

601. Montagu MFA: The origin of social life and the biological basis of cooperation. J Soc Psychol 29:267–284.

Biological and social cooperation originate in the process of reproduction. Social cooperation is a continuation of the maternal-offspring relationship.

602. Montagu MFA: Some psychodynamic factors in race prejudice. J Soc Psychol 30:175–188.

Racial prejudice is a real, not mythological, phenomenon. The roots of prejudice are integrated into the psychic structure of man. Prejudice patterns are created through denial of anxiety and substitution of aggression, affiliation with dominant group, elaboration of reaction formations and compensatory emotional drives, and renunciation of parts of the self-image and substituting a borrowed identity.

603. Maslow AH: Our maligned animal nature. J Psychol 28: 273–278.

Prejudices and misconceptions concerning the unconscious and primitive side of man and culture have contributed to the maligning of man's nature.

604. Pickford RW: The genetics of intelligence. J Psychol 28:129–146.

A simple genetic theory based upon groups of allelomorphic pairs of genes may represent the inheritance of intelligence. Where p is a gene tending to raise intelligence, and q is a gene tending to lower it, a $(p + q)^{20}$ expansion adequately duplicates the intelligence distribution curve.

605. Rank B: Aggression. Psychoanal Study Child 3:43–48.

The vicissitudes of aggression and its forms of expression depend on the relationship between the frustrating and frustrated forces. By providing an emotional climate favorable to the development of an ego that has the capacity to organize and to control drives, we may be able to modify or even eliminate the destructive element of aggression.

606. Rees L: The value of anthropometric indices in the assessment of body build. J Ment Science 95:171–179.

Body build is normally distributed along a leptomorphic-eurymorphic continuum in which the individual's position can be ascertained by Rees-Eysenk Body Index. The subjective procedure of somatoscopy can be effectively replaced by the objective method of using the index.

607. Roheim G: The magical function of the dream. Int J Psychoanal 30:172–176.

The psychological principles of magic derive from the libido and magic and epic incantation. The dream's magical function lies in solving difficulties that are illustrative of the conflict between id and superego.

608. Roheim G: The symbolism of subincision. Am Imago 6:321–328.

The ritual of subincision in Australia is aimed at separating young men from mothers and aggregating them to the group of fathers—the subincised penis symbolizes the vagina.

609. Roheim G: Technique of dream analysis and field work in anthropology. Psychoanal Q 18:471–479.

Interpretations of dreams obtained even by the analytically trained anthropologist can never be as detailed, as deep and as personal as those obtained in clinical analysis.

610. Rosenblith JF: A replication of "some roots of prejudice." J Abnorm Soc Psychol 44:470–489.

Allport and Kramer's findings are generally confirmed with data from South Dakota college students' correlates of prejudice.

611. Ruesch J, Bateson G: Structure and process in social relations. Psychiatry 12:105–124.

Social interaction systems are circular self-corrective systems tending toward a level of organization, or negative entropy, and stabilizing at a level that is characterized by a minimum rate of change.

612. Russell DH, Vaughn WT, King G: A contribution from child psychiatry towards a broader concept of constitution. Dis Nerv Syst 10:261–266.

There are intimate relationships between hereditary and developmental factors as determinants of constitution. A holistic viewpoint toward constitution is essential for proper evaluation of these factors.

613. Schirokauer A, Spitzer L: German words, German personality and Protestantism again. Psychiatry 12:185–187.

Some of the linguistic presuppositions of Thorner, in which he sees reflections of the German national character, rely on an apparent inadequate understanding of the German language and culture.

614. Sereno R: Boricua: a study of language, transculturation, and politics. Psychiatry 12:167–184.

Boricua, a Puerto Rican language, has undergone changes related to the passage from Spanish to American sovereignty. The language mutations affect personal integration and personal security.

615. Spitz RA: The role of ecological factors in emotional development in infancy. Child Dev 20:144–155.

The central psychosocial factor in the infant's life is its emotional interchange with its mother. This process is largely governed by culturally determined mores and institutions and by social and economic conditions.

616. Turquet PM: Aggression in nature and society. Br J Med Psychol 22:156–160.

The human organism is profoundly malleable, responding to cultural conditioning, and reflecting accurately and contrastingly different cultural conditions. The innate propensity of mankind to aggression is of less importance than its subsequent fate at the hands of the family and other social forces.

617. Vinacke WE: Stereotyping among national-racial groups in Hawaii: a study in ethnocentrism. J Soc Psychol 30:265–291.

Stereotyping among Japanese, Chinese, Haole, Korean, Filipino, Hawaiian, Samoan, and Negro groups is an extremely complex phenomenon marked by differences according to sex, ingroup perceptions, stereotype strength and favorable evaluations.

618. Ward THG: An experiment on serial reproduction with special reference to the changes in the design of early coin types. Br J Psychol 39:142–147.

The question of cultural and universal psychological influences as reflected in serial reproduction may be considered in terms of coin types and a laboratory series. Psychological forces play a large part in design changes. Such a technique may be of value to archaeologists interested in culture change.

619. White LA: A study of schizophrenic language. J Abnorm Soc Psychol 44:61–74.

Observations on identifying and sorting words and inverting sentences for normals and schizophrenics suggests that schizophrenic language is impersonal, involved, and complex.

620. Wolman B: Disturbances in acculturation. Am J Psychother 3:600–615.

The Zionist pioneers had hardly any acculturation problem with which to cope. Today they represent the most healthy and most happy part of the population of the modern state of Israel. The Oriental Jews in Israel have had many more acculturation problems.

1950

621. Abel TM, Joffe NF: Cultural backgrounds of female puberty. Am J Psychother 4:90–113.

Attitudes vary widely among European countries and ethnic groups in regard to menstruating women. Such negative attitudes as disgust, fear, and embarassment are common, although their method of expression varies according to the local culture. The American girl's attitude toward menstruation is that it is a nuisance to be put up with, rather than a danger or threat.

622. Baker SJ: Language and dreams. Int J Psychoanal 31: 171–178.

Polynesian languages provide examples of dream symbolism in terms of lexemes, manifest, and latent images. Word taboos in society demonstrate that language has sexualized origins.

623. Bettelheim B, Sylvester E: Notes on the impact of parental occupations: some cultural determinants of symptom choice in emotionally disturbed children. Am J Orthopsychiatry 20: 785–795.

Children who early and extensively are damaged do not develop enough closeness to those around them to discern the fine points of parental attitudes and are relatively untouched by the reality of the parent's occupational activities.

624. Black P, Atkins RD: Conformity versus prejudice as exemplified in white-Negro relations in the South: some methodological considerations. J Psychol 30:109–122.

Analyses of prejudice toward Negro and other groups must be considered in relation to the sociocultural behavior patterns of the local community or region. A modified Thurstone-type scale for measuring prejudice is suggested.

625. Carlson HB, Henderson N: The intelligence of American children of Mexican parentage. J Abnorm Soc Psychol 45:544–551.

Lower intelligence scores are found among Mexican-American children, but environmental factors cannot be ruled out. Standardization of scores must be relevant to the specific culture.

626. Cattell RB: The principal culture patterns discoverable in the syntal dimensions of existing nations. J Soc Psychol 32:215–253.

Factor analysis of 80 variables for 69 nations yields 12 dimensions of national syntality (personality) constricted into culture pattern profiles. Clusters may be established that describe culture pattern families that are historically, geographically, linguistically, religiously, and racially related.

627. Cooper JB: Learning and social behavior: a point of view. J Soc Psychol 32:31–44.

Learning is not a defined, self-contained process. Learning is a facility by which animals modify patterns of response in terms of past experience, thus permitting different degrees of differentiation of the regions within the life space. Learning can be seen as only one abstracted aspect of adjusted behavior.

628. Daly CD: The psychobiological origins of circumcision. Int J Psychoanal 31:217–236.

The object of cultural circumcision practices in puberty rites is to reinforce appropriate sexual identification.

629. Davidson KS, Gibby RG, McNeil EB, Segal SJ, Silverman HA: Preliminary study of Negro and white differences on Form I of the Wechsler-Bellevue Scale. J Consult Clin Psychol 14:489–492.

Poorer showings by Negroes on Arithmetic and Performance subtests may be due to slower performance of psychomotor perceptual functions, which are due in turn to lack of motivation derived from their social setting.

630. Devereux G: Catastrophic reactions in normals. Am Imago 7:345–349.

Anthropological and historical material provides examples of sets of incidents of human behavior derived from identical motivation, in support of the concept of the psychic unity of mankind.

631. Devereux G: Psychodynamics of Mohave gambling. Am Imago 7:55–65.

Gambling, a formal affair among the Mohave, represents a temporary return of repressed omnipotence fantasies and oral and anal elements, rather than a neurosis or addiction.

632. Devereux G: The psychology of feminine genital bleeding: an analysis of Mohave Indian puberty and menstrual rites. Int J Psychoanal 31:237–257.

Specific anthropological data demonstrate that the psychological link between all forms of female genital bleeding may be a central aggressive fantasy that coitus is a means of robbing the maternal body of its contents, with consequent genital hemorrhage.

633. Devereux G: Status, socialization, and interpersonal relations of Mohave children. Psychiatry 13:489–502.

The Mohave child develops those psychological capacities that are dependent upon the closeness of a living adult, as well as those that are a by-product of contact with other children. The final product is a well-adjusted and secure personality type that manages to resist acculturation to an alien way of life, while freely accepting the material advantages and devices of the intrusive American culture.

634. Farber ML: The problem of national character: a methodological analysis. J Psychol 30:307–316.

Methodologies of national character represent the convergence of projective techniques and cultural anthropological methods for literate society. A science of national character is methodologically feasible.

635. Fraiberg L, Fraiberg S: Hallow'en: ritual and myth in a children's holiday. Am Imago 7:289–328.

The children's holiday has faithfully preserved the customs and rituals of ancient new year festivals with respect to sacrifice, atonement, and license. Children's games and holidays are a museum of early religious beliefs.

636. Freedman LZ, Ferguson VM: The question of "painless childbirth" in primitive cultures. Am J Orthopsychiatry 20:363–372.

The pain of childbirth can be diminished and in some cases eliminated by the application of suitable techniques even of a rather simple and superficial nature, as is evidenced in some primitive cultures. The psychological dynamics of these techniques, however, are not thoroughly understood.

637. Gross L: A hypothesis of feminine types in relation to family adjustment. Am J Orthopsychiatry 20:373–381.

The roles that women assume within the home are channelized and patterned by observable somatic, gestural, and verbal responses. These responses can be divided into erotic, masked erotic, and maternal composites of personality and social characteristics.

638. Hallowell AK: Values, acculturation and mental health. Am J Orthopsychiatry 20:732–743.

The Flambeau Indian, because of a frustration of maturity, represents a regressive version of the personality structure of the northern Ojibwa. Due to the acculturation process there is little of genuine integrative value that the old culture can offer the individual in the structuralization of personality.

639. Hartmann H: The application of psychoanalytic concepts to social sciences. Psychoanal Q 19:385–392.

It would be desirable to create a common conceptual language, or to define sociological problems in terms of their psychological meaning, and to formulate psychological problems in direct relation to the social structure.

640. Heine RW: The Negro patient in psychotherapy. J Clin Psychol 6:373–376.

Problems related to minority group membership and stereotypic behavior are encountered in psychotherapy of Negro patients. The therapist must view the patient as an individual, not as a racial representative.

641. Holt LP: Identification: a crucial concept for sociology. Bull Menninger Clin 14:164–173.

Freud tried to describe man's capacity for forming an emotional tie to his fellows. Identification made possible man's creation of society, morality, religion, and art.

642. Honigman JJ: Culture patterns and human stress. Psychiatry 13:25–34.

Cultures induce personal anxieties and conflicts in their carriers; however, cultures also include mechanisms by which the members of a social group may obtain relief from tension. Social engineering needs to create cultural climates that will not only induce a minimum of tension, but that will also provide nondyscrasic channels for the relief of personal stress.

643. James HEO, Tenen C: How adolescents think of peoples. Br J Psychol 41:145–172.

Adolescent girls' attitudes toward Germans, Italians, Japanese, Chinese, Americans, Negroes, and Indians vary in terms of personal contact versus secondary evidence. Generally, peoples are thought of in the same fashion as individuals.

644. Karpman B: Aggression: tension, growth and reproduction in relation to aggression. Am J Orthopsychiatry 20:694–718.

Aggression is derived from instincts, and society's chief task is the control and taming of aggression. A progressive educational approach combined with a progressive social reorientation may result in a society in which there is a minimal expression of primary, destructive aggression.

645. Kline NS, Ashton MT: Constitutional factors in the prognosis of schizophrenia. Am J Psychiatry 107:434–441.

Significant correlations exist between somatotype and psychiatric diagnosis: mesomorphs tend to be paranoid, while ectomorphs tend to be hebephrenic.

646. Landes R, Aborowski M: Hypotheses concerning the Eastern European Jewish family. Psychiatry 13:447–464.

Shtetl families differ from those in the United States in that men do not hope to be outstripped by their sons, and the authority of the father rests primarily upon his status as an exponent of the religious and scholarly tradition. Women possess status only in the home, even though they may be effective wage earners.

647. Lantis M: The symbol of a new religion. Psychiatry 13:101–113.

The basic symbols system in Christianity and Judaism is weakening and there is a possibility of a successor to these religions that may manifest itself in a far different manner. New threats will drive man to seek new guides. Understanding or science may be designated—far in the future—as the ultimate power. Until then, however, a search for more personal symbols will continue.

648. Lee D: Lineal and nonlineal codifications of reality. Psychosom Med 12:89–97.

In contrast to our own lineal phrasing, the people of the Trobriand Islands have a nonlineal apprehension of reality. A careful analysis and study of the Trobriand code, and of the culture to which it belongs, should lead us to concepts that are ultimately comprehensible, and thus can lead us to aspects of reality from which our own code excludes us.

649. Lee D: Notes on the concept of the self among the Wintu Indians. J Abnorm Soc Psychol 45:538–543.

There is no fragmenting of self by the Wintu; the self is a concentration without definable limits, as can be seen by linguistic analysis. The universe is not centered on the self for the Wintu.

650. MacCurdy JT: Psychopathology and social psychology: hierarchies of interest. Br J Psychol 41:1–13.

The concepts of values, interests, belief, and reality all have implications for social psychology. There must be greater recognition of psychiatric and anthropological approaches to the study of political problems.

651. MacCurdy JT: Psychopathology and social psychology: personality and ethos. Br J Psychol 40:175–186.

The origin, evolution, and nature of social groups, social ideals, and ethos provide insight into human society and unconscious levels. Ethos is analogous to personality.

652. Mayo GD, Kinzer JR: A comparison of "racial" attitudes of white and Negro high school students in 1940 and 1948. J Psychol 29:397–406.

White and Negro groups in 1948 expressed more favorable attitudes toward Negroes than groups in 1940 but were more different from each other on issues involving interracial relations. The latter is due to a greater shift in Negro attitudes.

653. Murray VF, Joseph A: The Rorschach test as a tool in action research: a study of acculturation phenomena in a group of young Chamorro women. J Proj Techniques 14: 362–384.

Female teachers in the native school evidence stress and emotional disturbance more than females in other occupations. A brief historical and cultural outline indicates the influences upon general anxiety for the Saipan population, and especially for female teachers.

654. Newell HW: Interpretation of early Fiji customs. J Soc Psychol 31:39–67.

Customs related to secret societies, totemism, and cannibalism may be psychodynamically interpreted. Neurotic and psychotic behavior surfaces in ritual behavior and religious beliefs.

655. Parsons T: Psychoanalysis and the social structure. Psychoanal Q 19:371–384.

Psychoanalytic theory is important to sociology and vice versa. The analyst in fact is dealing with social systems.

656. Penrose LS: Genetic influences on the intelligence level of the population. Br J Psychol 40:128–136.

The level of intelligence of a population is based upon a stable genetical system, though subject to environmental changers. The fertile, though least scholastic, part of the population is necessary to group genetic stability.

657. Prasad J: A comparative study of rumours and reports in earthquakes. Br J Psychol 41:129–143.

The projection theory of rumours is inadequate. Congruency between external sociocultural material, the Indian cultural heritage, and attitudes gives rumour its specific form and content.

658. Radke M, Trager H: Children's perceptions of social roles of Negroes and whites. J Psychol 29:3–34.

Children's perception of social roles may be studied through their play manipulations of dolls, costumes, and houses. Children's responses clearly reflect the values of adult culture.

659. Razran G: Ethnic dislikes and stereotypes. J Abnorm Soc Psychol 45:7–27.

Attitudes toward Jews, Italians, and Irish may be separated into a global-affective component of dislike, and the segmental and cognitive components of stereotypes. Possibilities for decrease of ethnic prejudice are generally favorable.

660. Rees L: Body size, personality and neurosis. J Ment Science 96:168–180.

Using a body-size index to divide subjects into micro-, meso-, and macro-somatic reveals that while there are complex relationships between physical and mental characteristics, the degree of association is too low to be of clinical diagnostic or prognostic values.

661. Rees L: A factorial study of physical constitutions in women. J Ment Science 96:619–632.

A new index for female body build utilizing stature, symphysis height, chest and hip circumference, allows division of subjects into body-type classes convenient for clinical practice and research.

662. Roheim G: Fire in the dragon. Am Imago 7:163–172.

Swallowed-hero myths are a representation of mastery over an anxiety situation and body destruction fantasies. The oral-genital and aggression-libido entities of these fantasies are often fused in reality.

663. Roheim G: The psychology of patriotism. Am Imago 7:3–19.

The unconscious symbolic content of patriotism appears in the integration of the group and in the psychologic frontiers of ingroup versus outgroup.

664. Spiro ME: A psychotic personality in the South Seas. Psychiatry 13:189–204.

The Ifaluk ethos is characterized by nonaggression in interpersonal relations. In reaction to cruelties imposed by foreign culture a person may retreat to his privately constituted world. The natives of Ifaluk know of no instance of malebush prior to the Japanese occupation.

665. Thorner I: German word, German personality and Protestantism again: a rejoinder. Psychiatry 13:511–514.

Criticisms disputing the idea that the German title of address, *Herr,* has certain implications regarding the power of orientation are inadequate and in some cases corroborate the author's original analysis of the German personality type as one oriented toward power.

666. von Allesch J: German psychologists and national-socialism. J Abnorm Soc Psychol 45:402.

Accusations against German psychologists are unfair and nonfactual.

667. Wallace AFC: A possible technique for recognizing psychological characteristics of the ancient Maya from an analysis of their art. Am Imago 7:239–258.

The personality of precontact Maya may be inferred from three codices. Comparison with contemporary Rorschach protocols and historical observations shows some discrepancies but an overall agreement in outline.

668. Weakland JH: The organization of action in Chinese culture. Psychiatry 13:361–370.

Chinese behavior is organized into stages of preparation and culmination. The preparatory stages involve planning, may be comparatively lengthy, and are private. Go-betweens are used extensively in Chinese culture. The formal patterns of behavior can be related to Chinese child-rearing practices.

669. Weider A, Noller PA: Objective studies of children's drawings of human figures: sex awareness and socioeconomic level. J Clin Psychol 6:319–325.

Socioeconomic level is related to number of covert characteristics in figures of both sex drawn by boys, but is not related to overt verbal responses. Socioeconomic level and characteristics in female figures are related among girls' drawings.

670. Werner H, Kaplan E: Development of word meaning through verbal context: an experimental study. J Psychol 29:251–258.

Meaning and structure are interdependent in a test of contexts for an artificial word.

671. Williams AH: A psychiatric study of Indian soldiers in the Arakan. Br J Med Psychol 23:130–181.

The family life of the Arakans is protective, rich, and secure, and there is a high capacity for and dependence on group relationships in their culture. Because military life is a group phenomenon, it suits Indians very well. However, they encounter difficulty in living and fighting as individuals.

672. Williams PH, Straus R: Drinking patterns of Italians in New Haven: utilization of the personal diary as a research technique. Introduction and diaries 1 and 2. Q J Stud Alcohol 11:51–91.

Personal diaries that record type and amount of drink, and the circumstances surrounding the decision to drink reveal, in terms of time continuum and cultural interrelationship, facts about drinking patterns.

673. Williams PH, Straus R: Drinking patterns of Italians in New Haven: utilization of the personal diary as a research technique. Diaries 3, 4 and 5. Q J Stud Alcohol 11:250–308.

Personal diaries that record type and amount of drink and the circumstances surrounding the decision to drink reveal, in terms of time continuum and cultural interrelationship, facts about drinking patterns.

674. Williams PH, Straus R: Drinking patterns of Italians in New Haven: utilization of the personal diary as a research technique. Diaries 6 and 7. Q U Stud Alcohol 11:452–483.

Personal diaries that record type and amount of drink and the circumstances surrounding the decision to drink reveal, in terms of time continuum and cultural interrelationship, facts about drinking patterns.

675. Williams PH, Straus R: Drinking patterns of Italians in New Haven: utilization of the personal diary as a research technique. Diaries 8, 9 and 10. Q J Stud Alcohol 11:586–629.

Personal diaries that record type and amount of drink and the circumstances surrounding the decision to drink reveal, in terms of time continuum and cultural interrelationship, facts about drinking patterns.

1951

676. Arlow JA: A psychoanalytic study of a religious initiation rite: Bar Mitzvah. Psychoanal Study Child 6:353–374.

Bar Mitzvah combines the fusion of a religious component of induction into Judaism with an unconscious but more general component epitomizing ambivalent intergenerational attitudes. The initiate renounces remnants of his oedipal wishes for the demands of group loyalty and studiousness.

677. Bacon SD: Studies of drinking in Jewish culture: general introduction. Q J Stud Alcohol 12:444–450.

The development of an organized body of relevant data concerning the phenomena of alcoholic beverage use by American Jewry, college students, Italians, and Italian-Americans would increase understanding of alcohol addiction. The Yale Center of Alcohol Studies is such a broad, long-term program.

678. Barbee JN, Sumner FC: Psychological aspects of vitiligo in Negroes. J Soc Psychol 34:125–138.

The outbreak of a skin condition in Negro subjects gives rise to various forms of emotional stress, accentuating already present personality traits. Feelings of inferiority are evident in each case.

679. Barber TX: Death by suggestion. Psychosom Med 23:153–155.

Black magic, sorcery, or suggestion have not

been demonstrated to be direct causes of death among nonliterate people. Poisoning, organic illnesses, and starvation and/or dehydration of persons who believe that death is inevitable have been attributed to "voodoo death."

680. Barschak E: A study of happiness and unhappiness in the childhood and adolescence of girls in different cultures. J Psychol 32:173–216.

The family is the main source of happiness or unhappiness for English, American, Swiss, and German girls. Although the data are not conclusive with respect to national differences, some group tendencies in the area of school and social attitudes and leisure activities can be noted.

681. Bayer LM, Reichard S: Androgyny, weight, and personality. Psychosom Med 13:358–374.

The degree of somatic sexuality gives an important clue to the strength of the libidinal vector. A masculine direction in androgyny favors muscular activity and independence.

682. Bayley N: Some psychological correlates of somatic androgyny. Child Dev 22:47–60.

In normal adolescents, androgynic variables in body form are significantly related to strength, and, in some degree, to weight. Somatic androgyny is only one of a multiplicity of factors that may influence the direction of a person's interests.

683. Berndt RM: Subincision in a non-subincision area. Am Imago 8:165–179.

Esoteric meaning found for subincision in areas adjacent to western Arnhem Land is in general agreement with Roheim's data for central Australia and illustrates how a sacred rite in one region may become secularized in another culture.

684. Bernfield SC: Freud and archaeology. Am Imago 8:107–128.

Freud's archaeological interests are represented his mastery of the death problem and ability to live in mental security without religion. In his psychoanalytic work he became an excavator of earlier memories.

685. Bird C, Monachesi ED, Burdick H: Infiltration and the attitudes of white and Negro parents and children. J Abnorm Soc Psychol 47:688–699.

White residents in neighborhoods undergoing an influx of Negroes express very different racial attitudes. Negro children's attitudes toward non-Jewish children are more favorable than their attitudes toward Jewish children.

686. Bremer J: A social psychiatric investigation of a small community in northern Norway. Acta Psychiatr Neurol Supp 62:10–166.

While war neurosis and immigration patterns contribute to some degree to the number of psychic exceptionals in a Norwegian community, the admixture of persons of Lapp and Kvaen race are of no demonstrable influence. The patients' mental health forms a dominant environmental factor that influences the mental health of their children.

687. Brown GG: Culture, society and personality: a restatement. Am J Psychiatry 108:173–175.

Culture and society interact with personality, and one of the meeting grounds of the various behavioral science disciplines is in the area of this interaction.

688. Devereux G: Cultural and characterological traits of the Mohave related to the anal stages of psychosexual development. Psychoanal Q 20:398–422.

The structure of Mohave character supports psychoanalytic theories regarding the characterological influence of the anal stage of development, validates these theories by means of cross-cultural data, and lends support to the role of fantasy in the formation of character and the etiology of neurosis.

689. Devereux G: Three technical problems in the psychotherapy of Plains Indian patients. Am J Psychother 5:411–423.

The glaringly obvious influence that cultural factors exert upon the course, goals, and outcome of psychotherapy with Plains Indians can be thought of as a demonstration *in vitro* of the less conspicuous, though equally decisive, influence of cultural factors that the psychiatrist encounters, day after day, *in situ,* even when he treats native-born whites whose cultural, socioeconomic, religious, and professional backgrounds deviate somewhat from the therapist's own social heritage.

690. Eaton JW, Weil RJ: Psychotherapeutic principles in social research: an interdisciplinary study of the Hutterites. Psychiatry 14:439–452.

As demonstrated by a project in which social-anthropological, psychological, and psychiatric data were collected in Hutterite colonies, there is much similarity between the processes of the psychiatrist-patient relationship in psychotherapy and the scientist-informant relationship in social research.

691. Ellsworth RB: The regression of schizophrenic language. J Consult Psychol 15:387–391.

The hypothesis that schizophrenic regression to childhood would be reflected in terms of parts of speech percentages as compared with normal adult speech is confirmed. The language of schizophrenics is more similar to that of fifth graders than to adult language. Schizophrenic regression is closely related to thought disorganization.

692. Erikson EH: Differences in the play configurations of pre-adolescents. Am J Orthopsychiatry 21:667–692.

The interrelations of verbal, thematic, and spatial expressions in play indicate a most significant overall sex differentiation. In boys the outstanding variables are height and downfall, and motion and its channelization or arrest (policeman); in girls, static interiors, which are open, simply enclosed, or blocked and intruded upon. In boys these configurational tendencies are connected with a generally greater emphasis on the outdoors and the outside, and in girls, with an emphasis on house interiors.

693. Esman AH: Jazz—a study in cultural conflict. Am Imago 8:219–226.

The unspoken protest, kinesthetic release, and stimulation of repressed erotic drives are qualities of jazz music that appeal to those who seek liberation and individuality within the repressed aspects of American culture.

694. Eysenck HJ: Primary social attitudes and the "social insight" test. Br J Psychol 42:114–122.

A hypothesis relating radicalism with a high degree of social insight is accepted. Social insight is independent of education.

695. Farber ML: English and Americans: a study in national character. J Psychol 32:241–250.

Recent anthropological studies of national character are overly impressionistic. A comparison of the same occupational group, insurance clerks, in England and the United States reveals certain personality differences that may be moderately valid with respect to the nations.

696. Frenkel-Brunswik E: Patterns of social and cognitive outlook in children and parents. Am J Orthopsychiatry 21:543–558.

Prejudiced children are immature and show conflict and anxiety concerning their social, sexual, and personal roles.

697. Garn SM, Moorrees CFA: Stature, bodybuild, and tooth emergence in Aleutian Aleut children. Child Dev 22:261–270.

In stature, Aleutian Aleut children fall slightly below the norms for American whites, and above the norms for Japanese, Mexican, and American-born children of Chinese and Japanese descent. Tooth emergence is markedly advanced as compared to whites. Stunting or retardation did not occur as a result of the wartime experiences.

698. Gold HR: Observations on cultural psychiatry during a world tour of mental hospitals. Am J Psychiatry 108:462–468.

The attitudes of local culture toward psychiatry are reflected in mental hospitals visited throughout the world.

699. Hallowell AI: The use of projective techniques in the study of the socio-psychological aspects of acculturation. J Proj Techniques 15:27–44.

Three levels of acculturation (least to most) among the Inland, Lakeside, and reservation Flambeau Ojibwa are indicated by Rorschach results. The major psychological contrast is between the Berens River population as a whole and the Flambeau Ojibwa.

700. Henry J: The inner experience of culture. Psychiatry 14:87–103.

Patients' statements are frequently taken for granted because they seem so commonplace, however, they should be examined in the light of the cultural settings. The mental health worker must think about what he thinks about in order that he may think about what the patient thinks about.

701. Hofstaetter PR: A factorial study of cultural patterns in the U.S. J Psychol 32:99–114.

Three factors—urban comfort vs. rural fertility, emphasis on education, and absence of racial discrimination—account for almost two-thirds of the average variance on parameters for 48 states.

702. Hsu EH: The neurotic score as a function of culture. J Soc Psychol 34:3–30.

Neurotic score, as measured by Thurstone's Neurotic Inventory, for Chinese and Chinese-American subjects may be seen as a function of culture. A trait may be termed neurotic only when examined with reference to the standard of a given culture.

703. Kaldegg A: A study of German and English teacher-training students by means of projective techniques. Br J Psychol 42:56–113.

The findings of an attitudes projective test and a Rorschach test show that English women students react in a more direct and objective way, while German women students react in a more indirect and subjective way.

704. LaBarre W: Pediatrics, paranoia, and peace. Am Imago 8:99–105.

Child rearing and socialization are of central importance to the formation of the character structure in a group. Cultures are man-made and as such man must consider the moral implications of this responsibility.

705. Lepley WM, Korbrick JL: Word usage and synonym representation in the English language. J Abnorm Soc Psychol 47:572–573.

Synonym representation covaries with frequency of word use, giving support to the hypothesis that a principle of reactive inhibition operates in the development of language.

706. Moloney JC: Some simple cultural factors in the etiology of schizophrenia. Child Dev 22:163–183.

The mother is the infant's first and strongest love-object, and the prototype of all later love relations. If a mother neglects the head end or anal end of an infant, one might predict the immediate development of marasmus, or a later schizophrenic disintegration of the ego.

707. O'Connor P: Ethnocentrism, "intolerance of ambiguity," and abstract reasoning ability. J Abnorm Soc Psychol 47:526–530.

Ethnocentrism is positively associated with intolerance of ambiguity and related to inability to reason abstractly.

708. Roheim G: Mythology of Arnhem Land. Am Imago 8:180–187.

Two myths in Arnhem Land reflect unconscious conflicts that are incidental to every life, while a third is based upon the inner pressure of retold and acted out dreams.

709. Sereno R: Observations on the Santa Claus custom. Psychiatry 14:387–396.

The custom of Santa Claus as observed in a Midwestern district shows that children are its innocent victims and that the adults, unable to give or receive spontaneous love and affection, attach artificial importance to an "exchanged gift." Protected by taboo, the damaging custom continues.

710. Snyder CR, Landman RH: Studies of drinking in Jewish culture. II. Prospectus for sociological research on Jewish drinking patterns. Q J Stud Alcohol 12:444–450.

A delineation of actual drinking ways among New Haven Jews is being obtained by sociological field research. Data gathered principally from intensive interviews of Jewish adults are supplemented by less intensive interviews with Jewish children, and by questionnaires. Research on the role of alcoholic beverages in different epochs adds historical perspective to the study.

711. Snyder LL: Nationalistic aspects of the Grimm brothers' fairy tales. J Soc Psychol 33:209–224.

The Grimm fairy tales played a significant role in the development of modern German nationalism. The Grimm brothers were convinced that the strength of their writings derived from the German fatherland.

712. Spiro ME: Culture and personality: the natural history of a false dichotomy. Psychiatry 14:-19–46.

The concepts of personality and of culture cannot be separated empirically, and the dichotomy that is held to obtain between them is a consequence of Western intellectual history, on the one hand, and of contemporary fallacies of thinking about them, on the other.

713. Stewart B: Some determinants of social change. J Soc Psychol 33:33–50.

The role of the individual in large-scale social movements is quantitatively small, but important nevertheless. Cultures are not self-contained systems that determine human behavior, but are in turn determined by other sources.

714. Thompson L: Perception patterns in three Indian tribes. Psychiatry 14:255–263.

The study of the group structure of Papago, Hopi, and Navaho Indian tribes illustrates the need for recognition of cultural and psychological diversity of local groups by administrators, planners, teachers, and social workers who often assume quite erroneously that members of other groups perceive the world as they do.

715. Vinacke WE, Smith NVO: Reactions to humorous stimuli of different generations of Japanese, Chinese, and Caucasians in Hawaii. J Soc Psychol 34:69–96.

Caucasians, Japanese, and Chinese differ in their

reactions to humorous stimuli. There is less difference between older and younger groups of the same national ancestry than between the three national groups.

716. Warburton FW: The ability of the Gurkha recruit. Br J Psychol 42:123–133.

On the whole, Gurkha performance is lower than British standards and is characterized by passivity and slowness of movement. Problems raised by the research, however, indicate that conventional tests have limited applicability for primitive peoples, and further research is required.

717. Wolman B: Sexual development in Israeli adolescents. Am J Psychother 5:531–559.

Physical maturation in Israel and America are similar. School, home, and youth organizations do not discourage early emotional ties, but they do discourage early intercourse and even petting. Masturbation data in Israel are comparable to Kinsey's total male population; however, in Israel the peak seems to be age 14–16 and afterward shows a decline that is not evident in Kinsey's data.

718. Wolman B: Spontaneous groups of children and adolescents in Israel. J Soc Psychol 34:171–182.

Spontaneous groups, or gangs, are usually formed by maladjusted individuals and are a sign of infantile regression. Gang activities are characteristic for the age level of eight to twelve years.

719. Yap PM: Mental diseases peculiar to certain cultures: a survey of comparative psychiatry. J Ment Science 97:313–327.

There are basic pathological processes to be found in insanity everywhere. However, the detailed symptomatology of these broad syndromes may vary from one culture to another, reflecting as they do prevailing beliefs, customs, interests, and conflicts.

1952

720. Aberle DV: Middle-class fathers' occupational role and attitudes toward children. Am J Orthopsychiatry 22:366–378.

Efforts to educate parents regarding socialization practices must include intensive efforts to understand why parents use particular practices and their fears regarding changing them. Without such understanding, reactions to change will be met with ambivalence, overcomplicated performance, resistance, or complete rejection.

721. Argyle M: Methods of studying small social groups. Br J Psychol 43:269–279.

Basic psychological designs that are applied to the study of individuals may also be applied to groups. An evaluation of the validity of conclusions derived from such studies must be considered separately from the validity of the results.

722. Bettelheim B: Mental health and current mores. Am J Orthopsychiatry 22:76–88.

The degree to which mores encourage or impede interpersonal relations determines the degree of mental health and happiness that is available in a society.

723. Boag TJ: The white man in the Arctic. Am J Psychiatry 109:444–449.

Observations on psychological stresses of Arctic life must distinguish between situations involving direct exposure to climatic stress and those in which such exposure is avoided.

724. Bonaparte M: Some biopsychical aspects of sado-masochism. Int J Psychoanal 33:373–383.

The determinants of sado-masochism derive from the fact that internal impregnation of mammals occurs during coitus. The cerebellar activities of man enable him to moralize such trends.

725. Boyd GF: The levels of aspiration of white and Negro children in a non-segregated elementary school. J Soc Psychol 36:191–196.

As a result of environmental factors, subjects of the Negro group have a higher level of aspiration that the white group.

726. Deutsch KW: Communication theory and social science. Am J Orthopsychiatry 22:469–483.

Cybernetics offers social scientists an approach toward a theory of growth. Its philosophy is orientated toward research, observation, experiment, and ultimately measurement.

727. Devereux G: Psychiatry and anthropology: some research objectives. Bull Menninger Clin 16:-167–177.

A culturally neutral system of psychotherapy based upon an understanding of the nature of culture per se, so that a psychiatrist can treat with equal efficiency a refined Southern lady, an Eskimo seal hunter, and a Filipino scout, is needed. The task of developing a "trans-cultural" psychotherapy belongs to anthropologists.

728. Epps P, Parnell RW: Physique and temperament of women delinquents compared with women undergraduates. Br J Med Psychol 25:249–255.

Corresponding differences in physique and temperament for delinquent and nondelinquent groups can be found, using modern techniques, which confirm Sheldon's results.

729. Fishman JA: Degree of bilingualism in a Yiddish school and leisure time activities. J Soc Psychol 36:155–166.

Given the general aims and influences of Yiddish schools in the United States, voluntary leisure-time activities are not affected by degree of bilinguality.

730. Friedman J, Gassel S: Odysseus: the return of the primal father. Psychoanal Q 21:215–223.

The collective unconscious and the theme of the return of the primal father is clearly revealed in the Odysseus myth.

731. Greenberg P, Gilliland AR: The relationship between basal metabolism and personality. J Soc Psychol 35:3–9.

The neurotic triad, as measured by the Minnesota Multiphasic Personality Inventory, is positively related to basal metabolic rate, and the psychotic triad is negatively related to BMR. Further research on the validity of personality inventories, and with extreme deviates, is indicated.

732. Harding VV: Time schedule for the appearance and fusion of a secondary accessory center of ossification of the calcaneus. Child Dev 23:181–184.

A second small accessory center of the calcaneus appears regularly, superior to and considerably later than the first. The center is important for assessment of osseus development because it appears and develops during a period in which relatively few other centers are useful.

733. Hare EH: The ecology of mental disease: a dissertation on the influence of environmental factors in the distribution, development and variation of mental disease. J Ment Science 98:579–594.

At the present time conditions of modern Western civilization are becoming increasingly important in the etiology of mental disease. The principal causative factor in these conditions is lack of the sense of security and worth that an individual must derive from a social group.

734. Henry J, Boggs JW: Child rearing, culture and the natural world. Psychiatry 15:261–271.

Personality, partly through child-rearing prac-

tices, develops into a capacity to maintain the culture in a steady state. The greatest obstacle to understanding personality development is the absence of good observations of infant behavior.

735. Henry J, Winokur G: Some aspects of the relationship between psychoanalysis and anthropology. Am J Orthopsychiatry 22:644–648.

The alliance between anthropology and psychiatry is marked by inadequaces: (a) conceptualization of the fields of study; (b) understanding of proper areas of overlap; and (c) more efficient modes of interaction. Studies productive of clear observational data can differentiate between a patient's culturally produced aberrations and those produced by inner disturbances.

736. Inskip WM, Brody VA: A study in bio-semantics: an organismic approach to meaning. J Psychol 34:3–20.

The human tissue plays a role in the meaning process and is expressed by four types of tissue movements: organic, skeletal, epicortical, and cortical. The development of meaning parallels the growth of these tissues. Meaning depends upon the type of participating tissues, individual maturity, experience, education, and personality.

737. Jacobson A, Berenberg AN: Japanese psychiatry and psychotherapy. Am J Psychiatry 109:321–329.

Japanese psychiatrists tend to view maladaptive behavior as character neuroses that can be overcome by the development of "a calm and well regulated mind." This view is a goal of Zen Buddhism, not modern psychiatry. Morita's therapy, which is the method of achieving this goal, also is patterned closely after the precepts of Buddha.

738. Klatskin EH: Shifts in child care practices in three social classes under an infant care program of flexible methodology. Am J Orthopsychiatry 22:52–61.

Parental child-care practices are capable of modification through instruction, and it is possible to alter the influence of social class membership on child care. Although there is some variation among classes, there is a general shift toward leniency in child-care practices.

739. Kline NS, Oppenheim AN: Constitutional factors in the prognosis of schizophrenia. Am J Psychiatry 108:909–911.

A significant relationship exists between mesomorphy and paranoid schizophrenia, and between ectomorphy and hebephrenic schizophrenia.

740. Landman RH: Studies of drinking in Jewish culture: drinking patterns of children and adolescents attending religious schools. Q J Stud Alcohol 13:87–94.

The reduction of any element of excitement or thrill that might accompany a more tense handling of alcohol in the home may be a factor in the dissociation between drinking and inebriety that Jewish adolescents evince.

741. Lee RH: Delinquent, neglected, and dependent Chinese boys and girls of the San Francisco Bay region. J Soc Psychol 36:15–34.

Juvenile delinquency among Chinese-Americans is a result of cultural conflicts between parents and native-born children, broken homes, and longing for self-expression. Juvenile delinquents are taking devious routes toward more acceptable forms of acculturation.

742. Lolli G, Serianni E, Banissoni F, Golder G, Mariani A, McCarthy RG, Toner M: The use of wine and other alcoholic beverages by a group of Italians and Americans of Italian extraction. Q J Stud Alcohol 13:27–48.

Italians and Italian-Americans are exposed to wine from childhood and appreciate its value and dangers. Wine is a constant of their luncheon and dinner menu, and the psychological effects are not sought after.

743. Mandy AJ, Mandy TE, Farkas R, Scher E: Is natural childbirth natural? Psychosom Med 14:431–438.

The benefits claimed for natural childbirth are primarily psychologic. When adapted to the needs of the individual patient, however, it can serve as a useful obstetrical adjunct, but it cannot be expected to bring about, through regimentation, universally successful reforms.

744. Meredith HB, Goldstein MS: Studies on the body size of North American children of Mexican ancestry. Child Dev 23:91–110.

Present knowledge of the body size of children of Mexican ancestry is fairly adequate as regards central tendency statistics covering the late childhood and adolescent years. There are systematic differences in means associated with geographic region, socioeconomic level, and secular period.

745. Ogden CK: Word magic. Psyche 18:19–26.

We must fully understand the influence of super-stitions concerning the power of words across many cultures in order to better understand ourselves.

746. Olden C: Notes on child rearing in America. Psychoanal Study Child 7:387–392.

The respect for the child in America has been not a respect for the child as child, but a respect for the man in the child, for the future citizen, moneymaker, politician. Because the seed of psychoanalytic principles has been sown in such infertile soil, the results have been less than desirable.

747. Parsons T: The superego and the theory of social systems. Psychiatry 15:15–25.

The psychoanalytic concept of superego is a point at which it is possible to establish direct relations between the theory of personality and the theoretic analysis of culture and of the social system.

748. Pieris R: Character formation in the evolution of the acquisitive society. Psychiatry 15:53–60.

Human nature is not immutable, as is demonstrated by character changes in Ceylonese following the adoption of European clothing, economic attitudes, and athletic games.

749. Prothro ET: Cultural determinism: a challenge to action research. J Soc Psychol 35:205–215.

The science of culture and the study of determinant relationships can make valuable contributions to understanding human behavior. However, a complete determinism as expressed by Leslie White is an unnecessary assumption given the occurrence of divergent phenomena in human history.

750. Riesman D: Some observations on the study of American character. Psychiatry 15:333–338.

People are both more and less than their social roles at any one time and can fool the investigator as well as themselves by changing, even late in adult life.

751. Roe A: Analysis of group Rorschachs of psychologists and anthropologists. J Proj Techniques 16:212–224.

Differences in group Rorschach responses are found for psychologists, anthropologists, physical scientists, and biologists. Psychologists and anthropologists are concerned with people, and show very little concern for ordering their responses logically.

752. Roheim G: The anthropological evidence and the Oedipus complex. Psychoanal Q 21:537–542.

Anthropological data from Arnhem Land, Lesu

in New Ireland, Pilaga Indians, and the Fan in West Africa substantiate the Oedipus complex.

753. Roheim G: The panic of the gods. Psychoanal Q 21:92–106.

In Rido-Germanic and some Semitic mythologies the gods, presumably the most powerful of beings, are helpless.

754. Schmidl F: Freud's sociological thinking. Bull Menninger Clin 16:1–13.

Freud's treatment of sociological problems was methodologically inadequate and at times incorrect, but this does not preclude the hope that some psychoanalytic concepts may prove useful in sociological studies.

755. Sinha D: Behavior in a catastrophic situation: a psychological study of reports and rumours. Br J Psychol 43:200–209.

Inaccuracies in reporting a landslide in Darjeeling, India, are generally exaggerations due to anxiety produced by a feeling of insecurity.

756. Smith M: Different cultural concepts of past, present and future. Psychiatry 15:395–400.

The concept of ego extension may be used to contrast cultural concepts of time and perception among Western, Hindu, Chinese, and Coast Salish (Pacific Northwest) egos.

757. Spindler GD: Personality and peyotism in Menomini Indian acculturation. Psychiatry 15:151–159.

Members of a peyote cult are variants of a transitional acculturative type. A close relationship exists between cult-defined behaviors and psychological processes that suggest the identity of personality and culture.

758. Stainbrook E: Some characteristics of the psychopathology of schizophrenic behavior in Bahian society. Am J Psychiatry 109:330–335.

Based on the study of diagnosed schizophrenics in Bahia, assessment of the incidence of behavior disorder is a function of one's case-finding techniques and depends upon the relatively long-term application of anthropological skills in knowing and describing the community.

759. Stendler CB: Critical periods in socialization and overdependency. Child Dev 23:3–12.

The end of the child's first year of life and later when his parents begin to increase their demands

upon the child may constitute the two critical periods in the socialization process for the beginnings of overdependency. The timing of the disturbance with regard to dependency needs may influence ego and superego development in particular ways.

760. Straus EW: The upright posture. Psychoanal Q 26:529–561.

Upright posture, which is as original as any drive, determines man's mode of being-in-the-world. Human physique reveals human nature. Some expressive attitudes of man are related to his basic orientation in the world as an upright creature.

761. Strong EK: Interests of Negroes and whites. J Soc Psychol 35:139–150.

There is no clear-cut evidence that Negro differences in interests derive from frustration-arousing interest in denied activities. The manner in which frustration influences interests requires further explanation.

762. Wedge BM: Occurrence of psychosis among Okinawans in Hawaii. Am J Psychiatry 109:255–258.

Okinawan immigrants to Hawaii, who have mothering practices similar to those of native Okinawans, show a significantly high rate of psychosis. Mothering practices carried out in a different cultural context do not necessarily result in the ability to adjust satisfactorily to the new situation.

763. Wiesel C, Arny M: Psychiatric study of coal miners in eastern Kentucky area. Am J Psychiatry 108:617–624.

The cultural and social background of eastern Kentucky coal miners helps to explain the "miner's syndrome," characterized by numerous somatic complaints, a passive dependent attitude, and lack of anxiety.

764. Wolf K: Growing up and its price in three Puerto Rican subcultures. Psychiatry 15:401–433.

By examining major areas of stress as both a product of a culture and a clue to its functioning, it is apparent that there is no one uniform Puerto Rican personality type, in spite of the fairly uniform cultural tradition.

765. Woodruff AD: The roles of value in human behavior. J Soc Psychol 36:97–108.

The interrelationships and development of four value roles—major functional values, major verbalized values, functional process-concepts, and verbalized process-concepts—require further testing.

766. Wretmark G: The peptic ulver individual: a study in heredity, physique and personality. Acta Psychiatr Neurol Scand Supp 84:9–183.

Individuals with duodenal ulcers statistically show a preponderence of vertical over horizontal growth as compared with controls of the same age. The more tall-narrow the body build, the worse the course. There may exist an inherited predisposition for duodenal ulcer and nonsubstability is an essential factor in this predisposition.

767. Yap PM: The Latah reaction: its pathodynamics and nosological position. J Ment Science 98:516–564.

Latah is a specialized form of fright neurosis, with minimal hysterical features, culturally maintained and found only in persons whose powers of mastery and defense are limited by the level of their own cultural development. Outside of the Malay Archipelago, the neurosis is know by a variety of names.

768. Zubek JP: The Doukhobors: a genetic study on attitudes. J Soc Psychol 36:223–240.

The current antisocial behaviors of the Doukhobors, members of a Russian religious sect living in Canada, have a basis in their religious credo. Findings on Canadian prejudices and stereotypes of Doukhobor behavior have an important bearing on the process of Doukhobor assimilation.

1953

769. Adelson J: A study of minority group authoritarianism. J Abnorm Soc Psychol 48:477–485.

The constituents of Jewish authoritarianism include those who view the Jewish as composed of ingroups and outgroups, the latter being seen as violators of middle-class standards and nonconformists.

770. Adinarayan SP: Before and after independence: a study of racial and communal attitudes in India. Br J Psychol 44:108–115.

As measured by the Bogardus Social Distance test, South Indian Hindus show a more favorable attitude toward Britain following independence, and a more disfavorable attitude toward Muslims after the creation of Pakistan.

771. Anastasi A, deJesus C: Language development and nonverbal IQ of Puerto Rican preschool children in New York City. J Abnorm Soc Psychol 48:357–366.

Although the Puerto Rican sample was inferior to Negro or white samples in educational and occupational level of parents, scores of Puerto Rican children did not differ significantly on Draw-A-Man test and were superior in mean sentence length and maturity of sentence structure.

772. Bennett EM: A socio-cultural interpretation of maladjustive behavior. J Soc Psychol 37:19–26.

Western civilization emphasizes success through personal competence. The individual therefore adjusts his perception and recall to retain those elements that enhance self-competence and rejects those that do not.

773. Carpenter ES: Witch-fear among the Aivilik Eskimos. Am J Psychiatry 110:194–199.

Social factors, when projected into witch-fear in Aivilik culture, determine the content of psychoses, increase their incidence, and hinder their resolution.

774. Chess S, Clark KB, Thomas A: The importance of cultural evaluation in psychiatric diagnosis and treatment. Psychiatr Q 27:102–114.

Evaluation of the healthy or morbid psychological aspects of an individual can be made only in terms of what is appropriate and effective functioning in the specific cultural milieu. The psychiatrist may err in using his own status as the norm and that of the patient, if different, as the deviation from the norm.

775. Devereux G: Cultural factors in psychoanalytic therapy. J Am Psychoanal Assoc 1:629–655.

Though the human psyche and culture are functionally inseparable, the insight afforded by psychoanalysis and anthropology are not additive but complementary. Data from the psychoanalysis of a Plains Indian woman reveal technical rules for use with culturally alien patients.

776. Dudycha GJ: Race attitudes and esthetic preferences. J Soc Psychol 37:61–68.

The presence of race prejudice does not influence esthetic judgments of the majority of a student sample.

777. Eysenck HJ: Primary social attitudes: a comparison of attitude patterns in England, Germany, and Sweden. J Abnorm Soc Psychol 48:563–568.

Intercorrelations of items on a social attitude inventory administered to German subjects are factor analyzed. The resulting factors are very similar to those obtained for other populations, indicating that the structure of attitudes in the four countries is similar, if not identical.

778. Farber ML: English and Americans: values in the socialization process. J Psychol 36:243–250.

The study of child socialization in two countries may be approached through adults' verbalized values and expectations concerning their children.

779. Ferreira AJ: A note on the concepts of culture and human nature. Psychiatry 16:401–403.

Melford Spiro has described objections to David Bidney's concepts of culture and human nature. In learning and culture change, a circular process is formed, which requires both a social heritage and the emergence of personal culture.

780. Freeman HE, Showel M: The role of the family in the socialization process. J Soc Psychol 37:97–101.

A lack of relationship between the number of siblings in the consanguineal family and number of children in the conjugal family suggests that the role of the family in the socialization process has been overestimated.

781. Gray JS, Thompson AH: The ethnic prejudices of white and Negro college students. J Abnorm Soc Psychol 48:311–313.

Ratings for social distance of 24 ethnic groups show that Negroes rate all groups except their own lower than do white students. Acquaintance with members of the ethnic group tends to raise the social distance rating of both whites and Negroes.

782. Hammer EF: Frustration-aggression hypothesis extended to socio-racial areas: comparison of Negro and white children's H-T-P's. Psychiatr Q 27:597–607.

The relatively greater incidence of aggression and hostility found in a "normal" sampling of Negro children suggests that the clinician must be cautious in interpreting the projective protocols of a Negro subject. The frustration-aggression hypothesis may be extended to the social-racial area.

783. Hammer EF: Negro and white children's personality adjustment as revealed by a comparison of their drawings (H-T-P). J Clin Psychol 9:7–10.

Negro children show a greater incidence of emotional maladjustment than white children.

784. Hamza M: The dynamic forces in the personalities of juvenile delinquents in the Egyptian environment. Br J Psychol 44:330–338.

Differences in intensity, duration, and frequency of stress are evident from TATs given to juvenile delinquents and controls. The importance of the child's home environment is clearly indicated.

785. Horowitz MW, Perlmutter HV: The concept of the social group. J Soc Psychol 37:69–96.

A scientific treatment of the concept of group must incorporate definitions of group perceptions and change and development of these perceptions, to derive laws of group organization.

786. Hsu EH: Note on factor analysis of American culture. J Soc Psychol 38:137–140.

Hofstaetter's results and interpretations of a factor analysis of American culture are only tentative.

787. Klausner SZ: Social class and self concept. J Soc Psychol 38:201–206.

There are modally different self concepts between socioeconomic groups. Members of the same socioeconomic group have more homogeneous self-concepts.

788. Klineberg O: Cultural factors in personality adjustment of children. Am J Orthopsychiatry 23:465–471.

Studies regarding children's personality adjustment should include examination of the effect of training procedures on the child, of the relation between cultural factors in the life of a child and the personality of adults in the community.

789. Langfeldt G: The importance of constitution in psychiatry. Am J Psychiatry 110:261–268.

The diagnosis and differentiation of constitutional types enable one to understand the personality itself, as well as the pathological reactions, without any deeper analysis being necessary.

790. Laufer LG: Cultural problems encountered in the use of the Cornell Index among Okinawan natives. Am J Psychiatry 109:861–864.

The Cornell Index, validated for a different group, appears inappropriate for the current study. Anthropological knowledge of the culture would have facilitated defining neurosis among the Okinawans.

791. Lin T: A study of the incidence of mental disorder in Chinese and other cultures. Psychiatry 16:313–336.

In a psychiatric and sociological survey, it appears that the low incidence of psychopathic personality, psychoneurosis, and alcoholism in Formosa may be related to Chinese emphasis on filial piety, conformity to the traditional social pattern, and the mutual dependence and high tolerance of the extended-family system.

792. Lolli G, Sevianni E, Golder G, Balboni C, Mariani A: Further observations on the use of wine and other alcoholic beverages by Italians and Americans of Italian extraction. Q J Stud Alcohol 14:395–405.

Drinking exclusively with meals prevails among Italians but is rare among Italian Americans. The number of Italians who never use alcohol in excess is greater than the number of Italian Americans who never use alcohol in excess.

793. McGurk FCJ: On white and Negro test performance and socioeconomic factors. J Abnorm Soc Psychol 48:448–450.

Explanations generally offered for lower Negro test performance include an inability to handle culturally loaded material, or lower socioeconomic status. Data from matched white and Negro students do not support either explanation: there is no evidence that culturally loaded material discriminates against the Negro or that test score differences decrease as socioeconomic status is raised.

794. Michael DN: A cross-cultural investigation of closure. J Abnorm Soc Psychol 48:225–230.

No significant differences are found in the perception of closure in Navahos, who have a culture stressing nonclosure, and Americans, who stress closure in both values and design. The indeterminateness of many cultural factors that may have contributed to the results require further investigation.

795. Milner E: Some hypotheses concerning the influence of segregation on Negro personality development. Psychiatry 16:291–297.

Segregation practices fundamentally affect Negro personality development to the extent that these practices have a destructive effect on Negro family functioning and relationships.

796. Moloney JC: Understanding the paradox of Japanese psychoanalysis. Int J Psychoanal 34:291–303.

Japanese psychoanalysts, since they regard the individual as an integral part of the Japanese nation,

attempt to adjust the individual to the environment. The nationalistic characteristics of Japan are thus supported at the expense of the individual.

797. Moran LJ: Vocabulary knowledge and usage among normal and schizophrenic subjects. Psychol Monographs 67:1–19.

The schizophrenic is less precise in understanding of word meaning, less able to use words as conceptual instruments, and shows impaired ability to integrate words meaningfully.

798. Newland ET: Chicago Non-Verbal Examination results on an east Tennessee Negro population. J Clin Psychol 9:44–46.

At all age levels, Negro children are approximately two years below the norm for performance.

799. Radke-Yarrow M, Lande B: Personality correlates of differential reactions to minority group-belonging. J Soc Psychol 38:253–272.

The Jewish-American individual's reactions to minority group members are partly the expression of underlying personality trends.

800. Redlich FC, Hollingshead AB, Roberts BH, Robinson HA, Freedman LZ, Myers JK: Social structure and psychiatric disorders. Am J Psychiatry 109:729–734.

Significant relationships in New Haven exist between social level and (1) prevalence of psychiatric patients, (2) types of psychiatric disorders in the patient population, and (3) types of therapy given.

801. Roe A: A psychological study of eminent psychologists and anthropologists, and a comparison with biological and physical scientists. Psychol Monographs 67:1–55.

Anthropologists tend to obtain their degrees at a later age than psychologists. Differences between the two groups may be found on spatial and mathematical tests, though differentiation on verbal tests is slight. TATs for both groups show a tendency toward dependent parental relationships associated with guilt. Rorschach responses by professionals are very productive and demonstrate great interest in people.

802. Roheim G: Hansel and Gretel. Bull Menninger Clin 17–18:90–92.

"Hansel and Gretel" is a folktale directly derived from a dream, dreamed by someone, somewhere, and many times told and retold till only rudiments of the dream origin remain.

803. Rohrer JH: The research team concept and the cultural pattern of science. Am J Psychiatry 109:677–683.

Scientific theories, definitions, variables, and coordinating definitions are integral parts of cultural pattern that must be clearly recognized and effectively utilized if the necessary multidisciplinary approach to studying human behavior is to succeed.

804. Ruesch J: Synopsis of the theory of human communication. Psychiatry 16:215–243.

Communication, which is an organizing principle of nature and the backbone of mental health, may be viewed on the interpersonal, group, and social levels.

805. Sclare AB: Cultural determinants in the neurotic Negro. Br J Med Psychol 26–27:278–288.

Racial prejudice is important in the formation of character and the nature of neurotic patterns in Negroes. Recent improvement in Negro-white relationships may lead to elimination of some of the distorting influence which results from prejudice.

806. Segy L: Initiation ceremony and African sculptures. Am Imago 10:57–82.

Initiation ceremonies are socialization and psychotherapeutic institutions which give rise to African art.

807. Sillman L: The genesis of man. Int J Psychoanal 34:146–152.

Anatomical and behavioral transformations in man and the shift from the Paleolithic to the Neolithic are associated with division of the instinctual and counter-instinctual drives.

808. Slotkin JS: Social psychiatry of a Menomini community. J Abnorm Soc Psychol 48:10–16.

Menomini mores inhibit social opposition, producing symptoms of cultural inadequacy. Inhibited drives probably tend to vary with different cultures.

809. Spiro ME: Ghosts: an anthropological inquiry into learning and perception. J Abnorm Soc Psychol 48:376–382.

The acquisition of Ifaluk belief in malevolent ghosts cannot be explained by theories of cultural determinism or learning. The belief is learned by the child according to certain principles of perception and cognition and represents a pragmatic cognitive truth. The belief continues to persist into adulthood because it is re-created in Ifaluk psychodynamics.

810. Stein MI: Creativity and culture. J Psychol 36:311–322.

The extent to which creativity is present depends upon the influence of culture upon freedom of the individual in interaction with his environment, and upon the degree of diversity and ambiguity permitted.

811. Williams JR, Scott RB: Growth and development of Negro infants: IV. Motor development and its relationship to child rearing practices in two groups of Negro infants. Child Dev 24:102–121.

Negro infants from families in low socioeconomic groups show significant gross motor acceleration when compared to Negro infants from families in high socioeconomic groups. Infants from permissive, accepting environments score significantly higher on the Gesell Development schedules than infants from rigid, rejecting environments.

1954

812. Ariga K: The family in Japan. Marriage Fam Living 16:362–368.

The Japanese family is a particularly idealized institution stressing continuity with the past and the future, patriarchal power, and little personal freedom. Postwar changes have promoted personal mate selection but have not abolished the family system.

813. Behrens ML: Child rearing and the character structure of the mother. Child Dev 25:225–238.

The mother's character structure is an important causative factor in the wide variation in both child rearing and child adjustment within cultural subgroups in our society.

814. Benedict PK, Jacks I: Mental illness in primitive societies. Psychiatry 17:377–389.

A literature survey reveals that mental disorders known to Western psychiatry do occur among primitive peoples throughout the world, although there are differences in incidence rates and symptomatology. This universality of occurrence does not per se point to any particular etiological hypothesis.

815. Brown RW, Lennenberg EH: A study in language and cognition. J Abnorm Soc Psychol 49:454–462.

An experiment of English and Zuni codability of

colors suggests that lexical differences may be indicative of cognitive differences as indicated by the Whorfian hypothesis.

816. Burgess EW: Economic, cultural, and social factors in family breakdown. Am J Orthopsychiatry 24:462–470.

Economic conditions underlie causes of juvenile delinquency and family disintegration. Individualism, competition, and democracy weaken the institutional bonds of the family. The urban way of life is an unfavorable environment for the family and a new form is evolving—the companionship family.

817. Carpenter ES: External life and self-definition among the Aivilik Eskimos. Am J Psychiatry 110: 840–843.

Aivilik Eskimos assert that death is a beginning of a new phase in a never-ending cycle. By not admitting death they need no Divine Redeemer or culture-hero to conquer it.

818. Carstairs GM: Daru and bhang: cultural factors in the choice of intoxicant. Q J Stud Alcohol 15:220–237.

In a village in northern India (Rajasthan), members of the two highest caste groups, Rajput and Brahmin, differ in their choice of intoxicant. Choices are influenced by the psychological effects of the intoxicants, and by the different values stressed by each group.

819. Ceccaldi D: The family in France. Marriage Fam Living 16:326–330.

The French family is strongly influenced by traditional emphasis on a stable, hierarchical family based on heritage, social convention, and respectability.

820. Centers R, Blumberg GH: Social and psychological factors in human procreation. J Soc Psychol 40:245–258.

There is a negative relationship between sociological variables and desire to have children, but some psychological variables—religion, happiness, attitudes, beliefs—are significantly related to desire for children.

821. Chandrasekhar S: The family in India. Marriage Fam Living 16:336–342.

The Hindu joint family that was typical a half a century ago is today breaking up into numerous small biological families.

822. Chien I: The environment as a determinant of behavior. J Soc Psychol 39:115–128.

A comprehensive theoretical model of the geobehavioral environment may be useful in predicting and understanding human behavior. Anthropological and sociological findings contain much material relevant to the schema.

823. Cohn TS, Carsch H: Administration of the F scale to a sample of Germans. J Abnorm Soc Psychol 49:471.

German data on the F scale, as a reflection of authoritarian personality trends, appears to support its validity.

824. Douglass JH, Douglass KW: Aspects of marriage and family living among Egyptian peasants *(Fellaheen)*. Marriage Fam Living 16:45–48.

Patterns of familial relationships among the Egyptian peasants seem relatively impersonal, unromantic, contractual, nonegalitarian, and static.

825. Eisen NH: The influence of set on semantic generalization. J Abnorm Soc Psychol 49:491–496.

Variations in kind of set, method of inducing set, and prior experience with generalization stimuli do not seem to influence semantic generalization. Generalization occurs randomly and without regard to relationship of the stimulus.

826. Frumkin RM: Attitudes of Negro college students toward intrafamily leadership and control. Marriage Fam Living 16:252–253.

Most Negro college students seem to reflect the middle-class equalitarian family ideal, though they come from families in which leadership is either maternal or paternal.

827. Garma A: The Indo-American winged or feathered serpent, the step coil and the Greek meander. Am Imago 11:115–145.

American Indian, Greek, Roman, Arabic, and early Christian serpent representations are symbolic of male genitalia and anal excrement.

828. Geiger K, Inkeles A: The family in the U.S.S.R. Marriage Fam Living 16:397–404.

The general direction for development of the Soviet family is consistent with trends that have been observed for Western industrial nations.

829. Gini C, Caranti E: The family in Italy. Marriage Fam Living 16:350–361.

The fundamental characteristic of the Italian

family is its stability deriving from lack of the institution of divorce and difference in the position of men and women in the family and society. In view of an accelerated process of equalization many typical features are now purely of ethnographic interest.

830. Grossack MN: Perceived Negro group belongingness and social rejection. J Psychol 38:127–130.

Negroes support the concept of belongingness as a social norm and reject deviants.

831. Hayner NS: The family in Mexico. Marriage Fam Living 16:369–373.

Mexico has a strong tradition favoring the dominance of the male, and traditional courtship practices like chaperonage persist, though in modified forms.

832. Henry J: The formal social structure of a psychiatric hospital. Psychiatry 17:139–151.

An administrator might ask himself whether a poorly functioning person in a hospital setting might be affected by a defect in the organizational structure. Even well-integrated persons cannot function without stress in a poorly conceived organization.

833. Himes JS: A value profile in mate selection among Negroes. Marriage Fam Living 16:244–247.

Value systems influencing mate selection among Negroes reflect prevailing cultural as well as racial values.

834. Hobbs AH, Kephart WM: Professor Kinsey: his facts and his fantasy. Am J Psychiatry 110:614–620.

The methodology of data collection and interpretation by Kinsey in his volumes *Sexual Behavior in the Human Female* and *Sexual Behavior in the Human Male* are questionable.

835. Hofstaetter PR: Note on factor analysis of American culture: a rejoinder. J Soc Psychol 39:143–146.

Hsu's criticism lacks justification and constructiveness. Any application of factor analysis in new areas is bound to be tentative.

836. Jahoda G: A note on Ashanti names and their relationship to personality. Br J Psychol 45:192–195.

Possession of particular Ashanti names, which are given according to the day on which the child is born, appears to be related to delinquency rates. Ashanti beliefs on the connection between personality and names may enhance latent traits.

837. Levy LH: Sexual symbolism: a validity study. J Consult Psychol 18:43–46.

Studies with children do not support Freud's hypothesis of sexual symbolism for pointed and round objects.

838. Lorr M, Fields V: A factorial study of body types. J Clin Psychol 10:182–185.

A study of male psychotic patients demonstrates the existence of three groups with trait patterns that resemble patterns descriptive of Sheldon's components, and shows that Sheldon's 76 somatotypes can be defined as measurements on only two type factors.

839. McConnell J: Abstract behavior among the Tepehuan. J Abnorm Soc Psychol 49:109–110.

Inferences in the literature that primitive peoples' thought patterns are more concrete, while modern man's are more abstract, are not supported by data from the Tepehuan tribe. Tepehuan subjects can perform at the abstract level almost as well as the Weschler-Bellevue normative populations.

840. McGaugran LS: Predicting language behavior from object sorting. J Abnorm Soc Psychol 49:183–195.

The degree of interrelatedness found to exist between language and conceptual behavior suggests the presence of general behavior potentials that may be called reality-fixing and autism.

841. Mead M: Some theoretical considerations on the problem of mother-child separation. Am J Orthopsychiatry 24:471–483.

Tools for sufficiently precise recording of the interaction between mother and child are now available to replace the "impressionistic" and "intuitive" reports of clinicians and anthropologists.

842. Melikian L, Prothro ET: Sexual behavior of university students in the Arab Near East. J Abnorm Soc Psychol 49:59–64.

First sexual experience occurs later for Arab male students than for American students. More Arab students have positive histories of homosexual and heterosexual intercourse than Americans.

843. Mogey J: The family in England. Marriage Fam Living 16:319–325.

The size of the English family has been declining due to increased use of birth-control methods. The incidence of divorce and premarital sex has increased somewhat, and there is a trend toward more equal responsibility between spouses.

844. Nahas MK: The family in the Arab world. Marriage Fam Living 16:293–300.

The Arab family is distinguished by pride in large family size, subordination of women, and strong kinship orientations.

845. Ni E: The family in China. Marriage Fam Living 16:315–318.

The Communist regime in China has worked to accelerate the family from an institution to a companionship.

846. Nimkoff MF: The family in the United States. Marriage Fam Living 16:390–396.

Freedom of mate selection and individualistic self-determination in American youth reflect the subordinant role of the American family.

847. Osgood CE, Luria Z: A blind analysis of a case of multiple personality using the semantic differential. J Abnorm Soc Psychol 49:579–591.

Administration of the semantic differential to each of the three personalities of a woman proves to be an interesting test of the validity and sensitivity of the instrument. In general, all three personalities utilize the semantic scales in the same ways; but differences are noted.

848. Osgood CE, Sebeok T (eds): Psycholinguistics: a survey of theory and research problems. J Abnorm Soc Psychol Supp 49:1–203.

Three theoretical models of language process—the linguistic, learning theory, and information theory approaches—and various research problems which may be experimentally approached may be considered in the context of synchronic, sequential, and diachronic psycholinguistics.

849. Pearl D: Ethnocentrism and the self concept. J Soc Psychol 40:137–148.

Pre- and post-psychotherapy self concepts of mental patients indicate that ethnocentrism tends to be reduced as the self condept changes toward greater self awareness and increased conscious anxiety.

850. Peixotto HE: The Bender Gestalt Visual Motor Test as a culture free test of personality. J Clin Psychol 10:369–372.

Since different protocols are produced by different ethnic groups, the technique is not completely culture free.

851. Pierson D: The family in Brazil. Marriage Fam Living 16: 308–314.

Three types of family—that of the landed proprietors, the slaves, and the lower class—and a system of compadrio have been an integral part of Brazilian history.

852. Prothro ET: Studies in stereotypes: Lebanese stereotypes of America as revealed by the sentence completion technique. J Soc Psychol 40:39–42.

Sentence-completion responses by Lebanese girls reveal a generally favorable view of the United States. Comments on freedom and women's equality reflect significant problems within Lebanon.

853. Prothro ET: Studies in stereotypes: cross-cultural patterns of national stereotypes. J Soc Psychol 40:53–60.

Armenian student minority members in Lebanon have similar stereotypes of English, Jews, Americans, Russians, Negroes, and Italians. Differences in stereotypes are related to degree of social contact and may be useful in estimating social tensions.

854. Prothro ET: Studies in stereotypes: Lebanese businessmen. J Soc Psychol 40:275–280.

The stereotypes of businessmen are quite similar to those held by university students in Beirut.

855. Prothro ET, Melikian LH: Studies in stereotypes: Arab students in the Near East. J Soc Psychol 40:237–244.

Stereotypes of Arab students in Beirut are similar to those of American students in definiteness toward disfavored and familiar groups.

856. Roberts BH, Myers JK: Religion, national origin, immigration and mental illness. Am J Psychiatry 110:759–764.

Schizophrenia and psychosis with mental deficiency are not related to the social variables of religion, national origin, and immigrational status, but most other forms of psychopathology are.

857. Robinson HA, Redlich FC, Myers JK: Social structure and psychiatric treatment. Am J Orthopsychiatry 24:307–316.

Psychotherapeutic methods are applied in disproportionately high degree to patients in the upper social levels and organic therapies to the small business, white-collar, skilled, and semiskilled workers. Custodial care is given in largest measure to patients of lowest social status.

858. Schelsky H: The family in Germany. Marriage Fam Living 16: 331–335.

The view of the German family as essentially having a patriarchal-authoritarian structure cannot be maintained in light of contemporary research showing a transition to the partnership principle.

859. Schneck JM: The hypnotic trance, magico-religious medicine, and primitive initiation rites. Psychoanal Rev 41:182–190.

Different concepts—death, rebirth, and sexuality—can merge in the same individual in relation to the trance experience, as shown in an examination of patients, primitive medicine men, and initiation rites.

860. Skeels D: The function of humor in three Nez Perce Indian myths. Am Imago 11:249–261.

Humor allows unconscious identification, while enforcing aesthetic distance and relieving the audience's deep tensions associated with the castration themes of three myths.

861. Sommer R, Killian LM: Negro-white relations. J Soc Psychol 39:237–244.

The extent of divergence of the white attitude to Negroes and the Negro attitude to Negroes gives rise to interactional conflicts between races. Negro attitudes reflect a reaction against mass media stereotypy.

862. Straus MA: Subcultural variation in Ceylonese mental ability: a study in national character. J Soc Psychol 39:129–141.

The hypothesis that subcultural differences in personality are equivalent to or greater than differences between major cultures may be examined through verbal and nonverbal test performance. In spite of the complex nature of subcultural patterns, differences between the Sinhalese, Ceylon Tamil, and Burgher students are not significant. A general pattern of better performance on verbal tests lends support to concepts of basic personality or national character.

863. Strauss AL: Strain and harmony in American-Japanese warbride marriages. Marriage Fam Living 16:99–106.

The strains incurred in war-bride marriages are more like those occurring in more endogamous than exogamous marriages.

864. Svalastoga K: The family in Scandinavia. Marriage Fam Living 16:374–380.

Scandinavian society has not yet quite adapted to the situation of the woman working outside the home. Child-rearing attitudes have changed in the direction of development of the resources of the child, rather than stressing conformity.

865. Szekely L: Biological remarks on fears originating in early childhood. Int J Psychoanal 35:57–67.

The concordance between fear-release in infancy and animal key stimulus reflects a phylogenetic survival.

866. Talmon-Garber Y: The family in Israel. Marriage Fam Living 16:343–349.

A new type of family in Israel, the nonfamilistic organization of communal settlements, merits attention.

867. Teicher MI: Three cases of psychosis among the Eskimos. J Ment Science 100:527–535.

The cases suggest a basic schizophrenic process similar to that found in patients from Western society. The hallucinations and delusions, while expressed in terms compatible with Eskimo culture, could otherwise readily be duplicated on the wards of any mental hospital.

868. Thamavit V, Golden R: The family in Thailand. Marriage Fam Living 16:381–389.

The rural family shows no pronounced changes or trends in function or orientation, while the urban Thai family is beginning to exhibit some of the disintegrating influences of Westernization.

869. Tomasic DA: The family in the Balkans. Marriage Fam Living 16:301–307.

Households in the Dinaric Alps are characterized by eldest male autocracy and are basically a joint family system. In the agricultural lowlands the zadruga community household is found.

870. Wallis RS: The overt fears of Dakota Indian children. Child Dev 25:185–192.

Overt fears of Dakota children fall within the usual categories and are similar to those of rural white children. However, certain types of fear (particularly with regard to methods of toilet training) reflect characteristics of Dakota culture.

871. Watson G, Comrey AL: Nutritional replacement for mental illness. J Psychol 38:251–264.

A statistically significant improvement in emotionally disturbed individuals, as measured by the MMPI, is obtained by employing a particular formula in nutrition replacement therapy.

872. Wretmark G: Body-build of the male duodenal ulcer individual. Psychiatr Neurol Scand 29: 229–235.

Individuals with duodenal ulcers have a relatively smaller chest breadth than others. This difference is not due to a difference in stature. Lindegard's methods, because they permit a more detailed analysis than hitherto possible, should be used in future investigations of the relationship between body-build, personality pattern, and susceptibility to disease.

873. Wright GO: Projection and displacement: a cross-cultural study of folk tale aggression. J Abnorm Soc Psychol 49:523–528.

Analysis of folk tale data supports the essential features of approach-avoidance theory and its extension for displacement and projection in folk tales. Consistency of trends in child-rearing practices and folktale aggression is a significant phenomenon.

874. Young FM, Bright HA: Results of testing 81 Negro rural juveniles with the Wechsler Intelligence Scale for Children. J Soc Psychol 39:219–226.

According to Weschler norms, the performance of rural Negro children falls into the feeble-minded classification and therefore appears inapplicable to the sample since the norms are based upon white performance.

875. Young FM, Collins JJ: Results of testing Negro contact-syphilitics with the Wechsler-Bellevue Intelligence Scale. J Soc Psychol 39:93–98.

The syphilitic group is classed as borderline in terms of Wechsler's norms. The control groups show possible deterioration, while the experimental group shows definite deterioration. This outcome may be accounted for by cultural restrictions rather than pathological impairment.

1955

876. Block J: Personality characteristics associated with fathers' attitudes toward child-rearing. Child Dev 26:41–48.

Restrictive fathers tend to be constricted, submis-

sive, suggestible individuals with little self-assurance. Permissive fathers are self-reliant, ascendant, and function effectively. The restrictive father, acting upon the residues of his own childhood anxieties, is avenging himself upon the wrong generation, which results in a self-perpetuating but self-defeating cycle of personality.

877. Bowman CC: Loneliness and social change. Am J Psychiatry 112:194–198.

The decline in primary-group contacts, the impersonality of modern bureaucracy, and increased as well as vertical mobility result in the psychiatric phenomenon of loneliness. This social condition is alterable.

878. Brown RW, Black AH, Horowitz AE: Phonetic symbolism in natural languages. J Abnorm Soc Psychol 50:388–393.

Agreement and accuracy in the translation of foreign words can be explained as the result of a cultural conception of phonetic symbolic values and some universal phonetic symbolism deriving from the origin of speech.

879. Carothers JC: The nature-nurture controversy. Psychiatry 18:301–304.

Climate, nutritional, infective, and cultural factors play their part in forming the constitution of humanity in Africa, and the effects of each of these are not likely to have been the same as their effects in Europe. These remarks apply to bodies, but there is no evidence that they apply to minds. These factors may affect the mind directly, but there is a striking lack of evidence that adaptation to them has influenced the genetic basis of mentation.

880. Carstairs GM: Attitudes to death and suicide in an Indian cultural setting. Int J Soc Psychiatry 1:33–41.

"Suttee" is now a rarity in India and the warrior virtues are losing their old significance, but the basic values of Brahmanical Hinduism are still supreme in the minds of country people in Rajasthan. The villagers do not regard death as final but as one incident in a long series of existences. Death is regarded not as a solitary act but as a part of the series of domestic rites and ceremonies in which whole families are required to play their several parts.

881. Cohen YA: Character formation and social structure in a Jamaican community. Psychiatry 18: 275–296.

Rocky Roads, British West Indies, is a community in which a sense of collective unity of community is lacking not only in actual behavior but even on the purely verbal or ideal level. There is an absence of both leadership and ties of mutual obligation, and the population is characterized by deep-seated, rarely expressed hostilities.

882. De Liz Ferreira AJ: A note on Carothers' book. Psychiatry 18:99–101.

Carothers's failure to explain his empirical data on African mentality, intellect, and intelligence in terms of an acceptable theory of personality has led to widely different reactions to his book, *The African Mind in Health and Disease,* as is illustrated by the conflicting views of Margaret Mead and Jules Henry.

883. Dennis W: Are Hopi children noncompetitive? J Abnorm Soc Psychol 50:99–100.

Although Hopi culture is not characterized by expressions of overt competition, test performance by Hopi children indicates levels of competition that exceed those for white norm groups.

884. Dexter ES, Stein B: The measurement of leadership in white and Negro women students. J Abnorm Soc Psychol 51:219–221.

Small but statistically significant differences exist between leaders and nonleaders in a college that are greater than Negro-white differences.

885. Diaz-Guerrero R: Neurosis and the Mexican family structure. Am J Psychiatry 112:411–417.

The cultural assumptions of the supremacy of the father, and the absolute self-sacrifice of the mother, in the dominant Mexican family pattern are related to the development of neurosis.

886. Edinger ED: Archetypal patterns in schizophrenia. Am J Psychiatry 112:354–357.

Jung's theory of archetypes may be applied to schizophrenic delusions such as the prophet and religious savior, death and rebirth, and cosmic dualism.

887. Ferguson-Rayport SM, Griffith RM, Straus EW: The psychiatric significance of tattoos. Psychiatr Q 29:112–131.

Schizophrenics reiterate primitive attitudes as to the magical significance and potency of their tattoo choice and at the same time express their estrangement from the normal world. In personality disorder patients, tattoos express inner conflicts and satisfy inner needs, and evaluated as a social

phenomenon, signify another deviation from the mores of our culture.

888. Field MJ: Witchcraft as a primitive interpretation of mental disorder. J Ment Science 101:826–833.

Neurosis is displayed in the Gold Coast by both depressed "witches" and persons believing themselves bewitched. An increase in neurosis, attributable to social and economic changes, has led to increased preoccupation with witchcraft.

889. Fitt AB: A study of racial attitudes during and after the war by the Thurstone technique. Br J Psychol 46:306–309.

Changes in Australian attitudes as would be expected during war and peace are found with respect to Germans and Japanese. Attitudes toward the Maoris became more favorable.

890. Froeschels E: Grammar, a basic function of language-speech. Am J Psychother 9:43–53.

Both dreams and transition states use the grammar and modulation of the waking mind. Grammar and modulation are, as a rule, not added to the already selected word, but seem to represent a deep layer in the process of speaking into which the words are molded.

891. Gervais TW: Freud and the culture-psychologists. Br J Psychol 46:293–305.

Critiques of Freud's ignorance of sociocultural factors are exaggerated. On the whole, Freud's opponents betray grosser defects in these areas than Freud himself.

892. Goffman E: On face-work: an analysis of ritual elements in social interaction. Psychiatry 18:213–231.

Through rituals societies mobilize their members as self-regulating participants in social encounters.

893. Graham TF: Doll play phantasies of Negro and white primary school children. J Clin Psychol 11:29–32.

The quantitative differences between the fantasies of Negro and white school children are due to sex, development, and individuation.

894. Hamilton RV: Psycholinguistic analysis. J Soc Psychol 41:271–286.

An understanding of the manner in which the individual makes use of interpretive processes provides a basis for understanding individual value judgments. C. W. Morris's interpretive functions are expanded to include the categories of designaters, appraisers, prescripters, formaters, identifiers, and subjectifiers.

895. Hebb D: The mammal and his environment. Am J Psychiatry 111:826–831.

The greater the development of intelligence the greater the vulnerability to emotional breakdown. Culture provides a protective cocoon against mental breakdown.

896. Hill R: Courtship in Puerto Rico: an institution in transition. Marriage Fam Living 17:26–35.

The pattern of involving and committing young people to marriage in Puerto Rico is predominantly Spanish, but the system is ideologically oriented toward the beliefs of North America.

897. Hollingshead AB, Redlich FC: Social mobility and mental illness. Am J Psychiatry 112:179–185.

Psychoneurotics and schizophrenics are more upwardly mobile than the average population. The downward-drift hypothesis of schizophrenia is questionable.

898. Kaplan B: Reflections of the acculturation process in the Rorschach test. J Proj Techniques 19:30–35.

Rorschachs obtained from young Navaho, Zuni, Mormon, and Spanish-Americans show that the latter two groups are as different from American culture as the Navaho and Zuni.

899. Keehn JD: An examination of the two-factor theory of social attitudes in a Near-Eastern culture. J Soc Psychol 42:13–20.

A test of Eysenck's theory of organization of social attitudes (Radicalism-Conservatism, Tough-mindedness-Tendermindedness) in Near East culture shows the R-C factor to be a special case of a more general phenomenon, while the cross-cultural validity of the To-Te factor is upheld.

900. Kubie LS: Dr. Kinsey and the medical profession. Psychosom Med 17:172–184.

While Kinsey made important contributions, his book *Sexual Behavior in the Human Female,* has serious shortcomings that could have perhaps been prevented had Kinsey made use of the theoretical and clinical concepts as well as the essential sophistication that could have been provided by cultural anthropologists, sociologists, psychiatric social workers, clinical psychologists, psychiatrists, and particularly psychoanalytic psychiatrists.

901. Lambert WE: Measurement of the linguistic dominance of bilinguals. J Abnorm Soc Psychol 50:197–200.

The reaction-time method for measuring bilingualism shows reliable differences in predicted directions given language experiences. The method allows for statistical analysis of language dominance, which is related to cultural and personality characteristics.

902. Lambo TA: The role of cultural factors in paranoid psychosis among the Yoruba tribe. J Ment Science 101:239–266.

Paranoid psychosis in the rural, nonliterate tribe resembles a hypothetical mental disease lying midway between psychotic and neurotic illnesses in Euro-American cultures. Paranoid psychosis in the Westernized, literate group of the tribe does not differ from that seen in European cultures.

903. Lawlor M: Cultural influences on preference for designs. J Abnorm Soc Psychol 51:690–692.

The preferences of African and English students for West African designs are distinct for each group, showing considerable within-group agreement. Aesthetic preference is related to cultural influence.

904. Leighton AH: Psychiatric disorder and social environment: an outline for a frame of reference. Psychiatry 18: 357–383.

Interference with striving may lead to a disturbance of the essential psychical condition. Patterns of striving may be interfered with by difficulties in the individual, in the environment, or in the objects themselves. Social disorganization interferes with the definition of adequate objects and the development of adequate essential patterns. The social organization-disorganization approach has been given emphasis in the Stirling County Study.

905. Lorenz M: Expressive behavior and language patterns. Psychiatry 18:353–366.

Language expresses a person's selection and organization of the inner and outer reality that he perceives. The hysteric prefers to sift reality through emotional impression, the obsessive-compulsive through evaluation and judgments, the manic represents literally, and the schizophrenic abandons representation of outward reality for a presentation of his inward reality. These language characteristics may be present in "normal" people.

906. Montagu MFA: Man and human nature. Am J Psychiatry 112:401–410.

The historical perspective demonstrates that the Western view of man is incorrect. The doctrine of "original sin" must be replaced by a humanistic philosophy. Human aggression is caused by human nurture and not human nature.

907. Mozak HH: Language and the interpretation of sexual symbolism. J Consult Clin Psychol 19: 108.

Freud's contention that language should bear the stamp of unconscious processes cannot be supported by the translation of nouns that are supposedly sexual symbols into their equivalents in languages with genders for nouns.

908. Opler MK: Cultural perspectives in mental health research. Am J Orthopsychiatry 25:51–59.

Each culture has a typical life-cycle organization from infancy to death in which anxiety-producing experiences occur with different frequencies, at different stages, and often differentially for the two sexes.

909. Pasamanick B, Knobloch H: Early language behavior in Negro children and the testing of intelligence. J Abnorm Psychol 50:401–402.

Negro children are found to have lower language scores on third examination at two years of age, apparently due to lack of verbal responsiveness rather than poor comprehension. The implications for ethnic group psychology of this earlier awareness of racial difference are great.

910. Priestley KE: Education and mental health in South East Asia. Int J Soc Psychiatry 1:55–62.

The culture of the Chinese family may break down under the influence of Western rationalism. Any substantial advance in education and mental health must be thought of in terms of generations and in terms of the production of an indigenous body of scientific knowledge related to the races of South East Asia, and adapted to the local setting.

911. Prothro ET: An alternative approach in cross-cultural intelligence testing. J Psychol 39:247–252.

Intelligence tests can be adapted for cross-cultural use in the Near East, if there is a criterion of intelligence shared by the cultures. Adapted tests can be as effective in measuring intelligence as culture-free tests.

912. Prothro ET: Arab-American differences in the judgment of written messages. J Soc Psychol 42: 3–12.

The hypothesis that Arab speech is overassertive in comparison to American speech and that messages seen as extreme by Americans will be judged neutral by Arabs is supported by the data. The implications for cross-cultural communication are clear.

913. Prothro ET, Melikian LH: Studies in stereotypes: familiarity and the kernel of truth hypothesis. J Soc Psychol 41:3–10.

Increased familiarity and contact with an American group resulted in addition of personality traits to the American stereotype held by Arabian students. Agreement between groups on the American stereotype has implications for national-character studies.

914. Rabin AI, King GF, Ehrmann JC: Vocabulary performance of short-term and long-term schizophrenics. J Abnorm Soc Psychol 50:255–258.

Although no differences are found between short-term schizophrenics and normals on measures of vocabulary performance, the long-term schizophrenics are significantly lower than the other two groups.

915. Richman ML, Schmeidler GR: Changes in a folk dance accompanying cultural change. J Soc Psychol 42:333–336.

During a period of Israeli national solidarity and international conflict, changes symbolizing aggressive initiative and group solidarity were spontaneously integrated into the Hora.

916. Ruesch J: Nonverbal language and therapy. Psychiatry 18:323–330.

The combination of verbal and nonverbal codifications opens up possibilities of communication that otherwise would be closed to the average man, and particularly to the psychiatric patient. Therapy, therefore, has as one aim the achievement of a balanced, complementary use of both forms of language.

917. Slotkin JS: Culture and psychopathology. J Abnorm Soc Psychol 51:269–275.

A cultural relativist viewpoint in diagnosis has theoretical validity, since man's responses are profoundly influenced by his cultural milieu. Anthropology can make significant contributions to symptomatology and psychodynamics.

918. Smith HP: Do intercultural experiences affect attitudes? J Abnorm Soc Psychol 51:469–477.

An unstructured heterogeneous experience does not have a great impact on social attitudes, but the student establishing personal ties is more likely to engage in internationally oriented activities.

919. Snyder CR: A study of drinking patterns and sociocultural factors related to sobriety among Jews: Jewish drinking patterns. Q J Stud Alcohol 16:101–177.

While the Jews on the whole are a sober people, there is a range of variation in intoxication among Jews.

920. Snyder CR: A study of drinking patterns and sociocultural factors related to sobriety among Jews: cermonial orthodoxy and Jewish sobriety. Q J Stud Alcohol 16:263–289.

Orthodox Judaism, as a normative or cultural system, has a sobering influence on its members. This effect may depend upon continuing participation in the ceremonial and ritual activities of the traditional religious community.

921. Snyder CR: A study of drinking patterns and sociocultural factors related to sobriety among Jews: regional background, generation, and class. Q J Stud Alcohol 16:504–532.

Religious orthodoxy is more decisive for sobriety than regional background, generation, and class.

922. Snyder CR: A study of drinking patterns and sociocultural factors related to sobriety among Jews: in group—out group relations. Q J Stud Alcohol 16:700–742.

Through the ceremonial use of alcohol, religious Jews learn how to drink in a controlled manner. Through constant reference to the hedonism of outsiders, in association with a broader pattern of religious and ethnocentric ideas and sentiments, Jews also learn how not to drink.

923. Spiro ME: Education in a communal village in Israel. Am J Orthopsychiatry 25:283–292.

"Collective education" develops psychological characteristics such as identification with, and a sense of security with, the group, the absence of intense acquisitive drives and of intense "success" strivings, and a willingness to assume social responsibilities. These attitudes are necessary for the survival of a communal society.

924. Spitz RA: A note on extrapolation of ethological findings. Int J Psychoanal 36:162–165.

Observations of children contradict Szekely's notion that the infant reacts with fear to the mother's face. It is risky to draw conclusions about human behavior from animal behavior.

925. Starer E: Cultural symbolism: a validity study. J Consult Clin Psychol 19:435–454.

There may be symbolisms in any particular culture that are generally accepted. Inability of the individual to adopt or accept the cultural symbolism may result in emotional disturbance.

926. Vinacke WE, Fong RW: The judgment of facial expression by three national-racial groups in Hawaii: Oriental faces. J Soc Psychol 41:185–196.

Japanese, Chinese, and Caucasian groups demonstrate greater agreement on Oriental facial expression when the situational context is shown with the face.

1956

927. Abdelhalim IH: Factors related to the attitudes of adults towards relations between the sexes in a specific culture. Int J Soc Psychiatry 2:196–206.

Quantitative sex differences exist in relation to psychological factors associated with the attitudes of Egyptian adults toward male-female relationships. The major significant factors are a tendency towards heterodoxy, equality versus emancipation, matrimo-sexual versus sociopolitical alterationism, and realism versus humanism.

928. Abel TM: Cultural patterns as they affect psychotherapeutic procedures. Am J Psychother 10: 728–739.

Therapists need formal training in cultural anthropology so that they will understand cultural groups with whom they are working. They also need to understand their own cultural background. It would be valuable for therapists to do some research or at least give some thought to the role cultural regularities play in the therapeutic process and when interpretations of cultural patterns are indicated.

929. Albino RJ, Thompson VJ: The effects of sudden weaning on Zulu children. Br J Med Psychol 29:178–210.

The effect of Zulu weaning varies in intensity, form, duration, and permanence from child to child, though it is an event that produces great changes in a child's social relationships. Aggression is the most persistent of all immediate reactions to weaning.

930. Appel KE: Anxiety problems within cultural settings. Am J Psychiatry 113:526–529.

Ego, id, and superego anxiety manifestations may result from reactions to cultural pressures.

931. Asthana HS: Some aspects of personality structuring in India (Hindu) social organization. J Soc Psychol 44:155–163.

Rorschach findings suggest a pattern leaning toward introversion as a product of early permissiveness, later rigidity, and status role. The authoritarian family and Indian socialization are responsible for the development of rigid control and withdrawal mechanisms.

931a. Bateson G, Jackson DD, Haley J, Weakland J: Toward a theory of schizophrenia. Behav Sci 1:251–264.

Schizophrenia may be analyzed in terms of communication theory. The double-bind situation, in which conflicting messages of love-hate are transmitted to the individual, can create a confusion of logical types and ultimately may result in the manifestation of schizophrenic symptoms.

932. Berne E: Comparative psychiatry and tropical psychiatry. Am J Psychiatry 113:193–200.

Comparative psychiatry needs not only the clinician but also the geographer, anthropologist, sociologist, and epidemiologist.

933. Birch HG: Sources of order in the maternal behavior of animals. Am J Orthopsychiatry 26:279–284.

Patterned behavior need not be the product of a specific, hereditable patterned neural organization. This is exemplified in maternal rate behavior that suggests that in mammalian organisms the relation of the mother to her offspring may be an extension of her acquired relation to herself.

934. Bishop MM, Winokur G: Cross-cultural psychotherapy. J Nerv Ment Dis 123:369–375.

The problems of cross-cultural psychotherapy include the dangers of mutual misunderstanding, and of an attempt of the therapist to impose values and goals which, although appropriate in his society, might be unsuitable for the patient. In the Japanese culture of particular importance is the concept of what it means to "take one's proper station."

935. Carstairs GM: Hinjra and Jiryan: two derivatives of Hindu attitudes to sexuality. Br J Med Psychol 29:128–138.

Upper-caste Hindu attitudes toward the hinjra (homosexuals) and jiryan (loss of sperm) derive from emotional complexes formed during early childhood and reflect Hindu religion and interpersonal interaction.

936. Chaudhuri AKR: A psychoanalytic study of the Hindu mother goddess (Kali) concept. Am Imago 13:123–146.

The Kali image represents the projection of the child's view of the good-bad ambivalence of the mother. Kali provides psychological help for the individual and is a stabilizing influence on society in that she represents the resolution of the Oedipus complex by providing socially accepted outlets for aggression and sexuality.

937. Christopherson VA: An investigation of patriarchal authority in the Mormon family. Marriage Fam Living 18:328–333.

The Mormon doctrine of patriarchal authority has become institutionalized and has survived as a religious concept, but in the pattern of day-to-day living it has been adapted and modified to meet the needs of the family in changing society.

938. Earle A, Earle BV: Mental illness in British Guiana. Int J Soc Psychiatry 1:53–58.

The higher admission rate of Africans in British Guiana compared with East Indians is due to a greater incidence of schizophrenia. Affective disorders among the East Indian population follow the European pattern except that in the depressions, guilt, and self-deprecation are less striking and paranoid features more in evidence. The Portuguese have the highest first-admission rate. The illnesses of patients of mixed race are similar both in incidence and clinical picture to those of the Africans.

939. Essen-Moller E: Individual traits and morbidity in a Swedish rural population. Acta Psychiatr Scand [Suppl] 99:3–160.

Mental differentiation is accomplished, not by the influence of human relations exclusively, but by an interaction of such influence with basic individual biological differences.

940. Firth R: Rumor in a primitive society. J Abnorm Soc Psychol 53:122–132.

Though rumor is rarely neutral and often potentially destructive, it may be said to have a positive social function. Rumor becomes a social instrument for improving the social status of individuals or groups.

941. Fish MS, Horning EC: Studies on hallucinogenic snuffs. J Nerv Ment Dis 124:33–37.

Hallucinogenic snuffs were used by natives of the New World. Priests and medicine men performed better under the influences of snuffs. Modern enzymatic experiments with these snuffs focus on tryptophan metabolism.

942. Gerard RW, Kluckhohn C, Rapoport A: Biological and cultural evolution: some analogies and explorations. Behav Sci 1:6–34.

The biological evolutionary approach and methods may be profitably used in the study of culture. Experimentation with laboratory microcultures offers control over variables significant in cultural and linguistic evolution.

943. Gibb CA: Changes in the culture pattern of Australia, 1906–1946, as determined by p-technique. J Soc Psychol 43:225–238.

Isolation of five dimensions of cultural change—growth, depression, war, urban slum conditions, expansive ease of living—for Australia conforms in some respects with previous studies of Great Britain and the United States.

944. Gillin J: The makings of a witch doctor. Psychiatry 19:131–136.

The people of San Luis (Guatemala) believe that one who suffers from magical fright has lost his soul, and only a specialist who has the confidence of the mischievous spirits who kidnap souls can get it back. The process by which one becomes a witch doctor is a long one, but the nature of the tie between the supernatural and the witch doctor is uncertain.

945. Gupta NN: Influence of Hindu culture and social customs on psychosomatic disease in India. Psychosom Med 18:506–510.

Differences toward life, toward its frustrations, and toward the lapses of the inhibitions and taboos imposed on sex between the rural and urban peoples of northern India lead to an almost complete absence of psychosomatic problems in rural areas. A contributing factor in rural areas is the hard physical work, which serves as an outlet for hostility and agression.

946. Harvey WA: Changing syndrome and culture: recent studies in comparative psychiatry. Int J Soc Psychiatry 2:165–171.

Social order has much to do with the adequacy of opportunity for the constructive discharge of an individual's urges and impulses. The social environment is connected in ways not yet fully explained, to the development and form of mental illness.

947. Henry J: A report on "The African Mind in Health and Disease." Am J Orthopsychiatry 26:190–192.

J. C. Carother's book, published under the auspices of the World Health Organization, is an oversimplified picture of African cultures that makes little use of the entire field of dynamic psychiatry, ignores recent ethnographic reports on Africa, and asserts conclusions for which there is no evidence.

948. Horton D, Wohl RR: Communication and para-social interaction: Observations on intimacy at a distance. Psychiatry 19:215–229.

A parasocial relationship is one in which the illusion of face-to-face relationships with the performer are given as in radio, television, and the movies. Although parasocial interaction is analogous to, and in many ways resembles, social interaction in ordinary primary groups, it has certain differences that are worthy of a great deal more study.

949. Jahoda G: Assessment of abstract behavior in a non-Western culture. J Abnorm Soc Psychol 53:237–243.

Application of Goldstein-Scheerer Cube Test to Ga, Ewe, and Akan boys shows that tests of abstract ability are no more culture free than intelligence tests.

950. Jahoda G: Sex differences in preferences for shape: a cross-cultural replication. Br J Psychol 47:126–132.

The finding among Scottish children that boys prefer round shapes (symbolizing females) while girls prefer rectilinear shapes (symbolizing males) is also confirmed for less sexually repressed African culture.

951. Josselyn IM: Cultural forces, motherliness and fatherliness. Am J Orthopsychiatry 26:264–271.

Motherliness and fatherliness have both been crippled by recent social attitudes. The meanings of the mother-child, father-child, and mother-father relationship should be studied more intensively for the sake of both the child and the parents.

952. Kaplan B, Rickers-Ousiankiana MA, Joseph A: An attempt to sort Rorschach records from four cultures. J Proj Techniques 20:172–180.

Rorschach results of Spanish Americans, Navahos, Zunis, and Mormons are sorted by two workers; one without knowledge of the groups and one with partial knowledge. Results suggest that Rorschachs are different enough to be sorted with some success, though differentiation is more possible with some cultures.

953. Keehn JD, Prothro ET: National preferences of university students from twenty-three nations. J Psychol 42:283–294.

Data from twenty-three nations reveal three national preference patterns; generally the British, American, and Swiss are the most preferred groups.

954. Klatskin EH, Jackson EB, Wilkin LC: The influence of degree of flexibility in maternal child care practices on early child behavior. Am J Orthopsychiatry 26:79–93.

Deviant maternal practices in sleep during the first year are associated with problem behavior in the child, although no relationships are found between mother practices and behavior in the areas of feeding, toileting, and socialization.

955. Kubie LS: Influence of symbolic processes on the role of instincts in human behavior. Psychosom Med 18:189–208.

Symbolic functions introduce differences both in degree and in kind into the role of the biogenetic ingredients in the constellation of instinctual derivatives in human psychology. If the role of these symbolic processes is overlooked, then the comparative study of instinctual processes in different animal species may mislead us about human life instead of informing us.

956. Kuppuswamy B: A statistical study of attitude to the caste system. J Psychol 42:169–206.

More than half of the students sampled in South Indian colleges view the caste system as intolerable. Brahmins and women express greater satisfaction with the caste system than non-Brahmins and men. Village and joint family life also contribute to intolerance of the caste system.

957. Lambert WE, Taguchi Y: Ethnic cleavage among young children. J Abnorm Soc Psychol 53: 380–382.

Ethnic cleavage does exist among young children when choices of associates become significant.

958. Lemert EM: Alcoholism: Theory, problem and challenge: alcoholism and the sociocultural situation. Q J Stud Alcohol 17:306–317.

The process of alcohol addiction should be studied in relation to the parallel operation of social controls as well as attitudes of community, spouses, and other family members. The internalization of symbolic associations as they affect the self, and the variable way culture affects self-conceptions, merits far more attention from those occupied with the analysis of addictive drinking.

959. Lemert F, Maxwell MA, O'Hollaren P: Sociological survey of 7,828 private patients treated for alcoholism. J Nerv Ment Dis 123:281–285.

The typical private patient treated for alcoholism would tend to be a male, laborer, businessman, or executive of approximately 40 years of age. He would come from an urban community. His religion would be Protestant. He would be married with one or no children and referred by a former patient or doctor.

960. Lewis O, Lewis R: A day in the life of a Mexican peasant family. Marriage Fam Living 18:3–13.

A presentation of Mexican daily family life may convey the vividness of the culture and the individual role in a way that is not encountered in the traditional anthropological monograph.

961. Mackay DM: Toward an information-flow model of human behavior. Br J Psychol 47:30–43.

The manner of concept formation and manipulation can be viewed within an information-flow system. The correlate of perception is an activity that organizes matching responses to signals. This organizing activity consists of adaptive representations of signal features.

962. Maltzman I, Morrisett L, Brooks LO: An investigation of phonetic symbolism. J Abnorm Soc Psychol 53:249–251.

Subjects could match English and Japanese equivalents and English and Croatian words at a level beyond chance expectancy; however, the correct equivalents among Japanese and Croatian word pairs were not matched beyond a level of chance. The findings are contrary to the hypotheses of gestalt trace systems, phonetic symbolism, and physiognomic language.

963. Malzberg B: Marital status and mental disease among Negroes in New York State. J Nerv Ment Dis 123:457–465.

Among Negroes, separation and divorce are more significant factors in relation to mental disease for females than for males. Widowers have the highest standardized rate for total first admissions and rank highest for general paresis, alcoholic psychoses, psychoses with cerebral arteriosclerosis, and senile psychoses.

964. Malzberg B: Mental disease among Puerto Ricans in New York City, 1949–1951. J Nerv Ment Dis 123:262–269.

The higher rate of first admissions to mental hospitals among Puerto Ricans is associated in large part with difficult circumstances of life. Migration is probably also an important factor. A person of Puerto Rican origin has a greater probability of developing a mental disease during a lifetime than an average member of the entire population.

965. Malzberg B: Mental disease in relation to economic status. J Nerv Ment Dis 123:257–261.

There is a qualitative association between economic status and the relative distribution of the psychoses. Psychoses of clearly organic origin appear disproportionately in the lower economic levels. The influence of the economic factor is most apparent in the psychoses of old age.

966. Melikian LH: Some correlates of authoritarianism in two cultural groups. J Psychol 42:237–248.

Students from the authoritarian Arab Middle Eastern culture tend to be significantly more authoritarian and hostile than American students.

967. Miller RE, Murphy JV: Social interactions of rhesus monkeys: food-getting dominance as a dependent variable. J Soc Psychol 44:249–256.

Dominance hierarchies are stable over a period of fifteen months for ten young rhesus monkeys.

968. Montagu A: Contributions of anthropology to psychosomatic medicine. Am J Psychiatry 112:977–983.

The psychosomatic study of the patient indispensibly involves the study of the culturization process. Psychiatrists and anthropologists should collaborate to solve the problems of the sick patient in a sick environment.

969. Murphy G: The boundaries between the person and the world. Br J Psychol 47:88–94.

The data from physiology, genetics, and psychology suggest that the organism and environment are not sharply distinguished but grade into one another.

970. Opler MK: Cultural anthropology and social psychiatry. Am J Psychiatry 113:302–311.

Content and dynamics are always interrelated and have cultural connections of an etiological sort. Cross-cultural etiological studies are needed.

971. Opler MK, Singer JL: Ethnic differences in behavior and psychopathology: Italian and Irish. Int J Soc Psychiatry 2:11–23.

Differences between Italian and Irish behavior and psychopathology are related to the cultural system, its values, language, economy, expressive symbolism, and kinds of interpersonal relationships.

972. Pasamanick B, Knobloch H, Lilienfeld AB: Socioeconomic status and some precursors of neuropsychiatric disorder. Am J Orthopsychiatry 26:594–601.

Positive and probably etiologic relationships exist between low socioeconomic status and prenatal and paranatal abnormalities, which may in turn serve as precursors to retarded behavioral development and to certain neuropsychiatric disorders of childhood.

973. Place UT: Is consciousness a brain process? Br J Psychol 47:44–50.

Consciousness might be identified with a given pattern of brain activity by providing a physiological explanation of introspective observations.

974. Posinsky SH: Yurok shell money and "pains": a Freudian interpretation. Bull Menninger Clin 30:598–632.

Yurok shell money and "pains" are respectively the positive and negative aspects of an infantile introject, the breast and/or penis. Being reinforced at the different stages of psychosexual development, the symbolism is overdetermined in each case. The tense and heavily ritualized Yurok society is marked by a collective "compulsion neurosis" with a variable admixture of "conversion hysteria" which is most pronounced among the shamans.

975. Prothro ET, Keehn JD: The structure of social attitudes in Lebanon. J Abnorm Soc Psychol 53:157–160.

Analysis of F-scale items distinguishes two general factors: cynicism and punitiveness or authoritarian aggression.

976. Rennie TAC, Srole L: Social class prevalence and distribution of psychosomatic conditions in an urban population. Psychosom Med 18:449–456.

Tension-anxiety is not highly correlated with socioeconomic status, but it is highly correlated with multiple somatic ailments. In most somatic conditions both sociological and psychological variables are vitally involved.

977. Roheim G: The individual, the group, and mankind. Psychoanal Q 25:1–10.

Because of man's prolonged biological and psychological infancy, sex has become independent of its original goal of procreation. Dependency has been prolonged. Fantasy and memory—the past—determine man's actions.

978. Sayres WC: Ritual drinking, ethnic status and inebriety in rural Colombia. Q J Stud Alcohol 17: 53–62.

The Coconuco Indians, the Pueblo of Coconuco (mestizos), and the Zarzal (a status-transition community of mestizos tracing descent from Indians) are communities that are generally similar in cultural content but differ in terms of their respective status-value orientations. A comparison of these groups indicates that other factors besides ritual drinking must be considered when studying the varying tendencies toward inebriety of cultural groups.

979. Scarborough BB: Some mental characteristics of southern colored and white veneral disease patients as measured by the Wechsler-Bellevue test. J Soc Psychol 43:313–322.

The Wechsler-Bellevue Scale has doubtful validity for studying the general intelligence of southern whites and Negroes of low socioeconomic level.

980. Schermerhorn R: Psychiatric disorders among Negroes: a sociological note. Am J Psychiatry 112: 878–882.

Early comparisons of Negro and white mental patients were partially blemished by racist interpretations or by limited samples. Modern comparisons are not possible because federal statistics do not note race. Many studies inadequately appreciate the sociological dimensions in differential racial environments.

981. Secord PF, Bevan W: Personalities in faces: a cross-cultural comparison of impressions of physiognomy and personality in faces. J Soc Psychol 43:283–288.

Similarities in the judgments of Norwegian and American students seem greater than differences. Impressions from photos are stable and widespread.

982. Seguin CA: Migration and psychosomatic disadaptation. Psychosom Med 18:404–409.

The man of Peru's sierra and the man of the coast differ physiologically as well as culturally. A psychosomatic maladjustment syndrome occurs when young Indians or mestizos migrate to Lima.

983. Siegman AW: A "culture and personality" study based on a comparison of Rorschach performance. J Soc Psychol 44:173–178.

Comparison of the performance of Yeshiva and college students on a group Rorschach shows significant differences that may be interpreted in terms of cultural influence on personality patterns.

984. Singer JL, Opler MK: Contrasting patterns of fantasy and mobility in Irish and Italian schizophrenics. J Abnorm Soc Psychol 53:42–47.

A study of Irish and Italian mental patients confirms the hypotheses that the Irish schizophrenics would have more fantasy tendency and motor control in comparison with Italian schizophrenics.

985. Singer SL, Stefflre B: A note on racial differences in job values and desires. J Soc Psychol 43: 333–338.

Negro adolescents express concern for secure over interesting jobs, perhaps as a result of awareness of limitations in the socioeconomic realm.

986. Smartt CGF: Mental maladjustment in the East African. J Ment Science 102:441–466.

African thinking is essentially based on sympathetic magic and is largely emotionally determined. Much of this emotionally determined thinking comes from primitive myths. The study of myths and rituals may bring us to a closer understanding of the African personality, particularly with regard to his attitude towards the European today.

987. Snyder CR: Studies of drinking in Jewish culture: a study of drinking patterns and sociocultural factors related to sobriety among Jews. Chapter 5: signs of alcoholism. Q J Stud Alcohol 17:124–143.

While the possible role of psychophysical processes cannot be denied, social and cultural phenomena, especially those related to normative or cultural traditions regarding drinking, appear to be essential for the emergence of drinking pathologies. Orthodox Jews demonstrate that every member of a group can be exposed to alcoholic beverages without the emergence of alcoholism.

988. Sundberg ND: The use of the MMPI for cross-cultural personality study: a preliminary report on the German translation. J Abnorm Soc Psychol 52:281–283.

German students have MMPI profiles significantly higher than those of American students. Since many elements appear to be involved, the reasons for the results are not yet clear.

989. Weakland JH: Orality in Chinese conceptions of male genital sexuality. Psychiatry 19:237–247.

The Chinese mother is fearful of active demands, although she will meet the child's passive-receptive oral needs abundantly if the child restricts his activity and autonomy. The satisfaction of both passive and active demands is necessary for a child's optimal development, including the development of "realistic" or "rational" thought.

990. Weigert E: Human ego functions in the light of animal behavior. Psychiatry 19:325–332.

Under natural living conditions the complex instinctual behavior of animals is not free from aberrations that are similar to human conflict symptomatology. Ethological theory can be extended to include human behavior, since animal behavior in many instances is very similar to that of the infant and young child who has not gained consciousness of those things that make him distinctly human, i.e. death.

991. Willis RH: Political and child-rearing attitudes in Sweden. J Abnorm Soc Psychol 53:74–77.

Predictions from hypotheses on the relationship between roles of authority and submission are verified by findings that parents with authoritarian child-rearing attitudes expect political authoritarianism, as a result of their authoritarian upbringing.

1957

992. Adinarayan SP: A study of racial attitudes in India. J Soc Psychol 45:211–216.

Political factors and attitudes have influenced color prejudice in Indian students and professionals.

993. Alexander T, Anderson R: Children in a society under stress. Behav Sci 2:46–55.

TATs illustrate the responses of submission and denial by Northern Cheyenne children to acculturative stresses.

994. Allport GW, Pettigrew TF: Cultural influence of the perception of movement: the trapezoidal illusion among Zulus. J Abnorm Soc Psychol 55:104–113.

Under optimal conditions the perception of movement of the rotating trapezoid is governed by nativistic determinants and/or unconscious utilization of residual experience. Under marginal conditions, meaning based upon cultural experience helps determine the nature of the movement. Rural Zulus, coming from circular styled environment, are less affected by the illusion than Europeans or urbanized Zulus.

995. Bagby JW: A cross-cultural study of perceptual predominance in binocular rivalry. J Abnorm Soc Psychol 54:331–334.

Mexican and American subjects presented with simultaneous scenes from each country show a tendency for the scenes from subjects' own culture to be perceptually dominant.

996. Barnette WL: Fulbright-fellows up against acculturation. J Soc Psychol 46:199–205.

Fulbright lecturers in Delhi experience culture shock in everyday life and in the classroom.

997. Barry H, Bacon MK, Child IL: A cross-cultural survey of some sex differences in socialization. J Abnorm Soc Psychol 55:327–332.

In many cultures, differentiation of sexes in infancy is unimportant. During childhood, however, greater pressure for nurturance, obedience, and responsibility is placed upon girls. Boys are pressured toward self-reliance and striving. The degree of this differentiation varies across cultures.

998. Beck DF: The changing Moslem family in the Middle East. Marriage Fam Living 19:340–347.

Less seclusion, greater education, and increasing interpersonal contact for women are bringing about a change in family structure, although in many areas traditional ways persist.

999. Bowlby J: Symposium on the contribution of current theories to an understanding of child development. I: an ethological approach to research in child development. Br J Med Psychol 30:230–240.

The biologically rooted science of ethology may offer a more parsimonious and consistent body of theory for psychoanalysis than does social learning. Learning theory, however, is complementary to ethology in understanding many of the processes of change to which the components of instinctive patterns are subject.

1000. Bowman CC: Normal deviations from reality. Am J Psychiatry 114:439–443.

Normal deviations from reality may promote mental health and high morale in a society. Deviations from cultural orthodoxy usually are not frequent enough to constitute a serious threat to group integrity and morale.

1001. Brown RW: Linguistic determinism and the part of speech. J Abnorm Soc Psychol 55:1–5.

English-speaking children take the part of speech of a word as a clue to its meaning. Differences between parts of speech may be diagnostic of cognitive differences.

1002. Buber M: What can philosophical anthropology contribute to psychology? Psychiatry 20:97–129.

Distance and relation (97–104)

The inmost growth of the self is accomplished in man's relation between men, that is, preeminently in the mutuality of the making present of another self and in the knowledge that one is made present in his own self by the other— together with the mutuality of acceptance, of affirmation, and of confirmation. It is from one man to another that the heavenly bread of self-being is passed.

Elements of the interhuman: the social and the interhuman (105–113)

The essential problem of the sphere of the interhuman is the duality of being and seeming. Personal making present, imposition and unfolding, as well as genuine dialogue are necessary to do today's work and prepare tomorrow's with clear insight.

Guilt and guilt feelings (114–129)

The duty of the therapist is to reach out beyond his familiar methods and conduct the patient, whose existential help of the self can begin.

1003. Bustamante JA: Importance of cultural patterns in psychotherapy. Am J Psychother 11:803–812.

The psychotherapist must be able to assess the cultural background of his patient, and have a thorough knowledge of his own culture as well, to be effective with polycultural patients.

1004. Cannon WB: "Voodoo" death. Psychosom Med 19:182–190.

"Voodoo death" has been reported in many cultures and can be explained as due to shocking emotional stress because of obvious or repressed terror. Simple clinical observations and laboratory tests would confirm that this is true, if performed upon a victim of "voodoo death" before his last gasp.

1005. Cantril H: Perception and interpersonal relations. Am J Psychiatry 114:119–126.

Perception and interpersonal relations are linked to various mind sets, such as political and religious systems upon which individuals rely.

1006. Cho JB, Davis RT: Preferences of monkeys for objects other than food. Am J Psychol 70:87–91.

The consistency of monkeys' preferences for lures is similar to monkeys' consistent preferences for different kinds of food and different visually explored environments.

1007. Cohen AK: Sociological research in juvenile delinquency. Am J Orthopsychiatry 27:781–788.

Sociologists have contributed to the identification, by statistical methods, of syndromes of delinquent behavior or types of delinquent personalities suggested by clinical theory and have correlated these syndromes to background or situational constellations.

1008. Davis JC: The scatter pattern of a Southern Negro group on the Wechsler-Bellevue Intelligence Scale. J Clin Psychol 13:298–300.

The distinct scatter pattern for a Negro sample may reflect a probable relationship between environmental factors and subtest difficulty.

1009. Dennis W: A cross-cultural study of the reinforcement of child behavior. Child Dev 28:431–438.

The critical incident technique demonstrates highly significant differences between American and Near Eastern (Arabs, Armenians, and Jews living in Beirut) groups, in terms of which different kinds of behavior are rewarded. While some differences exist among the groups, they have a considerable degree of similarity. Rewarding behavior and values is an important method of transmitting and inculcating social norms and values.

1010. Dennis W: Performance of Near Eastern children on the Draw-a-Man test. Child Dev 28:427–430.

There are cultural handicaps to Draw-a-Man performance in the Near East that affect children very strongly after age six. The former Islamic taboo against representation of the human figure may be the genesis of an attitude of little positive valuation of representative art.

1011. Dennis W: Uses of common objects as indicators of cultural orientations. J Abnorm Soc Psychol 55:21–28.

Five-year-old American, Lebanese, and Sudanese children differ in their concepts of the uses of common objects.

1012. De Wet JS: Evaluation of a common method of convulsion therapy in Bantu schizophrenics. J Ment Science 103:739–757.

The recovery rate in schizophrenia of Europeans and Africans, with and without ECT, probably does not differ appreciably, although it seems as if the prognosis in the Bantu is poorer. Features indicating a good or bad prognosis are similar for Europeans and Africans.

1013. Doob LW: An introduction to the psychology of acculturation. J Soc Psychol 45:143–160.

Psychological theory can be useful in anthropological studies of acculturation. A pilot study on three African societies (Ganda, Luo, Zulu) of education and leadership as contact variables can generate and test useful hypotheses.

1014. Dunham HW: Methodology of sociological investigations of mental disorders. Int J Soc Psychiatry 3:7–17.

Clinical, ecological, and cultural approaches must be utilized for sociological investigations of mental disorders. Central concepts include culture and cultural internalization, socialization, and social system. Empirically developed sociological generalizations must square with validated biological, psychological, and physiological findings.

1015. Erikson KT: Patient role and social uncertainty—a dilemma of the mentally ill. Psychiatry 20:263–274.

The sociologist looks at the patient from a special viewpoint; however, whenever a psychiatrist makes the clinical diagnosis of a need for treatment, society makes the social diagnosis of a changed status for one of its members. Recovery must depend not only on the inner-dynamic realities of the patient's illness, but also must be geared to the social realities of the patient's changed status.

1016. Freedman L, Hollingshead A: Neurosis and social class: social interaction. Am J Psychiatry 113:769–775.

Neurotic psychological symptoms and interpersonal manifestations are intimately linked with the social class and social role of the sufferer.

1017. French JRP, Zajonc RB: An experimental study of cross-cultural norm conflict. J Abnorm Soc Psychol 54:218–224.

Examinations of normative conflict for Indian students studying in the U.S. did not clarify hypotheses of resolution of intergroup conflict under two conditions of situational potency of membership.

1018. Gardner GE: Present-day society and the adolescent. Am J Orthopsychiatry 27:508–517.

Adolescents must be considered biosocially as well as from the viewpoint of their internal conflicts and processes. Further study of both the adolescent and his society will indicate possible constructive changes that can occur in both.

1019. Grossack MM: Attitudes towards desegregation of Southern white and Negro children. J Soc Psychol 46:299–306.

Negro children are more favorable to desegregation than white children. Stereotypes are influenced by the conflict situation arising during desegregation.

1020. Grossack MM: Some personality characteristics of Southern Negro students. J Soc Psychol 46:125–132.

Responses to the Edwards Personal Preference Schedule indicate modal personality differences between Negro males and females and between Negroes and normative group males and females.

1021. Hamilton RV: A psycholinguistic analysis of some interpretive processes of three basic personality types. J Soc Psychol 46:153–178.

Psycholinguistic analysis can determine in part the functioning of language in the behavior of cultural groups. The functioning of ascriptive behavior in interpretive process influences group and personal dynamics of Dakota, Hopi, and English speakers.

1022. Hanfmann E: Social perception in Russian displaced persons and an American comparison group. Psychiatry 20:131–149.

Test data on Russian subjects, when compared with test data from American subjects, reveal a number of intergroup differences that, although not always striking in magnitude, are consistent with each other and seem to form a pattern. The social perception of Russians is marked by richness, is relatively nonstereotyped, and is suffused with evaluations.

1023. Henry J: The culture of interpersonal relations in a therapeutic institution for emotionally disturbed children. Am J Orthopsychiatry 27:725–734.

Every institution develops its own culture of interpersonal relations that is dependent on the social structure. The formal structure of the contemporary hospital prevents workers from becoming involved, encourages lack of autonomy and dedication to the task, and discourages self-realization.

1024. Hinkle L, Plummer N, Metraux R, Richter P, et al: Factors relevant to the occurrence of bodily illness and disturbances in mood, thought and behavior in three homogeneous population groups. Am J Psychiatry 114:212–220.

Individuals experiencing difficulty in adapting to their social environment have disproportionately large occurrences of all the illness that occur among the adult population.

1025. Kosa J: The rank order of peoples: a study in national stereotypes. J Soc Psychol 46:311–320.

Rank ordering of different ethnic groups by Hungarian immigrants to Canada reflects various levels of prestige. High levels of prestige given to the English population reflect Hungarian goals in assimilation.

1026. Levin AJ: Oedipus and Samson, the rejected hero-child. Int J Psychoanal 38:105–116.

Universal myths, such as hero-child rejection, may be interpreted through a search for similarity of cultural residues, physiological origins, and individual experience.

1027. Mangin W: Drinking among Andean Indians. Q J Stud Alcohol 18:55–66.

There is consensus about drinking and little ambivalence or guilt associated with drunkenness. Drinking and drunkenness seem to create few social strains and do not interfere with an individual's performance of his various social roles. Drinking does not seem to be primarily associated with anxiety.

1028. Mead M: Changing patterns of parent-child relations in an urban culture. Int J Psychoanal 38:369–378.

The primitive and industrial cultures, the biologi-

cal propensities of man, as manifested in parent-infant relationships, can be compared.

1029. Meerloo JAM: Human camouflage and identification with the environment: the contagious effect of archaic skin signs. Psychosom Med 19:89–98.

Communication as a behavioral reply to an external event is the forerunner of speech and verbal communication. This phylogenetic, older system of warning and communication still plays an important role in the symbolic function of organs to produce such symptoms as fear melanosis and goose flesh, and in the way disease is used as a disguise or an appeal for help and pity.

1030. Melikian LH, Prothro ET: Goals chosen by Arab students in response to hypothetical situations. J Soc Psychol 46:3–10.

Arab students are more eager for academic, vocational, and political achievement than concerned with peace and family welfare. They emphasize inability to change themselves, whereas American students place greater stress on inability to control environment.

1031. Metraux R, Abel TM: Normal and deviant behavior in a peasant community: Montserrat, BWI. Am J Orthopsychiatry 27: 167–184.

This peasant culture allows for minor behavior differences and presents little opportunity for major differences to develop. Deviance is not striking when appraised either psychologically or anthropologically.

1032. Moloney JC: The precognitive cultural ingredients of schizophrenia. Int J Psychoanal 38: 325–340.

In the absence of an optimum cultural climate, the child cannot acquire his own identity and develops distorted spatial relationships. The world becomes the cosmic mother and eventually leads to delusions of devouring the sun, as examples from various cultures show.

1033. Murdock GP: Anthropology as a comparative science. Behav Sci 2:249–254.

The cross-cultural approach is necessary for a generally valid science of man, despite problems of sampling, diffused elements, and controlled comparison.

1034. Opler MK: Group psychotherapy: individual and cultural dynamics in a group process. Am J Psychiatry 114:433–438.

Group psychotherapy provides the therapist an opportunity to develop an awareness of differing family structures and role conflicts of various cultures and subcultures.

1035. Parnell RW: The Rees-Eysenck Body Index of individual somatotypes. J Ment Science 103:209–213.

The Rees-Eysenck Body Index average values are highest in Sheldon's extreme ectomorphs and lowest in mesomorphic ectopenes. Measurement of fat and muscle should be added to factors derived from the correlation matrices.

1036. Posinsky SH: The death of Maui. J Am Psychoanal Assoc 5:485–489.

The death of Maui, a Polynesian culture hero, is clarified by psychoanalysis. The universally desired return to mother is equivalent to immortality and omnipotence, but is consistently impossible and must result in death.

1037. Posinsky SH: The problem of Yurok anality. Am Imago 14:3–31.

Erikson's alimentary hypothesis, and Roheim's view of Yurok anality, suffer from the inadequate status of the Yurok data, though it may be shown that Yurok anality is a concept of descriptive and genetic validity.

1038. Prothro ET, Keehn JD: Stereotypes and semantic space. J Soc Psychol 45:197–210.

Factor analysis of connotative meanings describes the stereotypes held by Arab students in greater detail than does classical technique. The factors of evaluation, potency, and activity as found by Osgood are capable of describing these stereotypes.

1039. Rabin AI: Personality maturity of kibbutz (Israeli collective settlement) and non-kibbutz children as reflected in Rorschach findings. J Proj Techniques 21:148–153.

Kibbutz-reared children display greater overall maturity than non-kibbutz children. Kibbutz collective child practices do not result in greater uniformity of personalities.

1040. Ramirez S, Parres R: Some dynamic patterns in the organization of the Mexican family. Int J Soc Psychiatry 3:18–21.

Dynamic Mexican family tendencies that affect character structure and social psychopathology include an intense mother-child relationship in the first year of life, dilution of the father-child relationship, and traumatic rupture of the mother-child relationship at the birth of the next sibling.

1041. Rennie T, Srole L, Opler M, Langner T: Urban life and mental health. Am J Psychiatry 113:831–837.

Evidence from the Midtown study supports the hypothesis that prevalence of psychopathology varies inversely with socioeconomic status and accessibility of psychotherapy varies directly with such status.

1042. Rosen S: An approach to the study of aggression. J Soc Psychol 46:259–268.

A theoretical model of aggression should include the dimensions of aggression motive, anticipation of consequence, and action readiness. Aspects of interpersonal reference include attributed power motive and personal power motive.

1043. Russell C, Russell WMS: An approach to human ethology. Behav Sci 2:169–200.

Human behaviors and pathologies, intelligence, and instinct may be approached conceptually as a synthesis of animal ethology, psychoanalysis, cybernetics, and neuropsychology.

1044. Schnier J: The Tibetan Lamaist ritual: chod. Int J Psychoanal 38:402–407.

Religious rituals are similar to obsessive ceremonies. Many Buddhist concepts are like those of psychoanalysis, and chod may be a form of self psychotherapy.

1045. Schwartz MS: Contributions of social science to the administrative process in the mental hospital. Am J Psychiatry 114:493–497.

Through continuing observations and feedback, the social scientist can provide current, ongoing, and pertinent information to the administrator that will keep him in touch with the social processes about which he is making decisions.

1046. Scodel A, Austrin H: The perception of Jewish photographs by non-Jews and Jews. J Abnorm Soc Psychol 54:278–280.

Jews are more accurate than non-Jews and have a tendency to label more photos as Jewish.

1047. Sherwood ET: On the designing of TAT pictures, with special reference to a set for African people assimilating Western culture. J Soc Psychol 45:161–190.

Examination of the criteria and procedures in the design of TATs for the Swazi can acquaint researchers with the nature of the task of cross-culture TAT applications.

1048. Siegel AI: The social adjustments of Puerto Ricans in Philadelphia. J Soc Psychol 46:99–110.

A summary of principal findings of social adjustment by Puerto Ricans reflects part of a program to facilitate community integration of migrants.

1049. Smith HP: The effects of intercultural experience—a follow up investigation. J Abnorm Soc Psychol 54:266–269.

Events that occurred in Europe during a four-year period subsequent to the first visit had a greater impact on social attitudes than the intercultural experience itself. Attitude stability following intercultural experience derives from an initially more world-minded orientation.

1050. Steckler GA: Authoritarian ideology in Negro college students. J Abnorm Soc Psychol 54: 396–399.

Data on authoritarian ideologies indicate an attempt by Negro middle-class individuals to identify with stereotyped white middle-class values and to dissociate from other Negroes.

1051. Szekely L: On the origin of man and the latency period. Int J Psychoanal 38:98–104.

Psychosocial factors of the primate nature lead to the evolution of human latency. Primate ability to control and postpone instinctual impulses and to master libido and aggression are selected for, and eventually organize, the ego.

1052. Taft R: A cross-cultural comparison of the MMPI. J Consult Psychol 21:160–164.

MMPI items on some scales are not culture bound, as can be demonstrated by the comparison of Australian and American samples. Where differences between the groups can be found, it is not possible to determine if these are the consequence of cultural or personality differences.

1053. Trevett LD: Origin of the creation myth: a hypothesis. J Am Psychoanal Assoc 5:461–468.

An analogy exists between Creation, as described in Genesis, and the sequence of the earliest perceptions of the infant.

1054. Vesky-Warner L: An Irish legend as proof of Freud's theory of joint parricide. Int J Psychoanal 38:117–120.

The Irish story of Clothru is a near perfect mythological example of the theory of joint parricide. Only the totem feast is missing.

1055. Vinacke WE: Stereotypes as social concepts. J Soc Psychol 46:229–244.

Stereotypes are organized and developed just as any other concept systems with negative and positive functions.

1056. Watson G: Vitamin deficiencies in mental illness. J Psychol 43:47–64.

Vitamin and mineral deficiencies are apparently etiological factors of fundamental import in some kinds of experimental emotional disturbances.

1057. Wilson DC, Lantz EM: The effect of culture on the Negro race in Virginia, as indicated by a study of state hospital admissions. Am J Psychiatry 114:25–32.

The preponderance of mental disease in Negroes, as compared with whites, and its increase in ratio to the Negro population in Virginia are due to segregation and to uncertainty accompanying culture change.

1058. Winter WD, Prescott JW: A cross-validation of Starer's test of cultural symbolism. J Consult Psychol 21:22.

Starer's impressions that psychotics incorrectly match designs and names of sexual symbols are not substantiated in a study of mental patients.

1059. Woods WA, Toal R: Subtest disparity of Negro and white groups matched for intelligence on the Revised Beta Test. J Consult Psychol 21:136–138.

Negroes' performance is inferior to whites on the culturally loaded items and items requiring spatial visualization but is superior on items requiring perceptual speed and accuracy.

1958

1060. Alt H: Basic principles of child rearing in the Soviet Union: firsthand impressions of an American observer. Am J Orthopsychiatry 28:233–240.

Differences between Soviet and American methods in basic principles of education and child rearing are due to sharp and striking differences in the tolerance of social structures and in tolerating difference itself.

1061. Bell EC: Nutritional deficiencies and emotional disturbances. J Psychol 45:47–74.

While patients with neurotic symptoms are not necessarily nutritionally deficient, their nutritional status should be examined. According to present knowledge, vitamin therapy cannot be considered specific. These aspects require further investigation.

1062. Biesheuval S: Methodology in the study of attitudes of Africans. J Soc Psychol 47:169–184.

The problems of cultural background, rapport, and validity must be considered in the measurement of attitudes using the techniques of directed interview, group discussion, TAT, incomplete sentences, and attitude inventories.

1063. Biesheuval S: Objectives and methods of African psychological research. J Soc Psychol 47:161–168.

The adequacy of methods in African research must be judged according to research objectives and assumptions. Research programs should be directed toward measurement of the limits of modifiability of African behavior and toward defining environmental factors.

1064. Bradley M, Lucero R: Seasonal variations in the incidence of severely crippling mental disorders. Am J Psychiatry 115:343–345.

Rural hospital admissions are seasonally and monthly related to age and psychoneurosis, but not to marital status or psychosis.

1065. Brown DG: Sex-role development in a changing culture. Psychol Bull 55:232–242.

A major effect of the merging American cultural pattern is widespread interfamily variability in the sex roles of family members.

1066. Colby B: Behavioral redundancy. Behav Sci 3:317–322.

Language redundancy parallels behavioral redundancy. Behavior seeks an equilibrium between predicted-expected and organization-disorganization. Individual values are less redundant than cultural values.

1067. Danziger K: Children's earliest conceptions of economic relationships (Australia). J Soc Psychol 47:231–240.

Four stages in the development of economic concepts may be defined, which are analogous to the general development of kinship and social concepts.

1068. Danziger K: Self-interpretations of group differences in values (Natal, South Afric). J Soc Psychol 47:317–325.

White South African students display orientations toward private satisfaction that are self-interpreted in terms of a group-conflict theory. Nonwhite students are more oriented toward community goals that are explained in terms of nonconflict and economic theory.

1069. Danziger K: Value differences among South African students. J Abnorm Soc Psychol 57:339–346.

A negative attitude toward "white civilization" held by nonwhite South Africans is related to personal values emphasizing politics, the community, and social orientations.

1070. Devereux G: Cultural thought models in primitive and modern psychiatric theories. Psychiatry 21:359–374.

Sociologists of knowledge have not, as yet, studied psychiatric theories in a systematic manner. Psychiatric theories reflect the language in which they are conceived and develop, the culture in which they were produced, and the individuals who proposed them. At present a reculturalization of psychoanalysis is taking place.

1071. Doob LW: On the nature of uncivilized and civilized people. J Nerv Ment Dis 126:513–522.

Civilized people seek future rather than present goals to a greater degree than nonliterate people. This generalization serves to highlight a quantitative difference. To learn more about civilization, civilized man must be systematically compared with nonliterate and acculturating people as well as animals, children, literate people in an earlier historical period, and abnormal people.

1072. Dreikurs R: The cultural implications of reward and punishment. Int J Soc Psychiatry 4:171–178.

Reward and punishment reflect authoritarian cultural patterns and tend to preserve patterns in our present society. There is, however, a current shift from an autocratic to a democratic society with the development of mutual equality and mutual respect as the basis for interpersonal relationships.

1073. Engel G, O'Shea HE, Fischl MA, Cummins GM: An investigation of anti-Semitic feelings in two groups of college students: Jewish and non-Jewish. J Soc Psychol 48:75–82.

A Jewish group shows some of the same negative attitudes toward Jews as are held by the prejudiced majority. In both groups, mechanisms for eliminating negative attitudes may be found.

1074. Faigen H: Social behavior of young children in the kibbutz. J Abnorm Soc Psychol 56:117–129.

The daily routine of children and the role of the children's caretaker influence the development of group identity, sharing, and behavior for very young children.

1075. Fernandez-Marina R, Maldonado-Sierra ED, Trent RD: Three basic themes in Mexican and Puerto Rican family values. J Soc Psychol 48:167–181.

Mexican and Puerto Rican family values associated with affectional patterns, authority patterns, and male-female status evaluations tend to be more similar to those of the Mexican than to the mainland American. Puerto Rican family beliefs are undergoing a process of Americanization.

1076. Field MJ: Mental disorder in rural Ghana. J Ment Science 104:1043–1051.

Among the Akan tribes the commonest mental illnesses found at native shrines are depression, acute transient fear-psychosis, and schizophrenia. Spirit possession is part of the technique of priests and is used therapeutically by some African-controlled Christian communities. Many traditional magical procedures were invented by schizophrenics, thus indicating that schizophrenic modes of thought are independent of culture, although their assessment and acceptance by others is culturally determined.

1077. Fortes M: Malinowski and Freud. Psychoanal Rev 45:127–145.

Contrary to contemporary thought, Freudian theory was Malinowski's point of departure for kinship theory. The weakness of Malinowski's kinship approach derives from his unwillingness to see the meaning of kinship terminologies within the total social structure.

1078. Gaitonde MR: Cross-cultural study of the psychiatric syndromes in out-patient clinics in Bombay, India, and Topeka, Kansas. Int J Soc Psychiatry 4:98–104.

There is a high incidence of conversion reaction in Bombay, where the culture encourages massive sexual repression. In the obsessive-compulsive neurosis syndrome a striking similarity is found be-tween the two cities. Anxiety symptoms stem predominantly from superego and external reality in Topeka patients, whereas id seems to be the source of anxiety in Bombay.

1079. Geber M: The psycho-motor development of African children in the first year and the influence of maternal behavior. J Soc Psychol 47:185–195.

Precocious psychomotor development of African children may be closely related to warm and solicitous maternal behavior.

1080. Golan S: Behavior research in collective settlements in Israel. Am J Orthopsychiatry 28:549–556.

Collective education in a kibbutz has positive effects on mental health of children.

1081. Goodman ME: Japanese and American children: a comparative study of social concepts and attitudes. Marriage Fam Living 20:316–319.

The continuing emphasis in Japan on kinship and sociocultural traditions has advantages and disadvantages. American concepts of individual autonomy are on the rise in Japan but should not be forced upon the people.

1082. Gray PH: Theory and evidence of imprinting in human infants. J Psychol 46:155–166.

Certain experiences during the infantile period of fearfulness may provoke a personality distortion of a psychopathological nature.

1083. Hanfmann E, Beier H: The mental health of a group of Russian displaced persons. Am J Orthopsychiatry 28:241–255.

A group of Russian displaced persons scores comparably on personality tests to Americans as regards level of mental health. Those who are disturbed show a frightened pessimistic outlook on life.

1084. Heath DB: Drinking patterns of the Bolivian Camba. Q J Stud Alcohol 19:491–508.

Alcohol plays an integrative role in Camba society, where drinking is an elaborately ritualized group activity and alcoholism is unknown.

1085. Henton CL: A comparative study of the onset of menarche among Negro and white children. J Psychol 46:65–74.

Data based on the instrument used reveal no significant differences in the mean age of the onset of menarche for Negro and white children.

1086. Hes JP: Hypochondriasis in Oriental Jewish immigrants: preliminary report. Int J Soc Psychiatry 4:18–23.

Among hospitalized mental patients, Oriental Jewish immigrants have a higher incidence of hypochondriacal complaints than a matched Occidental group. Schizophrenia may be more manifest as hypochondriasis in Orientals.

1087. Howell RJ, Lavorn E, Downing LN: A comparison of test scores for the 16–17 year age group of Navaho Indians with standardized norms for the Wechsler Adult Intelligence Scale (Arizona and New Mexico). J Soc Psychol 47:355–360.

Navahos score lower (than the standardized group) on Verbal, Performance, and Full Scale scores but score slightly better on Block Design and Object Assembly. Valid comparisons of Navaho intellectual ability can only be made within a culture rather than between cultures.

1088. Inselberg RM: The causation and manifestations of emotional behavior in Filipino children. Child Dev 29:249–254.

Filipino adults are more indulgent toward children aged two to four than those aged five to seven years. Emotional behavior among the younger group is manifested vocally while among the older it is characterized by withdrawal and overt physical aggression against others. In Filipino culture, respect for elders is carried to the extreme of prohibiting expression of opinions by children, and submissiveness is equated with good behavior.

1089. Jahoda G: Child-animism: a critical survey of cross-cultural research. J Soc Psychol 47:197–212.

Most cross-cultural studies of animism report results that conform to general predictions derived from Piaget's theory: that younger children give animistic responses, the proportion of which decline with age. Mead's negative findings are a result of misunderstanding Piaget's concept of animism.

1090. Jahoda G: Child-animism: a study in West Africa. J Soc Psychol 47:213–222.

In comparison with findings from other semiliterate societies, an overall low incidence of animism is elicited. Traditional religious beliefs, magical ideas toward Western technology, and language are some of the cultural factors influencing responses.

1091. Jahoda G: Immanent justice among West African children. J Soc Psychol 47:241–248.

Beliefs of immanent justice exist among African children, but quantitative assessment must await further clarification of the concept.

1092. Keehn JD, Prothro ET: The meaning of "intelligence" to Lebanese teachers. Br J Psychol 49:339–342.

Among Lebanese teachers, the variables controlling the use of the word *intelligence* are often the same as those controlling use of *conscientious, thoughtful,* and *emotionally stable.* Factor analysis can be useful in approaches to meaning.

1093. Keri H: Ancient games and popular games. Am Imago 15:41–89.

Ancient and popular games in many cultures may be structurally and psychodynamically analyzed as experiences of clinging protection that also occur within a community.

1094. Knapen MTH: Some results of an inquiry into the influence of child-training practices on the development of personality in a Bacongo society (Belgian Congo). J Soc Psychol 47:223–229.

The development of Bacongo personality proceeds along lines different from that for Western culture. The Bacongo tribal group uses realistic techniques in encouraging normal behavior and in appealing to social duty. The collective spirit is associated with weak self-consciousness and low intensity of affective relations with many persons.

1095. Kosa J, Rachiele LD, Schommer CO: Psychological characteristics of ethnic groups in a college population. J Psychol 46:265–276.

Males show more marked ethnic differences on aptitude and achievement tests. The females do not display ethnic differences due to their special self-selectivity.

1096. LaBarre W: The influence of Freud on anthropology. Am Imago 15:275–328.

A statistical, historical, and bibliographical survey of anthropology and anthropologists suggests that approaches to psychoanalysis and acknowledgment of Freud's influence are tentative and generalized, at best.

1097. Lambert WE, Havelka J, Crosby C: The influence of language acquisition contexts on bilingualism. J. Abnorm Soc Psychol 56:239–244.

Learning experiences in separated contexts increase the associative independence of translated equivalents in a bilingual's two languages and also increase semantic differences.

1098. Leblanc M: Acculturation of attitude and personality among Katangese women. J Soc Psychol 47:257–264.

Sentence completion and TAT tests administered to Katangese groups confirm the hypotheses that acculturation is associated with change in attitudes toward women and that the woman's self-perceived role changes more rapidly than the man's view. Traditional attitudes appear to change before the determining personality variables are modified.

1099. Lee SG: Social influences in Zulu dreaming. J Soc Psychol 47:265–283.

Zulu dream content is superficially affected by the culture content situation but is generally psychodynamically appropriate to sex, age, status, and role.

1100. Lord E: The impact of education on non-scientific beliefs in Ethiopia. J Soc Psychol 47:339–353.

Education has had some impact upon unscientific beliefs, but more than half of the superstitions considered have been resistent to educational procedures in Ethiopia.

1101. Lovaas OI: Social desirability rating of personality variables by Norwegian and American college students. J. Abnorm Soc Psychol 57:124–125.

Edward's Personal Preference schedule may be used cross-culturally. Norwegian students rate aggression statements more favorably than do American students.

1102. Mann JW: The influence of racial group composition on sociometric choices and perceptions. J Soc Psychol 48:137–146.

Variable racial composition of mixed groups influences sociometric choices and perceptions of Negro and white groups.

1103. McClelland DC, Sturr JF, Knapp RH, Wendt HW: Obligations to self and society in the United States and Germany. J Abnorm Soc Psychol 56:245–255.

Obligation to self, for German students, appears as stress on an ego entity; and obligation to society appears as an imperative to place obligation of the impersonal other as an abstract code above selfish considerations. U.S. students perceive obligation to self as a need for achievement and obligation to society as participation in group activities.

1104. Milton GA: A factor analytic study of child-rearing behaviors. Child Dev 29:381–392.

Factors analysis of 44 parental child-rearing behaviors among suburban New England mothers reveals 5 factors that are stable dimensions relevant to developmental theory.

1105. Mischel W: Preference for delayed reinforcement: an experimental study of cultural observation. J Abnorm Soc Psychol 56:57–61.

Tests of delayed gratification in the Negro and East Indian populations of Trinidad support the anthropological observations indicating that the former prefer immediate small gains while the latter prefer larger delayed gains.

1106. Nelson B: Social science, utopian myths, and the Oedipus complex. Psychoanal Rev 45:120–126.

The culturalist attack on Freud originates in a misconception of Freud's method.

1107. Ombredane A, Bertelson P, Beniest-Noirot E: Speed and accuracy of performance of an African native population and of Belgian children on a paper-and-pencil perceptual task. J Soc Psychol 47:327–353.

The slowness of an African's performance on a perceptual task is not related to task difficulty, suggesting a general lack of interest in performance speed rather than slower mental functions.

1108. Pettigrew TF, Allport GW, Barnett EO: Binocular resolution and perception of race in South Africa. Br J Psychol 49:265–278.

Racial perception is partly determined by subjective variables and racial membership for Afrikaners, English, Coloreds, Indians, and Africans in South Africa. Whites tend to report representations of racial mixtures as pure, a tendency that is consistent among persons who are apprehensive over race relations.

1109. Posinsky SH: Instincts, culture and science. Psychoanal Q 27:1–37.

Freud's theory of culture has certain lacunae. His hypothesis about the correlation between repression and civilization has not been validated or refuted with any decisiveness.

1110. Prothro ET: Arab students' choices of ways to live. J Soc Psychol 47:3–8.

Arab students' preferences are for activity, group participation, and self-control. Comparison with students from seven other countries shows similarity of self-reliance, enjoyment, and introversion-extroversion factors among the Arab, American, and East Indian students.

1111. Rabin A: Behavior research in collective settlements in Israel. Am J Orthopsychiatry 28:577–586.

Intermittent mothering in kibbutzim causes no adverse effects on the mental health of the children.

1112. Rabin AI: Some psychosexual differences between kibbutz and non-kibbutz Israeli boys. J Proj Techniques 22:328–332.

A group of 27 kibbutz-reared boys shows less Oedipal intensity, more diffuse positive indentification, and less sibling rivalry than 27 boys from patriarchal families.

1113. Rado S: From the metaphychological ego to the bio-cultural action-self. J Psychol 46:279–286.

The action self is the systemic self-image of the organism in action and is the controlling unit of the entire apparatus. Conscience promotes achievement by self-reward. The appearance of automatic means of self-punishment signifies a failure of conscience.

1114. Rapaport D: Behavior research in collective settlements in Israel. Am J Orthopsychiatry 28:587–597.

Kibbutz education has a bearing on childhood development. Individuals who grow up in the kibbutz are, in general, adapted to this collective way of life.

1115. Rath R: A comparison of attitude scores of some politico-economic issues between two samples of college students in Orissa, India, after an interval of four years. J Soc Psychol 47:361–372.

Differences in attitude scores for a 1952 and 1956 sample are statistically significant for almost all 16 politico-economic issues. The shift in attitudes includes a trend in favor of Russian influence and against American influence.

1116. Rath R, Das JP: A study in stereotype of college freshmen and service holders in Orissa, India, toward themselves and four other foreign nationalities. J Soc Psychol 47:373–386.

Selection of stereotype traits by subjects for themselves and for Americans, British, Russians, and Chinese demonstrates a tendency to select more derogatory traits for the former two groups and almost no bad traits for the Russians and Chinese.

1117. Rosenfeld E: Behavioral research in collective settlements in Israel. Am J Orthopsychiatry 28:563–571.

The social scientist experiences role conflict while studying the kibbutz due to the situation itself, his criterion of judgment, inner conflicts, defenses, and biases.

1118. Schwartz R: Behavior research in collective settlements in Israel. Am J Orthopsychiatry 28:572–576.

Research techniques that minimize the opportunity for value biases should be used when studying "experiments in nature" such as the kibbutz.

1119. Siegman AW: The effect of cultural factors on the relationship between personality, intelligence and ethnocentric attitudes. J Consult Psychol 22:375–377.

Negative correlates of ethnocentric attitudes tend to decrease as the culture countenances these attitudes.

1120. Sherwood R: The Bantu clerk: a study of role expectations. J Soc Psychol 47:285–316.

Role expectations of the efficient clerk differ as perceived by white supervisors and Bantu clerks. The marginal position of the Bantu clerk is illustrated by his awareness of the role expectations of his primary and employment reference groups and his conflicting, ambivalent attitudes toward the groups.

1121. Simons HJ: Mental disease in Africans: racial determinism. J Ment Science 104:377–388.

Stereotypes about Africans, including some of Carothers's speculations, give an inadequate and erroneous description of mental illness. Africa is very diverse both culturally and genetically and hence no special "racial character" can be ascribed to the entire nation. Mental disorders are not rare among tribal Africans. However, Europeans' ignorance of the culture and such beliefs as *thwasa* help account for the mistaken idea that mental disorder is rare in Africans.

1122. Stennett RG, Thurlow M: Cultural symbolism: the age variable. J Consult Psychol 22:496.

A comparison of previous studies supports the hypothesis of cultural symbolism and points out the importance of the variable.

1123. Sutton PRN: The development of independent muscular control of separate eyelids in two racial groups, European and Polynesian. Br J Psychol 49:65–69.

There are no sex or national group differences in

ability to wink. Europeans who could only use one eye tended to use the left one. Winking ability increases with age.

1124. Szekely L: A comment on Dr. Bowlby's "ethological approach to research in child development." Br J Psychol 31:131–134.

Psychoanalytic interest in the extrapolation of ethological findings has existed for the past 37 years. Serious efforts have been made to deal with concrete analytical problems in the area. The literature dealing with the ethological approach to psychoanalysis appears to have escaped Bowlby's notice.

1125. Taniguchi M, deVos G, Murakami E: Identification of mother and father cards on the Rorschach by Japanese normal and delinquent adolescents. J Proj Techniques 22:453–460.

A delinquent adolescent group gives evidence of less positive and dependent affective content, especially with the father card.

1126. Terashima S: Schizophrenic Japanese Canadians and their socio-cultural backgrounds. Can Psychiatr Assoc J 3:53–62.

The development of schizophrenia in Nisei may be regarded as a "chain reaction" caused by the maladjustment of Issei parents within the socially "closed" family. External stress is of paramount importance for the etiology of schizophrenia.

1127. Triandis HC, Osgood CE: A comparative factorial analysis of semantic structures in monolingual Greek and American college students. J Abnorm Soc Psychol 57:187–196.

Factor analysis indicates a high degree of similarity in basic semantic dimensions used by Greek and American students, but differences in meaning for certain concepts are found. Certain aspects of human cognition are independent of language structures that are used to communicate.

1128. Verhaegen P, Laroche JL: Some methodological considerations concerning the study of aptitudes and the elaboration of psychological tests for African natives. J Soc Psychol 47:249–256.

Efficient utilization of behavioral, genetic psychology, and psychometric approaches in the study of African intellectual capacities must take group educational and cultural levels into account.

1129. von Bertalanfly L: Comments on aggression. Bull Menninger Clin 22:50–57.

Domestication may foster intraspecific aggression. The most pernicious phenomena of aggression are based upon man's capability of creating symbolic universes in thought, language, and behavior. Only a minor part of "essential destructiveness," such as crimes of violence, is purely on the level of the primary process. The much more devastating part is essentially connected with secondary processes.

1130. Wainwright WH: Cultural attitudes and clinical judgment. Int J Soc Psychiatry 4:105–107.

Comments by staff members of mental hospitals may reflect the cultural backgrounds, standards, and goals of the staff rather than a realistic appraisal of the patients' probable prognoses.

1131. Walters RH: The intelligence test performance of Maori children: a cross-cultural study. J Abnorm Soc Psychol 57:107–114.

Differences among three Maori groups reflect the influence of educational, socioeconomic, and adjustment factors. Some doubt is thrown upon the validity of nonverbal tests for culturally handicapped peoples.

1132. Warren JM, Maroney RJ: Competitive social interaction between monkeys. J Soc Psychol 48: 223–234.

Rhesus monkeys placed in a food competitive setting show that variation in quantity of the incentive has no effect on degree of dominance. The dominance hierarchy for each group is stable. Dominance behavior is not related to weight, sex, or level of spontaneous activity.

1133. Winograd M: Behavior research in collective settlements in Israel. Am J Orthopsychiatry 28: 557–562.

A positive identity is developed by the individual in a group of young children raised in a kibbutz.

1134. Wittkower ED, Fried J: Some problems of transcultural psychiatry. Int J Soc Psychiatry 3: 245–252.

Cultures differ significantly in incidence and symptomatology of mental illness. Such sociocultural variables as family and community organization, rapid changes, migration, population pressure, and political events are related to the etiology of mental illness.

1135. Yamamuro B: Japanese drinking patterns. Q J Stud Alcohol 19:482–490.

Drinking patterns in Japan can be studied by examining legends, history, and contemporary religions.

1136. Yap PM: Hypereridism and attempted suicide in Chinese. J Nerv Ment Dis 127:34–41.

Hypereridism, a morbid state of hostile tension, is present in Chinese female suicide attempters. The diagnosis of aggressive psychopathy rests on a designation of behavior as well as on an understanding of the cultural factors which influence frustration tolerance and the genesis of hypereridism.

1137. Yap PM: Suicide in Hong Kong. J Ment Science 104:266–301.

While "social disorganization" can help to explain suicide in Hong Kong, the direct influence of social and economic disturbance arising from events in adjoining China should not be overlooked. Changing sex and age trends in the Chinese suicide rate may be related to the dissolution and modernization of a traditionally patriarchal culture.

1138. Zaidi SM, Ahmed M: National stereotypes of university students in East Pakistan. J Soc Psychol 47:387–396.

Dacca students generally assign favorable traits to Americans, Turks, Arabs, Chinese, and Germans and unfavorable traits to British, French, and Russians. Groups of students from Lahore are more favorably disposed toward the British, a difference that is explainable in terms of historical events.

1959

1139. Abel TM, Metraux R: Sex differences in a Negro peasant community: Montserrat, B.W.I. J Proj Techniques 23:127–133.

Projective tests administered to 34 males and 33 females reflect the culturally shaped sex differences and characteristics of the general peasant population.

1140. Ainsworth LH: Rigidity, stress, and acculturation (Uganda). J Soc Psychol 49:131–136.

The degree of acculturative stress influences rigidity in problem solving. Less acculturated Ugandan subjects are more rigid than the more acculturated subjects.

1141. Alfert E: A multiple score personality test administered to German and Austrian students: cross-cultural vs. intra-cultural differences. J Soc Psychol 50:37–46.

Intercultural differences between female American, German, and Austrian students are less significant than personality differences within each group.

1142. Anderson CS, Himes JS: Dating values and norms on a Negro college campus. Marriage Fam Living 21:227–229.

Going steady is the most prevalent dating pattern.

1143. Anderson HH, Anderson GL, Cohen IH, Nutt FD: Image of the teacher by adolescent children in four countries: Germany, England, Mexico, United States. J Soc Psychol 50:47–56.

Use of Anderson Incomplete Stories in dominant-authoritarian cultures and integrative democratic cultures can reveal differences in teacher image and teacher-child interactions.

1144. Arkoff A: Need patterns in two generations of Japanese Americans in Hawaii. J Soc Psychol 50:75–80.

Personality needs for Japanese Americans are higher for deference, abasement, nurturance, order, and change than for the normative sample. Differences between third-generation Japanese Americans and the American norm group are not statistically significant.

1145. Berne E: Difficulties of comparative psychiatry: the Fiji Islands. Am J Psychiatry 116:104–109.

Psychiatric incidence and prevalence studies of the Fiji Islands create doubt about the cultural etiology of mental disorder. The differences between individuals in any culture seem to be greater than the differences between cultures.

1146. Bhaskaran K: A psychiatric study of schizophrenic reaction patterns in an Indian mental hospital. Int J Soc Psychiatry 5:41–46.

The high preponderance of dullness, apathy, depression, and lack of interest in surroundings in female schizophrenics in Bihar might be attributed to their extremely restrictive atmosphere in their early lives. Other sociocultural factors are important in determining variations in psychopathology, clinical picture, and response to therapy.

1147. Bowman KM: Culture and mental disease, with special reference to Thailand. Arch Gen Psychiatry 1:593–599.

There is no adequate answer to the question of the relation of culture to mental disease. There are now almost no uncontaminated cultures in which to study the problem.

1148. Brown LB: The "Day at Home" in Wellington, New Zealand. J Soc Psychol 50:189–206.

Children's responses to the Day at Home questionnaire indicate a similarity of daily activity patterns between Wellington and Australian families.

1149. Brown RW, Nuttall R: Method in phonetic symbolism experiments. J Abnorm Soc Psychol 59: 441–445.

In tests matching English and foreign words, the phonetic symbolism effect is sensitive to change in procedures in such a way that suggests phonetic symbolism may be limited to pairs naming extremes of continua.

1150. Bustamante JA: Cultural factors in some schizophrenic patterns. Int J Soc Psychiatry 5: 50–55.

The "bilongos" and the "guijes" are paranoid traits of personality within the Cuban's projective system which influence his nosologic patterns.

1151. Carothers JC: Culture, psychiatry and the written word. Psychiatry 22:307–320.

Literacy in a society, or the lack of it, plays an important part in shaping the minds of men and the patterns of their mental breakdowns.

1152. Carpenter ES: Alcohol in the Iroquois dream quest. Am J Psychiatry 116:148–151.

Seventeenth-century Iroquois used alcohol to stimulate their mystical faculties. Although the primary role of alcohol in Iroquois life has changed over the centuries, the early mystical association was never wholly superceded and may persist among some modern Iroquois.

1153. DeVos G, Wagatsuma H: Psycho-cultural significance of concern over death and illness among rural Japanese. Int J Soc Psychiatry 5:5–19.

The culturally conditional differences between Japanese and American Indian groups in their psychocultural meaning of concern over death and illness are an emphasis on the mechanisms of introjection and related masochistic defenses, fear of retaliation, and projection of hostile impulses.

1154. Diab LN: Authoritarianism and prejudice in Near-Eastern students attending American universities. J Soc Psychol 50:175–188.

Arab student authoritarianism is related to traditional family ideology. Authoritarianism is significantly related to prejudice toward Jews, but not to prejudice toward Americans, Kurds, or Circassians. Increased hostility toward the outgroup is not necessarily a function of personal loss at the hands of the outgroup.

1155. Eitinger L: The incidence of mental disease among refugees in Norway. J Ment Science 105: 326–338.

The incidence of mental illness among refugees is a result of an intensive interplay of premorbid personality and external stress.

1156. Ellenberger H: Aspects culturels de la maladie mentale. Can Psychiatr Assoc J 4:26–37.

Allegedly specific conditions, such as running amok in Malays, occur in other parts of the world in less conspicuous forms. Only through precise anthropological knowledge of the patient's culture can the psychiatrist recognize whether certain manifestations are normal or abnormal, and if abnormal, evaluate their severity.

1157. Eysenck HJ: The Rees-Eysenck Body Index and Sheldon's somatotype system. J Ment Science 105:1053–1058.

Sheldon's system is complicated, inadequate statistically, and theoretically not well founded. The Rees-Eysenck Body Index is simpler and superior.

1158. Fantl B: Cultural factors in family diagnosis of a Chinese family. Int J Soc Psychiatry 5:27–32.

Children of Chinese parents living in America, as well as the parents, may exhibit a high degree of role confusion. Alertness to possible cultural difference can greatly aid in communication with such families and thus aid them in their adaptive process.

1159. Fantl B, Schiro J: Cultural variables in the behaviour patterns and symptom formation of 15 Irish and 15 Italian female schizophrenics. Int J Soc Psychiatry 4:245–253.

Differences between Irish and Italian female patients reflect their cultural backgrounds. Impulsiveness, unruly behavior, and difficulties with authority figures are more pronounced in the Italian patients. Sex guilt is much higher in Irish patients.

1160. Feldman H: The problem of personal names as a universal element in culture. Am Imago 16: 237–250.

Consideration of contemporary and primitive

concepts of naming suggests that names are an expression of antagonism felt toward a person or object properly identified while being a means for acceptance.

1161. Fischer JL, Fischer A, Mahony F: Totemism and allergy. Int J Soc Psychiatry 5:33–40.

Guilt about violating sexual and aggressive prohibitions established by one's parents appears to be involved in producing physical symptoms resembling allergies in a fair proportion of those Ponapeans who violate totemic food taboos.

1162. Gilbert GM: Sex differences in mental health in a Mexican village. Int J Soc Psychiatry 5:208–213.

Since rural Mexican culture puts special value on male dominance and machismo, the exaggerated sex differences in role expectancies are more anxiety provoking for males than for females. Older males show strong morbid and hypochondriacal tendencies. Both cultural modifications of sex differences in temperament and differential effects of social crises have definite implications for personality adjustment and mental health.

1163. Goffman E: The moral career of the mental patient. Psychiatry 22:123–142.

The moral career of the mental patient has unique interest in that in casting off the raiments of the old self the person need not seek a new robe and a new audience before which to cower. Instead he can learn, at least for a time, to practice before all groups the amoral arts of shamelessness.

1164. Golan S: Collective education in the kibbutz. Psychiatry 22:167–177.

Collective education promotes belongingness and independence. Uniform educational conditions do not suffice to do away with individual differences. It is difficult to compare mental health among kibbutz, as compared to family, raised children; however, the good adjustment of the adult kibbutz-raised child would tend to follow from a well-adjusted childhood.

1165. Hitson HM, Funkenstein DH: Family patterns and paranoidal personality structure in Boston and Burma. Int J Soc Psychiatry 5:182–190.

There is a strong paranoid cast to Burmese personality that predisposes toward paranoidal forms of mental illness. The psychodynamic processes operative in many areas of Burmese life are similar to psychodynamic processes generally found in paranoid patients.

1166. Hoenig J, Sreenivasan U: Mental hospital admissions in Mysore State, India. J Ment Science 105:124–141.

Admissions are higher in large cities, in districts near the hospital, in men, in married persons, in younger age groups, and in Brahmins, Vyshias, and Indian Christians.

1167. Hoffman H: Symbolic logic and the analysis of social organization. Behav Sci 4:288–298.

Symbolic logic notation is a tool to concisely display kinship terms, relations, and rules. Its use is demonstrated in the reconstruction of an ethnographically unrecorded Pawnee marriage rule.

1168. Hunt RG: Socio-cultural factors in mental disorder. Behav Sci 4:96–106.

Research of psychogenic mental disorders involves demographic, ecological, cross-cultural, and psychiatric treatment studies.

1169. Jahoda G: Development of the perception of social differences in children from six to ten. Br J Psychol 50:159–175.

Scottish children's ability to perceive social differences increases with age. An incipient class concept can exist even when there is no facility for giving it verbal expression.

1170. Jahoda G: Nationality preferences and national stereotypes in Ghana before independence. J Soc Psychol 50:165–174.

Ranking of nationalities by Gold Coast Africans is similar to findings for Western Countries, probably due to contact and the British educational system. Divergences in stereotypes are found, however.

1171. Jensen AR: A statistical note on racial differences in the progressive matrices. J Consult Psychol 23:272.

In spite of interaction among the variables of race, socioeconomic level, age, and sex on a previous study, the racial differences are statistically significant.

1172. Klett CJ, Yaukey DW: A cross-cultural comparison of judgments of social desirability. J Soc Psychol 49:19–26.

Near Eastern, Japanese-American, and Norwegian groups show a high degree of agreement on socially desirable vs. undesirable behaviors. American student groups show the greatest agreement, while Norwegians show the greatest divergence.

1173. Kubie LS: Social forces and the neurotic process. J Nerv Ment Dis 128:65–80.

When considering the influence of varying social, economic, cultural, and educational influences on the neurotic process, the significant external stresses and emotional disturbances that arise in certain phases of the neurotic process should not be confused with the unique neurotic process itself. It is essential not to oversimplify the nature of the interdependence between individual psychopathology and the pathology of social structure and of cultural forces.

1174. LaBarre W: Religions, Rorschachs and tranquilizers. Am J Orthopsychiatry 29:688–698.

Past psychiatric and anthropological studies of religion have given man a clear naturalistic and secular understanding of the alleged sacred mysteries of religious behavior and belief. These tribal obsessional neuroses of societies must be treated to permit survival through the atomic age.

1175. Lambert WW, Triandis LM, Wolf M: Some correlates of beliefs in the malevolence and benevolence of supernatural beings: a cross-societal study. J Abnorm Soc Psychol 58:162–169.

Societies with beliefs in aggressive supernaturals are more likely to have punitive infant-rearing practices than societies with benevolent supernaturals. In the former societies, parents tend to emphasize independence and self-reliance.

1176. Levinson BM: A comparison of the performance of bilingual and monolingual native born Jewish preschool children of traditional parentage on four intelligence tests. J Clin Psychol 15:74–75.

Intelligence test results may be considered valid since good estimates of native bilingual children can be derived.

1177. Lewis O: Family dynamics in a Mexican village. Marriage Fam Living 21:218–226.

The analysis of two authoritarian families in a peasant community shows marked differences in family patterns, suggesting a range of variability in peasant communities and the need for a cross-cultural family typology. Differences in the two family configurations may be explained by spouses' personalities.

1178. Lorenz M: Language as an index to perceptual modes. J Proj Techniques 23:440–452.

Patterns of language responses to the Rorschach test can reveal the transformational process from real to ideational experience, while modes of representation indicate perception.

1179. Luria AR, Vinogradova OS: An objective investigation of the dynamics of semantic systems. Br J Psychol 50:89–105.

Human consciousness, as a system of semantic relationships, can be investigated by conditioned reflex methodology of alteration in brain functioning. The semantic systems of the individual, formed in childhood, become automatic and particular to the adult.

1180. Melikian L: Preference for delayed reinforcement: an experimental study among Palestinian Arab refugee children. J Soc Psychol 50:81–86.

No relationship may be found for age after six years and a preference for immediate or delayed reward. A difference with respect to IQ suggests that the more intelligent subjects prefer delayed reward.

1181. Melikian LH, Diab LN: Group affiliations of university students in the Arab Middle East. J Soc Psychol 49:145–160.

No relationship is found between the rank order of family, religion, citizenship, ethnicity, and political party and the variables of sex, religion, and political orientation. A strong culture core may determine the observed hierarchy.

1182. Mezey AG: Psychiatric aspects of human migrations. Int J Soc Psychiatry 5:245–260.

Adaptive difficulties are etiologically important in affective disorders occurring early after migration, while the inadequacy of social communication has a pathoplastic influence on paranoid and hysterical manifestations. Personality factors probably underlie the high incidence of schizophrenic disorders in migrants.

1183. Miller RD, Murphy JV, Mirsky IA: Relevance of facial expressions and posture as cues in communication of affect between monkeys. Arch Gen Psychiatry 1:480–488.

Communication of affect in monkeys is demonstrable even when all behavioral expression other than posture and facial expressions is eliminated.

1184. Mitchell JD: The Sanskrit drama *Shakuntala:* a psychologic sounding board for Hindu culture. Am Imago 16:328–348.

The Sanskrit drama reveals, aside from specific characteristics of fifth-century Hindu culture and conditioning environment, that the play functioned to mitigate classic Oedipal anxieties.

1185. Moloney JC: The origin of the rejected and crippled hero myths. Am Imago 16:271–328.

Rejected, crippled-hero myths, which appear in power cultures and reflect the human need to survive, have animistic origins in the minds of man attempting to learn the secret of immortality.

1186. Naroll R: A tentative index of culture-stress. Int J Soc Psychiatry 5:107–116.

A tentative index of culture-stress can be formed from data on four symptoms: protest suicide, defiant homocide, drunken brawling, and witchcraft attribution.

1187. Opler ME: Considerations in the cross-cultural study of mental disorders. Int J Soc Psychiatry 5:191–196.

The hypothesis that one kind of family pattern and socialization process, under chronic stress, will produce acutely depressed persons who have turned anger inward, while a markedly different type of family and socialization process will result instead in a paranoid type who turns anger outward, is difficult to reconcile with a comparative study of India and Burma.

1188. Opler MK: Cultural perspectives in research on schizophrenias: a history with examples. Psychiatr Q 33:506–524.

Differences in Irish and Italian culture result in different clinical manifestations of schizophrenic reactions between the two groups.

1189. Osgood CE, Walker EG: Motivation and language behavior: a content analysis of suicide notes. J Abnorm Soc Psychol 59:58–67.

Hypotheses that motivation level effects language encoding suggest that messages produced under heightened drive will show more stereotypy, disorganization, motivational nature, and competing motives. All of these are manifest in suicide notes, except for disorganization of encoding skills.

1190. Patal R: The Indian dowry system: a clinical study. Am J Psychoanal 19:216–219.

The hostile emotions generated by the caste system and dowry system are clearly brought out in psychotherapy. Concern over dowry gives rise to marital discord and some hostility toward female offspring.

1191. Popham RE: Some social and cultural aspects of alcoholism. Can Psychiatr Assoc J 4:222–229.

Sex and group cultural differences, as well as urban or rural origin, affect the prevalence and pattern of alcoholism. Jewish attitudes toward drinking may be characterized as ritualized while Irish attitudes are predominantly utilitarian.

1192. Prange AJ: An interpretation of cultural isolation and alien's paranoid reaction. Int J Soc Psychiatry 4:254–263.

Paranoid delusions among immigrant students who were not maladapted in their own country may be a result of cultural isolation. The isolated individual who perceives his environment as "bad" may people it with destroyers or, using wish fulfillment, may attempt restitution and people it with saviors.

1193. Rabin AI: Attitudes of kibbutz children to family and parents. Am J Orthopsychiatry 29:172–179.

Kibbutz children show more clearly positive attitudes toward the family than do nonkibbutz children; however, kibbutz girls less frequently show positive attitudes toward the father. Kibbutz boys show more frequent positive attitudes toward the mother than do nonkibbutz boys.

1194. Rabin AI: A comparison of American and Israeli children by means of a sentence completion technique. J Soc Psychol 49:3–12.

Israeli children tend to idealize family and mother less than American children, tend to be suspicious of friends, indicate reactions of guilt rather than objective anxiety, show less optimism and more concern with occupational and academic goals than American children. The greater continuity of child-adult roles in Israel may account for these findings.

1195. Rabin AI, Limuaco JA: Sexual differentiation of American and Filipino children as reflected in the Draw-a-Person test. J Soc Psychol 50:207–211.

Differences in American and Filipino cultural clarity of sex roles are reflected in drawings by Filipino children, which show a higher degree of sexual differentiation.

1196. Radzinski JM: The American melting pot: its meaning to us. Am J Psychiatry 115:873–886.

Overly liberal immigration laws will result in a

perpetuation of confusion and lawlessness, as the "melting pot" is already too full.

1197. Ratanakorn P: Schizophrenia in Thailand. Int J Soc Psychiatry 5:47–49.

Even though a high proportion of mentally ill patients in Thailand are schizophrenic, only one in two thousand of the population is mentally ill. This may be because the Buddhist way of life makes for a peaceful mind.

1198. Rath R: A comparison of attitude scores on some socio-cultural and educational issues between two samples of college students after an interval of four years (India). J Soc Psychol 50:57–64.

Retests of Bengali, Bihari, and Telugu students on various issues can reveal trends and shifts in attitudes related to transitional changes.

1199. Rettig S, Pasamanick B: Moral codes of American and Korean college students. J Soc Psychol 50:65–74.

With the exception of religious items, Korean students are more severe in their moral judgments than American students.

1200. Rodd WG: A cross-cultural study of Taiwan's schools. J Soc Psychol 50:3–36.

Test performance differences by sex and locality of school are more distinct than native origin for Chinese and Taiwanese groups. No significant differences between groups are found for Cattell's culture-free test and American mathematics tests, although on other tests the former show better critical and science ability than the latter group.

1201. Rosen E: A cross-cultural study of semantic profiles and attitude differences (Italy). J Soc Psychol 49:137–144.

The semantic differential technique may predict attitude differences between American and Italian groups, demonstrating its cross-cultural utility.

1202. Rubin V: Approaches to the study of national characteristics in a multicultural society. Int J Soc Psychiatry 5:20–26.

The survey method is a reliable technique for validating studies of normative values and their subcultural variants. The method has aided in the investigation of changing attitudes toward social organization and family among East Indians and Creoles in Trinidad.

1203. Santos RSI: The social conditions of psychotherapy in Indonesia. Am J Psychiatry 115:798–800.

Present attitudes toward psychotherapy and the difficulties encountered in adapting it to a non-Western culture are related to the Indonesian sociocultural environment.

1204. Scodel A: Some correlates of different degrees of Jewish identification in Jewish college students. J Soc Psychol 49:87–94.

Among Jewish students, ambivalent ethnic identifiers accept authoritarianism less than do low identifiers. The tendency to view persons in photographs as Jewish is greater among low identifiers.

1205. Sperrazzo G, Wilkins WL: Racial differences on progressive matrices. J Consult Psychol 23:273–274.

Race differences in "intelligence" are likely to be found in a test that is sensitive to socioeconomic background. A nonverbal test is demonstrably sensitive to socioeconomic level.

1206. Taft R: Ethnic stereotypes, attitudes, and familiarity (Australia). J Soc Psychol 49:177–186.

Stereotype consistency, preference, and familiarity with ethnic group are intercorrelated for Australian students.

1207. Valentine M: Psychometric testing in Iran. J Ment Science 105:93–107.

The low intelligence scores of Iranian school and university populations are due to lack of training in perceptual analysis and logical reasoning. In the general population neuroticism, with features of anxiety and hysteria, is very common.

1208. Wallace AFC: Cultural determinants of response to hallucinatory experience. Arch Gen Psychiatry 1:58–59.

Internalized cultural definitions of hallucinatory experience have a profound effect on the responses both of mentally ill and of normal persons. There is a wide range of cultural variations in conditions inducing, interpretations of and responses to hallucinatory experience.

1209. Whitacre J, Grimes ET: Some body measurements of native-born white children of seven to fourteen years in different climatic regions of Texas. Child Dev 30:177–209.

Climatic differences may influence the rate of children's growth. Differences in mean measurements of children's growth seem not to be related to age, possible difference in food consumption, differences in genetic background, or socioeconomic levels.

1210. Wittkower E, Fried J: A cross-cultural approach to mental health problems. Am J Psychiatry 116:423–428.

Major mental disorders occur ubiquitously, although they are distributed unevenly. Differences in the nosology, in the frequency, and in the nature of clinical manifestations are related to cultural differences.

1211. Wolff PH: Observation on newborn infants. Psychosom Med 21:110–118.

Differentiated reflex predecessors of several behavior forms are already distinguishable in the first few days after birth, although motor behavior in the neonatal period is justifiably considered undifferentiated.

1212. Zaidi SMH: Problems of human relations in industry in Pakistan: a preliminary report. J Soc Psychol 49:13–18.

Accidents, absenteeism, and neuroses in a Pakistani jute mill are indicative of difficulties between educated employees, illiterate workers, and management.

1960

1213. Abel TM: Differential responses to projective testing in a Negro peasant community: Montserrat, B.W.I. Int J Soc Psychiatry 6:218–224.

Negro peasants in Montserrat show individual differences in projective test responses, thus indicating idiosyncratic aspects of personality in a given cultural group.

1214. Anderson AW: Personality traits of Western Australian university freshmen. J Soc Psychol 51: 87–92.

American males and females appear to be more outgoing, relaxed, sociable, and group dependent than Western Australian males and females. Although there are variations, status and role of males and females are similar in both groups.

1215. Ausubel DP: Acculturative stress in modern Maori adolescence. Child Dev 31:617–631.

Young urban and rural Maori adolescents successfully assimilate the Pakeha (European) pattern of educational and vocational aspiration. Later, however, as relationships and communication with parents and the adult community improve, the influence of Maori cultural values, as mediated through parents and peers, begins to prevail. Significant Maori-Pakeha differences in achievement orientation may be reasonably anticipated for at least another generation.

1216. Ball JC: Comparison of MMPI profile differences among Negro-white adolescents. J Clin Psychol 16:304–306.

Findings of a high incidence of neurotic tendencies among Negro boys, and withdrawal and introversion among Negro girls, may be accounted for in terms of age, intelligence, socioeconomic status, broken homes, academic achievement, and educational retardation.

1217. Berne E: The cultural problem: psychopathology in Tahiti. Am J Psychiatry 116:1076–1081.

Emphasis on cultural factors in mental illness is an attempt to find a successor to such scapegoats as devils, autointoxication, etc., as etiological agents, and is an outcome of nostalgic illusions of the Golden Age, or the Blessed Isle, which was free of mental disorders.

1218. Berne E: A psychiatric census of the South Pacific. Am J Psychiatry 117:44–47.

The true prevalence of endogenous psychoses in the South Pacific maintains a constant ratio regardless of racial, cultural, geographical, and socioeconomic conditions. Psychiatric hospital figures are functions of variables other than true prevalence or incidence.

1219. Bernstein B: Aspects of language and learning in the genesis of the social process. J Child Psychol Psychiatry 1:313–324.

Speech is the major means through which the social structure becomes part of individual experience. The major role of speech is to sensitize the child progressively toward the demands that will be made upon him by the normative arrangements of his group.

1220. Bloom L: Self concepts and social status in South Africa: a preliminary cross-cultural analysis. J Soc Psychol 51:103–112.

African whites show concern for social change primarily in the direction of conventional socioeconomic success. Social change for nonwhite Africans (Africans, Coloreds, and Indians) has more political overtones and reflects a high degree of emotionality, insecurity, and frustration.

1221. Bowlby J: Ethology and the development of object relations. Int J Psychoanal 41:313–317.

Ethological concepts of instinctual response systems permit better understanding of biological processes and psychological concomitants, as exemplified in the significance of the instinctive attachment response in the mother-child relationship.

1222. Branch CHH, Anderson R: Clinical and research collaboration in psychiatry and anthropology. Int J Soc Psychiatry 6:247–251.

Interview collection of symbolates must be supplemented by community field research, for patients are a selected segment of the community. It is no more the proper task of the psychiatrist to sketch a culture than it is of the anthropologist to make a diagnosis.

1223. Brown F: Intelligence test patterns of Puerto Rican psychiatric patients. J Soc Psychol 52:225–230.

Examination of intelligence patterns for psychiatric patients shows the group as a whole is classifiable as dull-normal, but there are indications that there is more variation within the group than among members of the general population.

1224. Bustamante JA: The importance of cultural factors in mental hygiene. Int J Soc Psychiatry 6:252–259.

Mental hygiene must consider cultural factors, not only in order to comprehend the peculiar modalities of nosologic entities but also to facilitate its own application and development by making the proper allowances for characteristic features of the basic personality.

1225. Carstairs GM, Payne RW, Wittaker S: Rorschach responses of Hindus and Bhils. J Soc Psychol 51:217–222.

A blind analysis of Rorschach records for high-caste Hindus and Bhil tribesmen by psychologists indicates that there is no evidence that the Rorschach per se accounts for the significant differences obtained.

1226. Chapman LF, Hinkle LE Jr, Wolff HG: Human ecology, disease, and schizophrenia. Am J Psychiatry 117:193–204.

Diseases such as schizophrenia result in biological, cultural, and psychological adaptations.

1227. Chowdhury U: An Indian modification of the Thematic Apperception Test. J Soc Psychol 51:245–263.

Rorschach responses of Hindus and Muslims are congruent with a modified TAT which may be taken as a suitable test for Indian subjects.

1228. Curti MW: Intelligence tests of white and colored school children in Grand Cayman. J Psychol 49:13–28.

Colored inferiority in intelligence tests does not have a racial basis. Colored inferiority occurs only in young children whose age is not appropriate to the test, and on the most academic tests for older children.

1229. Danziger K: Choice of models among Javanese adolescents. Psychol Rep 6:346.

In Europe and the U.S. the ideal personalities chosen by adolescents are related to the culturally determined attitude of privatism. Java has a collectivistic tradition yet adolescents' choices there resemble the Western problem.

1230. Danziger K: Independence training and social class in Java, Indonesia. J Soc Psychol 51:65–74.

Mothers of the professional class tend to give lower ages for expected child independence than mothers of the working class. White-collar group mothers take an intermediate position. Rural-urban origin, education, mass media, and privacy of living conditions are some factors related to independence training.

1231. Danziger K: Parental demands and social class in Java, Indonesia. J Soc Psychol 51:75–86.

Of two ideal-typical patterns of parent-child relationships in Java, professional-class mothers tend to follow a pattern derived from Western middle-class culture in which the child is an individual. Working-class mothers follow a pattern corresponding to traditional Javanese norms, which emphasize child as part of a social collectivity. White-collar class mothers occupy an intermediate position.

1232. Davenport RK, Menzel EW: Oddity preference in the chimpanzee. Psychol Rep 7:523–526.

When presented with three objects, two of which are similar, chimpanzees demonstrate a clear preference for oddity, even though no food reward is offered.

1233. Dennis W: The human figure drawings of Bedouins. J Soc Psychol 52:209–219.

Bedouins have little exposure to realism in art. Their decorations are low in detail, geometric, simple and small, and shaded. Drawings of human figures basically conform to their traditional art in many respects.

1234. DeVos G: The relation of guilt toward parents to achievement and arranged marriage among the Japanese. Psychiatry 23:287–301.

The Japanese emphasis on achievement drive and on properly arranged marriage may be a derivative, not of "shame" orientation but rather of a deep undercurrent of guilt developed in the basic interpersonal relationship with the mother within the Japanese family.

1235. Doob LW: The effect of codability upon the afferent and efferent functioning of language. J Soc Psychol 52:3–15.

Examination of color codability among Ewe children in Ghana leads to the hypothesis that category codability is more likely to affect efferently the encoding of the perceived stimulus attribute, than afferently affect the selection of the attribute to be perceived.

1236. Dreger RM, Nuller KS: Comparative studies of Negroes and whites in the United States. Psychol Bull 57:361–402.

Many of the wide differences between Negro and white in many areas of psychological functioning may be the result of social class discrimination. Information from the U.S. must be supplemented by data from other cultures where caste differences are relatively nonexistent.

1237. Ehrenwald J: The return of Quetzalcoatl and doctrinal compliance: a case study of Cortez and Montezuma. Am J Psychother 14:308–321.

The legend of Quetzalcoatl's return played an important part in the downfall of Montezuma's empire. The meeting of Cortez and Montezuma involved the ubiquitous pattern of dominance versus submission, surpassing the boundaries of a given culture, race, or animal species.

1238. Eitinger L: The symptomatology of mental disease among refugees in Norway. J Ment Science 106:947–966.

The incidence of all psychoses among refugees in Norway is five times higher than among a comparable Norwegian population. Symptoms that appear to be of special importance among refugee patients in Norway are persecutory delusions, disturbances of consciousness, conversion symptoms, and ideas of jealousy.

1239. Etzioni A: Interpersonal and structural factors in the study of mental hospitals. Psychiatry 23:13–22.

In adopting the human-relations approach used in industrial theory to hospitals, some studies seem to overemphasize (1) the importance of communication, (2) the totality of the institution, and (3) the benefits of participation in decisionmaking conferences. In so doing, important structural factors are ignored.

1240. Ferreira AJ: The semantics and the context of the schizophrenic's language. Arch Gen Psychiatry 3:128–138.

The schizophrenic mismatches symbols with referents and shuffles their relation as well, to insure the privacy and safety of any communication considered dangerous otherwise. In the shelter of his secret code, the schizophrenic regains some of his self-assertion and independence.

1241. Fisher S, Fisher RL: A projective test analysis of ethnic subculture themes in families. J Proj Techniques 24:366–369.

Families have cross-generational themes of ethnic subcultural identification. Fourteen Texan families display concern with the themes of taking responsibility vs. wandering freely, while fourteen Jewish families demonstrate concern with inferiority vs. superiority.

1242. Gaier EL, Wambach HS: Self-evaluation of personality assets and liabilities of Southern white and Negro students. J Soc Psychol 51:135–144.

No significant differences in liabilities listed are found for white and Negro males and females. Socially oriented responses are more often listed as assets than liabilities, and are especially the more frequent response for white males.

1243. Green HB: Comparison of nurturance and independence training in Jamaica and Puerto Rico, with consideration of the resulting personality structure and transplanted social patterns. J Soc Psychol 51:27–63.

Differences in child-rearing patterns are the product of different values in the Spanish (Puerto Rico) and English (Jamaica) cultural traditions, in nurturance and independence training. When the people migrate, areas of conflict and strength remain the same.

1244. Gussow Z: Pibloktoq (hysteria) among the polar Eskimo: an ethnopsychiatric study. Psychoanal Study Society 1:218–236.

Case materials on the pibloktoq syndrome may be interpreted psychodynamically.

1245. Harlow H: Primary affectional patterns in primates. Am J Orthopsychiatry 30:676–684.

The affectional pattern of the neonate and infant monkey for the mother has four stages: reflex, attachment, security, and independence. These findings have high generality to the human baby.

1246. Herman SN, Schild E: Contexts for the study of cross-cultural education. J Soc Psychol 52:231–250.

The problems of learning and adjustment of American Jewish students in Israel may be seen in terms of the person in a new psychological situation, as a stranger in a host country and as a person in overlapping situations. Change in the cross-cultural environment may be viewed as re-education.

1247. Holmes MB: A cross-cultural study of the relationship between values and modal conscience. Psychoanal Study Society 1:98–184.

Detailed examination of American, French, Irish, and German modal personalities suggests a strong relationship between values and modal conscience.

1248. Horney K: Culture and aggression. Am J Psychoanal 20:130–138.

Destructive drives in man are not innate, as Freud maintains, but are acquired under specific conditions and can thus be modified. The emotional attitude of the parents is more significant than any other element of child-rearing.

1249. Hudson W: Pictorial depth perception in sub-cultural groups in Africa. J Soc Psychol 52:183–208.

Formal or informal training combines to supply an exposure threshold for the development of dimensional perception among Bantu groups, while cultural isolation retards or prevents the process.

1250. Hunt R: Social class and mental illness. Am J Psychiatry 116:1065–1069.

Psychotherapy may be a middle-class form of treatment. In the quest for alternative forms of treatment for alternative groups, psychiatrists should assume a sophisticated cross-cultural position.

1251. Jegard S, Walters RH: A study of some determinants of aggression in young children. Child Dev 31:739–747.

The guilt level of children and their level of frustration do not seem to have significant effects on the amount of aggression manifested, on the latency of the initial aggressive response, and on the incidence of displaced responses.

1252. Jellinek EM: Social, cultural and economic factors in alcoholism. Q J Stud Alcohol 21:565–578.

Social and economic factors not only greatly influence the drinking patterns and the magnitude of alcohol problems but also leave their stamp on the process of alcoholism and even on some aspects of its clinical picture.

1253. Joseph ED: Cremation, fire and oral aggression. Psychoanal Q 20:98–104.

The traditional prohibition of cremation in the Jewish religion is connected with beliefs about resurrection, with the ceremonial expression (or prohibition) of oral aggression, and with historical regression to ancient cannibalism.

1254. Kahn TC: A new "culture-free" intelligence test. Psychol Rep 6:239–242.

The Kahn Intelligence Test Experimental Form has clear value as an adjunct to other tests when a complicating verbal or cultural factor is suspected. Its advantages lie in the simplicity and availability of materials used, easy administration and scoring, and relative freedom from the influence of special cultural, educational, and language factors.

1255. Kaufman IC: Some ethological studies of social relationships and conflict situations. J Am Psychoanal Assoc 8:671–685.

Chickens demonstrate an early ontogenetic development of a social bond through social experience. Disruption of the bond by separation produces a state of distress. Further studies of separation reactions in animals might help clarify the relationship between separation, anxiety, and depression in humans.

1256. Kiev A: Primitive therapy: a cross-cultural study of the relationship between child training and therapeutic practices related to illness. Psychoanal Stud Society 1:185–217.

Childhood-training patterns and acquired drives influence the modalities and concept of medical therapy. Therapies may be related to specific motivational patterns.

1257. Kimmich RA: Ethnic aspects of schizophrenia in Hawaii. Psychiatry 23:97–102.

Cultural and sociological factors, such as a conflict between a wish to adhere to parental attitudes and a wish to adopt new cultural mores and behaviors, affect the emotional adjustment of children and grandchildren of immigrants to a different culture. The relation between ethnic factors and first psychiatric hospitalizations may provide a clue to the etiology of schizophrenia.

1258. Kleiner RJ, Tuckman J, Lavell M: Mental disorder and status based on race. Psychiatry 23: 271–274.

Concentration of low-status groups in paranoid and other schizophrenic reactions is not a chance occurrence. These mental disorders are reactions triggered by a frustrating environment. The greater vulnerability of the low-status group to mental breakdown suggests that its "frustration tolerance" is impaired earlier and more frequently.

1259. Lindgren HC, Lindgren F: Expressed attitudes of American and Canadian teachers toward authority. Psychol Rep 7: 51–54.

In an incomplete sentences test, Canadian teachers give significantly more hostile responses, especially in response to items concerned with figures in authority in the business world and with interaction with authority on an interpersonal level.

1260. Littunen Y, Gaier EL: Occupational values and modes of conformity (Turku, Finland). J Soc Psychol 51:123–135.

Findings of a significant relationship between personality liabilities and self-group control-initiative dimensions suggest that the concept of perceptual defense has particular relevance for Finnish culture, in which socialization is parent centered and inner-directed personalities are common. The individual subscribing to the inner-directed ideal of self-initiative or control tends to repress failure to live up to cultural ideals.

1261. Liu MC: General paresis of the insane in Peking between 1933 and 1943. J Ment Science 106:1082–1092.

Malaria was the cheapest form of fever therapy in Peking, during the decade from 1933–1943. Syphilis was often hopelessly advanced by the time of admission of patients to hospitals, due mainly to special social and family traditions and customs.

1262. Maldonado-Sierra ED, Trent RD: The sibling relationship in group psychotherapy with Puerto Rican schizophrenics. Am J Psychiatry 117:239–244.

A group psychotherapeutic process is made more culturally relevant by focusing on the close relationship among siblings, a common Peurto Rican phenomenon, to assist schizophrenics in verbalizing difficulties with mother and father figures.

1263. Maldonado-Sierra EDM, Trent RD, Marino RF: Neurosis and traditional family beliefs in Puerto Rico. Int J Soc Psychiatry 6:237–246.

Puerto Rican non-neurotics are signifcantly more accepting of traditional Latin American family beliefs than Puerto Rican neurotics.

1264. Mason AS, Tarpy EK, Sherman LJ, Haefner DP: Discharges from a mental hospital in relation to social class and other variables. Arch Gen Psychiatry 2:1–16.

Social-class position per se is not directly related to length of hospital care, but diagnosis and mental status are.

1265. Mason WA: A socially mediated reduction in emotional responses of young rhesus monkeys. J Abnorm Soc Psychol 60:100–104.

Presence of an adult monkey arouses emotional disturbance for a young monkey subject; however, while in the presence of a familiar partner or an age-peer such responses are less frequent.

1266. Metraux R: The dispersion of significance in a changing culture: Montserrat, B.W.I. Int J Soc Psychiatry 6:225–229.

In the Danio villager's culture, individual differences in experiences lead to continually recurring, inconclusive arguments or, alternately, to the suspension of judgment of ideas, feelings, or acts as a way of avoiding discord. Survival and dispersion of meaning are ever more closely linked in the process of change, as people move along in step with others only part of the time and seldom in step with everyone.

1267. Mezei TC, Rosen J: Dominance behavior as a function of infantile stimulation in the rat. Arch Gen Psychiatry 3:53–56.

Rats receiving systematic gentling during infancy are significantly more dominant than ungentled animals. The differences in dominance-submission behavior persist into the adult life of the rat.

1268. Mezey AG: Personal background, emigration and mental disorder in Hungarian refugees. J Ment Science 106:618–627.

Emigration stresses among Hungarian refugees

with psychiatric disorders do not play an important causal role in schizophrenic illness. Patients with affective disorders other than schizophrenia show a deterioration of the mean Index of Social Adaptation while in England.

1269. Michael ST: Social attitudes, socio-economic status and psychiatric symptoms. Acta Psychiatr Scand 35:509–517.

Persons with organic, psychotic, or deviations in personality pattern express less confidence in the effectiveness of voluntary social interaction and prefer authority and leadership that provide strict discipline and an uncompromising, harsh moral conformity. Those who have no significant symptoms, or whose symptoms are of neurotic character, express more trust and confidence in spontaneous, constructive social interaction, and tend not to agree with the imposition of strict discipline on themselves or their children. These characteristics are related to socioeconomic status.

1270. Miller MK, Windle C: Polygyny and social status in Iran. J Soc Psychol 51:307–311.

Marked variations in the occurrence of polygyny among Iranians are generally characterized by higher incidence of polygyny for higher occupational status, with lower incidence for higher education.

1271. Mohanna AI, Argyle M: A cross-cultural study of structured groups with unpopular central members. J Abnorm Soc Psychol 60:139–140.

Small group interaction studies in Oxford and Cairo show that popular central member groups have more effective communication than unpopular central member groups.

1272. Mosher DL, Scodel A: Relationships between ethnocentrism in children and the ethnocentrism and authoritarian rearing practices of their mothers. Child Dev 31:369–376.

Although there is a significant relationship between the ethnic attitudes of mothers and the attitudes toward authoritarian rearing practices of these mothers, the ethnic attitudes of children are related only to the ethnic attitudes of their mothers and not to the attitudes toward authoritarian rearing practices of their mothers.

1273. Mussen P, Distler L: Child-rearing antecedents of masculine identification in kindergarten boys. Child Dev 31:89–100.

High degrees of masculinity are fostered by affec-

tionate—and, by inference, frequent and intense—father-son interactions but are not significantly affected by mother-son relationships.

1274. Norman RD, Mead DF: Spanish-American bilingualism and the Ammon Full-Range Picture-Vocabulary Test. J Soc Psychol 51:319–330.

An investigation into bilingualism and performance on a test that does not require a verbal response, the Ammon FRPV test, shows a low negative association between level of schooling and bilingual background, urban-rural differences, and lower score by Spanish-Americans on the FRPV.

1275. Ostow M: Psychoanalysis and ethology. J Am Psychoanal Assoc 8:526–534.

In the overt performance of animals, ethology demonstrates behavior corresponding to psychoanalytically inferred unconscious impulses in humans and dissects out of total behavior discrete performances as integral components of instinctive mechanisms.

1276. Parsons A: Family dynamics in South Italian schizophrenics. Arch Gen Psychiatry 3:507–518.

South Italian schizophrenics tend toward a very close identity with family members rather than a drifting away into isolation.

1277. Patal R: Understanding culture through mythological stories. Am J Psychoanal 20:83–85.

Differences between stories of Krishna, Shiva, and Mahaviz (Jainism) reflect differing religious attitudes toward instincts. The followers of these religions also reflect these differences in everyday life. The psychoanalyst must take cultural-religious background into account when treating his patient.

1278. Prince R: The "brain fag" syndrome in Nigerian students. J Ment Science 106:559–570.

"Brain fag" is a common psychoneurotic syndrome occurring among students of southern Nigeria. The syndrome seems not to be directly related to genetic factors, intelligence, parental literacy, study habits, or family responsibilities. It may be in some way related to the imposition of European learning techniques upon the Nigerian personality.

1279. Prince R: Curse, invocation and mental health among the Yoruba. Can Psychiatr Assoc J 5:65–79.

Psychiatric disturbances and possibly deaths may result from Yoruba beliefs and practices relating to the magical power of words and language. Yoruba belief in the omnipotence of the word is a memory of one of the early phases of ego development.

1280. Prince R: The use of rauwolfia for the treatment of psychoses by Nigerian native doctors. Am J Psychiatry 117:147–149.

"Snake root" (rauwolfia) has been used for centuries in the treatment of psychoses in Nigeria. Contemporary witch-ridden Nigerian culture may be compared with the late Medieval European.

1281. Prothro ET: Patterns of permissiveness among preliterate peoples. J Abnorm Soc Psychol 61:151–154.

Factor analysis of Whiting and Child's data on primitive child rearing shows three unrelated dimensions of permissiveness: orality-sexuality, independence-anality, and aggression. Patterning of child-rearing norms may reflect parental motives, ecological variables, or ethnographic bias.

1282. Rashkis HA: Toward the operational definition of a biosocial system. Compr Psychiatry 1: 244–249.

Wards may be classed on the basis of consensus-disturbance functional relationship. Definition in terms of shared variance is appropriate for biosocial systems in general, and that classification may be possible in terms of the set of functions relating the variates. The type of ward on which a therapeutic procedure is tested may bear significantly on the results obtained.

1283. Rath R, Sircar NC: The cognitive background of six Hindu caste groups regarding low caste untouchables. J Soc Psychol 51:295–305.

The majority of high- and low-caste Hindus believe that untouchability is due to unlawfulness, tradition, and other social factors, rather than biological or mental deficiences. More high-caste members believe in a casteless society, but both groups prefer peaceful and gradual means to this end. Some inconsistency and confusion with regard to certain caste beliefs may be accounted for by the conflict between modernity and tradition.

1284. Rath R, Sircar NC: Inter-caste relationship as reflected in the study of attitudes and opinions of six Hindu caste groups. J Soc Psychol 51:3–25.

Upper-caste Hindus seem to be more liberal and in favor of drastic change in regard to the caste system. Lower-caste untouchables are more inclined to conform to social norms, have a sense of inferiority, and are intolerant of caste reform. Almost all are in favor of political and economic equality and believe that the caste system will disappear under these conditions.

1285. Rath R, Sircar NC: The mental picture of six Hindu caste groups about each other as reflected in verbal stereotypes. J Soc Psychol 51:277–294.

Of the trait names selected for study, two distinct groups of traits are rather consistently applied to high-caste groups vs. low-caste groups. Judgments made by own caste members tend to conform to the general pattern.

1286. Riesman D, Potter RJ, Watson J: Sociability, permissiveness, and equality. Psychiatry 23:323–340.

An overequalitarian ethos has the same effect on sociability as on schools: by denying differences of skill and motivation it compresses all into a limited range of possibility. Sociability, an art like any other, cannot be learned if the participants deny that there is anything to learn.

1287. Roen SR: Personality and Negro-white intelligence. J Abnorm Soc Psychol 51:148–150.

As a consequence of their sociohistorical background, Negroes may incorporate intellectually self-defeating personality traits that interfere with their intelligence-test performance.

1288. Rollman-Branch HS: On the question of primary object need: ethological and psychoanalytic considerations. J Am Psychoanal Assoc 8:686–702.

Ethological studies of animals indicate an instinctive need for attachment to others beyond the level of subsistence. Human infants also require contact and the infant's capacity to elicit maternal care plays an important role.

1289. Schonbar RA, Davitz JR: The connotative meaning of sexual symbols. J Consult Psychol 24: 483–487.

Denotative and connotative responses by students do not support the Freudian theory of sexual symbols. Culture rather than form determines the meaning of objects.

1290. Scofield RW, Sun CW: A comparative study of the differential effect upon personality of Chinese and American training practices. J Soc Psychol 52: 221–224.

Due to severity of Chinese child-rearing practices in the areas of orality, sexuality, dependence, and aggression, the personality of the Chinese student is more schizothemic than that of the American student. Since there is no difference in severity of anal training, no consequent differences in compulsivity, control, fridigity, or sociability are found between the two groups.

1291. Shah K: Attitudes of Pakistani students toward family life. Marriage Fam Living 22:156–161.

Male and female Pakistani students hold significantly different attitudes toward family life. Women tend to be more liberal in their attitudes toward education and equality and more orthodox in the remainder of their attitudes.

1292. Shapiro MB: The rotation of drawings by illiterate Africans. J Soc Psychol 52:17–30.

Illiterate Africans rotate considerably and significantly more than educated Africans, brain-damaged and normal English subjects, in accordance with the three laws of organization of target material.

1293. Sinha AKP, Upadhyaya OP: Change and persistence in the stereotypes of university students toward different ethnic groups during Sino-Indian border dispute. J Soc Psychol 52:31–39.

In the context of the Sino-Indian border dispute, stereotypes and characteristics assigned to the Chinese changed in a less favorable direction. Ranking for association is not entirely a function of stereotypes.

1294. Sinha AKP, Upadhyaya OP: Stereotypes of male and female university students in India toward different ethnic groups. J Soc Psychol 51:93–102.

Males and females demonstrate considerable agreement in their stereotypes of nine ethnic groups, the highest agreement assigned to the Russians and the minimum agreement to Americans, Germans, and French. Agreement is not necessarily based upon familiarity, as shown by lack of high agreement on Indians.

1295. Screenivasan U, Hoenig J: Caste and mental hospital admissions in Mysore State, India. Am J Psychiatry 117:37–43.

Case records of the Bangalore mental hospital are analyzed in relation to caste of patients and results correlated with census caste data. The Indian caste structure offers opportunities for both genetic and environmental research, especially because both mental hospitals and governmental census reports contain caste data.

1296. Sierra EDM, Trent RD, Marina RF: Neurosis and traditional family beliefs in Puerto Rico. Int J Soc Psychiatry 6:237–246.

Puerto Rican nonneurotics are significantly more accepting of traditional Latin-American family beliefs than are Puerto Rican neurotics. Converse results between Mexican and Puerto Rican subjects may be attributable to variations in the process of sociocultural change that have occurred within the two cultures and to the kinds of ego defenses that have developed to cope with accelerated societal change.

1297. Silva ACP: Infanto-juvenile criminality in Brazil. Int J Soc Psychiatry 6:190–194.

Family disintegration, lack of culture, absence of adequate schooling, transplantation of rural populations to the towns, toxicomanias, and the use of amphetamines play an undeniable part in the genesis of many cases of infantile criminality registered in Brazil.

1298. Sommers VS: Identity conflict and acculturation problems in Oriental-Americans. Am J Orthopsychiatry 30:637–644.

Two major sources of the problem of psychocultural neurosis and culture conflict are, first, the lack of secure parent-child relationships and opportunities for identification in early home life and, second, severe emotional conflict derived from culture contrasts, especially in family tradition. The psychotherapeutic approach with people of dual background should be culturally neutral.

1299. Suci GJ: A comparison of semantic structures in American Southwest culture groups. J Abnorm Soc Psychol 61:25–30.

Factor structures indicate that Hopi, Zuni, Spanish, and English speakers define a semantic space with similar evaluative and dynamic dimensions.

1300. Thass-Thienemann T: The talking teapot—a note on psycholinguistics. Compr Psychiatry 1:199–200.

Schizophrenics are sometimes like creative poets. They are able to revive "dead metaphors" out of the cemetery of forgotten associations and to rediscover pathways of associations that once were common but have been abandoned in the course of history.

1301. Tidd CS: Symposium on psychoanalysis and ethology: introduction. Int J Psychoanal 41:308–312.

Contributions by various ethologists on instincts

and drives show how problems in psychoanalysis may be clarified by reference to ethological studies on instincts and drives.

1302. Trent RD, Fernandez-Marina R, Maldonado-Sierra ED: The cross-cultural application of the Adjectival Check List Adjustment Index. J Soc Psychol 51:265–276.

A Spanish adjectival checklist clearly discriminates between Puerto Rican neurotic experimental subjects and healthier controls. This suggests that, with appropriate colloquial modifications, the checklist may be applied to other Latin American societies.

1303. Triandis HC, Triandis LM: Race, social class, religion, and nationality as determinants of social distance. J Abnorm Soc Psychol 61:110–118.

Race and social class are important determinants of social distance for whites. Negroes show less social distance than whites. Northern European immigrants show more social distance than Southern European immigrants.

1304. Veith I: Twin birth: blessing or disaster. A Japanese view. Int J Soc Psychiatry 6:230–236.

Multiple birth in Japan until recently was viewed with thorough distaste. The reported ratio of twin births in Japan is still very low and may reflect a continuation of the traditional desire to keep information concerning twin pregnancy out of official family registers which are generally inspected by the families of prospective marriage partners.

1305. Watson G, Currier WD: Intensive vitamin therapy in mental illness. J Psychol 49:67–82.

Some states that are psychologically diagnosed as mental illness may actually involve unsuspected nutritional deficiencies.

1306. Wheeler DK: Western Australian results on an educational attitudes scale. J Soc Psychol 51: 113–122.

Progressive and traditional attitudes toward education in Western Australia are similar to those held by comparable occupational groups in the United States.

1307. Woods PJ, Glavin KB, Kettle CM: A mother-daughter comparison on selected aspects of child rearing in a high socioeconomic group. Child Dev 31:121–128.

There is a general trend towards more permissiveness in child rearing as reflected in how daughters raise their children as compared to how they themselves were raised. Daughters are somewhat less concerned with modesty and are more permissive towards sex play. Daughters are also less severe in the socialization process in both sucking and feeding and toilet training.

1308. Yap PM: The possession syndrome: a comparison of Hong Kong and French findings. J Ment Science 106:114–137.

Hong Kong Chinese inpatients with symptoms of possession suffer from pseudopsychotic hysteria related to real environmental difficulties. This contrasts with data from French cases who frequently suffer from more highly structured psychoneuroses based on sexual conflicts. This difference may be due to contrasting cultural backgrounds, specifically the belief or absence of belief in possession by a primal satanic figure who is the source of all evil.

1309. Zaidi SMH: A study of cultural orientation of Pakistan children through their use of common objects. J Soc Psychol 52:41–49.

Data obtained from Pakistani children support previous hypotheses that the uses of common objects indicate general cultural patterns. Similarities between Arab children and differences with American children indicate the technique is useful in cross-cultural research.

1961

1310. Abramson JH: Observations on the health of adolescent girls in relation to cultural change. Psychosom Med 23:156–165.

Ill health, especially emotional disturbance, is associated in unmarried Hindu girls living in South Africa with a discrepancy between the traditionalism of the daughter and that of the mother. Ill health is also associated with a disharmony between role prescriptions and the actual role enactment in the home.

1311. Abu-Lughod J, Amin L: Egyptian marriage advertisements: microcosm of a changing society. Marriage Fam Living 23:127–136.

The appearance of marriage advertisements in the Egyptian media signifies the undermining of the traditional marriage institution, particularly for the marginal part of the population. Values in mate selection are reflected in such advertisements.

1312. Anderson HH, Anderson GL: Culture components as a significant factor in child development: image of the teacher by adolescent children in seven countries. Am J Orthopsychiatry 31:481–492.

The Anderson Incomplete Stories, a psychological instrument sensitive to cross-national similarities and differences, can be used validly to differentiate educational values and value systems in interpersonal relating.

1313. Arkoff A, Meredith G, Jones R: Urban-rural differences in need patterns of third generation Japanese-Americans in Hawaii. J Soc Psychol 53: 21–25.

No significant difference is found in need patterning between rural and urban Japanese-American groups, as measured by the Edwards Personal Preference schedule.

1314. Arlow JA: Ego psychology and the study of mythology. J Am Psychoanal Assoc 9:371–393.

The regressive representation of mythology in concrete, audible, and visual form in the mass media has important implications for ego structuring and fantasy formation during childhood and adolescence. In recent history, some frightening myths have been consciously and maliciously created and exploited.

1315. Barry H, Barry H Jr: Season of birth. Arch Gen Psychiatry 5:292–300.

The birthrate of schizophrenics is above the control group rate in the first trimester (January-April) and below the control in the second (May-August). The relationship between season of birth and psychosis merits further investigation.

1316. Becker E: A note on Freud's primal horde theory. Psychoanal Q 30:413–419.

By elaborating a rigorous kinship organization of mutual rights, duties, obligations, and taboos, primitive man created an unparalleled exploitative structure over the natural environment.

1317. Becker E: Private versus public logic: some anthropological and philosophical reflections on the problem of mental health. Am J Psychiatry 118:205–211.

By allowing mental deviants to live, modern society is threatened by the revelation of the transparency of the culturally fabricated meanings from which humans draw sustenance.

1318. Bellak L: Personality structure in a changing world. Arch Gen Psychiatry 5:183–185.

The future generation may have a "shallow" character, though of great cosmopolitan, urbane, smoothness, and no great sense of lack of belongingness. The "lonely crowd" may become the "uninvolved" one.

1319. Bloom L, De Crespigny ARC, Spence JE: An inter-disciplinary study of social, moral, and political attitudes of white and non-white South African university students. J Soc Psychol 54:3–12.

An independent survey generally confirms the conclusion reached by Gillespie and Allport that the majority of students, except for the Afrikaaner group, is desirous of racial equality. Many Colored students are pessimistic concerning the immediate outcome of this idealism.

1320. Brody EB: Social conflict and schizophrenic behavior in young adult Negro males. Psychiatry 24:337–346.

Schizophrenic Negro males share the following characteristics: (1) aggressive mothers and passive, absent, or remote fathers; (2) impotent relationships with slightly older or more successful male peers, and disruption of these relationships before the psychotic break; (3) psychoses with prominent elements of confusion and somatic concern; (4) a tendency to overt homosexual concern or a past history of homosexual interest or activity.

1321. Brown LB: English migrants' expectation of New Zealand. J Soc Psychol 53:3–11.

Expectations and attitudes are the mechanisms through which the migrant readjusts to the reality of the situation. Revision of expectations can be demonstrated, although it is not required over all areas.

1322. Brown R, Ford M: Address in American English. J Abnorm Soc Psychol 62:375–385.

The semantic rules governing the use of address terms in American English are revealed by three dyadic patterns: mutual title-last name use, mutual first name, and nonreciprocal use of the former and latter.

1323. Cattell RB, Warburton FW: A cross-cultural comparison of patterns of extraversion and anxiety. Br J Psychol 52:3–16.

American students have a significantly higher level of anxiety and extraversion than British students and are also more conservative and less sensitive, with high superego development.

1324. Cochrane R, Davis RT: Guided-choice training of young monkeys. Psychol Rep 9:223–226.

Rhesus monkeys trained with guided-choice trials on problems that resemble object-quality discrimination problems form a correct-response learning set.

1325. Cooper LR, Harlow HF: Note on a Cebus monkey's use of a stick as a weapon. Psychol Rep 8:418.

In the presence of two laboratory observers, a Cebus monkey used a stick as a weapon against another monkey.

1326. Davis R: The fitness of names to drawings: a cross-cultural study in Tanganyika. Br J Psychol 52:259–268.

African children ascribe nonsense names to abstract drawings in a highly consistent manner that is similar for an English control group. Structural similarities between sounds and shapes can be appreciated across cultures.

1327. Deane WN: The culture of the patient: an underestimated dimension in psychotherapy. Int J Soc Psychiatry 7:181–186.

Limitations in psychotherapy can be removed if therapists would take fuller account of patient culture and adjust therapy to it as the starting point, placing psychological and methodological points of view in the background to be used as required by the social reality of the situation.

1328. Easson WM, Steinhilber RM: Murderous aggression by children and adolescents. Arch Gen Psychiatry 4:27–35.

Murder and murderous violence committed by children and adolescents occur where there is parental fostering, albeit unconscious, of murderous assault.

1329. Elonen AS: Culture components as a significant factor in child development. Am J Orthopsychiatry 31:505–512.

Finnish culture has limited the number of socially acceptable channels for the expression of emotion, has encouraged indulgence in dramatic forms and the expression of personal needs through physical activity, and has provided the paradox of there being a few Finns not only capable of, but admiring, the use of extreme violence.

1330. Eron LD: Application of role and learning theories to the study of the development of aggression in children: use of theory in developing a design. Psychol Rep 9:292–301.

Socialization of aggression is a crucial aspect of child training. Research in this area should, through the use of interrelated hypotheses, provide a built-in set of validity studies of predictor and criterion measures. The study of aggression can become a testing ground for a theory of behavior.

1331. Farber IE: Application of role and learning theories to the study of the development of aggression in children: comments. Psychol Rep 9:313–322.

In the study of aggression many of the constructs are vague because the steps necessary to derive a prediction from theory have not been made.

1332. Feibleman JK: The cultural circuit in psychology and psychiatry. J Nerv Ment Dis 132:127–145.

Healthy as well as pathological behavior partakes of a neurophysiological, a psychological, and a cultural circuit. The concept of cultural circuit derives from cybernetics.

1333. Feibleman JK: Ecological factors in human maladaption. Am J Psychiatry 118:118–124.

The elimination of human maladaptation depends upon provision for a proper cultural environment.

1334. Fernandez-Marina R: The Puerto Rican syndrome: its dynamics and cultural determinants. Psychiatry 24:79–82.

The Puerto Rican syndrome is a hysterical attack that functions as a basic ego defense against a psychotic break. The cultural context in which the Puerto Rican syndrome manifests itself suggests possible "internal causes."

1335. Firth R: Suicide and risk-taking in Tikopia society. Psychiatry 24:1–17.

The notion of suicide in Tikopia society is seen as the outcome of a gamble. The incidence of suicide is not a simple variable that can be correlated directly with any single feature of the society. Not only the manner but also the fact of suicide may be socially determined.

1336. Freedman LZ: Sexual, aggressive and acquisitive deviates. J Nerv Ment Dis 132:44–49.

The acquisitive offender is much more typically a subcultural phenomenon, in that there is variance in the values of his entire group and those of the dominant sanctioning community. The sex and aggressive offender represents a personal anomie.

1337. Fried M, Lindemann E: Sociocultural factors in mental health and illness. Am J Orthopsychiatry 31:87–101.

Multidimensional variables, e.g., role satisfaction, which focus on social adaptation, may provide meaningful operational definitions of mental health and illness necessary for large-scale studies.

1338. Galvin JAV, Ludwig AM: A case of witchcraft. J Nerv Ment Dis 133:161–168.

Belief in witchcraft persists among many uneducated, rural, and low-income Spanish-Americans, and they are apt to interpret any personal or family misfortune as evidence of bewitchment. Witchcraft serves as the key to unlock, and thereby partially discharge, unconscious sexual feelings.

1339. Giovacchini PL: Ego adaptation and cultural variables. Arch Gen Psychiatry 5:37–45.

The variable of having been raised in two cultural settings concurrently has particular effects on the family and leads to certain specific characterological features of the second-generation immigrant patient.

1340. Glatt MM, Koon LH: Alcohol addiction in England and opium addiction in Singapore: some differences and similarities. Psychiatr Q 35:1–17.

Despite the differences arising from the differing natures of alcohol and opium, the differences in personality and in sociocultural backgrounds of addicts to the two drugs, there are important similarities. The attitudes of doctors, the layman, and the state toward the addicts are indifferent, and the addicts readily respond to an understanding, accepting attitude within a therapeutic community, whether the drug involved is alcohol or opium.

1341. Goldman AE: The classification of sign phenomena. Psychiatry 24:299–306.

A distinction must be made among the three classes of signs—signals, idiosymbols, and consensual symbols—in terms of developmental levels so as to provide a schema that can bring, within a single genetic conceptual framework, different levels of sign phenomena and the terms used to refer to them.

1342. Hinkle LE: Ecological observations of the relation of physical illness, mental illness, and the social environment. Psychosom Med 23:289–296.

Man's interaction with his "social" and "interpersonal" environment is relevant not just to his "emotional state" or to his "mental health" but to all the illness that he experiences. Those aspects of human biology that are "social" or "behavioral" are different from the remainder of the natural world only in degree, complexity, and order.

1343. Hood RW, Ginsburg GP: Cultural availability: an associative characteristic of Remote Associates Test items. Psychol Rep 25:443–446.

Difficulty of RAT items is related to the cultural availability of correct RAT item response to the stimuli composing the test.

1344. Hsu FLK, Watrous BG, Lord EM: Culture pattern and adolescent behavior. Int J Soc Psychiatry 7:33–54.

Compared with Chicago adolescents, Hawaiian adolescents have a smoother transition from childhood to adulthood. Their strivings are less rebellious; they experience fewer signs of autistic fantasy, less uncontrolled emotionality and bodily anxiety, more empathy, greater sensitivity to the needs of others, and more submissive acceptance of their roles. Adolescent unrest is one of the prices of the American type of culture.

1345. Huang LJ: Some changing patterns in the Communist Chinese family. Marriage Fam Living 23:137–145.

The traditional dating, marriage, and family patterns of China have been disrupted by the People's Party and replaced by a philosophy of the larger family of socialism.

1346. Jacobs RC, Campbell DT: The perpetuation of an arbitrary tradition through several generations of a laboratory microculture. J Abnorm Soc Psychol 62:649–658.

Significant remnants of an arbitrary cultural norm persist four of five generations beyond the last original group member but gradually deteriorate back to a natural norm thereafter.

1347. Jahoda G: Traditional healers and other institutions concerned with mental illness in Ghana. Int J Soc Psychiatry 7:245–268.

Traditional institutions in Ghana have adapted themselves to cope with new needs and new institutions. Wise men, religious leaders, and professional healers still exert a very beneficial activity, contrary to Leighton's claims.

1348. Jourard SM: Self-disclosure patterns in British and American college females. J Soc Psychology 54:315–320.

English females are less self-disclosing than American females, but both tend to self-disclose more to other females than to males.

1349. Kaffman M: Evaluation of emotional disturbance in 403 Israeli kibbutz children. Am J Psychiatry 117:732–738.

Children raised in kibbutzim fit into the normal range of behavior and, except for increased thumbsucking, have the usual percentage of mental disorders.

1350. Kauffman JH: Interpersonal relations in traditional and emergent families among Midwest Mennonites. Marriage Fam Living 23:247–252.

Some Mennonite families show a preponderance of traditional family traits, while others show the contrasting emergent traits. Emerging family patterns show a higher quality of interpersonal relationships than traditional, authoritarian families.

1351. Kiev A: Folk psychiatry in Haiti. J Nerv Ment Dis 132:260–265.

The therapeutic framework of voodoo is similar to that of Western psychiatry. The voodoo folk religion provides not only a reasonable theory and treatment method for the psychiatrically ill but also religious and spiritual guidance for the people.

1352. Kiev A: Spirit possession in Haiti. Am J Psychiatry 118:133–138.

Haitian possession is a culturally sanctioned and symbolical behavioral outlet for impoverished and suppressed peasants.

1353. Kitano H: Differential child-rearing attitudes between first and second generation Japanese in the United States. J Soc Psychol 53:13–19.

The Issei differ significantly from the Nisei in their child-rearing attitudes. Education and acculturation may furnish more varied models for patterning of attitudes and behavior among the Nisei.

1354. Klopfer B, Boyer LB: Notes on the personality structure of a North American Indian shaman: Rorschach interpretation. J Proj Techniques 25:170–178.

Protocols of a Mescalero Apache shaman show an hysterical personality disorder with oral and phallic fixations, confusion of sex roles, and deep anxieties characteristic of the average shaman.

1355. Knoff W: Role: a concept linking society and personality. Am J Psychiatry 117:1010–1015.

The concept of role may serve an important integrative function in the study of sociological and psychological phenomena.

1356. Landy D: An anthropological approach to research in the mental hospital community. Psychiatr Q 35:741–757.

The anthropological view of the social structure of the mental health community, the interprofessional competition for the patient, and the problems of controlled interprofessional research suggest that differing professional orientations require mutual respect.

1357. Laulicht JH: Application of role and learning theories to the study of the development of aggression in children: use of theory in developing measures. Psychol Rep 9:302–305.

A measure of overt aggressive behavior in school is the Aggression Index, a 26-item instrument designed to obtain specific rather than global ratings.

1358. Levine J: Regression in primitive clowning. Psychoanal Q 30:72–83.

Anthropological accounts of American Indian ceremonials reveal how humor permits the acting out of regressive and aggressive behavior.

1359. Lyons J, Davis JE, Murphy JP: Discriminating mental patients from normals. Psychol Rep 8:313–316.

Judges, regardless of training, are able to discriminate mental patients from normals appearing in motion-picture sequences.

1360. Mace DR: The employed mother in the U.S.S.R. Marriage Fam Living 23:330–333.

Although women in the Soviet Union are emancipated and can have economic independence, they must still work harder and longer than men, have less time for self-development, and carry the burden of domesticity.

1361. McCartney JL: Psychoneuroses as a world problem. Psychosomatics 2:23–27.

Emotional illness is on the increase around the world. The complexities of living in the modern civilized world have become too great for unstable personalities. The foundations of international relations are being undermined to a considerable degree by psychologically incompetent men in key positions.

1362. Mehlman RD: The Puerto Rican syndrome. Am J Psychiatry 118: 328–332.

Ataque, the Puerto Rican syndrome characterized by bizarreness, fright, agitation, and personal violence, is not a disease entity but rather a collection of disease processes that tend to be superficially and deceivingly similar in that culture.

1363. Meszaros AF: Types of displacement reactions among the post revolution Hungarian immigrants. Can Psychiatr Assoc J 6:9–19.

The solution of the adaptation conflict and the integration of the Hungarian immigrant with his new environment depend upon the degree of hostility that emerges after social displacement and upon the ways in which it is channeled and controlled.

1364. Miller WB, Geertz H, Cutter HSG: Aggression in a boys' street corner group. Psychiatry 24: 283–298.

Adolescent street-corner gangs are organized, efficient, dynamically balanced, and perform stabilizing and integrative functions for both the group and its members. They are an effective device for accommodating a universal human problem in a manner particularly well geared to the conditions of its cultural milieu.

1365. Miron MS: A cross-linguistic investigation of phonetic symbolism. J Abnorm Soc Psychol 62: 623–630.

Symbolic value accrues to inherent phonetic content, not to meaning via actual word associates. Affective meanings are highly similar across the English and Japanese languages and are suggestive of some universality.

1366. Mischel W: Delay of gratification, need for achievement, and acquiescence in another culture. J Abnorm Soc Psychol 62:543–552.

The expected positive relationship between preferred delayed larger reward and need achievement, and the inverse relationship between preferred delayed larger reward and acquiescence are illustrated by a Trinidad sample.

1367. Mischel W: Father absence and delay of gratification: cross-cultural comparisons. J Abnorm Soc Psychol 63:116–124.

Children in Trinidad show a greater preference for immediate over delayed reward than do children in Grenada. In both cultures, preference for immediate reward is associated with father absence for children from eight to nine years.

1368. Mitchell JD, Schwartz EK: A psychoanalytic approach to Kabuki: a study in personality and culture. J Psychol 52:269–280.

Japanese Kabuki theater reflects folk beliefs, piety, supersition, social and didactic problems, violence and sexuality, and human life in general. The audience closely identifies with the actors. Regression is facilitated through considerable unreality of pattern and style in Kabuki.

1369. Montagu A: Culture and mental illness. Am J Psychiatry 118:15–23.

Ifaluk, U.S., Nazi Germany, and Hutterite cultural patterns demonstrate not only the cultural influence on mental illness but also the influence of mental illness on cultures.

1370. Moreno JL: The role concept, a bridge between psychiatry and sociology. Am J Psychiatry 118:518–523.

Role is a concept that cuts across the sciences of physiology, psychology, sociology, and anthropology.

1371. Opler MK: Social psychiatry—evolutionary, existentialist and trans-cultural findings. Psychosomatics 2:430–434.

Purely individualistic or existentialist theories ignore areas of meanings and values that the anthropologist uses in discussing an environment. To promote positive mental health, social psychiatry must utilize cross-cultural methods while realizing the importance of primary groups within each culture.

1372. Parsons A: A schizophrenic episode in a Neapolitan slum. Psychiatry 24:109–121.

Freud's theories are far less culture bound than some anthropologists believe. For a unified model of personality that can be successfully used cross culturally, it will be necessary to amplify the definition of the ego to include both the honor ethic of the Neapolitan slum resident as well as the rationalist and introspective ethic of the psychoanalyst.

1373. Pease D: Some child rearing practices in Japanese families. Marriage Fam Living 23:179–181.

The Japanese family appears to be very child oriented, and lenient toward feeding and weaning needs. Data obtained on toilet training contradicts Gorer's conclusions and indicates little early disciplinary training.

1374. Pollock GH: Mourning and adaptation. Int J Psychoanal 42:341–361.

The mourning process is an adaptational adjustment of the internal to the external milieu. Human object relations become maladaptive when the object ceases to exist. The mourning process begins with an acute stage, also found in infrahuman primates, followed by a chronic stage. Formation of new object ties is adaptive and subject to selection.

1375. Prentice NM: Ethnic attitudes, neuroticism, and culture. J Soc Psychol 54:75–82.

The available empirical evidence does not support a significant relationship between ethnic attitudes and neuroticism or culture.

1376. Prince R: The Yoruba image of the witch. J Ment Science 107:795–805.

In Yorubaland, witchcraft is a feminine art sanctioned by the gods. The Yoruba may defend himself against malevolent witchcraft with the help of the native doctor, through membership in cults, and through organizing witch hunts and using trial by ordeal.

1377. Rabin AI: Culture components as a significant factor in child development: kibbutz adolescents. Am J Orthopsychiatry 31:493–504.

Kibbutz-reared adolescents, when compared with nonkibbutz-reared adolescents, are at least as well adjusted and intelligent and may be more spontaneous. They are less in conflict with parents and are more concerned with taboos on premarital sexuality.

1378. Radnitzky G: Some remarks on the Whorfian Hypothesis. Behav Sci 6:153–157.

Metascientific considerations of describing and explaining have philosophical implications for the study of the Whorfian effects on cognitive and noncognitive behavior.

1379. Reiss S: Language as a psychological phenomenon. Psychiatr Q 35:140–155.

Language should be regarded as a purely psychological product of the human mentality. An understanding of the unconscious psychological processes of language will lead to applications in such related fields as semantics, logic, mathematical foundations, and general philosophy, in all of which the role of the unconscious factor in the thought process itself has hitherto not been sufficiently appreciated.

1380. Rodman H: Marital relationships in a Trinidad village. Marriage Fam Living 23:166–170.

Three types of marital or quasi-marital relationships are evident in a Negro village in Trinidad: friending (or visitation), living, and married.

1381. Sanua VD: Sociocultural factors in families of schizophrenics: a review of the literature. Psychiatry 24:246–265.

Evidence of the importance of family factors in the background of schizophrenics is compelling; however, the patterns of the home environment need to be more clearly defined and isolated from home patterns that lead to other types of psychoses, neuroses, and antisocial behavior.

1382. Schlesinger B: The changing patterns in the Hindu joint family system of India. Marriage Fam Living 23:170–175.

The traditional joint family and its many functions are experiencing a dissolution in Indian society and a movement toward the nuclear family, resulting in a tension between the traditional ideal and the individualistic ideal.

1383. Schrier AM: Response latency of monkeys as a function of amount of reward. Psychol Rep 8:282–289.

Measurement of the response latencies of five rhesus monkeys on a single instrumental task reveals a significant nonlinear downward trend in mean log latency as a function of log reward.

1384. Shirasa T, Azuma T: The applicability of an American delinquency scale to Japanese subjects. J Clin Psychol 17:291–292.

The discriminative efficiency and reliability of a brief deliquency scale are as high in Japan as in America.

1385. Shoben EJ: Culture, ego psychology, and an image of man. Am J Psychother 15:395–408.

The history of the culture-building enterprise suggests that our understanding of the socialization process and our clinical effectiveness may be enlarged by attending rather more to the significance of ideals, the human capacity for rational thought and imagination, and the potentiality of men for forming wide-ranging identifications with one another.

1386. Siegman AW: A cross-cultural investigation of the relationship between ethnic prejudice, authoritarian ideology and personality. J Abnorm Soc Psychol 63:654–655.

Data from Israel indicates that not all ethnic prejudice is related to authoritarian ideology.

1387. Skinner J: Ritual matricide: a study of the origins of sacrifice. Am Imago 18:71–102.

Archaeological and ethnographic data on sacrifice ritual may be interpreted as a struggle with the Oedipus complex and the mother (Earth), and as a means of dealing with man's fear and envy of woman.

1388. Spiegel JP: Application of role and learning theories to the study of the development of aggression in children: comments. Psychol Rep 9:325–329.

Aggressive behavior includes a spectrum composed of the intermingling of the purely hostile and the purely assertive components. Studies of aggression must focus more on unconscious defense processes, especially displacement.

1389. Stamm JS: Social facilitation in monkeys. Psychol Rep 9:479–484.

Upon testing for dominance-submission, monkeys respond more often under social than under solitary settings. Emotional stability is an important determinant in social facilitation.

1390. Stunkard A: Motivation for treatment: antecedents of the therapeutic process in different cultural settings. Compr Psychiatry 2:140–148.

Motivation for therapy requires more than education in a theory of the "nonadapted state"; it also demands the adoption of an appropriate attitude toward one's condition. In any culture, learning what it means to be sick involves also learning how to get well.

1391. Triandis LM, Lambert WW: Pancultural factor analysis of reported socialization practices. J Abnorm Soc Psychol 62:631–639.

Ten factors that point up differences in various child-rearing practices may be extracted from data gathered from mothers in North India, Mexico, Okinawa, Philippines, Kenya, and New England.

1392. Triandis LM, Lambert WW: Sources of frustration and targets of aggression: a cross-cultural study: J Abnorm Soc Psychol 62:640–648.

A multicultural study of primitive societies and their views toward famine suggest that intrapunitive outlook is positively associated with extrapunitive response of coercion of the gods. Extrapunitive outlook and responsiveness, and impunitive outlook and responsiveness are associated.

1393. Turnbull CM: Some observations regarding the experience and behavior of the BaMbuti pygmies. Am J Psychol 74:304–308.

The art and music of the BaMbuti pygmies illustrate their perception of distance, size, and numbers.

1394. Vaughen GM, Thompson RHT: New Zealand children's attitudes towards Maoris. J Abnorm Soc Psychol 62:701–704.

Unfavorable attitudes toward Maoris increase among high- and low-contact subjects of 8 to 12 years, and among low-contact subjects of 12 to 16 years.

1395. Vogel EF, Vogel SH: Family security, personal immaturity, and emotional health in a Japanese sample. Marriage Fam Living 23:161–165.

Considerable family security and dependence is evident in six normal Japanese families. There are no serious personality disturbances in the children, even though they do not meet the Western ideal for independence from the family.

1396. Walder LO: Application of role and learning theories to the study of the development of aggression in children: an attempt at an empirical test of a theory. Psychol Rep 9:306–312.

Both fathers and mothers should be interviewed in order to obtain family data on aggression. The fathers of high-aggression boys punish more severely than the fathers of low-aggression boys.

1397. Ward TF: Immigration and ethnic origin in mental illness. Can Psychiatr Assoc J 6:323–332.

Age, rather than cultural and ecological difficulties, is an important determining factor in serious mental disease in the southern half of Saskatchewan. Foreign-born and Canadian-born groups, however, have different social characteristics on the basis of derivation from different cultures and present different forms of mental disease in the community.

1398. Wells WD, Siegel B: Stereotyped somatotypes. Psychol Rep 8:77–78.

When American adults rate silhouettes of physiques on personality-rating scales, clear stereotypes emerge linking physique and personality.

1399. Winthrop H: Cultural determinants of psychological research values. J Soc Psychol 53:255–270.

Culture has a Lebensstil of its own, and may

therefore influence the type of problem chosen by the researcher and weigh the type of outcome he expects. The nature-nurture controversy, for example, demonstrates the existence of implicit values.

1962

1400. Abel T: The dreams of a Chinese patient. Psychoanal Stud Society 2:280–310.

Case-study analysis of a Chinese-American demonstrates the way dreams reflect motivation, conflicts, and the difficulties of acculturation.

1401. Acord LD: Sexual symbolism as a correlate of age. J Consult Psychol 26:279–281.

The Freudian hypothesis of pointed elongated objects as male symbols, and round objects as female symbols, is supported for subjects older than 17 years but not under 14 years of age.

1402. Adelson D: Some aspects of value conflict under extreme conditions. Psychiatry 25:273–279.

Phenomenological evidence offered by victims of a concentration camp and a ghetto does not substantiate the view offered by either the ethical absolutist or the ethical relativist. The person's actions in a situation depend on the choices he has and on the degree of his own intellectual and emotional development.

1403. Ainsworth LH, Ainsworth MD: Acculturation in East Africa: attitudes toward parents, teachers and education. J Soc Psychol 57:409–415.

The more acculturated Ugandan and Kenyan students assign a higher value to education but are more critical of teachers.

1404. Ainsworth LH, Ainsworth MD: Acculturation in East Africa: political awareness and attitudes toward authority. J Soc Psychol 57:391–399.

The more acculturated Ugandan and Kenyan students are hostile to authority, politically aware, discontent, and nationalistic. Degree of acculturation is related to identification with Europeans and tendency to view them as dominant.

1405. Ainsworth MD, Ainsworth LH: Acculturation in East Africa: frustration and aggression. J Soc Psychol 57:401–407.

The more acculturated Ugandan and Kenyan students are more frustrated by authority; more aggressive, intropunitive, and need-persistent; and less fearful of aggression or rebellion.

1406. Ainsworth MD, Ainsworth LH: Acculturation in East Africa: summary and discussion. J Soc Psychol 57:417–432.

Traditional-modern, and subcultural differences in levels of acculturation in Uganda and Kenya allow the generation of new hypotheses, and give basic support to the initial hypotheses of the study.

1407. Anderson HH, Anderson GL: Social values of teachers in Rio de Janeiro, Mexico City, and Los Angeles County, California: a comparative study of teachers and children. J Soc Psychol 58:207–226.

The findings of Anderson Incomplete Stories for teachers and pupils generally support previous research hypotheses on dominant and integrative teacher-child relations.

1408. Arkoff A, Meredith G, Twahara S: Dominance-deference patterning in motherland-Japanese, Japanese-American, and Caucasian-American students. J Soc Psychol 58:61–66.

Japanese-Americans demonstrate patterns of low-dominance and high-deference in comparison to motherland-Japanese and Caucasians. No significant differences in patterning exist between the latter two groups.

1409. Becker E: Anthropological notes on the concept of aggression. Psychiatry 25:328–338.

Aggression may be regarded as an attempt toward self-affirmation by a fragmented ego and is manifest according to whether the means for this end have been variously supplied by the particular cultural context. A departure from the Freudian instinctive, destructive aggression concept is indicated.

1410. Becker E: The relevance to psychiatry of recent research in anthropology. Am J Psychother 16:600–611.

The cross-cultural approach of anthropology can broaden the field for transcultural psychiatry and place concepts of normality and relativity in a new perspective. Research on the biological basis of human sociability (ethology) contributes to understanding man when appropriately applied. The epistological presuppositions of psychiatry must also be examined.

1411. Becker E: Toward a comprehensive theory of depression: a cross-disciplinary appraisal of objects, games and meaning. J Nerv Ment Dis 135:26–35.

A focus on the ego and on self-esteem calls into

question a whole range of cultural phenomena. The psychiatrist dealing with ego phenomena must face up to the broad questions being posed by the other human sciences.

1412. Becker E: Toward a theory of schizophrenia. Arch Gen Psychiatry 7:170–181.

Schizophrenia represents a disparate private attempt to fabricate meaning in a world that is poor in complex objects. It is an attempt to build up an identity by motivational vocabularies that are divorced from the real interpersonal activities by which such an identity can be most convincingly fashioned. Schizophrenia is a poverty in external objects and consequently in selfhood and meaning.

1413. Benjamin LS: Nonnutritive sucking and dental malocclusion in the deciduous and permanent teeth of the rhesus monkey. Child Dev 33:29–35.

Infantile thumbsucking in rhesus monkeys is significantly correlated with malocclusion shown in both deciduous and permanent teeth.

1414. Bharucha-Reid RP: Appearance and reality in culture. J Soc Psychol 57:169–193.

The noncomparative and ahistorical approach leads to studies that are deficient in design, neglect significant variables, and generally misrepresent foreign cultures. The social scientist must take some responsibility for the status of foreign-exchange programs and international relations.

1415. Bloom BL: The Rorschach popular response among Hawaiian schizophrenics. J Proj Techniques 26:173–181.

Investigation of sociocultural and psychiatric dimensions of popular responses by 101 hospitalized patients demonstrates some differences in degree of popularity but no new popular responses.

1416. Bonte M: The reaction of two African societies to the Muller-Lyer illusion. J Soc Psychol 58:265–268.

Bashi Africans and Mbuti pygmies are not more susceptible to the illusion when measured with an apparatus like that employed by W. H. R. Rivers. However, the Bashi are significantly less susceptible and variable to a series of drawings prepared by M. J. Herskovits et al.

1417. Boyer LB: Remarks on the personality of shamans: with special reference to the Apache of the Mescalero Indian Reservation. Psychoanal Study Society 2:233–254.

Previous hypotheses of shamanistic hysterical personality disorders are supported. Present-day differences between nonshamans and shamans are a consequence of a complex interaction of status and supported imposture.

1418. Brenner AB: Onan, the levirate marriage and genealogy of the Messiah. J Am Psychoanal Assoc 10:701–721.

In the levirate marriage, as in the related "ghost marriage," the actual begetter of the child is a living mortal man; the status father is a dead man, a ghost, a spirit. The institution of the levirate marriage, as is indicated in the Bible, conveys archaic repressed notions that could not be given overt expression.

1419. Clark L: A comparative view of aggressive behavior. Am J Psychiatry 119:336–341.

Onychomys leucogaster, the northern grasshopper mouse, possesses unique qualities for the experimental study of agonistic behavior.

1420. Cryns AGJ: African intelligence: a critical survey of cross-cultural intelligence research in Africa south of the Sahara. J Soc Psychol 57:283–301.

Quantitative and qualitative differences in intelligence may be interpreted in terms of the nature-nurture controversy.

1421. Das JP: Ethnocentrism and stereotypes among Santhals. J Soc Psychol 57:79–84.

The Santhals of West Bengal are generally democratic and rational. They demonstrate a dislike of the Hindus with whom they have contact but borrow many Hindu ideals and customs of dress.

1422. Dubreuil G: Les bases psycho-culturelles du tabou de l'inceste. Can Psychiatr Assoc J 7:218–234.

Incest was rare and sporadic in primitive society due to life conditions that sharply limited its possibility. Incest taboo emerged in a situation where incest could occur only infrequently and like other exceptional acts was at the same time an offense, or a privilege and liberty reserved for exceptional people. Incest taboo and oedipal complex are both rooted in the culture and the individual.

1423. Fenz WD, Arkoff A: Comparative need patterns of five ancestry groups in Hawaii. J Soc Psychol 58:67–90.

Personality need patterns for Caucasians, Chinese, Filipinos, Hawaiians, and Japanese indicate a Caucasian profile distinct from a general non-Caucasian profile. Female groups' profiles are more similar than those of male groups.

1424. Field PB, Maldonado-Sierra ED, Wallace SE, Bodarky CJ, Coelho GV: An other-directed fantasy in a Puerto Rican. J Soc Psychol 58:43–60.

A student's unsatisfying formal, impersonal family relationships lead him to seek the informal relationships of a peer group and to achieve success through conformity and dependency. These features may be related to Puerto Rican cultural themes.

1425. Forster EB: The theory and practice of psychiatry in Ghana. Am J Psychother 16:7–51.

No homogeneous African culture exists, and to establish a school specifically to take cognizance of this fact will be difficult. However, future training in psychiatry should include sessions in anthropology, social psychology, and transcultural psychiatry. Some important customs observed in Ghana include lip pulling, Bladzoo, Dippo, and Bragro.

1426. Fowlie HC: The physique of female psychiatric patients. J Ment Science 108:594–603.

The relationship that Parnell has reported in depressed patients, between somatotype, psychiatric diagnosis, and duration of stay in a mental hospital, and between somatotype, civil state, family size, and the sex ratio of the children of female patients admitted to a mental hospital, is not statistically confirmed. The failure may be due to differences in the ethnic constitution of the two groups of patients.

1427. Frings H: Animal communication. Am J Psychiatry 118:872–880.

The transmission of information involves all animals, from slime molds to man.

1428. Gaier EL, Collier MJ: Adult reactions to preferred childhood stories: a Finnish-American comparison. Psychoanal Study Society 2:263–279.

Finnish males and females and American females share childhood preferences for instinct-gratifying fairy tales with happy endings, peer sharing, and encountering the story in the oedipal period. American males, however, prefer action fiction stories, not peer shared, and encountered in the latency period.

1429. Gardner GH: Cross cultural communication. J Soc Psychol 58:241–256.

The failure of many programs for development of underdeveloped areas may be in part due to failure of cross-cultural communication between the expert and the culture. A study of some perspectives of communication and the problems of matching cultural value systems may facilitate efficacious communication.

1430. Goff RM: Psychology and intercultural interaction. J Soc Psychol 58:235–240.

Successful intercultural interaction and learning of new attitudes is a function of skillful psychological management of cultural values.

1431. Grinker RR Sr, Grinker RR Jr, Timberlake J: "Mentally healthy" young males (homoclites): a study. Arch Gen Psychiatry 6:405–453.

Study of the character structure of a group of "mentally healthy" college students reveals some general characteristics and relative homogeneity. The students are middle-of-the-roaders in every way and plan to carry on their lives quietly in simple comfort, marry and raise their families, and retire on small pensions plus social security.

1432. Halpern H: Alienation from parenthood in the kibbutz and America. Marriage Fam Living 24:42–45.

Liberation from the traditional parental self-concept in the kibbutz and in America has its healthy aspects, although it may lead to less capacity for love and involvement with children.

1433. Harlow HF, Harlow MK: The effect of rearing conditions on behavior. Bull Menninger Clin 26:213–224.

Total isolation for two years of infant rhesus monkeys results in failure to display social or sexual behavior in the next two years, spent in joint living. Six months of isolation results in severe but not complete social deficits. Partial isolation produces behavioral aberrations and sexual inadequacy. The longer and the more complete the social deprivation the more devastating are the behavioral effects.

1434. Hayakawa SI: Conditions of success in communication. Bull Menninger Clin 26:225–236.

The fundamental motive of human behavior is not self-preservation, but preservation of the symbolic self. This concept can be extended to include groups. Preservation of the symbolic self, whether it be individual or group, as a purpose of a successful flow of communication is vital.

1435. Hendin H: Suicide in Sweden. Psychiatr Q 36:1–28.

Certain child-rearing practices in Sweden stimulate anger and deflate self-esteem while failing to promote the required control of anger and all strong affect. Such a combination provides fertile soil for suicide. The Swedish male's attitudes toward females further aggravate the situation.

1436. Hes JP, Levine J: Kibbutz humor. J Nerv Ment Dis 135:327–331.

Kibbutzim cartoons are a regulating force to drain off and to express tension. The sharing of laughter by the group members reinforces their mutual support and identification and thus brings them closer together.

1437. Huang LJ: Attitudes of the Communist Chinese toward interclass marriage. Marriage Fam Living 24:389–392.

The trend in mainland China of political homogamy frequently results in interclass marriage, often with the wife having a higher position than the husband. The political atmosphere emphasizes compatability.

1438. Jahoda G: Development of Scottish children's ideas and attitudes about other countries. J Soc Psychol 58:91–107.

Rate of development of national attitudes in children is significantly correlated with social class, individual differences being found within each class. Three general developmental trends may be noted for characteristic age levels, and the wide range of variation cannot be underemphasized.

1439. Kaplan B: Psychological themes in Zuni mythology and Zuni TATs. Psychoanal Stud Society 2:255–262.

Zuni myths and results of TATs do not reflect the full range of Zuni personality characteristics.

1440. Kiev A: Brief note: primitive holistic medicine. Int J Soc Psychiatry 8:58–61.

Haitian native doctors, who are voodoo priests and priestesses (hungans and mambos), have developed an amazingly large formulary and set of treatment techniques. The hungan's power to cure is amply supported by the community and he engages in ritual and symbolic maneuvers familiar to all his patients from early life.

1441. Kiev A: Psychotherapy in Haitian voodoo. Am J Psychother 16:469–476.

Native doctors, or hungans, treat patients with such techniques as magic, divination, ceremonials, exorcism, and trance states. Voodoo theory includes ideas on etiology of mental illness, heredity, patient responsibility, disease description, prognosis, and treatment.

1442. Kiev A: Ritual goat sacrifice in Haiti. Am Imago 19:349–359.

Voodoo sacrifice serves to maintain cultural suppression and control over man by preventing ego autonomy and freedom from instincts. Freud's notion of repetitive original parricide and Kyree's concept of ambivalence toward the diety are validated by examination of the interelationships among the voodoo participants.

1443. Kothari U: The animals and their symbolic meaning. Am Imago 19:157–162.

Animal figures in Hindu mythologies represent the inner conflict of id and ego for mankind by symbolizing instincts and character traits.

1444. Krupp GR: The bereavement reaction: a special case of separation anxiety: sociocultural consideration. Psychoanal Stud Society 2:42–74.

Cross-cultural variations in mourning practices and, specifically, American cultural patterns of bereavement, express important aspects of the cultures.

1445. Lambo TA: Malignant anxiety: a syndrome associated with criminal conduct in Africans. J Ment Science 108:256–264.

Malignant anxiety in its sporadic or epidemic form may lead to crimes akin to ritual murder, which in the past was prevalent in the whole continent of Africa. Mental maladjustment is more frequently seen in "marginal" Africans who are in the process of renouncing their age-old culture but have failed to assimilate the new.

1446. Leach ER: Pulleyar and the lord Buddha: an aspect of religious syncretism in Ceylon. Psychoanal Rev 49:81–102.

Pulleyar, both a potent warrior and an ascetic monk, is what Buddha is not. In Eastern religions consistency is provided by the totality of symbols rather than by theology.

1447. Lessler K: Sexual symbols, structured and unstructured. J Consult Psychol 26:44–49.

Female subjects identify more unstructured than structured symbols. The multiple dimensions of symbolism must be considered in order to properly evaluate the Freudian hypothesis.

1448. Levinson BM: A preliminary study of the Yeshiva College Subcultural Scale. J Clin Psychol 18:314–315.

The YCSS cannot serve as a scholastic predictor or as an indicator of intelligence.

1449. Li PC: Accuracy of male Chinese student's perception of traits women desire in a husband. Marriage Fam Living 24:285–286.

The majority of the male respondents have a distorted picture of the important qualities for mate selection by Chinese-American girls.

1450. Lynn R, Gordon IE: Maternal attitudes to child socialization: some social and national differences. Br J Soc Clin Psychol 1:52–55.

British middle-class mothers are more permissive toward children's unsocialized behavior but generally are less permissive and more punitive than American mothers.

1451. Malzberg B: Mental disease among Norwegian-born and native-born of Norwegian parentage in New York State, 1949–1951. Part I: born in Norway. Acta Psychiatr Scand 38:48–75.

In general, natives of Norwegian parentage have a lower rate of first admissions than all native whites of foreign parentage, with the exception of those in respect to general paresis and alcoholic psychoses. Norwegian-born have a lower rate than overall white foreign-born subjects and, in relation to general paresis and alcoholic psychoses, they compare favorably with native-born.

1452. Malzberg B: Mental disease among Swedish-born and native-born of Swedish parentage in New York State, 1949–1951. Part I: born in Sweden. Acta Psychiatr Scand 38:79–107.

Natives of Swedish parentage have, in general, a higher rate of first admissions than natives of native parentage; however, there are important differences with respect to generations. We may anticipate a lowering of the incidence of mental disease in New York State among those of Swedish ancestry.

1453. Mann JW: Race-linked values in South Africa. J Soc Psychol 58:31–42.

Nonwhite students value community service, public welfare, and full democracy rather than privatism.

1454. McDonald RL, Gynther MD: MMPI norms for southern adolescent Negroes. J Soc Psychol 58: 277–282.

Although there are configurational similarities between MMPI profiles for Negroes and whites, sufficient differences exist to warrant the construction of separate norms for Negroes, males, and females.

1455. McNeil EB: Patterns of aggression. J Child Psychol Psychiatry 3:65–77.

The behavioral interplay between aggressive action and reaction tends to be a function not only of the vicissitudes of an individual's history in learning to manage hostile impulses but also of the complexion of the group in which he must exist. Expressions of hostility should not be viewed as a unitary phenomenon that can be captured by means of a single, global estimate of "aggressiveness."

1456. Maupin EW: Zen Buddhism: a psychological review. J Consult Psychol 26:362–370.

The concept of regression in service to the ego seems relevant to Zen Buddhism. Relaxation therapy and attention are aspects of the training process. Morita therapy in Japan is akin to the viewpoint of Zen, which may be effective for those who do not employ other psychotherapy.

1457. Mehlman B, Volio AM, Jamieson BB, Gligor AM: Child-rearing practices in Kent, Ohio. Child Dev 33:391–401.

With the exception of the age at which diurnal bladder training is begun, social class does not affect child-rearing practices. A more universal child-personality as a result of greater similarity in child-rearing practices may be in the offing.

1458. Meyer JE: The theory and practice of psychiatry in West Germany. Am J Psychother 16: 484–508.

The geographical position of Germany in the center of Europe and its long struggle for national unity have led to a labile historical consciousness that fluctuates between an accentuated national pride and feelings of inferiority. The psychiatrist in West Germany is often in the spotlight of public criticism and discussion, and prejudice toward the mentally ill still exists.

1459. Mills LF: Epidemic in a Navajo school. Bull Menninger Clin 26:189–194.

The Kayenta Boarding School epidemic of an ulcerative gum infection, which threatened to reach pandemic proportions, may be attributable to the sudden introduction of children into a regimented authoritative environment without appropriate preparation. Lack of appreciation of Navajo culture in the school caused emotional and psychic distress in the children and resulted in the gingivitis.

1460. Nelson B: Sociology and psychoanalysis on trial: an epilogue. Psychoanal Rev 49:144–160.

The Existential Freudo-Marxist "Opposition" needs to be more respectful of the rights of the Morality of Thought. If the Two Logics are not joined in time, there may be no cultures left to bridge.

1461. Parsons T: Individual autonomy and social pressure: an answer to Dennis H. Wrong. Psychoanal Rev 49:70–79.

Sociological theory should be articulated with psychological theory. Human behavior is not "determined" by society as against the individual, nor is the obverse true.

1462. Pasamanick B: Prevalence and distribution of psychosomatic conditions in an urban population according to social class. Psychosom Med 24:352–356.

The interview method of securing information has profound limitations—limitations as serious as those of using available public records in epidemiological research.

1463. Peal E, Lambert WE: The relation of bilingualism to intelligence. Psychol Monographs 76:1–23.

French Canadian bilingual children perform significantly better than monolinguals on verbal and nonverbal intelligence tests. The bilingual group possesses a more diversified set of mental abilities and has more favorable attitudes toward English Canadians.

1464. Posinsky SH: Ritual, neurotic and social. Am Imago 19:375–390.

An analogy between neurotic-psychotic compulsive behavior and socially patterned ritual must carefully acknowledge the significant differences between the two phenomena.

1465. Prange AJ, Vitols MM: Cultural aspects of the relatively low incidence of depression in Southern Negroes. Int J Soc Psychiatry 8:104–112.

Depression is relatively uncommon in Southern Negroes, whose basic attitudes include stoicism and fundamental defiance and whose fundamental religion insists that he actively mourn his losses. As the Negro comes to share more fully the white man's culture, he will also share his malady—depression.

1466. Rainwater L: Social status differences in the family relationships of German men. Marriage Fam Living 24:12–16.

The upper middle class emphasizes individuality, the lower middle class has a familistic emphasis, and the upper- or lower-class working man is tangential and shows loose family ties. German men reflect more emotional family involvement at all levels than American men.

1467. Reiss PJ: The extended kinship system: correlates of and attitudes on frequency of interaction. Marriage Fam Living 24:333–339.

Degree of relationship and distance of residence are the most important variables of kin interaction for the middle class.

1468. Rin H, Lin TY: Mental illness among Formosan aborigines as compared with the Chinese in Taiwan. J Ment Science 108:134–146.

"Hsieh Ping" (Chinese), "Utox reaction" (Atayal), and "Imu" (Ainus) belong to the category of fright reactions, but they differ from each other in terms of the levels of the organization of symptoms and the levels of consciousness at which the fear complex operates. Mental disorder among Formosan aborigines differs from that among the Chinese, and even more so, from Western cultures in regards to onset, duration, and outcomes.

1469. Roheim G: The Western tribes of Central Australia: childhood. Psychoanal Study Society 2:195–232.

The cultural implications of childbirth, naming, infanticide, cannibalism, discipline, and play activities of Australian aborigines can be understood in psychodynamic terms.

1470. Rosen J, Wejtko J: Effects of delayed weaning on rat emotionality: related to dominance behavior in the rat. Arch Gen Psychiatry 7:77–81.

Delayed weaning has no significant effect on emotional elimination, timidity, and consumatory behavior in the albino rat. Normally weaned rats are more dominant in competitive feeding situations than ones weaned when they are somewhat older. Remaining with the mother beyond the normal weaning period diminishes the aggressive behavior of mice.

1471. Rosenblatt PC: Functions of games: an examination of individual difference hypotheses derived from a cross-cultural study. J Soc Psychol 58: 17–22.

Data do not support the hypothesis that those interested in mastering social environment prefer games of strategy, while those interested in mastering the supernatural prefer games of chance. Cross-cultural studies as sources of generalizations of individual differences have limited utility.

1472. Ross AO: Ego identity and social order: a psychosocial analysis of six Indonesians. Psychol Monographs 76:1–33.

Anthropological data and projective test results indicate areas of marginality in ego identity among a sample of Indonesians from Sumatra.

1473. Ruesch J: Human communication and the psychiatrist. Am J Psychiatry 116:881–888.

Therapeutic communications are regulatory processes whereby deviant patient messages are altered.

1474. Saler B: Unsuccessful practitioners in a bicultural Guatemalan community. Psychoanal Rev 49:103–118.

The Quiche Indians deal with two types of curers, Ladino spiritualists and Indian calendar shamans. Among the latter the Aj-Nawal Mesas are unsuccessful because of their antisocial manipulations.

1475. Schwitzgebel R: A comparative study of Zulu and English reactions to sensory deprivation. Int J Soc Psychiatry 8:220–225.

Zulus under sensory deprivation show significantly less variation in their ability to perform certain perceptual and cognitive tasks than do the English. The effects of major cultural variables should be examined more closely before assuming that sensory deprivation necessarily determines the modification commonly reported in Canadian and U.S. studies.

1476. Seay B, Hansen E, Harlow HF: Mother-infant separation in monkeys. J Child Psychol Psychiatry 3:123–132.

Mothers and infant monkeys show emotional disturbance in response to separation; however infants' disturbances are more intense and more enduring than those of the mothers. Such disturbance differentials are in accord with the human separation syndrome described by Bowlby.

1477. Singh NS, Retting S: Cross-cultural differences in habitual response preferences as an index of anxiety. J Soc Psychol 58:9–15.

Since the traditionally oriented Indian culture produces little anxiety in the child during socialization, two hypotheses concerning American and Indian students are supported: that Indians would prefer stimuli that signify lower anxiety and that frequency of response set differences is inversely related to structure of the stimuli.

1478. Stott DH: Delinquency and cultural stress. Br J Soc Clin Psychol 1:182–191.

Lower culture groups demonstrate greater evidence of behavior disturbances as a result of ecological differences and genetically based stress proneness.

1479. Sussman MB, Burchinal L: Kin family network: unheralded structure in current conceptualizations of family functioning. Marriage Fam Living 24:231–240.

The concept of the functional significance of the isolated nuclear family has been overestimated and the importance of the kin network overlooked.

1480. Szabo D: Problèmes de socialisation et d'integration socioculturelles: contribution á l'étologie de l'inceste. Can Psychiatr Assoc J 7:235–249.

In some families early incest barriers are not well established, with consequent continuing attachment to sexual objects within the family. Predisposing factors like the absence of the wife, provocative attitude of the daughter, alcoholism, and depression of the father are important. Incest is not completely intelligible from the light of individual psychopathology, but rather many factors must be taken into consideration.

1481. Teahan JE, Drews EM: A comparison of Northern and Southern Negro children on the WISC. J Consult Psychol 26:292.

The Southern Negro group is deficient on performance rather than verbal subtests; while the Northern Negro group does better on nonverbal tests.

1482. Tedeschi JT, Kian M: Cross-cultural study of the TAT assessment motivation: Americans and Persians. J Soc Psychol 58:227–234.

Results show no significant difference in need for achievement in either relaxed or aroused conditions of presentation of the TAT, indicating that TAT assessment of achievement motivation is culture free.

1483. Thomas A: Pseudo-transference reactions due to cultural stereotyping. Am J Orthopsychiatry 32:894–900.

Derogatory, culturally determined, stereotyped therapist attitudes may create disturbed, negative reactions in the patient which can be incorrectly interpreted as neurotic transference phenomena, resulting in significant distortions of the diagnostic and therapeutic process.

1484. Thompson DC: Development of attitudes in respect to discrimination. Am J Orthopsychiatry 32:74–85.

In New Orleans Negro society the middle class, matriarchy, gang, nuclear family, and marginality are the most significant social worlds, and it is from these segments that individual members receive their attitudes regarding self, other, skin color, sex, religion, race, family, and achievement.

1485. Triandis HC, Triandis LM: A cross-cultural study of social distance. Psychol Monographs 76: 1–21.

Nationality and religion are the most important variables of social distance for Greek subjects, while race and religion are most important for the American group. Insecure individuals in both samples illustrate the most social distance toward minority groups.

1486. van Mering O: Value dilemmas and reciprocally evoked transitions of patient and cures. Psychoanal Rev 49:119–143.

In a complex healing organization not only the individual patient but also the medical and administrative staff develop and rely upon nonmedical, sociocultural, and personal-emotional criteria for evaluating the available services.

1487. Washburn WC: The effects of physique and intrafamily tension on self-concepts in adolescent males. J Consult Psychol 26:460–466.

The absence of intrafamily tension results in a greater concept difference between linear and non-linear physique groups than does the presence of intrafamily tension.

1488. Weiner IB: Father-daughter incest: a clinical report. Psychiatr Q 36:608–632.

Incestuous fathers rarely show psychotic disturbance or neurotic symptom formation. Intellectualization, isolation, and reaction formation are primary modes of defense.

1489. Weintraub W, Aronson H: The application of verbal behavior analysis to the study of psychological defense mechanisms: methodology and preliminary report. J Nerv Ment Dis 134:169–181.

Patterns of verbal behavior reflect patient psychological defenses. These patterns can be measured.

1490. White LA: Symboling: a kind of behavior. J Psychol 53:311–318.

Man alone is capable of symboling, which is to be distinguished from signing. The somatic context of symbolates is human behavior, while the extrasomatic context of symbolates is culture.

1491. Whittaker JO: Alcohol and the Standing Rock Sioux tribe: the pattern of drinking. Q J Stud Alcohol 23:468–479.

Seventy percent of the tribe are drinkers. Sixty-eight percent have been arrested for drunkenness, and the overall proportion of problem drinkers is about twice that of the previous generation.

1492. Wrong DH: The over-socialized conception of man in modern society. Psychoanal Rev 49: 53–69.

All men are socialized but this does not mean that they have been completely molded by the particular norms and values of their culture.

1963

1493. Anisfeld M, Musioz SR, Lambert W: The structure and dynamics of the ethnic attitudes of Jewish adolescents. J Abnorm Soc Psychol 66: 31–36.

The structure of the factors of negative social orientation, attitudes toward parents and self may be linked by a manifest hostility.

1494. Arkoff A, Meredith G, Dong J: Attitudes of Japanese-American and Caucasian-American students toward marriage roles. J Soc Psychol 59: 11–15.

Japanese-American males are more male-dominant in their conception of marriage than Japanese-American females or Caucasian-Americans.

1495. Back KW: A model of family planning experiments: the lessons of the Puerto Rican and Jamaican studies. Marriage Fam Living 25:14–19.

A proposed model of family planning shows that

individuals can be influenced by different means in a particular society, and by high- and low-impact programs.

1496. Bacon MK, Child IL, Barry H: A cross-cultural study of correlates of crime. J Abnorm Soc Psychol 66:291–300.

Limitation of father-son identification is associated with theft and personal crimes. Socialization anxiety and status differences are associated with theft, and general adult destructiveness is associated with personal crime in nonliterate societies.

1497. Baggaley AR: Comparison of temperament scores of Jewish and Gentile male students. Psychol Rep 13:598.

As measured by the Guilford-Zimmerman Temperament Survey, the temperament of Jewish and Gentile male students is essentially similar, although Jewish students are characterized by slightly more Ascendance and slightly less Restraint.

1498. Benedek T: An investigation of the sexual cycle in women: methodologic considerations. Arc Gen Psychiatry 8:311–322.

The principles of psychoanalytic theory and technique can be applied to recorded psychoanalytic material. Data so derived have a high level of correlation with parallel data of a physiologic method of investigation.

1499. Benjamin LS, Mason WA: Effect of hunger on nonnutritive sucking in infant Rhesus monkeys. J Abnorm Soc Psychol 66:526–531.

Thumbsucking increases with hunger for infant rhesus monkeys.

1500. Bernstein IS: Social activities related to Rhesus monkey consort behavior. Psychol Rep 13:375–379.

Consort behavior among dominant rhesus monkeys is expressed primarily in increased proximity scores and consequent increases in all types of social interaction. Estrus females enjoy greater toleration by the male but may be attacked too, and show no change in dominance rank relative to other group members.

1501. Bing E: Effect of childrearing practices on development of differential cognitive abilities. Child Dev 34:631–648.

Discrepant verbal ability is fostered by a close relationship with a demanding and somewhat intrusive mother, while discrepant nonverbal abilities are enhanced by allowing children a considerable degree of freedom.

1502. Boehm L: The development of conscience of preschool children: a cultural and subcultural comparison. J Soc Psychol 59:355–360.

Whereas previous studies on Swiss and English preschoolers show an inability to judge an action by intention, more than one third of American preschoolers were able to do so with Piaget's Lost Story. Upper-middle-class subjects reveal more mature responses than working-class subjects.

1503. Bradburn NM: Achievement and father dominance in Turkey. J Abnorm Soc Psychol 67:464–468.

Father dominance is associated with low need achievement in American and Turkish junior executives, but not when measured by Turkish subjects' reported most influential life figure.

1504. Brody EB, Derbyshire RL: Prejudice in American Negro college students. Arch Gen Psychiatry 9:619–628.

Negro college students with the least marked antiforeign and anti-Semitic prejudice are those with less uncertainty and anxiety concerning their identities as members of the Negro group.

1505. Caldwell BM, Hersher L, Lipton EL, Richmond JB, Stern GA, Eddy E, Drachman R, Rothman A: Mother-infant interaction in monomatric and polymatric families. Am J Orthopsychiatry 33:653–664.

A closer emotional attachment is found in families where mothering is provided by only one person (monomatric) than those in which mothering is provided by more than one person (polymatric). This may be influenced by prenatal personality factors as well as by the exclusiveness of the postnatal mother-infant diad.

1506. Centers R, Centers L: Social character types and beliefs about child-rearing. Child Dev 34:69–78.

Other directedness has a small but statistically significant positive correlation with the tendency to believe in fostering independence and has a slight, but not statistically significant, positive correlation with the tendency to believe in strictness in child rearing.

1507. Christiansen JR: Contemporary Mormon's attitudes toward polygynous practices. Marriage Fam Living 25:167–170.

Polygynous practices of the early Mormons are generally condoned by contemporary Mormons, although the possibility of present and future practices are generally rejected. The attitudes of present and early Mormons show some similarities and indicate that even under approved circumstances few persons wish to practice polygyny.

1508. Coles MR: Southern children under desegregation. Am J Psychiatry 120:332–344.

Negro children have, in general, endured the stresses of initial desegregation in Southern cities without evidence of significant psychiatric illness.

1509. Cooper JG: Cultural and social correlates of teachers' attitudes toward their school. J Soc Psychol 61:35–41.

Mainland U.S. contract teachers and military dependent part-time teachers are more likely to be highly critical of Guam's schools than are local Guamanian teachers, possibly as a result of differential educational background.

1510. Coughlin RJ, Coughlin MM: Fertility and birth control among low income Chinese families in Hong Kong. Marriage Fam Living 25:171–177.

The desire to have male offspring is the strongest cultural obstacle to birth control among low-income Hong Kong Chinese. Lack of information and availability of devices seem to be due to the ineffective impact of the mass media on an illiterate population.

1511. Darlington CD: Psychology, genetics and the process of history. Br J Psychol 54:293–298.

The problems of genetics and psychology can be traced to a conflict derived from Galton and Freud's perspectives. For both disciplines history has four stages, from tribes to the present, which may be delimited in terms of heredity, class structure, and individuals.

1512. Davenport RK, Menzel EW: Stereotyped behavior of the infant chimpanzee. Arch Gen Psychiatry 8:99–104.

Stereotypes are phenomena unique to chimpanzee infants raised in restricted environments. These behaviors show marked resemblances to behaviors of human beings with certain pathological conditions.

1513. Derbyshire RL, Brody EB, Schleifer C: Family structure of young adult Negro male mental patients: preliminary observations from urban Baltimore. J Nerv Ment Dis 136:245–251.

The family structure of young adult Negro male mental patients constitutes an adaptation to a social situation that has provided no alternatives. The family structure is controlled by an inconsistent matriarch and is present oriented.

1514. Devereux G: Sociopolitical functions of the Oedipus myth in early Greece. Psychoanal Q 32:205–214.

The great crisis of Greek society was the struggle for supremacy of the patrilineal system over the matrilineal, which led to a blending of the two cultures. The Oedipus myth was a decisive element and served as a conservative political manifesto.

1515. Duhl LJ: The American character: crisis, change and complexity. J Nerv Ment Dis 137:124–134.

Strengths inherent to American society may provide means for preventing destructive patterns. Historically, the world perceives America to represent revolution. If the American character can provide revolutionary ways of looking at current world crises, the newly emerging shape of the world can be altered for the better.

1516. Dundes A: Summoning deity through ritual fasting. Am Imago 20:213–230.

Fasting has an infantile origin in association of parental succor at time of hunger. Fasting is thus also a means whereby a deity is summoned.

1517. Ellenberger H, Fried J, Murphy HBM, Wittkower ED: A cross-cultural survey of schizophrenic symptomatology. Int J Soc Psychiatry 9:237–249.

Schizophrenic symptoms vary in association with social, cultural, observational, and conceptual factors, thus throwing some doubt on the Western view of schizophrenic process.

1518. Enright JB, Jaeckle WR: Psychiatric symptoms and diagnosis in two subcultures. Int J Soc Psychiatry 9:12–17.

Although Japanese and Filipino patients are identified as identical by the American Psychiatric Association diagnostic system, they show distinct differences in the frequency of occurrence of concrete symptoms. Japanese and Filipino paranoid patients differ in specific ways. In comparison of psychiatric symptoms in non-Western ethnic groups reliance on diagnostic categories developed in a Western culture conceals clear and important differences.

1519. Ervin SM, Landar H: Navaho word-associations. Am J Psychol 76:49–57.

Navaho verbs strongly elect the nouns that precede them. Contextual variety is a fundamental variable in association.

1520. Finney JC: Psychiatry and multiculturality in Hawaii. Int J Soc Psychiatry 9:5–11.

Hawaiian ethnic groups are differentially prone to various psychological illnesses. Differences between the groups are reflected on psychological questionnaire response scales.

1521. Forbes GS: Some observations of family life education in India. Marriage Fam Living 25:466–468.

Family life education, especially its biological aspects, is not generally an accepted topic for school curricula in India, although the foundation is currently being put down for teaching the subject in Indian schools.

1522. Freymann MS: Population control in India. Marriage Fam Living 25:53–61.

Population in India has been on the rise due to more continuous food supplies, disease controls, and rural health programs. The move among Indian intellectuals and in the government to sponsor family planning programs may hasten an overall decline in birthrate.

1523. Gaier EL, Collier MJ: Theme appeal in the preferred childhood stories of Finnish men: a longitudinal approach. Int J Soc Psychiatry 9:110–120.

Swedish-speaking Finnish males overwhelmingly prefer fairy tales as their favorite story of childhood. The appeal of different characters in childhood stories varies between high school boys and university men. The variations may reflect developmental stage shifts in psychological orientation as well as changes in Finland's culture while moving from an agrarian economy to one of industrial urbanization.

1524. Gelfand S: The relation of birth order to pain tolerance. J Clin Psychol 19:406.

No significant relationship between birth order and pain tolerance and placebo response can be found for nursing students.

1525. Ghei SN: The reliability and validity of Edwards Personal Preference Schedule: a cross-cultural study. J Soc Psychol 61:241–246.

The reliability coefficients for the EPPS variables of a sample of Indian liberal arts students are significant at less than the .01 level. The EPPS effectively differentiates the former sample from both student nurses and student teachers.

1526. Gladstone R, Gupta GC: A cross-cultural study of the behavioral aspects of the concept of religion. J Soc Psychol 60:203–211.

Indian and American students' conception of the behavior of religious persons is homogeneous within each group, with the Indian students conceiving of a religious person's actions dealing with human relations more than nonhuman relations. Assumptions on the actions of religious persons in another country may help shape the individual's attitudes toward that country.

1527. Goldberg EM, Morrison SL: Schizophrenia and social class. Br J Psychiatry 109:785–802.

Schizophrenics suffer "downward drift" attributable to the disease process. Gross socioeconomic deprivation is unlikely to be of major etiological significance in schizophrenia. Occupational factors, yet to be defined clearly, appear to exert some influence on the course of the disease.

1528. Gottesman II: Heritability of personality: a demonstration. Psychol Monographs 77:1–21.

MMPI and Cattell's HSPQ assessments of personality of monzygotic and dizygotic twins indicate that psychopathology has a genetic component, and introversion is most heavily influenced by genetic factors.

1529. Grinder RE, McMichael RE: Cultural influence on conscience development: resistance to temptation and guilt among Samoans and American Caucasians. J Abnorm Soc Psychol 66:503–507.

Samoan children are less likely to resist temptation or be susceptible to guilt manifestations after transgression than American children.

1530. Gussow Z: A preliminary report of Kayak-Angst among the Eskimo of West Greenland: a study in sensory deprivation. Int J Soc Psychiatry 9:18–26.

Kayak hunting under specific conditions of sea and weather represents a sensory deprivation and isolation environment. Kayak-angst reactions may be analyzed in terms of the more general Eskimo tendency to withdraw in the face of specific types of stress. Cultural factors may exacerbate the condition.

1531. Hall C, Dornhoff B: Aggression in dreams. Int J Soc Psychiatry 9:259–267.

Freud's data led him to place emphasis on the male figure and on aggression. Dream narratives with aggressive interactions obtained from male and female college students support Freud's conclusions.

1532. Hall C, Dornhoff B: A ubiquitous sex difference in dreams. J Abnorm Soc Psychol 66:278–280.

Men dream more about men, while females dream more about both sexes in equal proportions. These findings are in accord with conflict theory and Freud's Oedipus complex.

1533. Hall KRL: Observational learning in monkeys and apes. Br J Psychol 54:201–226.

Observational evidence indicates that young monkeys and apes acquire certain tendencies and avoidance habits by following and experiencing the manner in which mothers and other group members behave toward objects and places. The affectional situation is crucial to this learning.

1534. Heuscher JE: Cinderella, eros and psyche. Dis Nerv Syst 24:286–292.

Genuine folk-fairy-tales, in simple but beautiful pictures, transmit a rich heritage of deep insights into human nature. They may, especially to the child, be an indispensable nourishment that offsets or balances the overly rational or natural-scientific influences of our times.

1535. Hoffs JA: Anthropophagy (cannibalism) and its relation to the oral stage of development. Psychoanal Rev 50:187–214.

The cannibalism of primitive man parallels that of the infant. Derivatives of cannibalism are found in the mental life of all civilized people. The decline of cannibalism was associated with assimilation into religious and political structure, and with increasing taboos.

1536. Huang LJ: The problem child and delinquent youth in the Communist Chinese family. Marriage Fam Living 25:459–465.

Chinese youth are clearly experiencing some frustrations and insecurity related to the changing patterns of the new regime. Delinquency is generally attributed by the political regime to a capitalist and feudalistic past. Parent-teacher cooperation, friendly persuasion, and group efforts are brought to bear on the problem of misbehavior; but the country must recognize and place greater emphasis on the family factor in child education if the problem is to be controlled.

1537. Huang LJ: A re-evaluation of the primary role of the Communist Chinese woman: the homemaker or the worker. Marriage Fam Living 25:162–166.

The Communist Chinese woman frequently experiences a conflict between the role of worker and the role of homemaker. However, working for the common cause of social reconstruction and contribution to the people's large family may provide the women with new incentives and loyalties.

1538. Kiev A: Beliefs and delusions of West Indian immigrants to London. Br J Psychiatry 109:356–363.

West Indian schizophrenics in English mental hospitals reveal a predominance of religious and magical themes, related to a fundamentalist approach to the Bible, the phenomenon of charismatic personalities, and the notions of obeah, ghosts, and religious healing. There are distinct differences in the use of culturally derived materials by the normal and psychotic groups.

1539. Kline NS: Psychiatry in Indonesia. Am J Psychiatry 119:809–815.

Attitudes toward and the influence of culture on mental illness in Indonesia are linked to the dearth of mental health facilities and psychiatrists.

1540. Koranyi EK, Kerenyi AB, Sarwer-Foner GJ: On adaptive difficulties of some Hungarian immigrants: clinical considerations and the process of acculturation. Am J Orthopsychiatry 33:760–763.

One of the best correlations to adaptation among Hungarian-speaking psychiatric patients in Montreal is the capacity to learn English. Patients unable to adapt functioned inadequately in their native country.

1541. Kuethe JL, Stricker G: Man and woman: social schemata of males and females. Psychol Rep 13:655–661.

Shared social learning, rather than sex-linked response sets, may account for the overall similarity of major schemata employed by males and females. Differences in idiosyncratic responses may reflect differences in conventionality or "creativity" between males and females.

1542. Leighton AH, Lambo TA, Hughes CC, Leighton DC, Murphy JM, Macklin DB: Psychiatric disorder in West Africa. Am J Psychiatry 120: 521–527.

Mental health problems and social disintegration components are found among the Yoruba in the western region of Nigeria. Findings can be compared with the North American Stirling County study, which utilized many of the same methods.

1543. Leuba C: Comments on Isaac's "Evidence for a sensory drive in monkeys." Psychol Rep 12:14.

The concept of a drive or a drive state as espoused by W. Isaac seems unnecessary and, in some of its main implications, misleading.

1544. LeVine RA: Child rearing in sub-saharan Africa: an interim report. Bull Menninger Clin 27: 245–256.

Variations in African child-rearing practices that might have a significant effect on the social behavior of the individual are age of weaning, parent-child separation, and training in sociability, aggression, and sexual behavior. Three common patterns are: (1) "casual nurturance" in infant care; (2) emphasis on obedience and responsibility in child training; (3) the use of corporal punishment.

1545. Lilly JC: Productive and creative research with man and dolphin. Arch Gen Psychiatry 8: 111–116.

The large, complex brain of the dolphin implies large, complex capabilities and great mental sensitivity. Such capabilities and sensitivities can exist as in yet unrealized forms. When encouraged, dolphins make valiant efforts to use humanoid sounds, apparently in (to them) an appropriate fashion.

1546. Lindgren HC, Guedes HDA: Social status, intelligence, and educational achievement among elementary and secondary students in Sao Paulo, Brazil. J Soc Psychol 60:9–14.

Social and sociometric status, intelligence, and academic success are positively, significantly intercorrelated for Brazilian elementary school children. Social status, intelligence, and academic success are positively correlated for secondary-school students, but the correlation with social status is not as high as for elementary students.

1547. Lindgren HC, Singer EP: Correlates of Brazilian and North American attitudes toward child-centered practices in education. J Soc Psychol 60: 3–7.

North American and Brazilian attitudes of educators and advanced students toward modern of child-centered education are positively correlated with attitudes of independence of judgment and negatively correlated with authoritarian attitudes.

1548. Locke N: The early Maya: a repressed society. Am Imago 20:49–59.

The material remains of the Maya suggest that Mesoamerica as a whole was a repressed society, with the Maya at its extreme. Maya culture was predominantly male, sexuality was denied, and self and other-directed aggression was encouraged.

1549. Luria Z, Goldwasser M, Goldwasser A: Response to transgression in stories by Israeli children. Child Dev 34:271–280.

Kibbutz children confess more readily than Moshav children. Israeli and Jewish American children do not show any significant pattern of sex differences in frequency of confession but Gentile American children do. The warmth in mother-child contacts among Jews plus the high value put on verbal facility may undercut some of the basis for sex differences in a verbal measure like confession.

1550. McHugh AF: H-T-P proportion and perspective in Negro, Puerto Rican, and white children. J Clin Psychol 19:312–313.

Negro children draw houses and trees close to the left margin and persons narrow and away from the right margin. Puerto Rican children draw shorter persons than white children. There is little evidence for greater space restriction, frustration, or aggression for Negroes, and no evidence of this for Puerto Ricans.

1551. Mahler I, Bhargava VP: Professional desirability in India. J Soc Psychol 61:233–240.

Indian students, like American students, conceive of occupational desirability as determined by popular prestige first, material reward second, and personal satisfaction last. There are cultural differences, however, in the ranking of various occupations in terms of these general determinants.

1552. Maltz HE: Ontogenetic change in the meaning of concepts as measured by the semantic differential. Child Dev 34:667–674.

The semantic differential measures a change in the meaning of concepts to the child as he grows older. The change becomes more apparent the greater the differences in age between studied groups. The meaning of concepts to younger children is not as consistent as it is to older ones.

1553. Masserman JH, Aarons L, Wechkin S: The effect of positive-choice conflicts on normal and neurotic monkeys. Am J Psychiatry 120:481–484.

An impasse between positive, but mutually exclusive, goal-seeking responses can also induce significant deviations of conduct. Although six previously normal monkeys exhibited neurotic behavior after ten days, it remained below that of six neurotic monkeys.

1554. Mason WA, Sponholz RR: Behavior of Rhesus monkeys raised in isolation. J Psychiatr Res 1:299–306.

Two monkeys kept in isolation until early adolescence were severely and persistently handicapped in their ability to cope with other monkeys and with novel situations. Their most common reactions to social contact were submission or flight.

1555. Maudlin WP: Population and population policy in Pakistan. Marriage Fam Living 25:62–68.

The current family-planning programs of Pakistan must be intensified and expanded in order to achieve some success in controlling the birthrate.

1556. Mead M: Totem and taboo reconsidered with respect. Bull Menninger Clin 27:185–199.

Freud's theories of totemism were based on secondary sources. Instead of a "collective mentality," the concept of survival may be invoked—biological survival in the constitution of the individual, and social survival in the cultural tradition. The psychoanalytic concepts of "primitive" and "archaic" refer to impulses and modes of thought and functioning that have survived from a far more ancient period than 20,000 years ago.

1557. Mednick SA, Shaffer JBP: Mother's retrospective reports in child-rearing research. Am J Orthopsychiatry 33:457–461.

Retrospective mothers' reports regarding their children's development tend to be unreliable when compared with reports made by the mothers to their pediatrician at the time of the unfolding of their children's development.

1558. Meerloo JAM: Four hundred years of witchcraft, projection, and delusion. Am J Psychiatry 120:83–86.

Johannes Wier (b. 1515), the father of modern clinical psychiatry, introduced the concept of delusion into medical history, wrote an elaborate treatise against the persecution of witches, and proposed a cure for hysterical paralysis and malingering.

1559. Mercado SJ, Guerrero RD, Gardner RW: Cognitive control in children of Mexico and the United States. J Soc Psychol 59:199–208.

Cultural differences in concept formation between Mexican and U.S. children of 9 to 11 years are suggested by a pilot study, but definitive results are not obtained. Differences are revealed between the sexes for the Mexican group but not the U.S. group. Mexican girls' preference for low levels of abstraction may be suggestive of culturally defined sex roles in the development of cognitive structures.

1560. Miller RE, Banks JH, Ogawa N: Role of facial expression in "Cooperative-Avoidance Conditioning" in monkeys. J Abnorm Soc Psychol 67: 24–30.

Identification of various specific facial expressions and their affects between rhesus monkeys is permitted within the context of the cooperative conditioning paradigm.

1561. Mishler EG, Scotch NA: Sociocultural factors in the epidemiology of schizophrenia. Psychiatry 26:315–343.

The social etiology of schizophrenia is an area in which few studies are available; concepts and methods are unclear and unstandardized, findings are inconsistent, and speculation abounds in the absence of reliable empirical knowledge. Epidemiologists must build into their designs the types of controls and measuring instruments that will permit alternative and competing interpretations to be evaluated.

1562. Moloney JC: Carnal myths involving the sun. Am Imago 20:93–104.

Ancient man, through the use of myths, converted the sun into a foil upon which he projected many of his methods of coping with anxiety—processing the sun as if it were a gastrointestinal or a vaginal continent.

1563. Mobray JB, Wolf RC, Beckett P, Frohman C, Gottlieb J: Schizophrenic-like mechanisms in monkeys. Am J Psychiatry 119:835–842.

Rhesus monkeys reared in conditions of social isolation and tactile monotony show evidence of metabolic disturbance consistent with the presence of a factor found in schizophrenic patients. The biochemical defect is not correlated with disturbed behavior in the monkeys.

1564. Murphy HBM: Juvenile delinquency in Singapore. J Soc Psychol 61:201–231.

Juvenile delinquency in Singapore is closely related to the cultural values of the society. Effective prevention calls for the changing of these cultural values.

1565. Murphy HBM, Wittkower ED, Fried J, Ellenberger H: A cross-cultural survey of schizophrenic symptomatology. Int J Soc Psychiatry 9: 237–249.

The distribution of schizophrenic symptoms appears to vary in association with social, cultural, observational, and conceptual factors. Delusional symptoms, which are the most familiar feature of chronic schizophrenia in Euro-American hospitals, may be culturally conditioned attempts by the personality to "make sense" of a process that might be dealt with differently in Eastern cultures.

1566. Ohara K: Characteristics of suicides in Japan, especially of parent-child double suicide. Am J Psychiatry 120:382–385.

Parent-child suicides are seldom seen except in a few Asian countries. Cultural tendencies influence the characteristics of Japanese suicide.

1567. Orme JE: Intelligence, season of birth and climatic temperature. Br J Psychol 54:273–276.

Season of birth is associated with level of intelligence among adult subnormals, possibly as a result of climatic temperature changes during pregnancy. Summer and autumn births are associated with later higher intelligence than winter and spring births.

1568. Otten MW, Van de Castel RL: A comparison of Set "A" of the Holtzman inkblots with the Rorschach by means of the semantic differential. J Proj Tech Pers Assessment 27:452–460.

Responses to Holtzman cards differ in some respects from Rorschach card responses.

1569. Otterbein KF: Marquesan polyandry. Marriage Fam Living 25:155–159.

The apparently anomalous Marquesan system of polyandry-polygyny becomes clear when seen in terms of household types. Viewing household types in terms of composition permits an examination of the manner in which a household type changes through time.

1570. Pond DA, Ryle A, Hamilton M: Social factors and neurosis in a working-class population. Br J Psychiatry 109:587–591.

There are large social and economic achievement differences within the working-class population that show no correlation with neuroticism.

1571. Porkoney AD, Davis F, Harberson W: Suicide, suicide attempts and weather. Am J Psychiatry 120:377–381.

Suicide and suicide attempts in Houston are not significantly related to weather phenomena.

1572. Posinsky SH: Navaho infancy and childhood. Psychiatr Q 37:306–321.

Kluckholn's idyllic view of Navaho infancy and childhood must be balanced by a consideration of Kluckholn's biases and of maladaptive behavior in the Navaho.

1573. Prange AJ, Vitols MM: Jokes among Southern Negroes: the revelation of conflict. J Nerv Ment Dis 136:162–167.

The Southern Negro is enormously preoccupied with the fact of being Negro as is shown by Negro humor.

1574. Rettig S, Jin-Sook L: Differences in moral judgments of South Korean students before and after the Korean revolution. J Soc Psychol 59:3–9.

Following the Korean revolution, the religious moral judgments of Korean students declined in severity, and economic moral judgments increased in severity.

1575. Richards BW: Intelligence and culture. Can Psychiatr Assoc J 8:281–286.

Mental retardation must be defined in terms of both the capacity of the subject and the demands of society. The social environment may influence mental development directly.

1576. Rizk H: Social and psychological factors affecting fertility in the United Arab Republic. Marriage Fam Living 25:69–73.

The current population growth of the United Arab Republic will have an adverse effect on attempts to maintain economic independence. Programs of action to alleviate this situation must include social change, educational and health programs, clarification of religious interpretations, and research and experimentation.

1577. Roberts JM, Sutton-Smith B, Kendon A: Strategy in games and folk tales. J Soc Psychol 61:185–199.

Cross-cultural studies of games of strategy have indicated a link with cultural complexity. Folktales with strategic outcomes are associated with games of strategy in the same cultures and may be explained by a conflict-enculturation hypothesis.

1578. Ross AO, Bruner EM: Family interaction at two levels of acculturation in Sumatra. Am J Orthopsychiatry 33:51–59.

Interview and projective data of a Batak peasant family in a mountain village, compared with an acculturated family from a seacoast town, reveal similarities in dominance patterns of the spouses and in the dependency needs of adolescent daughters. Education is the major variable determining the way children handle aggression and guilt.

1579. Roy B: A cross-cultural study of persons within the industrial belt of Calcutta. J Soc Psychol 60:195–201.

Social perceptions growing out of needs and achievements take shape amidst international exchanges, as reflected in preferences for other nations of the Mideast and West by university students in Calcutta.

1580. Sanua VD: The socio-cultural aspects of schizophrenia: comparison of Protestant and Jewish schizophrenics. Int J Soc Psychiatry 9:27–36.

Protestant fathers and Jewish mothers of schizophrenics belonging to the lower social classes are more disturbed than their mates.

1581. Segall MH: Acquiescence and "Identification with the Aggressor" among acculturating Africans. J Soc Psychol 61:247–262.

Methodological difficulties encountered in comparing attitudes of Ugandan Banyankole tribal members toward their own ethnic group with Europeans' attitudes toward that tribe emphasize the need for careful analysis of response styles and the relationship among questionnaire terms. However, the findings suggest that anti-African attitudes expressed by Africans reflect superficial acquiescence to the beliefs of the dominant group rather than a profound indentification with such beliefs.

1582. Sinha AKP, Ojha H: An experimental study of the operation of prestige suggestion in extraverts and introverts. J Soc Psychol 61:29–34.

Extravert Indian students are more likely to change their judgments under the influence of prestige than introvert students.

1583. Stein WW: Patterns of a Peruvian mental hospital. Int J Social Psychiatry 9:208–215.

Traditional Latin-American conceptions of social class are relevant to the understanding of the kind of hospital structure that exists in Peru. Doctors are directively fatherlike in their relations with patients and with patients' families. While Peru shares in Western prescientific and scientific medical traditions, some aspects of Peruvian medical ideology are unique.

1584. Stuart IR: Minorities vs. minorities: cognitive, affective and conative components of Puerto Rican and Negro acceptance and rejection. J Soc Psychol 59:93–99.

The Negroes and Spanish-American workers in a garment industry are perceived by others to be immoral, devious, combative, sly, deceitful, and many other adjectival components of aspects of intergroup relations. Economic competition is the locus for these perceptions.

1585. Tabah L: A study of fertility in Santiago, Chile. Marriage Fam Living 25:20–26.

Santiago is currently in the transition away from collective opposition to birth control, so conditions favorable for declining birthrate are on the increase.

1586. Takeshita JV: Population control in Japan: a miracle or secular trend. Marriage Fam Living 25:44–52.

Postwar legislation in Japan facilitated the diffusion of fertility control in the population, but this trend, which accompanied industrial-urban transformation of Japan, was advanced prior to government advocacy.

1587. Talerico M, Brown F: Intelligence test patterns of Puerto Rican children seen in child psychiatry. J Soc Psychol 61:57–66.

Results on the WISC show consistent dull normal intelligence pattern for Puerto Rican children with better perceptual organization than verbal comprehension. The adolescent group, however, shows increased IQ possibly associated with cultural influences and loose home ties. Further research on sociological factors with stratified samples are indicated.

1588. Terhune KW: An examination of some contributing demographic variables in a cross-national study. J Soc Psychol 59:209–219.

Multifactorial analysis of content of written stories on interpersonal conflict and material versus interpersonal aspects from the U.S., Norway, and Germany reveals differences associated with demographic variables on various scales, but overall variations of the samples are not affected. The non-orthogonal multivariate method may have value for showing the effects of demographic variables on personality.

1589. Tien HY: Induced abortion and population control in Mainland China. Marriage Fam Living 25:35–43.

The prospects for the use of induced abortion as a means of population control in Mainland China are reduced by professional opposition and lack of any strong spokesman in favor of this practice.

1590. Trethowan WH: The demonopathology of impotence. Br J Psychiatry 109:341–347.

In medieval demonological literature, a classification of impotence relates remarkably closely to some current psychodynamic hypotheses. The convergence of the Christian ascetic ideal and Ritual Witchcraft led to the emergence of a delusional belief that witches had power to interfere with sexual relationships.

1591. Walker RN: Body build and behavior in young children: body build and parents' ratings. Child Dev 34:1–23.

Mothers depict girls as mesomorphic and boys as energetic. The ectomorphic girl is depicted as uncooperative, anxious, and aloof while the ectomorphic boy is seen as similarly unsocial but cooperative and unaggressive. There is a low correlation between parents' and teachers' rating. Physique-behavior associations arise from many sources, including those within the child's physical organism, those in his life experiences, and those in the observers' reactions.

1592. Weissberg NC, Proshansky HM: The Jewish anti-Semite's perceptions of fellow Jews. J Soc Psychol 60:139–151.

The anti-Semitic Jewish student's perception of his Jewish instructor is influenced by the student's authoritarian personality and general tendency to stereotype. He perceives the instructor in terms of his position as teacher and his ethnic background and determines the degree of relevancy of particular traits to these social attributes of the instructor.

1593. Whittaker JO: Alcohol and the Standing Rock Sioux tribe: psychodynamics and cultural factors in drinking. Q J Stud Alcohol 24:80–90.

Social sanctions against the heavy drinker do not exist. The basic insecurity of life on the reservation,

the break up of Sioux culture, and repressed aggression and hostility are factors in producing problem drinking.

1594. Winick C: Taboo and disapproved colors and symbols in various foreign countries. J Soc Psychol 59:361–368.

Colors and objects are salient in the self-perception of nationals of many countries. Blue is the only color not disapproved of when by itself. Political and religious factors may be relevant to some negative preferences. Hotter climates seem to be related to dislike of dark colors, and colder climates to light colors.

1595. Wittkower ED, Bijou L: Psychiatry in developing countries. Am J Psychiatry 120:218–221.

Native beliefs affect psychiatric treatment in Haiti.

1596. Yang KS, Tzou HY, Wu CY: Rorschach responses of normal Chinese adults: the popular responses. J Soc Psychol 60:175–186.

Cross-cultural comparison of popular responses reveals at least one popular response that is unique to normal Chinese adults.

1597. Yaukey D: Some immediate determinants of fertility differences in Lebanon. Marriage Fam Living 25:27–34.

The factors that contribute to differences in fertility rates between village, city, uneducated, and educated couples include the age of woman at marriage, induced abortion, conception control, voluntary, and involuntary differences.

1964

1598. Adinarayan SP, Swaminathan M: Attitudes and adjustment problems of African students in India. J Soc Psychol 63:65–72.

African students have more prejudice against Indians in general and high negative prejudice toward Afrikaners. Political rights are more highly valued by African students than rights to intermarry. Africans perceive that Indians are strongly prejudiced against them and experience a deterioration in favorable attitudes toward Indians as a result of their experiences.

1599. Anisfeld M, Lambert WE: Evaluational reactions of bilingual and monolingual children to spoken languages. J Abnorm Soc Psychol 68:89–97.

French-Canadian children's personality characterizations of English and French recorded speakers reflect actual stereotyped reactions to these two groups.

1600. Antonovsky HF, Ahent L: Cross-cultural consistency of children's preferences for the orientation of figures. Am J Psychol 77:295–297.

Iranian and American children respond similarly to geometric cards.

1601. Arkoff A, Meredith G, Iwahara S: Male-dominant and equalitarian attitudes in Japanese, Japanese-American, and Caucasian-American students. J Soc Psychol 64:225–229.

Japanese and Japanese-American males reveal more male-dominant attitudes to marriage, and the females show more egalitarianism. No significant sex differences are found in the marriage-role attitudes of Caucasian-American students.

1602. Arnhoff FN, Leon HV, Lorge I: Cross-cultural acceptance of stereotypes towards aging. J Soc Psychol 63:41–58.

The acceptance of predominantly negative stereotypes of the aged and aging, and similarity of these attitudes across the U.S., Great Britain, Greece, Japan, and Puerto Rico, places these attitudes in their proper perspective. American attitudes toward aging are clearly not unique and are often more favorable than in other countries.

1603. Badri MB, Dennis W: Human-figure drawings in relation to modernization in Sudan. J Psychol 58:421–426.

Children's attributions of modern vs. traditional appearance to human-figure drawings is a reflection of the degree of group adoption of modern lifestyles.

1604. Bernstein IS: Group social patterns as influenced by removal and later reintroduction of the dominant male Rhesus. Psychol Rep 14:3–10.

Removal of a dominant male monkey in a rhesus monkey group results in increased social activities of the remaining males. Resumption of his former position by a dominant monkey reduces the activity of other males.

1605. Biernoff A, Leary RW, Littman RA: Dominance behavior of paired primates in two settings. J Abnorm Soc Psychol 68:109–113.

Social hierarchies have strong transsituational features but are not monolithic, as shown by the behavior of three species of monkeys in two settings.

1606. Blum G: Defense preferences among university students in Denmark, France, Germany, and Israel. J Proj Tech Pers Assessment 28:13–19.

A follow-up study of male students indicates as much within-group variability as between-group variability for defense modes with some national differences. Danes prefer avoidance while the French prefer intellectualization.

1607. Bock PK: Patterns of illegitimacy on a Canadian Indian reserve: 1860–1960. J Marriage Fam 26:142–148.

Fluctuations in the number of illegitimate births on an Indian reserve are the result of structural factors of changing socioeconomic conditions that affect community integration and thus affect adherence to norms.

1608. Bodarky CJ: Chaperonage and the Puerto Rican middle class. J Marriage Family 26:347–348.

Although the custom has been relaxed, attitudes toward chaperonage are still favorable and viewed as functional.

1609. Bolardos AC: Validation of the Maudsley Personality Inventory in Chile. Br J Soc Clin Psychol 3:148.

Results from normal and neurotic subjects are consistent with predictions from the original MPI theory.

1610. Botha E: Some value differences among adults and children in South Africa. J Soc Psychol 63:241–248.

Low sustentative value scores are linked with higher standards of living and vice versa. Adults of two colored groups score higher on benevolence category than the children in general of the white groups. Malevolence and religious scores are low through all groups. An adult Afrikaans group and an adult Bantu group, two opposites in power, differ significantly on six of seven value categories, and these differences increase with age.

1611. Boyer LB: Psychological problems of a group of Apaches: alcoholic hallucinosis and latent homosexuality among typical men. Psychoanal Study Society 3:203–277.

The acculturative difficulties and traumatic experiences during infancy are manifest in personal identity problems.

1612. Boyer LB, Boyce RM, Brawer FB, Kawai H, Klopfer B: Apache age groups. J Proj Tech Pers Assessment 28:397–402.

Rorschach protocols, in conjunction with anthropological and psychoanalytic observations, demonstrate that acculturative effects are less disruptive to personalities of old-aged traditionalists than to young and middle-aged Mescalero and Chiricahua Apaches.

1613. Boyer LB, Klopfer B, Brawer FB, Kawai H: Comparisons of the shamans and pseudo-shamans of the Apaches of the Mescalero Indian Reservation. J Proj Tech Pers Assessment 28:173–180.

Shamans possess hysterical personality features, show a high degree of reality testing potential, sharper awareness of peculiarities, and a capacity to regress in the ego's service. Pseudoshamans, lacking the prominent shamanistic characteristics and marginal to Apache norm groups, are unfulfilled personalities.

1614. Brody EB: Color and identity conflict in young boys: observations of white mothers and sons in urban Baltimore. Arch Gen Psychiatry 10:354–360.

Growing up in a segregated community contributes to the development of problems in self-perception in majority-group children insofar as minority-group individuals come to represent fearful or unacceptable aspects of themselves.

1615. Brody EB: Some conceptual and methodological issues involved in research on society, culture and mental illness. J Nerv Ment Dis 139:62–74.

Attention must be given to social-control mechanisms, institutionalized behavior patterns, social status and role, influence of sociocultural factors upon the doctor and patient, and cross-cultural comparison of behavior in assessing the nature of the research.

1616. Cowen EL, Frankel G: The social desirability of trait-descriptive terms: applications to a French sample. J Soc Psychol 63:233–239.

Although there are some stylistic differences, there is a high degree of constancy across American, French, and Japanese samples in the relative ordering of adjectives describing properties of social desirability. This indicates the constancy of good and bad perceptions in modern societies.

1617. Davies ADM: Season of birth, intelligence and personality measures. Br J Psychol 55:475–476.

In a population of normal adults, season of birth has no effect on two intelligence tests or two measures of personality.

1618. Derbyshire RL, Brody EB: Marginality, identity and behaviour in the American Negro: a functional analysis. Int J Soc Psychiatry 10:7–13.

The "marginal" Negro is unacceptable both to the white social world, which sees him as a nonconformist, and to the Negro social world, from which he has become alienated because of his upward strivings. The consequent problem in self-definition, which is a function of his varying perceptions of those aspects of the white social world with which he comes into contact, constitutes an important aspect of his marginal state.

1619. Dien DS, Vinacke WE: Self-concept and parental identification of young adults with mixed Caucasian-Japanese parentage. J Abnorm Soc Psychol 68:463–466.

Males, but not females, of mixed parentage have smaller self-ideal and overall score discrepancy than those of homogeneous parentage. Self-concept is correlated with youth's concept of the same sex parent.

1620. Domey RG, Duckworth JE, Morandi AJ: Taxonomies and correlates of physiques. Psychol Bull 62:411–426.

There is probably closer correspondence between anthropometric data and function than is reported in the literature. Taxonomies may be improved by various techniques.

1621. Dunham HW: Social class and schizophrenia. Am J Orthopsychiatry 34:634–642.

There is a heavy concentration of schizophrenics in the lowest among five social classes; however, there are no significant differences in its incidence among the other four classes.

1622. Ervin S: Language and TAT content in bilinguals. J Abnorm Soc Psychol 68:500–507.

Achievement, aggression, and autonomy-withdrawal themes shift with language for French-Canadian bilinguals in two TAT sessions.

1623. Foa UG: Cross-cultural similarity and difference in interpersonal behavior. J Abnorm Soc Psychol 68:517.

Cross-cultural distinctions between European Israelis and Mideast Israelis may be traced to socialization sequences of the development of interpersonal concepts and cultural values.

1624. Fried M: Effects of social change on mental health. Am J Orthopsychiatry 34:3–28.

Mental health is inherent not in the individual but in the relationship between the individual and his immediate environment. Greater and more widespread well-being relies upon more effectively planned social action and more broadly conceived psychotherapeutic intervention.

1625. Garmize LM, Rychlak JF: Role-play validation of a sociocultural theory of symbolism. J Consult Psychol 28:107–115.

A theory of symbolism in Rorschach content is supported by a study in which students rely upon the same cultural experience that Rorschach analysts rely upon in making hypotheses about personality.

1626. Green HB: Socialization values in the Negro and East Indian subcultures of Trinidad. J Soc Psychol 64:1–20.

Low-income Negro mothers in Trinidad value extrafamily involvement, autonomous independence, and direct expression more than East Indian mothers in Trinidad. Socialization, as the major means of maintaining cultural values, is an important determinant in the perpetuation of cultural disparity.

1627. Grinder RE, Spotts WS, Curti MW: Relationships between (Goodenough Draw-A-Man) test performance and skin color among preadolescent Jamaican children. J Soc Psychol 62:181–188.

When tests are conducted within the middle ranges of social-class strata, equating environmental conditions, measures of skin color, and intelligence are independent for Jamaican children.

1628. Hall C, Domhoff B: Friendliness in dreams. J Soc Psychol 62:309–314.

There is more friendliness in male than female dreams. For male dreamers the highest ratio obtains for friendly interactions with female characters, the lowest ratio for male characters. Older dreamers show the least friendliness for all characters.

1629. Heath DB: Prohibition and post-repeal drinking patterns among the Navaho. Q J Stud Alcohol 25:119–135.

Drinking patterns among the Navaho Indians have shown little change since 1941 despite the repeal of federal and state prohibition laws applicable to Indians during that time. The nature of the drinking population and the composition of the drinking groups remain unchanged.

1630. Himes JS: Some reactions to a hypothetical premarital pregnancy by 100 Negro college women. J Marriage Fam 26:344–347.

Negro attitudes toward illegitimacy are not permissive but tend to follow white middle-class norms.

1631. Himes JS: Some work-related cultural deprivations of lower class Negro youths. J Marriage Fam 26:447–449.

Exclusion of lower-class Negroes from the work force deprives them of relevant work models and affects their job performance.

1632. Howe ES: Three-dimensional structure of ratings of exploratory responses shown by a semantic differential. Psychol Rep 14:187–196.

A broad range of exploratory responses will yield three dimensionality among ratings of this variable. The primary dimension is sufficiently large and variable to make it significant for theoretical approaches to exploratory verbal behavior.

1633. Iwawaki S, Cowen EL: The social desirability of trait-descriptive terms: applications to a Japanese sample. J Soc Psychol 63:199–205.

The Japanese relative ordering of perceived social desirability is similar to American ordering, though less extreme ratings are used than among Americans. The American group shows more variability than the Japanese group.

1634. Iwawaki S, Cowen EL: The social desirability of trait-descriptive terms: further applications to a Japanese sample under a personal set. J Soc Psychol 63:207–214.

The relative ordering of trait terms is highly constant for American and Japanese cultural groups. A personal set of social-desirability ratings produces more variable rating for both groups.

1635. Jalota S: Some data on the Maudsley Personality Inventory in Punjabi. Br J Soc Clin Psychol 3:148.

Neuroticism and extraversion can be measured among East Indian students using the MPI.

1636. Johnston FE: Individual variation in the rate of skeletal maturation between five and eighteen years. Child Dev 35:75–80.

There is no basis for the assumption that if a child is skeletally retarded at 8 years he will be retarded at 10, 12, and so on. The time clock which governs the developmental process in children is an individual one.

1637. Kaplan HB, Boyd I, Bloom SW: Patient culture and the evaluation of self. Psychiatry 27:116–126.

The therapeutic process and the negative image of "the mental patient" influence changes in self-concepts and self-evaluations. The patterns that comprise the patient culture arise in response to the patient's needs and should be carefully studied before structuring of informal aspects of patient life is attempted.

1638. Kiev A, Francis JL: Subud and mental illness: psychiatric illness in a religious sect. Am J Psychother 18:66–78.

Subud is an Indonesian religious sect that mainly attracts middle-class individuals with intellectual and humanist interests. Its aim is to bring people closer to the Divine Spirit through a process of purification. Although Subud may temporarily slow the course of illness in patients with psychological conflicts and provide some relief for their distress, it ultimately contributes to the development of their illnesses through the excessive anxiety and conflict it arouses.

1639. Kitano H: Inter- and intragenerational differences in maternal attitudes towards child rearing. J Soc Psychol 63:215–220.

Discrepancies in child-rearing attitudes between age-generation sets in the same country, and non-significant differences across national boundaries, suggest that common role positions produce attitudes that transcend boundaries while there is a structural conflict based on age within the same country.

1640. Klapman H, Morino I: Conformist or deviant: children's character problems and local culture. Int J Soc Psychiatry 10:276–281.

There is a definite relationship between local culture and psychopathology. Man expresses and channels his drives through culture. Separating deviance and mental illness in each culture is crucial to understanding the problems of the community, as well as those of the individuals residing there.

1641. Klausner SZ: Inferential visibility and sex norms in the Middle East. J Soc Psychol 63:1–29.

The premarital sexual behavior of immigrants from Iraq to Israel tends to approach that of the receiving population. The learning that accompanies this sexual acculturation may be partly accounted for in the concept of inferential visibility.

1642. Klausner SZ: Sacred and profane meanings of blood and alcohol. J Soc Psychol 64:27–43.

The relationship between religious and secular drinking is an indirect one. The association of alcohol in a religious ceremony reflects a sanctity that is symbolically equivalent to the sanctity of blood, especially revealed in severe menstrual taboos. Societies in which blood is very sacred will avoid it in secular situations and have corresponding moderate secular drinking, with use of alcohol in religious situations.

1643. Knox JB: The corporation: some Argentine and American attitudes. J Soc Psychol 63:221–232.

More Argentines believe the government should stimulate or eliminate corporations, while U.S. respondents believe that government should restrict corporations.

1644. Koyano S: Changing family behavior in four Japanese communities. J Marriage Fam 26:149–159.

Urban Japanese families have adopted nuclear family structure but attitudes and values have changed from the rural pattern to a lesser degree.

1645. Kumasaka Y: A culturally-determined mental reaction among the Ainu. Psychiatr Q 38:733–739.

The Imu reaction, a subdivision of the latah syndrome, has shown dramatic decrease among the Ainu in the last quarter century. This is suggestive of a highly sensitive form of mental reaction to a changing environment.

1646. Lambert WE: Cultural comparison of boy's occupational aspirations. Br J Soc Clin Psychol 3:56–65.

Filial aspiration indexes correlate significantly with cultural attitudes toward achievement among 11 cultures.

1647. Lantz D, Stefflre V: Language and cognition revisited. J Abnorm Soc Psychol 68:472–281.

The influence of language on nonverbal behavior is evidenced by the accuracy of communication of color from person to person. Communication accuracy is positively correlated with recognition, but not with naming agreement or brevity of communication.

1648. Laycock F, Caylor JS: Physiques of gifted children and their less gifted siblings. Child Dev 35:63–74.

The standard description of the gifted—generally taller and heavier than others—has ignored the superior home care that may also be theirs. Bright children are not larger than ordinary children from the same homes.

1649. Lesse S: The relationships between socioeconomic and sociopolitical practices and psychotherapeutic techniques. Am J Psychother 18:574–583.

Socioeconomic and sociopolitical factors must be considered in the selection of specific psychotherapeutic techniques. The very nature of a psychotherapeutic technique will aid or hinder a patient in his adaptation to a given economic or political milieu. It would be a gross error to assume that all persons should adjust or should be adjusted by their psychotherapists to their culture.

1650. Lessler K: Cultural and Freudian dimensions of sexual symbols. J Consult Psychol 28:46–53.

Sexual symbols are complex and are sorted by students with respect to the cultural referent, when discernable, and the Freudian referent when the former is minimized.

1651. Levert EM: Drinking in Hawaiian plantation society. Q J Stud Alcohol 25:689–713.

Difference in drinking and changes in drinking patterns among the "Caucasian," Portugese, Puerto Rican, Hawaiian, Japanese, and Filipino ethnic groups in the Hawaiian plantation community appear to be the product of culturally persistent patterns of drinking, position in the social structure, psychic stress, group interaction, and social control. Except for Hawaiians, the number of beverages drunk by a group is a measure of their acculturation, secularization, and range of social participation acquired by their social status.

1652. Levitt M, Rubenstein B: Some observations on the relationship between cultural variants and emotional disorders. Am J Orthopsychiatry 34:423–435.

The increasing "absurdity" of life results in little communication among family members, lack of love, and an increase in fantasy as a place to hide. The child-centered world of permissive child rearing fosters the demise of parental influence, degrades the parental role, and denies children parents upon whom they can depend.

1653. Locke KD, Locke EA, Morgan GA, Zimmerman RR: Dimensions of social interactions among infant Rhesus monkeys. Psychol Rep 15:339–349.

In infant monkeys, dominance and submission are independent rather than opposite poles of a single dimension. In contrast to studies of interpersonal behavior among humans, in infant monkeys there is no evidence of a dimension of love-hostility. Individual differences in behavior cannot be explained consistently by differences in sex, age, or weight.

1654. Low WD, Chan ST, Chang KSF, Lee MMC: Skeletal maturation of Southern Chinese children. Child Dev 35:1313–1336.

Skeletally more advanced children reach their adult size at earlier ages than the skeletally less mature children. Children from the high socioeconomic stratum are skeletally more advanced than children from other socioeconomic groups.

1655. McCaldon RJ: Aggression. Can Psychiatr Assoc J 9:502–511.

The Dobu and Mundugumor of New Guinea exhibit psychosocially conditioned hostile aggressiveness. It may not be that the will to destroy drives us but rather the will to live forces us to destroy.

1656. McGinnies E: Attitudes toward civil liberties among Japanese and American university students. J Psychol 58:177–186.

Japanese youth show greater concern with civil liberties than American youth, despite the authoritarian political atmosphere of Japan's recent history.

1657. McMichael RE, Grinder RE: Guilt and resistance to temptation in Japanese- and white-Americans. J Soc Psychol 64:217–223.

Although Japanese-Americans may depict guilt in different ways from American children, there is a basic similarity in conscience development in terms of resistance to temptation and guilt responses between the two groups. This similarity may be due to the effect of American culture on the former.

1658. Macoby M, Modiana N, Lander P: Games and social character in a Mexican village. Psychiatry 27:150–162.

The roots of authoritarian, noncooperative attitudes and conflicts between the sexes can be explored through the study of play and games based on a sociopsychological analysis. New games will not reform character and society, but they appear to support the process of culture change.

1659. Maguigad L: Psychiatry in the Philippines. Am J Psychiatry 121:21–25.

The character structure and culture of the Filipino people affect the incidence and expression of mental disorders.

1660. Masserman J, Wechkin S, Terris W: Altruistic behavior in Rhesus monkeys. Am J Psychiatry 121:584–585.

Most rhesus monkeys refrain from operating a device for securing food if this causes another monkey to suffer an electric shock. Such "succorance" behavior is observable throughout the animal kingdom and deserves greater cognizance in psychiatric theory and therapy.

1661. Mead M: Cultural factors in the case and prevention of pathological homicide. Bull Menninger Clin 28:11–22.

Cultural taboos and torturing living creatures are reinforced during childhood. Violent punishment for breaking these taboos can be as disastrous as no punishment. Children must be provided with cultural cues and taught appropriate behavior toward living animals.

1662. Melikian LH: The use of selected TAT cards among Arab university students: a cross-cultural study. J Soc Psychol 62:3–19.

Ten selected TAT cards have generally equal stimulus value for both Arab and American students. Significant differences in the frequencies of themes for each card may be considered principally in terms of cultural differences.

1663. Mintz NL, Schwartz DT: Urban ecology and psychosis: community factors in the incidence of schizophrenia and manic-depression among Italians in greater Boston. Int J Soc Psychiatry 10:101–118.

The incidence of both schizophrenia and manic-depression among Italians is inversely related to the density of Italians in greater Boston communities. There is no correlation between community incidence of psychosis and community monthly rental.

1664. Morgenthaler F, Parin P: Typical forms of transference among West Africans. Int J Psychoanal 45:446–449.

The Dogon ego takes advantage of differentiated oral tendencies. All subjects show good capacity for transference and mechanisms which permit identification entry and re-emergence with the analyst.

1665. Muensterberger W: Remarks on the function of mythology. Psychoanal Stud Society 3:94–97.

Mythology controls instinctual drives, organizes ego and superego, and provides a stabilizing influence on the individual and his group.

1666. Naka S, Kawakita Y: Psychiatry in Japanese culture. Dis Nerv Syst 25:298–304.

Religion, habits and customs, and housing influence the personality structure of the Japanese. As Japan becomes increasingly westernized the resulting profound changes are associated with much emotional disturbance and many mental problems.

1667. Narain D: Growing up in India. Fam Process 3:127–154.

Review of the literature on child rearing, socialization, and family relationships and the nuclear and joint family will further understanding of the family in India.

1668. Nelson LG, Tadlock LD, Dawes JW, Hipple JL, Jetmalani NB: Screening for emotionally disturbed students in an Indian boarding school: experience with the Cornell Medical Index Health Questionnaire. Am J Psychiatry 120:1155–1159.

Forty-seven adolescent Indian boarding-school students were administered the Cornell Medical Index Health Questionnaire to determine its validity. The value of the CMI in detecting psychoanalytic disturbance was confirmed. The Cornell Medical Index Health Questionnaire is valid in detecting psychiatric disturbances among adolescent Eskimo boarding-school students.

1669. Opler MK: Socio-cultural roots of emotional illness. Psychosomatics 5:55–58.

Mental illness is a social reality. The issue is no longer whether culture influences mental health epidemiology, but rather, how does culture help or harm in each milieu.

1670. Parin P, Morgenthaler F: Ego and orality in the analysis of West Africans. Psychoanal Study Society 3:197–202.

A summary of the psychodynamics of adult Dogons and an evaluation of psychoanalytic techniques provide further information on ego functions and instinctual drives.

1671. Parsons A: Is the Oedipus complex universal? The Jones-Malinowski debate revisited and a South Italian "nuclear complex." Psychoanal Study Society 3:278–328.

Comparison of a South Italian nuclear family complex to Freud's patriarchal and the Trobriand matrilineal case raises theoretical and methodological questions. The question of the universality of the Oedipus complex is not a meaningful one.

1672. Perry HS: Nature in the world view of the Russian nation: a psychological and cultural analysis. Psychiatry 27:28–51.

Russia's world view of the sea, the ocean, and the sky is different from our own. Understanding of this difference is important to an analysis of our own national behavior vis-à-vis Russian national behavior since both affect the well-being of the international community.

1673. Pitfield M, Oppenheim AN: Child rearing attitudes of mothers of psychotic children. J Child Psychol Psychiatry 5:51–57.

In terms of stated attitudes, mothers of mongol children are more detached and somewhat stricter than mothers of normal children, whereas mothers of psychotic children are more lax, indulgent, and more uncertain of their attitudes.

1674. Polidora VJ, Schneider IJ: Preferences of monkeys for automatically dispensable rewards. Psychol Rep 15:55–64.

A paired-comparison method provides a better estimate of initial preference in rhesus monkeys than does an operant response rate procedure.

1675. Prince RH, Wittkower ED: The care of the mentally ill in a changing culture (Nigeria). Am J Psychother 18:644–648.

The Yoruba of West Africa deal with the mentally ill through the utilization of native healers. Currently modern psychiatric facilities are becoming available, although acceptance of modern treatment procedures in psychiatry is bound up with a shift from religio-magic thinking to pragmatic thinking, which will take a long time to materialize.

1676. Rabin AI: Kibbutz mothers view "collective education." Am J Orthopsychiatry 34:140–142.

Most kibbutz mothers fully accept collective education. Those who indicate ambivalence or negative overall attitudes are concerned with separation from, and insufficient contact with, their children. "Maternal drive" seems to be gratified by kibbutz education and criticism of it may be culturally bound.

1677. Rainwater L: Marital sexuality in four cultures of poverty. J Marriage Fam 26:457–466.

Marital relations in poverty groups in the U.S., England, Puerto Rico, and Mexico are characterized by a high degree of role segregation with consequent dissatisfaction of wives, and lack of close sexual relationship.

1678. Rank O, Sachs H: The significance of psychoanalysis for the humanities. Am Imago 21:6–134.

The unconscious and its expressed forms may be applied to the study of myths, legends, religion, ethnology, linguistics, art, ethics, and law.

1679. Reece MM: Masculinity and femininity: a factor analytic study. Psychol Rep 14:123–139.

The current college stereotype of the male is of strength but not harshness. The ideal female is regarded as vigorous, industrious, but delicate and graceful. There is no support for the notion that the behavior of females in our culture is becoming more assertive and aggressive in the attempt to attain a status equal to males.

1680. Rinder ID: New directions and an old problem: the definition of normality. Psychiatry 27:107–115.

An understanding of diverse sociocultural systems and their characterological requirements confuses the delineation of any single ideal type of positive mental health; rather, an array of types is required by an array of systems representing stages of social and technological development.

1681. Roheim G: The Western tribes of Central Australia: the alknarintja. Psychoanal Study Society 3:173–198.

The worldly and ritual roles of the *alknarintja,* a mythical and sometimes real female character, have psychodynamic implications.

1682. Rothenberg A: Puerto Rico and aggression. Am J Psychiatry 120:962–970.

Sociocultural and psychoanalytic interpretations can explain why the Puerto Rican people have difficulty in dealing with aggressive impulses.

1683. Rule C: A biologically based theory of human behavior and its implications for psychiatry. Am J Psychiatry 121:344–352.

Study of the social behavior of nonhuman primates leads to speculations about a biologically rooted theory of human behavior. The three fundamental patterns of social behavior that lead to the maturation of the individual are mothering behavior, peer or play behavior, and reproductive behavior.

1684. Scheflen AE: The significance of posture in communication systems. Psychiatry 27:316–331.

According to the level of behavior, postures indicate the beginnings and endings of units of communicative behavior, the ways in which participants are related to each other, and the steps in a "program." They have great value in identifying the participants' location in a flow of social events and the nature of their relationships.

1685. Seay B, Alexander BK, Harlow HF: Maternal behavior of socially deprived Rhesus monkeys. J Abnorm Soc Psychol 68:345–354.

Socially deprived monkeys become very inadequate mothers, although their offspring show normal development. Normal maternal care is manifest by three inadequate mothers for their second offspring.

1686. Schorr AL: The nonculture of poverty. Am J Orthopsychiatry 34:907–912.

A realistic response to the facts of poverty is found in the attitudes prevalent in poverty. However, as demonstrated by the civil-rights movements, these attitudes contain unrecognized affirmatives that can be utilized in an effective manner in altered circumstances.

1687. Seguin CA: The theory and practice of psychiatry in Peru. Am J Psychother 18:188–211.

Each of Peru's three regions has its own social organization and a way of life. *Susto* is a syndrome found on the sierra and in the selva, and is often treated by the magic of the curandero. Other special syndromes include *coqueo* and psychosomatic disadaptation syndrome.

1688. Seward GH: Sex identity and the social order. J Nerv Ment Dis 139:126–136.

Our current society has built value conflicts into the very definition of the sex roles, resulting in serious confusions in sex identity. It behooves the psychiatric worker to become aware of the underlying cultural factors.

1689. Shell SA, O'Mally JM, Johnsbard KW: The semantic differential and inferred identification. Psychol Rep 14:547–558.

Semantic differential can be used to measure difference between normal and neurotic groups using a "distance from positive concept" interpretation.

1690. Skeels DR: Eros and Thantos in Nez Percé river mythology. Am Imago 21:103–110.

River myths, an ambivalent psychological bipolarity symbol for the Nez Percé, demonstrate that the death instinct is as basic as the love instinct. Water is the symbol of the womb, and the river is ultimately destructive.

1691. Skolnick A: Some psychiatric aspects of the "new Soviet child." Bull Menninger Clin 28:120–144.

Russian psychotherapy attempts to reach the emotionally disturbed individual with ego strengthening measures, often supplied by mobilization of the collective. It is important to recognize that character changes have been initiated in Russia, to follow their continuing development, and to anticipate the reciprocal effect of such altered personalities upon the character of Russian society.

1692. Sobel R, Ingalls A: Resistance to treatment: explorations of the patient's sick role. Am J Psychother 18:562–573.

The medical role model of patient behavior calls for passive, submissive, and dependent behavior while the psychiatric role model calls for more independence, activity, and self-direction. State hospital patients follow the medical role model, whereas private psychiatric patients are closer to the psychiatric role model.

1693. Sommers VS: The impact of dual-cultural membership on identity. Psychiatry 27:332–344.

There is an intimate interdependence and cross influence of psychological and sociocultural processes in personality functioning, particularly with regard to identity disorders. A depreciated or deceptive self-image can become the keystone of an entire defense system.

1694. Stern MM: Ego psychology, myth and rite: remarks about the relationship of the individual and the group. Psychoanal Study Society 3:71–93.

Prehistoric man's poor bodily and mental capabilities gave rise to group formation. Myth and ritual originated in attempts to control reality by the group. These attempts had many psychodynamic ego developmental consequences for man.

1695. Sweeney DR, Zegers RT, Collins WE: Color blindness in male Negro children. J Soc Psychol 62:85–91.

Negro populations reveal a greater incidence of blue-yellow color defectives than Caucasian populations, and the age factor may be important in color-vision screening tests.

1696. Thaver F, Arkoff A, Elkind L: Conceptions of mental health in several Asian and American groups. J Soc Psychol 62:21–27.

Two American groups, students and psychologists, and four Asian student groups (Chinese, Japanese, Filipino, and Thai) reveal significant differences across cultures on conceptions of mental health. The greatest discrepancy between Americans and Asians is reflected in the latter's beliefs that mental health can be achieved through will power and pleasant thoughts, while the former rejects the efficacy of will power in this realm.

1697. Varela JA: A cross-cultural replication of an experiment involving birth order. J Abnorm Soc Psychol 68:456–457.

First-born Uruguayan students tend to volunteer for psychological experiments more than later borns. The potential impact of this phenomenon on experimental sample structure should not be ignored.

1698. Vaughn GM: The effect of ethnic grouping of the experimentor upon children's responses to tests of an ethnic nature. Br J Soc Clin Psychol 3:66–70.

The defensive reaction of older Maori children who favor white figures on an attitude test when the experimenter is white indicates that interviewers of their own race should be an automatic control in testing.

1699. Walters RH: On the high-magnitude theory of aggression. Child Dev 35:303–304.

The high-magnitude theory of aggression does not involve the claim that any and every high-magnitude response will be classified as aggressive; it claims only that the production of high-magnitude responses increases the probability that the agent will be regarded as behaving in an aggressive manner.

1700. Waters E, Crandall VJ: Social class and observed maternal behavior from 1940 to 1960. Child Dev 35:1021–1032.

Coercive maternal behavior is class linked: the higher the family social status, the less likely mothers are to employ coercive suggestions, restrictive regulations, or severe penalties for misbehaviors. The current trend is away from such coercive maternal behavior.

1701. Wright BR: Social aspects of change in the Chinese family pattern in Hong Kong. J Soc Psychol 63:31–39.

The quest for higher education is accelerating cultural modifications taking place in Hong Kong. The atmosphere of schools and the traditional family patterns present a cultural conflict for the Chinese student. Disruption of the extended family and movement away from dependence on the family are accompanied by social mobility and development.

1702. Zaidi SMH: National stereotypes of university students in Karachi. J Soc Psychol 63:73–85.

Students in Karachi rate Arabs most favorably, the Japanese second, and the Indians least favorably. An increased percentage of bad traits assigned to Americans may be explained in terms of American lack of sympathy to Pakistan's defense programs. The only bad trait assigned to own cultural group is laziness, which may be a carryover from earlier political admonitions with respect to British domination.

1965

1703. Aall-Jilek LM: Epilepsy in the Wapogoro tribe in Tanganyika. Acta Psychiatr Scand 41: 57–86.

Epilepsy has high prevalence and is recognized as a disease by the Wapogoro people, who follow preventative and curative measures as prescribed by native doctors.

1704. Arthur AZ: Clinical use of the semantic differential. J Clin Psychol 21:337–338.

The routine clinical use of the semantic differential is limited by the necessity of complex calculations and procedures for a view of the semantic space. A simple method is to plot the average scores of the dimensions (usually evaluation, potency, and activity) directly on a chart.

1705. Asuni T: Suicide in Western Nigeria. Int J Psychiatry 1:52–63.

Nigeria, with the lowest world reported suicide rate, demonstrates a greater suicide rate in rural rather than urban areas, and among persons who have remained in their native settings.

1706. Atzet J, Gerard HB: A study of phonetic symbolism among native Navaho speakers. J Pers Soc Psychol 1:524–527.

Navahos are unable to match antonyms with equivalents provided by Chinese and Hindi informants.

1707. Baasher T: Treatment and prevention of psychosomatic disorders: psychosomatic diseases in East Africa. Am J Psychiatry 121:1095–1102.

Symbolic expression of the psychosomatic concept is deeply enmeshed in the culture of certain East African countries as revealed by epidemiological psychiatric studies and scientific therapeutic practices.

1708. Badri MB: The use of finger drawings in measuring the Goodenough quotient of culturally deprived Sudanese children. J Psychol 59:333–334.

Five-point differences in the Draw-A-Man IQ indicate that the hypothesis, rural children's performance may be handicapped by the use of the unfamiliar pencil, deserves more consideration.

1709. Barnett LD: The kibbutz as a child-rearing system: a review of the literature. J Marriage Fam 27:348–349.

Research evidence indicates no marked differences in deviant behavior rates between individuals reared in conjugal families or in Israeli kibbutzim.

1710. Bender D: The development of French anthropology. J Hist Behav Sciences 1:139–151.

Anthropology in France, under the influence of Levi-Straus, has not yet completely integrated physical anthropology and prehistory with ethnology.

1711. Berrien FK: Japanese vs. American values. J Soc Psychol 65:181–191.

Japanese personal values are not much different from those that characterized the post-Meiji era Japanese. These retained values are not necessarily incompatible with a nominal democracy comparable to that of the U.S.

1712. Boyer LB: Stone as a symbol in Apache mythology. Am Imago 22:14–39.

Variations of two myths reflect pre-oedipal and oedipal conflicts arising from reported Apache child-rearing practices. They illustrate the multifaceted symbolism of the stone (father, labia, teeth, penis).

1713. Boyer LB, Klopfer B, Boyer RM, Brawer FB, Kawai H: Effects of acculturation on the personality traits of the old people of the Mescalero and Chiricahua Apaches. Int J Soc Psychiatry

Rorschach responses of Apaches reveal significant perceptual and cognitive differences between the old Mescaleros and Chiricahuas. The Mescaleros are more secure in their personal identities and more capable of establishing meaningful object relationships than the Chiricahuas, whose reactions to the test stimuli are more like those expected from American whites.

1714. Broderick CB: Social heterosexual development among urban Negroes and whites. J Marriage Fam 27:200–203.

Negro boys show a higher level of preadolescent heterosexual interest and disenchantment with the concept of marriage than white boys of 10–13 years, possibly as a result of cultural influences.

1715. Cameron A, Storm T: Achievement motivation in Canadian Indian, middle- and working-class children. Psychol Rep 16:459–463.

There is a significant interaction between subculture and reward condition. Middle-class whites perform better than Indian or working-class white children under nonmaterial reward but not under material reward. Middle-class children differ from the other groups in achievement motivation measures.

1716. Cawte JE: Ethnopsychiatry in Central Australia. I: traditional illnesses in the Eastern Aranda people. Br J Psychiatry 111:1069–1077.

An unusual incidence of mental disturbance as reported among the Yowera of Central Australia may be considered in terms of traditional illnesses (associated with aboriginal belief) and transitional illnesses (arising from acculturative pressures).

1717. Cawte JE, Kidson MA: Ethnopsychiatry in Central Australia. II: the evolution of illness in a Walbiri lineage. Br J Psychiatry 111:1079–1085.

The evolution in patterns of mental illness occurring in aboriginal lineages in Central Australia may reflect the historical adaptational process of aborigines to the white man.

1718. Cerny J: Chinese Psychiatry. Int J Psychiatry 1:229–239.

Psychiatry in Mainland China emphasizes prevention and makes extensive use of traditional medical techniques in addition to modern scientific treatment.

1719. Chang SC: The cultural context of Japanese psychiatry and psychotherapy. Am J Psychother 19:593–606.

Certain Japanese clinical entities, such as anthropophobia, homosexuality and psychopathy, and Morita psychotherapy, can be better appreciated by understanding the relationship among mental illness, psychotherapy, and culture in Japan.

1720. Coles R: The lives of migrant farmers. Am J Psychiatry 122:271–285.

Migrants are suspicious and guarded toward intruders, but they are exceptionally close knit with their young children, who progressively learn a sense of their own weakness and inadequacy. The physical health of migrants is poor, and they are especially susceptible to psychiatric symptoms.

1721. Coles R: Observation or participation: the problems of psychiatric research on social issues. J Nerv Ment Dis 141:274–284.

Psychiatric participation in social issues is desirable if it is done mindful of the daily influence of social, political, and economic institutions upon human beings.

1722. Croog SH, New PKM: Knowledge of grandfather's occupation: clues to American kinship structure. J Marriage Fam 27:69–77.

Differences in knowledge of grandfather's occupation reflect kindred orientations that vary according to social status.

1723. Dai B: Culture and delusional systems of some Chinese patients. Int J Soc Psychiatry 11: 59–69.

The delusional systems of Chinese patients are attempts to satisfy biosocial needs and preserve human identity under the stress of culture conflict. They are simply an attempt to disguise gratification of instinctive drives.

1724. Deutsch M: The role of social class in language development and cognition. Am J Orthopsychiatry 35:78–88.

Lower-class and minority-group status are associated with poorer language functioning. This association is stronger for fifth than for first-grade children indicating that remedial and enrichment programs should be introduced at the earliest possible time in order to arrest the cumulative deficit.

1725. Devereux G: The voices of children: psychocultural obstacles to therapeutic communications. Am J Psychother 19:4–19.

Adults have great difficulty in truly understanding the communications of children. Through a discontinuity in cultural conditioning, we teach our children childish behavior.

1726. Diers CJ: Social-desirability ratings of personality items by three subcultural groups. J Soc Psychol 67:97–104.

Similarities in value judgment between social classes across nationalities may be greater than across social classes within a nation. Canadian and American students show no differences in their need rating. Hungarian immigrants to Canada value order above other needs and highly value aggression.

1727. Doob L: Exploring eidetic imagery among the Kamba of Central Kenya. J Soc Psychol 67: 3–22.

Twenty percent of Kamba adolescents and adults possess eidetic imagery, an incidence that is higher than found in the West, but similar to an Ibo sample. Almost all Kamba report having picture imagery, which is claimed to be useful in daily life. Eidetic imagery may help people recall the past more vividly, but not more accurately.

1728. Dovenmuehle RH, McGough WE: Aging, culture and affect: predisposing factors. Int J Soc Psychiatry 11:138–146.

Negro and lower-class subjects have a higher incidence of disabling depression than commonly assumed. Age makes no significant difference in the older group, but the incidence of depression is higher than would be expected in younger individuals.

1729. Dow TE: Social class and reaction to physical disability. Psychol Rep 17:39–62.

There is no consistent social-class bias in either the reaction to disability or the emphasis attached to physique.

1730. Eisenberg L, Neubauer PB: Mental health issues in Israeli collectives: kibbutzim. J Am Acad Child Psychiatry 4:426–442.

The kibbutz society is a remarkable human success. Kibbutz life, with its well-defined society and ideology, its distinct structure, and clearly outlined value systems that permit the isolation of factors, presents an extraordinary opportunity for research.

1731. Farnsworth PR: A social effect on the perception of facial resemblance. J Soc Psychol 65: 222–223.

Tests of facial resemblance of Caucasian to Japanese and Chinese faces, conducted in 1942 and 1962, indicate that perception of resemblance may be affected by the degree of friendliness toward the racial group in question.

1732. Fong SLM: Cultural influences in the perception of people: the case of Chinese in America. Br J Soc Clin Psychol 4:110–113.

As Chinese students become more assimilated to Western culture and removed from their ethnic background, there is an increase in internalization of Western affective-cognitive norms.

1733. Freed DX: Ethnic identification of hospitalized Jewish psychiatric patients: an exploratory study. Int J Soc Psychiatry 11:110–115.

When Jewish nonpsychiatric patients are compared with Jewish psychiatric patients, significant differences between the groups are not found on the Geismar's Scale of Ethnic Identification and Srole's Anomie Scale. The psychiatric patients are more defensive and tend to overstress their Jewish identity.

1734. Gallagher OR: Drinking problems of tribal Bihar. Q J Stud Alcohol 26:617–628.

The present-day emphasis by the Oraon and other Bihar tribes is on drinking to get drunk, on social rather than ritual drinking. Under conditions of full employment, drinking is limited to specific ceremonial occasions and to weekend social drinking.

1735. Glicksman M, Wohl J: Expressed values of Burmese and American university students. J Soc Psychol 65:17–25.

Essays written by business students reveal that Americans use the categories of economic security, marriage and children, and religion, while Burmese use education and social concern value categories.

1736. Gordon EB: Mentally ill West Indian immigrants. Br J Psychiatry 111:877–887.

The reactive nature of mental illness among West Indian immigrants is substantiated by a low incidence of psychiatric disorder prior to migration and by predominantly negative family histories.

1737. Gough HG: Cross-cultural validation of a measure of asocial behavior. Psychol Rep 17:379–387.

Use of the socialization scale of the California Personality Inventory in eight languages in ten countries indicates a significant difference in every

instance. The inventory places a theoretical emphasis on folk concepts found in all cultures and societies.

1738. Green RF, Goldfried MR: On the bipolarity of semantic space. Psychol Monographs 79:1–21.

Analysis of concept ratings on a single adjective form of the semantic differential fails to indicate the model of semantic space described by Osgood and his associates. Some adjective pairs may be more functionally bipolar than others.

1739. Guterman RD: Notes from the field: testing Eskimos in Alaska. Am J Orthopsychiatry 35:798–801.

In light of the rapid change in population characteristics it seems wiser to adapt current testing instruments rather than to develop tests appropriate to contemporary Eskimos.

1740. Hagstron WO, Hadden JK: Sentiment and kinship terminology in American society. J Marriage Fam 27:324–332.

Children do not tend to use intimate address terms for opposite-sex parents, nor are sentiments highly correlated with preferred address terms. Uncles and aunts are more likely to be addressed by kin terms by females if they are mother's siblings and not well liked.

1741. Hallowell AI: The history of anthropology as an anthropological problem. J Hist Behav Sciences 1:24–38.

The events and conditions that led up to the period when anthropological questions became the concern of special disciplines require historical investigation as an anthropological problem.

1742. Hamer JH: Acculturation stress and the functions of alcohol among the Forest Potawatomi. Q J Stud Alcohol 26:285–302.

The Forest Potawatomi, subjected to the pressures of acculturation stress, have institutionalized drinking to the point where it constitutes an outlet for certain psychological needs and provides a means of repatterning social functions. The adaptive aspects of heavy and frequent consumption of alcohol are recognized by these people as outweighing the social costs.

1743. Harmsworth HC: Family structure on the Fort Hall Indian reservation. Fam Life Coordinator 14:7–9.

The functions served by Fort Hall family structure include use of kinship ties in times of need, mediation between individual and the community, and a bulwark against acculturation.

1744. Heise DR: Semantic differential profiles for 1,000 most frequent English words. Psychol Monographs 79:1–31.

A dictionary includes semantic differential factor scores on evaluation, potency, and activity dimensions for 1,000 English words, as well as a list of derived scores (polarization, N affiliation, and N achievement).

1745. Helper MM, Garfield SL: Use of the semantic differential to study acculturation in American Indian adolescents. J Pers Soc Psychol 2:817–822.

Semantic differences can be used to assess relative acculturation.

1746. Johnson DL, Sikes MP: Rorschach and TAT responses of Negro, Mexican-American and Anglo psychiatric patients. J Proj Tech Pers Assessment 29:183–188.

Rorschach tests measure group differences in hostility. The persistence of cultural values is illustrated by Mexican-American group differences, especially for perception of family themes.

1747. Joshi V: Personality profiles in industrial and preindustrial cultures: a TAT study. J Soc Psychol 66:101–111.

The primary differences between an educated urban sample and uneducated rural sample in India lie in the areas of parental authority, interpersonal relations, family roles, and relationships. The former are insecure, nonconformist, experimental, and progressive, while the latter are secure, conformist, conventional, and resistant to change.

1748. Kaffman M: A comparison of psychopathology: Israeli children from kibbutz and from urban surroundings. Am J Orthopsychiatry 35:509–520.

With the exception of psychopathic disturbances that do not appear in the kibbutz group, there is a surprisingly similar distribution and percentage of diagnostic entities among kibbutz and nonkibbutz disturbed children. Emotional pathology is consistently less severe among kibbutz children in the majority of diagnostic categories.

1749. Kaufmann H: Definitions and methodology in the study of aggression. Psychol Bull 64:351–364.

The study of the form of social interaction termed *aggression* has been hampered by major conceptual difficulties. A flowchart studying aggression as the end result of a variety of stimuli, dispositional, and reward variables may prove helpful.

1750. Kaunitz PE, Tec L: Unsuccessful initiation rites among adolescent boys. J Nerv Ment Dis 140:175–179.

Operation of automobiles in a maladaptive manner by adolescent boys, in contrast to initiation rites in primitive societies, may represent attempts to overcome the fear of injury and to indicate strength and valor. Through such activities, the wish is expressed for the powerful genital hidden within the frail exterior.

1751. Kiev A: Psychiatric morbidity of West Indian immigrants in an urban practice group. Br J Psychiatry 111:51–56.

West Indian immigrants in London share common concepts and attitudes toward medical care with Englishmen.

1752. Kiev A: The study of folk psychiatry. Int J Psychiatry 1:524–540.

Folk therapeutic methods are relative to culturally prescribed relationships among patient, healer, and group. The study of folk beliefs and treatment aids the Western psychiatrist in understanding his own therapy systems.

1753. Kline LY: The psychotherapy of two Nigerian students. Am J Psychother 19:641–649.

The strongly patriarchal nature of the Nigerian family might account for the importance of "oedipal" conflicts in that culture.

1754. Langness LL: Hysterical psychosis in the New Guinea Highlands: a Bena Bena example. Psychiatry 28:258–277.

The Bena Bena and the Gururumba differ with respect to their interpretation of and reaction to psychotic behavior. The Bena lack insight into the behavior, provide no special ritual to reintegrate the person after an attack, and stress its being outside the realm of human control.

1755. Leon RL: Maladaptive interaction between Bureau of Indian Affairs staff and Indian clients. Am J Orthopsychiatry 35:723–728.

Authoritarian responses from Bureau of Indian Affairs staff in reaction to Indian passive-aggressive behavior can defeat present-day program goals. To break this maladaptive circular interaction the agency must consciously and deliberately reverse the authority pattern.

1756. Lewis L: Terms of address for parents and some clues about social relationships in the American family. Fam Coordinator 14:43–46.

American terms of address, as an index of affective quality of social relationships, are determined by sex of speaker and social context (casual, neutral, intimate, and conflict) rather than sociological variables.

1757. Lindgren HC, Lindgren F: Creativity, brainstorming, and orneriness. J Soc Psychol 67:23–30.

Group brainstorming may facilitate creativity among English-speaking Lebanese students. Some positive correlations between self-reported symmetrical preference and creativity obtain for the U.S. but not for Middle Eastern students.

1758. McEwan PJW: Climate and intelligence. Br J Soc Clin Psychol 4:8–13.

Significant differences in intelligence may be obtained for children from different countries of origin and differing length of ancestral stay in Southern Rhodesia. Higher intelligence is associated with colder countries of origin.

1759. McGinnies E: A cross-cultural comparison of printed communication vs. spoken communication in persuasion. J Psychol 59:1–8.

Contrary to most reports on media effectiveness, printed persuasive communications are more influential for Japanese students than vocal communications.

1760. Maretzki TW: Suicide in Okinawa: preliminary explorations. Int J Soc Psychiatry 11:256–263.

Neurotic suicide is more typical for Okinawa than rational or irrational suicide. Suicides in the younger age group may well be similar in their underlying dynamics to the Japanese type. Women are less affected by the suicidal trend because they can express nurturance needs, as well as aggression, through a religious role not open to men.

1761. Meadow A, Stoker D: Symptomatic behavior of hospitalized patients: a study of Mexican-American and Anglo-American patients. Arch Gen Psychiatry 12:267–277.

Mexican-American females are more acutely and affectively disturbed than Anglos, while the males are more assaultive and alcoholic. Both have a tendency toward catatonic symptomatology.

1762. Miles AL: Some aspects of culture amongst sub-normal hospital patients. Br J Med Psychol 38:171–176.

Informal stratification, inability to form mutual friendships, and conformity to hospital norms are some aspects of culture in mentally handicapped patients.

1763. Melikian L: Sexual symbolism: a cross cultural study. Int J Soc Psychiatry 11:226–229.

The psychoanalytic theory of sexual symbols is valid cross-culturally as determined by the response of Arab boys to a sexual symbolism test.

1764. Mishler EG, Scotch NA: Sociocultural factors in the epidemiology of schizophrenia. Int J Psychiatry 1:258–295.

Greater incidence of schizophrenia is found among the lowest socioeconomic class. No evidence is found with regard to differential rates across cultures or in settings of culture change.

1765. Moss HA: Methodological issues in studying mother-infant interaction. Am J Orthopsychiatry 35:482–486.

Indirect approaches provide highly fallible information about mother-infant relations. Direct observation is a more reliable method, and methodological problems can be allayed through the use of certain tactics.

1766. Nanda PC, Das JP, Mishra HK: Discrimination of geometrical patterns in tribal, rural, and urban children. J Soc Psychol 67:197–200.

Although speed of learning is not significantly different among three groups in India, the total number of subjects failing to discriminate geometric figures is greater among tribal groups and least among urban groups.

1767. Nash J: The father in contemporary culture and current psychological literature. Child Dev 36:261–297.

Western industrial society appears to be decidedly matricentric. The relative neglect of the father in our society may have distorted our understanding of the dynamics of development and have adversely affected the rearing of males.

1768. Nataraj P: Social distance within and between castes and religious groups of college girls. J Soc Psychol 65:135–140.

The Sindhi caste is most distant from other castes, the Brahmins least distant. Social distance is more pronounced among religious groups than among castes in one religious group, with Muslims most distant. Lingayets, Vysyas, Ursus, Hindus, and Jains are more conservative than Muslims, Sindhis, and Vakkaligas.

1769. Orme JE: Ability and season of birth. Br J Psychol 56:471–476.

For subnormal and supernormal adult subjects, in the British Isles, the relationship between season of birth and intelligence holds.

1770. Parhad L: The cultural-social conditions of treatment in a psychiatric out-patient department in Kuwait. Int J Soc Psychiatry 11:14–19.

The cultural background of clinic patients in Kuwait with its restraints on open expression of aggression, particularly in women, is psychodynamically related to the psychosomatic reactions observable in the majority of these patients.

1771. Pavenstedt E: A comparison of the child-rearing environment of upper-lower and very low-lower class families. Am J Orthopsychiatry 35:89–98.

Children raised in stable upper lower-class homes adjust and learn in first grade because of normal personality adjustment. Deviations in personality development among children of "multi-problem" low lower-class families interfere with learning. An altered self-image among low lower-class parents is a necessary prelude to their finding value in their children.

1772. Pavenstedt E: Observations in five Japanese homes. J Am Acad Child Psychiatry 4:413–425.

In Japan the importance of the family has superseded the importance of the individual. Children are offered few avenues for the displacement of aggressive and libidinal drives. Because of their concept of the merging of the individual spirit with the whole, it is difficult for individuals to ever reach the differentiation that is desirable in Western culture.

1773. Piedmont EB: Ethnicity as a variable in mental disorder research. Community Ment Health J 1:91–98.

Research investigating sociocultural variables has paid particular attention to social status and economics. Ethnicity, a concept linked with value systems, is an important, easily operationalized intermediate variable.

1774. Plog SC: The disclosure of self in the United States and Germany. J Soc Psychol 65:193–203.

Americans are more self-revealing than Germans, but there is no sex difference in self-disclosure within each culture.

1775. Posinsky SH: Yurok shamanism. Psychiatr Q 39:227–243.

The Yurok shaman, usually a woman, diagnoses and treats most personal physical and psychological ailments not associated with changing personal status. The formulist functions in rites of passage require extrafamilial ritual direction. Both must undergo training and initiation.

1776. Price-Williams DR: Displacement and orality in Tiv witchcraft. J Soc Psychol 65:1–15.

Among the Tiv of central Nigeria, the blame for illnesses is attributed to an offence by the sick person or to witchcraft. Illness ceremonies function to cure the person, alleviate guilt, and restore imbalances caused by supernatural forces. Tiv socialization practices and folktales reveal a central aggressive theme with emphasis on oral factors. Tension between kinsmen is alleviated by the ceremonies that displace overt kin conflict into the covert realm of supernatural agencies.

1777. Proenza L, Strickland BR: A study of prejudice in Negro and white college students. J Soc Psychol 67:278–281.

Negro students are more favorable toward the concepts "Negro" and "integration" than whites on a semantic differential. The former are also more favorable to the concept "Negro."

1778. Rabbie JM: A cross-cultural comparison of parent-child relationships in the United States and West Germany. Br J Soc Clin Psychol 4:298–310.

American parents are reported by high-school graduates to be less strict and confer more autonomy than German parents. Parental roles are more differentiated in Germany than the U.S. The American mother is more child-achievement directed and the German father more strict than their counterparts.

1779. Rafi AA: The Maudsley Personality Inventory: a cross-cultural study. Br J Soc Clin Psychol 4:266–268.

An Arabic MPI and other tests of Lebanese students reveal a similarity with the original standardization group and absence of notable influence from cultural factors.

1780. Riegel KF: Age and cultural differences as determinants of word associations: suggestions for their analysis. Psychol Rep 16:17–78.

New norms for the Kent-Rosanoff word-association test revive methodological problems in the analysis of developmental and cultural changes. In enumerating the degree of approximation of a simplex the age of subjects is a more important determinant than time of testing.

1781. Reiss IL: The universality of the family: a conceptual analysis. J Marriage Fam 27:443–453.

The nurturant socialization function of the family, not the nuclear family per se, is universal and is a functional prerequisite for human society that must be fulfilled by some small kinship structured group. Cross-cultural, primatological, and studies of mother separation are evidence for this premise.

1782. Rin H: A study of the aetiology of koro in respect to the Chinese concept of illness. Int J Soc Psychiatry 11:7–13.

In China, koro is related to the marked emphasis on orality as well as the basic concept of Chinese sexuality which stems from the male-female principle, yin and yang. Koro is still a geographically localized disease, but it will appear among any people who are deeply steeped in the aforementioned concepts.

1783. Sackett GP: Effects of rearing conditions upon the behavior of Rhesus monkeys (Macaca Mulatta). Child Dev 36: 855–868.

Stimulus deprivation during rearing can produce monkeys that are inactive, prefer visual and manipulatory stimuli of low complexity, show little exploration of the environment, are sexually and maternally abnormal, and generally withdraw from social contact. Such behavior can be explained by a complexity dissonance preference theory, which assumes normal behavioral development proceeds by a gradual process of paced increments in environmental complexity.

1784. Schmidt KE: Communication problems with psychiatric patients in the multi-lingual society of Sarawak. Psychiatry 28:229–233.

While verbal communications with patients are very important, nonverbal communication can be used effectively when it is impossible to rely on verbal means. This is especially important in an area such as Sarawak where each river tributary group speaks its own dialect.

1785. Schneiderman L: The cult of Osiris in relation to primitive initiation rites. Psychoanal Rev 52:38–50.

Obsession with death is basic to the cult of Osiris and the mystery of primitive initiation. The so-called lasting verities to which Osiris bears witness are really primitive intuitions of fear, adumbrations of apocalypse and death.

1786. Schneidermann I: Social class, diagnosis and treatment. Am J Orthopsychiatry 35:99–105.

The middle-class-oriented technology that directs our nation's health and welfare is culture bound and severely limits is availability to impoverished individuals and families in need of professional services.

1787. Scott R: Social-class correlate of selected cognitive functions. Psychol Rep 17:63–68.

There are no social-class differences to average need level of word associations. In IQ testing of culturally deprived students, greater emphasis should be placed on cognitive functions that can be executed on lower need levels, such as physiological need and safety.

1788. Sethi BB, Sachdev S, Nag D: Sociocultural factors in the practice of psychiatry in India. Am J Psychother 19:445–454.

Indian society as a whole is reluctant to give the same recognition to mental disorders as to other illnesses. In an appreciable segment of the community, these disorders are looked upon as a punishment rather than a disease. Changing patterns of behavior have brought along new conflicts that have generated substantial stress for the community.

1789. Skinner JC: Symptom and defense in contemporary Greece: a cross-cultural inquiry. J Nerv Ment Dis 141:478–489.

The "Evil Eye" affects both private and public Greek behavior, is incorporated in a variety of institutions and customs, and persists even in the face of scientific and psychological sophistication. The particular geography and history of Greece have precipitated "interruptions" in childhood that are handled by institutional methods.

1790. Skottowe I: Somatometry—a second look. Br J Psychiatry 111:4–9.

Somatometry is capable of giving information that is helpful in the practical management of many individual patients. Aside from formal illness, somatometry can provide a useful guide to prognosis in biological adaptation.

1791. Smith WG, Hansell N, English JT: Values and mental health in a college population: a follow-up report. J Nerv Ment Dis 140:92–95.

Highly developed "social values" tend to preserve interpersonal function in face of intrapsychic breakdown, while behaviorally expressed "social engagement" tends to maintain social role function in face of subjective psychiatric symptoms.

1792. Solomon F, Walker WL, O'Connor GJ, Fishman JR: Civil rights activity and reduction in crime among Negroes. Arch Gen Psychiatry 12:227–236.

Negroes release long dammed-up resentment of segregation by asserting themselves (directly or vicariously) in direct action for civil rights. Such emotional expression, when it occurs in a framework of community organization, may reduce the need for violent outbursts, thus reducing the incidence of such crimes.

1793. Somerville RM: The family in Yugoslavia. J Marriage Fam 27:350–362.

The changing structure and function of the Yugoslav family that accompanies industrialization and new ideologies must be considered within the total social framework.

1794. Stocking GW: From physics to ethnology: Franz Boas' arctic expedition as a problem in the historiography of the behavioral sciences. J Hist Behav Sciences 1:53–66.

Following Boas from physics to ethnology (1880–1887) illustrates that he experienced a gradual realization of the significance of culture, continuing his interest in epistemological problems. From the conditions of the physicist's knowledge of the external world he turned to man's knowledge of himself.

1795. Stocking G: Religion and personality in the anthropology of Henry Schoolcraft. J Hist Behav Sciences 1:301–313.

Schoolcraft, assuming a paternal role in his relationship with Indians, expected the Indians to adopt and appreciate his authoritarian form of Christianity. When they failed to do so, he rejected them, just as he rejected his own son, for ingratitude. He saw himself as a stern father advising his children on the road to survival.

1796. Tanaka Y, Osgood C: Cross-culture, cross-type, and cross-subject generality of affective meaning systems. J Pers Soc Psychol 2:143–153.

Testing of American, Finnish, and Japanese groups using perceptual signs of colors, line-forms, and color-form combinations and an examination of meaning space structure indicate four important semantic factors: dynamism, evaluation, warmth, and weight.

1797. Treisman AM: The effects of redundancy and familiarity on translating and repeating back a foreign and a native language. Br J Psychol 56:369–380.

Increased information rate decreases the efficiency of repetition of two languages and simultaneous translation tasks. Familiarity affects the performance on the former task of shadowing. Translation proves more difficult than shadowing with the higher information of the passage.

1798. Trent RD: Economic development and identity conflict in Peurto Rico. J Soc Psychol 65:293–300.

Female students show more identity conflict than do male students, although the latter show great conflict with respect to the ideal Puerto Rican male model and are more resistant to self-change. Identity shifts are occurring the direction of U.S. cultural models.

1799. Trethowan WH, Conlon MF: The couvade syndrome. Br J Psychiatry 111:57–66.

Aspects of the couvade syndrome are related to ritual couvade.

1800. Triandis HC, David EE, Takezawa S: Some determinants of social distance among American, German, and Japanese students. J Pers Soc Psychol 2:540–551.

Social distance is defined in terms of differing relative importance of race, occupation, religion, and nationality among subjects in Germany, Illinois, and Japan.

1801. Tsujioka B, Cattell RB: Constancy and difference in personality structure and mean profile in the questionnaire medium, from applying the 16 P.F. Test in American and Japan. Br J Soc Clin Psychol 4:287–297.

Factor analysis of variables from 16 P.F. scales yields highly congruent structures for Americans and Japanese, suggesting that these personality source traits are universal. Significant differences on factor levels, however, may be due to greater introversion among the Japanese.

1802. Woodbury MA, Friedman R, Palacios ES, Thosmas W: Psychiatric care at the Albert Schweitzer Hospital. Ment Hospitals 16:145–150.

A ward therapeutic community is helpful to Gabonese patients, many of whom suffer from transcultural anomie. This anomie may be a major cause of paranoid resolutions of African national conflicts.

1803. Yap PM: Koro—a culture-bound depersonalization syndrome. Br J Psychiatry 111:43–50.

Koro is an unique example of a depersonalization syndrome whose form and content, and indeed occurance and distribution, are determined by a combination of social and cultural factors acting on predisposed personalities.

1804. Yarrow LJ, Goodwin MS: Some conceptual issues in the study of mother-infant interaction. Am J Orthopsychiatry 35:473–481.

Scientific study of the "normal environment," as opposed to focusing on maternal pathology, can increase understanding of significant variables of maternal care and of reciprocal influences in mother-infant interactions.

1966

1805. Alker HA: A psycholinguistic investigation of a rule theory of "sense." Br J Psychol 57:397–404.

Sommer's proposition that the sense of term sets may be represented uniquely and unequivocally by a topological tree is supported by test of equivocation of terms not fitting on a tree.

1806. Alvarez GA: Socio-cultural aspects of British Guiana: colonialism superstitions and obeah in the West Indies. Dis Nerv Syst 27:127–131.

Obeah practice in British Guiana is striking in its cleverness and its formidable therapeutic impact on patients and/or their families. The obeah man treats people from all classes, both with physical and psychological problems. The success of the obeah man points out that there is no clear cleavage between the organic and the functional.

1807. Amir Y, Kohen-Raz R, Rabinowitz G: The effect of non-personality factors on ink-blot responses in a cross cultural study. J Proj Tech Pers Assessment 30:247–249.

Western and Eastern origin Israeli officer candidates initially demonstrated highly significant response differences. These differences vanish, however, in a second test with control for educational level.

1808. Angelini A: Measuring the achievement motive in Brazil. J Soc Psychol 68:35–40.

A projective measure of achievement motivation yields results similar to those for the United States. Achievement imagery can be increased by manipulated success and failure in Brazilian women, although negative results along these lines were obtained in the United States by previous researchers.

1809. Arkoff A, Weaver HB: Body image and body dissatisfaction in Japanese-Americans. J Soc Psychol 68:323–330.

Japanese American females express greater dissatisfaction with bodily dimensions than males or Caucasian American females, and a great desire to be taller.

1810. Babayan SY, Budayr B, Lindgren HC: Age, sex, and culture as variable in food aversion. J Soc Psychol 68:15–17.

Armenian and Arab students in Lebanon confirm findings that food aversions decline with age during adolescence, and girls tend to reject more foods than boys. A greater frequency of food aversion in Armenians may be due to a higher level of anxiety in problems of adjustment.

1811. Barnett LD: Opinion and knowledge of child-rearing professionals and non-professionals regarding three child-rearing systems. Fam Coordinator 15:101–106.

Professional and nonprofessionals are equally knowledgeable about (1) American middle class, (2) Russian, and (3) kibbutz child-rearing systems, indicating that professionals need greater ethnological background. Evaluation of the system is most related to its degree of meeting the needs of the children.

1812. Bartlett EW, Smith CP: Childrearing practice, birth order and the development of achievement-related motives. Psychol Rep 19:1207–1216.

First-born children have a higher need for achievement than later children. The achievement tendencies of first borns are due to the greater involvement, encouragement, and urging of their parents.

1813. Bazzoui W, Al-Issa I: Psychiatry in Iraq. Br J Psychiatry 112:827–832.

Despite the Moslem influence in Iraq, beliefs concerning mental illness are deeply rooted in superstition. There is a similarity between the incidence and classification of mental illness in Iraq and the West but the manifestations of mental illness are somehow different.

1814. Behar I: Response latency in simian learning set performance. Psychol Rep 19:403–406.

The study of reacquisition of learning set is an attempt to define when "hesitations" occur in learning set performance and the relation between response speed and accuracy.

1815. Bendeim OL: Psychiatry in Yucatan: medical archaeology in Mexico. Hosp Community Psychiatry 17:167–169.

Mayan medicine, like all primitive medicine, was intimately bound to magic. Nowhere in the world do we find such naturalistic descriptions of human pathology as in the ceramic art of the Mayan and other pre-Columbian Indians. Through artifacts such as tools, human and animal remains, and architectural structures of medical or paramedical use, the exciting history of Mayan medicine can be traced.

1816. Bernard J: Note on educational homogamy in Negro-white and white-Negro marriages, 1960. J Marriage Fam 28:274–276.

When an interracial marriage is not educationally homogamous, there is a tendency for Negroes, especially females, to marry up; and whites, especially males, to marry down.

1817. Berrien FK: Japanese and American values. Int J Psychol 1:129–142.

Differences between the values of young Japanese and American students suggest that postwar democracy in Japan is not well supported by appropriate personal values that would facilitate the operation of democratic structures.

1818. Berrien FK: Japanese values and the democratic process. J Soc Psychol 68:129–138.

Comparison of Japanese and American performance on the EPPS suggests that the persistence of traditional values in Japan, reflected in dependence on authority, abasement, hard work, and acceptance of control, provides little support for democratic processes.

1819. Berry JW: Temne and Eskimo perceptual skills. Int J Psychol 1:207–230.

Temnes differ significantly from Eskimos and Scottish subjects on tests of discrimination and spatial skills. Wider ecological and cultural factors account for these differences in analytic behavior, in addition to mode of parental discipline.

1820. Blauner R: Death and social structure. Psychiatry 29:378–394.

Death weakens the social group and calls forth personal anxieties. In response, members of a society cling closer together. Modern societies control death through bureaucratization and encourage the segregation of death from the more workaday social territory.

1821. Blehert SR: Pattern discrimination learning with Rhesus monkeys. Psychol Rep 19:311–324.

There is a progressive elimination of responses to irrelevant aspects of the discriminanda until only the correct cue is chosen.

1822. Boehm L: Moral judgment: a cultural and subcultural comparison with some of Piaget's research conclusions. Int J Psychol 1:143–150.

Comparative research with children of differing backgrounds supports Piaget's three stages of morality. Although a child may consider extenuating circumstances involved in transgression, he is still subject to adult constraints.

1823. Bolman WM, Katz AS: Hamburger hoarding: a case of symbolic cannibalism resembling Wihtico psychosis. J Nerv Ment Dis 142:424–428.

"Wihtico" psychosis is an obsessive cannibalistic conflict found among Cree and Ojibwa Indians. It is psychodynamically similar to hamburger hoarding.

1824. Brody EB: Recording cross-culturally useful psychiatric interview data: experience from Brazil. Am J Psychiatry 123: 446–456.

Standardized observation and recording systems are necessary in cross-cultural data gathering. The Initial Interview Inventory: Cross-cultural Instrument has validity in recording such useful data.

1825. Brody EB: Cultural exclusion, character and illness. Am J Psychiatry 122:852–858.

Population segments and social subsystems are being excluded from complete participation in the culture of the large societies to which they belong. The consequences of exclusion may be identity problems, hostility, and psychosis.

1826. Brown LB: Egocentric thought in petitionary prayer: a cross-cultural study. J Soc Psychol 68:197–210.

Children in the United States, Australia, and New Zealand show a consistent trend in disbelief of the causal efficacy of prayer with increasing age. Belief in the appropriateness of prayer is more influenced by adult requirements.

1827. Burt C: The genetic determination of differences in intelligence: a study of monozygotic twins reared together and apart. Br J Psychol 57:137–154.

Monozygotic twins reared apart show high correlations for intelligence. Supplementary data also confirm the largely genetic component of intelligence.

1828. Callieri B, Frighi L: Social psychiatry and criteria of normality. Soc Psychiatry 1:142–143.

The danger of cultural relativism is that the formal aspects of psychopathology are disregarded. The most important contribution of cultural psychiatry is the identification of potential conflicts which are inherent in the structure of a society and of the degree of tolerance shown by different societies toward mental disorders.

1829. Carlson LD: A comparison of Negro and Caucasian performances on the Bender-Gestalt Test. J Clin Psychol 22:96–98.

Cultural factors do not significantly influence performance on the Bender-Gestalt Test. Significant differences between Negro and white groups on Figures 4, 6, 7, and 8 of the Bender-Gestalt indicate that cultural factors may influence test performance significantly.

1830. Carstairs GM: Psychiatric problems of overdeveloped countries. Am J Psychiatry 122:1406–1414.

Changes in psychiatry in the United States and United Kingdom may be contrasted with psychiatric practices and problems in India.

1831. Caudill WA, Plath DW: Who sleeps by whom? Parent-child involvement in urban Japanese families. Psychiatry 29:344–366.

In Western eyes, Japanese cosleeping patterns

may appear to be pathogenic, or a denial of maturation and individuation.

1832. Cawte JE, Djagamara N, Barrett MG: The meaning of subincision of the urethra to aboriginal Australians. Br J Med Psychol 39:245–253.

There is some significance to the "marsupial" origin of subincision. However, other functions, such as provision of a site for ritual bloodletting could serve to reinforce the practice among the Walbiri.

1833. Cesa-Bianchi M: The development of social attitudes as studied in two cross-cultural research projects. Int J Psychol 1:59–64.

The significance of cross-cultural research is demonstrated by results of two studies of socialization processes in compliance, coping style, and achievement.

1834. Davenport RK, Menzel EW, Rogers CM: Effects of severe isolation on "normal" juvenile monkeys. Arch Gen Psychiatry 14:134–138.

Three wild-born, and initially mother-raised, young monkeys placed in extreme isolation for six months show good health, weight gain, and do not evidence the stereotyped motor patterns often found among chimpanzees isolated as infants.

1835. Denko JD: How preliterate peoples explain disturbed behavior. Arch Gen Psychiatry 15:398–409.

Allowing for differences in cultural patterns, explanations for disturbed behavior are similar in many ways across dissimilar cultures.

1836. Doob L: Eidetic imagery: a cross-cultural will-o'-the-wisp? J Psychol 63:13–34.

Eidetic imagery is reported in similar terms across five African societies, although its incidence varies. Eidetic images do not significantly aid in recall, nor are they significantly related to any psychological or demographic factors. This type of concrete magic may well have been part of man's earlier adaptive repertoire that is activated when he experiences difficulty coping with the environment.

1837. Dozier EP: Problem drinking among American Indians: the role of sociocultural deprivation. Q J Stud Alcohol 27:72–87.

A deep sense of inadequacy and inferiority, growing from relations with the white man, is an important factor in Indians' excessive drinking problem. Drinking is a recognized evil in all Indian communities. Traditional controls are somctimes effective, but often the problem of inebriety arises with the breakdown of traditions.

1838. Foa UG, Triandis HC, Katz EW: Cross-cultural invariance in the differentiation and organization of family roles. J Pers Soc Psychol 4:316–327.

The process of role development is invariant across American, Greek, Hawaiian-Japanese, and Japanese cultures.

1839. Foulkes SH: Illness as a social process. Psychother Psychosom 14:217–225.

The form illness assumes depends on the cultural and social (class) background. Human behavior can only be fully understood as part of an interactional process comprising a number of people (a "network").

1840. Frijda N, Jahoda G: On the scope and methods of cross-cultural research. Int J Psychol 1:109–128.

Cross-cultural research must face the mcthodological issues of equivalent category systems, comparability of procedure and sampling, multiple variables, and alternative interpretations. Native assistants may facilitate research and testing.

1841. Ghei SN: A cross-cultural study of need profiles. J Pers Soc Psychol 3:580–585.

The degree of congruence between individual personality structure and group personality profile may be determined by discriminant function analysis of data from urban middle-class subjects in the United States and India.

1842. Ghei SN: Needs of Indian and American college females. J Soc Psychol 69:3–11.

EPPS data on systematic and significant need differences between American and Indians are consistent with previous research and are indicative of the utility of multivariate statistical procedures in cross-cultural studies.

1843. Gluckman LK: Aspects of the background of Maori children. Br J Med Psychol 39:319–327.

History, sociology, education, and psychology are all aspects of the clinical picture of the Maori people and their ethnic identity.

1844. Gordon LV, Kakkar SB: A cross-cultural study of Indian and American interpersonal values. J Soc Psychol 69:339–340.

Mean differences, reflecting cultural value differences, found between American and Indian teacher trainees in another study are mirrored in a sample of Indian and American students.

1845. Gordon LV, Kikuchi A: American personality tests in cross-cultural research—a caution. J Soc Psychol 69:179–183.

Criterion-oriented tests should not be used for cross-cultural research; construct-oriented tests are more appropriate. However, construct relevance and translatability are important considerations in making cross-cultural comparisons.

1846. Griffin GA, Harlow HF: Effects of three months of total social adjustment and learning in the Rhesus monkey. Child Dev 37:533–547.

Totally socially isolated rhesus monkeys exhibit a drop in oral and manual exploration of their cages when removed from isolation and show an increase of self-directed orality and extreme withdrawal. No differences in social learning behaviors are found between three-month total social isolates when compared with three-month partial social isolates.

1847. Grosser GS, Walsh AA: Sex differences in the differential recall of taboo and neutral words. J Psychol 63:219–228.

Although males and females have equal recall ability, males verbalize more taboo words and females verbalize more neutral words. Presentation order does not effect recall.

1848. Guanche-Padron J, Torres-Castro J: Psychiatry in Yucatan: old culture, new programs. Hosp Community Psychiatry 17:162–163.

The majority of the people in Yucatan have been exposed to a variety of social and cultural influences that have brought about great changes. However, there is still a nucleus of Indians whose mores and way of life have not altered much and who speak only Mayan. Psychiatry is fairly new to Yucatan and has not had time to develop.

1849. Guthrie GM: Structure of maternal attitudes in two cultures. J Psychol 62:155–165.

Indications of superficially similar behavior for American and Philippine mothers belies the evidence that these behaviors have different underlying meanings.

1850. Gutmann D: Mayan aging—a comparative TAT study. Psychiatry 29:246–259.

The Mayan results of TAT studies differ from American findings in that American men, as they age, are more troubled by problems of conscience and retribution. These transcultural findings tend to bear out Carl Jung's observation that the second half of life is compensatory for the first.

1851. Heer DM: Negro-white marriage in the United States. J Marriage Fam 28:262–273.

Negro-white intermarriage is relatively high in less segregated residential areas with minimal status differences.

1852. Herreid CF II, Herried JR: Differences in MMPI scores in native and nonnative Alaskans. J Soc Psychol 70:191–198.

MMPI comparisons of Alaskan students show natives and nonnatives to be more deviant in mean scale scores than U.S. college groups. Differences in groups of most to least deviant for males (Aleuts, Eskimos, Indians) and females (Aleuts, Indians, Eskimos) may reflect differing degrees of acculturation to U.S. society.

1853. Hes JP: From native healer to modern psychiatrist. Soc Psychiatry 1:117–120.

Less prejudice about mental illness and its treatment is found among Afro-Asian immigrants to Israel than among immigrants of Polish origin. The high position of intellectual functioning in the value system of the Polish Jews is an important factor in their desire to remedy loss of intellectual function.

1854. Hes JP: From native healer to modern psychiatrist: Afro-Asian immigrants to Israel and their attitudes towards psychiatric facilities. Part II: attitudes of relatives towards the hospital. Int J Soc Psychiatry 13:21–27.

Responses to a questionnaire by husbands of former mental patients indicate that among Yemenite and Moroccan immigrants to Israel, acculturation results only in partial acceptance of Western culture-derived stereotypes concerning the nature of psychiatric hospitalization. Such patients, in contrast with a Polish control group, are frequently discontent with treatment offered at Western type hospitals and resort to native healers.

1855. Hilton AM: Homo faber, homo sapiens, and homo poeta. Am J Psychother 20:627–635.

The cybercultural revolution, far from being merely a revolution in production methods, is a revolution in which man is changing the cybernetic relationships in his universe. As of yet he has given little thought to changing the relationships in himself. There is no obstacle left to keep man from evolving into a truly human being but his own blind fear.

1856. Hoepfner R, Nihara K, Guilford JP: Intellectual abilities of symbolic and semantic judgment. Psychol Monographs 80:1–47.

Symbolic and semantic evaluation factors are hypothesized to be distinct within a structure of intellect model, and from factors in other domains of the model. The model has the potential of discovering differentiable intellectual aptitudes.

1857. Hunt RG, Smith ME: Cultural symbols and response to thematic test materials. J Proj Tech Pers Assess 30:587–590.

Comparison of responses to modified TAT cards suggests the need to distinguish between individual personality characteristics and cultural patterns in the assessment of culture and personality.

1858. Hutt C, Ounsted C: The biological significance of gaze aversion, with special reference to childhood autism. Behav Sci 11:346–356.

The social encounters of autistic children are suggestive of a signaling function of gaze aversion, similar to animal appeasement postures.

1859. Iga M: Relation of suicide attempt and social structure in Kamakura, Japan. Int J Soc Psychiatry 12:221–232.

Components of the Japanese social structure that make for dependency, the wish for self-assertion, and insecurity reinforce and intensify such elements in suicidal Japanese youths.

1860. Irvine EE: Children in kibbutzim: thirteen years after. J Child Psychol Psychiatry 7:167–178.

Family relations in the kibbutz are typically warm and affectionate and many opportunities for occasional unplanned contact even during the working day are provided. Every care is taken to give the child as rich and stimulating an environment as possible.

1861. Iwao S, Child IL: Comparison of esthetic judgments by American experts and by Japanese potters. J Soc Psychol 68:27–33.

The esthetic judgments of Japanese potters on artistic representations are in greater agreement with those of American experts than are the judgments of American nonexperts, most probably due to the interests of the Japanese potters and cross-cultural similarity of esthetic criteria.

1862. Jahoda G: Geometric illusions and environment: a study in Ghana. Br J Psychol 57:193–200.

Overall significant expected differences in the Muller-Lyer illusion obtain for British and Ghanaian subjects, but findings for Ghanaian subgroups on the horizontal-vertical illusion are inconsistent with a simple ecological interpretation.

1863. Jahoda G: Impressions of nationalities—an alternative to the "stereotype" approach. Br J Soc Clin Psychol 5:1–16.

Content analysis of verbal reports indicates judgments of nationality are made on various bases, and suggest modes of impression formation.

1864. Jakobovits LA: Comparative psycholinguistics in the study of cultures. Int J Psychol 1:15–38.

Responses associated with emotional, purposive, and motivational dynamics show evidence of generality across twenty cultures. Similarities and dissimilarities in affective meaning systems across cultures are also evident.

1865. Janowsky DS, Gorney R, Kelley B: The curse—vicissitudes and variations of the female fertility cycle: evolutionary aspects. Psychosomatics 7:283–287.

There is evidence of emotional and behavioral disturbance associated with cyclic ovulatory function. Unconscious recognition of menstrual pathology may have contributed powerfully to formation of group-protecting menstrual taboos. Nonsexual psychological and social disruptions could result from decreased menstrual frequency.

1866. Jay EJ: Religious and convivial uses of alcohol in a Gond village of middle India. Q J Stud Alcohol 27:88–96.

Among the Hill Maria Gond villagers, drinking has both religious and convivial implications. Alcohol is used as a libation, as a sacrifice to the gods, and as an intoxicant by shamans. The fact that the villagers abstain from drinking alcohol at times of anxiety contradicts Horton's hypothesis that the strength of drinking response varies directly with the level of anxiety.

1867. Kahn MW, Hyun-soo L, Jones NF, Jin SK: A comparison of Korean and American mental patients' attitudes towards mental illness and hospitalization. Int J Soc Psychiatry 13:14–20.

American patients' attitudes concentrate on issues of authoritarian control and restrictive penal victimization. Korean attitudes are concentrated in opposing constellations: a positive, cheerful view of the mental hospital and treatment and a negative, fearful, pessimistic view.

1868. Kakkar SB, Gordon LV: The interpersonal values of Indian trainees. J Soc Psychol 69:341–342.

Indian trainees score lower on the Survey of Interpersonal Values for Support and Recognition, and higher on Conformity and Benevolence than their American counterparts. Indian males also score lower on Independence than American males.

1869. Kalish RA, Maloney M, Arkoff A: Cross-cultural comparisons of college student marital-role preferences. J Soc Psychol 68:41–47.

Japanese-American, Japanese, Caucasian, and especially Japanese-American males are male dominant in their attitudes toward the marriage role. Females, especially Japanese university students, are more egalitarian.

1870. Karr C, Wesley F: Comparison of German and U.S. child-rearing practices. Child Dev 37:715–723.

German parents punish more severely and are more controlling than American parents in such areas as toilet training, table manners, and school and homework. American parents exercise more control with regard to personal hygiene, sex behavior, sports, and church and youth organizations.

1871. Kassarjian WM: A cross-cultural study of social character. Psychol Rep 19:966.

German college students, even in large cities, are not as other-directed as U.S. students.

1872. Keenan B: Psychiatry in Yucatan: the hospital Ayala, Merida. Hosp Community Psychiatry 17:164–166.

Mental illness in Yucatan is tolerated by the community to a much greater extent than in the United States and is brought to medical attention only when it is grossly disruptive. In a few of the more primitive sectors of the state, witch doctors still practice.

1873. Kent C: Roots of violence in modern man. Psychoanal Rev 53:555–575.

The Freudian school emphasizes the inborn instinctive feature of aggression, while Bender emphasizes the inhibition of a biological maturation process.

1874. Kent DP: Social and cultural factors influencing the mental health of the aged. Am J Orthopsychiatry 36:680–685.

Changes in role and status that occur in old age lack the social support and rewards given to other times of transition and mitigate against good mental health in the aged.

1875. Kidson MA, Jones IV: Psychiatric disorders among aborigines of the Australian Western desert. Arch Gen Psychiatry 19:413–417.

Functional psychoses, personality disorders, organic and exotic possession syndromes are found among Warburton Range and Walbiri aborigines; but no classical neuroses, psychosomatic illnesses, or suicides are detected.

1876. Kline NS: A theoretic framework for transcultural psychiatry. Am J Psychiatry 123:85–87.

The basic disorders (psychoses) presume an organic substrate, while compensatory mechanisms imply a culturally conditioned layer of response and behavior. This heurism permits an understanding of the cross-cultural sameness of the structure of disorders with differences in content and expression.

1877. Knudsen AK, Gorham DR, Moseley EC: Universal popular responses to inkblots in five cultures: Denmark, Germany, Hong Kong, Mexico, and United States. J Proj Tech Pers Assessment 30: 135–142.

General universality of response to certain inkblots illustrates more commonality than differences in perception across five cultures. The core concept "person" accounts for more instances of populars than other concepts.

1878. Krush T, Bjork J, Sindell P, Nelle J: Some thoughts on the formation of personality disorder: study of an Indian boarding school population. Am J Psychiatry 122:868–876.

Frequency of movement and the necessity to conform to changing standards lead to confusion and disorganization of a child's personality. Although this is a problem among American Indians, it is also a problem among children of other deprived cultures.

1879. Kumasaka Y: Soka Gakkai: group psychologic study of a new religio-political organization. Am J Psychother 20:462–470.

Soka Gakkai is a new religio-political organization that originated in Japan and has spread to the United States, particularly to the West Coast. The household is the standard unit of Soka Gakkai, and an individual member is usually reclassified so as to belong to a household unit. In Japan it gained its initial stronghold among families of miners.

1880. Kurokawa M: Family solidarity, social change, and childhood accidents. J Marriage Fam 28:498–506.

The extended family may serve to better protect the child from mishap. Acculturated Oriental-American children have more accidents, although families with tension and conflict in general are not suited for coping with potential hazards.

1881. Lambo TA: Neuro-psychiatric syndromes associated with human trypanosomiasis in tropical Africa. Acta Psychiatr Scand 42:474–484.

There is no mental syndrome or psychosis that cannot be caused by the endemic disease, cerebral trypanosomiasis. The mental symptoms do not seem to depend on any specific type of lesion of the CNS; however, at least some of the psychiatric syndromes are due to changes in the anatomo-physiological complexes of the CNS.

1882. Lazarus RS, Tomita M, Opton E, Kodama M: A cross-cultural study of stress-reaction patterns in Japan. J Pers Soc Psychol 4:622–633.

Japanese and American distress responses to benign and stressful films are similar except for differences in respect to interaction between MMPI-scaled personality disposition and defensive orientations.

1883. Levine DN: The concept of masculinity in Ethiopian culture. Int J Soc Psychiatry 12:17–23.

The Amhara ideal of masculinity refers primarily to aggressive capacity. The traditional military ethic takes the form of a cult of the hero. The Amhara rank masculinity very high in their hierarchy of values and regard it as a crucial component of their general cultural identity.

1884.

Lewis DG: Commentary on "The genetic determination of differences in intelligence: a study of monozygotic twins reared together and apart." Br J Psychol 57:431–434.

The need for further assessment of environmental conditions and the evolution of genetic-environmental factor interactions is evident.

1885. Little RB: Oral aggression in spider legends. Am Imago 23:169–179.

Spider tales from various cultures are symbolic of male-female conflict and general oral aggressive fears and impulses.

1886. Liu PYH, Meredith GM: Personality structure of Chinese college students in Taiwan and Hong Kong. J Soc Psychol 70:165–166.

Chinese students in Taiwan and Hong Kong, particularly for the female samples, are noticeably different on several personality dimensions as measured by the Sixteen Personality Factor Questionnaire.

1887. Liu WT: Family interactions among local and refugee families in Hong Kong. J Marriage Fam 28:314–323.

Chinese families in Hong Kong are characterized by a generally strong support pattern between father-son-wife. The content of interpersonal relationships in local and refugee families reflects strengths of position and response tendencies. Among refugee family members, there is a higher value consistency than among local families.

1888. Lomas P: Ritual elements in the management of childbirth. Br J Med Psychol 39:207–213.

Rituals of childbirth—which include segregation of the mother, sacrifice of the first born, and couvade—may be viewed in terms of envy of woman's creative success and anxiety toward growth and change.

1889. Malev M: The Jewish orthodox circumcision ceremony: its meaning from direct study of the rite. J Am Psychoanal Assoc 14:410–517.

The Jewish circumcision ritual, in its symbolizations and displacements, is a condensed defensive maneuver on the part of the father against his own castration anxieties, recalled from regression by the birth of his son.

1890. Mann JW: Family values in overlapping cultures. J Soc Psychol 69:209–222.

Although Hindus in South Africa show evidence of limited Westernization, Hindu family values are resistant to this process. Hindu perception of the typical English white values and of their own Westernization are quite exaggerated.

1891. Marais HC: Attitudes of Bantu mine workers toward a communication medium. Psychol Rep 19:107–111.

Bantu mine workers show significantly favorable attitudes toward a specific radio program in their native languages that includes music, serials, news, religion, and talks on mining.

1892. Markman R: Juvenile delinquency in Israel. Am J Psychiatry 123:463–469.

Rising rates of juvenile delinquency are directly related to ethnic origin and indirectly to immigration. Juveniles of Afro-Asian origin have the highest rates. Immigration leads to family anomie.

1893. Marks IM: Semantic differential uses in psychiatric patients: a study of obsessive, psychopath and control inpatients. Br J Psychiatry 112:945–951.

The semantic-differential technique is useful for psychiatric problems to which meaning or attitude is relevant. Psychiatric patients use semantic differential scales differently from control, but the scores are stable and they parallel clinical events.

1894. Marks Breenfield P, Bruner JS: Culture and cognitive growth. Int J Psychol 1:89–108.

Value complexes and education influence cognitive development and level. Various levels of cognitive development are also the result of biological-cultural constraints.

1895. McGinn NF: Marriage and family in middle class Mexico. J Marriage Fam 28:305–313.

Sex roles formed during courtship carry over into Mexican marital relationships. There is a cyclic tendency for the discontinuity of role expectations by women to be reflected in child-rearing practices, in turn creating male-female role dichotomies.

1896. McGinnies E: Studies in persuasion: an attempt to induce both direct and generalized attitude change in Japanese students. J Soc Psychol 70:69–75.

Unless a significant amount of change occurs in the target attitude, generalized attitude change toward a specific and logically related issue is not likely to occur. Neutrality in attitudes does not necessarily indicate increased susceptibility to persuasion in different cultures.

1897. McGinnies E: Studies in persuasion: primacy-recency effects with Japanese students. J Soc Psychol 70:77–85.

The primacy of a first persuasive argument and the recency of second argument appear irrelevant to a sample of subjects with neutral attitudes, who are generally uninfluenced by either pro or con positions on cold war issues.

1898. McGinnies E: Studies in persuasion: reaction of Japanese students to one-sided and two-sided communications. J Soc Psychol 70:87–93.

Measures of attitude change, convincingness, and

speaker impressions indicate that two-sided communication is more effective than one-sided communication in generating attitude shift among those opposed to the position advocated. The one-sided argument seems to be slightly more influential for subjects favoring the position advocated.

1899. McMichael RE, Grinder RE: Children's guilt after transgression: combined effect of exposure to American culture and ethnic background. Child Dev 37:425–431.

There is decreasing assimilation to American standards of conduct among Japanese-, Hawaiian-, and Caucasian-American children as one goes from relatively great to lesser degrees of community dominance by American culture. Expression of guilt varies with ethnic background and degree of exposure to American culture.

1900. Meier GW, Garcia-Rodriques C: Development of conditioned behaviors in the infant Rhesus monkey. Psychol 19:1159–1169.

Instrumental learning to noxious reinforcement develops rapidly in the newborn rhesus monkeys and to a response level indistinguishable from that of one- and two-month-old monkeys.

1901. Meredith GM: Amae and acculturation among Japanese-American college students in Hawaii. J Soc Psychol 70:171–180.

An introversion-anxiety pattern for Sansei Japanese-American students, indicated by analysis of 16 P.F. scales, parallels L. T. Doi's theory of amae (a basic dependency need) at the center of Japanese core personality. Factors in the early social environment of Japanese-Americans maintain this pattern.

1902. Meredith GM, Meredith CGW: Acculturation and personality among Japanese-American college students in Hawaii. J Soc Psychol 68:175–182.

Second-order analysis of 16 P.F. patterns for Sansei students indicates Japanese-American males are higher in introversion and females higher on anxiety than Caucasian-American students.

1903. Mitchell WE: The baby disturbers: sexual behavior in a childhood contraculture. Psychiatry 29:367–377.

Precipitating social factors in the formation of a preadolescent male contraculture appear to be: the segregation of a group of socially stigmatized children, their denial of the stigmatizing mental-patient role, the presence of imaginative and persuasive in-

novators, a permissive ward system, and group solidarity. When these conditions exist, a group of children in latency is as capable of creating a sustained contraculture as are adolescents or adults.

1904. Mora G: The history of psychiatry: a cultural bibliographical survey. Int J Psychiatry 2:335–356.

Increased concern with the history of psychiatry indicates the need for more investigation into classic psychiatric texts, the cultural background of psychiatric concepts, and the psychological implications of specific cultural topics.

1905. Mukherjee BN: "Social desirability" and "anxiety" variables in three measures of anxiety. Br J Soc Clin Psychol 5:310–312.

Investigation of three measures of anxiety in India suggests that inference from one scale cannot be generalized to another when anxiety is the relevant variable.

1906. Mukherjee BN, Verma S: A cross-cultural comparison of judgments of social desirability for items of a forced-choice scale of achievement motivation. J Soc Psychol 69:337–338.

Indian students show a tendency to attribute certain failures to environment, emphasize cleanliness and healthy atmosphere, and rate social conformity and faithfulness more highly than their American counterparts.

1907. Mundy-Castle AC: Pictorial depth perception in Ghanaian children. Int J Psychol 1:289–300.

Ghanaian children identify familar objects more frequently than abstractions and show some three-dimensional discrimination with greater age on Hudson's Depth Perception test. Degree of pictorial experience may be important in the development of pictorial depth perception.

1908. Munoz L, Marconi J, Horwitz J, Naveillan P: Cross-cultural definitions applied to the study of functional psychoses in Chilean Mapuches. Br J Psychiatry 112:1205–1215.

There is relatively a greater proportion of oneiriform psychoses in individuals having an indigenous (Mapuche) culture than in a Chilean control group with a predominantly Western European culture.

1909. Miyekawa AM: Authoritarianism in an authoritarian culture: the case of Japan. Int J Soc Psychiatry 12:283–288.

Authoritarianism in Japan is characterized by acquiescence. Ideologically consistent authoritarianism does not seem to be an important part of authoritarianism in Japan. Cross-cultural evidence is lacking for the establishment of the universal syndrome of an authoritarian or acquiescent personality.

1910. Parker S, Kleiner RJ: Characteristics of Negro mothers in single-headed households. J Marriage Fam 28:507–513.

Mothers of broken homes have poorer psychological adjustment and less goal involvement for self and male offspring than mothers in intact homes. The implications for the achievement attitudes of children raised in broken homes are important considerations.

1911. Paul SK: Worldminded attitudes of Panjab university students. J Soc Psychol 69:33–37.

High-income students, with political inclinations toward Congress, and background and occupational intentions toward defense services tend to be more worldminded than their counterparts.

1912. Petrus EP: The Golem: significance of the legend. Psychoanal Rev 53:63–68.

The possible sources of the Golem myth are: a flight into fantasy in order to adapt to painful reality, an individual's desire for power, and a repetition-compulsion mechanism.

1913. Podell L: Sex and role conflict. J Marriage Fam 28:163–165.

Role conflicts for females have been exaggerated in the literature. Alternative marital patterns may be generated by the various adaptations of females and males to value and occupational systems respectively.

1914. Preble E: Social and cultural factors related to narcotic use among Puerto Ricans in New York City. Int J Addict 1:30–41.

Narcotic use is one solution to the social and psychological problems of male Puerto Ricans under acculturative stresses.

1915. Prothro ET: Socialization and social class in a transitional society. Child Dev 37:219–228.

Greek peasant mothers are most permissive with infants, but middle-class mothers are more permissive with young children. Middle-class mothers are warmer, more given to "love-oriented" discipline, and more active in family decisions. The Greek pattern of class differences may be common in transitional societies.

1916. Rabin AI, Goldman H: The relationship of guilt to intensity of identification in kibbutz and non-kibbutz children. J Soc Psychol 69:159–163.

Due to diffuse and less intense identification, kibbutz children show less severity of guilt for norm violation than do nonkibbutz children.

1917. Rao S: Caste and mental disorders in Bihar. Am J Psychiatry 122:1045–1055.

Schizophrenia is conspicuous among Brahmin and Kayastha patients. Single, female Kayastha patients have higher mental hospital admission rates than other Kayastha patients, as do eldest siblings.

1918. Rao S: Culture and mental disorder: a study in an Indian mental hospital. Int J Soc Psychiatry 12:139–148.

The rarity of senile disorders among patients admitted to Indian mental hospitals affects such traditional values as respect for age and the protection afforded by an extended family system. A harmonious integration of old values and new ideals, rather than a destruction of old values, is essential for the preservation of Indian mental health.

1919. Rao S: A note on the investigation of the MMPI with different occupational groups in India. Br J Soc Clin Psychol 5:274–275.

Overall high neuroticism and extraversion scores for Indian students suggest that occupational role determines personality tendencies.

1920. Rastogi GD: Social psychology of Chinese aggression. J Soc Psychol 68:49–55.

The Indian nation must build its morale, counteract Chinese propaganda, and develop a strong defensive attitude with the help of other nations in order to stand against aggressive actions by the Chinese nation.

1921. Rin H, Chu H, Lin T: Psychophysiological reactions of a rural and suburban population in Taiwan. Acta Psychiatr Scand 42:410–473.

Rates of psychophysiological reactions differ significantly when analyzed according to age, marital status, social classes, period of migration, and types of religion. People who are incapable of adjusting to modern life and who greatly lessen their traditional value identity show a significantly high rate of psychophysiological disorder.

1922. Rosenblatt PC: A cross-cultural study of child-rearing and romantic love. J Pers Soc Psychol 4:336–338.

Childhood frustration of oral needs in 19 societies corresponds with concern for affection as adults (romantic love).

1923. Sallery RDH, Lindgren HC: Arab attitudes toward authority: a cross-cultural study. J Soc Psychol 69:27–31.

Attitudes toward authority are specific and vary with cultural background. Arab students, as compared to American and Canadian subjects, show greater hostility toward institutions and less toward interpersonal relations.

1924. Schneiderman L: A theory of repression in the light of archaic religion. Psychoanal Rev 53: 220–232.

Since the promotion of fertility is a primary focus of primitive religious life, it can be argued justly that sex divorced from fertility is taboo, and therefore subject to repression.

1925. Senay EC: Toward an animal model of depression: a study of separation behavior in dogs. J Psychiatr Res 4:65–71.

Separation is associated with increases in object seeking for animals of the approach temperament and increases in object avoidance and aggressive behavior for animals of the avoidance temperament. Reunion is associated with deviations from preseparation patterns. Models of separation and depression can be constructed in experimental animals.

1926. Sinha TC: Development of psycho-analysis in India. Int J Psychoanal 47:427–439.

Dr. G. Bose was a pioneer in psychoanalysis. His correspondences with Freud reflect their differences in consideration of the concept of repression, which Bose viewed as the opposition of infantile wishes.

1927. Spencer-Booth Y, Hinde RA: The effects of separating Rhesus monkey infants from their mothers for six days. J Child Psychol Psychiatry 7:179–197.

Infant rhesus monkeys display disturbed behavior after having been separated for six days from their mothers. The extent of the disturbances varies with the kind of relationship between mother and infant before the separation.

1928. Stage TB, Keast TJ: A psychiatric service for Plains Indians. Hosp Community Psychiatry 17:74–76.

Many Plains Indians are more psychologically minded and insightful than the usual white patient, although they appear to be quite reserved and taciturn in social situations. Any evaluation of Indian patients must take into the account the conflict caused by the impingement of white culture on the Indian culture.

1929. (Deleted)

1930. Stefflre V, Vales VC, Morley L: Language and cognition in Yucatan: a cross-cultural replication. J Pers Soc Psychol 4:112–115.

Munsell color chips may be used as stimuli for Spanish and Yucatec speakers to determine the correspondence between communication and memory.

1931. Stocking GW: The history of anthropology: where, whence, whither? J Hist Behav Sciences 2: 281–290.

The history of anthropology must be studied both historically and anthropologically.

1932. Stott DH: Commentary on "The genetic determination of differences in intelligence: a study of monozygotic twins reared together and apart." Br J Psychol 57:423–430.

A congenital explanation that postulates special intrauterine genetics-environment interactions may be offered for the mental similarity of monozygous twins.

1933. Straus MA: Westernization, insecurity, and Sinhalese social structure. Int J Soc Psychiatry 12: 130–138.

A latent dysfunction of Sinhalese society is a high level of anxiety and insecurity. The more Westernized students in this society have the fewest indicators of psychological disability.

1934. Suchman EA: Medical "deprivation." Am J Orthopsychiatry 36:665–672.

Cultural, social, psychological, economic, and medical conditions create a situation in which lower income groups suffer medical deprivation. Modification of middle-class oriented treatment approaches and education of low-income clients are necessary prerequisites to improvement of medical care among the socially deprived.

1935. Suchman RG: Cultural differences in children's color and form preferences. J Soc Psychol 70:3–10.

The typical Euro-American relationship between age and color-form preferences is not found for a sample of students at a Koranic school in Nigeria. Greater color preference is revealed by test scores, but all age levels are represented and no developmental transitions from color to form are indicated.

1936. Szasz TS: Psychotherapy: a sociocultural perspective. Compr Psychiatry 7:217–223.

Psychotherapy can be described in different terms: instrumental, institutional, entrepreneurial, bureaucratic, and coerced. Psychotherapy as education for social conformity or deviance is a continuation of what Benda called "the treason of the intellectuals."

1937. Tanner RES: Drug addiction in East Africa. Int J Addict 1:9–29.

Attitudes toward drug use and the legal backgrounds for Kenya, Uganda, and Tanzania may be examined with respect to use of hemp by students and prisoners.

1938. Thorne FC: A factorial study of sexuality in adult males. J Clin Psychol 22:378–386.

Sexuality in young adult males may be studied reliably and validly utilizing an objective questionnaire (The Sex Inventory) consisting largely of obvious-direct items.

1939. Thorne FC: Scales for rating sexual intercourse. J Clin Psychol 22:404–407.

Much has been written concerning orgastic experiencing, but there have been no objective studies of its nature across population. Some objective scales have been developed for the operational definition of the dimensions of climactic sex experiences. Difficulties introduced by cultural stereotypes engendered by local and colloquial differences in expressing sex symbolically can be overcome.

1940. Thorne FC: The Sex Inventory. J Clin Psychol 22:367–374.

"The Sex Inventory" is a 200-item self-report questionnaire for the study of sex interests, drives, attitudes, adjustment, conflict, cathexes, controls, and sociopathic tendencies and represents an attempt to objectify direct questioning methods in the form of an inventory.

1941. Thorne FC, Haupt TD: The objective measurement of sex attitudes and behavior in adult males. J Clin Psychol 22:395–403.

College and medical students when compared with convicted homosexuals, rapists and murderers, and property-crime felons, are sexually liberal and psychologically healthy. Drug addicts and psychotherapy patients are extremely liberal but psychologically unhealthy. Objective methods of measuring sex attitudes are valid.

1942. Toker E: Mental illness in white and Bantu populations of the Republic of South Africa. Am J Psychiatry 123:55–65.

Urbanization and detribalization have resulted in increased mental illness among the Bantu, who are generally treated by medicine men or in state institutions. Men are more likely to be found in state hospitals than women, since it is they who tend to move toward urban centers.

1943. Triandis HC, Tanaka Y, Shanmugam AV: Interpersonal attitudes among American, Indian and Japanese students. Int J Psychol 1:177–208.

A behavioral differential applied to three groups of students yields responses that differ cross-nationally. Marital, respect, and friendship factors are found for all three groups.

1944. Tuckman J, Ziegler R: Language usage and social maturity as related to suicide notes. J Soc Psychol 68:139–141.

The hypothesis that persons committing suicide show social immaturity is not supported by the distribution of self-reference and self-other reference pronouns in simulated and genuine suicide notes.

1945. Vaillant GE: Parent-child cultural disparity and drug addiction. J Nerv Ment Dis 142:534–539.

Both minority status and parental—rather than individual—cultural mobility is positively correlated with the incidence of drug addiction among individuals from lower socioeconomic groups.

1946. Vincent CE: Familia Spongia: the adaptive function. J Marriage Fam 28:29–36.

Social change is mediated by the family through the socialization process. The general adaptability of the family is principally due to an absence of institutionalized organization that might resist change; this facet of the family cannot be ignored by researcher.

1947. Vosburgh P: Kenya's only mental hospital. Hosp Community Psychiatry 17:104–107.

Mathari is a cottage-style hospital, which serves the city of Nairobi. There seems to be a greater incidence of mental disorder among African men than among women. However, in any African village or settlement there are many obviously psychotic women who are apparently well tolerated by the tribe.

1948. Warren N: Social class and construct systems: an examination of the cognitive structure of two social class groups. Br J Soc Clin Psychol 5: 254–263.

Repertory grid data for middle-class and working-class subjects provide some support for the theory that differences in linguistic coding are associated with social class groupings, with consequent differences in cognitive process organization.

1949. Wesley F, Karr C: Problems in establishing norms for cross-cultural comparisons. Int J Psychol 1:257–262.

German and U.S. research indicates that data standardized in one culture cannot be appropriate in assessing another. Use of native raters may eliminate bias, and many variables in each culture must be isolated in order to make valid comparisons.

1950. White JH: Some attitudes of South African nurses: a cross-cultural study. J Soc Psychol 69: 13–26.

Although Africans are more authoritarian than whites, there is no evidence for the prejudiced assertion that African nurses lack sympathy for their patients.

1951. Wober M: Sensotypes. J Soc Psychol 70:181–189.

Sensotypes, or the patterns of relative importance of different sense that structure perception and development of abilities, may differ across cultures, with respect to analytic abilities in different sensory realms. Southern Nigerian performance on the Rod and Frame test is not as closely related to visual tests of analytic functioning as found in Westernized groups. This performance is related to work efficiency ratings, however.

1952. Yamamoto J, Goin MK: Social class factors relevant for psychiatric treatment. J Nerv Ment Dis 142:332–339.

Sociological evaluation is relevant in the treatment of psychiatric patients in a clinic setting if treatment consonant with the patients' expectations is to be offered.

1967

1953. Adler LL: A note on cross-cultural preferences: fruit-tree preferences in children's drawings. J Psychol 65:15–22.

The overall majority of children from 13 countries favor apple trees in their drawings, but tend to draw trees that grow in their own local environment.

1954. Aldous J: Intergenerational visiting patterns: variation in boundary maintenance as an explanation. Fam Process 6:235–253.

Kinship interaction can be studied in terms of the impact of boundary maintenance upon the stability and well-being of the nuclear family.

1955. Al-Issa I: Effects of literacy and schizophrenia on verbal abstraction in Iraq. J Soc Psychol 71:39–44.

Level of education (literacy) and schizophrenic illness are significant variables for level of abstract thinking in non-Western and Western cultures.

1956. Al-Issa I, Dennis W: Cultural orientations and the use of common objects in Iraq. J Psychol 66:315–319.

The results of a Uses test in Baghdad are consistent with predictions that may be derived from the culture.

1957. Allen MG: Childhood experience and adult personality: cross-cultural study using the concept of ego strength. J Soc Psychol 71:53–68.

Many variables of childhood experience and anxiety are directly related to adult personality adjustment. The sexual aspects of early experience correlate most strongly with the cultural measure of adult ego strength.

1958. Arnold CB: Culture shock and a Peace Corps field mental health program. Community Ment Health J 3:53–60.

A field mental health program based upon group therapy precepts in order to minimize the effects of adjustment dilemmas among Bolivian Peace Corps personnel was effective. However, there are some limitations to such a program.

1959. Asuni T: Nigerian experiment in group psychotherapy. Am J Psychother 21:95–104.

Psychotherapy alone, without the use of some organic treatment, or at least placebos, is not likely to be accepted in Nigeria. The tendency to externalize and the apparent lack of introspection may hinder the progress of nondirective, informal, and loosely knit kinds of group psychotherapy.

1960. Beaubrun MH: Treatment of alcoholism in Trinidad and Tobago, 1956–1965. Br J Psychiatry 113:643–658.

Negroes and East Indians form subcultures of comparable size, yet highest rates of alcoholism come from the Indians with stable family units and male role models, while the matrifocal Negro group seems less vulnerable. Sociocultural deprivation seems the likely explanation. Cultural acceptance of the disease concept of alcoholism is important to therapy.

1961. Belcher JC: The one-person household: a consequence of the isolated nuclear family? J Marriage Fam 29:534–540.

An increase in the number of single-person households in the United States is partly a consequence of the dominance of the small nuclear family.

1962. Bennett FJ, Mugalula-Mukiibi A: An analysis of people living alone in a rural community in East Africa. Soc Sci Med 1:97–115.

Many of the young single men and older age inhabitants of homesteads in Ganda villages are observing local customs by living alone. Middle-aged solitary inhabitants are most likely to be ill or have personality problems. Where solitary residence is associated with isolation and is not merely a reflection of a socially required pattern of residence, a pattern of morbidity exists as shown elsewhere in the world.

1963. Berardo FM: Kinship interaction and communications among space-age migrants. J Marriage Fam 29:541–554.

Despite geographic mobility, extended family identification can be maintained in the United States. Women are the principle actors in maintaining such communications.

1964. Berger H: Conference on narcotic addiction. Int J Addic 2:283–290.

The impact of use of hemp and opium derivatives upon the East Indian population indicates the programs for control must consider the cultural setting.

1965. Berger SM: Social structure and mediated learning. J Pers Soc Psychol 7:104–107.

Knowledge of social structure such as learning new rank insignia in Israeli soldiers produces a cognitive structure that mediates learning.

1966. Berglund GW: A note on intelligence and season of birth. Br J Psychol 58:147–152.

No significant differences are obtained between season of birth and intelligence for Swedish children, but subnormal children born during autumn show the highest mean IQ of that group.

1967. Berrien FK: Methodological and related problems in cross-cultural research. Int J Psychol 2:33–44.

Sampling and instrument comparability, the effect of ethnocentrism, and ethnic influences are some of the methodological considerations of cross-cultural research.

1968. Berrien FK, Arkoff A, Iwahara S: Generation difference in values: Americans, Japanese-Americans, and Japanese. J Soc Psychol 71:169–176.

The hypothesis that value patterns, which might contribute to generational conflict, would be more different between Japanese college students and their parents than in any other settings, is not confirmed by the data. The findings suggest that there is a social maturational process that contributes to shaping of values and overshadows cultural differences.

1969. Berry JW: Independence and conformity in subsistence level societies. J Pers Soc Psychol 7:415–518.

A conformity test of degree of acceptance of a group norm shows that Sierra Leone Temne intensive agriculturalists are dependent and group reliant, while Baffin Island Eskimo hunters and fishers are independent and self-reliant.

1970. Boyer LB, Boyer RM: Some influences of acculturation on the personality traits of the old people of the Mescalero and the Chiricahua Apaches. Psychoanal Study Society 4:170–182.

Subjected to different processes of acculturation, the more secure Mescalero retain traditional cognitive and value patterns, while the Chiricahua more resemble white cognitive and value orientations.

1971. Boyer LB, Boyer RM, Kawai H, Klopfer B: Apache "learners" and "nonlearners." J Proj Tech Pers Assessment 31:22–29.

Differences in cognitive and perceptual patterns are found for old-age Mescalero and Chiricahua Apaches. Nonlearner children and the aged, less acculturated Mescalero have similar responses to Rorschach stimuli.

1972. Bradley N: Primal scene experience in human evolution and its phantasy derivatives in art, proto-science and philosophy. Psychoanal Study Society 4:34–79.

The ubiquitous effects of the primal scene appear throughout man's history, from Paleolithic art to Butler's Erewhon.

1973. Brody EB: Transcultural psychiatry, human similarities, and socioeconomic evolution. Am J Psychiatry 124:616–622.

The mental health of underprivileged groups may be evaluated in terms of general health, economic powerlessness, and social alienation.

1974. Buric O, Zecevic A: Family authority, marital satisfaction and the social network in Yugoslavia. J Marriage Fam 29:325–336.

In Greece and Yugoslavia, the husband's higher social position is associated with lower traditional family authority; while higher social position is related to greater family authority in the United States and France.

1975. Burt C: The genetic determination of intelligence: a reply. Br J Psychol 58:153–162.

Although Stott and Lewis's alternative explanations may be conceivable, they have not been shown to be more probable than the original explanation that is grounded in empirical evidence.

1976. Camilleri C: Modernity and the family in Tunisia. J Marriage Fam 29:590–595.

The influence of modernity on the traditional Tunesian patriarchal model is complex, yet fluid. Change is accompanied by a series of reactions that tend to minimize their impact and create unexpected compromises.

1977. Carstairs GM: The limitations of "instant research." Int J Psychiatry 3:15–17.

Cross-cultural research requires a more scientific approach than evaluation of questionnaire responses of nonrandom groups.

1978. Cawte JE, Kiloh LG: Language and pictorial representation in aboriginal children: implications for transcultural psychiatry. Soc Sci Med 1:67–76.

Because language influences representation of the physical world by aboriginal children, it will need to be taken into account in future work on their mental and personality disorders, and on their psychology in general.

1979. Chamove A, Harlow HF, Mitchell G: Sex differences in the infant-directed behavior of pre-adolescent Rhesus monkeys. Child Dev 38:329–335.

Sexually immature female monkeys exhibit maternallike affiliative patterns toward infants, whereas sexually immature males exhibit patterns of indifference or hostility. To a considerable extent, cultural variables can override biological variables in the human being, but the relative importance of these two factors in various developmental stages remains unresolved.

1980. Chu GC: Sex differences in persuasibility factors among Chinese. Int J Psychol 2:283–288.

Culturally prescribed sex differentiated norms may give rise to differences in persuasibility factors for male and female Taiwan Chinese students.

1981. Claeys W: Conforming behavior and personality variables in Congolese students. Int J Psychol 2:13–24.

Congolese and American performances are comparable in conformity situations. Independent students handle stress more easily than conforming students, but the two do not differ on extraversion and need for social approval.

1982. Clarke AH: The dominant matriarch syndrome. Br J Psychiatry 113:1069–1071.

In a three-female generation complex dominated by the grandmother, emotional and psychosomatic illness in the younger members are prominent presenting features. In such a situation, it is unlikely that psychiatric referral will be of much help; too much of the cause is situational and yet unrecognized and therefore is not reported to the consultant by the patient or parent.

1983. Collumb H: Methodological problems in cross-cultural research. Int J Psychiatry 3:17–19.

Cross-cultural inquiries should pertain to individuals of similar cultures or, in the case of different cultures, should include psychosociologists and ethnologists in a multidisciplinary team.

1984. Crockett WH, Nidorf LJ: Individual differences in responses to the semantic differential. J Soc Psychol 73:211–218.

Although an evaluative factor is evident for all subjects, there is some indication that individual differences in interpreting various subscales are not accounted for by the technique that generates three scores for conceptual connotative meaning.

1985. Curley RT: Drinking patterns of the Mescalero Apache. Q J Stud Alcohol 28:116–131.

Blitz drinking behavior is common and serves as a substitute for the various forms of institutionalized activity and group relationships that have been lost to the Apache during a hundred years of deculturation.

1986. David KH, Bochner S: Immediate vs. delayed reward among Arnhemland aborigines. J Soc Psychol 73:157–159.

Irrespective of age, one-half of aborigine children chose immediate reward, and the other half chose delayed reward. This contrasts with the situation in Western cultures and may be due to the fluidity of time perspective in Australian aborigine culture.

1987. Dawson JLM: Cultural and physiological influences upon spatial-perceptual processes in West Africa. Int J Psychol 2:115–128.

Witkin's hypothesis relating severe socialization and maternal dominance to spatial-perceptual ability is supported among two tribal groups with differing socialization practices and field-dependence.

1988. Dawson JLM: Traditional versus Western attitudes in West Africa: the construction, validation, and application of a measuring device. Br J Soc Clin Psychol 6:81–96.

The validity and usefulness of an attitude scale is demonstrated in two research studies in Sierra Leone, controlling for traditional and Western attitudes in the study of tribal distance and habits of perceptual inference.

1989. DeBrabander B: A comparison of interaction patterns of North American and Colombian face-to-face groups. J Soc Psychol 71:309–310.

Cross-culturally the interactions are very similar. The main difference between the American and Colombian patterns is the greater solidarity displayed by Colombians.

1990. Deregowski JB: The horizontal-vertical illusion and the ecological hypothesis. Int J Psychol 2:251–268.

Results obtained from Lusaka boys give some support to the proposition that the horizontal-vertical illusion has effects that may be attributed to verticality and line intersection. The role of carpentered environment can only be measured with an L-type figure.

1991. Diaz-Guerrero R: Socio-cultural premises, attitudes and cross-cultural research. Int J Psychol 2:79–88.

Sociocultural premises, which are permanent group determinants in contrast to attitudes, differently affect the thinking and feeling of individuals reared in Mexico and the United States.

1992. Dobbelaere K: Ideal number of children in marriage in Belgium and the U.S.A. J Marriage Fam 29:360–367.

A status congruency theory states that individuals of high social status and church integration seek to further church status by adhering totally to Roman Catholic ideology and hence have a large family.

1993. Dohrenwend BS, Dohrenwend BP: Field studies of social factors in relation to three types of psychological disorder. J Abnorm Soc Psychol 72:369–378.

Analysis of community rates of psychoses, neuroses, and personality disorder across age, sex, and social class reveals that psychosis, in general, is not consistently related to these variables, but schizophrenia and manic-depressive psychosis relate to social class in various ways. Neurosis rates are higher for females, and personality disorders higher for males and low social class.

1994. Duff DF, Arthur RJ: Between two worlds: Filipinos in the U.S. Navy. Am J Psychiatry 123:836–843.

High rates of hypochondriasis and paranoia among Filipinos in the U.S. Navy may result from certain cultural conditions that encourage strong feelings of obligation and shame, and from child-rearing practices that emphasize passivity.

1995. Dumon WA: The problem of sampling and instrument construction in a study of the entrepreneurial family in Belgium and the United States: some methodological problems of minor importance. J Marriage Fam 29:368–373.

The main problem for cross-cultural research is the reconceptualization of the research problem for each different country.

1996. Earle MJ: Bilingual semantic meaning and an aspect of acculturation. J Pers Soc Psychol 6:304–312.

Semantic differential ratings for Chinese-English bilinguals correspond to the degree of similarity of beliefs with either the second- or native-language community. Acceptance of second-language community beliefs may result in a transformation from a coordinate to a compound bilingual system.

1997. Eisenman R: Scapegoating the deviant in two cultures. Int J Psychol 2:133–138.

Scapegoating, a cultural universal, may be integrative or disintegrative for the Eskimo and Navaho. Reactions to deviance in other cultures may further an understanding of reactions in our own culture.

1998. El-Eslam MF: The psychotherapeutic basis of some Arab rituals. Int J Soc Psychiatry 13:265–268.

The psychotherapeutic effect of the Sheikh-visiting and Zaar rituals is due to the satisfaction of unconscious needs to submit to a parent-figure transferred to imaginary "Master" figures.

1999. Fabrega H, Wallace CA: How physicians judge symptom statements: a cross-cultural study. J Nerv Ment Dis 145:486–491.

American physician groups scale patients higher on the Midtown Mental Health Questionnaire than do Mexican physician groups. Male patients receive higher symptom scores. Conceptual and methodological biases may be present in cross-cultural psychiatric studies that use structured symptom questionnaires.

2000. Field GR: Persons admired by Turkish university students. Psychol Rep 21:443–444.

Although Turks head the lists of persons admired, persons drawn from international life predominate. Religious figures or persons drawn from the immediate range of experience are rarely mentioned.

2001. Field MG: Soviet psychiatry and social structure, and ideology: a preliminary assessment. Am J Psychother 21:230–243.

Russian culture, as manifested by collectivism, humanitarianism, rejection of sexuality, and isolation, has greatly affected the concepts and practice of human psychiatry. In the Soviet view, the handling of mental illness is considered strictly a medical function in which medical personnel do something to patients and are responsible both to society and the patient.

2002. Fischer R: Acquiescent response set, the Jesness Inventory, and implications for the use of "foreign psychological tests." Br J Soc Clin Psychol 6:1–10.

English and American differences in performance on the Jesness Inventory are not reflections of personality but of differing test-taking techniques

related to an acquiescent response set among English boys.

2003. Freeman D: Shaman and incubus. Psychoanal Study Society 4:315–343.

An eye-witness account of demon slaying by an Iban (Borneo) shaman illustrates his role as a healer of emotional problems and defender of psychic integrity.

2004. Freeman D: Totem and taboo: a reappraisal. Psychoanal Study Society 4:9–33.

Evidence from anthropology, primatology, and genetics does not support Freud's theory of the primal deed, though the essential elements of the oedipal situation (sexual drives, dominance, aggression, and fear) are basic to man's nature.

2005. Garsee JW, Glixman AF: Samoan interpersonal values. J Soc Psychol 72:45–60.

Values held by Samoan students as measured by the Gordon Survey of Interpersonal Values are consistent with anthropological observations. There is evidence that the Samoan value system is changing under the influence of contact with industrial society.

2006. Georgas JG, Vassiliou V: A normative Rorschach study of Athenians. J Proj Tech Pers Assessment 31:31–38.

A representative sample of 200 adults shows a tendency to internalize. Except for greater productivity in females, no significant variations are found for age, sex, education, or income.

2007. Gibby RG, Gabler R: The self-concept of Negro and white children. J Clin Psychol 23:144–148.

Similar groups of Negro and white children do differ significantly on self-concept as measured by self-rating on intelligence and on measures of Discrepancy and Self-Discrepancy, but not on Ideal-Discrepancy. The magnitude and direction of such differences are dependent on the sex and IQ level of the children.

2008. Ginsburg KN: The "meat-rack": a study of the male homosexual prostitute. Am J Psychother 21:170–185.

The homosexual prostitute has never learned to relate to people; it is only with his body that he relates at all. The selection of the homosexual object as the preferred choice is quite consistent with a life pattern that has incorporated few cultural mores, social controls, or moral imperatives.

2009. Gold D: Psychological changes associated with acculturation of Saskatchewan Indians. J Soc Psychol 71:177–184.

Patterns of preference for delayed reward are more similar between urban Indians and whites than reserve Indians (Cree, Chippewa) and whites, with these patterns falling along a continuum according to degree of acculturation. Socioeconomic, urbanization, ethnics, and cultural factors all determine gratification patterns.

2010. Goldscheider C, Goldstein S: Generational changes in Jewish family structure. J Marriage Fam 29:267–276.

Generational changes in family structure and acculturation, as well as an overall stability, are evident in the Jewish-American family.

2011. Gordon LV: Q-typing of Oriental and American youth: initial and clarifying studies. J Soc Psychol 71:185-196.

The Q-typing approach, for describing individuals and groups in terms of personality types, has been found to yield meaningful cross-cultural results.

2012. Graham PJ, Meadows CE: Psychiatric disorder in the children of West Indian immigrants. J Child Psychol Psychiatry 8:105–116.

West Indian immigrant boys show less neurotic disorder than controls, while girls show antisocial disorder. The high rate of antisocial disorders may be related to the fact that in the West Indies, bolder and more aggressive behavior is acceptable in a girl than is the case in the United Kingdom.

2013. Grimshaw AD: Social epithet in India: a Hindi example. J Soc Psychol 72:189–196.

Use of a modified semantic differential and factor analysis of interregional imagery indicate that factors for various regions are complex and stereotypes are multidimensional. Though language ratios may vary, there is a greater proportion of negative epithet in the lexical inventory of languages.

2014. Guggenheim F, Hoem A: Cross-cultural and intracultural attitudes of Lapp and Norwegian children. J Soc Psychol 73:23–36.

The semantic differential and Draw-A-Person test for Lapp and Norwegian children indicate that inter- and intragroup attitudes are favorable across communities; and there are no differences in self-esteem for communities with different degrees of intercultural contact.

2015. Gutierrez J: A note on juvenile delinquency: the gamin problem in Colombia. Contemp Psychoanal 3:173–176.

Gamin are Colombian children living in the large cities who lead an unsettled life alternating between beggary and delinquency. Family disintegration, alcoholic parents, and other delinquents in the family are common psychosocial characteristics of the milieu from which gamin come.

2016. Gutmann D: Aging among the highland Maya: a comparative study. J Pers Soc Psychol 7:28–35.

Highland Mayan men develop lessening autonomy and objectivity with increasing age, as do urban American and Lowland Mayan men.

2017. Haavio-Mannila E: Sex differentiation in role expectations and performance. J Marriage Fam 29:568–577.

Finnish norms concerning sexual equality are adhered to more in public than private life.

2018. Harford TC, Willis CH, Deabler HL: Personality correlates of masculinity-feminity. Psychol Rep 21:881–884.

Masculinity is associated with aloofness, unpretentiousness, tough poise, guilt proneness, anxiety, and neurotic tendencies. Low M-F scores are associated with warmth, Bohemianism, sensitivity, sophistication, acceptance, responsive emotionality, and anesthetic values.

2019. Hashimoto A: Kaiun-Tokyujutsu and its modern interpretation. J Hist Behav Sciences 3:236–255.

Tenegenjutsu, a Japanese version of astrological characterology, was developed into a kind of ethical and religious teaching called Kaiun-Tokyujutsu.

2020. Heckscher BT: Household structure and achievement orientation in lower-class Barbadian families. J Marriage Fam 29:521–526.

The Barbadian Negro-American mother's concern for child's future is most closely associated with differences in household structure (presence or absence of father).

2021. Hemsi LK: Psychiatric morbidity of West Indian immigrants. Soc Psychiatry 2:95–100.

West Indian migrants show higher morbidity for both the major functional psychoses and the personality and neurotic disorders. An investigation of West Indians who return to their homelands after a psychiatric illness in Britain may allow for a better evaluation of the respective roles of individual predisposition and of external difficulties in leading to illness in the migrants.

2022. Henderson NB: Cross-cultural action research: some limitations, advantages, and problems. J Soc Psychol 73:61–70.

The treatment program for Navaho problem drinkers reveals the limitations (sampling, role perceptions, inconsistency of aims, worker training), advantages (culture and personality dimensions, combining study and service), and problems (cultural relativism, ethnocentrism, and stereotypy) of action research.

2023. Huescher JE: Mythologic and fairy tale themes in psychotherapy. Am J Psychother 21:655–665.

Although myths and fairy tales in some respects are comparable to dreams, they are free from the dream's secondary distortions caused by the dreamer's individual problems. Themes of myths and fairy tales can be used effectively in psychotherapy if the patient feels unreservedly accepted by the therapist.

2024. Hudson W: The study of the problem of pictorial perception among unacculturated groups. Int J Psychol 2:89–108.

The efficacy of a representation depends upon its form and the group perceiving it; pictorial meaning varies according to level of acculturation.

2025. Iwawaki S, Sumida K, Okuno S, Cowen E: Manifest anxiety in Japanese, French, and United States children. Child Dev 38:713–722.

There is significantly less anxiety in Japanese children and significantly more anxiety in Japanese adults than in American and French samples. Anxiety item content needs to be broadened for cross-cultural research. Specific content areas need to be evaluated in terms of what we know about the cultures.

2026. Kamii CK, Radin NL: Class differences in the socialization practices of Negro mothers. J Marriage Fam 29:302–310.

Middle-class and lower lower-class Negro mothers differ considerably more in their socialization practices than in their child-rearing goals.

2027. Karr C: Reciprocal rating for cross and subcultural comparisons. Psychol Rep 20:68.

Cross-cultural studies may be facilitated by asking individuals who have been reared in one culture and lived in another to compare the two cultures on a variety of topics.

2028. Kaufman IC, Rosenblum LA: The reaction to separation in infant monkeys: anaclitic depression and conservation-withdrawal. Psychosom Med 29:648–675.

Infant monkeys have a greater chance of survival without a mother figure than humans because of their greater locomotor ability, which appears to initiate recovery from the depressed state. Their styles of reaction are adaptive and especially related to dominance-heirarchical regulatory influences.

2029. Kidd CB, Kingham J: An anthropological study of the elderly patient in an adult psychiatric clinic. Int J Soc Psychiatry 13:115–125.

By utilizing the anthropological methods of observation, intent analysis of interactions, and unstructured interviewing, it was noted that staff expectations for elderly patients in treatment favored outgroup formation of the elderly within the therapeutic community. The expectations of the elderly patients in regards to the treatment service also favored outgroup formation.

2030. Kiev A: Opening up communication channels. Int J Psychiatry 3:20–21.

Further research using the world-wide questionnaire approach will continue to clarify the issues and needs within international psychiatry.

2031. Kitano H: Japanese-American crime and delinquency. J Psychol 66:253–267.

Low rates for crime and delinquency may be explained in terms of the ability of the Japanese-American subculture to provide alternatives to these directions.

2032. Kline P: The use of the Cattell 16 P.F. Test and Eysenck's E.P.I. with a literate population in Ghana. Br J Soc Clin Psychol 6:97–107.

Rotated factor analysis shows the Sixteen Personality Factor Questionnaire and Eysenck's Personality Inventory are valid among literate Ghanaians.

2033. Klingelhofer EL: Occupational preferences of Tanzanian secondary school pupils. J Soc Psychol 72:149–160.

Similarities of occupational interest for individual sexes, regardless of African or Asian background, have implications for manpower planning in Tanzania.

2034. Klingelhofer EL: Performance of Tanzanian secondary school pupils on the Raven Standard Progressive Matrices test. J Soc Psychol 72:205–215.

Differences in mean level of performance are associated with African or Asian ethnic group, sex, and age of student, but are independent of grade level, tribe, or community groupings.

2035. Koenigsberg RA: Culture and unconscious fantasy: observations on courtly love. Psychoanal Rev 54:36–50.

The form of Courtly Love was not caused by socioeconomic variables but rather by unconscious conflict. The ultimate rapprochement between sociology, history, and psychoanalysis will involve the identification of the infantile root of social institutions.

2036. Korson JH: Dower and social class in an urban Muslim community. J Marriage Fam 29:527–533.

Dower in Pakistan is the wife's insurance of economic security should marital separation occur. Upper-class Muslims commit the largest amount of dower, the lower class the smallest amount, and the middle class an intermediate amount.

2037. Krupinski J: Sociological aspects of mental ill-health in migrants. Soc Sci Med 1:267–281.

In Victoria, Australia, psychiatric disorders, particularly schizophrenic states, occur more frequently in non-British immigrants, especially in those from Eastern Europe, than in Britons and Australian-born. Stresses of migration may play a contributory part.

2038. Kumasaka Y: Iwakura: early community care of the mentally ill in Japan. Am J Psychother 21:666–676.

Iwakura, a farming village, has been known for the past 900 years for care of the mentally ill. Kindness and hospitality were considered necessary ingredients for recovery. The practice rapidly deteriorated during World War II and has not revived.

2039. Kuttnes RE, Lorincz AB, Swan DA: The schizophrenia gene and social evolution. Psychol Rep 20:407–412.

A tendency toward schizophrenia may offer protection from stresses of social interaction. Like many other beneficial traits, however, when fully expressed, the individual is handicapped and loses the benefit of the gene.

2040. Langness LL: Hysterical psychosis: the cross-cultural evidence. Am J Psychiatry 124:143–52.

An interdisciplinary approach is needed to appreciate the similarities and differences in cases of hysterical psychosis in Bena Bena, Puerto Rican, Malaysian, Eskimo, and Ainu cultures.

2041. Lee SC, Brattrud A: Marriage under a monastic mode of life: a preliminary report on the Hutterite family in South Dakota. J Marriage Fam 29:512–520.

The cohesion and stability of the Hutterite colony is perpetuated by its special, stable pattern of family life. Each family unit is auxiliary to the colony, not a conjugal family as such. Church control supplants the economic and child-training functions of the family.

2042. Lemert EM: Secular use of kava in Tonga. Q J Stud Alcohol 28:328–341.

While the tradition of kava drinking has been continuously reinforced in Tongan society, liquor has remained a marginal cultural alternative. Increased kava drinking suggests a cultural reaction formation that allows for psychic detachment from the immediate situation and a retreat to older Tongan values.

2043. Leon RL, Martin HW, Gladfelter JH: An emotional and educational experience for urban migrants. Am J Psychiatry 124:381–384.

Education in urban living within a modified therapeutic community may be applied at a center for reducing the stress encountered by urban migrants.

2044. Levison PK, Findley JD: Counting behavior in baboons: an error-contingency reinforcement schedule. Psychol Rep 20:393–394.

Baboons can respond appropriately to mixed contingencies demanding both "correct" and "incorrect" solutions without suffering general disruption to a complex performance.

2045. Luchterhand E: Prisoner behavior and social system in the Nazi concentration camps. Int J Soc Psychiatry 13:245–264.

The carry-over by individual prisoners of pre-camp beliefs and attitudes aided in the development of conduct norms. The very nature of human socialization assisted renorming by the common tendency, in all but the most antisocial prisoners, for reciprocal acceptance of duties and rights in pair relations.

2046. MacArthur RS: Sex differences in field-dependence for the Eskimo: replications of Berry's findings. Int J Psychol 2:139–140.

An independent sample of Eskimo children also shows no sex differences on the Embedded Figures Test, thus supporting Berry's findings. Social or environmental aspects may influence sex differences in other cultures.

2047. Madaus GF: A cross-cultural comparison of the factor structure of selected tests of divergent thinking. J Abnorm Soc Psychol 73:13–21.

The difference of higher scores on measures of divergent thinking for American over Irish adolescents may be explained in terms of cultural factors, bilingualism, and relevancy; however, the high cross-cultural similarity requires further explanation.

2048. Malzberg B: Internal migration and mental disease among the white population of New York State, 1960–1961. Int J Soc Psychiatry 13:184–191.

When associated with minority status, migration is characterized by a degree of insecurity that may have as a consequence a higher incidence of mental disorder. This is evidenced in a comparison of French-Canadian and British rates of first hospital admissions in Quebec and Ontario.

2049. Marks IM, Sartorius NH: A contribution to the measurement of sexual attitude: the semantic differential as a measure of sexual attitude in sexual deviations. J Nerv Ment Dis 145:441–451.

A simple two-dimensional (6 scale) measure of sexual attitude can be used as a clinical aid in assessing the therapeutic progress of sexual deviants.

2050. Mason EP: Comparison of personality characteristics of junior high students from American Indian, Mexican, and Caucasian ethnic backgrounds. J Soc Psychol 73:145–155.

Female responses on subtests of the California Personality Inventory reflect a consistently negative pattern. Mexican and Indian males show lower social presence than Caucasian males. Mexican male scores on social responsibility, tolerance, and intellectual efficiency are higher than for males of the other groups.

2051. Masuda M, Holmes TH: The social readjustment rating scale: a cross-cultural study of Japanese and Americans. J Psychosom Res 11:227–237.

Japanese and Americans show essential similarities in their attitudes towards life events, but there are some differences that reflect cultural variation. The Japanese, for example, regard changes in church activities as less meaningful than do Americans.

2052. Mead M: Ethnological aspects of aging. Psychosomatics 8:33–37.

In primitive society, one does not see old people who are reduced to a vegetable state. From comparisons with other societies, we ought to be able to construct a society where the process of aging is different; where the expectation of learning is high; where we recognize that older people can continue to learn and produce.

2053. Meade RD: An experimental study of leadership in India. J Soc Psychol 72:35–43.

Morale and productivity is higher for North Indian Hindu boys under the direction of authoritarian, rather than democratic, leadership.

2054. Meade RD, Whittaker JO: A cross-cultural study of authoritarianism. J Soc Psychol 72:3–7.

Authoritarian scores increase for the United States, Brazil, Arabia, Hong Kong, Rhodesia, and India, in that order. This characterization has cross-cultural implications for personality, leadership, and social relations.

2055. Meeks JE: Some observations on adolescent group leaders in two contasting socioeconomic classes. Int J Soc Psychiatry 13:278–286.

Volunteers working with adolescents of middle and upper classes do not feel alienated from society at large and are not as critical of the social order and its deficits as of their own. Group leaders working with adolescents of lower class and minority people tend to be critical of the social order and feel that hostile attitudes toward society are justified.

2056. Melikian LH: Social change and sexual behavior of Arab university students. J Soc Psychol 73:169–175.

The incidence of various reported sexual behaviors did not differ significantly in 1963 from reports obtained in 1952, although more of the subjects in the later study reported masturbation and a decline in patronizing prostitutes.

2057. Mercer C: Interrelationships among family stability, family composition, residence, and race. J Marriage Fam 29:456–460.

Variations in family patterning are best understood in terms of the total interrelatedness of stability, living patterns, residence, and race.

2058. Michael ST: Social class and psychiatric treatment. J Psychiatr Res 5:243–254.

Social class significantly influences the occurrence, duration, and success of psychiatric treatment. Psychoneurotic reactions prevail in upper socioeconomic status patients, and psychotic, organic and character disorder reactions in patients of low SES. Treatment rates are conspicuously higher in the upper SES third, even though impairment from symptoms are more severe in the low.

2059. Michel A: Comparative data concerning the interaction in French and American families. J Marriage Fam 29:337–344.

Trends in husband's authority are similar between the United States and France, but marital satisfaction differs with husband's income between the two countries.

2060. Miles J: The psychiatric aspects of the traditional medicine of the British Columbia Coast Indians. Can Psychiatr Assoc J 12:429–431.

Primitives saw all disease as a manifestation of the supernatural. Indians of the British Columbia coast reflect this in their medicine and intuitive therapeutic use of trance, suggestion, and confession.

2061. Miller RE, Caul WF, Mirsky IA: Communication of affect between feral and socially isolated monkeys. J Pers Soc Psychol 7:231–239.

Rhesus monkey isolates are incapable of employing facial expressions in order to perform avoidance responses in a cooperative-avoidance situation.

2062. Mizushima K, DeVos G: An application of the California Psychological Inventory in a study of Japanese delinquency. J Soc Psychol 71:45–52.

Similar results obtained with a Japanese translation of the California Psychological Inventory suggest that this inventory illuminates social attitudes of general relevance and may be successfully used cross-culturally.

2063. Mohan RP: Factors to motivation towards sterilization in two Indian villages. Fam Life Coordinator 16:35–38.

While some individuals in two Indian villages are aware of the advantages of smaller family size, knowledge of the operation and adverse group opinion function to resist family-planning programs.

2064. Moloney JC: Oedipus Rex, Cu Chulain, Khepri and the ass. Psychoanal Rev 54:201–247.

Oedipus Rex is a dramatization of the mythic description of the ritualized birth and death of the son. The Oedipus myth is like a thematic apperception story, like the psychic elaborations of a Rorschach test upon which is projected an anthropomorphic animation.

2065. Morioka K: Life cycle patterns in Japan, China, and the United States. J Marriage Fam 29:595–606.

A developmental framework for the conjugal family, the changing Japanese stem family, and the Chinese joint family points out characteristic role complexes.

2066. Morris P: Individual achievement and family ties: some international comparisons. J Marriage Fam 29:763–771.

Conceptualizations of family relationships adapt to economic circumstances as suggested by data from Nigeria, Kenya, Britain, and the United States. Resistance to change cannot be attributed solely to traditional family structures. Community opportunities and obligations effect the structure of attitudes toward individual achievement.

2067. Morsbach H, Morsbach G: A cross-cultural investigation of occupational stereotypes in three South African groups. J Soc Psychol 73:53–59.

The influence of Western culture and norms may account for the high similarity between white and colored groups in the hierarchical ranking of occupations; while differences between the white and colored groups are mainly due to the politically enforced separation of the groups.

2068. Muensterberger W, Kishner IA: Hazards of culture clash: a report on the history and dynamics of a psychotic episode in a West African exchange student. Psychoanal Study Society 4:99–123.

The impact of transition from the African to American cultural environment upon a Nigerian student suggests that government should provide a more suitable environment for non-Western students.

2069. Mukherjee BN: A cross-cultural study of social desirability judgments. Int J Psychol 2:25–32.

Indian students view simplicity, social conformity, constraint, and faithfulness as more desirable than their American counterparts.

2070. Mukherjee BN: A cross-validation of the Marlowe-Crowne Social Desirability Scale on an Indian sample. J Soc Psychol 72:299–300.

Item analysis shows a sex difference in India that may be explained in terms of differing male-female standards.

2071. Mundy-Castle AC: An experimental study of prediction among Ghanaian children. J Soc Psychol 73:161–168.

Successful prediction of simple dot patterns is low for children of 5 to 6 years and significantly higher among chindren of 7 to 10 years. Analysis indicates the conditions that must be fulfilled as a prerequisite to successful prediction.

2072. Murphy HBM, Wittkower ED, Chance NA: Crosscultural inquiry into symptomatology of depression. Int J Psychiatry 3:6–15.

Frequency of psychotic depression is more related to level of community cohesion than to specific cultures. Symptoms such as thought retardation and self-depreciation appear to be culturally specific, indicating that therapy must be culturally specific.

2073. Niederland WG: Clinical aspects of creativity. Am Imago 24:6–34.

Clinically observed psychological features common to certain creative individuals and examination of prehistoric and historic creativity processes illuminate the persistent difficulties encountered by psychoanalytic investigations with the phenomenon of creativity.

2074. Nye FI: Values, family and a changing society. J Marriage Fam 29:241–248.

Changing family structure and interactions accompany changes in instrumental values, the former are therefore major considerations for social change.

2075. Oliensis DG: East African psychological patterns. J Am Acad Child Psychiatry 6:551–572.

The traditional African tribes are very efficiently organized to maintain themselves in a relatively static context. Their culture is not so well organized, however, so as to be able to cope with the rapid changes induced by Westernization. Education will do much to shape African ingestion and assimilation of cultural invasions.

2076. Otto HA, Anderson RB: The hope chest and dowry: American custom? Fam Life Coordinator 16:15–19.

The hope chest, mostly associated with higher income levels, and the dowry equivalent (gifts) have become a larger part of American marriage culture than previously assumed.

2077. Pal SK: Values of students in four professions under Indian conditions. J Soc Psychol 72:297–298.

Value differences exist for students of engineering, law, medicine, and teaching in India.

2078. Pattison EM: Psychiatry and anthropology: three models for a working relationship. Soc Psychiatry 2:174–179.

Social and community psychiatry and applied anthropology have the opportunity to contribute to community dialogue that will eventuate in community change.

2079. Peck RF, Diaz-Guerrero R: Two core-culture patterns and the diffusion of values across their border. Int J Psychol 2:275–282.

Mexican students attach more authoritarian meaning to the concept of respect than do American subjects. Subjects from the Mexican-American border areas show more diffuse and differentiated value patterns.

2080. Peterson DR, Migliorino G: Pancultural factors of parental behavior in Sicily and the United States. Child Dev 38:967–991.

There are few differences between Sicilian and American parents as regards parental affection, but there are striking differences in parental control. Sicilian culture seems to be more repressive than American as far as overt sexuality among children is concerned.

2081. Press I: Maya aging: cross-cultural projective techniques and the dilemma of interpretation. Psychiatry 30:197–202.

Comparison of TAT protocols collected in Yucatan and in Kansas City suggests the need for cooperation between anthropologists and psychologists. Without such cooperation, no full range of alternative interpretations can be established.

2082. Rabin AI, Limuaco JA: A comparison of the connotative meaning of Rorschach's inkblots for American and Filipino college students. J Soc Psychol 72:197–204.

Use of the semantic differential to indicate connotative meaning of Rorschach inkblots indicates differences in meaning for Americans and Filipinos that seriously question the universality of Rorschach interpretive procedures.

2083. Ramirez M: Identification with Mexican family values and authoritarianism in Mexican-Americans. J Soc Psychol 73:3–11.

Mexican-American family attitude patterns show some Americanization in comparison to Mexican and Puerto Rican values, particularly in the decreased authority of the male. The basic agreement on Mexican family values of conformity, strict child rearing, and authoritarian submission suggests acculturative stress and cognitive dissonance in the area of civil rights.

2084. Raser JR: Cross-cultural simulation research. Int J Psychol 2:59–68.

If subject responses and model structures mirror the real world, then simulation research may enhance the understanding of very complex social situations.

2085. Robinson IE, Clune FJ: Sexual symbolism and archeology Psychoanal Rev 56:468–480.

Ancient Mayan-Toltec artistic work is a direct expression of man's confusion of reality with analogy. Symbols for fertility, such as the serpent and the circle, were commonly used and the Toltec-Mayan ball game is some form of fertility rite.

2086. Rodgers DA, Ziegler FJ, Levy N: Prevailing cultural attitudes about vasectomy: a possible explanation of postoperative psychological response. Psychosom Med 29:367–375.

Erosive cultural attitudes substantially contribute to adverse self-concept change and to negative emotional reactions of couples utilizing vasectomy.

2087. Rodman H: Marital power in France, Greece, Yugoslavia, and the United States: a cross-national discussion. J Marriage Fam 29:320–324.

A positive relationship between male educational, occupational, and income status in the United States and France in terms of marital power contrasts with a negative relationship between these variables for Greece and Yugoslavia. The interaction between marital resources and cultural expectations accounts for these differences.

2088. Rosenthal BG, Miller D, Teryenyi F: The measurement of social interaction among Negro and white children in a housing community. J Soc Psychol 71:27–28.

Negro children or their parents show considerable fear or anxiety in a new interracial situation, manifest in smaller numbers appearing in play areas, restriction of movement, and higher propor-

tion of adults accompanying children during various activities.

2089. Ruesch J: Technological civilization and human affairs. J Nerv Ment Dis 145:193–205.

A nontechnical orientation suitable for the majority of the population must be developed so that the 75 percent of the population who find symbolic systems and the gadgets of the technological civilation too difficult to master will not be dominated and disfranchised by the minority of "machine people."

2090. Safilios-Rothschild C: A comparison of power structure and marital satisfaction in urban Greek and French families. J Marriage Fam 29:345–352.

For Greece, in contrast to more industrialized countries, a high socioeconomic position for the husband tends to decrease his family authority.

2091. Sargent MJ: Changes in Japanese drinking patterns. Q J Stud Alcohol 28:709–722.

The traditional pattern of Japanese drinking is a concrete example of the cultural integration theory of drinking. In the present transitional stage, Japan is more permissive of drinking, more protective of the drunken, then almost any other complex society.

2092. Sarlin CN: Identity, culture and psychosexual development. Am Imago 24:181–247.

The cultural environment, specifically child-rearing practices, influences the psychosexual development for the Arapseh, Alorese, Southern Chinese, Balinese, Yurok, and Sioux.

2093. Saucier JF: Anthropologie et psychodynamique du deuil. Can Psychiatr Assoc J 12:477–496.

The behavior sequence of the young child following the mother's departure can be compared to the prototypical sequence of mourning behavior in adults (following the final departure of a parent), not only in Western culture but in all human societies. Throughout the world there are institutionalized funeral rituals similar to the many separation reactions of the young child.

2094. Savage C, Prince R: Depression among the Yoruba. Psychoanal Study Society 4:83–98.

Socially determined depression is prominent among students, menopausal and barren women, occurring when self-esteem is lowered and when defensive denial through magical practice fails.

2095. Schuch AJ, Quesada CC: Attitudes of Filipino and American college students assessed with the semantic differential. J Soc Psychol 72: 301–302.

Students in the Philippines and the United States perceive their educational environments in different ways but have similar self-evaluations.

2096. Schwarzweller HK, Seggar JF: Kinship involvement: a factor in the adjustment of rural migrants. J Marriage Fam 29:662–671.

In certain situations, a greater degree of involvement with kin in the recipient community facilitates the rural-urban migrant's personal stability and alleviates potential tensions.

2097. Shanas E: Family help patterns and social class in three countries. J Marriage Fam 29:257–266.

The social class of the elderly individual has an impact on the magnitude and direction of family help patterns in Denmark, Britain, and the United States.

2098. Shuval JT, Antonovsky A, Davies AM: The doctor-patient relationship in an ethnically heterogeneous society. Soc Sci Med 1:141–154.

Physicians in the Kupat Holim clinics in Israel tend to "give" more status to Rumanian rather than to Moroccan clients. Physicians in urban practices are under greater professional scrutiny and therefore are more likely than their rural counterparts to conform to the norms of their profession.

2099. Silverman W, Hill R: Task allocation in marriage in the United States and Belgium. J Marriage Fam 29:353–359.

Spouse availability best explains American task allocation. A developmental theory, which places availability into a life-cycle framework, explains differences in Belgian and American task allocation.

2100. Silverstein A: The prediction of individual association-hierarchies from cultural frequencies. Am J Psychol 80:88–94.

The norms of cultural free association reflect individual associative hierarchies as measured by the probability of repetition.

2101. Simon HA: An information-processing explanation of some perceptual phenomena. Br J Psychol 58:1–12.

Various phenomena of visual perception may be accounted for by a mechanism of information encoding that provides an internal representation characterized by efficiency of information processing and retrieval.

2102. Snell JE: Hypnosis in the treatment of the "hexed" patient. Am J Psychiatry 124:311–316.

A modern Southern cultural phenomenon, the hexing belief, is coming to the attention of psychiatrists. Hypnosis is the treatment of choice.

2103. Stoodley BH: Normative family orientations of Chinese college students in Hong Kong. J Marriage Fam 29:773–782.

Chinese students have adopted the Western norm of individual mate selection while retaining traditional concepts of parental respect and obligation. The resultant structural cohesion favors the extended solidarity of nuclear families, which may be especially functional in the urban setting.

2104. Stricker G, Takahashi S, Zax M: Semantic differential discriminability: a comparison of Japanese and American students. J Soc Psychol 71: 23–26.

The cross-cultural stability of methods of utilizing semantic space support the utility of the semantic differential in comparing meaning among different groups.

2105. Szalay LB, Brent JE: The analysis of cultural meanings through free verbal associations. J Soc Psychol 72:161–187.

Measures of word relatedness and content analysis of responses that reflect priority orders and meaning components point up the quantitative utility of free verbal association analysis of group-specific meaning content. The method has relevance for intercultural communication.

2106. Tamaradze V: Statistical differentiation of four African sculptural styles: a preliminary report. J Soc Psychol 71:163–168.

Quantitative procedures for discriminating Yoruba, Ibo, Ibibo, and Fang art styles are feasible and, in conjunction with ethnographic inquiry, may reflect some behavioral patterns.

2107. Taylor AJW: Culture conflict and student performance. Int J Soc Psychiatry 13:307–312.

Psychological, social, and cultural factors, rather than a conflict between arts and sciences, underlie the symptoms of university students from different backgrounds at home or overseas. Asian students are under particular stress, as evidenced by the case of a Fijian student in New Zealand.

2108. Tecson MP: Traditional magic and medicine, and the history of modern psychiatry in the Philippines. Can Psychiatr Assoc J 12:223–225.

Traditional Philippine magic rested in beliefs in religion, in the future life, mourning customs, black magic, and superstitions. Psychiatry, which had its modest beginnings from 1800 to 1910 when the care of mental cases was taken over by the religious charities and interests of the clergy, has progressed as far as the founding of The Philippine Society of Psychiatry and Neurology in 1940 and the organization of a Mental Health Association in 1950.

2109. Tinling DC: Voodoo, root work, and medicine. Psychosom Med 29:483–490.

Voodoo has evolved into a rural Southern practice in America called "root work." The migration of the Negro has brought root work to the industrial North. Patients presenting what appear to be organic or psychological symptoms may have a problem strictly related to a belief in being hexed. The cultural belief in root work also may confuse and complicate another disease process.

2110. Toker E: Mental illness in the white and Bantu populations of the Republic of South Africa. Am J Psychiatry 123:56–65.

Cultural differences between the white and Bantu populations of the Republic of South Africa account for differing incidences and modes of treatment of mental disorder between the groups. The effects of Westernization, including population movement to urban areas by the Bantu males, are particularly important.

2111. Torrey EF: The Zar cult in Ethiopia. Int J Soc Psychiatry 13:216–223.

There are three major types of the Zar "possession" cult in Ethiopia—conversion, seer, and group therapy. The group therapy Zar doctors could become analogous to the "mental health aids" now being trained to staff community clinics in the United States.

2112. Umunna I: The drinking culture of a Nigerian community: Onitsha. Q J Stud Alcohol 28: 529–537.

Compared to the people of surrounding districts, Onitshas take more drinks but appear to stay sober. Their sobriety may be due to the nature of their social organization.

2113. van den Ban AW: Family structure and modernization. J Marriage Fam 29:771–773.

Extended or highly familial families are not necessarily slow to accept technological innovations or modern attitudes.

2114. Vatuk VP, Vatuk SJ: *Chatorpan:* a culturally defined form of addiction in North India. Int J Addict 2:103–113.

Analysis of an addictive condition, characterized by excessive consumption of sweets and salty-spicy snacks, with associated deviant behavior patterns, indicates basic cultural value orientations and normative cognitive categories.

2115. Wassink MWG: Opinion survey on mixed marriages in Morocco. J Marriage Fam 29:578–589.

Moroccan male-European female intermarriage elicits negative attitudes by Arabic speakers and positive attitudes by French speakers. Both groups clearly regard mixed marriage as an important factor in social change.

2116. Whittaker JO: Attitudes toward civil liberties: a cross-cultural study. J Psychol 65:145–152.

Many factors, including race and religion, affect students' responses to items on civil liberties, though all groups studied are on the favorable side of the continuum.

2117. Whittaker JO, Meade RD: Sex and age as variable in persuasibility. J Soc Psychol 73:47–52.

Chronological age and sex for adolescents appear to be related to persuasibility for American culture. A cross-cultural comparison of young adults shows that only the Chinese reflect the sex differences in persuasibility as observed among American adolescents.

2118. Whittaker JO, Meade RD: Sex of the communicator as a variable in source credibility. J Soc Psychol 72:27–34.

In Brazil, Hong Kong, and India, male sources of oral presentations are judged more credible than female sources.

2119. Whittaker JO, Meade RD: Social pressure in the modification and distortion of judgment: a cross-cultural study. Int J Psychol 2:109–114.

Brazilian, Arabian, and Chinese students perform like Americans in terms of the effects of social pressure on conformity; while Rhodesians show greater conformity than the others.

2120. Wignall CM, Koppin LL: Mexican-American use of state mental hospital facilities. Community Ment Health J 3:137–148.

Although the specific causes of the differences in Mexican-American usage of state mental hospital facilities are not known, it seems clear that these differences must be the end products of economic and social discrimination.

2121. Williams JE, Carter DJ: Connotations of racial concepts and color names in Germany. J Soc Psychol 72:19–26.

Replication of an American study among German subjects shows that the designation of racial groups by color names, through color coding, influences the manner in which the groups are perceived.

2122. Wintrob RM: A study of disillusionment: depressive reactions of Liberian students returning from advanced training abroad. Am J Psychiatry 123:1593–1598.

Liberian students may experience depressive reactions upon returning to their rapidly developing homeland after advanced study in a developed country.

2123. Witkin HA: A cognitive style approach to cross-cultural research. Int J Psychol 2:233–250.

Tasks designed for the assessment of cognitive style are constructed so as to assess cultural influences rather than eliminate them; results may be subject to differing interpretations, however. Consistency in scoring and orientation is necessary in cross-cultural tests.

2124. Wober M: Adapting Witkin's field independence theory to accommodate new information from Africa. Br J Psychol 58:29–38.

Nigerian manual workers, especially sensitive to the proprioceptive field, show different patterns of scoring on the rod-and-frame test (which contains visual and proprioceptive idioms) than on the embedded figures test, which is essentially visual. The sameness of cognitive style through all fields does not occur for Africans as it may for Americans.

2125. Woodbury MA, Palacios ES, Thomas W: The village care system in Nigeria. Hosp Community Psychiatry 18:28–30.

An innovative psychiatric Nigerian village-care system follows several principles: the patient and his family are treated as a sociocultural unit, the mental health program provides tangible assistance to the community at large, the chief of each village remains chief of the therapeutic community, existing traditional beliefs and concepts are used rather than ignored.

2126. Yamamoto J, James QC, Bloombaum M, Hattem J: Racial factors in patient selection. Am J Psychiatry 124:630–636.

A study of 594 outpatient admissions reveals that psychiatric outpatients are treated differently by therapists on racial ethnocentric factors.

2127. Yamane Y, Nonoyama H: Isolation of the nuclear family and kinship organization in Japan: a hypothetical approach to the relationships between the family and society. J Marriage Fam 29:783–796.

The Dozuku-like occupational system of Japan attempts to counter the potential development of family anomie in the isolated nuclear family of the urban middle class.

2128. Zaidi SMH: A study of social distance as perceived by students of Karachi University. J Soc Psychol 71:197–208.

Responses to the Bogardus Social Distance Scale indicate that Pakistani students have the highest social proximity with other Pakistanis, and then with a general Muslim population, and finally with Asians as opposed to non-Asians.

2129. Zax M, Takahasi S: Cultural influences on response style: comparisons of Japanese and American college students. J Soc Psychol 71:3–10.

While many observed differences are not significant, the greater frequency of neutral responses to inkblots suggests that Japanese subjects are generally less extreme than their American counterparts. Response style differences may help verify qualitative evaluations of Japanese cultures.

2130. Zegans L: An appraisal of ethological contributions to psychiatric theory and research. Am J Psychiatry 124:729–739.

Ethology can contribute to the study of man by describing the process of communication of motivational and affective messages in a natural setting.

2131. Zern D: The influence of certain developmental factors in fostering the ability to differentiate the passage of time. J Soc Psychol 72:9–17.

A cross-cultural study of societies from Africa, South America, Oceania, Asia-Russia, and North America suggests that overall child indulgence, with maternal interaction secondary, is of primary importance in the development of an undifferentiated sense of time for the adult.

2132. Zippel B, Fink RT, Bessemer DW: Semantic differential profiles and free-association norms. Psychol Rep 20:1259–1263.

Semantic generalization is one determinant of the associative response hierarchy established by the free-association technique.

1968

2133. Adler LL: A note on the cross-cultural fruit-tree study: a test-retest procedure. J Psychol 69: 53–61.

Even in test-retest procedures, representations of apple trees outnumber all others and remain stable throughout.

2134. Ahmad FZ: Family and mental disorders in Pakistan. Int J Soc Psychiatry 14:290–295.

In Pakistan there is no statistically significant relationship found among mental disorders and marital status, family system, siblings, parental loss in childhood, children, and mother's age at birth. Parents of psychotics, however, are closer together in age than parents of neurotics. There is more psychopathology in the families of psychotics than neurotic patients.

2135. Amara IB: Detribalization and neuroses among the Africans. Bull Menninger Clin 32:291–300.

The fabric of African tradition is based upon group solidarity, the continuity of existence, and the basic religion of animism. African cultural traditions are threatened by education, industrialization, migration, increasing avoidance of initiation ceremonies by the young, and the changing role of women. Detribalization seems to lead to increasing neurosis.

2136. Al-Issa I: Cross-cultural studies of symptomatology in schizophrenia. Can Psychiatr Assoc J 13:521–538.

A more rigorous system of classification is needed to differentiate between normal and schizophrenic behavior in different cultures or in the same culture. Cross-cultural studies suggest that some test responses are more amenable to the influence of culture than others.

2137. Beall L: The psychopathology of suicide in Japan. Int J Soc Psychiatry 14:213–225.

Suicide today is more masochistic and reflects the highly masochistic Japanese culture where aggression is turned inward against the self, where motivation is basically "other-directed," and where obligation and indebtedness are anchored in a complicated system of *on* and *giri.*

2138. Belcher LH, Campbell JT: An exploratory study of word associations of Negro college students. Psychol Rep 23:119–134.

The responses of Negro college students to word-association lists show similar results with previous normative studies. A number of responses indicates reading difficulty or misunderstanding of the word.

2139. Beloff H, Coupar S: Some transactional perceptions of African faces. Br J Soc Clin Psychol 7:169–175.

The hypotheses that those with negative attitudes toward black people would set African faces farther away than European ones, while those with positive attitudes would show no differences, are confirmed.

2140. Bennett FJ, Saxton GA: Family structure and health at Kasangati. Soc Sci Med 2:261–282.

The dispersed nature of the kinship group is the outstanding feature of the family structure in Ganda villages. Poor school examination results by the children may be the result of the effects of frequent moves, broken homes, and several stepmothers.

2141. Berrien FK: Cross-cultural equivalence of personality measures. J Soc Psychol 75:3–9.

It is unproductive to speculate about instruments of factorial differences between cultures unless the problem of cross-cultual concepts of constructs is considered, and a pooling of items from instruments and samples across cultures is performed.

2142. Berry JW: Ecology, perceptual development and the Muller-Lyer illusion. Br J Psychol 59:205–210.

Appropriate sampling of Eskimo and Temne populations demonstrates the presence of a confounding of ecological and developmental variables and the influence of each on susceptibility to the Muller-Lyer illusion.

2143. Biller H: A note on father absence and masculine development in lower-class Negro and white boys. Child Dev 39: 1003–1006.

Underlying sex-role orientation is more influenced by both father absence and family background than are more manifest aspects of masculinity. Studies comparing Negro and white father-present and father-absent boys at several age levels and with a variety of measures are called for if we are to better understand the effects of father availability and sociocultural background on masculine development.

2144. Bochner S, David KH: Delay of gratification, age and intelligence in an aboriginal culture. Int J Psychol 3:167–174.

Contrary to expectations, North Territory aborigine youths show no association between age and delay of gratification and a negative association with intelligence. These results may be consistent with the exigencies of uncertain day-to-day subsistence.

2145. Bolman WM: Cross-cultural psychotherapy. Am J Psychiatry 124:1237–1244.

Cross-cultural psychotherapy may be used effectively in non-Western, developing nations following a model that utilizes cross-cultural relationships with traditional healers.

2146. Botha E: Verbally expressed values of bilinguals. J Soc Psychol 75:159–164.

Significantly different value scores appear from other groups, when French-Arabic bilinguals use French in a test of values.

2147. Boyer LB, Boyer RM, Klopfer B, Scheiner SB: Apache "learners" and "nonlearners" II: quantitative Rorschach signs of influential adults. J Proj Tech Pers Assessment 32:146–159.

The hypothesis that Apache learner children identify with the more acculturated Chiricahua Apache adults is not verified. Learner children are influenced by those adults with balanced approaches to Rorschach stimuli.

2148. Breen M: Culture and schizophrenia: a study of Negro and Jewish schizophrenics. Int J Soc Psychiatry 14:282–289.

The symptoms of schizophrenia are in part exaggerations of ego types that may vary considerably from culture to culture. Whatever the particular coping style and whatever the particular culture, there is always the possibility that the techniques designed to mold personality, once they are overused, create instead a self-perpetuating bizarre caricature.

2149. Brewer MB: Determinants of social distance among East African tribal groups. J Pers Soc Psychol 10:279–289.

Variation of social distance in Kenyan, Ugandan, and Tanzanian tribes is found most strongly with perceived similarity of outgroup, next with distance of outgroup, and to some extent with educational-economic advancement of the outgroup.

2150. Bringmann W, Rieder G: Stereotyped attitudes toward the aged in West Germany and the United States. J Soc Psychol 76:267–268.

Highly unrealistic beliefs about older persons are held by younger women in both countries, although in Germany the negative and positive stereotypes seem balanced.

2151. Bronson GW: The development of fear in man and other animals. Child Dev 39:409–431.

Studies of humans, other primates, and dogs provide evidence for describing three stages in the development of the fear of novelty. The development of normal patterns of fear behavior in later periods depends upon successful transitions through preceding stages.

2152. Brotman J, Senter RJ: Attitudes toward feminism in different national student groups. J Soc Psychol 76:137–138.

American culture is characterized by a heterogeneity of sexual attitudes, whereas European attitudes are apparently more stable.

2153. Bruhn HG, Wolf S, Lynn TN, Bird HB, Chandler B: Social aspects of coronary heart disease in a Pennsylvania German community. Soc Sci Med 2:201–212.

As a group, coronary patients in Nazareth, Pennsylvania have a difficult time adapting to environmental and individual change.

2154. Burton A: Culture and healing. Psychother Res Theory Practice 5:55–57.

The basic human problem is how to remain individual and human in a culture that grinds every personality into the dust of conformity. With a relative disregard of the past and a concentration on the phenomenology of the moment, it is possible to see more of the patient's true bondage than our conventional techniques reveal. The psychotherapist may be the means by which a new culture will erect itself.

2155. Bustamante JA: Cultural factors in hysterias with schizophrenic clinical picture. Int J Soc Psychiatry 14:113–118.

Transcultural studies may follow an epidemiologic approach or an anthropologic-clinical approach. Studies of patients from two Cuban provinces illustrate the relationship between the *santeria* religious cult and a Catholic-Yourba syncretism, and hysterias with schizophrenic clinical picture.

2156. Bychowski G: A brief visit to India: observations and psychoanalytic implications. Am Imago 25:59–76.

The ego feelings of many schizophrenics are analogous to the results and practices of the Indian ascetic.

2157. Caldwell MB, Smith TA: Intellectual structure of Southern Negro children. Psychol Rep 23:63–71.

There are regional differences in Negro intellectual performance.

2158. Cansever G: The achievement motive in Turkish adolescents. J Soc Psychol 76:269–270.

Turkish children coming from authoritarian family or strict educational environments have high achievement scores; democratic environment has a positive effect on Turkish females and little effect on males.

2159. Caruth E: Hercules and Superman: the modern-day mythology of the comic book. J Am Acad Child Psychiatry 7:1–12.

Superman owes his effect to the vanishing remnants of ancient mythology, that collective memory of mankind that has been combined with Utopian anticipation. Superman readers regress to the pre-logical state in order to relax for a while and become all the more logical thereafter.

2160. Chekki DA: Mate selection, age at marriage, and propinquity among the Lingayats of India. J Marriage Fam 30:707–711.

Marriage in India is still largely characterized by traditional subcaste endogamy, and hypergamy, preferred kin marriage, parental control of mate selection, and low age at first marriage. Subcaste endogamy is greatly influenced by residential propinquity.

2161. Child I, Iwao S: Personality and esthetic sensitivity: extension of findings to younger age and to different culture. J Pers Soc Psychol 8:308–312.

Esthetic sensitivity is related to personality variables of cognitive independence and openness for American and Japanese subjects.

2162. Clare DA: Language medium and responses to the semantic differential. J Soc Psychol 76:271–272.

Occupational role is an important determinant of semantic judgments, and language is a mediator in judgments of relevant concepts within a single occupation.

2163. Cole M, Gay J, Glick J: A cross-cultural investigation of information processing. Int J Psychol 3:93–102.

Comparisons between American and Kpelle African performance on number recognition of random and patterned dots provide data on culturally different informational processing.

2164. Coles R: Northern children under desegregation. Psychiatry 31:1–15.

Northern Negro children who are sent to white schools experience no significant medical or psychiatric "harm" or injury. Both white and Negro children have trouble reconciling religious, ethical, social, and racial attitudes they receive in such abundance and contradiction from their parents.

2165. Copeland JRM: Aspects of mental illness in West African students. Soc Psychiatry 3:7–13.

Persecutory delusions occur in nearly all West African students admitted to a London mental hospital. They have diagnostic significance for schizophrenia only when they are Western in content.

2166. Coyle FA Jr, Eisenman R: Negro performance on the Hooper visual organization test: impairment or artifact? J Soc Psychol 75:269–271.

Low scores by Southern Negro college students on a test for organic pathology probably reflect the use of different subjects in standardization. Caution in diagnosis across ethnic and regional bounds is therefore indicated.

2167. Dennis W: Racial change in Negro drawings. J Psychol 69:129–130.

An increasingly favorable self-image is reflected in the greater incidence of drawing Negro figures by Negroes.

2168. Deregowski JB: Difficulties in pictorial depth perception in Africa. Br J Psychol 59:195–204.

Passive exposure to material has only a small role

in determining depth perception as demonstrated by a sample of children and a sample of servants on Hudson's pictorial perception test and a construction test. Two-dimensional responses to Hudson's, in contrast to three-dimensional constructions, may be due to inability to organize the presented materials.

2169. Deregowski JB: On perception of depicted orientation. Int J Psychol 3:149–156.

Presentation angle, subject-apparatus positions, and connotative meaning of the material may effect the amount of error in depth perception by Bantu children.

2170. Derogatis LR, Gorham DR, Moseley EC: Structural vs. interpretive ambiguity: a cross-cultural study with the Holtzman inkblots. J Proj Tech Pers Assessment 32:66–73.

Findings from Mexican, German, Taiwan-Chinese, U.S. student samples, and a sample of psychologists indicate an inverse relationship between structural and interpretive ambiguity measures.

2171. Dixon PW, Fukuda NK, Berens AE: The influence of ethnic groups on SCAT, teacher's ratings, and rank in high school class. J Soc Psychol 75:285–286.

The superiority of Japanese females over other ethnic or sex groupings in Hawaii on school measures may be due to their high need for achievement and degree of clinical anxiety.

2172. Diab LN, Prothro ET: Cross-cultural study of some correlates of birth order. Psychol Rep 22:1137–1142.

First-born Arab students do not attend college in greater numbers than later borns. There is no significant relationship between birth order and level of academic achievement among Arabs.

2173. Douglas M: The relevance of tribal studies. J Psychosom Res 12:21–28.

The social dimensions of tribal rituals can be illuminating. Tribal rituals function in terms of social coercion and expression of society's essential nature. Public ritual expresses social concerns and needs rather than individual ones.

2174. duPreez PD: Social change and field dependence in South Africa. J Soc Psychol 76:265–266.

Subjects who had traveled performed more accurately on the rod-and-frame test. Traveling to obtain work is a reflection of psychological aggressiveness and ability to cope with social change.

2175. (Deleted)

2176. Elsarrag ME: Psychiatry in the Northern Sudan: a study in comparative psychiatry. Br J Psychiatry 114:945–948.

Cultural patterns account for the differences between Northern Sudanese and British psychiatry. *Grande hysterie,* organ neurosis, and puerperal septic delerium are common in the Northern Sudan, while obsessive-compulsive neurosis and chronic alcoholism are rare.

2177. Entwisle DR: Subcultural differences in children's language development. Int J Psychol 3:13–22.

Rural-urban and ethnic (Amish, Negro, Caucasian) differences in language development suggest a language deficit-environmental deprivation relationship that needs further investigation.

2178. Fabrega H Jr, Metzger D: Psychiatric illness in a small Ladino community. Psychiatry 31:339–351.

In the highlands of Chiapas, Mexico, illness is a social affair, and the care of the psychiatrically ill is initiated and carried out by neighbors and important leaders of the community using measures that have local meaning. Some of the current attitudes, foci, and goals of "community psychiatry" could be said to be embodied and applied in this setting.

2179. Fabrega H, Swartz JD, Wallace CA: Ethnic differences in psychopathology: specific differences with emphasis on a Mexican American group. J Psychiatr Res 6:221–235.

Mexican-American schizophrenics are more chronic, regressed, and disorganized than their Negro and Anglo counterparts. Reported differences in psychopathology between ethnic groups may reflect an association that ethnicity has with particular social status features and may not be a direct result of unique cultural values or patterns. The schizophrenic process may diminish differences in behavior that are culturally determined.

2180. Farley FH: Season of birth, intelligence and personality. Br J Psychol 59:281–284.

No differences between intelligence, personality, and season of birth are associated in a sample of adolescent males. The relationship is most likely only for subnormal persons.

2181. Feldman M: Eidetic imagery in Ghana: a cross-cultural will-o'-the-wisp? J Psychol 69:259–269.

Differences between village and town Ghanaian groups, between test and retest, and between behavioral measures and interview probing point up the inadequacies of the test and the problems of cross-cultural research.

2182. Field MJ: Chronic psychosis in rural Ghana. Br J Psychiatry 114:31–33.

Rural Ghana has had an explosive increase in schizophrenia, especially the paranoid type, within the last 20 years. Acute trypanosomiasis treated too late to avert permanent brain damage can produce identical clinical symptoms.

2183. Figelman M: A comparison of affective and paranoid disorders in Negroes and Jews. Int J Soc Psychiatry 14:277–281.

Negroes tend to have more paranoid, and Jews more affective, disorders based on a sociocultural theory of mental illness. It is possible that when outlets for acting out, whether by means of alcohol or antisocial behavior, are available to Negroes, there are fewer paranoid disorders.

2184. Freeman D: Thunder, blood and the nick-naming of god's creatures. Psychoanal Q 37:353–399.

The ritual beliefs and practices of the Semang and other peoples are parts of psychological projective systems. Mocked-at objects are symbolic representations of paternal genitalia.

2185. Friedman L: Japan and the psychopathology of history. Psychoanal Q 37:539–564.

The neurotic nature of Japan's reaction to Western aggression, her hostile intent, and attempt to rewrite the past are not different from the way all cultures are organized and transformed.

2186. Gaddes WH, McKenzie A, Barnsley R: Psychometric intelligence and spatial imagery in two Northwest Indian and two white groups of children. J Soc Psychol 75:35–42.

Analysis shows no superiority or inferiority of spatial imagery of Indian children compared with white children on largely culture-free tests. Theoretically, a truly culture-free test might reveal slight spatial superiority for Indian children.

2187. Garcia-Esteve J, Shaw ME: Rural and urban patterns of responsibility attribution in Puerto Rico. J Soc Psychol 74:143–149.

Youngest or rural subjects attribute more responsibility than older or urban subjects. Urban subjects attribute more responsibility for negative outcomes and show higher differentiation between levels of causality than those in the rural environment of Puerto Rico.

2188. Gardiner HW: Attitudes of Thai students toward marriage roles. J Soc Psychol 75:61–65.

Thai males are high on a scale of male-dominant attitudes, and Thai females high on egalitarianism. Thai females show higher egalitarianism than Japanese-American or white American females.

2189. Gardiner HW: Dominance-deference patterning in Thai students. J Soc Psychol 76:281–282.

A similarity in deference patterning for Thai males and females and a dissimilarity between the sexes in dominance patterning cannot yet be explained within the scope of this research.

2190. Gardiner HW: Dominance-deference: a cross-cultural comparison. J Soc Psychol 75:287–288.

Thai students, rather than Japanese-American students, have dominance-deference scores that approximate Caucasian-American scores.

2191. Geismer LL, Gerhart UC: Social class, ethnicity, and family functioning: exploring some issues raised by the Moynihan report. J Marriage Fam 30:480–487.

Social status is more salient in determining the nature of family functioning than is ethnicity.

2192. Gerwitz HB, Gerwitz JL: Visiting and caretaking patterns for kibbutz infants: age and sex trends. Am J Orthopsychiatry 38:427–443.

A small kibbutz sample exemplifies the methods of data organization and analysis in the context of child rearing.

2193. Giel R, Gezahegn Y, Van Luijk JN: Faith-healing and spirit-possession in Ghion, Ethiopia. Soc Sci Med 2:63–79.

The Orthodox Church teaches that certain illnesses are caused by evil spirits. Numerous people in Ghion and the surrounding area share this belief and go to a priest for treatment. The state of possession is more often a learned absent-mindedness than a hysterical dissociative reaction and occurs in the mentally normal as well as mentally ill people.

2194. Giel R, Van Luijk JN: On the significance of a broken home in Ethiopia. Br J Psychiatry 114:957–961.

Thirty-seven percent of schoolchildren in Ethiopia come from broken homes. In more than half of these cases the disturbance of family life occurred before the age of five. Coming from a broken home does not appear to affect school performance in a negative way.

2195. Gillis LS, Lewis JB, Slabbert M: Psychiatric disorder amongst the coloured people of the Cape Peninsula: an epidemiological study. Br J Psychiatry 114:1575–1587.

Except for some culturally determined manifestations (poltergeist and special dissociative phenomena) Cape colored people have the same types of illness as other populations. There is three times as much psychiatric illness in persons in the lowest social class as in the highest.

2196. Gordon LV: Comments on "cross-cultural equivalence of personality measures." J Soc Psychol 75:11–19.

Berrien's solution of master-item pooling incorporates previously mentioned problems associated with translations and additional problems as well.

2197. Gotts EE: A note on cross-cultural age-group comparisons of anxiety scores. Child Dev 39:945–947.

Japanese children receive lower anxiety scores on the Children's Manifest Anxiety Scale than do either French or American children. They also receive consistently lower Lie scores than other groups. Anxiety increases among Japanese and decreases among American and European children as they move from middle childhood toward young adulthood.

2198. Gough HG, Chun K, Chung Y: Validation of the CPI femininity scale in Korea. Psychol Rep 22:155–160.

Although the femininity scale functions validly in Korea, its level of efficiency is lower than in previous applications in other cultures.

2199. Grant EC: An ethological description of non-verbal behaviour during interviews. Br J Med Psychol 41:177–184.

Ethological methods can be used to make a sequential analysis of nonverbal behavior shown during face-to-face discussion. There is an essential similarity in the structure of such behavior despite variations in situations and degree of mental breakdown of subjects.

2200. Grunfeld B, Salversen C: Functional psychoses and social status. Br J Psychiatry 114:733–737.

Social backgrounds of schizophrenics do not differ significantly from status distributions in the general population. Reactive psychotics come from a significantly lower social background than expected. Both schizophrenics and reactive psychotics show a decline in social status when compared with their fathers.

2201. Haffter C: The changeling: history and psychodynamics of attitude to handicapped children in European folklore. J Hist Behav Sciences 4:55–61.

The abnormal child was regarded as a changeling in Europe from the Middle Ages to the Enlightenment. The changeling was the instrument of a vengeful God and the result of internalized blame. The sins of the parents first resulted with the child being exchanged for another, and when the parents thoughts were against the child, the devil took the child in punishment.

2202. Hammond KR, Bonaiuto GB, Faucheux C, Moscovici S, Frohlich WD, Joyce C, DiMajo G: A comparison of cognitive conflict between persons in Western Europe and the United States. Int J Psychol 3:1–12.

Europeans placed in a conflict situation show different patterns of cognitive difference reduction and are less compromising than Americans.

2203. Hare RT, Hare AP: Social correlates of autonomy for Nigerian university students. J Soc Psychol 76:163–168.

Younger Yoruba and Ibo students are higher on autonomy, as are those students whose fathers are not farmers. Ibo Protestants are more autonomous than Ibo Catholics, but there are no differences between Ibo and Yoruba.

2204. Henderson RW, Merritt CB: Environmental backgrounds of Mexican-American children with different potentials for school success. J Soc Psychol 75:101–106.

A greater variety of intellectually stimulating experiences is included in the preschool environment of high-potential Mexican-American children than in the environments of low-potential subjects.

2205. Heron A: Studies of perception and reasoning in Zambian children. Int J Psychol 3:23–29.

Perceptual and reasoning differences between Zambian and Western children are due to cultural and motivational differences; the use of such measurements must account for cultures in which time and error number are not significant to performance.

2206. Hicks JM, Goldman M, Kang J: Attitudes toward Negroes and stereotypes about Americans among Chinese students in Taiwan and the United States. J Soc Psychol 76:139–141.

Chinese in the United States show more negative attitudes toward Negroes than Chinese in Taiwan as a reflection of American attitudes. However, greater duration of stay in the United States results in increased favorable attitudes, perhaps due to increased interminority group contact.

2207. Jackson SW: Aspects of culture in psychoanalytic theory and practice. J Am Psychoanal Assoc 16:651–670.

Behavior is ultimately determined by the instinctual drives, but the environment coordinates their direction and provides the sociocultural conditions for adaptive measures. Any particular patient must be assessed in terms of his own cultural context.

2208. Jaffe FS, Polgar S: Family planning and public policy: is the "culture of poverty" the new cop-out? J Marriage Fam 30:228–235.

A cultural-motivational approach in family planning is often employed to rationalize slow progress. The culture of poverty may lend dangerous scientific sanction to a eugenics movement.

2209. Jew CC, Brody SA: Mental illness among the Chinese. I: hospitalization rates over the past century. Compr Psychiatry 8:129–134.

The hospitalization rate of Chinese males in California has gradually increased over the past 100 years. The incidence of mental disease is higher among the older age groups than among the younger. Chinese males have lower rates of first admission to mental hospitals in California than males of all other races combined.

2210. Jordan JE, Friesen EW: Attitudes of rehabilitation personnel toward physically disabled persons in Columbia, Peru, and the United States. J Soc Psychol 74:151–161.

In general, the disabled are viewed more positively in modern than traditional societies, and progressive educational attitudes are associated with the more modern spot on the socioeconomic-educational continuum.

2211. Kawwa T: A survey of ethnic attitudes of some British secondary school pupils. Br J Soc Clin Psychol 7:161–168.

British children living in an area with a higher percentage of black and Cypriot immigrants show more negative attitudes, without a concomittant belief in their inferiority, than do children in areas with few immigrants.

2212. Kellaghan T: Abstraction and categorization in African children. Int J Psychol 3:115–120.

Irish boys perform better on color-form sorting and cube tests than their Yoruba counterparts who do well on familiar object sortings. Westernization and familiarity with test material may influence Yoruba performance.

2213. Koenigsberg RA: Culture and unconscious phantasy: observations on Nazi Germany. Psychoanal Rev 55:681–696.

In Nazism the oedipal struggle is revived with emphasis on destruction of the father and defense of the mother.

2214. Kohn ML: Social class and schizophrenia: a critical review. J Psychiatr Res Supp 7:155–173.

The relationship of class to schizophrenia is probably real. The greater stress suffered by lower-class people may be relevant to the etiology of schizophrenia, and perhaps lower- and working-class patterns of family relationships are broadly conducive to schizophrenia.

2215. Kollar E, Edgerton R, Beckwith W: An evaluation of the behavior of ARL Colony chimpanzees. Arch Gen Psychiatry 19:580–598.

ARL Colony chimpanzees, due to social deprivation at critical periods, show a high incidence of atypical behavior. Approximating wildlife conditions is a prerequisite for behaviorally normal animals and should be pursued with renewed vigor.

2216. Korson JH: Residential propinquity as a factor in mate selection in an urban Muslim family. J Marriage Fam 30:518–526.

Family arrangements and interests still predominate in Pakistani Muslim society. Residential propinquity between mates is greater for lower-class families and less for upper-class families.

2217. Korson JH: The roles of the dower and dowry as indicators of social change in Pakistan. J Marriage Fam 30:696–707.

Most Pakistani male and female students intend

to conform to current practices, although they express negative attitudes toward the institutionalized dower-dowry system.

2218. Krauss HH, Krauss BJ: Cross-cultural study of the thwarting-disorientation theory of suicide. J Abnorm Soc Psychol 73:353–357.

A multicultural ethnographic analysis confirms the hypotheses that suicide takes place in contexts where a person experiences the frustration associated with disruption or threat to his social position as a consequence of actions of his own or others. The more a society permits the occurrence of thwarting disorientation, the higher its suicide case rate.

2219. Kurokawa M: Lineal orientation in child rearing among Japanese. J Marriage Fam 30:129–135.

For Japanese, and Japanese-Americans, a lineal orientation, rather than an individualistic principle, is dominant in parent-child relationships.

2220. Leighton A, Prince R, May R: The therapeutic process in cross-cultural perspective: a symposium. Am J Psychiatry 124:1171–1184.

The social, cultural, psychological, and physical factors of emergence into a disorder-free state may be exemplified in a study of contrasting Yoruba and Navaho patterns of therapy and the treatment process in history.

2221. Leon R: Some implications for a preventive program for American Indians. Am J Psychiatry 125:232–236.

The bio-psycho-social disorganization that exists among Indians may be dealt with by a process that involves the Indian throughout in determining his own fate. Consultants and other experts should be in the service of the Indian people, as should the Bureau of Indian Affairs.

2222. Lerner J, Noy P: Somatic complaints in psychiatric disorders: social and cultural factors. Int J Soc Psychiatry 14:145–150.

Among Israeli psychiatric outpatients there is a converse relation between somatization and level of education. No correlation is established between degree of somatization and ethnic origin.

2223. Lesse S: The influence of socioeconomic and sociotechnologic systems on emotional illness. Am J Psychother 22:569–576.

The urgent need for the development of trained psychosociologists who will comprehend the interrelationships between broad sociodynamic and psychodynamic forces is illustrated by Japan and India, countries in which the emergence from a centuries-old traditional culture into the scientific-industrial era has precipitated changes in the types of emotional illnesses seen.

2224. Little K: Cultural variations in social schemata. J Pers Soc Psychol 10:1–7.

Mediterranean contact cultures show closer social interaction distances in doll placement than North European noncontact cultures.

2225. Lloyd BB: Choice behavior and social structure: a comparison of two African societies. J Soc Psychol 74:3–12.

Ethnographically observed Gusii and Yoruba differences in sex status, age status, and initiation ceremonies as associated with sex-role identification allow the generation of hypotheses that predict the choice behavior of children on a projective test, the Pretend Game.

2226. Loh WD, Triandis HC: Role perceptions in Peru. Int J Psychol 3:175–182.

Factors of rejection, respect, formal friendship, marital acceptance, and subordination are revealed in a role differential for Peruvian male students. Low to high status interactions differ across cultures, from more to less egalitarian societies.

2227. MacArthur R: Some differential abilities of Northern Canadian native youth. Int J Psychol 3:43–51.

Eskimo and Indian-Metis have developed abilities that facilitate adaptation to their own environments and different developmental potentials for adaptation to technological-educational environments.

2228. Makita K: The rarity of reading disability in Japanese children. Am J Orthopsychiatry 38:599–614.

The prevalence of dyslexia in Japan is ten times lower than in Western countries. Specificity of the used language is the most potent contributing factor and indicates that reading disability is more of a philological than a neuropsychiatric problem.

2229. Margetts EL: African ethnopsychiatry in the field. Can Psychiatr Assoc J 13:521–538.

There is a long list of "phenomena" that must be taken note of in African cultures in order to conceive of a local psychology and thence psychiatry. These phenomena include native psychology, conceptions of magic, death and burial customs, social hierarchy, religion, birth and child rearing, genital customs, education, etc. The methodology by which information can be gained about these phenomena include observation, interview, language, tales and myths, art, the study of artifacts, photography, sound recording, and special laboratory aids.

2230. Mariategui J, Samanez F: Sociocultural change and mental health in the Peru of today. Soc Psychiatry 3:35–40.

The traditional and telluric life of the upland Indian forms a contrast with the assimilation of Western culture in the capital. The confrontation between the passivity typical of the mestizo and the competitive and hostile world into which he finds himself hurled at the time of migration calls forth early frustrations, increases insecurity, threatens his life plan, and produces in him a permanent source of anxiety.

2231. McCandless F: Suicide and the communication of rage: a cross-cultural case study. Am J Psychiatry 125:197–205.

African populations have a low frequency of suicide attempts as compared to the East Indian population. East Indians in Guyana, without culturally sanctioned techniques for the discharge of aggression, are trapped in their own retroflexed rage.

2232. McGinnies E: Studies in persuasion: source credibility and involvement as factors in persuasion with students in Taiwan. J Soc Psychol 74:171–180.

National origin, involvement, and communicator credibility are significant sources of variance, but a lack of interaction between these and the influence of source credibility on attitudes are more consistent with assimilation-contrast theory than cognitive dissonance theory.

2233. McGinnies E, Turnage TW: Verbal association by Chinese and American students as a function of word frequency and mode of presentation. Psychol Rep 23:1051–1060.

Americans produce more associations than do Taiwanese under all conditions.

2234. McGuire MT, Lorch S: Natural language conversation modes. J Nerv Ment Dis 146:239–248.

Conversation modes are aggregates of behavior rules that guide two-person conversations. The understanding of mode behavior helps the therapist

understand the patient as well as helping him to teach the patient new language behavior.

2235. McNickle D: The sociocultural setting of Indian life. Am J Psychiatry 125:219–223.

Workshops for American Indian students demonstrate that young Indians may support their traditional society by utilizing skills acquired from the majority white culture.

2236. Meade RD: Psychological time in India and America. J Soc Psychol 76:169–174.

Subjects with high achievement motivation (Americans, Kshatryas, Sikhs, Parsees) estimate a time period involving progress as shorter than an equal time period with no action than do subjects with lower achievement motivation (Brahmins, Vaisyas, Sudras, Muslims).

2237. Meade RD: Realism of aspiration levels in Indian and American college students. J Soc Psychol 75:169–173.

Higher goal discrepancy scores on two tests of aspiration indicate that Indian students are less realistic and pay more attention to affective factors than American students.

2238. Meerloo JAM: Human violence versus animal aggression. Psychoanal Rev 55:37–56.

Violence and aggression are culturally inspired. Man's aggression is the result of a disorganization of drives provoked by manifold inner and outer factors and by lack of cultural transformation and control.

2239. Melamed L: Race awareness in South African children. J Soc Psychol 76:3–8.

When the cues of skin color, hair type, lip shape, and nose shape are provided, skin color is most frequently used by white children to distinguish between people, indicating that by age six they have assumed the primary cue as used in South African society.

2240. Miller C, Knapp SC, Daniels CW: MMPI study of Negro mental hygiene clinic patients. J Abnorm Soc Psychol 73:168–173.

Negro patients, in comparison to white patients, tend to conform more to middle-class norms, deny anxiety and sensitivity, focus on physical symptoms, and project anxiety and hostility onto impersonal, distant objects.

2241. Mumford E: The use of medical sociology on a psychiatric service: research and application. Am J Psychiatry 124:892–899.

Attempts at explaining the individual by describing his society may be as misleading as attempts at explaining society by psychological mechanisms.

2242. Murphy HBM: Cultural factors in the genesis of schizophrenia. J Psychiatr Res Supp No 1: 137–153.

The rates and genesis of schizophrenia among the Tamilians of South India, Catholics in Canada, the Southern Irish, and the people of northwest Croatia indicate that culture may be one of a host of variables that can confront the schizophrenic-prone individual with a particular class of experience able to evoke his disease.

2243. Orgel S: Comment on Dr. Sinha's paper. Int J Psychoanal 49:417–419.

Yogic philosophy has loftier aims than Freudian psychoanalysis with respect to the ego.

2244. Opler MK, Small SM: Cultural variables affecting somatic complaints and depression. Psychosomatics 9:261–266.

Depressive states, of which suicide is a symptom, are affected by age, sex, race, class, and ethnicity. Short-term and supportive modes of treatment of various kinds may be utilized in brief psychotherapy of depressive states. The effectiveness of such therapy will depend upon ethnic and class variables and the age and sex differentiations.

2245. Orr DW: Anthropological and historical notes on the female sexual role. J Am Psychoanal Assoc 16:601–612.

Sherfey's ideas about the insatiable sexuality of prehistoric women are probably not valid. Any statement about the sexual role of women should be in the context of race, class, social, and economic position in any given culture and historical era.

2246. (Deleted)

2247. Pal SK: Personality needs of engineering, law, medical, and teacher-training students in an Indian university. J Soc Psychol 74:135.

TAT scores indicate that there are differences in needs between engineering, law, medical, and education students.

2248. Pande SK: The mystique of "Western" psychotherapy: an Eastern interpretation. J Nerv Ment Dis 146:425–432.

Cultural sensitivities and the structure of Western consciousness obscure the recognition of some of the basic needs that psychotherapy, as a cultural institution, serves and that lie veiled behind the quest for health and self-understanding.

2249. Pandey RE: The suicide problem in India. Int J Soc Psychiatry 14:193–200.

There is a strong belief in India that most suicides are committed under the influence of the tamas guna, because it is the root of all sin. Women are believed to commit suicide more often than men, although this is not true, because they are more frequently dominated by Tamas and Rajas.

2250. Pareek U, Singh YP: Sociometry and communication network in an Indian village. Int J Psychol 3:157–165.

Interpersonal influence concerning the adoption of agricultural innovations is closely related to individual popularity and charisma, and number and frequency of communication acts.

2251. Penalosa F: Mexican family roles. J Marriage Fam 30:680–689.

Mexican family roles are primarily determined by male dominance over females and the submission of younger to elder.

2252. Pfeil E: Role expectations when entering marriage. J Marriage Fam 30:161–165.

Traditional interpretations of the marriage role prevail among young people in Hamburg, although there is a trend toward family partnerships.

2253. Phillips DL: Social class and psychological disturbance: the influence of positive and negative experiences. Soc Psychiatry 3:41–46.

Low SES in New England is associated with the presence of high stress and the absence of positive experiences. An individual may experience considerable stress in his environment but still not have these "presses" produce psychological disturbance if, at the same time, he experiences a high number of positive feelings.

2254. Pivnicki D, Christie RG: Body build characteristics in psychotics. Compr Psychiatry 9:574–580.

A definition or delineation of any kind of static body-build types in the present state of our knowledge is impossible, and efforts to set up rigid constructs would be a hindrance to further understanding.

2255. Prince R, Leighton AH, May R: The therapeutic process in cross-cultural perspective—a symposium. Am J Psychiatry 124:1171–1183.

Clinical psychiatry and cultural anthropology are bound together by a common orientation and procedure in order to examine several questions: What makes psychotherapy work? What are the social, cultural, psychological, and physical factors that enhance the emergence of a person from a disorder to a disorder-free state?

2256. Prothro ET, Diab LN: Birth order and age at marriage in the Arab Levant. Psychol Rep 23: 1236–1238.

A study of Christian and Moslem college students in Beirut reveals no significant differences in mean actual ages at marriage between first-born and latter-born wives or husbands.

2257. Rabin AI: CAT findings with kibbutz and non-kibbutz preschoolers. J Proj Tech Pers Assessment 32:420–424.

By age five, kibbutz children have higher intellectual productivity, a positive relationship with parental figures, and a high level of ego coping behavior. However, they also have developed a stronger oral dependency and reliance on denial.

2258. Richer S: The economics of child rearing. J Marriage Fam 30:462–466.

An exchange model of parent-child resources and power can contribute to the analysis of family interactions.

2259. Riegel KF: Comparison of restricted associations among six languages. J Soc Psychol 75:67–78.

The application of restricted association tests in foreign languages has demonstrated feasibility. The method is useful in pointing out interlingual differences in response variability and response differentiation, as well as quantification of meaning similarity or substitutability of stimuli.

2260. Risso M, Boker W: Delusions of witchcraft: a cross cultural study. Br J Psychiatry 114:963–972.

Belief in magic, love philtres, and death potions is widespread in Southern Italy and is a pathoplastic factor in psychiatric illnesses of migrant workmen. A response to conflicts among Italian laborers working in German-speaking Switzerland may result in a psychoticlike syndrome in which symptoms are attributed to witchcraft.

2261. Rodgers RR, Bronfenbrenner U, Devereux EC Jr: Standards of social behavior among school children in four cultures. Int J Psychol 3:31–41.

U.S. and European girls assign more value to a manners factor; while boys assign more value to a masculinity factor. Americans more than the English, and Soviets more than the Swiss, tend to give socially desirable answers.

2262. Roos LL: Frustration and attitude change among Turkish villagers. J Soc Psychol 74:163–169.

Economic and political change in Turkey from 1962 to 1963 may account for attitude changes that reflect increased frustration and higher levels of regression and aggression.

2263. Rosenblum LA, Kaufman IC: Variations in infant development and response to maternal loss in monkeys. Am J Orthopsychiatry 38:418–426.

The gregarious quality of group interaction in bonnet, as compared to pigtail, monkeys vitiates the potentially debilitating effects of the loss of the real mother. Behavior thought to have a specific genetic base, may be highly influenced by ontogenetic factors.

2264. Rosenmayer L: Family relations of the elderly. J Marriage Fam 30:672–679.

The classic theory of the isolation of the nuclear family in industrialized society is contradicted by evidence for frequent elderly parent-adult offspring interactions in Europe.

2265. Saenger G: Psychiatric outpatients in America and the Netherlands: a transcultural comparison. Soc Psychiatry 3:149–164.

American and Dutch outpatients display cultural differences in symptom choice. Depressed Dutch patients show more apathy, guilt feelings, and psychomotor retardation. Complaints about feelings of inadequacy are more marked among American patients. Americans feel more lonely and complain about social isolation.

2266. Safilios-Rothschild C: Deviance and mental illness in the Greek family. Fam Process 7:100–117.

Greek findings suggest that the greater degree of normal spouse satisfaction, the lesser the tendency to label spousal alleviance as mental illness and the better the chance for rehabilitation of spouse. Greek culture defines mental illness as violent or hallucinatory behavior, while other symptoms are accepted as mere idiosyncrisies.

2267. Safilios-Rothschild C: "Good" and "bad" girls in modern Greek movies. J Marriage Fam 30: 527–531.

Female movie figures are generally portrayed in terms of an inverse relationship between wealth and morality.

2268. Salisbury RF: Possession in the New Guinea highlands. Int J Soc Psychiatry 14:84–95.

"Possession" in New Guinea is usually characterized by a general anticipation by other people that a case of possession might occur. Every unexpected death is followed by a case of possession in about two weeks. This culturally sanctioned dissociational state is a mechanism whereby an individual can make abrupt changes in his behavioral pattern.

2269. Sallery RDH: Artistic expression and self-description with Arabs and Canadian students. J Soc Psychol 76:273–274.

Subjects using self-descriptive adjectives that emphasize the extraordinary, primitive, and sensual also show greater degree of complexity of drawings as measured by the House-Tree-Person Drawing.

2270. Saslow H, Harrover M: Research on psychosocial adjustment of Indian youths. Am J Psychiatry 125:224–231.

A failure in psychosocial development of Indian youth during the latency and early pubertal years contributes heavily to the high incidence of problem behavior. Indian and non-Indian value systems must be harmonized in a school system prior to the offering of an education.

2271. Schlesinger B: Family patterns in Jamaica: review and commentary. J Marriage Fam 30:136–148.

Many of the gaps in Jamaican family research should be filled by West Indian social scientists.

2272. Schlesinger B: Family patterns in the English-speaking Caribbean. J Marriage Fam 30:149–153.

In the English-speaking parts of the West Indies, family patterns ranging from visiting to marriage are evident.

2273. Schmidt KE: Some concepts of mental illness of the Murut of Sarawak. Int J Soc Psychiatry 14:24–31.

The Murut have developed comprehensive theories of personality structure, therapy, etiology of

mental illness, and nomenclature of psychopathology. Some Murut syndromes are comparable to Western entities, e.g., Ruden Talai has the features of paranoid schizophrenia.

2274. Schneck J: Freud and Kronos. Am J Psychiatry 125:692–693.

Freud mistakenly wrote that Zeus had castrated his son, Kronos. Freud's false recollection of mythology may be attributed to an unconscious effort to reinforce his own view regarding the special role of castration fear as part of the father-son relationships and the oedipal constellation.

2275. Schwab JJ, Brown JM, Holzer CE, Sokolof M: Current concepts of depression: the sociocultural. Int J Soc Psychiatry 14:226–234.

It is hazardous to specify strict cause-and-effect relationships between sociocultural factors and the etiology of mental illness. Demographic groups formerly considered less susceptible to depression, when examined closely, give greater evidence of its frequency. Diagnosis may be obscured by class condition.

2276. Sechrest L, Flores L, Arellano L: Language and social interaction in a bilingual culture. J Soc Psychol 76:155–161.

A local dialect is used in casual conversation on a Philippine university campus with English as the instructional language. English is more likely to be used when the couples speaking are of mixed sex.

2277. Senay EC, Redlich FC: Cultural and social factors in neuroses and psychosomatic illness. Soc Psychiatry 3:89–97.

Basic syndromes occur in widely different settings but are modified by them in form and course. Subcultural variables contribute more to variance than culture.

2278. Sethi BB, Thacore VR, Gupta SC: Changing patterns of culture and psychiatry in India. Am J Psychother 22:46–54.

India is passing through a phase of far-reaching socioeconomic, sociophilosophical, and cultural changes. Revolutionary changes have unfolded and set in motion instability and uncertainty. The prevalence of psychiatric disorders is high. To be effective in India, psychiatry must fit the cultural pattern.

2279. Shaw ME, Briscoe ME, Garcia-Esteve J: A cross-cultural study of attribution of responsibility. Int J Psychol 3:51–60.

Cubans show more causal differentiation than Americans and Puerto Ricans, although the latter join Cubans in greater sophistication for positive outcomes. Differences may be due to family and child-rearing patterns.

2280. Sharma KL, Sinha SN: A note on cross-cultural comparison of occupational ratings. J Soc Psychol 75:283–284.

An apparent similarity between 1967 Indian rankings of occupations and a 1947 American sample may be the result of a time lag or a general tendency to rank white-collar over blue-collar occupations.

2281. Shiloh A: The interaction between the Middle Eastern and Western systems of medicine. Soc Sci Med 2:235–248.

Despite apparent striking differences between the Middle Eastern and Western systems of medicine, interaction between the two can be of a positive nature with only limited culture conflict. The essentially empirical attitude of the Middle Eastern system of medicine has allowed many persons to accept certain new medical practices.

2282. Siegel IE, Perry C: Psycholinguistic diversity among "culturally deprived" children. Am J Orthopsychiatry 38:122–126.

The phrase "culturally deprived" is not only derogatory but psychologically inaccurate. The test behavior of underprivileged children shows a great diversity. Failure to recognize this diversity may result in educational and service disservice.

2283. Simmons OG: The sociocultural integration of alcohol use: a Peruvian study. Q J Stud Alcohol 29:152–171.

In the Lunahuana community of Peru, the annual round of religious and secular ceremonies, the celebration of rites of passage, and the use of informal leisure time are all intimately associated with the use of alcohol. Drinking is utilized to express social identification and solidarity.

2284. Sinha JBP: The construct of dependence proneness. J Soc Psychol 76:129–131.

The cognitive view of the dependence-proneness construct holds for the sample of Indian students.

2285. Sinha TC: Observation on the concept of ego. Int J Psychoanal 49:413–416.

The concept of ego may be viewed from the treatment given it in Yoga.

2286. Skipper JK, Hadden JK, Tucker GD: Three dimensions of parental kinship terminology: situation, subgroup identity, and sentiment. J Marriage Fam 30:592–596.

Schneider and Homan's proposition of various alternative kinship terms in American culture can be supported. Variation in kin terminology along three dimensions may reflect differences in parent-child relationships.

2287. Sollenberger RT: Chinese-American child-rearing practices and juvenile deliquency. J Soc Psychol 74:13–23.

From interview responses and participant observation in Chinatown it appears that the low delinquency rate among Chinese-Americans may be due to (1) high nurturance that generates security and trust-facilitating acceptance of demands for conformity, (2) discouragement of physical aggression, (3) mutual respect between child and family, and (4) presence of good behavioral models in the community.

2288. Sommer R: Intimacy ratings in five countries. Int J Psychol 3:109–114.

American, European, and Pakistani judgments of seating closeness reflect cultural differences in views of spatial arrangement that may hinder or facilitate social interactions.

2289. Straus J, Straus MA: Family roles and sex differences in creativity of children in Bombay and Minneapolis. J Marriage Fam 30:46–53.

Children in Bombay, and the Indian family background of conformity, have lower creativity scores than American children. Scores for girls are lower than for boys in both cultures.

2290. Straus MA: Society as a variable in comparative study of the family by replications and secondary analysis. J Marriage Fam 30:565–577.

A cross-cultural approach that utilizes secondary analysis of previous research or replication of studies on single societies is heuristically valuable for pointing to cross-cultural inconsistencies.

2291. Strodtbeck FL, Creelan PG: The interaction linkage between family size, intelligence, and sex-role identity. J Marriage Fam 30:301–307.

Complex parent-child and sibling-sibling relationships may, in conjunction with the birth interval, account for sex role identity and intelligence.

2292. Styn AF, Rip CM: The changing urban Bantu family. J Marriage Fam 30:499–517.

Movement away from the stabilizing influences of the tribe and into the unstructured urban setting has brought about a change in urban Bantu family structure. The urban family is characterized by loss of control and weakening of functions in socialization, production, and other areas and is a reflection of social disorganization and instability.

2293. Sundberg N, Ballinger T: Nepalese children's cognitive development as revealed by drawings of man, woman, and self. Child Dev 39:969–985.

Nepalese schoolchildren show decreasing IQ's based on American normals as evidenced on drawings of man, woman, and self. While American norms are unfair to Nepalese children, the renorming of Nepalese drawings might be useful for rough screening purposes.

2294. Szalay LB, Windle C: Relative influence of linguistic versus cultural factors on free verbal associations. Psychol Rep 22:43–51.

Study of the continued free word associations of Koreans in Korean and in English, and a U.S. group in English, reveals the influence of cultural background is at least as great as that of language.

2295. Tharp RG, Meadow A, Lennhoff SG, Satterfield D: Changes in marriage roles accompanying the acculturation of the Mexican-American wife. J Marriage Fam 30:404–412.

Marriage roles take on a more egalitarian-companionate pattern, and move away from a segregate role pattern, for the acculturating Mexican-American.

2296. Thimmesch N: Puerto Rico and birth control. J Marriage Fam 30:252–262.

Given Puerto Rico's growing economy and some liberalization in attitudes, widespread family planning is necessary to maintain the present standard of living.

2297. Tomeh AK: Moral values in a cross-cultural perspective. J Soc Psychol 74:137–138.

Students in the Mideast tend to be more severe in their moral judgments than American students and tend to regard some codes as intrinsically moral where American students might view them as secondary aspects of morality. American restrictions reflect the individualistic aspect of the society, while Mideastern restrictions reflect authoritarian tradition.

2298. Treffers PE: Family-size, contraception, and birth rate before and after the introduction of a new method of family planning. J Marriage Fam 30:338–345.

The introduction of effective family planning and oral contraceptives in the Netherlands relieved some of the tension created by the conflict over a discrepancy between desired and actual family size.

2299. Triandis HC, Vassilious V, Nassiakou M: Three cross-cultural studies of subjective culture. J Soc Psychol Monograph Supplement 8:1–42.

Four common factors—affect, intimacy, dominance, and hostility—may be derived from examination of role perception, behavioral intent, and perception of social behavior in American and Greek subjects.

2300. Vitols MM: Culture patterns of drinking in Negro and white alcoholics. Dis Nerv Syst 29:391–394.

The pattern of drinking in the Negro reflects the inseparability of the historical social and cultural factors from the psychodynamic aspect. The Negro shows a specific adaptive mechanism, and one might predict that the more the Negro comes to fully share the white man's culture and society the more he will also share the patterns of drinking of the white alcoholic.

2301. Wagner NN: Birth order of volunteers: cross-cultural data. J Soc Psychol 74:133–134.

The relationship of birth order to volunteering behavior does not appear in a Malaysian sample, although the sample does not replicate a study of the higher incidence of first borns in medical school.

2302. Waldman RD: Neurosis and the social structure. Am J Orthopsychiatry 38:89–93.

Attempts to coerce, to communicate indirectly, and to rely excessively on the past may be responses to contemporary social order limitations which result in the frustration of human behavioral possibilities.

2303. Wang RP: A study of alcoholism in Chinatown. Int J Soc Psychiatry 14:260–267.

Confucianism and Taoism influence the pattern of drinking in their emphasis on moderation and nonviolence. The emphasis on intellectuality among the Chinese may also lead to a fear of alcoholic intoxication. The emphasis for the individual to seek harmony with the environment may be important in the selection of opium over alcohol.

2304. Wilkening EA, Pinto JB, Pastore J: Role of the extended family in migration and the adaptation in Brazil. J Marriage Fam 30:689–695.

Contact with the extended family increases in accordance to length of migrant's residence. This is positively associated with occupational status in both rural and urban areas.

2305. Wintrob R: Sexual guilt and culturally sanctioned delusions in Liberia, West Africa. Am J Psychiatry 125:89–95.

As a culturally sanctioned way of dealing with feelings of worthlessness and guilt, Liberian women may develop delusional systems concerning snakes and genii.

2306. (Deleted)

2307. Yamamuro B: Origins of some Japanese drinking customs. Q J Stud Alcohol 29:979–982.

Japanese drinking customs are related to customs of prehistoric origin as well as incidents related in epic poems, Kabuki plays, and traditional songs.

2308. Young FW, Young RC: The differentiation of family structure in rural Mexico. J Marriage Fam 30:154–160.

Principle components analysis of structural measures differentiating rural Mexican families demonstrates the presence of one main factor, although another, labeled "farm continuity," also appears.

2309. (Deleted)

2310. Veness H, Hoskin JO: Psychiatry in New Britain: a note on the "fruit-tree experiment" as a measure of the effect of language on association processes. Soc Sci Med 1:419–422.

Fruit-tree experiments with Tolai (New Guinea) children parallel those in Central Australia and show that trains of association set in motion by a stimulus in one language will differ from those set in train by a stimulus in the other. The "fruit-tree" experiments provide a convenient practical measure of the effect of language in a given transcultural situation.

1969

2311. Adams PL: Puberty as a biosocial turning point. Psychosomatics 10:343–349.

Puberty is not a conspicuous feature of human transition in our society, and puberty rites of passage are not in evidence.

2312. Adams-Webber JR: Cognitive complexity and sociality. Br J Soc Clin Psychol 8:211–216.

Cognitively complex persons infer others' personal constructs in social situations more effectively than do cognitively simple persons.

2313. Ahmed F: Age at marriage in Pakistan. J Marriage Fam 31:799–807.

Female age at marriage in Pakistan, though early, is not as low as previously supposed. Male age at first marriage is similar to that for the United States. Regional and rural-urban differences in marriage age are more pronounced for females than males.

2314. Al-Issa I: Problems in the cross-cultural study of schizophrenia. J Psychol 71:143–151.

Physiological responses are minimally influenced by culture and may be used as a baseline in comparing schizophrenics and normals within and across cultures.

2315. Asuni T: Homicide in Western Nigeria. Br J Psychiatry 115:1105–1113.

Many mentally disturbed persons in Western Nigeria are executed if they commit a homicide. There is a geographical correlation between suicide and homicide. Murderers mainly come from the lower classes.

2316. Attneave CL: Therapy in tribal settings and urban network intervention. Fam Process 8:192–210.

The processes of network therapy can be better understood through examining a case study of an American Indian natural network-clan.

2317. Averill JR, Opton EM Jr, Lazarus RS: Cross-cultural studies of psychophysiological responses during stress and emotion. Int J Psychol 4:82–102.

Although Japanese subjects differ in skin conductance and show the same level of response throughout a subincision film, results are similar to American responses. Similarities in reactions, stress, and emotions are particularly significant to psychological processes.

2318. Babow I: The singing societies of European immigrant groups in San Francisco: 1851–1953. J Hist Behav Sciences 5:10–24.

The singing societies aid immigrants in maintaining cultural ties with the homeland and give symbolic expression to community cohesion and homogeneity. They have fostered the formation of nonimmigrant singing societies and thus implanted a culture trait in American national culture.

2319. Balter L: The mother as source of power. Psychoanal Q 38:217–274.

The Perseus myth prompted the patriarchal orientation of ancient Greece. The Oedipus and Jason legends propounded a matriarchal orientation for the male.

2320. Barry H III: Cross-cultural research with matched pairs of societies. J Soc Psychol 79:25–34.

The method of matched pairs can maximize the degree of independence of different pairs in relation to the similarity between pair members. It also lessens the likelihood that differences will be caused by a common relationship with a third variable. The method is exemplified in a study of subsistence and child training.

2321. Bash KW, Bash-Liechti JB: Studies on the epidemiology of neuropsychiatric disorders among the rural population of the Province of Khuzestan, Iran. Soc Psychiatry 4:137–143.

Out of a population of 7,485 persons, 72 were found with significant psychiatric disturbance.

2322. Bean LL, Afzal M: Informal values in a Muslim society: a study of the timing of Muslim marriages. J Marriage Fam 31:583–588.

Selection of the month in which an Islamic marriage is to take place is largely influenced by religious considerations, while selection of the day of that month is a socioeconomic consideration.

2323. Bell RR: Some comments in Christensen's "Normative theory derived from cross-cultural family research." J Marriage Fam 31:223–224.

Intracultural comparison and analyses are as important as cross-cultural studies and may be more realistic than the idealized search for cultural universals.

2324. Berrien FK: Familiarity, mirror imaging and social desirability in stereotypes: Japanese vs. Americans. Int J Psychol 4:33–39.

Ideal cross-cultural research is investigatively international, researches common concerns, contains methodological comparability, and pools data for responsible interpretations.

2325. Berry JW: Ecology and socialization as factors in figural assimilation and the resolution of binocular rivalry. Int J Psychol 4:271–280.

Data from Scottish, Eskimo, and Temne subjects provide support for direct and indirect culture-personality relationships. The former refers to culturally structured sensory ecology, while the latter pertains to social, personality, and developmental mediation.

2326. Berry JW: On cross-cultural comparability. Int J Psychol 4:119–128.

Frameworks for cross-cultural studies should proceed from a demonstration of behavioral functional equivalence, generation of comparative description from specific description, and application of instruments to assess behavior in the two settings.

2327. Bhushan LI: A comparison of four Indian political groups on a measure of authoritarianism. J Soc Psychol 79:141.

Mean F scores for four political groups and for the overall sample prove the validity of the scale in terms of the evidence for the tradition-oriented, authoritarian Indian culture.

2328. Biaggio AMB: Internalized versus externalized guilt: a cross-cultural study. J Soc Psychol 78:147–149.

North American preadolescents, and girls in general, are higher in internalization of guilt than Brazilian preadolescents and males.

2329. Bowden E: Perceptual abilities of African and European children educated together. J Soc Psychol 79:149–154.

Europeans are superior to Africans in perceptual discriminative ability when age-connected, discriminative scores are positively related to age.

2330. Brill N, Weinstein R, Garrat J: Poverty and mental illness: patients' perceptions of poverty as an etiological factor in their illness. Am J Psychiatry 125:1172–1179.

A majority of state hospital patients reported having experienced poverty at some time during their lives and feeling that poverty contributed to their illness. Poverty may signify an accepted way of life for lower social classes but is more of an emotional stress for patients of higher social origins.

2331. Butts HF: White racism: its origins, institutions, and the implications for professional practice in mental health. Int J Psychiatry 8:914–928.

Institutional racism, as part of the white psychosocial character, has given rise to adaptive coping patterns by blacks. The mental health profession must be aware of the problems of black adaptations.

2332. Bynder H: Emile Durkheim and the sociology of the family. J Marriage Fam 31:527–533.

Durkheim's conceptual and methodological approach and his views on the dysfunctions of divorce should be given more consideration by American sociology.

2333. Chekki DA: Social legislation and kinship in India: a sociolegal study. J Marriage Fam 31:165–172.

The impact of contemporary social law upon the Lingayat caste of Mysore State has led to a rupturing of kinship relations. In the absence of social security programs the majority still depends upon family and kin ties in times of crisis.

2334. Chopra GJ: Man and marijuana. Int J Addict 4:215–247.

Analysis of historical, ethnological, and etiological aspects of hemp use indicates differing patterns of abuse between the East and the West.

2335. Choungourian A: The Maudsley Personality Inventory: extraversion and neuroticism in the Middle East. Br J Soc Clin Psychol 8:77–78.

Marked differences on English and Arabic forms of the MPI suggest the two forms may not be interchangeable.

2336. Christensen HT: Normative theory derived from cross-cultural family research. J Marriage Fam 31:209–222.

Value-behavior discrepancies have negative affects. In restrictive societies, greater deviation from local standards has greater negative consequences than in permissive societies.

2337. Chu H: A note to utilizing Murdock's ethnographic survey materials for cross-cultural family research. J Marriage Fam 31:311–314.

Combining three of Murdock's family types (extended, lineal, stem) for analytic purposes reduces rather than strengthens the extent of association between family types and other variables.

2338. Chu H, Hollingsworth JS: A cross-cultural study of the relationships between family types and social stratification. J Marriage Fam 31:322–327.

The lineal, rather than independent, family is positively associated with complex systems of social stratification.

2339. Comer J: White racism: its root form and function. Am J Psychiatry 126:802–806.

The development of white racism in the United States may be traced back to the Protestant Reformation in sixteenth-century Europe and the later period of the American revolution. Racism results from the projection of "bad impulses."

2340. Coombs RH: Problems in mate selection. Fam Coordinator 18:293–296.

Mate selection must take into account social change and role behaviors that are culturally determined.

2341. Cooper J, Kendell R, Gurland B, Sartorius N, Farkas T: Cross-national study of diagnosis of the mental disorders: some results from the first comparative investigation. Am J Psychiatry (Supp) 125:21–29.

Comparisons are made between the frequencies of diagnoses given to patients consecutively admitted to an American state mental hospital and to an English area mental hospital. National differences exist not only in the use of diagnostic terms by American and English mental hospital psychiatrists, but genuine clinical differences are present between the patient populations as well.

2342. Crandall VC, Gozali J: The social desirability responses of children of four religious-cultural groups. Child Dev 40:751–762.

Catholic and fundamentalist children have higher Children's Social Desirability scores than children of other faiths. This might be accounted for by their more frequent use of denial or repression defense mechanisms.

2343. Dawson JLM: Attitudinal consistency and conflict in West Africa. Int J Psychol 4:39–53.

Results from a traditional-western scale in Sierra Leone support a consistency theory indicating adaptive alteration toward midcontinuum traditional-western attitudes in the face of attitude conflict.

2344. Dawson JLM: Exchange theory and comparison level changes among Australian aborigines. Br J Soc Clin Psychol 8:133–140.

The effects of urbanization on Australian aborigines may be viewed in terms of exchange theory.

Australian aboriginal comparison level for expectations rises with increased exposures to urban influences.

2345. Day LH, Day AT: Family size in industrialized countries: an inquiry into the socio-cultural determinants of levels of childbearing. J Marriage Fam 31:252–256.

Family size varies according to availability of alternatives that satisfy interests fulfilled by having children. Size also varies according to the influence of culture and social setting upon the individuals' expectations for satisfying the interest of parents and children.

2346. deAndrade D, de Godoy Alves D, Ford JJ: A comparison of North-American and Brazilian college students' personality profiles on 16 PF questionnaire. Int J Psychol 4:55–58.

Second-order analysis of 16 PF data reveals more introversion, anxiety, spontaneity, and creativity for Brazilians. Brazilian males and American females are higher on superego strength than their other cultural counterparts.

2347. deBie P, Presvelou C: Young families: a survey of facts and guiding images in the European and American literature. J Marriage Fam 31:328–338.

A review of the sociological literature indicates that the subject of young families has been inadequately treated and that there are still conceptual difficulties to overcome.

2348. deLemos MM: The development of conservation in aboriginal children. Int J Psychol 4:255–269.

Piaget's stages for conservation are generally supported, although aboriginal children tend to develop them later than European children or sometimes not at all. An invariant order of development for weight and quantity conservation is not found.

2349. Deutscher I: A comment on Straus's "Phenomenal identity and conceptual equivalence." J Marriage Fam 31:240–241.

Straus's work is a welcome addition to methodology of family sociology.

2350. Devereux EC, Bronfenbrenner U, Rodgers RR: Child-rearing in England and the United States: a cross-national comparison. J Marriage Fam 31:257–270.

Generally, parent-child relationships in America

are more strong, salient, and binding than in England where they are somewhat attenuated and strained.

2351. Dick DH: The measurement of aggression and other attitudes in psychosomatic disorders by means of the semantic differential. J Psychosom Res 13:299–305.

Notions concerned with the expression and reception of aggression give rise to different strength of associations on the semantic differential in psychosomatic patients than with neurotic and control patients. The semantic differential is likely to prove a useful tool in psychosomatic research.

2352. Dingman HF, Paulson MJ, Eyman RK, Miller C: The semantic differential as a tool for measuring progress in therapy. Psychol Rep 25:271–279.

Progress through therapy can be evaluated by a factor analysis of responses to a semantic rating scale.

2353. Dobkin M: Folk curing with a psychedelic cactus in the North Coast of Peru. Int J Soc Psychiatry 15:23–32.

San Pedro, a psychedelic cactus, is employed to diagnose illness and effect cures. Folk healing cements together a system of social relationships and results in mutual benefits, both material and spiritual, which accrue to the members of the community.

2354. Doi LT: Cannot transcultural psychiatry be "transcultural"? Int J Psychiatry 8:825–827.

A hypothesis in which mental illness is defined as a manifestation of aborted or twisted dependency need can account for the difference between shame and guilt cultures and provide a true transcultural perspective.

2355. Doob LW, Foltz WJ, Stevens RB: The fermeda workshop: a different approach to border conflicts in Eastern Africa. J Psychol 73:249–266.

Although the main objective of the workshop was not achieved and no original solution to the disputes involved, from a research point of view attitudes and complex processes were revealed that were not obtainable through standard techniques.

2356. Dornhoff GW: Historical materialism, cultural determinism, and the origin of the ruling classes. Psychoanal Rev 56:271–287.

Priests and cities are symbols of man's desperate

attempt to deal with his guilt. Money evolved out of guilt-alleviating sacrifices and the profit motive became the driving force of Western man.

2357. Dow TE: Family planning: theoretical considerations and African models. J Marriage Fam 31:252–256.

Substantial interest in contraception in Africa is not generally associated with effective use, due to the transitional character of the population.

2358. Dyer D: Human problems in an Indian culture. Fam Coordinator 18:322–325.

A discussion group may consider problems of alcoholism, causes of communication breakdowns, sex education, motivation, hostility, and cultural values of a Sioux reservation.

2359. Earle MJ: A cross-cultural and cross-language comparison of dogmatism scores. J Soc Psychol 79:19–25.

The mean dogmatism score of Hong Kong students is higher than the mean score of British students. Chinese-English bilingual mean scores are higher on a Chinese translation than mean scores on the English scale.

2360. Edwards JN: Familial behavior as social exchange. J Marriage Fam 31:518–526.

Generating testable relationships and a theory of homogamous mating illustrate the value of consistent application of a social exchange framework to family studies.

2361. Ekman P, Friesen WV: Nonverbal leakage and clues to deception. Psychiatry 32:88–106.

Within deception interactions, differences in neuroanatomy and cultural influences combine to produce specific types of body movements and facial expressions that escape efforts to deceive and emerge as leakage or deception clues.

2362. El-Islam MF: Depression and guilt: a study at an Arab psychiatric clinic. Soc Psychiatry 4: 56–58.

A majority of depressed Arab patients at a Cairo clinic had guilt feelings. This study does not confirm earlier reports supporting the rarity of guilt and self-reproach in African, Arab, and non-Christian depressions.

2363. El-Islam MF, El-Deeb HA: The educational and occupational correlates of psychiatric disorder (a study at an Arab psychiatric clinic). Int J Soc Psychiatry 15:288–293.

Among psychiatric outpatients in Cairo schizophrenia is overrepresented in the illiterate. The educational difference between medical and psychiatric patients in this milieu is significant only in males, so that the relation of environmental factors to psychiatric disorders seems to show sex differences. Hysteria is overrepresented among the less intelligent illiterate patients.

2364. eSilva ACP: A lance broken on behalf of transcultural psychiatry. Int J Psychiatry 8:828–830.

Transcultural psychopharmacology is capable of providing valuable information on folk treatment of mental illness, therefore yielding new data for psychiatry.

2365. Evans JL, Segall MH: Learning to classify by color and by function: a study of concept-discovery by Ganda children. J Soc Psychol 77:35–53.

Learning to sort by physical appearance is easier for Ganda children, especially with color as the attribute, than learning to sort by function. Both tasks are more difficult for rural children than urban children. Educational experience is a critical factor in the development of conceptual functioning.

2366. Fabrega H: Social psychiatric aspects of acculturation and migration: a general statement. Compr Psychiatry 10:314–326.

The conceptual and methodological subset issues of acculturation and migration may be examined from the psychiatric standpoint. The strict epidemiological approach is somewhat simplistic in terms of the complexity of these issues of changing cultural environment.

2367. Fernando SJM: Cultural differences in the hostility of depressed patients. Br J Med Psychol 42:67–74.

Minority-group status alone is unlikely to be of importance in explaining Jewish-Protestant differences in direction of hostility. Close kinship ties with relatives in Jewish families may be important in this context, as well as cultural differences in childhood. Protestant-Catholic difference is not statistically significant.

2368. Fischer J: Negroes and whites and rates of mental illness: reconsideration of a myth. Psychiatry 32:428–446

Higher differential frequency of the occurrence of mental illness in the Negro population may be more apparent than real. While some differences in mental health may exist between the races, there is no indication that they are due to "inferiority" or "superiority."

2369. Flapan M: A paradigm for the analysis of childbearing motivations of married women prior to birth of the first child. Am J Orthopsychiatry 39:402–417.

Thirteen perspectives for delineating childbearing motivations form a psychosocial framework for the investigation of differential family size preferences, child-spacing intentions, female reproductive reactions, and patterns of maternal behavior.

2370. Foa UG, Mitchell TR, Lekhyananda D: Cultural differences in reaction to failure. Int J Psychol 4:21–25.

Americans show greater cognitive flexibility than Far Eastern students with respect to reported failure.

2371. Fong SL, Peskin H: Sex-role strain and personality adjustment of China-born students in America: a pilot study. J Abnorm Soc Psychol 74:563.

China-born female students feel alienated and in defiance of the norms of traditional culture in which females generally do not become students. The naturalized Chinese female accepts a Chinese model of feminine role, while the visa student rejects this model.

2372. Friedman N: African and the Afro-American: the changing Negro identity. Psychiatry 32:127–136.

Despite all his efforts, the American Negro has not been accepted as a Negro American. His new relationship to Africa is in the process of breaking the power of the white man's view of the Negro over the Negro's inner life, as he exchanges a domestic for an international identity.

2373. Gardiner HW: A cross-cultural comparison of hostility in children's drawings. J Soc Psychol 79:261–264.

Differences in children's drawings can differentiate a broad range of cultural groups on the variable of hostility.

2374. Geen RG, George R: Relationship of manifest aggressiveness to aggressive word associations. Psychol Rep 25:711–714.

Aggressive word associations may be used as a measure of aggression, which is a function of several antecedent conditions.

2375. German GA, Arya OP: Psychiatric morbidity amongst a Ugandan student population. Br J Psychiatry 115:1323–1329.

Makere University College students have a prevalence rate for psychiatric morbidity of 11.5 percent, a figure similar to figures from British universities. The basic diagnostic patterns are similar to those reported from British universities, although the pathoplastic effects on symptomatology of local cultural preoccupations are present.

2376. Goddard D, deGoddard SN, Whitehead PC: Social factors associated with coca use in the Andean region. Int J Addict 4:577–590.

Attitudes about coca use and patterns of social transmission of coca use are related to extent of coca use, which is generally considered to be a normative practice.

2377. Goffman E: The insanity of place. Psychiatry 32:357–388.

The philosophy of community containment is desirable but has serious implications for significant "others" in the patient's life.

2378. Gondor LH, Gondor EI: Changing times. Am J Psychother 23:67–76.

Children's drawings are a valuable source of information, especially when the parents are uncooperative or unavailable. Children from deprived families and minority groups whose manifest behavior patterns differ from middle-class patients show marked difficulty in verbalizing and are generally uncommunicative and suspicious. These children can express themselves by drawing and painting specific topics introduced by the therapist.

2379. Gurland B, Fleiss J, Cooper J, Kendell R, Simon R: Cross-national study of diagnosis of the mental disorders: some comparisons of diagnostic criteria from the first investigation. Am J Psychiatry (Supp) 125:30–39.

Psychiatric clinical diagnoses made in New York and London reflect the psychopathology of the patient more accurately than is generally acknowledged.

2380. Haavio-Mannila E: The position of Finnish women: regional and cross-national comparisons. J Marriage Fam 31:339–347.

The discrepancy between formal and informal

behavior and attitudes on women's equality leads to strain for Finnish women, who are generally active but not very strong or appreciated.

2381. Harley RE: Children's perceptions of sex preference in four cultural groups. J Marriage Fam 31:380–387.

Responses to an adoption story by Hawaiian whites, Japanese-Americans, New Zealand whites, and Maori children suggest that young children do not perceive culturally determined male sex favoritism or cross-sex preference on the part of adults.

2382. Hartley SM: Illegitimacy among "married" women in England and Wales. J Marriage Fam 31:793–798.

The ratio of illegitimacy fertility rates of unmarried women to total fertility of married women increases sharply with age.

2383. Heeren HJ, Moors HG: Family planning and differential fertility in a Dutch city. J Marriage Fam 31:588–594.

The decline in the birthrate of the Netherlands since 1965 can be seen in terms of actual and desired number of offspring, religious affiliation, education, socioeconomic status, and housing variables. In terms of desired number of children, the Netherlands is intermediate in the movement from a negative to positive correlation between SES and fertility.

2384. Hendershor GE: Familial satisfaction, birth order, and fertility values. J Marriage Fam 31: 27–33.

Size preferences for the family of procreation vary with the size of family of orientation and familial satisfaction. This association is greater for first-born women.

2385. Herson A, Simonsson M: Weight conservation in Zambian children. Int J Psychol 4:281–292.

Approximately one-half of urban Zambian children increasingly fail to demonstrate weight conservation by ages 10–15, although for earlier ages the proportions are comparable to those obtained for European children.

2386. Hinde RA: The bases of aggression in animals. J Psychosom Res 13:213–219.

Frustrations are part of animal life and some aggression is inevitable. This, however, need not discourage attempts to reduce undesirable aggressiveness, and it would seem most profitable to focus on developmental issues to this end.

2387. Hiniker PJ: Chinese reactions to forced compliance: dissonance reduction or national character. J Soc Psychol 77:157–176.

Chinese and American reactions to forced compliance differ. The Chinese may overtly comply with authority, but increased inducement will have no observable effect on internalized attitudes.

2388. Holthouse RJ, Kahn MW: A study of the influence of culture on the personality development of the Hausas of Kano City. Int J Soc Psychiatry 15:107–119.

The culture and personality of Moslem Hausas may be conceptualized in terms of Erikson's social-psychoanalytic stages. What emerges is a picture of a society and a personality that is a curious blend of primitive indulgence of impulses existing along with strict moral rituals and a deep sense of sin and of need for atonement.

2389. Hoskin JO, Friedman MI, Cawte JE: A high incidence of suicide in a preliterate-primitive society. Psychiatry 32:200–210.

The Kandrian district of Southwest New Britain has a suicide rate of double that usually given for Western countries. This challenges the belief that suicide is a product of civilization and is rare in preliterate countries.

2390. Hoskin JO, Kiloh LG, Cawte JE: Epilepsy and guria: the shaking syndromes of New Guinea. Soc Sci Med 3:39–48.

Guria, a shaking syndrome found in New Guinea, represents a culturally determined expression of a variety of excitatory themes, including physical illness and interpersonal and ecological tensions.

2391. Irvine SH: Factor analysis of African abilities and attachments: constructs across cultures. Psychol Bull 71:20–32.

Although tests tend to group in ways that can be explained in terms of Western constructs, sources of variance exist that are unique to the society. Cross-cultural analysis must be considered in terms of the logic of contructs; the concept of intelligence, for example, is part of a value system that has limited cultural transferability.

2392. Irvine SH: Figural tests of reasoning in Africa: studies in the use of Raven's Matrices across cultures. Int J Psychol 4:217–228.

Cultural differences in item difficulty and individual differences in problem-solving strategy are indicated among African cultural groups. Exposure to Western value systems produces test-score patterns that are near to those for Western groups.

2393. Iwao S, Child IL, Garcia M: Further evidence of agreement between Japanese and American esthetic evaluation. J Soc Psychol 78:11–15.

Japanese artists' esthetic judgments on prints show a significant tendency toward agreement with U.S. experts, but no significant agreement is shown on abstract paintings. There is growing evidence that esthetic evaluations in different cultural settings may tend toward agreement.

2394. Iwawaki S, Zax M, Mitsuoka S: Extremity of response among Japanese and American children. J Soc Psychol 79:257–260.

Japanese twelfth-grade students make fewer extreme responses than their American counterparts, but such differences are not found among a sample of younger children. This finding appears consistent with that pattern of early Japanese child rearing.

2395. Jahoda G: Understanding the mechanism of bicycles: a cross-cultural study of developmental change after 13 years. Int J Psychol 4:103–108.

Long-term improvement in the understanding of bicycle mechanisms by Ghanaian boys may be due to educational and technological advances, while the lack of improvement for girls may reflect different educational environments.

2396. Jenkin N, Vroegh K: Contemporary concepts of masculinity and femininity. Psychol Rep 25:679–697.

Based upon adjective endorsements, masculinity and femininity are not opposite ends of a bipolar variable. Gender is not a sufficient criterion for selecting groups for the study of masculinity and femininity.

2397. Jensen GD, Bobbitt RA, Gordon BN: Patterns and sequences of hitting behavior in mother and infant monkeys (Macaca Nemestrina). J Psychiatr Res 7:55–61.

In a rich environment the mother's hitting is effective in inducing the infant to leave. In a privation environment, in which infants characteristically did more climbing-on, hitting was ineffective in instigating independence.

2398. Jones IV: Subincision among Australian Western Desert aborigines. Br J Med Psychol 42:183–190.

Subincision is a powerful means of producing group cohesion by endowing status on those who have the operation performed. Hygiene is not an entirely satisfactory explanation for the act. Subincision may have become incorporated into the culture of the society in much the same manner as circumcision.

2399. Josephson E: The matriarchy: myth and reality. Fam Coordinator 18:268–278.

American fathers continue to play an effective, perhaps more democratic, role. Paternal deprivation is not the sole cause of lower-class pathologies. The matriarchy is as much myth as exaggeration.

2400. Kandel D, Lesser GS: Parent-adolescent relationships and adolescent independence in the United States and Denmark. J Marriage Fam 31:348–358.

Authoritarian family decisionmaking patterns are more frequent in the United States, and democratic patterns more frequent in Denmark.

2401. Karno M, Ross RN, Caper RA: Mental health roles of physicians in a Mexican-American community. Community Ment Health J 5:62–69.

Family physicians in the Los Angeles Mexican-American community are by far the most active and available service for sustaining mental health in this low-income, ethnic area with its poverty of formal psychiatric facilities.

2402. Katchadourian HA, Churchill CW: Social class and mental illness in urban Lebanon. Soc Psychiatry 4:49–55.

In urban Lebanon a statistically significant association exists between class position, as determined by estimated family income, and the prevalence of psychiatric disorders. A significant association is also found between class position and types of psychiatric disorders. Neurotic disorders are overrepresented in the upper class, and psychotic disorders in the lower class.

2403. Kato M: An epidemiological analysis of the fluctuation of drug dependence in Japan. Int J Addict 4:591–621.

Since World War II, a fluctuation from methamphetamine and heroin to hypnotics and analgesics has occurred, along with increased alcohol consumption.

2404. Keith RA, Varranda EG: Age independence norms in American and Filipino adolescents. J Soc Psychol 78:285–286.

Social custom, religion, family structure, and economic opportunity contribute to differences in age norms for independence behaviors between America and the Phillippines.

2405. Kendon A, Cook M: The consistency of gaze patterns in social interaction. Br J Psychol 60:481–494.

Duration, frequency, and action patterns of gazing are all related. Long gazes have more favorable receptions than short, frequent gazes. Sex and personality differences may be defined.

2406. Kennedy JG: Psychosocial dynamics of witchcraft systems. Int J Soc Psychiatry 15:165–178.

Witchcraft produces fear and stress rather than satisfaction. The anthropological notion of witchcraft as a "positive philosophy" that functions to maintain social order and continuity seems no longer useful.

2407. Khatri AA, Siddiqui BB: "A boy or a girl?" Preferences of parents for sex of offspring as perceived by East Indian and American children: a cross-cultural study. J Marriage Fam 31:388–392.

The adoption story used by Harley et al. in India failed to confirm same sex preference of the story mother figure. Cross-cultural differences may be considered in light of Indian culture.

2408. King K: Adolescent perception of power structure in the Negro family. J Marriage Fam 31:751–755.

Negro adolescents view the family power structure as syncratic and report same sex parental participation as the strongest. Both males and females indicate stronger father decisionmaking than previously reported.

2409. Kline L: Some factors in the psychiatric treatment of Spanish-Americans. Am J Psychiatry 125:1674–1681.

Spanish Americans identify psychiatry as "Anglo" and therefore not a possible source of understanding and support. Community resistance to treatment may be overcome by developing services with the participation of community leaders and traditional healers. Ethnic resistance to treatment may be overcome when the patient learns that he can express ordinarily unacceptable feelings about Anglos without fearing retaliation by the therapist.

2410. Kline P: The anal character: a cross-cultural study in Ghana. Br J Soc Clin Psychol 8:201–210.

Ghanaian students score higher on a test of anal characteristics than their British counterparts.

2411. Korson JH: Student attitudes toward mate selection in a Muslim society. J Marriage Fam 31:153–163.

Male West Pakistani university students are more liberal and more likely to initiate social change than female students. An important segment of the student population supports traditional mate selection practices, while a significant number are ready to challenge traditional norms.

2412. Kramer M: Cross-national study of diagnosis of the mental disorders: origin of the problem. Am J Psychiatry (Supp) 125:1–11.

Patients with affective disorders, schizophrenia, and psychosis with cerebral arteriosclerosis have vastly different rates of first admissions to mental hospitals in England and the United States.

2413. Kurokawa M: Acculturation and mental health of Mennonite children. Child Dev 40:689–705.

Due to natural increase, group contact, and other factors, the Mennonite society has been pressured toward change. Orthodox Mennonite children are not immune to stresses and show symptoms of covert maladjustment. Transitional Mennonite children show symptoms of mental disturbances, indicating that the adaptive change undertaken by the church is not adequate for the prevention of personality disturbance.

2414. Lalli M: The Italian-American family: assimilation and change, 1960–1965. Fam Coordinator 18:44–48.

Variations in the process of assimilation traceable to different regional origins of Italian families provide a cautionary note concerning generalization about the typical "Italian family" and demonstrate the importance of cultural background for understanding behavior.

2415. Lamouse A: Family roles of women: a German example. J Marriage Fam 31:145–152.

Urban Münster family attitudes are traditional in power allocation; however, the degree of power balance is relatively high. The wife's influence in decisionmaking varies according to husband's social status and her external role experiences.

2416. Lauriat P: The effect of marital dissolution on fertility. J Marriage Fam 31:484–493.

Overall loss of fertility is greatest for divorced women who do not remarry, intermediate for remarried women, and least for widowed women.

2417. Lazarus JR, Kessel FS, Botha E: Cultural differences in n-ach externality between white and colored South African adolescents. J Soc Psychol 77:133–134.

The mean n-ach score for the colored sample is significantly lower than for the white sample. However, the hypothesis that coloreds would show a greater tendency than whites to believe that reward is externally controlled could not be confirmed.

2418. Leon C: Unusual patterns of crime during La Violencia in Colombia. Am J Psychiatry 125:1564–1575.

La Violencia refers to the professionalization of criminal behavior from 1940 to the 1960s. The bandalero criminal prototypes of the period typically were raised in a childhood environment characterized by social, economic, religious, and familial repression. When these repressive forces began to collapse as a result of social and political change, the bandalero, his intense destructive rage unleashed, committed atrocious crimes.

2419. Lesse S: Revolution, vintage 1968: a psychosocial view. Am J Psychother 23:584–598.

To understand the current revolution, the concept of sociocultural rate of change must be considered. The rate of change that has occurred technologically, socioeconomically, sociopolitically, and sociophilosophically since the end of World War II has accelerated to a degree that never before has been experienced in all of recorded history.

2420. Levak MD: Eidetic images among the Bororo of Brazil. J Soc Psychol 79:135–138.

Eidetic imagery in clear form is totally absent from a sample of Bororo males and females, although females from a less acculturated group experience the imagery in a weaker form.

2421. Lewis IM: Some strategies of non-physical aggression in other cultures. J Psychosom Res 13:221–227.

From the empirical evidence in many tribal societies it is possible to infer a hierarchy of increasingly direct styles of aggressive behavior. These range from spirit possession at one extreme, through witchcraft, to open litigation and fighting at the other end of the spectrum.

2422. Liu WT, Rubel AJ, Yu E: The urban family of Cebu: a profile analysis. J Marriage Fam 31:393–402.

Kin solidarity is a function of class and ethnic variations. The bilateral mestizo and Filipino family is more adaptive to the political structure than the Chinese family clan system. The peer-group system and sex-segregated friendships influence conjugal roles and relations. Segregated nuclear family roles give the wife greater domestic autonomy.

2423. Lomas P: Taboo and illness. Br J Med Psychol 42:33–39.

Taboo that exists in advanced as well as primitive societies is a beneficial means of avoiding psychic, personal, and social confusion, a means of separating incompatible parts. Taboos on illness are prevalent in contemporary society.

2424. Lorr M, Klett CJ: Cross-cultural comparison of psychotic syndromes. J Abnorm Soc Psychol 74:531–543.

In most cases, each of twelve psychotic syndromes are confirmed in samples from England, France, Germany, Italy, Japan, and Sweden.

2425. Lubart JM: Field study of the problems of adaptation of Mackenzie Delta Eskimos to social and economic change. Psychiatry 32:447–458.

The Mackenzie Delta Eskimos face the ordeal of adapting to a radically different culture. The stress of this adaptation has given rise to clinical and psychodynamic manifestations of social pathology.

2426. Luckey EB, Nass GD: A comparison of sexual attitudes and behavior in an international sample. J Marriage Fam 31:364–379.

North American students, and women in general, have more conservative views on sex roles and courtship than European students. Sexual attitudes in England and Norway are more liberal than in the other countries surveyed.

2427. Lupri E: Contemporary authority patterns in the West German family: a study in cross-national validation. J Marriage Fam 31:134–144.

A spouse's relative participation in the external system determines his/her power position in the family.

2428. Mason EP: Cross-validation study of personality characteristics of junior high students from American Indian, Mexican, and Caucasian ethnic backgrounds. J Soc Psychol 77:15–24.

Significant ordered ethnic differences on the California Personality Inventory are obtained, with Caucasians highest and Indians lowest, and evidence for a generalized more negative response for all females is validated. The consistently negative attitudes of American Indian male and female responses is significant.

2429. Mazer M, Ahern J: Personality and social class position in migration from an island: the implications for psychiatric illness. Int J Soc Psychiatry 15:203–208.

Values and beliefs associated with social position may be more influential than personality in determining migration based upon economic and related considerations. Data from Martha's Vineyard do not support the selection hypothesis of the relation of migration to the occurrence of psychiatric disorder.

2430. Meadow A, Bronson L: Religious affiliation and psychopathology in Mexican-American populations. J Abnorm Soc Psychol 74:177–180.

A lower rate of pathological responses by Protestant subjects may be due to the social support offered by a strong leader and small, close congregation; as opposed to the Catholic Mexican-American.

2431. Melikian LH: Acculturation, time perspective, and feeling tone: a cross-cultural study in the perception of the days. J Soc Psychol 79:273–276.

Exposure to other cultures seems to increase future orientation, whereas nonexposure appears to favor past orientations among Saudi Arab college students.

2432. Melikian LH, Wahab AZ: First drawn picture: a cross-cultural investigation of the DAP. J Proj Tech Pers Assessment 33:539–541.

Similar findings for Afghan and American college students indicate that more females than males draw a picture of the opposite sex person first.

2433. Meredith GM: Sex temperament among Japanese-American college students in Hawaii. J Soc Psychol 77:149–156.

Although Caucasians score in the most masculine direction, few differences between Chinese, Japanese-American, and Caucasian males are found. Comparison of females shows the Japanese-American to be highest in the feminine direction. Intergroup differences may be discussed in terms of sex-role strategies and a Japanese-American distinction between Meiji-type and Haole-type females.

2434. Michael G, Willis FN: The development of gestures in three subcultural groups. J Soc Psychol 79:35–42.

American and German children exposed to both cultures learn the gestures of both cultures. However, accuracy of gesture use could not be predicted from amount of exposure of Americans in Germany and Germans to American culture.

2435. Michel A, Feyrabend FL: Real number of children and conjugal interaction in French urban families: a comparison with American families. J Marriage Fam 31:359–363.

Marital satisfaction and agreement in France and the United States are more related to realized number of desired children than to actual number of children. Excessive fertility has a greater negative impact on conjugal interaction than negative fertility.

2436. Milner E: Extreme cultural discontinuity and contemporary American adolescent behavior: a relational analysis. Int J Soc Psychiatry 15:314–318.

American girls and young women are reacting to culturally based ego-formation threat in both adaptive-constructive and unadaptive-self-destructive ways. Afro-American girls, a special subgrouping among American women, are taking consistently greater advantage of continuing education towards occupational and marital mobility than are their white social-class counterparts.

2437. Mitchell GS: Paternalistic behavior in primates. Psychol Bull 71:399–417.

The roles of kinship, social change, sex and age of infant, dominance status, number of adult males, consort relations, delivery season, cultural propagation, and orphaned infants are profitable areas for laboratory research on primate paternalistic behavior.

2438. Mogey JM: Research on the family: the search for world trends. J Marriage Fam 31:225–232.

Content analysis of 800 bibliographic items indicates a need for use of more advanced methodology of data collection and analysis.

2439. Mountjoy PT, Bos JH, Duncan MO, Verplank RB: Neglected aspect of the history of psychology. J Hist Behav Sciences 5:59–67.

A prescientific technology of animal behavior preceded and influenced the development of a science of animal behavior. The concept of imprinting was described in A.D. 1250 in relation to falconry.

2440. Muensterberger W: Psyche and environment: sociocultural variations in separation and individuation. Psychoanal Q 38:191–216.

In primitive cultures inhibitions and restraint depend more heavily on external than on internal influence, on a psychic organization that relies for support on the force of outside demands instead of stable introjects.

2441. Munroe RL, Munroe RH, Daniels RE: Effect of status and values on estimation of coin size in two East African societies. J Soc Psychol 77:25–34.

The fewer the number of father's cattle, the larger the coin size estimate by Kipsigis children; and the less land held the larger the size estimate by Logoli children. The relationship between wealth and the estimation of coin sizes is supported, with indications that cultural factors in status determination are also important.

2442. Murphy HBM: Handling the cultural dimension in psychiatric research. Soc Psychiatry 4:11–15.

Diversification is the safest approach to cross-cultural research. Until the types of cultural influence are known it is safe and potentially much more informative to keep cultures distinct and to make separate comparisons within each than to compare between many cultures.

2443. Nash D: The domestic side of a foreign existence. J Marriage Fam 31:574–583.

American families in Spain respond to their setting with increased family cohesiveness, ethnocentrism, and increased valuation of American culture. Although women and children may adopt new roles, they do so reluctantly and with difficulty.

2444. Okong MO: The differential effects of rural and urban upbringing on the development of cognitive style. Int J Psychol 4:293–305.

Nigerian university students from urban, literate backgrounds are more field-independent than those from rural, illiterate backgrounds. Differences between rural and urban Nigerian males and New York females point out the role of cultural factors in perceptual field independence.

2445. Opler MK: International and cultural conflicts affecting mental health. Am J Psychother 23:608–620.

Cultures of violence breed violence in individuals. Schizophrenia in nonliterate cultures is often cured by group or cultural technique. The appearance of serious mental illness in advanced societies represents a human reaction to social distortions that reach down deeply into family systems.

2446. Osmund MW: A cross-cultural analysis of family organization. J Marriage Fam 31:302–310.

A multicultural analysis of family organization indicates that family type is significantly related to variables of social organization. The limited family type is more characteristic of complex societies than the general family type. A family typology that emphasizes economic household responsibility may be more useful than the independent-extended family dichotomy.

2447. Ostheimer JM: Measuring achievement motivation among the Chagga of Tanzania. J Soc Psychol 78:17–30.

Test results of n ach and attitudes of Tanzanian subjects are compared to levels of academic and economic achievement, but the results fail to support hypotheses concerning these interrelationships.

2448. Parker S, Kleiner RJ: Social and psychological dimensions of the family role performance of the Negro male. J Marriage Fam 31:500–506.

Discrepancies in family role performance are part of a perceived failure in the larger arena of goal-striving behavior.

2449. Parker S, Kleiner RJ, Needelman B: Migration and mental illness: some reconsiderations and suggestions for further analysis. Soc Sci Med 3:1–9.

Contrary to predictions based on the culture shock hypothesis, urban migrants show higher rates of mental illness than rural migrants. There is, however, a relationship between mental illness and high goal-striving stress, high reference group discrepancy, and low self-esteem among Philadelphia Negroes.

2450. Person ES: Racism: evil or ill. Int J Psychiatry 8:929–933.

In all varieties of tribalism, perception of difference is linked to negative value judgments. White racism is a social evil rather than social illness, and change depends upon a merger of morality and self-interest.

2451. Petersen KK: Kin network research: a plea for comparability. J Marriage Fam 31:271–280.

An unsuccessful attempt to compare Egyptian and American data on network size and extensiveness points out the need for a consensus on concepts, measurements, and analytic modes in kinship studies.

2452. Petroni FA: Social class, family size, and the sick role. J Marriage Fam 31:728–735.

Socioeconomic status and family size are inversely related to perceived right to assume the sick role. Frequency of reported illness and physician visits are inversely related to family size in lower classes, but not related to socioeconomic status.

2453. Pinderhughes CA: The origins of racism. Int J Psychiatry 8: 934–941.

Understanding the primitive origins and group dynamics of racism is a prerequisite to changing the nature of group behavior.

2454. Pollitt E, Ricciuti H: Biological and social correlates of stature among children in the slums of Lima, Peru. Am J Orthopsychiatry 39:735–747.

Differences in slum children's stature may reflect nutritional background, but they also reflect differences in other biological and social factors associated with, or capable of, influencing intellectual development.

2455. Pope H: Negro-white differences in decisions regarding illegitimate children. J Marriage Fam 31:756–764.

Patterns of decisionmaking with respect to illegitimacy suggest perhaps Negroes are less committed to the legitimacy norm and have less reason and desire to marry than whites. Due to conceptual inadequacies and lack of data, these interpretations are not definitely supported, however.

2455a. Preble E, Casey J: Taking care of business. The heroin user's life on the street. Int J Addictions 4:1–24.

An ethnographic account of lower class heroin users in New York City details the history of heroin use; and the social hierarchy from importer to street dealer and juggler.

2456. Prince J: An anthropometric comparison of psychiatric patients and their siblings. Br J Psychiatry 115:435–442.

Comparison of patients and healthy siblings of same sex on various anthropometric measures shows no difference in the groups by sex and diagnosis.

2457. Rahe RH: Multi-cultural correlations of life change scaling: America, Japan, Denmark and Sweden. J Psychosom Res 13:191–195.

Despite many cross-cultural differences, similarities between twentieth-century cultures are far more pronounced.

2458. Ramirez M: Identification with Mexican-American values and psychological adjustment in Mexican-American adolescents. Int J Soc Psychiatry 15:151–156.

Whenever a person, caught between two opposing sets of values, decides to reject one of the sets he becomes overwhelmed by feelings of guilt and self-derogation. Mexican-Americans exhibit such values and the resultant problems.

2459. Rodman H, Nichols FR, Voydanoff P: Lower-class attitudes toward "deviant" family patterns: a cross-cultural study. J Marriage Fam 31:315–321.

Data on nonlegal marriage in Trinidad and Detroit indicate that the greater the pressure upon a group to maintain conventional values, the less the members will accept deviant behavior patterns.

2460. Rosen VH: Introduction to panel on language and psychoanalysis. Int J Psychoanal 50: 113–116.

The issue of the relationship between language and the thought process is a central interdisciplinary pursuit. Whorf's linguistic relativity principle has important implications for unconscious mental processes.

2461. Rosenthal TL, Henderson RW, Hobson A, Hurt M: Social strata and perception of magical and folk-medical child-care practices. J Soc Psychol 77: 3–13.

Cultural milieu and socioeconomic level affect acceptance of healing practices, non-Anglo groups in the Southwest are more accepting than Anglo groups and higher SES level groups.

2462. Rubin D: Parental schemata of Negro primary school children. Psychol Rep 25:60–62.

For Negro children placement of "self" on a field in relation to parental figures is only a function of achievement.

2463. Safilios-Rothschild C: Family sociology or wive's family sociology? A cross-cultural examination of decision-making. J Marriage Fam 31:290–301.

There is not always a congruence between husband's and wife's perception of familial decision-making, as shown in an examination of Detroit and Athenian couples.

2464. Safilios-Rothschild C: Psychotherapy and patients' characteristics: a cross-cultural examination. Int J Soc Psychiatry 15:120–128.

Data from Greece indicate that while a selective process operates cross-culturally in determining who will be offered psychotherapy, the nature of this process varies with predominant cultural values, sociocultural conditions, the personal characteristics and the hierarchical ranking of therapists, and the patient's diagnosis.

2465. Safilios-Rothschild C: Sociopsychological factors affecting fertility in urban Greece: a preliminary report. J Marriage Fam 31:595–606.

Generation and level of education are the most important predictors of family size for working and nonworking Athenian women.

2466. Sarnoff CA: Mythic symbols in two Pre-Columbian myths. Am Imago 26:3–20.

Verbal representations of Pre-Inca and Mayan stone reliefs suggest that Pre-Columbian and Western peoples have the potential for drive gratification through the same core fantasies.

2467. Schluderman S, Schluderman E: Social role perceptions of children in Hutterite communal society. J Psychol 72:183–188.

Hutterite responses to a semantic differential show no clear cut indication of a stable EPA semantic space for any age-sex group.

2468. Schluderman S, Schluderman E: Developmental study of social role perception among Hutterite adolescents. J Psychol 72:243–246.

The principle factor matrix for Hutterite adolescents is almost as undifferentiated as that for Hutterite children.

2469. Schluderman S, Schluderman E: Scale checking style as a function of age and sex in Indian and Hutterite children. J Psychol 72:253–261.

Age effects in terms of extreme, middle, or neutral ratings are significant in both groups, and sex differences are obtained for the Indian group only. Results may be seen in terms of cognitive differentiation and levels of judgmental process.

2470. Schluderman S, Schluderman E: Factorial analysis of semantic structures in Hutterite adults. J Psychol 73:267–273.

A few basic dimensions underlie adult Hutterite perception of social roles; the failure to obtain these dimensions for children and adolescents is due to the delaying effects of social influences on the development of cognitive differentiation.

2471. Schmitt RC: Age and race differences on divorce in Hawaii. J Marriage Fam 31:48–50.

Interracial marriage and divorce in Hawaii involve a disproportionate number of couples in which one spouse is much older than another. Divorce rates are higher when the wife is older than her husband.

2472. Schoenfeld E: Intermarriage and the small town: the Jewish case. J Marriage Fam 31:61–64.

Endogamy and exogamy do not appear to be salient factors in Jewish identity. To adapt to high rates of interethnic marriage, the Jewish community changes from its ideology of compulsory endogamy to "preferred" endogamy.

2473. Schuch AJ, Trexler JT, Quesada CC: Filipino and American college student preferences for working conditions. J Soc Psychol 78:281–282.

Preferences for desirable working conditions are noticeably different between the United States and the Philippines. A greater frequency in sex differences in job condition preferences is found in the American group.

2474. Sechrest L, Flores L: Sibling position of Philippine psychiatric patients. J Soc Psychol 77:135–137.

The representation of younger or older children in the psychiatric patient sample differs according to family size.

2475. Sechrest L, Flores L: Homosexuality in the Philippines and the United States: the handwriting on the wall. J Soc Psychol 79:3–12.

A sample of U.S. graffitti is higher in homosexual content than a Philippine sample, which has higher frequency of hostility and disapproval of sexual ideation.

2476. Serpell R: Cultural differences in attentional preference for colour over form. Int J Psychol 4:1–8.

Developmental increases in form-dominance for Zambian and Indian schoolchildren are absent in a rural sample and more pronounced in a university sample than an illiterate sample.

2477. Serpell R: The influences of language, education, and culture on attentional preference between colour and form. Int J Psychol 4:183–194.

Preferences for form over color are evident with increasing age, among boys more than girls, and among the Western educated. Color preference is shown by active males, adult schizophrenics, and Zambian subjects.

2478. Shaffer M, Sundberg ND, Tyler LE: Content differences on word listing by American, Dutch, and Indian adolescents. J Soc Psychol 79:139.

Spontaneous word naming and frequencies may reflect situational and cultural activities and habits.

2479. Shainess N: Images of woman: past and present, overt and obscured. Am J Psychother 23:77–97.

Most of the theoretical concepts relating to feminine psychology were evolved by men, who have tended to have a self-serving perspective of women and have taken for granted the superior position they have occupied in most societies. Women have also tended to accept their allotted place. Freud's phallocentric bias has led to misunderstanding of feminine behavior.

2480. Shakman R: Indigenous healing of mental illness in the Philippines. Int J Soc Psychiatry 15:279–287.

The indigenous healer is the primary provider of psychiatric therapy to the vast majority of Filipinos who are geographically or culturally remote from psychiatric treatment administered by physicians. Some healers are aware of the psychological basis of many somatic complaints and of the need to refer individuals with organic disease to physicians.

2481. Shapira A, Madsen MC: Cooperative and competitive behavior of kibbutz and urban children in Israel. Child Dev 40:609–617.

Kibbutz children show more cooperative behavior than city children in Israel. This may be because kibbutz children grow up in such a competitive atmosphere that they must develop cooperative tendencies so that the group can continue to function.

2482. Sharma KL: Dominance-deference: a cross-cultural study. J Soc Psychol 79:265–266.

American males are more dominant than Indian males, who are in turn more dominant than Japanese-Americans. Indian females are more dominant than American and Thai females.

2483. Shepher J: Familism and social structure: the case of the kibbutz. J Marriage Fam 31:567–573.

Research of different housing systems reveals a positive association between the familistic system and (1) polarized sexual division of labor in housework and public activity, (2) less social activity, and (3) anticollective trends in consumption patterns.

2484. Singh NP: N/Ach among successful-unsuccessful and traditional-progressive agricultural entrepreneurs of Delhi. J Soc Psychol 79:271–272.

High n/Ach is the special feature of a successful agricultural entrepreneur; perhaps by developing n/Ach among Indian farmers agricultural input and output may be enhanced.

2485. Sinha D: Study of motivation in a developing country: concept of happy life among Indian farmers. J Soc Psychol 79:89–98.

Villagers are generally concerned with immediate economic values and needs that do not transcend their personal or familial spheres. Farmers from a more developed village are more reality oriented and show greater clarity than other farmers.

2486. Smith HC: The triple choice: social, political, cultural. Am J Orthopsychiatry 39:16–22.

Man lives in a political, social, and cultural environment and needs to rebuild the community in the social sphere, to revitalize democracy in the political sphere, and to update culture through relevant art.

2487. Spitz RA: Aggression and adaptation. J Nerv Ment Dis 149:81–90.

Psychiatry is indebted to Konrad Lorenz for the concept of drive regulation through "the parliament of instincts." Psychiatrists must explore the devices that will make it possible for man to domesticate aggression, to find how to reorient it and how to place it in the service of the survival of the species and its development.

2488. Stanley G: Australian students' attitudes to Negroes and aborigines on the Multifactor Racial Attitude Inventory (MRAI). J Soc Psychol 77:281–282.

A sample of white Australian university students did not view aborigines less favorably than American Negroes, and thus the predicted difference based on Rokeach's theory of prejudice is not confirmed.

2489. Staples RE: Research on the Negro family: a source for family practitioners. Fam Coordinator 18:202–209.

The Negro family has undergone adaptive changes and yet has survived as an important social unit and bulwark against racism. Family life educators must gain greater understanding of the Negro family in order to facilitate its role.

2490. Steinmann A, Fox DJ: Specific areas of agreement and conflict in women's self-perception and their perception of men's ideal woman in two South American urban communities and an urban community in the United States. J Marriage Fam 31:281–289.

North and South American women believe man's ideal woman to be submissive and family oriented. North American women do tend to seek achievement more aggressively and feel that a career can be integrated into family life.

2491. Straus MA: Phenomenal identity and conceptual equivalence of measurement in cross-national comparative research. J Marriage Fam 31:233–239.

Phenomenal identity of procedure does not necessarily lead to conceptual equivalence in measurement. A taxonomy of measurement equivalence and their applications may be suggested: culturally universal, culturally modified, culturally ipsatized, and culturally specific.

2492. Sundberg N, Sharma V, Wodtli R, Tohila P: Family cohesiveness and autonomy of adolescents in India and the United States. J Marriage Fam 31:403–407.

Adolescents in India emphasize greater family cohesiveness, while their U.S. counterparts emphasize autonomy. Indian fathers are perceived as influential.

2493. Sussman MB: Cross-cultural family research: one view from the "catbird seat." J Marriage Fam 31:203–208.

Some of the objectives of previous cross-cultural research require further work and application.

2494. Thoma H: Some remarks on psychoanalysis in Germany. Int J Psychoanal 50:683–692.

The history of psychoanalysis in Germany from

1933 to the present indicates an increasing relevancy and importance of the discipline in that country.

2495. Thomas DR: Social distance between Fijians and Fiji-Indians in Suva, Fiji. J Soc Psychol 79:269–270.

Indians show less social distance to Fijians than Fijians show toward Indians. The viewpoint that one or the other group is becoming more liberal in attitudes, and toward differences in religion, has some influence on social distance.

2496. Tin-Yee Hsieh T, Shybut J, Lotsof EJ: Internal versus external control and ethnic group membership: a cross-cultural comparison. J Consult Clin Psychol 33:122–124.

Chinese, Chinese-American, and Anglo-American cultural orientation is closely related to personal belief in internal vs. external control.

2497. Tomeh AK: Birth order and kinship affiliation. J Marriage Fam 31:19–26.

First-born women in the Mideast tend to exceed last borns in kinship participation and may therefore be conservers of traditional culture.

2498. Tsushima WT: Responses of Irish and Italians of two social classes on the Marlowe-Crowne social desirability scales. J Soc Psychol 77:215–219.

Irish and Italian-Americans from lower and lower-middle classes have similar responses on the social desirability scale. A caution must be noted that the scale may simply contain only those values that are shared by the nature of its construction.

2499. Turner C, Davenport R, Rogers C: The effect of early deprivation on the social behavior of adolescent chimpanzees. Am J Psychiatry 125:1531–1536.

Adolescent chimpanzees reared during early life in environments with social and perceptual restrictions behave differently than chimpanzees reared by their mothers in a natural habitat. Their atypical social behavior is very resistant to "therapeutic" modification efforts.

2500. Walkey FH, Boshier R: Changes in semantic differential responses over two years. Psychol Rep 24:1008–1010.

The evaluation scale elicits responses that vary most over a two-year period, while the potency scale elicits responses that vary least.

2501. Walsh D: Social class and mental illness in Dublin. Br J Psychiatry 115:1151–1161.

The relatively unfavorable socioeconomic and medical background of Local Authority hospitals in Dublin has social, medical, and administrative implications.

2502. Weinstein EA, Eck RA, Lyerly OG: Conversion hysteria in Appalachia. Psychiatry 32:334–341.

Violence is an important source of identity and a significant component of social relationships in the Appalachian subculture. There is a high incidence of conversion hysteria in societies in which physical violence is a major channel of communication.

2503. Wittkower ED: Perspectives of transcultural psychiatry. Int J Psychiatry 8:811–824.

Psychiatry, anthropology, and epidemiology must work together to resolve methodological difficulties, identify cultural factors of mental illness, and recognize the beliefs, attitudes, and therapeutic procedures concerning mental illness in other cultures.

2504. Wober M: The meaning and stability of Raven's Matrices test among Africans. Int J Psychol 4:229–235.

When administered to Nigerians, there was greater correlation between scores on the Embedded Figures Test and Matrices retest than on the initial test. The testing situation, communication method, and means of information manipulation are important considerations.

2505. Wolff HH: The role of aggression in the psychopathology of illness. J Psychosom Res 13:315–320.

The positive and constructive aspects of the aggressive drive contribute to the maintenance of health. Mutuality in interaction is essential if the aggressive drive is not to lead to dissatisfaction and illness in one or more persons in a family or group.

2506. Wymae LC: Methodologic prerequisites for cross-cultural conclusions. Int J Psychiatry 8:831–833.

Greater methodologic rigor is required in cross-cultural research, particularly with respect to specifying anthropological research as opposed to anecdotal impressions, diagnostic labels, and study of cultural subgroups.

2507. Wysocki BA, Wysocki AC: Cultural differences as reflected in Wechsler-Bellevue Intelligence Test. Psychol Rep 25:95–101.

In comparison with whites, Negro veterans score higher on the verbal than the performance parts of the scale. Comparisons of racial groups based solely on intelligence-test scores should be treated with caution.

2508. Yamamoto J, Okonogi K, Kwasaki T, Yoshimura S: Mourning in Japan. Am J Psychiatry 125:1660–1665.

The work of mourning in Japan is facilitated by the custom of ancestor worship. Widows who adhere to the cultural custom of ancestor worship are less depressed and anxious than widows who do not.

2509. Yap PM: A search for order in diversity. Int J Psychiatry 8:834–839.

The theory-oriented comparative aspect of transcultural psychiatry and the pragmatic aspect of application must be defined in order to delimit the field and conserve resources and foci.

2510. Zern D: The relevance of family cohesiveness as a determinant of premarital sexual behavior in a cross-cultural sample. J Soc Psychol 78:3–9.

A lineal orientation of values and attitudes is related to the negative value ascribed to premarital pregnancy and premarital intercourse in society.

2511. Zung W: A cross-cultural survey of symptoms in depression. Am J Psychiatry 126:116–121.

The Zung Self-Rating Depression Scale yields comparable results when translated and given to patients in Japan, Australia, Czechoslovakia, England, Germany, and Switzerland.

1970

2512. Adams BN: Isolation, function, and beyond: American kinship in the 1960's. J Marriage Fam 32:575–597.

A review of findings, debates, and questions on American kinship in the 1960s shows that the task of specifying, interpreting, and comparing U.S. kinship must continue into the 1970s.

2513. Adams HL, Mason EP, Blood DF: Personality characteristics of American and English bright and average college freshmen. Psychol Rep 26:831–834.

Published norms for personality tests appear to be outmoded, probably because of changes in student personality characteristics in the past decade. "Abnormal" test scores of the bright may simply indicate that they are more creative.

2514. Adevai G, Silverman AJ, McGough WE: Ethnic differences in perceptual testing. Int J Soc Psychiatry 16:237–239.

An emphasis upon the abstract, the educational, and the cultural, perhaps accompanied by an underemphasis on the first-hand data of the senses, may explain the preponderance of field-dependency in male Jewish students.

2515. Adler LL: The "Fruit Tree Experiment" as a measure of retarded children's preferences of fruit trees under varied conditions of color availability. J Psychol 76:217–222.

When no color, or only red, is available to retarded children, apple trees are the most frequent tree drawn. When only orange is available, orange trees are mostly drawn. Retarded and normal children tend most often to draw apple, orange, and cherry trees in that order.

2516. Al-Issa I, Al-Issa B: Psychiatric problems in a developing country: Iraq. Int J Soc Psychiatry 16:15–22.

Despite ethnic and religious diversity of the population in Iraq, there is a general pattern of common habits and beliefs. The advent of Westernization has brought about many psychological problems relevant to conflicts between the old and the new systems. The functions of the extended family have been partly taken over by the government.

2517. Anant SS: Self- and mutual perception of salient personality traits of different caste groups. J Cross-Cultural Psychol 1:41–52.

Urban East Indian subjects answering a stereotype checklist on traditional caste groups indicate acceptance of some stereotypes similar to others' perception of the group.

2518. Anant SS: Caste prejudice and its perception by Harijans. J Soc Psychol 82:165–172.

Caste Hindus report liberal interactions with Harijans but maintain traditional attitudes in areas of intimate interactions such as food acceptance. Harijan perception of caste attitude and interaction is similar to those held by caste Hindus.

2519. Anderson R: The history of witchcraft: a review with some psychiatric comments. Am J Psychiatry 126:1727–1735.

The main theme of witchcraft was perverse sexuality treated by sadistic aggression. The witch-hunt was a self-propagating delusion that supplied its own evidence. The narrowness of our cultural adaptability is demonstrated by the defensive response of a whole civilization to a change in life patterns.

2520. Ando H, Hawegawa E: Drinking patterns and attitudes of alcoholics and non-alcoholics in Japan. Q J Stud Alcohol 31:153–161.

In Japan drinking acts as an important medium for social interaction, and alcohol is an essential for ceremonial occasions. Egocentric and dependent attitudes and short-circuit behavior concerning drinking are characteristic traits of many Japanese alcoholics.

2521. Axelson LJ: The working wife: differences in perception among Negro and white males. J Marriage Fam 32:457–464.

Negro and white males have marked differences in their perception of the working wife and her relationship to her husband and her husband's career. The Negro male is generally more indecisive in his evaluation of the working wife.

2522. Barron F, Young HB: Personal values and political affiliation within Italy. J Cross-Cultural Psychol 1:355–368.

The influence of Roman Catholicism in custom and morality is a source of divisiveness in political realms. The Left splits on matters of divorce and sexual freedom, the Center is less dogmatic but still conservative, while the Right emphasizes formalism and central authority.

2523. Barron F, Young HB: Rome and Boston: a tale of two cities and their differing impact on the creativity and personal philosophy of Southern Italian immigrants. J Cross-Cultural Psychol 1:91–114.

Young men in a sample group from Boston have more religious orthodoxy and conventional social values than a Rome sample that exibits religious skepticism, social relativism and liberalism, and greater creativity in terms of fluency, originality, and flexibility.

2524. Bates BC, Sundberg ND, Tyler LE: Divergent problem solving: a comparison of adolescents in India and America. Int J Psychol 5:231–244.

Indian rural youths are less successful on divergent tasks than their American counterparts, with Indian girls more productive than Indian boys. Urban youths from Delhi are almost as divergent as American subjects, suggesting an urbanization explanation.

2525. Bateson G: A systems approach. Int J Psychiatry 9:242–244.

Viewing the family as a system can ultimately apply to the individual patient.

2526. Bazzoui W: Affective disorders in Iraq. Br J Psychiatry 117:195–203.

Iraqi patients who suffer depression do not feel or show the sadness of Western depressed patient, and in mania they lack the infective joyous mood. These differences can be explained culturally.

2527. Berrien FK: A super-ego for cross-cultural research. Int J Psychol 5:33–39.

Ideal cross-cultural research is international, addresses common concerns, employs comparable methods, and pools data for appropriate interpretations.

2528. Berry JW: Marginality, stress and ethnic identification in an acculturated aboriginal community. J Cross-Cultural Psychol 1:239–252.

Investigation of an acculturated aboriginal Australian community partly supports marginality theory. The more traditionally oriented display the most psychological marginality and reaffirm rather than retain traditional values as a response to the dominant white society.

2529. Bhagat M, Graser WI: Young offenders' images of self and surroundings: a semantic inquiry. Br J Psychiatry 117:381–387.

Young Glasgow offenders from traditional slum areas have an identical perception of concepts relevant to deliquency as offenders reared in new housing estates. Nonoffenders show less negative attitudes to all concepts and significantly so to self, love-affection, and environs.

2530. Bianchi GN, Cawte JE, Kiloh LG: Cultural identity and the mental health of Australian aborigines. Soc Sci Med 3:371–387.

Neither acquisition nor emulation of Western patterns by Australian aborigines is related to the incidence of psychiatric symptomatology. The retention of traditional beliefs is, however, associated with high symptom scores. The relationship between retention of traditional beliefs and psychological disability merits further examination in other populations.

2531. Bianchi GN, McElwain EW, Cawte JE: The dispensary syndrome in Australian aborigines: origins of their bodily preoccupation and sick role behaviour. Br J Med Psychol 43:375–382.

The dispensary syndrome is a neurotic phenomenon with pursuit of the nursing sisters for medicines and consolation as its way of becoming manifest to European observers. Somatization and attention seeking indicate how burdened Yolngu aborigines feel by life.

2532. Binitie AO: Attitude of educated Nigerians to psychiatric illness. Acta Psychiatr Scand 46:391–398.

In general, educated Nigerians view the mentally ill with disfavor and are unwilling to interact with them in close social situations, especially in marriage and employment.

2533. Blane HT, Yamamoto K: Sexual role identity among Japanese and Japanese-American high school students. J Cross-Cultural Psychol 1:345–354.

Higher femininity of Japanese males is a reflection of East vs. West masculinity models. Lower femininity of Japanese women may be due to changing conceptions of femininity in the East, while higher femininity of Hawaiian Japanese-American women may be a subcultural expression.

2534. Blizard PJ: The social rejection of the alcoholic and the mentally ill in New Zealand. Soc Sci Med 4:513–526.

The alcoholic and the mentally ill are rejected because their behavior deviates from institutionally expected ways of behaving within a specified culture. Attitudes are shaped not by the actual (or reputed) psychiatric severity of the behavior but by the visibility and social repercussions of the pathology.

2535. Boag TJ: Mental health of native peoples of the Arctic. Can Psychiatr Assoc J 15:115–120.

Traditional patterns of psychopathology in the peoples native to the Arctic are rapidly being obscured by culture change. Many of the more articulate spokesmen of the native peoples are expressing their resistance to the wholesale adoption of Western value systems, and they voice the need to devise compromises that might allow them to cope successfully with a modern industrial society without abandoning their traditional cultural roots.

2536. Bock EW, Iutaka S: Social status, mobility, and premarital pregnancy: a case of Brazil. J Marriage Fam 32:284–292.

Significant variables for premarital pregnancy among women in Rio de Janeiro are educational attainment, social status, and social mobility. Premarital conception may result in downward social mobility for women seeking mates.

2537. Born DO: Psychological adaptation and development under acculturative stress: toward a general model. Soc Sci Med 3:529-547.

Primary stress is derived from relative deprivation and withdrawal of status respect. Adaptation to socially induced stress approximates four modes: retreatism, reconciliation, innovation, and withdrawal. Innovation and withdrawal are improbable in the tradition-oriented society. Both retreatism and reconciliation can lead to successful psychocultural adaptation.

2538. Borude RR: Cross-cultural study of the communality of certain word responses. Int J Psychol 5:255–260.

Word response communality is not appreciably affected by geographic, cultural or linguistic distinctions, or isolation. There is 60 percent agreement between Indian student choices of the 1970s and American choices from the 1940s.

2539. Botha E: The effect of languages on values expressed by bilinguals. J Soc Psychol 80:143–146.

Fewer significant differences in expressed value systems are present when there is no marked difference in the value or status of the bilingual's languages.

2540. Brar HS: Rorschach content responses of East Indian psychiatric patients. J Proj Tech Pers Assessment 34:88–94.

The tendency of different categories of patients to select content of a specific nature demonstrates the significance of content analysis to diagnosis and study of personality disorders.

2541. Brehmer B, Hammond KR, Azuma H, Kostron L, Varonos DD: A cross-national comparison of cognitive conflict. J Cross-Cultural Psychol 1: 5–20.

Interpersonal conflict experiments in Czechoslovakia, Greece, Japan, Sweden, and the United States demonstrate a slow rate of conflict reduction with no significant cross-national differences.

2542. Brislin RW: Back-translation for cross-cultural research. J Cross-Cultural Psychol 1:185–216.

Investigation of factors of translation quality conducted with bilinguals representing ten languages demonstrates that translation quality can be predicted and functional equivalence evaluated among translations.

2543. Brodsky CM: The culture of the small psychiatric unit in a general hospital. Am J Psychother 24:246–257.

The small psychiatric unit presents evidence of "role drift" and improvised value systems and resembles in many ways certain types of "transient cultures" that assume responsibility for the custody and rapid processing of people.

2544. Brodsky CM: Macrocosm and microcosm: the interface of anthropology and clinical psychiatry. Compr Psychiatry 11:482–491.

In our fascination with individual differences that can seem monumental when people are studied intensively as discrete, socially dissociated units, we often fail to see the common humanity, the common culture, that has bred and sustains us all.

2545. Brody EB: Recording cross-culturally useful psychiatric interview data: experience from Brazil. Am J Psychiatry 123:446–456.

Interview data on the behavior of lower-class psychiatric patients in Rio de Janeiro may be recorded by the use of the Initial Interview Inventory: Cross-Cultural Instrument, an instrument designed with the aim of providing information that can be compared with some degree of validity to similar studies in Baltimore, Maryland.

2546. Brooksband BWL, MacSweeney DA, Johnson AL, Cunningham AE, Wilson DA, Coppen A: Androgen excretion and physique in schizophrenia. Br J Psychiatry 117:413–420.

There is no significant difference between male schizophrenic patients and normal men in the androgyny score. There is a significant positive correlation coefficient between urinary testosterone and urinary androstenol excretion rates in schizophrenics and combined schizophrenic control groups.

2547. Burch TK, Gendall M: Extended family structure and fertility: some conceptual and methodological issues. J Marriage Fam 32:227–236.

Fertility studies must distinguish between individual and aggregate analysis levels, coresidence and kin interaction, define types of family structure that are congruent with time reference of fertility, and account for age at marriage, celibacy, and opposing causal forces.

2548. Burton-Bradley BG: Transcultural psychiatry in Papua and New Guinea. J Cross-Cultural Psychol 1:177–183.

Some of the cultural factors that must be considered in cross-cultural studies are the definition of mental disorder, communication, recognition of customary behavior, knowledge of social relationships, supernatural beliefs, acculturative impacts, and the role of native specialists.

2549. Cameron P, Robertson D: A comparison of the cultural values of Scot and U.S. children. Int J Psychol 5:135–139.

Similarities in values are greater than dissimilarities, but the Scottish children tend to value career, happiness, health, and biological satisfactions more than American children.

2550. Chan LMV: Foot binding in Chinese women and its psychosocial implications. Can Psychiatr Assoc J 15:229–231.

Foot binding disappeared when Chinese women threw off their social bondage and found other outlets for vanity. This ancient custom may be likened to modern foot and shoe fetishism.

2551. Chen PCY: Classification and concepts of causation of mental illness in a rural Malay community. Int J Soc Psychiatry 16:205–215.

Indigenous Malay psychotherapy is a logical consequence of indigenous concepts about the causation of mental illness. Exorcism, carried out in illnesses perceived to be due to spirit possession and witchcraft, is an elaborate ritual during which the *bomoh* mobilizes the elements of shared traditions and incorporates such elements as group participation and support of the emotionally disturbed individual.

2552. Cheng JCC: Psychiatry in traditional Chinese medicine. Can Psychiatr Assoc J 15:399–401.

Naturalistic and animistic thought merges and interacts in Chinese medicine. Disease may be explained in terms of Tao, Yin-Yang, and disequilibrium of five elements. Mental illness is also conceptualized within these general schemes.

2553. Cheyne WM: Stereotyped reactions to speakers with Scottish and English regional accents. Br J Soc Clin Psychol 9:77–79.

It is difficult to separate the effects of perceived nationality from perceived social class on stereotyped reactions, although differing reactions to different speakers, and to same speaker pairs with different regional accents, are evident.

2554. Christensen HT, Gregg CF: Changing sex norms in America and Scandinavia. J Marriage Fam 32:616–627.

Attitudes concerning premarital coitus have become considerably liberalized, but changes in premarital coital behavior have been less dramatic, resulting in a decline in value-behavior discrepancy.

2555. Christiansen T, Livermore G: A comparison of Anglo-American and Spanish-American children on the WISC. J Soc Psychol 81:9–14.

Ethnic origin and social class are related to general intelligence and verbal abilities, whereas only social-class membership is related to nonverbal abilities, perceptual organization, and concentration.

2556. Clement DE, Sistrunk F, Guenther ZC: Pattern perception among Brazilians as a function of pattern uncertainty and age. J Cross-Cultural Psychol 1:305–313.

For Brazilian students, as for U.S. students, pattern preference and goodness are the function of pattern uncertainty. The encoding process is the same for both with slower development in Brazil than in the United States.

2557. Cosneck BJ: Family patterns of older widowed Jewish people. Fam Coordinator 19:368–373.

Independence from children, reluctance to remarry, satisfaction with the marriage spouse and with continued sensitivity to the loss of spouse characterize Jewish widows and widowers.

2558. Crisp AH, Priest RG: Nature of complaint in relation to social class. Psychother Psychosom 18:216–225.

There is no straightforward linear or monotonic relationship between the variables of social class and somatic complaints: on the contrary, the direction and magnitude of the correlation change continuously with age.

2559. Cundick BP: Measures of intelligence on Southwest Indian students. J Soc Psychol 81:151–156.

Although nearly normal IQs are indicated after one year of schooling, lack of increase in verbal IQ after the second grade may be due to increased instructional speed, language, or negative predictions and expectancy for the child.

2560. Cunningham CE: Thai "injection doctors" antibiotic mediators. Soc Sci Med 4:1–24.

Unlicensed rural Thai "injection doctors" do a broad range of treatment but do not practice a unique form of therapy. Their technology does not parallel "ancient" protective tattooing by a needle, though folk interpretations of the effect of injection medicine may parallel "ancient" approaches to an illness by drawing lines along the body or striking with a knife.

2561. Davis CM: Education and susceptibility to the Muller-Lyer Illusion among the Banyankole. J Soc Psychol 82:25–34.

The complex relationship between education and illusion susceptibility is indicative of the need for more precise indexes and examination of the role of literacy, carpenteredness, and sophistication.

2562. Davis CM, Carlson JA: A cross-cultural study of the Muller-Lyer Illusion as a function of attentional factors. J Pers Soc Psychol 16:403–410.

An attentional interpretation of cross-cultural differences is partially supported by the results of adult males in Uganda and the United States in taking an illusion test with differing instructions.

2563. Davis RWL: Comment on H. S. Brar, "Rorschach content responses of East Indian psychiatric patients." J Proj Tech Pers Assessment 34:95–97.

Despite some methodological difficulties, Brar's findings should be seriously considered. Meaning of content responses and scoring procedures must be examined in future studies.

2564. de Lacey PR: A cross-cultural study of classificatory ability in Australia. J Cross-Cultural Psychol 1:293–304.

Environmental differences account for the differences in performance on classificatory tests of high and low socioeconomic European children and high- and low-contact aboriginal children. A subsample of high-contact aboriginal children performed as well as European children of similar environments.

2565. Deregowski JB: Effect of cultural value of time upon recall. Br J Soc Clin Psychol 9:37–41.

Rural African women have inferior recall of numbers relating to temporal phenomena when compared to urban African schoolboys.

2566. Deregowski JB, Byth W: Hudson's pictures in Pandora's box. J Cross-Cultural Psychol 1:315–323.

Difficulties of pictorial perception in a Zambian sample may be due to interpretative and perceptual difficulties. Europeans respond with depth perception to Pandora's Box procedure when it contains overlap and familiar size cues.

2567. Distler L: The adolescent "hippie" and the emergence of a matristic culture. Psychiatry 33:362–371.

The hippie movement provided the vanguard for a trend away from patristic-instrumental culture and toward a more matristic-expressive culture.

2568. Doob LW: Correlates of eidetic imagery in Africa. J Psychol 76:223–230.

Eidetic imagery is reported for half the sample of Hutu in Rwanda. A hypothesis regarding a kwashiorkor-eidetic imagery relationship could not be adequately tested. Tanzanian and Kamba (Kenya) students express the reality EI has for them, with a significant relation between interview responses of the latter group and subsequent EI tests. Except for a negative association with age and acculturation, consistent EI-demographic interactions could not be ascertained.

2569. Draguns JG, Phillips L, Broverman IK, Caudill WA: Social competence and psychiatric symptomatology in Japan: a cross-cultural extension of earlier American findings. J Psychol 75:68–73.

Symptomatology and social competence appear to be associated in a similar manner in Japan and the United States. Cultural differences across sex lines and in the clustering of symptoms are important.

2570. Dube KC: A study of prevalence and biosocial variable in mental illness in a rural and an urban community in Uttar Pradesh—India. Acta Psychiatr Scand 46:327–359.

Illiteracy and lower education, nonearning status, joint family structure, addiction to habitual use of intoxicants, neurotic traits, special strains, severe anxiety, and certain caste groups are associated with higher prevalence of mental disease. Mental disease is found more in the urban area as compared to the rural. Punjabi refugees have difficult experiences during the period of migration and have more mental illness than both Sindhi refugees and normals.

2571. duPreez P, War DG: Personal constructs of modern and traditional Xhosa. J Soc Psychol 82: 149–160.

Modern Xhosa show more homogeneity and permeability of self-constructs and greater consistency between ideal and self. Disintegration may be indicated by the greater diversity of constructs in the traditional group.

2572. Dyer ED: Upward social mobility and nuclear family integration as perceived by the wife in Swedish urban families. J Marriage Fam 32:341–350.

Nuclear family integration is negatively associated with differential husband-wife mobility orientations, differential role models for spouses, and differential generational husband-wife mobility.

2573. Eaton RL: An historical look at ethology. J Hist Behav Sciences 6:176–187.

Biological theory in the hands of ethologists has led to a rapid growth of evidence on the importance of heredity in behavior.

2574. Edgerton RB, Karno M, Fernandez I: Curanderismo in the metropolis: the diminished role of folk psychiatry among Los Angeles Mexican-Americans. Am J Psychother 24:124–134.

While curanderismo is present in the East Los Angeles community, its importance has diminished greatly. There is no evidence to suggest that the reported underrepresentation of Mexican-Americans in psychiatric treatment facilities is due to the wide-spread practice of folk psychiatry.

2575. Edwards J: The Koro pattern of depersonalization in an American schizophrenic patient. Am J Psychiatry 126:1171–1173.

The Koro syndrome has two components: experience of shrinkage of the penis, and the cultural interpretation of this experience. The folk illness Koro is endemic in certain Eastern countries, while the Koro pattern of depersonalization is probably universal in its distribution and more common than generally supposed.

2576. Eisenman R, Foulks EF: Usefulness of Mussens' TAT scoring system: I. differences among Guatemalan Indians, Ladinos, and Menjala on a modified TAT; II. attitudes towards the physically disabled. Psychol Rep 27:179–185.

Use of culturally modified TAT confirms the hypothesis that Ladinos have higher need achievement and need autonomy, while Indians have higher need affiliation. Press lack and press physical danger are frequent themes in all three groups.

2577. Engebretson D, Fullmer D: Cross-cultural differences in territoriality: interaction distances of native Japanese, Hawaii Japanese, and American Caucasians. J Cross-Cultural Psychol 1:261–269.

Personal relationship and culture significantly determine dyadic distance, while sex and conversational content do not. Native Japanese have greater distance than Hawaii Japanese or American Caucasians; but no differences are found between Hawaii Japanese and American Caucasians.

2578. England GW, Koike R: Personal value systems of Japanese managers. J Cross-Cultural Psychol 1:21–40.

Value orientations are primarily pragmatic and secondly moral and ethical. There is a feedback between personal values and related organizational behavior.

2579. Fabrega H, Metzger D, Williams G: Psychiatric implications of health and illness in a Maya Indian group: a preliminary statement. Soc Sci Med 3:609–626.

Among the Maya Indians of Tenejapa, Mexico, a person can have a "strong" illness, or a "weak" one. The existence of disease is linked directly to the belief that man is imperfect, corruptible, and has a propensity to misbehave and do harm. Individuals with long-standing unusual behavioral manifestations are not usually regarded as suffering from an illness, but are simple viewed as strange or different.

2580. Fabrega H, Silver D: Some social and psychological properties of Zinacanteco shamans. Behav Sci 15:471–486.

Zinacanteco shamans and nonshamans are similar when compared using projective tests and social parameters.

2581. Ferguson F: A treatment program for Navaho alcoholics: results after four years. Q J Stud Alcohol 31:898–919.

Navahos arrested for drunkenness respond well to a treatment program that includes probation, disulfiram, detoxification, and continued follow-up.

Characteristics associated with successful treatment include high arrest rate, older age, less education, and less facility with English.

2582. Foley Meeker B: An experimental study of cooperation and competition in West Africa. Int J Psychol 5:11–19.

Tribal Africans of varying degrees of Westernization show differential cooperation on Prisoner's Dilemma game but not a Maximizing Difference game.

Both traditional and Westernized Africans show greater partner similarity on the latter game. Results suggest the influence of situational structure on interaction and the importance of individualism vs. conformity.

2583. Frager R: Conformity and anti-conformity in Japan. J Pers Soc Psychol 15:203–210.

Traditionalism is most related to conformity, and anticonformity is most related to alienation.

2584. Frankel SA, Frankel EB: Nonverbal behavior in a selected group of Negro and white males. Psychosomatics 11:127–132.

Negro patients are more inhibited than white patients in autistic and communicative nonverbal behavior. This may reflect general differences in behavior of the two races or might result from the situation of Negroes interacting with white professionals in an institution of white society.

2585. Gardiner HW, Lematawekul D: Second-generation Chinese in Thailand: a study of ethnic identification. J Cross-Cultural Psychol 1:333–344.

Study of adolescent ethnic identification demonstrates a higher degree of identification for those who use Chinese rather than Thai family names and those who attend Chinese schools.

2586. Gardner RA: A four-day diagnostic-therapeutic home visit in Turkey. Fam Process 9: 300–317.

An intimate diagnostic experience brings home the necessity for the therapist to understand the sociocultural milieu of the patient and his family.

2587. Giel R, Van Luijk JN: Psychiatric morbidity in a rural village in South-Western Ethiopia. Int J Soc Psychiatry 16:63–71.

Psychiatric illness, mainly psychoneurosis and personality disorder, is no less common among the Kafa than the townspeople, although the differences between life in the village and in the towns are considerable.

2588. Giel R, Van Luijk JN: Psychiatric morbidity in 50 juvenile delinquents in Addis Ababa. Soc Psychiatry 5:183–186.

In Addis Ababa, there is no correlation between broken homes and mental illness in children. In Ethiopia, the broken home is so common that it appears to establish a pattern of life.

2589. Ginsburg GP, McGinn NF, Harburg E: Recalled parent-child interaction of Mexican and United States males. J Cross-Cultural Psychol 1: 139–152.

A Parent Image Differential yields several dimensions of child-perceived parent-child interaction, some of which appear across parents and cultures (potency and ambivalence) and some of which indicate parental sex-role and cultural differences (justice and support). Almost all differences are specific to context of interaction.

2590. Greene JM: The semantic function of negatives and passives. Br J Psychol 61:17–22.

Natural semantic functions, rather than unnatural functions, facilitate decisions of meaning of syntactic constructions.

2591. Gregson ED, Gregson RAM: A note on a seventeenth-century distinction between feral man and man-like apes. J Hist Behav Sciences 6:159–161.

A. Kircher's 1667 text distinguishes between ape-like animals and wild men in a manner consistent with modern views. Linnaeus's classification was a retrograde step.

2592. Groen JJ: Influence of social and cultural patterns on psychosomatic diseases. Psychother Psychosom 18:189–215.

Every society or culture tends to preserve its homeostasis by feed-back mechanisms that consist in the psychosocial interactions of the members of its cultural and social subgroups. Support for the thesis that psychosomatic disorders are culture induced is derived from clinical transcultural experience and from observations during World War II in Holland and in the concentration camps.

2593. Gurland BJ, Fleiss JL, Cooper JE, Sharpe L, Kendell RE, Roberts P: Cross-national study of diagnosis of mental disorders: hospital diagnoses and hospital patients in New York and London. Compr Psychiatry 11:18–25.

Hospital staffs in New York tend to diagnose all kinds of patients (excluding alcoholics, drug addicts, and patients with organic disorders) as schizophrenic, whereas in London some kinds of patients are diagnosed mainly as schizophrenic and others mainly as affective disorder.

2594. Harmon DK, Masuda M, Holmes TH: The Social Readjustment Rating Scale: a cross-cultural study of Western Europeans and Americans. J Psychosom Res 14:391–400.

There is a high concordance among French, Belgian, and Swiss samples on the SRR as well as between the combined European and corresponding American sample. That the relative order of importance assigned to life events by Americans and Europeans is highly concordant is understandable in the light of the cultural contributions of Western Europe to America.

2595. Harwood BT: Substantive significance of the linguistic relativity hypothesis when using translations of written personality measures. J Soc Psychol 81:3–8.

Principle components analysis of a Samoan interest inventory results indicate a strong component for each sex and a weak component for language. This suggests that the linguistic relativity principle is not reason enough to change the language form of the research instrument.

2596. Hayashi T, Lynn R, Rim Y: A test of McClelland's theory of achievement motivation in Britain, Japan, Ireland and Israel. Int J Psychol 5:275–277.

In countries with high economic growth (Japan and Israel) university students show greater commitment to career success than those in countries with low growth (Britain, Ireland).

2597. Hellon CP: Mental illness and acculturation in the Canadian aboriginal. Can Psychiatr Assoc J 15:135–139.

The presence of folklore within delusional systems of the Indian, Metis, and Eskimo population of Alberta and the Western Arctic does not protect significantly against the expression of violence to others. Further research along epidemiological lines is essential before any rational provisions can be made to ensure the well-being of the Canadian aboriginal.

2598. Hinde RA, Spencer-Booth Y: Individual differences in the responses of Rhesus monkeys to a period of separation from their mothers. J Child Psychol Psychiatry 11:159–176.

Individual differences in the responses of rhesus infants at each stage during and after a period of maternal deprivation can be related to those at preceding stages and to the nature of the mother-infant relationship before separation.

2599. Hocking F: Extreme environmental stress and its significance for psychopathology. Am J Psychother 24:4–26.

Extreme forms of environmental stress, such as semistarvation, sensory deprivation, natural disasters, military combat, concentration camps, labor camps, and nuclear bombing, may result in permanent psychologic disability. Constitutional factors, patterns of child rearing, and preexisting personality characteristics may do no more than determine how long an individual can withstand prolonged extreme stress.

2600. Hofman JE, Debbing S: Religious affiliation and ethnic identity. Psychol Rep 26:1014.

Use of a semantic differential suggests that to be an Arab means first of all to be a Moslem.

2601. Hood RW, Ginsburg GP: Cultural availability: a cross-culturally stable determinant of performance on Remote Associates Test items. Psychol Rep 26:755–758.

Difficulty is greatest for those items with answers not readily available in the local culture as associates to the stimulus words of the item.

2602. Hughes CC, Hunter JM: Disease and "development" in Africa. Soc Sci Med 3:443–493.

Coordination of development activities within a comprehensive ecologic framework is necessary if there is to be an overall betterment of social and economic conditions of life in Africa.

2603. Hutter M: Transformation of identity, social mobility, and kinship solidarity. J Marriage Fam 32:133–137.

The hypothesis that the occupationally based pressure for transformation of identity leads to weakening of kinship solidarity is supported by an American sample but not by a Japanese sample.

2604. Irwin MH, McLaughlin DH: Ability and preference in category sorting by Mano schoolchildren and adults. J Soc Psychol 82:15–24.

Elementary students and illiterate adults show preference and ability to sort by color and number over form. Ability to shift sorting scheme and sort by form is related to schooling. Adult rice sorting exceeds student card sorting. Cultural motivations in classification are probably reflected in these sorting orientations.

2605. Irvine SH: Affect and construct—a cross-cultural check on theories of intelligence. J Soc Psychol 80:23–30.

Various theories of intelligence must be considered incomplete unless the role of affect and values in the formation of human abilities in different societies are incorporated, as shown in a study of the Mashona of Central Africa.

2606. Jahoda G: Supernatural beliefs and changing cognitive structures among Ghanian university students. J Cross-Cultural Psychol 1:115–130.

Higher scores on external control are related to higher scores on an index of supernatural belief. Older students display an inverse relationship between modernity and supernatural beliefs, while the younger sample illustrates movement toward coexistence of African and Western beliefs.

2607. Jaques ME, Linkowski DC, Sieka FL: Cultural attitudes toward disability: Denmark, Greece, and the United States. Int J Soc Psychiatry 16:54–62.

Greeks report more contacts with disabled persons than Americans or Danes. Americans report closer relationships with the disabled than do the other two groups. Each of the three cultures shows a unique pattern of relationship between the sex of the subjects and reactions to the Attitudes Towards Disabled Persons scale. In the United States there is no observable difference between males and females; in Denmark males are more positive than females; and in Greece females are more positive than males.

2608. Kagitcibasi C: Social norms and authoritarianism: a Turkish-American comparison. J Pers Soc Psychol 16:444–451.

Americans have higher correlations between authoritarian attitudes and the authoritarian syndrome than Turks. The difference between the two groups in core authoritarianism is less than the difference in respect for authority and patriotism.

2609. Kanter I: Extermination camp syndrome: the delayed type of double-bind (a transcultural study). Int J Soc Psychiatry 16:275–282.

The double-bind theory of Bateson may apply not only to the schizophrenic processes but to a number of other psychiatric disturbances including the extermination camp syndrome. The stronger the ethnic identification of the victim, the less he was prone to be caught by the double-bind situations created by the Nazis with the intent to destroy his spirit.

2610. Kearney M: Drunkness and religious conversion in a Mexican village. Q J Stud Alcohol 31:132–152.

Drunkenness is endemic in the Zapotec-Mestizo town of Ixtepeji, Oxacaca. Conversion to a religious sect that requires abstinence is of important therapeutic value.

2611. Kelly R, Cazabon R, Fisher C, Laroque R: Ethnic origin and psychiatric disorders in a hospitalized population. Can Psychiatr Assoc J 15:177–182.

There are differences among the hospitalized Canadian population in the distribution of patients among the major diagnostic classifications as a function of ethnic background. The Canadian population may offer considerable potential for research into the relationship between cultural factors and mental illness.

2612. Kikuchi A, Gordon LV: Japanese and American personal values: some cross-cultural findings. Int J Psychol 5:183–187.

Japanese students are higher in orderliness and goal orientation than their American counterparts and tend to consider goals in social group terms. Results are generally consistent with anthropological observations.

2613. Kitano HHL: Mental illness in four cultures. J Soc Psychol 80:121–134.

Although there are some subcultural differences, the reactions and resources of Japanese schizophrenics from Okinawa, Los Angeles, Hawaii, or Japan are quite similar, perhaps due to the nature of the illness. Acculturation may be less significant in the treatment of the severely mentally ill.

2614. Kraus RF: Implications of recent developments in primate research for psychiatry. Compr Psychiatry 11:328–335.

Primatological data on dominance behavior for confined primates may be extended to the study of dominance hierarchy among boys in psychiatric hospitals.

2615. Krauss HH: Social development and suicide. J Cross-Cultural Psychol 1:159–167.

A cross-cultural sample of 58 societies demonstrates a significant relationship between social complexity and frequency of suicide. Suicide is possibly produced through some manner of interaction between thwarting disorientation and degree of social integration.

2616. Kubany ES, Gallimore R, Buell J: The effects of extrinsic factors on achievement-oriented behavior: a non-Western case. J Cross-Cultural Psychol 1:77–84.

Hawaiian-Filipino male high school students demonstrate more achievement-oriented behavior in performing a public rather than a private task, pointing out the importance of distinguishing between intrinsic and extrinsic motives and the effects of situational variables.

2617. Kumasaka Y, Saito H: Kachigumi: a collective delusion among the Japanese and their descendants in Brazil. Can Psychiatr Assoc J 15:167 175.

At the end of the World War II some of the Japanese people living in Brazil maintained that Japan had won the war. This group called the Kachigumi suffered from a collective delusion that is understandable in light of the sociocultural background of the Japanese community in Brazil.

2618. Kundu CL: Comparison of intelligence test scores of Bhil and high caste Hindu delinquents. J Soc Psychol 81:265–266.

Bhil and Hindu nondelinquents have higher mean intelligence quotients than delinquents.

2619. Kuttner RE: Comparative performance of disadvantaged ethnic and racial groups. Psychol Rep 27:372.

Evidence of genetic components in group performance can be obtained without the necessity of equating all human and suspected environmental factors.

2620. Larkin F, Owen C, Rhodes K: The differentiation of households in a Ghanian community. J Marriage Fam 32:304–314.

The concept of structural differentiation requires modification in terms of individual attributes, communication stability, and ease in order to be more meaningfully applied to the Ghanaian data.

2621. Lauterbach A: Psychocultural roots of America's self-image. Am J Psychother 24:627–642.

The mental wall of Americans toward understanding others comes from childhood training in wishful images of society, a training that has had its roots in the immigration background of the population. An image guided by a fixation of childhood fears as well as an unresolved contradiction between Christian values and acquisitive compulsions has prevented Americans from understanding other nations or being accepted by them.

2622. Lebra TS: Logic of salvation: the case of a Japanese sect in Hawaii. Int J Soc Psychiatry 16:45–53.

Mechanisms used by converts to the Dancing Religion are emotionally reassuring and logically contradictory. Sociologically, salvation logic is learned, sustained, and elaborated through the continuous transmission of information between pairs of interactors. Psychologically, receptivity to the logic may be explained by guilt and shame derived from the sense of responsibility for what has happened to the ego.

2623. LeCompte W, LeCompte G: Effects of education and intercultural contact on traditional attitudes in Turkey. J Soc Psychol 80:11–22.

Data from Istanbul support the hypothesis that less traditional attitudes are associated with more education and with foreign school attendance. However, there is some interaction between these effects and different issues pertaining to family interactions.

2624. Lee SD, Temerlin MK: Social class, diagnosis, and prognosis for psychotherapy. Psychother Res Theory Practice 7:181–185.

The capacity to function effectively in intimate social relationships is much more indicative of personal integrity than sociological effectiveness. Because of the class bias applied in the diagnosis of neurosis and psychosis, the question of covariation between the phenomena of mental illness and social class cannot be answered.

2625. Lent RH: Binocular resolution and perception of race in the United States. Br J Psychol 61:521–534.

Further research is necessary to explain the generality of the role of group membership in the resolution of binocular conflict beyond the bounds of South Africa.

2626. Lester D: Adolescent suicide and premarital sexual behavior. J Soc Psychol 82:131–132.

Analysis of many cultures provides no significant support for Kluckholn's suggestion that adolescent suicide occurs in the environment of severe punishment for premarital sexual intercourse.

2627. Lester D: Social disorganization and completed suicide. Soc Psychiatry 5:175–176.

The incidence of suicide is high in socially disorganized areas of Edinburgh. A study of Buffalo, New York, fails to replicate this finding and may indicate that the types of people who kill themselves differ in the two cities.

2628. Levin J, Karni ES: Demonstration of cross-cultural invariance of the California Psychological Inventory in America and Israel by the Guttman-Lingoes Smallest Space Analysis. J Cross-Cultural Psychol 1:253–260.

Correlation of .92 is obtained between the Smallest Space Analysis interpoint distances of the American and Israeli data, demonstrating cross-cultural invariance of the pattern of the CPI scale intercorrelations.

2629. Long BH, Ziller RC, Kanisetti RV, Reddy VE: Self-description as a function of evaluative and activity rating among American and Indian adolescent. Child Dev 41:1017–1024.

The effect of social desirability upon self-description is higher for Teluga Indians than Americans, while "activity" has a greater value for Americans. Sex differences in self-perceptions are greater among Americans.

2630. Lorenz K: The enmity between generations and its probable ethological causes. Psychoanal Rev 57:333–337.

Our culture is in immediate danger of extinction by a complete break in its tradition caused by a tribal war between two generations. This war is caused by a mass neurosis that may be cured by making its subconscious roots accessible to conscious understanding.

2631. Lowenfeld H, Lowenfeld Y: Our permissive society and the superego: some current thoughts about Freud's cultural concepts. Psychoanal Q 39:590–608.

Freud's ideas about the development of civilization and its dilemma between freedom and restriction of drives have been remarkably confirmed by the change of the cultural climate of the last 50 years.

2632. Lubchansky I, Egri G, Stokes J: Puerto Rican spiritualists view mental illness: the faith healer as a paraprofessional. Am J Psychiatry 127:312–321.

Puerto Rican spiritualists in New York City are functioning healers with a distinctive method. Some therapeutic techniques include use of short sentences, a specific vocabulary, and encouragement of hallucinatory experiences.

2633. Mai FMM, Pike A: Correlation of Rhesus (Rh) and personality factors. Br J Soc Clin Psychol 9:83–84.

No significant differences are found on various scales, indicating that previously suggested relationships between positive Rh donors, anxiety, and tender mindedness are invalid.

2634. Mapstone JR: Familistic determinants of property acquisition. J Marriage Fam 32:143–149.

Integrated family work groups and mutual aid by kinsmen contribute to land purchasing power among Macedo-Slav settlers in Australia.

2635. Martins C: Poverty and mental health. Can Psychiatr Assoc J 15:159–166.

Poverty brings with it malnutrition, illiteracy, and sickness, together with primitive processes of world interpretation, and prolongs magic-religious rituals. Conflicts between cultural patterns, enhanced by the exaggerated socioeconomic disparity, aggravate the communication difficulties between the group in need of help and the technicians.

2636. Masuda M, Matsumoto GH, Meredith GM: Ethnic identity in three generations of Japanese Americans. J Soc Psychol 81:199–208.

Ethnicity decreases as acculturation increases. Age, education, occupational status, and religion are salient factors for ethnicity.

2637. Matsumoto GM, Meredith GA, Masuda M: Ethnic identification: Honolulu and Seattle Japanese-Americans. J Cross-Cultural Psychol 1:63–76.

Ethnic identification for three generations of Japanese-Americans in the Honolulu sample is less than the Seattle sample possibly due to historical, personality, and assimilation differences.

2638. McCulloch JW, Alistair EP: The social prognosis of persons who attempt suicide. Soc Psychiatry 5:177–182.

Demographic, social, and personality factors are important in the social prognosis of persons who attempt suicide. Many attempted suicides appear to lack a very basic social skill, the ability to relate to people in a mutually satisfactory way. Their problems seem to stem from a failure to develop aspects of personality, emotional maturity, self-control, and awareness of social mores.

2639. Meade RD: Leadership studies of Chinese and Chinese-Americans. J Cross-Cultural Psychol 1:325–332.

In group and individual ranking of critical issues, authoritarian leadership produces a greater degree of cohesiveness among Chinese subjects. A high level of group cohesion is produced among Chinese-American subjects in both democratic and authoritarian leadership situations.

2640. Meade RD, Singh L: Motivation and progress effects on psychological time in subcultures of India. J Soc Psychol 80:3–10.

Time estimates are related to progress under conditions of high motivation for some Indian subcultural communities that are thought to have high achievement motivation, but not for others.

2641. Meers DR: Contributions of a ghetto culture to symptom formation: psychoanalytic studies of ego anomalies in childhood. Psychonal Study Child 25:209–230.

Social indifference collides with professional ignorance of "cultural deviance" to obscure a broad range of psychopathology, including severe psychotic, atypical, and psychoneurotic disorders. Contemporary ghetto life compounds academic problems since daily experience is fraught with instinctual trauma, not least of these being the realities of terrifying, real danger and interminable discontinuities of residence and caretakers.

2642. Mehryar AH: Some data on the Persian translation of the EPI. Br J Soc Clin Psychol 9: 257–263.

Iranian subjects score higher than their British counterparts on neuroticism and lie scales of the Persian translation of the Eysenck Personality Inventory. The translation is considered reliable and valid.

2643. Mehryar AH: A cross-cultural investigation of Eysenck's hypothesis regarding the relationship between personality and attitudes. Br J Soc Clin Psychol 9:216–221.

Studies of British and Iranian students demonstrate no correlation between extraversion and ten-

der mindedness, but a positive relationship between the latter and religionism.

2644. Messing SD: Social problems related to the development of health in Ethiopia. Soc Sci Med 3:331–337.

Public health programs in Ethiopia cannot be expected to overcome the linked problems of economic fatalism, poverty, traditional reliance on destructive health attitudes, practices and healers, and feudalistic patterns of human behavior.

2645. Meyer AE, Otte H: The semantic differential as a measure of the patients' image of their therapist. Psychother Psychosom 18:56–60.

The semantic differential is a powerful tool to measure the doctors' image in the doctor-patient relationship. Results of anorexia patients given the semantic differential favor the hypothesis that they see the therapist as a raping male.

2646. Michel A: Wife's satisfaction with husband's understanding in Parisian urban families. J Marriage Fam 32:351–359.

Interactional aspects of communication, the power structure, family life planning, and agreement are clearly associated with wife's satisfaction with husband's understanding.

2647. Middendorp CP, Brinkman W, Koomen W: Determinants of premarital sexual permissiveness: a secondary analysis. J Marriage Fam 32:369–378.

Reiss's hypothesis of negative relationship between social class of conservatives and sexual permissiveness is challenged by data from the Netherlands. Religion, age, and residence are isolated as determinants of premarital sexual permissiveness.

2648. Miller MJ, Brehmer B, Hammond KR: Communication and conflict reduction: a cross-cultural study. Int J Psychol 5:75–87.

Full communication facilitates conflict reduction for Swedish and American undergraduate students; but no cross-cultural differences are obtained.

2649. Miller P: Social activists and social change: the Chicago demonstrators. Am J Psychiatry 126: 1752–1759.

Activists can be understood in terms of their youthlike style and culture. It is likely that social activists and social activism will continue to grow as long as youths believe that the general culture is not accommodating to them.

2650. Money J, Cawte JE, Bianchi GN, Nurcombe B: Sex training and traditions in Arnhem Land. Br J Med Psychol 43:383–399.

Yolngu society imposes limits, regulations, or taboos on sexual expression that are at least as stringent as our own, but they are different restrictions and are imposed at a different age in a child's development. Lack of abnormal sexual behavior may result from the fact that sex itself is not tabooed but rather certain selections of a partner.

2651. Murphy L, Murphy G: Perspectives in cross-national research. J Cross-Cultural Psychol 1:1–4.

Cross-national research may be understood by regarding issues, goals, and future research areas.

2652. Musaph H: The influence of social and cultural patterns on psychosomatic disorders. Psychother Psychosom 18:239–242.

Transcultural psychosomatic medicine is based on the working hypothesis that in a disorder, transpersonal processes play an important role and that each individual is a point of junction in the family network. The influence of social and cultural patterns on psychosomatic disorders can be demonstrated by studies of kibbutz children in Israel as compared with nearby children in traditional family settings.

2653. Newton N: The effect of psychological environment on childbirth: combined cross-cultural and experimental approach. J Cross-Cultural Psychol 1:85–90.

A cross-cultural survey of birth patterns suggests that the psychological environment may influence the effectiveness of labor. Mice in labor have increased fetal mortality in adverse psychological environments.

2654. Nielson J, Tsuboi T: Correlation between stature, character disorder and criminality. Br J Psychiatry 116:145–150.

Patients with tall stature (181 cm. +) have a comparatively pronounced disposition to character disorder and criminality.

2655. Noesjirwan J: Attitudes to learning of the Asian student studying in the West. J Cross-Cultural Psychol 1:393–397.

Analysis of components of a learning attitudes questionnaire given Indian students points out three factors, two of which discriminate between Asian students who are more authority dependent, have less independence of thought, and depend more on memorization than Australian students.

2656. Nordenstreng K: Changes in the meaning of semantic differential scales: measurement of subject-scale interaction effects. J Cross-Cultural Psychol 1:217–237.

Transformation analysis is an efficient way of analyzing changes in meaning in studies of the influence of subject group and language translation on qualifier meaning.

2657. Noshpitz JD: Certain cultural and familial factors contributing to adolescent alienation. J Am Acad Child Psychiatry 9:216–233.

The current generation of adolescents is alienated both by being cut off from the magical wellsprings of cultural energy and by having thrust upon them forms of magical pressure that they find distasteful. For a young person caught in the swirl of change, there is nothing as reassuring as a sense of parental strength and stability.

2658. Obeyesekere G: The idiom of demonic possession: a case study. Soc Sci Med 4:97–111.

In Ceylon, demonic possession permits regression, abreactions, and the release of primary process material. Through a mutually comprehensive religious idiom, the priest, family, and community support the patient and tolerate his "bizarre" behavior. The patient knows that whatever he does, there will be others in the environment who will care for him. This allows for "regression under the control of the environment."

2659. Olusanya PO: A note on some factors affecting the stability of marriage among the Yoruba of Western Nigeria. J Marriage Fam 32:150–155.

Marital stability in two Yoruba towns is significantly influenced by age at first marriage, type of marriage contract, educational status, and particularly by number of cowives.

2660. Oppong C: Conjugal power and resources: an urban African example. J Marriage Fam 32:676–680.

Decisionmaking modes differ significantly with respect to the variables of age, educational levels, and occupation of spouses.

2661. Orpen C: Authoritarianism in an "authoritarian" culture: the case of Afrikaans-speaking South Africa. J Soc Psychol 81:119–120.

Afrikaaners have largely internalized authoritarian norms in their basic personality structure and are receptive to prejudiced attitudes that are prevalent in South Africa.

2662. Ozturk OM: Critique of Gardner's paper. Fam Process 9:318–321.

Gardner's understanding of the cultural setting is lacking and his analysis colored by preconceived analytic formulas.

2663. Paredes A, West LJ, Snow CC: Biosocial adaptation and correlates of acculturation in the Tarahumara ecosystem. Int J Soc Psychiatry 16: 163–174.

The Tarahumara Indians of northern Mexico have utilized autochthonous techniques to adapt to the rugged mountainous terrain. Community feeling, uniformity of culture, and effective communication are achieved through the institution of the "tesguinada," a periodic celebration in which groups of men and women work and drink together, forming overlapping social networks that constitute the molecules of their social body.

2664. Pauker JD, Sines JO, Owen DR, Baker EA: A comparison of black and white children on an objective, non-verbal test of personality. J Oper Psychiatry 1:61–64.

SES and cultural factors, independent of race, may be associated with white-black differences on the Missouri Children's Picture Series (MCPS). The MCPS offers a basis for a culture-free intelligence test.

2665. Paydarfar AA, Sarram M: Differential fertility and socioeconomic status of Shirazi women: a pilot study. J Marriage Fam 32:692–699.

Findings among married Iranian women demonstrate an inverse relationship between three measures of SES (occupation, education, income) and fertility patterns. Shirazi couples of high SES prefer smaller families.

2666. Pepitone A, Maderna A, Caporicci E, Tiberi E, Iacono G, diMajo G, Perfetto M, Asprea A, Villone G, Fua G, Tonicco F: Justice in choice behavior: a cross-cultural analysis. Int J Psychol 5:1–10.

Italians tend to maximize gain when self-estimate is low and equalize payoffs. Americans maximize gains when self-estimate is high and maintain consistency in rewarded merit positions. Both groups reduce inequity when one member is arbitrarily rewarded.

2667. (Deleted)

2668. (Deleted)

2669. Pflanz M, Rohde JJ: Illness: deviant behaviour of conformity. Soc Sci Med 4:645–653.

Medical sociologists should be open to recognize aspects of conformity in illness so as to refine their conceptual and analytical tools in the course of a constant dialogue between theory and empirical observation.

2670. Pinderhughes CA: The universal resolution of ambivalence by paranoia with an example in black and white. Am J Psychother 24:597–610.

Nonpathologic paranoid patterns aggrandize one side and denigrate the other side of a conflict situation and are thus employed to resolve ambivalence and stabilize relationships between individuals and between members of groups. Interpretations and actions related to the expression or correction of nonpathologic paranoia are the source of most of the misunderstanding, conflict, neglect, repression, exploitation, and violence among people throughout the world.

2671. Pivnicki D: Aggression reconsidered. Compr Psychiatry 11:235–241.

We are not precise in our differentiation of the faculty to be aggressive and the aggressive act itself. By suppressing some aggressive acts we may harm and even destroy the energies man needs to survive.

2672. Prestude AM: Sensory capacities of the chimpanzee. Psychol Bull 74:47–67.

Although the chimpanzee has long been considered similar to man and is often employed as a human surrogate in research, investigation of the chimpanzee's sensory processes has been limited mainly to vision and audition.

2673. Rabkin L: Parties and cultural values: a kibbutz example. Psychiatry 33:482–493.

A social party is a small social world in which the core values, as well as the submerged tensions, of a culture are expressed.

2674. Read M: Medical education. Soc Sci Med 4:163–167.

The concepts and techniques inherent in medical anthropology are relevant to contemporary medical education; however, their value in different geographical and cultural areas differs widely.

2675. Reiss IL: Comments on Middendorp's "determinants of premarital sexual permissiveness." J Marriage Fam 32:379–380.

The Middendorp et al. study suffers from drawbacks due to inadequate measurement of dependent and control variables and misunderstanding of Reiss's position.

2676. Resner G, Hartog J: Concepts and terminology of mental disorder among Malays. J Cross-Cultural Psychol 1:369–381.

Concepts and terminology of urban and rural Malays parallel modern concepts of mental disorder, suggesting universal bases and clues to labeling and to treatment.

2677. Roberts KH: On looking at an elephant: an evaluation of cross-cultural research related to organizations. Psychol Bull 74:327–350.

Most studies are based on poorly conceived surveys and deal with individual behavior in organizations. Organizations are rarely viewed as parts of their environment, yet understanding organizational-environmental interactions seems a major practical reason for cross-cultural research.

2678. Rosenberg S: Hospital culture as collective defense. Psychiatry 33:21–35.

Hospital social structure is an intricately interwoven system integrated around a set of shared unconscious problems, defenses, and myths.

2679. Rosenberg SD: The disculturation hypothesis and the chronic patient syndrome. Soc Psychiatry 5:155–165.

The potential for regression under strong situational stress (facilitated by cultural inducement) is a general human characteristic that varies in degree rather than quality. While individuals who are more autonomous may vacate the patient role in fairly short order, even in the state hospital, there is obviously a group of more marginal individuals whose movement into the disculturation syndrome is largely dependent on situational factors.

2680. Ross BM, Millson C: Repeated memory of oral prose in Ghana and New York. Int J Psychol 5:173–181.

Ghanaian children perform better at remembering oral prose across one-week intervals than American children, probably because of their strong oral tradition.

2681. Roy C, Choudhuri A, Irvine D: The prevalence of mental disorders among Saskatchewan Indians. J Cross-Cultural Psychol 1:383–392.

Prevalence of mental disorder is significantly higher in Indian than non-Indian rural communities, with the Indian sample containing higher numbers of schizophrenics and mental retardates.

2682. Safilios-Rothschild C: The influence of the wife's degree of work commitment upon some aspects of family organization and dynamics. J Marriage Fam 32:681–691.

Greek women with a high work commitment are generally more satisfied with their marriages, and perceive themselves as prevailing in decisionmaking and having more freedom of behavior. Women with low work commitment must of necessity perceive an egalitarian model of family dynamics.

2683. Safilios-Rothschild C, Georgiopoulos J: A comparative study of parental and filial role definitions. J Marriage Fam 32:381–389.

The Parsonian typology of clearly defined instrumental and expressive roles is not supported by American and Greek data, which suggest that parents of both sexes define roles in terms of both types of components. Furthermore, Greek spouses hold less differentiated role definitions than their American counterparts.

2684. Sanua VD: A cross cultural study of cerebral palsy. Soc Sci Med 4:461–512.

As evidenced by the responses to psychological tests of cerebral palsy victims in eight European countries, sociocultural as well as psychological forces affect the individual's response to cerebral palsy and its resulting disability.

2685. Sarwer-Foner GJ: Human territoriality and its cathexis. Dis Nerv Syst 31:82–87.

The dimension of territoriality is observable in man as well as in lower mammalian forms. Man cathects not only literal geographic space, but also symbolized personal "space." This symbolized form of human territoriality permits speculations on some of the ways in which human instincts can cathect the biological apparatus and are, in their turn, channeled onto an object by this apparatus.

2686. Schneider JM, Parsons OA: Categories on the locus of control scale and cross-cultural comparisons in Denmark and the United States. J Cross-Cultural Psychol 1:131–138.

Findings from locus of control scale measures on Danish and U.S. students support the assumption that categories are useful for examining differences and stereotypes.

2687. Schwab J, McGinnis N, Norris L, Schwab R: Psychosomatic medicine and the comtemporary social scene. Am J Psychiatry 126:1632–1642.

Psychosomatic medicine may be examined in terms of (1) the frequency and distribution of the illness, (2) the demographic characteristics of the afflicted, (3) the changing patterns of individual and group susceptibility, and (4) the emergence of newer forms of illness and the waning of others. Because our natural environment is increasingly man-made, psychosomatic medicine, in order to be relevant, must meaningfully integrate ecologic principles with the knowledge of psychic and physical processes.

2688. Seelye HN, Brewer MB: Ethnocentrism and acculturation of North Americans in Guatemala. J Soc Psychol 80:147–156.

Actual contact with a foreign culture, rather than resistant attitudinal positions, and the individuals' increased security and reduced ingroup orientation have more influence on acculturation. Degree of cultural contact has socioeconomic determinants.

2689. Settlage CF: Adolescence and social change. J Am Acad Child Psychiatry 9:203–215.

Social change can cause a lack of consensus and conviction regarding values on the part of society. This tends to deprive parents of conviction and support in their child-rearing practices and to deprive their children of the benefit of relatively clear-cut limits and guidelines for their impulses and behavior.

2690. Sherman R: Culture and strategic choice. J Psychol 75:227–230.

The extent of preference for competitive strategies in hypothetical circumstances varies with cultures, and varies within a culture for risk attitudes. British subjects show greater preference for competitive strategic choices than Americans.

2691. Silverstone JT: Obesity and social class. Psychother Psychosom 18:226–230.

In both New York and London, increasing social class is associated with a decreasing prevalence of obesity. Most people tend to put on weight as they grow older, but those in the upper socioeconomic groups take dietary steps to remedy the situation, while those in the lower social classes do not.

2692. Singh NP: Creative abilities: a cross-cultural study. J Soc Psychol 81:125–126.

Socioeconomic advantage may play a more significant role in creative abilities than culture.

2693. Singh NP: Risk-taking and anxiety among successful and unsuccessful, traditional and progressive agricultural extrepreneurs of Delhi. Br J Soc Clin Psychol 9:301–308.

Traditional entrepreneurs show higher anxiety scores than progressive ones. Extremes of risk taking (high and low) are found among successful and unsuccessful entrepreneurs, respectively.

2694. Singh NS: n/Ach among agricultural and business entrepreneurs of Delhi. J Soc Psychol 81:145–150.

Higher mean n/Ach scores for Indian business entrepreneurs over agricultural entrepreneurs may be ascribed to greater motivation and economic opportunities for the former.

2695. Singh SP: Sex and age differences in persuasibility. J Soc Psychol 82:269–270.

An Indian student sample confirms previous findings of greater persuasibility attached to females and younger age groups.

2696. Singh SP, Pareek U: Discriminant function in a profile pattern of key-communicators in an Indian village. Int J Psychol 5:99–107.

Key communicators in an Indian village are higher in socioeconomic status than noncommunicators. Their position as leaders is continually reinforced in this authoritarian culture.

2697. Sisley E: The breakdown of the American image: expansion of stereotypes held by college students over four decades. Psychol Rep 27:779–786.

Comparison of adjectives used by college students to assign traits to America in 1932, 1950, and 1970 reveals that today's youth views its country and its people very differently from students tested a few decades ago.

2698. Sistrunk F, Clement DE: Cross-cultural comparisons of the conforming behavior of college students. J Soc Psychol 82:273–274.

Brazilian males conform to an external influence source while females conform to own nationality.

2699. Slochower H: Psychoanalytic distinction between myth and mythopoesis. J Am Psychoanal Assoc 18:150–164.

Mythopoesis takes the pivotal step by which magical and religious reality is transformed into symbolic and psychological reality. It exemplifies the process of "a change in function" in its relation to mythology, a change that renders the hero in mythopoesis at once tragically guilty and redeemable.

2700. Sloggett BB, Gallimore R, Kubany ES: A comparative analysis of fantasy need achievement among high and low achieving male Hawaiian-Americans. J Cross-Cultural Psychol 1:63–62.

Filipino-American, Japanese-American, and native Hawaiian male high school students' Need Achievement scores and findings challenge the notion that Hawaiian children do poorly in school because they lack Need Achievement motive.

2701. Spence DP: Human and computer attempts to decode symptom language. Psychosom Med 32: 615–625.

"Marker words," which are embedded in idiomatic contexts, are redundant additions to the manifest content that are systematically inserted into the thought stream by the pressure of dynamic forces and can be revealed by careful analysis of protocols and patient records. The words *up* and *down* are the two best single predictors of symptom frequency.

2702. Stacey BG: An evaluation of an ethnocentrism scale with reference to item content and response style. Psychol Rep 26:595–602.

A British ethnocentrism scale is reliable and has stable characteristics, though it does not have a high level of acceptability in the population at large and its factorial structure is psychologically uninterpretable.

2703. Stark S, Kugel Y: Toward an anthropology of dogmatism: maladjustment, modernization and Martin Luther King. Psychol Rep 27:291–309.

The more democratic, open-minded, pluralistic, and tolerant a society, the more maladjusted it will be to traditional man, an example of whom is Martin Luther King.

2704. Steinmann A, Fox DJ: Attitudes toward women's family role among black and white undergraduates. Fam Coordinator 19:363–367.

Black and white women's perceptions of ideal self did not differ; however, the groups do differ on perception of man's ideal woman.

2705. Sundberg ND, Rohila PK, Tyler LE: Values of Indian and American adolescents. J Pers Soc Psychol 16:374–397.

There is greater commonality than divergence in expressed values between North Indian and American youths. Traditional-modern, spiritual-material value dichotomies have little use for cultural generalization.

2706. Sundberg ND, Tyler LE: Awareness of action possibilities of Indian, Dutch, and American adolescents. J Cross-Cultural Psychol 1:153–157.

Questionnaire responses of boys and girls illustrate greater awareness of occupations by the Dutch, American concern with free-time activities and peer culture, and family orientation of East Indian girls. The findings suggest a relationship between school and environmental influences and individually perceived possibilities.

2707. Suomi SJ, Harlow HF, Domek CJ: Effect of repetitive infant-infant separation of young monkeys. J Psychol 76:161–172.

Short-term infant-infant separations produce results similar to mother-infant separations; the reactions perpetuate without infant adaptation; and finally, arrest of maturation of social development occurs.

2708. Surawicz FG, Sandifer MG: Cross-cultural diagnosis: a study of psychiatric diagnosis, comparing Switzerland, the United States and the United Kingdom. Int J Soc Psychiatry 16:232–236.

Cross-national differences for schizophrenia and grouped depressive disorders are not so varied as might be supposed. Providing a sufficiently large and heterogenous group of diagnosticians is used, cross-national comparisons should be reasonably valid.

2709. Tajifel H, Nemeth C, Jahoda G, Campbell JD, Johnson N: The development of children's preference for their country: a cross-national study. Int J Psychol 5:245–253.

Assessment of European children's assignments of photos to national groups indicates a tendency to assign best-liked photos to own nation that decreases with age.

2710. Teele JE: Sociocultural factors relating to mild mental retardation. Soc Sci Med 3:363–369.

An assessment of the relationship between sociocultural factors and mild mental retardation in the United States should, at a minimum, include a consideration of social-class factors, social-class composition of schools, racial composition of schools, interracial acceptance, home conditions, and the need for achievement.

2711. TenHoutcn W: The black family: myth and reality. Psychiatry 33:145–173.

The Moynihan thesis of black male subdominance in conjugal and parental roles is contradicted by research data.

2712. Tenzel J: Shamanism and concepts of disease in a Mayan Indian community. Psychiatry 33:372–380.

Guatemalan shamans are not psychotic and effectively treat physical as well as psychological diseases.

2713. Termansen PE, Tyan J: Health and disease in a British Columbian Indian community. Can Psychiatr Assoc J 15:121–127.

Indian patients in British Columbia do not differ significantly from the rest of the mental hospital patients and exhibit no unique patterns of illness. The low prevalence of mental disorders as reflected in admission data to hospitals may reflect a difference in ways of defining and dealing with disturbed behavior.

2714. Terry RL: Primate grooming as a tension reduction mechanism. J Psychol 76:129–138.

Primatological studies of grooming events and their correlates provide support for the hypothesis that grooming is more than biologically or socially functional. Grooming is a response to tensions generated by an event that threatens individual-group integration. Research projects designed to measure the concomitants of grooming are needed.

2715. Tomeh AK: Birth order and friendship associations. J Marriage Fam 32:360–369.

Last-born girls in the Mideast tend to interact more frequently with friends, possibly as a result of changing family functions.

2716. Tomeh AK: Reference-group supports among Middle Eastern college students. J Marriage Fam 32:156–166.

Women college students consider the familial group to be most important in various areas of interest, while the friendship group is important only in the social world, thus emphasizing the importance of family solidarity in Middle Eastern societies.

2717. Tseng W, Hsu J: Chinese culture, personality formation and mental illness. Int J Soc Psychiatry 16:5–14.

Chinese focus on culture is oriented to age, stresses the importance of filial piety, and emphasizes tradition and the past. Chinese patients are seldom confused in the choice of sexual object and seldom manifest homosexual problems because the gender roles of Chinese adults are clearly differentiated. Chinese people handle and manifest their problems in ways that are provided for and channeled by their culture.

2718. Varga K: The view of life of Hungarian students: an international comparison. J Cross-Cultural Psychol 1:169–176.

Hungarians value creative-humanistic life-styles and reject religious lifeways. Hungarian students are more similar to U.S. students in their evaluation of activity and consumer orientation and their disapproval of conformity and introversion but differ from Americans in being more inflexible and collective minded.

2719. Ulmer RA: Token-economy mental hospital society: an American operant sub-cultural society for cross-cultural studies. Int J Psychol 5:269–274.

The token economy, which can serve as a basis for acculturating schizophrenics into general society, provides a reliable data base for studying personality functioning in a culture.

2720. Vassiliou G: Critique of Gardner's paper. Fam Process 9:324–328.

Gardner's analysis consists of subjective interpretations rather than a specific approach through an operational milieu.

2721. Wakil PA: Explorations into the kin-networks of the Punjabi society: a preliminary statement. J Marriage Fam 32:700–707.

The functions and implications of the Punjab *biraderi* kinship system are an important consideration for the approach to resolving the conflict between kin requirements and national development in Pakistan.

2722. Weidman HH, Sussex JN: Cultural values and ego functioning in relation to the atypical culture-bound reactive syndromes. Int J Soc Psychiatry 17:83–100.

The theoretical factors that might predispose a population to paranoid and hysterical disorders are present in Burma. Beliefs in witchcraft and sorcerers exist, as do beliefs in spirit influence and intrusion. Repression, denial, and projection are paramount modes of defense.

2723. Weiss MS: Selective acculturation and the dating process: the patterning of Chinese-Caucasian interracial dating. J Marriage Fam 32:273–278.

Chinese-American boys' and girls' divergent expectations and/or dating behavior may be related to cultural and psychological factors. Chinese-American females prefer Caucasian courtship behavior.

2724. Werner E, Muralidharan R: Nutrition, cognitive status and achievement motivation of New Delhi nursery school children. J Cross-Cultural Psychol 1:271–281.

Physical and cognitive measures of lower-middle-class preschoolers indicate greater variability for inadequately nourished children and lower mean scores for inadequately nourished girls than boys.

2725. Weston PJ, Mednick MT: Race, social class and the motive to avoid success in women. J Cross-Cultural Psychol 1:283–291.

Responses to verbal TAT cues support the hypothesis that black women show less motive to avoid success than white women, but no differences between social classes are found.

2726. Wilkinson C: The destructiveness of myths. Am J Psychiatry 126:1087–1092.

While early American myths held that black persons were genetically inferior to whites, current myths focus on a sociopathological basis of inferiority. Black persons would be helped in establishing a sense of worthwhileness for themselves if such myths were corrected and new myth formulations and symbols developed.

2727. Wilkinson CB: Racism and the acquisition of prejudice. J Oper Psychiatry 1:55–60.

Racism is psychohistorically based, augmented by misconceptions brought about by the separation of races, and is psychologically rooted in individuals. Alteration of child-rearing practices and basic transformation in societal systems and institutions provide possibilities for change.

2728. Williams JE, Morland JK, Underwood WL: Connotations of color names in the United States, Europe, and Asia. J Soc Psychol 82:3–14.

General agreement in the ranking of ten color names on the evaluative, activity, and potency dimensions of the semantic differential supports the generality of connotative meaning of color names.

2729. Wintrob RM: Mammy Water: folk beliefs and psychotic elaborations in Liberia. Can Psychiatr Assoc J 15:143–157.

About 10 percent of the male patients in Liberia's only psychiatric facility reveal a system of delusions relating to possession by Mammy Water—a female water spirit of exceptional power and beauty. Mammy Water may represent a fusion of fantasies relating to the ultimate desired but prohibited object—mother.

2730. Wittkower ED: Trance and possession states. Int J Soc Psychiatry 16:153–160.

Trance and possession states in Liberia, Brazil, and Haiti play a part in religious rituals and have an important distress-relieving, integrative, and adaptive function. They may be of prophylactic value for mental illness. A revival and reinforcement of traditional practices is noticeable in many developing countries.

2731. Wittkower E: Transcultural psychiatry in the Carribean: past, present and future. Am J Psychiatry 127:162–166.

The frequency, distribution, and symptomatology of mental disorders in the Carribean is linked to the ethnography of the area.

2732. Wolman C: Group therapy in two languages, English and Navaho. Am J Psychother 24:677–685.

Alcoholism, a disease introduced by white men to the Navaho, is resistant to "traditional" cures and the white doctor is expected to treat it. Group therapy, using both the Navaho and English languages, may be effective.

1971

2733. Ablon J: Bereavement in a Samoan community. Br J Med Psychol 44:329–337.

Samoan family and community behavior at times of death is a social system with a remarkable program of immediate services for acute crisis periods. Culturally determined attitudes toward death and misfortune serve to mitigate the severe grief reaction that Americans consider to be "normal."

2734. Aiello JR, Jones SE: Field study of the proxemic behavior of young school children in three subcultural groups. J Pers Soc Psychol 19:351–356.

Cultural and sex-role differences exist in the use of space as measured by interactions among white, black, and Puerto Rican children.

2735. Alexander CA, Shivaswamy MK: Traditional healers in a region of Mysore. Soc Sci Med 5:595–601.

There are some common structural features between the indigenous system of medicine in the villages and modern medicine as practiced in India's cities.

2736. Anant SS: Stereotypes of educated North Indians about different ethnic groups. Int J Psychol 6:313–321.

A relationship between frequency of contact and sterotype is not confined for rank ordering of different nationalities, but it is clear that attributes associated with acceptable or rejected groups are favorable or unfavorable, respectively.

2737. Anant SS: Ethnic stereotypes of educated North Indians. J Soc Psychol 85:137–138.

The favorability of national stereotypes may be a result of the acceptability of the national group as influenced by social and political factors.

2738. Ayabe HI: Deference and ethnic differences in voice levels. J Soc Psychol 85:181–185.

Japanese-American and Caucasian-American female university students show no differences from each other in voice level when speaking normally before an authority figure or loudly before a peer. The Japanese-American female, however, is inhibited in speaking loudly before an authority figure.

2739. Bagley C: The social aetiology of schizophrenia in immigrant groups. Int J Soc Psychiatry 17:292–304.

Ethnic minorities have higher rates of schizophrenia than the major population. Social stress and particularly status striving in a climate of limited opportunity are significantly associated with schizophrenia among West Indian immigrants to England.

2740. Beck S: Cosmic optimism in some Genesis myths. Am J Orthopsychiatry 41:380–389.

Genesis myths provide rationalizations for harsh toil for sustenance, woman's pain in childbirth, the unequal struggle against conscience, punishment for murder, and world destruction and rebirth.

2741. Bergman RL: Navojo peyote use: its apparent safety. Am J Psychiatry 128:695–699.

The use of peyote by Indian members of the Native American Church of North America, indicates that the use of hallucinogens, when channeled by

church practices and beliefs, may result in ego strengthening. Built-in cultural safeguards result in a low incidence of adverse reactions to peyote.

2742. Berkowitz WR: A cross-national comparison of some social patterns of urban pedestrians. J Cross-Cultural Psychol 2:129–144.

National tendency to form groups is found in the following order: Turkey, Iran, Afghanistan, England, West Germany, Sweden, Italy, and the United States. Italians, West Germans, and Englishmen show more physical contact than Americans, Swedes, and Moslems, though there are few national differences in interaction frequency.

2743. Berry JW: Muller-Lyer susceptibility: culture, ecology, or race? Int J Psychol 6:193–197.

A positive correlation exists between perceptual differentiation and Muller-Lyer susceptibility. Some support for the ecological hypothesis and a strong relationship between skin pigmentation and susceptibility between Temne, Eskimo, aborigine, and Scottish samples are obtained.

2744. Bice TW, Kalimo E: Comparisons of health-related attitudes: a cross-national factor analytic study. Soc Sci Med 5:283–318.

The existence of six health-related attitudes in seven countries is corroborated. These attitudes are highly independent dimensions and may be used as variables in health-related, cross-national studies.

2745. Bloom L: The formation of friendships among Zambian university students. Int J Psychol 6:157–162.

Sociopsychological factors (age, sex, academic interest) are more salient to the establishment of friendships than spatial relations among Zambian students. Religion has a strong influence on friendship choice, while linguistic and tribal factors are not as important as belonging to an elite student group.

2746. Bochner S, Perks RW: National role evocation as a function of cross-national interaction. J Cross-Cultural Psychol 2:157–164.

Awareness of national role has an implication for race relations. More ethnic responses occur in cross-national interaction conditions, with Asians giving more ethnic responses than Australians, and feeling more ethnically conspicuous.

2747. Botha E: The achievement motive in three cultures. J Soc Psychol 85:163–170.

South African and Arab student achievement scores reflect shared cultural values rather than values that are sex differentiated.

2748. Braun C, Klassen B: A transformational analysis of oral syntactic structures of children representing varying ethnolinguistic communities. Child Dev 42:1859–1871.

A monolingual community reflects marked superiority over bilingual communities in control of syntactic complexity. Bilingual French communities appear to exceed bilingual German communities in such control.

2749. Brein M, David KH: Intercultural communication and the adjustment of the sojourner. Psychol Bull 76:215–230.

Intercultural communication is both an integrating and crucial factor for understanding the adjustment of the sojourner.

2750. Brislin RW: Interaction among members of nine ethnic groups and belief-similarity hypothesis. J Soc Psychol 85:171–179.

Similarity of beliefs leads to friendship choices among heterogeneous groups of students at the University of Guam. Students view culture and language as most salient in interpersonal interaction.

2751. Brislin RW, Baumgardner SR: Non-random sampling of individuals in cross-cultural research. J Cross-Cultural Psychol 2:397–400.

Careful definition and precision in the use of non-random samples will facilitate validity estimates and cross-cultural comparability.

2752. Britton JH, Britton JO: Children's perceptions of their parents: a comparison of Finnish and American children. J Marriage Fam 33:214–218.

A considerable similarity between national groups, ages, and sexes may be found in perceptions of parents by Finnish and American children. All groups see the mother as understanding and comforting and the father as dominative and fear provoking.

2753. Calogeras RC: Geza Roheim: psychoanalytic anthropologist or radical Freudian. Am Imago 28:146–157.

Roheim, an anthropologist rather than radical Freudian, was devoted to demonstrating a causal relationship between infantile psychosexual and aggressive phases and cultural forms and an understanding of the development of culture by the same mechanisms of individual development.

2754. Cancian FM: Affection and dominance in Zinacantan and Cambridge families. J Marriage Fam 33:207–213.

Interaction in Zinacantan and Cambridge families shows that affection elicits affection, all group members illustrate the same degree of affection, and there is homogeneity of dominance for unequal dyads.

2755. Carlaw RW, Reynolds R, Green LW, Khan NI: Underlying sources of agreement and communication between husbands and wives in Dacca, East Pakistan. J Marriage Fam 33:571–583.

Marital communication patterns in Pakistan suggest three dimensions of relationships: role empathy, husband dominance, and shared values. Consideration of sociopsychological aspects and various types of interspouse relationships are warranted.

2756. Carlson JA, Davis CM: Cultural values and the risky shift: a cross-cultural test in Uganda and the United States. J Pers Soc Psychol 20:392–399.

Ugandans are more conservative and less disposed to risk taking than Americans.

2757. Chiu LH: Manifested anxiety in Chinese and American children. J Psychol 79:273–284.

Chinese children score higher than Americans on anxiety and lie scales. Girls are more anxious than boys, and some geographic regional differences may be found.

2758. Ciborowski T, Cole M: Cultural differences in learning conceptual rules. Int J Psychol 6:25–37.

The Kpelle of Liberia show a similar relationship between conjunctive and disjunctive concept difficulty as found for American groups.

2759. Clay MM: Polynesian language skills of Maori and Samoan school entrants. Int J Psychol 6:135–145.

Testing of native and school language comprehension shows Maori children are monolingual in English while Samoan children are bilingual. Language planning and educational programs must take the home background of the child into account.

2760. Collett P: On training Englishmen in the non-verbal behavior of Arabs. Int J Psychol 6:209–215.

Arab students are more favorably inclined toward English students manifesting Arab-like nonverbal behavior, but the reverse phenomenon is not evident, indicating that Arabs place more emphasis on nonverbal behaviors in assessing their fellows than do Englishmen.

2761. Consalvi C: Some cross- and intra-cultural comparisons of expressed values of Arab and American college students. J Cross-Cultural Psychol 2:95–107.

Though significant differences are found between Arab and American university students' median ratings of morality situations, there is an overall similarity of values in terms of level of severity and ranking of situations. Within Arab subgroups the similarities are also greater than the differences.

2762. Cox DR: Child rearing and child care in Ethiopia. J Soc Psychol 85:3–5.

Data on child-rearing practices elicited from education students suggest an Ethiopian pattern of extensive infant contact and security, indulgent weaning and toilet training, restriction of aggressive expression, and extensive use of physical punishment.

2763. Craddick RA, Thumin FJ: A semantic differential study of the Yin-Yang symbol. J Pers Assess 35:338–343.

The semantic qualities of the symbol support the Yin-Yang archetype and are consistent with Jung's concept of the anima and animus.

2764. Crocetti G, Spiro H, Siassi I: Are the ranks closed? Attitudinal social distance and mental illness. Am J Psychiatry 127:1121–1127.

Blue-collar workers are almost unanimous in considering mental illness an illness requiring a physician's care and are optimistic about the outcome of psychiatric treatment. Blue-collar workers do not reject the mentally ill.

2765. Dawson JLM, Law H, Leung A, Whitney RE: Scaling Chinese traditional-modern attitudes and the GSR measurement of "important" versus "un-important" Chinese concepts. J Cross-Cultural Psychol 2:1–28.

Attitude inconsistency is resolved by maintaining important concepts through social reinforcement. A higher level of traditional-modern attitude conflict and higher GSR arousal are associated with attitude change for the more important topics.

2766. De Fundia TA, Draguns JG, Phillips L: Culture and psychiatric symptomatology: a comparison of Argentine and United States patients. Soc Psychiatry 6:11–20.

Differences of considerable scope and magnitude exist in the symptomatology recorded in the United States and Argentina. Psychopathology is an exaggeration and caricature of normal, culturally mediated modes of adaptations.

2767. de Lacey PR: Classificatory ability and verbal intelligence among high-contact aboriginal and low-socioeconomic white Australian children. J Cross-Cultural Psychol 2:393–396.

Despite lower verbal IQ scores, Australian aboriginal children tend to show a similar level of performance on two classificatory tests as that of white urban children.

2768. Dempsey AD: Time conservation across cultures. Int J Psychol 6:115–120.

Results from conservation of simultaneity and order of events tasks given to Mexican-American, Anglo, Hopi, Pima, Papago, Apache, and Navaho children indicate that the acquisition of formal reasoning may occur at a later age than has been proposed by Piaget.

2769. Deregowski JB: Responses mediating pictorial recognition. J Soc Psychol 84:27–33.

Aside from previous findings of Zambian difficulties with pictorial material, additional difficulties in operating across levels of abstraction are evident.

2770. Deregowski JB: Orientation and perception of pictorial depth. Int J Psychol 6:111–114.

Unlike Scottish children, Zambian children do not differentiate between vertical or skewed presentation material. Although older Zambians show increase in depth perception, there is no age or educational progression discrimination of orientation.

2771. Deregowski JB, Serpell R: Performance on a sorting task: a cross-cultural experiment. Int J Psychol 6:273–281.

Zambian children more frequently sort models by color than Scottish children; but no difference is obtained for sorting colored photographs. The salience of color may vary according to the nature of the stimuli.

2772. DeRios MD: Ayahuasco—the healing vine. Int J Soc Psychiatry 17:256–269.

The use of ayahuasco, an alkaloid with psychedelic effects, in Indian groups living in a Peruvian urban slum continues to be an integral part of healing procedures, permitting the curer to determine the magical cause of illness and to neutralize evil magic.

2773. Dershowitz Z: Jewish subcultural patterns and psychological differentiation. Int J Psychol 6: 223–231.

Anglo children show greater psychological differentiation than traditional Jewish children, with acculturated Jewish children midway. Many factors that may be differentially affected by the environment contribute to psychological differentiation.

2774. Douglas M: Do dogs laugh? A cross-cultural approach to body symbolism. J Psychosom Res 15: 387–390.

The Pygmies, living in the equatorial Congo forest, are not under obvious social pressure. Haitians are part of a modern police state at a low level of economic development. Both peoples seem to use the full bodily range of expression for grief and joy. Comparisons of laughter should take account of the load of social meaning that the body has to carry. Variations in the strength and permanence of social relations have significance for bodily expressions.

2775. Draguns JG, Leaman L, Rosenfeld JM: Symptom expression of Christian and Buddhist hospitalized psychiatric patients of Japanese descent in Hawaii. J Soc Psychol 85:155–161.

Christian and Buddhist Japanese-American patients differ in sphere dominance patterns but not in individual symptoms or roles. Affect dominance is prevalent among Christian males, somatization among Buddhist males, and thought dominance among Christian females.

2776. Dunham HW: Sociocultural studies of schizophrenia. Arch Gen Psychiatry 24:206–214.

Two major approaches to schizophrenia derive from the soft diagnosis—which has roots in psychoanalysis, learning, socialization, and anomie theory—and hard diagnosis, stemming from Kraepelin's classical work. Cross-cultural studies have provided little conclusive data, and new levels of synthesis are required.

2777. Eckhardt W: Conservationism, East and West. J Cross-Cultural Psychol 2:109–128.

An 18-nation student survey shows a general similarity between the Eastern pattern of conservatism and that of the West, though the former are less militaristic, nationalistic, and racialistic than the latter.

2778. Eckhardt W: Eastern and Western religiousity. J Cross-Cultural Psychol 2:283–292.

A generally similar pattern for the East and West suggests that religiosity is a function of personal conservatism and conformity.

2779. Ekman P, Friesen WV: Constants across cultures in the face and emotion. J Pers Soc Psychol 17:124–129.

A pancultural association exists between particular facial patterns and discrete emotions.

2780. El-abd HA: Application of the Minnesota Teacher Attitude Inventory (MTAI) to British and East African diploma students. J Cross-Cultural Psychol 2:203–204.

East African students are as efficient at teaching practice as British students, though the former show less progressive attitude responses on the MTAI.

2781. El-Islam MF, Ahmed SA: Traditional interpretation and treatment of mental illness in an Arab psychiatric clinic. J Cross-Cultural Psychol 2:301–308.

Somatic psychiatric symptoms are usually attributed to a general physical weakness and may be treated by vitamins and tonics at the hands of less well trained physicians. On the other hand, among illiterate peoples, behavioral changes are attributed to external agents and are treated by various rituals that may be psychologically satisfying.

2782. Elnegar NM, Promila M, Rao MN: Mental health in an Indian rural community. Br J Psychiatry 118:499–503.

There is a high prevalence of mental disorder in West Bengali neighborhood communities, with significant variation in rates and diagnostic patterns for three groups. Higher prevalences are found among the illiterate, those from 15 to 54 years, among cultivators, and for functional psychoses rather than neuroses.

2783. Engel M, Marsden G, Pollock SW: Child work and social class. Psychiatry 32:140–155.

The prevalence of child work varies with social class. There may be an initial late-middle childhood period for becoming a working boy.

2784. Erwin J, Mobaldi J, Mitchell G: Separation of Rhesus monkey juveniles of the same sex. J Abnorm Soc Psychol 78:134–139.

Separation between juvenile monkeys is similar

in effect to that of mother-infant separation. Where mother and infant usually return directly following separation, however, juveniles initially ignore or avoid one another at reunion.

2785. Eysenck HJ, Souief MI: Cultural differences in aesthetic preferences for polygonal figures. Int J Psychol 6:293–298.

Although no differences in mean preferences between British and Egyptian comparison groups are found, cultural differences are indicated in the tendency for British artists to prefer simple figures and British nonartists to prefer complex figures. Egyptian artists prefer complex over the simple figures also preferred by Egyptian nonartists.

2786. Forrest DV: Vietnamese maturation: the lost land of bliss. Psychiatry 34:111–139.

The study of child-rearing practices, legends, and customs aids in understanding the Vietnamese personality, a major determinant of which occurs at age 6–7 when the permissiveness regarding free play and bodily pleasures changes to strong obligations and taboos.

2787. Furby L: A theoretical analysis of cross-cultural research in cognitive development: Piaget's conservation task. J Cross-Cultural Psychol 2:241–255.

Formulation of a theoretical framework for analysis of the conservation task and relevant cognitive processes permits the prediction of conservation performance of children cross culturally.

2788. Georgas JG, Vassiliou V, Katakis H: The verbal intelligence of Athenians. J Soc Psychol 83:165–173.

The properties of three verbal subtests of the Wechsler Adult Intelligence Scale are similar across American and Greek culture, although sex role and cultural effects are evident.

2789. Gerson M: Women in the kibbutz. Am J Orthopsychiatry 41:566–573.

Women's social status changes in the kibbutz have many advantages but also have led to tensions and necessary adjustments.

2790. Golden M, Birns B, Bridger W, Moss A: Social-class differentiation in cognitive development among black preschool children. Child Dev 42:37–45.

The same pattern of social-class differentiation in cognitive development that emerges during the third year of life, previously reported for white children, can be demonstrated with black children. Since SES differences in cognitive development emerge during a period of rapid language growth, it seems reasonable to assume that these differences may be due to language.

2791. Golden M, Birns B: Social class, intelligence, and cognitive style in infancy. Child Dev 42:2114–2116.

Social-class differences in intellectual development or cognitive style are probably not present during the sensorimotor period. SES differences emerge somewhere between 18 and 36 months of age, when language enters the picture.

2792. Gorney R: Interpersonal intensity, competition, and synergy: determinants of achievement, aggression, and mental illness. Am J Psychiatry 128:436–445.

Interpersonal bonding may be necessary for such disparate human behaviors as cultural achievement, aggression, and mental illness. A reduction in intrasocial competition and an increase in synergy in contemporary society may be the basis for minimizing aggression and mental disorder, while providing the impetus for a high level of cultural achievement.

2793. Goodman FE: Glossolalia and single-limb trance: some parallels. Psychother Psychosom 19:92–103.

The same trance behavior is seen in the single-limb trance of preliterate society as in the graphic automatism of literate society. In the same manner as glossolalia, single-limb trance shows distinct characteristics depending on the energy level producing the manifestation. Single-limb trance occurs in the Navaho in connection with a divining curing strategy called hand trembling.

2794. Gough K: The origin of the family. J Marriage Fam 33:760–771.

Evidence from infrahuman primate ethology, hominoid evolution, hunting and gathering societies, and the role of women in these societies can provide clues to the development and maintenance of the family, its role in the social structure, and the function of the sexual division of labor.

2795. Green HB: Socialization values in West African, Negro and East Indian cultures: a cross-cultural comparison. J Cross-Cultural Psychol 2:309–312.

Negro mothers' attitudes rank highest in social

breadth as a socialization value. West African mothers rank highest in autonomy and expressionism, while East Indian mothers rank lowest for all three indexes.

2796. Greenglass ER: A cross-cultural comparison of maternal communication. Child Dev 42:685–692.

Italian mothers, when compared with Canadian mothers, tend to use more requests for orientation, more imperatives, and fewer justifications in addressing their sons and daughters. As their children increase in age, both Italian and Canadian mothers use more justifications in communicating with them.

2797. Grey A, Kalsched D: Oedipus East and West: an exploration via manifest dream content. J Cross-Cultural Psychol 2:337–352.

The percentage of opposite sex figures in the dreams of Indian students is less than that for Americans and varies with traditional or Westernized background. The findings support a phenomenological-cultural theory rather than a classical psychoanalytic theory of dreams.

2798. Griffitt W, Veitch R: Hot and crowded: influences of population density and temperature on interpersonal affective behavior. J Pers Soc Psychol 17:92–98.

Personal, social, and nonsocial affective behavior is negatively influenced by conditions of environmental stress.

2799. Grimmett SA: The influence of ethnicity and age on solving twenty questions. J Soc Psychol 83:143–144.

SES and residence may have a stronger effect than ethnicity on strategy, categorization, and conceptual tempo respectively.

2800. Gupta BS: Adaptation of a Hindi version of the Junior Eysenk Personality Inventory. Br J Soc Clin Psychol 10:189–190.

The Hindi version gives results similar to those obtained for England.

2801. Guthrie GM: Unexpected correlations and the cross-cultural method. J Cross-Cultural Psychol 2:315–324.

Individual differences, differences in variable definition variables, and researcher biases may introduce errors into cross-cultural studies. It is necessary to demonstrate that unexpected correla-

tions are lower than those correlations consistent with the investigated theory.

2802. Guthrie GM, Bennett AB Jr: Cultural differences in implicit personality theory. Int J Psychol 6:305–312.

Filipino and American data support the concept that within a culture behavior is considered predictable and consistent; while between cultures, behavior is considered erratic and unpredictable due to differential theories of personality. The two groups show marked differences in factor structure of personality scales.

2803. Guthrie GM, Sinaiko HW, Brislin T: Nonverbal abilities of Americans and Vietnamese. J Soc Psychol 84:183–190.

Persistent lower performance, in comparison to Americans, by Vietnamese mechanics on spatial and mechanical knowledge tests may reflect failure to learn Western dimensional representations.

2804. Guttmacher S, Elinson J: Ethno-religious variation in perceptions of illness: the use of illness as an explanation for deviant behavior. Soc Sci Med 5:117–125.

Eight ethnoreligious groups in New York City differently perceive deviant behavior as illness. The marked difference between Puerto Ricans and others is a cultural phenomenon.

2805. Hamburg DA: Aggressive behavior of chimpanzees and baboons in natural habitats. J Psychiatr Res 8:385–398.

Situations that elicit threat and attack patterns in baboons involve either protection of, or access to, vital resources. Both chimpanzees and gorillas show more elaborate aggressive displays than any other primate species. In chimpanzees, "technology" is more advanced than in baboons and attachments based on kinship and group traditions strongly influence behavior over a large part of the life span.

2806. Hamilton JW: Some cultural determinants of intrapsychic structure and psychopathology. Psychoanal Rev 59:279–294.

As American culture has developed, the superego system has become less meaningfully internalized. The doctrine of pseudo-equality will give rise to unresolved dependency strivings and to primitive oral-anal rage leading to violent forms of acting-out behavior.

2807. Harasym CR, Boersma FJ, Maguire TO: Semantic differential analysis of relational terms used in conservation. Child Dev 42:767–779.

Children with conservation status have a greater understanding of relational terms used in conservation testing than children who do not conserve. The ability to conserve and the ability to distinguish qualitative and quantitative differences seem to develop together in young children.

2808. Hartman J: Psychological conflict in Negro American language behavior: a case study. Am J Orthopsychiatry 41:627–635.

Programs designed to teach standard English to Negro Americans should do so without inherent assumptions of the inferiority or pathology of the dialect.

2809. Henderson NB, Butler BV, Goffeney B, Saito CH, Clarkson QD: Sex of person drawn by Japanese, Navajo, American white and Negro 7-year olds. J Pers Assess 35:261–264.

Within the general tendency for seven-year-olds to draw their own sex, girls draw self-sex more frequently than boys. Of the cultural groups, the tendency to draw self-sex is strongest among the Japanese.

2810. Henshel AM: The relationship between values and behavior: a developmental hypothesis. Child Dev 42:1997–2007.

Older French-Canadian children show a stronger value-behavior relationship than younger children. The increased strength of the relationship with age is not accompanied by an increase in honesty value orientation with age, although such an increase appears for behavior after the fourth-grade level.

2811. Heron A: Concrete operations, 'g' and achievement in Zambian children. J Cross-Cultural Psychol 2:325–336.

Zambian children display a wide range of performance on nonverbal tests. No significant differences may be found between performance and weight-conservation behavior status. Research into the relationship between Piagetian theory of intelligence and the traditional psychometric approach is indicated.

2812. Hossain ASMT: Sexual behavior of male Pakistanis attending venereal disease clinics in Great Britian. Soc Sci Med 5:227–241.

In comparison to other immigrants, those who utilize a venereal disease clinic have a history of early sexual activity. Sexually active in Pakistan, they remain active in Britain, especially with prostitutes.

2813. Hughes PH, Craseford GA, Barker NW, Schumann S, Jaffe JH: The social structure of a heroin copping community. Am J Psychiatry 128:551–557.

A one-year study of 127 heroin dealers and consumers who were members of a "copping area" in Chicago resulted in the differentiation of the group into different roles. Different roles are assumed by heroin dealers and consumers of a Chicago "copping area." Psychosocial functioning and treatability among the subgroups vary widely, indicating that "copping areas" may be more amenable to public health intervention than previously thought.

2814. Jahoda G: Retinal pigmentation, illusion susceptibility and space perception. Int J Psychol 6:199–208.

Investigation into retinal pigmentation, spatial perception, and Muller-Lyer susceptibility shows that the Malawi Africa susceptibility is influenced by red and blue materials, but no difference is found for Scottish subjects.

2815. Jamias MF, Pablo RY, Taylor DM: Ethnic awareness in Filipino children. J Soc Psychol 83:157–164.

Ethnic group identification is greater for own regional group, Tagalog, than for the national group, Filipino. Picture recognition is more accurate for the more familiar Chinese than American representations.

2816. Jones IH: Stereotyped aggression in a group of Australian Western Desert aborigines. Br J Med Psychol 44:259–265.

Stereotyped spearing, clubbing, and magical procedures are aggressive acts. The stereotyped form may be changed in various pathological states or inhibited by placatory gestures. Ethological models may be applied to such a community without claiming that the behavior described is homologous with that shown in lower animals.

2817. Jones SE: A comparative proxemics analysis of dyadic interaction in selected subcultures of New York City. J Soc Psychol 84:35–44.

Within black, Peurto Rican, Italian, and Chinese subcultures women are more direct in shoulder orientation than men. Interaction distance is similar across subcultures, indicating that there is some general homogeneity among poverty groups.

2818. Kadri ZN: The use of the MMPI for personality study of Singapore students. Br J Soc Clin Psychol 10:90–91.

Similarity of personality profiles for American groups and Singapore groups suggests common knowledge of desirable answers and internalization of norms of Western culture.

2819. Kakkar S: The theme of authority in social relations in India. J Soc Psychol 84:93–101.

Particularly salient to authority themes in three Indian states are family authority, the traditional-moral source for authority, the autocratic superior who provides emotional reward while arousing the guilt of the subordinate, and submissive acceptance of authority.

2820. Jabejar S, Mukerjee S: Personality variables among three communities in India. J Soc Psychol 84:305–306.

There are no significant differences between Maharashtrians, Bengalis, and Madrasis on neuroticism, authoritarianism, and misogyny variables, although differences are obtained on the extraversion variable.

2821. Karno M, Morales A: A community mental health service for Mexican-Americans in a metropolis. Compr psychiatry 12:116–121.

Mexican-American patients respond well when offered professionally expert treatment in a context of cultural and linguistic familiarity and acceptance. Alleged "cultural factors" may often be over-interpreted in a stereotypic manner to the detriment of an adequate understanding of the Spanish-speaking patient by the Anglo therapist.

2822. Kelvin P: Socialization and conformity. J Child Psychol Psychiatry 12:211–222.

An individual can be made to comply with the behavioral expectations of others, but he cannot be forced to share the values of others. Behavioral conformity does not provide an adequate criterion either for socialization or for the evaluation of treatment, as it can only be regarded as a possible first step towards socialization in terms of values.

2823. King M, King J: Some correlates of university performance in a developing country: the case of Ethiopia. J Cross-Cultural Psychol 2:293–300.

Prediction of academic success on the basis of tests using a nonnative instructional language may not be an adequate measure of a student's other aptitudes and potentials. Motivation is an important factor in performance.

2824. Kjell ER: Stockholm and Los Angeles: a cross-cultural study of the communication of suicidal intent. J Consult Clin Psychol 36:82–90.

Although greater concern for the victim is verbalized in Stockholm than in Los Angeles, most suicidal individuals in both countries identify themselves to available listeners in a similar manner.

2825. Klingelhofer EL: What Tanzanian secondary school students plan to teach their children. J Cross-Cultural Psychol 2:189–195.

Respondents across sex and ethnic (Asian or African) subgroups emphasize obedience and traditional aspects of child rearing. The results may indicate persistence of a form after functional meaning has been lost in modern technological societies.

2826. Krohn A, Gutmann D: Changes in mastery style with age: study of Navajo dreams. Psychiatry 32:289–300.

Navajo men's dreams move from an active-productive (alloplastic) orientation in younger men to receptive, accommodating (autoplastic), and magical (omniplastic) orientations in older men. Only when a cluster of dream measures points in the same direction can their central tendency be taken as an indicator of personality parameters.

2827. Korten DC: The life game: survival strategies in Ethiopian folktales. J Cross-Cultural Psychol 2:209–224.

Content analysis of behavior patterns in folktales suggests that Ethiopians view the everyday life game as zero-sum, nonshared sum, and with a limited payoff. Survival strategies of self-protection, deception, and revenge are oriented toward self-advancement at others' expense or perpetuating the status quo.

2828. (Deleted)

2829. Kunitz SJ, Levy JE, Odoroff CL, Bollinger J: The epidemiology of alcoholic cirrhosis in two Southwestern Indian tribes. Q J Stud Alcohol 32:706–720.

In comparison with the general U.S. population, liver cirrhosis deathrates among the Hopi Indians are over four times higher, but among the Navaho, the age-adjusted rate is slightly less. Contrasting drinking patterns, rather than acculturation stress, may account for the difference.

2830. La Belle TJ: Differential perceptions of elementary school children representing distinct sociocultural backgrounds. J Cross-Cultural Psychol 2: 145–155.

Semantic differential tests of meaning differences of school-related concepts for fifth-grade students demonstrate more positive perception of school-related concepts by females and by students with middle and high socioeconomic status. More similarities than differences are found for Anglo and Spanish-American students.

2831. Lambrechts E: Religiousness, social status and fertility values in a Catholic country. J Marriage Fam 33:561–566.

Although mutual contamination of the factors seems great, the influence of religiousness and Roman Catholic education on fertility values in Belgium is clearly indicated.

2832. Laosa LM, Swartz JD, Moran LJ: Word association structures among Mexican and American children. J Soc Psychol 85:7–15.

The close similarity of American and Mexican samples is indicated by the same factor structure representing the same associative modes, and by analysis of grammatical variables. Basic association structures may be common to language users in general.

2833. Larsen KS: An investigation of sexual behavior among Norwegian college students: a motivation study. J Marriage Fam 33:219–227.

Predictable sex and national group differences in sexual arousal to a pornographic movie indicate that sexual appetite is a more important factor in sexual arousal in comparison to a drive index.

2834. Leighton DC, Hagnell O, Leighton AH, Harding JS, Kellert SR, Danley RA: Psychiatric disorder in a Swedish and a Canadian community: an exploratory study. Soc Sci Med 5:189–209.

Comparison of psychiatric and selected demographic sociocultural data demonstrates that age, sex, education, and occupation are related to the prevalence of psychiatric disorder in the cultures. In the Swedish sample, the lowest occupational class group also has the lowest prevalence of psychiatric disorder.

2835. Leininger M: Some anthropological issues related to community mental health programs in the United States. Community Ment Health J 7: 50–61.

Current cultural and social forces affect an individual patient's illness. Sociocultural data must be incorporated into existing mental health programs.

2836. Lester D: The incidence of suicide and the fear of the dead in non-literate societies. J Cross-Cultural Psychol 2:207–208.

In 33 societies, correlations between ratings of incidence of suicide and the beliefs of illness caused by spirits of the dead are not significant.

2837. Lester D: Suicide and homicide rates and the society's need for affiliation. J Cross-Cultural Psychol 2:405–406.

Although no strong associations between national motives and deaths from suicide and homicide have been obtained from various studies, some trends are indicated that may be illuminated by larger sample sizes.

2838. Levin J, Karni ES: A comparative study of the CPI Femininity Scale: validation in Israel. J Cross-Cultural Psychol 2:387–392.

The validity of the CPI Femininity Scale in Israel is one of the highest established for the scale next to those results obtained in the United States.

2839. Levitt M, Rubenstein B: The student revolt: totem and taboo revisited. Psychiatry 34:156–167.

Life-styles of student radicals give psychoanalytic clues to their basic character structure, but to concentrate on this to the exclusion of the social goals involved is a futile intellectual exercise.

2840. Lindgren HC, Tebcherani A: Arab and American auto- and heterostereotypes: a cross-cultural study of empathy. J Cross-Cultural Psychol 2:173–180.

Adjectives selected as descriptive of Arab and American respondents were used to construct a questionnaire of contrasting adjective pairs. Arab students are more successful at identifying typical American responses than Americans at identifying Arab responses, illustrating more empathy on the part of a lower power group for a high power group.

2841. Littig LW: Motives of Negro Americans who aspire to traditionally open and closed occupations. J Cross-Cultural Psychol 2:77–86.

In a middle-class college context Negro students' aspiration to open and closed occupations is related to weak and strong affiliation motivation respectively. In the working-class college context strong achievement and power motivation are related to aspiring to closed occupations.

2842. Lloyd BB: Studies of conservation with Yoruba children of differing ages and experience. Child Dev 42:415–428.

Universal factors of a biological or social nature are important among children about eight years of age, be they American, Tiv, Yoruba, or Wolof, in regards to conserving responses. However, particular educational experiences are important also.

2843. Lloyd BB: The intellectual development of Yoruba children: a re-examination. J Cross-Cultural Psychol 2:29–38.

Yoruba subjects from traditional and educated homes display no evidence of convergence of intellectual development. A coefficient indicates a steeper growth curve under five years for traditional subjects, and over five years for elite subjects.

2844. Lueschen G, Blood RO, Lewish M, Staikof Z, Stolte-Heiskanne V, Ward C: Family organization, interaction and ritual: a cross-cultural study in Bulgaria, Finland, Germany and Ireland. J Marriage Fam 33:228–234.

More modern societies have a somewhat higher frequency of ritual interaction and kin visits at the Christmas ritual than less modern societies. The data give very little support to Durkheim's law of contraction.

2845. Madsen MC: Developmental and cross-cultural differences in the cooperative and competitive behavior of young children. J Cross-Cultural Psychol 2:365–372.

Experimental results suggest a higher level of cooperation among Mexican children and an increase in nonadaptive competition along with age for American children.

2846. Manaster GJ, Ahumada I: Cultural values in Latin and North American cities. J Cross-Cultural Psychol 2:197–202.

Functions of common objects as described by San Juan, Puerto Rico, adolescents are indicative of cultural values. Comparison with the Latin passive pattern of Buenos Aires adolescents, and the North American active pattern of Chicagoan adolescents, shows that the San Juan group's orientation is midpoint between North and South American cultural orientation.

2847. Mace DR, Mace VD: Training family life leaders in developing countries: a seminar approach. Fam Coordinator 20:23–29.

A seminar for native trainees includes a session in which the trainees instruct their leaders in the cultural values and customs of their country.

2848. McKinney W, Suomi S, Harlow H: Depression in primates. Am J Psychiatry 127:1313–1320.

Behavioral manifestations of depression may be produced in monkeys less than a year old, regardless of their early training experiences. Induction methods include the use of mother-infant separation, peer separation, and the vertical chamber.

2849. McKissack IJ: Comformity in Ghana. Br J Soc Clin Psychol 10:87.

Testing conformity in other cultures using the Asch procedure suggests that Africans are particularly susceptible to face-to-face interaction pressures.

2850. McNeill D, Yukawa R, McNeill NB: The acquisition of direct and indirect objects in Japanese. Child Dev 42:237–249.

Japanese children are guided in their behavior by certain universals of language. These give rise at times to "supernormal" sentences analogous to the supernormal stimuli of ethology.

2851. Marino C: Cross-national comparisons of Catholic-Protestant creativity differences. Br J Soc Clin Psychol 10:132–143.

Highly authoritarian Roman Catholic students in the United States and Ireland perform less well on tests of creativity factors than do Protestants of the same country.

2852. Melikian L, Ginsberg A, Cuceloglu D, Lynn R: Achievement motivation in Afghanistan, Brazil, Saudi Arabia and Turkey. J Soc Psychol 83:183–184.

Achievement motivation scores are comparatively high in developing countries and may underlie economic growth rates.

2853. Miller MH, Yeh EK, Alexander AA, Klein MH, Tseng KH, Workneh F, Chu HM: The cross-cultural student: lessons in human nature. Bull Menninger Clin 35:128–131.

International students associate mostly with fellow nationals. Their warm, intimate, dependent, personally satisfying contacts are almost exclusively limited to their conational group. Their relations with host nationals rarely go beyond superficial pleasantries. They are rather discouraged about any prospects for deep cross-cultural friendships.

2854. Miller SI, Schoenfeld LS: Suicide attempt patterns among the Navajo Indians. Int J Soc Psychiatry 17:189–193.

Suicide and suicide attempt is a problem for the Navaho people; however, it is no greater than for other people. If culture plays a part it may be the culture of a socioeconomically depressed group, rather than anything specifically Indian or Navaho.

2855. Mosena PW, Stoeckel J: The impact of desired family size upon family planning practices in rural East Pakistan. J Marriage Fam 33:567–570.

Rural Pakistani women whose desired and actualized family size are relatively matched tend to practice family planning more frequently than women whose actual family size is less than desired.

2856. Mote TA, Natalicio LFS, Rivas F: Comparability of the Spanish and English editions of the Spielberger State-Trait Anxiety Inventory. J Cross-Cultural Psychol 2:205–206.

High correlations between A-State and A-Trait scales in English and Spanish versions indicate good translations and comparable validities.

2857. Munroe RH, Munroe RL: Household density and infant care in an East African society. J Soc Psychol 83:3–13.

The ecological variables of high-density households among the Logoli Kenyans result in greater infant contact and indulgence in socialization, although the mother may be less available due to her greater economic responsibilities.

2858. Munroe RL, Munroe RH: Effect of environmental experience on spatial ability in an East African society. J Soc Psychol 83:15–22.

Sex-role differences and the greater tendency for males to encounter environments beyond the household may account for the greater skill in spatial tasks of Logoli boys over girls.

2859. Munroe RL, Munroe RH: Male pregnancy symptoms and cross-sex identity in three societies. J Soc Psychol 84:11–25.

Male pregnancy symptomatology in the United States, among the Black Carib of British Honduras, and among the Kenya Logoli can be related to covert femalelike responses and hypermasculine over-responses on various measures, and may therefore serve as an indication of cross-sex identity.

2860. Munroe RL, Munroe RH: Overrepresentation of firstborns in East African secondary schools. J Soc Psychol 84:151–152.

Among more selective secondary schools, Kenya Gusii, Kipsigis, and Logoli first borns are over-represented, although second-born females appear more frequently than expected.

2861. Murphy HBM, Raman AC: The chronicity of schizophrenia in indigenous tropical peoples: results of a twelve-year follow-up survey in Mauritius. Br J Psychiatry 118:489–497.

Although the incidence for schizophrenia approaches British rates, the percentage of normally functioning, symptom-free individuals is greater than for comparable British samples, with lower number of relapse as well. The question of chronicity among tropical peoples should be further examined.

2862. Musil J: Some aspects of social organization of the contemporary Czechosolovak family. J Marriage Fam 33:196–206.

There is more variety of family types and social organization in Czechoslovakia than is generally assumed for socialist countries.

2863. Naroll R, Benjamin EC, Fohl FK, Fried MJ, Hildreth RE, Schaefer JM: Creativity: a cross-historical pilot survey. J Cross-Cultural Psychol 2:181–188.

Four hypothesized causes of creative productivity of given societies—wealth, geographic expansion, degree of governmental centralization, and degree of external challenge—are unsupported. Tentative support is found for the hypothesis that the more the political fragmentation of a civilization, the higher its creativity level.

2864. Nelson C: Self, spirit possession and world view: an illustration from Egypt. Int J Soc Psychiatry 17:194–209.

The zar is a spirit possession cult whose members are predominantly women and that has little or no relation to formal Islamic practices. Both the zar and marriage are parallel institutions which involve placating a superior. The zar symbolizes the conjugal role and self-image of women.

2865. Nelson TM, Allan DK, Nelson J: Cultural differences in the use of colour in Northwest Canada. Int J Psychol 6:283–292.

Canadian-Indian, Hutterite, white secular, and Roman Catholic children indicate color preferences as a sensory phenomenon. Color appears to indicate the degree of social direction of individual communication.

2866. Nerlove SB, Munroe RH, Munroe RL: Effect of environmental experience on spatial ability: a replication. J Soc Psychol 84:3–10.

Comparison of Kenya Gusii and Logoli children indicates that boy children who are further away from home than girls are more skillful at certain spatial tasks, such as copying geometric figures.

2867. Neumann AK, Bhatia JC, Andrews S, Murphy AKS: Role of the indigenous medicine practitioner in two areas of India: report of a study. Soc Sci Med 5:137–149.

Interviews in Kerala State and Punjab State do not support the stereotype of the indigenous medicine practitioners as one using traditional herbs, oils, and incantations and having little to do with modern medicine.

2868. Neumarket P: Amos Tutuola: emerging African literature. Am Imago 28:129–143.

The modern African literary scene is dominated by mythopoeic activity, while Tutuola's paranoid works seem to be the voice of a literary and psychological antithesis and a man unable to cope with his situation.

2869. Nicol AR: Psychiatric disorder in the children of Caribbean immigrants. J Child Psychol Psychiatry 12:273–287.

A high proportion of disturbed girls and of girls with conduct disorders are found among children in Britain who were born West Indian. Unlike boys, conduct disorder in West Indian girls is not associated with the disturbance of migration.

2870. Ogunlade JO: National stereotypes of university students in Western Nigeria. J Soc Psychol 85:309–310.

Favorability of national stereotypes held by Nigerian students appears to be a function of differing support given during the civil war by the national group.

2871. Okano Y, Spilka B: Ethnic identity, alienation and achievement orientation in Japanese-American families. J Cross-Cultural Psychol 2:273–282.

Although Buddhist Japanese-American mothers are more ethnically identified than Christian mothers, maternal and child ethnic identity are independent of achievement orientation and alienation.

2872. Okonji OM: A cross-cultural study of the effects of familiarity on classificatory behavior. J Cross-Cultural Psychol 2:39–49.

Nigerian Ibusa and Glasgow children's performance on two classificatory tasks is influenced by familiarity with classificatory objects. Overall developmental trends are similar for both samples.

2873. Okonji OM: Culture and children's understanding of geometry. Int J Psychol 6:121–128.

Ugandan children who attend school have better performance on conservation length and angular measurement but do not differ from unschooled children on point location.

2874. Olesen V: Contest and posture: notes on socio-cultural aspects of women's roles and family policy in contemporary Cuba. J Marriage Fam 33:548–560.

Recent trends in Cuba include greater occupational opportunities for women and their emergence into the labor force, liberalized marital laws, and family planning. Some traditional culture themes are still present, however, and include sex-role distinctions as sustained in the concepts of machismo and hidalgoism, or courtly honor and values.

2875. Olsen NJ: Sex differences in child training antecedents of achievement motivation among Chinese children. J Soc Psychol 83:303–304.

Independence training may be significantly related to achievement motivation in Taiwan-Chinese boys but is not related for girls.

2876. Orpen C: The effect of cultural factors on the relationship between prejudice and personality. J Psychol 78:73–80.

Cultural norms rather than deep authoritaristic personality trends determine degree of prejudiced views in a prejudiced climate.

2877. Orpen C: Prejudice and adjustment to cultural norms among English-speaking South Africans. J Psychol 77:217–218.

The relationship between prejudice and cultural values points out the importance of the cultural milieu in shaping and providing sanction for white African attitudes.

2878. Ozturk OM, Volkan VD: The theory and practice of psychiatry in Turkey. Am J Psychother 25:240–271.

In 1925 all religious and quasi-religious educational and therapeutic institutions were abolished in Turkey and since then the practice of folk healing has been outlawed and prosecuted. However, these practices continue in the traditional segments of society. There is a traditional tolerant attitude toward mental illness; however, the majority of both urban and rural subjects see mental illness as a shameful social stigma.

2879. Papajohn JC, Spiegel JP: The relationship of culture value orientation change and Rorschach indices of psychological development. J Cross-Cultural Psychol 2:257–272.

Degree of internalization of American value orientations is related to psychological stress for second-generation Greek-Americans. Increased correlations between culture change and psychological stress follow the acculturation continuum of lower-class females, middle-class females, lower-class males, and middle-class males.

2880. Papanek H: Purdah in Pakistan: seclusion and modern occupations for women. J Marriage Fam 33:517–530.

The purdah system in India and Pakistan is related to status, division of labor, dependency, social distance, and maintenace of moral standards. These factors may be conceptualized as "separate worlds" and "symbolic shelter." Because of special needs of a sex-segregated system, medicine and teaching are high-prestige occupations for educated women in Pakistan.

2881. Phillips BN, Martin RP: Factorial structure of the Children's School Questionnaire in American and Solvenian samples. J Cross-Cultural Psychol 2:65–76.

Responses by children to a questionnaire indicate common factors: school anxiety sex role, school aspirations, and feelings of inadequacy—which are influenced by nationality, social status, and sex differences.

2882. Pirojnikoff LA, Hadar I, Hadar A: Dogmatism and social distance: a cross-cultural study. J Soc Psychol 85:187–193.

Kibbutz members, American Jews, and non-Jews are less dogmatic than Israeli city dwellers, although the Israeli samples in general are less inclined to experience interaction with outgroups than the American samples.

2883. Polednak AP: Body build of paranoid and non-paranoid schizophrenic males. Br J Psychiatry 119:191–192.

Univariate and multivariate statistical tests show little difference in body measures between paranoid and nonparanoid subgroups.

2884. Rahe RH, Lundberg U, Bennett L, Theorell T: The Social Readjustment Rating Scale: a comparative study of Swedes and Americans. J Psychosom Res 15:241–249.

Swedish samples give higher life-change-unit (LCU) scores to most life-change events than do their American counterparts. Cultural differences between Swedes and Americans appear in the life-change category of work items and are consistent with Hendin's findings that the Swedish male shows an exceptionally high drive for achievement and success in his work, as well as placing high priority upon his achievement of a professional identity.

2885. Raybin JB: Aggression, mythology, and the college student. Am J Psychiatry 128:446–472.

The need among college students to face conflicts about aggression commonly results in family "myths," such as (1) to be aggressive is to be bad, (2) to be aggressive is to love, (3) to be aggressive is to be masculine, and (4) to be aggressive is to be free.

2886. Resnik H, Diznang L: Observations on suicidal behavior among American Indians. Am J Psychiatry 127:882–887.

In addition to high suicide rates on some reservations a distinguishing characteristic of Indian suicidal behavior is its almost unique occurrence in those ages 35 or younger. An Indian adolescent has a double identity crisis—the expected adolescent turmoil plus a cultural crisis.

2887. Richardson A: Predicting socio-economic satisfaction levels among British immigrants in Australia. J Cross-Cultural Psychol 2:51–64.

Levels of socioeconomic satisfaction are predictable from preresidence questionnaire responses. Empirical evidence supports the predictive value of adaptive capacity and situational stress as theoretical constructs.

2888. Robbins MC, Kilbride PL: Sex differences in dreams in Uganda. J Cross-Cultural Psychol 2:406–408.

The dreams of Bantu students indicate a tendency for males to dream more about males and for females to dream about both sexes. Male figures do dominate in the dreams of both sexes, perhaps reflecting the patricentric focus of the society. Some support is given to the concept that dreams tend to universally reflect conflict and anxiety.

2889. Schenflen AE: Living space in an urban ghetto. Fam Process 10:429–450.

The temporal and spatial arrangements of urban Puerto Rican and Afro-American households in the Bronx can be examined in terms of territorial defense behavior.

2890. Schludermann S, Schludermann E: Adolescent perception of parent behavior (CRPBI) in Hutterite communal society. J Psychol 79:29–40.

While boys describe parents as higher in Firm Control and lower on Acceptance dimensions than girls, in other respects parents are described in a similar way by adolescents.

2891. Schludermann S, Schludermann E: Adolescent's perception of themselves and adults in Hutterite communal setting. J Psychol 78:39–48.

Girls tend to have a more favorable view of teens and adults than boys, while both tend to rate adults more favorably than teens. Ratings of teenagers by adults were more favorable than expected.

2892. Schludermann S, Schludermann E: Maternal childrearing attitudes in Hutterite communal society. J Psychol 79:169–178.

Young and old Hutterite mothers have quite similar parental attitudes, which tend to conform to traditional Hutterite values.

2893. Schludermann S, Schludermann E: Paternal attitudes in Hutterite communal society. J Psychol 79:41–48.

Several dimensions of paternal attitudes—male dominance, authoritarian discipline, paternal responsibility, and power assertion—indicate general authoritarian attitudes to child rearing.

2894. Seifert JA, Draguns JG, Caudill WA: Role orientation, sphere dominance, and social competence as bases of psychiatric diagnosis in Japan: a replication and extension of American findings. J Abnorm Soc Psychol 78:101–106.

The symptom styles of role and sphere dominance are significantly related to diagnosis; however, these relationships differ in specific respects from those established in the United States. The greater cultural variability between spheres and roles and diagnosis, than between social competence and either of the former, constitutes a paradox.

2895. Serpell R: Preference for specific orientation of abstract shapes among Zambian children. J Cross-Cultural Psychol 2:225–239.

Two experiments and comparisons of Zambian to Western-educated school children provide limited support for "familiarity" as a determinant of orientation preferences. Features intrinsic to the shapes result in specific orientation preferences, regardless of cultural background.

2896. Sharan S, Weller L: Classification patterns of underprivileged children in Israel. Child Dev 42:581–594.

Different configurations of grouping behavior are associated with major background variables. Lower-class children are less able to achieve conceptual breadth than are their middle-class peers. Children of Middle Eastern ethnic background give fewer descriptive responses and fail to cope with the fundamental requirement of grouping as well as their peers of Western ethnic background.

2897. Sharma KL: Attitudes of Indian students towards marriage roles. J Soc Psychol 83:299–300.

Consistent male-dominant attitudes by males and equalitarian attitudes by females appear across Indian, Asian-American, and Asian samples.

2898. Seigler M, Osmond H: Goffman's model of mental illness. Br J Psychiatry 119:419–424.

Goffman gives the impression that a mental hospital is a concentration camp because it fails to describe the rights and duties of patients, i.e., the sick role. Peculiar difficulties of maintaining psychiatric patients in the sick role result in the demoralized hospitals he so vividly describes.

2899. Snelbecker BE, Fullard W, Gallagher JM: Age related changes in the pattern prediction—a cross-cultural comparison. J Soc Psychol 84:191–196.

Comparison of data from American children and Mundy-Castle's report on African children confirms the latter's findings of a developmental shift in pattern prediction and perception, although the American data provides differing information on the age level at which such a shift occurs.

2900. Solway KS: Freudian and cultural symbolism. J Clin Psychol 27:516–518.

Only adults clearly respond to anatomical symbols in the manner Freud hypothesized. Male anatomical symbols produce associations in agreement with Freudian theory significantly more often than do female anatomical symbols. Symbols with cultural referents, regardless of congruence or incongruence with anatomical referents, are recognized at a statistically significant level.

2901. Staples R: Towards a sociology of the black family: a theoretical and methodological assessment. J Marriage Fam 33:119–138.

The imposition of ethnocentric values, and concomitant myths and stereotypes, on research of the black family obstructs the application of current theory to the development of a viable sociology of the black family. The value of theories of black family life is diminished by the application of weak methodology.

2902. Stedman JM, McKenzie RE: Family factors related to competence in young disadvantaged Mexican-American children. Child Dev 42:1602–1607.

There is a moderate relationship between behavioral adjustment and linguistic ability among Mexican-American children. Families of children who have achieved high language adjustment view the Anglo teacher as assigning positive and potent qualities to their children, and perhaps as willing to give the Mexican-American child at least an even break.

2903. Stephan WG, Stephan C: Role differentiation, empathy, and neurosis in urban migrants and lower-class residents of Santiago, Chile. J Pers Soc Psychol 19:1–6.

Urban-born subjects and migrants are similar in empathy, but the former are high in role differentiation and low in neurosis.

2904. Swanson DW, Bratrude AP, Brown EM: Alcohol abuse in a population of Indian children. Dis Nerve Syst 32:835–842.

The most apparent cause of childhood abuse of alcohol is the Indian respect for individual autonomy which, combined with permissiveness, allows the child to determine how much alcohol he will drink. The Indians' own lack of concern and a tendency to regard alcohol abuse as a somewhat humorous inevitability interferes with treatment.

2905. Taub JM: The sleep-wakefulness cycle in Mexican adults. J Cross-Cultural Psychol 2:353–364.

There may be culturally specific sleep-related behaviors. The importance of anthropological and biological factors in the human sleep requirement should be considered.

2906. Teja JS, Narang RL, Aggarwal AK: Depression across cultures. Br J Psychiatry 119:253–260.

Somatic symptoms, hypochondriasis, anxiety, and agitation are present in a significantly larger percentage of Indian than in British depressives. Obsessional and paranoid symptoms are significantly less frequent among Indian depressives. Sociocultural environment may account for these differences in symptoms.

2907. Tenzel JH: Student activism: a problem of cultural transmission. Am J Psychother 25:553–563.

Student activism is representative of a problem of cultural transmission. The increasing difficulty in achieving adult status, with the concomitant interminable prolongation of adolescence resulting from changes in adult models, is a major factor in student demonstrations. However, the legitimate social grievances present should not be ignored.

2908. Terry RL: Dependence nurturance and monotheism: a cross-cultural study. J Soc Psychol 84:175–181.

Multicultural data from simple and complex societies provide strong indications for an inverse relationship between monotheism and dependence nurturance.

2909. Thiagarajan KM, Lukas PA: Personal values across cultures: a study of managers and students in India and the United States. J Soc Psychol 85:139–140.

Cultural effects on personal values are most dominant across the United States and India.

2910. Ticho GR: Cultural aspects of transference and countertransference. Bull Menninger Clin 35:313–326.

The distinction of stereotypes from transference manifestations may be more difficult when patient and analyst come from different cultures. Cultural differences may stir up countertransference manifestations that may not be easily distinguishable from reactions to the foreign culture and may render self-analysis more difficult. These problems do not require a change in the analytic techniques.

2911. Walker C, Torrance EP, Walker TS: A cross-cultural study of the perception of situational causality. J Cross-Cultural Psychol 2:401–404.

Cross-cultural differences in the perception of situational causality are found for American and Indian children. There is a developmental gradient for American children but not for Indian children.

2912. Wasserman SA: Values of Mexican-American and Anglo blue-collar and white-collar children. Child Dev 42:1624–1628.

Mexican-American, Negro, and Anglo children internalize certain success and humanitarian values in differing degrees. Minority children, in particular, may experience value conflict in school.

2913. Weick KE, Gilfillan DP: Fate of arbitrary traditions in a laboratory microculture. J Pers Soc Psychol 17:179–191.

Arbitrary traditions of easy and difficult strategies achieve differential compliance over time. Warranted arbitrary traditions are perpetuated while unwarranted traditions decrease.

2914. Weidman HH: Trained manpower and medical anthropology: conceptual, organizational, and educational priorities. Soc Sci Med 5:15–36.

Medical anthropology is following very closely the pattern of development of its sister discipline, medical sociology. It is important to delineate priorities for enlarging the corps of specialists in medical anthropology.

2915. Weller L, Aharan S: Articulation of the body concept among first-grade Israeli children. Child Dev 42:1553–1559.

Western Jews raised in a subculture stressing verbal-intellectual achievement with a concomitant neglect of body awareness for its male members manifest greater sex differences in body articulation than Iranian and Iraqi Jews whose subculture lacks such emphasis. However, Middle-Eastern children, whose ethnic background is more typical of a traditional society in regard to social sex roles, do not show greater sex differences in body articulation.

2916. Westermeyer J: Use of alcohol and opium by the Meo of Laos. Am J Psychiatry 127:1019–1023.

The Meo is a tribal group of Asian mountaineers who raise opium as a cash crop. Alcohol is used within rigid social constraints, and alcoholism as defined in Western culture does not occur. Opium is found in almost every home, and few users are addicted. Opium use may contribute to an integrated Meo society by allowing certain stressed individuals to continue to live in and contribute to Meo society.

2917. Whitney RE: Agreement and positivity in the pleasantness ratings of balanced and unbalanced social situations. J Pers Soc Psychol 17: 11–14.

The determinants of pleasantness in social situations as rated by Hong Kong Chinese students are interpersonal agreement and positivity rather than balance.

2918. Williams JI: Disease as deviance. Soc Sci Med 5:219–226.

The major determinants that affect the life chance of becoming deviant are the background characteristics of people who display symptoms or cues, the type of disabling conditions, and the type of rehabilitation facility.

2919. Wittmer J: Perceived parent-child relationships: a comparison between Amish and non-Amish young adults. J Cross-Cultural Psychol 2: 87–94.

Perception of Amish parents' behavioral characteristics differs significantly from perception of non-Amish parents. Amish parents are seen as being less rejecting, less neglecting, less casual, less likely to reward directly or to use symbolic punishment.

2920. Wolier M: Adapting Dawson's Traditional versus Western Attitudes Scale and presenting some new information from Africa. Br J Soc Clin Psychol 10:101–103.

An adaptation of Dawson's device differs in method of presentation and comprehension, changes in scale, logicality of responses, and lack of high correlation between Western attitudes and rated work efficiency.

2921. Woon T, Masuda M, Wagner NN, Holmes TH: The social readjustment rating scale: a cross-cultural study of Malaysians and Americans. J Cross-Cultural Psychol 2:373–386.

Malaysian medical students score higher than Americans on items pertaining to personal habits and religious activities.

2922. Za'rour GI: The conservation of number and liquid by Lebanese school children in Beirut. J Cross-Cultural Psychol 2:165–172.

Ability to conserve increases significantly with age, though Lebanese youngsters lag behind American children of a middle-class school. This difference is possibly due to child-rearing practices that stress obedience and conformity and a less rich educational environment.

2923. Zegans LS: Toward a unified theory of human aggression. Br J Med Psychol 44:355–365.

Primary and secondary inhibiting mechanisms have been ineffective in checking man's destructive powers. There is now a need to consider a third form of control over aggression. This would involve a reinterpretation and change in those signals that provoke our rage rather than a blocking or redirection of our violence.

1972

2924. Adinolfi AA, Klein RE: The value orientations of Guatemalan subsistence farmers: measurements and implications. J Soc Psychol 87:13–20.

Pragmatic orientations characterize Ladino farmers with a high coping effectiveness. The impact of acculturation is illustrated in comparison of Spanish-American "being" value orientations and Ladino "doing" orientations.

2925. Aleksandrowicz M: The art of a native therapist. Bull Menninger Clin 36:596–608.

Um-Razzia, an illiterate Iraqui-Jewish indigenous healer practicing in Israel, successfully treats neurosis and psychosomatic illness in villagers. Among her techniques are magic rituals, encouragement of regression, increasing and then rapidly alleviating anxiety, and blaming Jinns (spirits) for causing problems.

2926. Allen MG: A cross-cultural study of aggression and crime. J Cross-Cultural Psychol 3:259–272.

Indirect, displaced aggression is more likely in cultures with permanent settlement patterns exhibiting high anxiety, deviance-conformity, crime, suicide, and mental illness; and having dependence socialization that creates anxiety and low indulgence. High crime frequencies occur in larger societies with high levels of political integration, social stratification, and indirect displaced aggression and high achievement training in socialization.

2927. Anwar MP, Child IL: Personality and esthetic sensitivity in an Islamic culture. J Soc Psychol 87:21–28.

Correlates of esthetic sensitivity-tolerance of complexity, independence, and regression in service of ego provide support for the cross-cultural generality of esthetic interests and judgments.

2928. Aronow E: Comment on Raychaudhuri's "Relation of creativity and sex to Rorschach M responses." J Pers Assess 36:303–304.

Inadequate controls for intelligence and education render Raychaudhuri's findings on Indians ineffective in terms of proving a creativity-sex-Rorschach relationship.

2929. Assael MI, Namboze JM, German GA, Bennett FJ: Psychiatric disturbances during pregnancy in a rural group of African women. Soc Sci Med 6:387–395.

The high rate of psychiatric disturbances among rural Ugandan pregnant women may be the result of unfavorable social, economic, and domestic patterns inherent in the present transition between traditional and urbanized patterns of life. Modern antenatal care must take into account the traditional beliefs and anxieities of rural African women, and seek to deal with these as they arise.

2930. Ayabe HI, Santo S: Conceptual tempo and the Oriental American. J Psychol 81:121–124.

Japanese- and Chinese-American children produce less errors in performance under fast testing conditions than other groups, possibly as a function of traditional emphasis on perseverance and reservedness.

2931. Baron A: Aggression as a function of ambient temperature and prior anger arousal. J Pers Soc Psychol 21:183–189.

Aggression is inhibited rather than facilitated by high temperatures, regardless of prior anger arousal.

2932. Barzilai S, Davies AM: Personality and social aspects of mental disease in Jerusalem women. Int J Soc Psychiatry 18: 22–28.

Hospitalized mentally ill Jewish married women in Jerusalem are characterized by earlier marriages and lower social status as indicated by their husbands' occupations. The lower educational and occupational levels are a result, rather than a cause, of their psychopathology.

2933. Bastiaans J: General comments on the role of aggression in human psychopathology. Psychother Psychosom 20:300–311.

Many syndromes of psychiatry and psychosomatic medicine reveal the failure of healthy problemsolving on the level of socio-psycho-biological adaptation and aggression regulation. Instrumental, situational, and obediential aggression can be used for the reinforcement of the feeling states of safety, freedom, and completeness.

2934. Bat-Hall MA, Mehryar AH, Sabharwal B: The correlation between Piaget's conservation of quantity tests and three measures of intelligence in a select group of children in Iran. J Psychol 80: 197–202.

Positive correlations between three measures of intelligence and Piaget's conservation tasks for an Iranian sample suggest the presence of a common general factor.

2935. Baumrind D: An exploratory study of socialization effects on black children: some black-white comparisons. Child Dev 43:261–267.

If black families are viewed by white norms they appear authoritarian, but unlike their white counterparts, the most authoritarian black families produce the most self-assertive and independent girls.

2936. Beier E, Zautra A: Identification of vocal communication of emotion across cultures. J Consult Clin Psychol 39:166.

Results from American, Polish, and Japanese samples indicate intracultural information can be transmitted on a nonverbal vocal channel, although some noise enters the system.

2937. Beiser M, Ravel JL, Collomb H, Egelhoff C: Assessing psychiatric disorder among the Serer of Senegal. J Nerv Ment Dis 154:141–151.

It is possible to develop a standardized instrument for gathering data about psychiatric illness in a "primitive" culture. When the Serer speak of "illness of the spirit" they mean approximately what a psychiatrist does when he speaks of "mental disorder."

2938. Belcher JC, Vasquez-Calcerrada PB: A cross-cultural approach to the social functions of housing. J Marriage Fam 34:750–762.

Family functions are influenced by the characteristics of the home. There are culturally specific differences in house functions as perceived in terms of a dream home for rural Georgians, Puerto Ricans, and Dominicans, but generally the higher the SES of the group, the more functions satisfied within the home.

2939. Bennett M: Predictions and determinants of educational performance in the South Pacific. J Soc Psychol 88:145–146.

The predictive value of a test for rural and urban Fijian children is inversely related to the internal strength of the text where there are variations in the experience of the children.

2940. Berger B, Hackett B, Millar RM: The communal family. Fam Coordinator 21:419–428.

A typology of communes on an urban-rural and creedal-noncreedal basis clarifies the concept of commune.

2941. Beshai JA: Content analysis of Egyptian stories. J Soc Psychol 87:197–204.

School reading books reflect the rise in achievement imagery across three periods of social change and reflect certain semantic inconsistencies that accompany differences between the views of Western and developing countries.

2942. Bloom JD: Population trends of Alaska natives and the need for planning. Am J Psychiatry 128:998–1002.

Current cross-cultural contacts and changes will increase among Indians, Eskimos, and Aleuts as the population, due to improved medical care, becomes increasingly skewed toward the young.

2943. Bloomberg SG: The present state of suicide prevention: an African survey. Int J Soc Psychiatry 18:104–108.

The African's spontaneous reaction to stress and his expression of aggression are extrapunitive in nature and have tended to lead him toward homicidal rather than suicidal behavior. Suicide does not constitute a serious problem in Black Africa. However, with Africa's economic progress, suicide may before long present a major social problem. Organizations like the South African Suicide Prevention Centre can do much both to aid individuals and to prepare for what could become an increasing problem.

2944. Bock EW: Aging and suicide: the significance of marital, kinship and alternative relations. Fam Coordinator 21:71–80.

Study of suicides in a retirement community indicates that older marrieds need kinship, friendship, and community interaction to combat their greater isolation.

2945. Borke H, Su S: Perception of emotional responses to social interaction by Chinese and American children. J Cross-Cultural Psychol 3:309–314.

Chinese children perceive more angry reactions in social interaction situations, while American children perceive more sad reactions. These differences may be related to differing child-rearing practices.

2946. Borude RR, Rajkarne CG, de Souza TA, Janbandhu DS: Rural-urban and sex differences in the valuation of fifty activities: a cross-cultural study. Int J Psychol 7:191–195.

Indian activity preferences differ from American preferences with respect to recreational activities; although there is general agreement between cultures, sexes, and rural-urban groups.

2947. Bruhn HG, Philips BU, Wolf S: Social readjustment and illness patterns: comparisons between first, second and third generation Italian-Americans living in the same community. J Psychosom Res 16:387–394.

Roseto, Pennsylvania, has been undergoing rapid acculturation into the conventional American pattern over the past seven to ten years. Changes in community and family ties are reflected in the Holmes Social Readjustment Rating Questionnaire. Generational groups differ with respect to the type of life change they experience.

2948. Burr WS: Role transition: a reformulation of theory. J Marriage Fam 34:407–416.

Reworking of theoretical propositions provides a model that permits the formulation of deductions about factors that influence variations in the ease of role transitions.

2949. Calestro KM: Psychotherapy, faith healing, and suggestion. Int J Psychiatry 10:83–113.

The use of therapeutic suggestibility by shamans and faith healers and its importance to Western psychotherapy must be further researched.

2950. Cawte JE: Discussion of psychiatric pluralism. Int J Psychiatry 10:47–52.

Anthropological evidence from Australia supports psychiatric pluralism as a medical aim, in spite of some reservations concerning feasibility.

2951. Chandra S: An assessment of perceptual acuity in Fiji: a cross-cultural study with Indians and Fijians. J Cross-Cultural Psychol 3:401–406.

Performance on a perceptual acuity test is significantly correlated with age and is related to sex. Differences between Fijian and Indian youths and between delinquents and nondelinquents are insignificant.

2952. Chiu LH: A cross-cultural comparison of cognitive styles in Chinese and American children. Int J Psychol 7:235–242.

Chinese and American comparisons indicate that cultural differences in attitudes, values, and modes of thinking are as important as differences in child-rearing practices in structuring cognitive style.

2953. Chiu TL, Tong JE, Schmidt KE: A clinical and survey study of latah in Sarawak, Malaysia. Psychol Med 2:155–165.

Latah, a predominately female behavioral phenomenon occurring mainly in the Maylay archipelago, is characterized by echolalia, echopraxia, and command automatism. Latah never occurs in social isolation, and the condition will probably become less prevalent with increased education of the population.

2954. Chopra GS: Sociological and economic aspects of drug dependence in India. Int J Addict 7:57–69.

Patterns of drug abuse of opium, cannabis, and alcohol have changed little during the last decades. Drug abuse is associated with urbanization, industrialization, poor living conditions, and unfavorable working conditions.

2955. Chrzanowski G: Transcultural psychiatry. Contemp Psychoanal 8:194 196.

To obtain more reliable data in the area of transcultural psychiatry we need: (1) a sharper distinction between sustained, disciplined research and travelogues, (2) a clarification of nosological entities in diagnostic evaluations, (3) a consideration of variables with respect to age, sex, education, and socioeconomic factors, and (4) the maintenance of ongoing research collaboration.

2956. Ciborowski T, Cole M: A cross-cultural study of conjunctive and disjunctive concept learning. Child Dev 43:774–789.

The performances of Americans and Liberians on concept-formation experiments are strikingly similar. Evidence of cultural differences centers on measures of the way stimuli are classified into subclasses and the relation between learning and verbalization.

2957. Cohen RE: Principles of preventive mental health programs for ethnic minority populations: the acculturation of Puerto Ricans to the United States. Am J Psychiatry 128:1529–1533.

The differences between Puerto Rican migrant value systems and those of the larger culture can cause difficulties in adjustment for both the migrant and the institutions that serve him.

2958. Collett P: Structure and content in cross-cultural studies of self-esteem. Int J Psychol 7:169–179.

Investigations of structure may be preferable and more illuminating than investigations of content in cross-cultural studies of self-esteem, as shown in various investigations of English-Arab comparison groups.

2959. Conco WZ: The African Bantu traditional practice of medicine: some preliminary observations. Soc Sci Med 6:283–322.

The doctor working in Africa must have a thorough and sympathetic understanding of the extent and strength of traditional African medicine. Understanding of African medical beliefs must begin with a systematic and true account in subjective terms of what some Africans do, think, entertain, and fear in problematic situations, sickness, and disease.

2960. Consalvi C: An item and factor analysis of Danish, Lebanese, and United States college students' responses to the Marlowe-Crowne Social Desirability Scale. J Cross-Cultural Psychol 3:361–372.

Factor analysis indicates only a moderate similarity among the groups. In general, findings support the use of the Marlowe-Crowne Scale among Lebanese and Danish student groups.

2961. Crowther B: Patterns of drug use among Mexican Americans. Int J Addict 7:637–648.

Mexican-Americans, valuing drugs for their escape properties, experiment with drugs much less than do Anglo drug addicts.

2962. Dasen PR: Cross-cultural Piagetian research: a summary. J Cross-Cultural Psychol 3:23–40.

Descriptive studies, which attempt a cross-cultural verification of Piaget's stages, may be examined according to three interpretations of these stages. More quasi-experimental research is needed in order to relate the qualitative and quantitative aspects of operational development to cultural factors.

2963. Dasen PR: The development of conservation in aboriginal children: a replication study. Int J Psychol 7:75–85.

European and aboriginal children do not differ on qualitative aspects of operative development, although development is slower for aboriginal children. No quantity-weight reversal or genetic differences are found for full or part aborigine subjects.

2964. Davidoff J: The effect of colour distraction on a matching task in Ghanaian children: a methodological note. Int J Psychol 7:141–144.

Unschooled Ghanaian children tend to give color rather than form responses; whereas nursery-school children give an unexpectedly high proportion of

form responses. The latter finding brings into question the effect of the apparatus and questions used.

2965. Davidson JRT: Post-partum mood change in Jamaican women: a description and discussion on its significance. Br J Psychiatry 121:659–663.

Nearly two thirds of Jamaican women experience some emotional upset during the first 11 days post-partum. In form the "blues" do not differ from the condition reported in other cultures, but they have a different meaning in this population.

2966. Davidson L: "Devi" and transcultural psychiatry. Contemp Psychoanal 8:173–179.

An analysis of the Indian film *Devi*, the story of an Indian girl born and married into high caste Bengal Brahmin society 100 years ago, reveals parallels between her life and role with that of women in contemporary Western society.

2967. Dawson JLM: Temne-Arunta hand-eye dominance and cognitive style. Int J Psychol 7:219–233.

Conformist Temne culture reflects a low incidence of left-handedness, while more permissive Arunta and Eskimo cultures have a relatively high incidence of left-handedness. Mixed hand-eye dominance subjects show field-dependent style on all tests.

2968. Dawson JLM, Ng W, Cheung W: Effects of parental attitudes and modern exposure on Chinese traditional-modern attitude formation. J Cross-Cultural Psychol 3:201–208.

Children in an agricultural village have more traditional attitudes than those of older adolescents. Students attending a Chinese middle school are influenced by parental attitudes, while students at an Anglo-Chinese school in Hong Kong are influenced by parental attitudes and mass media.

2969. Dawson JLM, Whitney RE, Lau RTS: Attitude conflict, GSR, and traditional-modern attitude change among Hong Kong Chinese. J Soc Psychol 88:163–176.

Level of traditional-modern attitude conflict is related to the importance of beliefs for Hong Kong Chinese. Attitude change that reduces discrepancy between peers is correlated with pre-GSR when conflict and importance are high, but not when low.

2970. Dean SR, Thong D: Shamanism versus psychiatry in Bali, "Isle of the Gods": some modern implications. Am J Psychiatry 129:59–62.

Analogies may be drawn between the therapeutic practices of Balinese native healers and modern concepts of treatment.

2971. deLacey PR: A relationship between classificatory ability and verbal intelligence. Int J Psychol 7:243–246.

Data from Australian children's test performance suggest that correlation between Piagetian classificatory ability and verbal-intelligence may be a function of environmental enrichment.

2972. Deregowski JB: Drawing ability of Soli rural children: a note. J Soc Psychol 86:311–312.

Assessments of Zambian children's drawings (grades 5–7) generate low marks for awareness of perspective and high marks for artistic merit assuming a specific grade level. Comparison to English pupils suggests that the higher age of Zambian students fails to compensate entirely for various handicaps.

2973. Deregowski JB: Reproduction of orientation of Kohs-type figures: a cross-cultural study. Br J Psychol 63:283–296.

Zambian difficulties with a Kohs-type task verify the hypothesis that stability of the model is of primary importance over symmetry. An Icelandic sample made few errors and could not therefore be used to evaluate the hypothesis.

2974. Deregowski JB: The role of symmetry in pattern reproduction by Zambian children. J Cross-Cultural Psychol 3:303–308.

The only significant difference obtained in a study of the influence of symmetry is in number of errors for stimuli showing symmetry about the vertical axis, and vertically repeated symmetry. The nature of matrix pattern difficulties for Zambian children is probably similar to the difficulties observed for Western cultures.

2975. DuCette J, Wolk S, Friedman S: Locus of control and creativity in black and white children. J Soc Psychol 88:297–298.

Internals are more creative and efficient than externals, but neither race nor dependent variable interactions are significant.

2976. Ellsworth PC, Carlsmith JM, Henson A: The stare as a stimulus to flight in human subjects: a series of field experiments. J Pers Soc Psychol 21:302–311.

Staring at pedestrians and motorists at a traffic light results in shorter crossing time by subjects, thus suggesting some correspondence with primate staring.

2977. Eswara HS: Administration of reward and punishment in relation to ability, effort, and performance. J Soc Psychol 87:139–140.

Performance and effort, but not ability, are effective in influencing the distribution of reward and punishment by East Indian students. Cultural belief in ability as God-given and unchanging may account for this particular outcome.

2978. Fabrega H: The study of disease in relation to culture. Behav Sci 17:183–203.

A perspective for studying health and illness cross-culturally is suggested by different conceptual frameworks for describing disease and applying traditional sociomedical approaches in preliterate contexts.

2979. Feitelson D, Weintraub S, Michaeli O: Social interactions in heterogeneous preschools in Israel. Child Dev 43:1249–1259.

When children from disadvantaged and privileged homes are brought together during free play school time, their respective home environments do not seem to contain enough common elements to make joint participation in play themes possible. Teachers can sometimes overcome obstacles to mutual play by providing shared experiences.

2980. Figa-Talamanca I: Inconsistencies of attitudes and behavior in family planning studies. J Marriage Fam 34:336–344.

Favorable attitudes to family planning are often inconsistent with actual behaviors. Cultural and personal situational factors and social change must be considered as a prerequisite to fertility control programs.

2981. Foggitt RH, Mangan GL, Law H: Cognitive performance and linguistic codability. Int J Psychol 7:155–161.

Differences in factor content for European and aboriginal performance in the Queensland subtests suggest that individuals of different cultures may apply different abilities to the same problem. Intercultural comparisons using this type of test may be inappropriate.

2982. Freedman AM: Drugs and society: an ecological approach. Compr Psychiatry 13:411–420.

A sense of injustice, entwined with a feeling of

powerlessness, contributes to the wide use of drugs among young people. Psychopathologists must play a role in developing techniques that provide a sense of personal worth and dignity to populations at risk.

2983. Frost BP, Iwawaki S: Argentinian, Canadian, Japanese and Puerto Rican norms on the Frost Self Description Questionnaire. J Cross-Cultural Psychol 3:215–218.

The English and Japanese versions of the Frost Questionnaire are valid and reliable, but the Spanish-language version requires further investigation.

2984. Garcia AB, Zimmerman BJ: The effect of examiner ethnicity and language on the performance of bilingual Mexican-American first graders. J Soc Psychol 87:3–12.

A Mexican-American examiner elicits higher response levels from Mexican-American children. Praise given in English is more effective when it follows praise given in Spanish.

2985. Gardner HW: The use of human figure drawings to assess a cultural value: smiling in Thailand. J Psychol 80:203–204.

Drawings of smiling human figures are common among Thai youths and reflect the degree to which smiling is culturally approved or valued.

2986. Gardner RC, Kirby DM, Gorospe FH, Vielamin AC: Ethnic stereotypes: an alternative assessment technique, the stereotype differential. J Soc Psychol 87:259–267.

The stereotype differential is advantageous in providing an individual difference measure of extent of adoption of stereotype.

2987. Garza JM, Rao N: Attitudes toward employment and employment status of mothers in Hyderabad, India. J Marriage Fam 34:153–155.

Dissatisfaction with husband's level of income, desire for material comfort, educational aspirations for offspring, desire for increased social contact, and perceived image of working mother are significantly related to mother's employment status.

2988. German GA: Aspects of clinical psychiatry in Sub-Saharan Africa. Br J Psychiatry 121:461–479.

Psychiatric disorders are no less frequent in Africa than in developed countries. Although the general picture of mental illness is similar to other parts of the world, differences are determined by physiological deprivations and physical disease and by cultural differences and widespread illiteracy.

2989. Gharagozlu-Hamadani H: Psychiatric evaluation of 100 cases of suicidal attempts in Shiraz, Iran. Int J Soc Psychiatry 18:140–144.

In Shiraz, poverty is not an important reason for attempting suicide. However, inability to express aggression following a quarrel is an important motivation for suicide.

2990. Gibson G: Kin family network: overheralded structure in past conceptualization of family functioning. J Marriage Fam 34:13–23.

The case against the isolated nuclear family and in favor of the extended-kin system has not yet been satisfactorily demonstrated. A study of disability applicants concludes that the household is the basic family system for nuclear families and for the non-married the extended-kin network is basic.

2991. Giora Z, Esformes Y, Barak A: Dreams in cross-cultural research. Compr Psychiatry 13:105–114.

Factorial analysis of recalled dreams of Israeli and Arab high school students show differences regarding the internalization of social values. Dreams are a valuable tool in cross-cultural research.

2992. Gitter AG, Mostofsky DI, Satow Y: The effect of skin color and physiognomy on racial misidentification. J Soc Psychol 88:139–143.

Black children tend to misidentify race more than white children, and physiognomy is more salient in misidentification than skin color. The effect of new black race awareness is yet to be determined.

2993. Glidden HW: The Arab world. Am J Psychiatry 128:984–988.

The Arab value system demands complete solidarity, thus preventing any Arab nation from proposing compromise with Israel. It also encourages rivalry among Arab nations because they fear one group may achieve dominance over the others. This cultural conflict is a major reason for the seeming insolubility of the difficulties between Israel and the Arab nations.

2994. Goldstine T, Gutmann D: A TAT study of Navajo aging. Psychiatry 35:373–384.

TAT responses of Navaho men shift from an active orientation in younger men to a passive and magical orientation in older men, thus supporting a developmental theory of aging.

2995. Gordon CP, Gallimore R: Teacher ratings of behavior problems of Hawaiian-American adolescents. J Cross-Cultural Psychol 3:209–213.

Two factors are extracted from teachers' responses to a behavior problem checklist for Hawaiian and part-Hawaiian students—disruptiveness and passive withdrawal. Due to typical school situations, behavior problems reported by teachers are very similar across situations and cultures.

2996. Gould KH: Parsis and urban demography: some research possibilities. J Marriage Fam 34: 345–352.

Alleged lack of rural-urban fertility differential in India may be due to conceptual difficulties of the urban variable. Studies of Parsis and other pure urban groups may provide a more accurate picture of urban fertility.

2997. Granzberg G: Hopi initiation rites—a case study of the validity of the Freudian theory of culture. J Soc Psychol 87:189–196.

Hopi initiation rites change disruptive behavior into nondisruptive, conforming behavior. This is consistent with predictions from Whiting's Freudian interpretation of initiation and culture-serving individual needs. Symbolic interaction interpretations and Freudian theory may be compatible.

2998. Greenglass ER: A comparison of maternal communication style between immigrant Italian and second-generation Italian women living in Canada. J Cross-Cultural Psychol 3:185–192.

Communication style for Italian immigrant mothers is characterized by direct imperatives. Canadian mothers rely on indirect forms for control, and second-generation Italian mothers are most likely to employ justifications.

2999. Greenspan S: Leaving the kibbutz: an identity conflict. Psychiatry 35:291–304.

Internal conflict is fostered in young kibbutzniks by their parents' emphasis on independence and individual fulfillment versus kibbutz unity and loyalty.

3000. Groen JJ: The study of human aggression. Psychother Psychosom 20:312–315.

Human aggressive behavior during a brawl between students and police suggests that at least some components of human aggression are controlled by nervous systems that can function more or less independently from those that control speech, conscious thinking, and reflection.

3001. Haavio-Mannila E: Cross-national differences in adoption of new ideologies and practices in family life. J Marriage Fam 34:525–537.

Families at the center of a valley boundary between Sweden and Finland adopt more new practices and ideologies than families at the periphery. Differences between the countries are greater at the center than at the periphery, possibly due to the more rapid economic and social development of Sweden.

3002. Harding VSV: A method of evaluating osseous development from birth to 14 years. Child Dev 23:247–271.

Children tend to maintain a fairly constant rate of osseous development over long periods of time. By the use of X-rays and specialized charts, osseous development can be simply estimated.

3003. Hartog J: The intervention system for mental and social deviants in Malaysia. Soc Sci Med 6: 211–220.

Intervention systems for mental and social deviants in Malaysia operate through two distinct channels: in one, primarily medical and psychiatric, the village folk healer (bomoh) plays a pivotal role; in the other, for the criminal, delinquent, and insane, the village headman (ketua) and higher government officers are most influential. Folk healers are being discredited and may die out. More humane psychiatric treatment units and outpatient clinics are being established.

3004. Hautaluoma JE, Loomis RJ: Perception of visual illusions in a sample of Afghan boys. J Soc Psychol 87:143–145.

With the exception of the Sander parallelogram, data on Nuristani Afghan boys are consistent with other findings that Western samples are more likely than Eastern samples to see the Muller-Lyer and less susceptible to horizontal-vertical illusions.

3005. Hayes DP, Sievers S: A sociolinguistic investigation of the dimensions of interpersonal behavior. J Pers Soc Psychol 24:254–261.

The study of English and Spanish-language lexemes suggests a parabolic, rather than an independence, model of affect and prominence in interpersonal behavior.

3006. Henderson DJ: Incest: a synthesis of data. Can Psychiatr Assoc J 17:299–313.

Although incest itself is uncommon, the incest taboo, which has cultural variations, is universal. Drastic role shifts accompany overt incest in a dysfunctional family setting. Desertion anxiety is a recurrent theme in the psychodynamics of incest.

3007. Hendrie H, Hanson D: A comparative study of the psychiatric care of Indian and Metis. Am J Orthopsychiatry 42:480–489.

Indian and Metis patients in Winnipeg with the diagnosis of personality disorder received fewer follow-up outpatient appointments and had a shorter hospital stay than did control patients. The difference may be attributed to staff attitudes.

3008. Hinde RA: Mother-infant separation in Rhesus monkeys. J Psychosom Res 16:227–228.

Mother-infant interaction and infant behavior return more rapidly to normal after reunion in infant-removed infants than in mother-removed ones. This is presumably because the prime determiner of the relationship, the mother, suffers less trauma and is less disturbed than the mother of the mother-removed infant.

3009. Hinde RA, Davies L: Removing infant Rhesus from mother for 13 days compared with removing mother from infant. J Child Psychol Psychiatry 13:227–237.

Infant monkeys removed from their mothers are less disturbed than infants left in a familiar environment whose mothers are removed from them. This may be because infant-removed infants have no unpleasant experience in the home pen, or it may be due to the fact that infant-removed mothers suffer less trauma and thus can participate in a more rapid restoration of normal relations with their infants.

3010. Hobart CW: Sexual permissiveness in young English and French Canadians. J Marriage Fam 34:292–304.

Factorial analysis of permissive attitudes and behavior demonstrates a significant increase in reported intercourse experience by women, especially among English students, and the emergence of a new sexual morality.

3011. Ibsen CA, Klobus P: Fictive kin term use and social relationships: alternative interpretations. J Marriage Fam 34:615–620.

Contemporary American society utilizes fictive kin terms (1) to address persons assuming a supplementary of replacement kin status; (2) as a form of address to express familiarity in a personal relationship; and mostly (3) as a public validation of a special kind of association.

3012. Iwawaki S, Lynn R: Measuring achievement motivation in Japan and Great Britain. J Cross-Cultural Psychol 3:219–220.

Differences in the means between Japanese and British male students on achievement motivation are not statistically significant, suggesting that the economic growth rates of the two countries should converge in the next few decades.

3013. Jackson JJ: Comparative life styles and family and friend relationships among black women. Fam Coordinator 21:477–486.

A great similarity between married and spouseless women is demonstrated, but the need for further data is great. Greater contact frequency and satisfaction with friends rather than with children is shown for both groups.

3014. Jackson JJ: Marital life among aging blacks. Fam Coordinator 21:21–28.

Interview data from low-income, Southern, urban, aged blacks indicate matriarchy is not the dominant pattern.

3015. Jilek-Aall LM: What is a Sasquatch—or, the problematics of reality testing. Can Psychiatr Assoc J 17:243–247.

Investigation of belief in the Sasquatch legend indicates that it is more difficult for the people in isolated remote areas to distinguish hearsay and imagination from reality. Formal education and urban residence play a part in belief phenomena.

3016. Jones IH: Psychiatric disorders among aborigines of the Australian Western desert. Soc Sci Med 6:263–267.

The principal differences in the type of psychiatric illness seen between the aborigines of the Australian Western desert and Western communities is the absence of suicide and homosexuality, the virtual absence of "free floating anxiety," and the occurrence of possession syndromes. The principal personality disorders are characterized by excessive aggressive behavior, an exaggeration of an already prominent cultural trait.

3017. Jones RR, Popper R: Characteristics of Peace Corps host countries and the behavior of volunteers. J Cross-Cultural Psychol 3:233–246.

Early termination of Peace Corps volunteers is more likely in countries with high linguistic standardization, socioeconomic development, and cultural exposure. In countries with low cultural exposure, volunteers may be more successful as agents of change due to their unusualness.

3018. Kaffman M: Characteristics of the emotional pathology of the kibbutz child. Am J Orthopsychiatry 42:692–709.

Kibbutz children and youth do not reveal any specific personality type developmental deviations or distinctive psychiatric syndromes.

3019. Kaffman M: Family conflict in the psychopathology of the kibbutz child. Fam Process 11:171–188.

A distinct pattern of family malfunctioning is one of the central etiological factors influencing the psychopathology of the kibbutz-reared child, despite the socializing functions of the kibbutz educators.

3020. Kagan S, Madsen MC: Rivalry in Anglo-American and Mexican-American children of two ages. J Pers Soc Psychol 24:214–220.

Anglo children are more rivalrous than Mexican-American children and develop increasing male rivalry with age.

3021. Kagitcibasi C: Application of the D 48 test of general intellectual ability in Turkey. J Cross-Cultural Psychol 3:169–176.

The D 48, or Dominoes, test of general intellectual ability has high predictive validity for school achievement in Turkey.

3022. Kalant OJ: Report of the Indian Hemp Drugs Commission, 1893–94: a critical review. Int J Addict 7:77–96.

The depth, scope, and objectivity of an early British government investigation in India are relevant to contemporary issues.

3023. Kandal DB, Lesser GS: Marital decision-making in American and Danish urban families: a research note. J Marriage Fam 34:134–138.

In both countries marital power does not always positively correlate with spouses' resources. Wife's employment does, however, contribute to her decisionmaking power in the household.

3024. Kanekar S, Mukerjee S: Intelligence, extraversion, and neuroticism in relation to season of birth. J Soc Psychol 86:309–310.

Summer-born Indian students have higher intelligence scores than winter-born students, but no association between extraversion or neuroticism and season of birth is evident.

3025. Kang TS: Name and group identification. J Soc Psychol 86:159–160.

Shifts in social identity are reflected in name changing by more outgroup oriented Chinese students.

3026. Kar SB: Opinion towards induced abortion among urban women in Delhi, India. Soc Sci Med 6:731–736.

An overwhelming majority of currently married urban women in Delhi approve induced abortion as a family-planning method under the following ranking conditions: rape, deformed offspring, and unwed pregnancy. Previous experience of abortion and contraception are significantly related with approval of abortion.

3027. Kassees AS: Cross-cultural comparative familism of a Christian Arab people. J Marriage Fam 34:538–544.

Familistic attitudes are more pronounced among immigrants to U.S. individualistic culture than among those Christian Arabs remaining in Palestine (occupied Jordan).

3028. Kelleher MJ: Cross-national (Anglo-Irish) differences in obsessional symptoms and traits of personality. Psychol Med 2:33–41.

The Irish possess more obsessional symptoms and traits of personality than the English. There may be a relationship between the attitudes to sex in Irish culture and the higher obsessional scores of Irish subjects.

3029. Kershner JR: Ethnic group differences in children's ability to reproduce direction and orientation. J Soc Psychol 88:3–13.

Cognitive style for Chicano children is analytic-spatial and for Anglo children is global-verbal.

3030. Khatri AA: The Indian family: an empirically derived analysis of shifts in size and types. J Marriage Fam 34:725–734.

Most of the households are of a nuclear family type, while a female child averaging 14.10 years is found exposed to 6.14 shifts in family figures. The occurrence of extended and joint family types raises questions concerning the life cycle of the Indian family and the use of the nuclear family type as a reference point in cross-cultural analysis.

3031. Kinzie D, Sushama PC, Lee M: Cross-cultural family therapy—a Malaysian experience. Fam Process 11:59–68.

Some of the problems of cross-cultural family therapy are exemplified by a case study of a family in Malaysia.

3032. Kinzie JD: Cross-cultural psychotherapy: the Malaysian experience: an open system model. Am J Psychother 26:220–231.

Therapy in Malaysia exemplifies the difficulties in cross-cultural treatment. When cultural differences are recognized and handled directly, a stable system of interaction can often be established in which there is progression to a new level of interaction that may be independent of the initial preconceptions of the two participants.

3033. Kinzie JD, Shore JH, Pattison EM: Anatomy of psychiatric consultation to rural Indians. Community Ment Health J 8:196–207.

An active mental health consultation program can be developed with a rural, isolated, Indian community. The development of mental health services must be developed within the political, social, geographical, and economic parameters of the community.

3034. Kraus RF: A psychoanalytic interpretation of shamanism. Psychoanal Rev 59:19–32.

The shaman differs little in general characteristics from others in his population, but is exquisitely sensitive to environmental cues and is capable of regression in service of the ego to primary process levels of thinking and perception.

3035. Kriger SF, Kroes WH: Child-rearing attitudes of Chinese, Jewish, and Protestant mothers. J Soc Psychol 86:205–210.

Chinese mothers are higher on control or restrictive attitudes than Jewish and Protestant mothers, but on a rejection scale no significant differences are obtained between the three.

3036. Kugelmass S, Lieblich A, Erlich C: Perceptual exploration in Israel Jewish and of Israeli-Bedouin children. J Cross-Cultural Psychol 3:345–352.

An investigation of the effects of Arabic language structure and exposure to printed materials upon the perceptual exploration of the Israeli-Bedouin children suggests that the greater the right-left directionality of the environment, the lower the frequency of left-right patterns of organization.

3037. Kuiper PC: Some theoretical remarks about the theme aggression. Psychother Psychosom 20:260–267.

Aggressive behavior comes into being when libidinal and ego forces are frustrated. The libido-versus-aggression hypothesis is an excellent tool in psychotherapy for investigating the fantasies of the patient and expressing his instinctual forces.

3038. Kuvlesky WP, Obordo AS: A racial comparison of teen-age girls' projections for marriage and procreation. J Marriage Fam 34:75–84.

Both black and white girls desire and expect small families, but more black girls desire later marriage and employment opportunities *after* arrival of children.

3039. Lange A: Possible determinants of aggression. Psychother Psychosom 20:241–248.

Contrary to the thinking of the last decades, frustration cannot simply be held as a major determinant of aggressive behavior. The situation, the kind of frustration, and the pattern of acquired reactions of the victim determine what the results of frustration will be.

3040. Langgalung H, Torrance EP: The development of causal thinking of children in Mexico and the United States. J Cross-Cultural Psychol 3:315–320.

American children are more causally oriented than their Mexican counterparts. Sixth graders and advantaged children are more causally oriented than fourth graders or disadvantaged children.

3041. LaPierre YD: Koro in a French Canadian. Can Psychiatr Assoc J 17:333–334.

Although cultural factors are usually significant in the development of the koro syndrome, which is most common in Asia, in the case of a French-Canadian the symptoms are possibly due to psychogenic depersonalization arising from operative or postoperative stress.

3042. Larsen KS: Determinants of peace agreement, pessimism-optimisim, and expectation of world conflict: a cross-national study. J Cross-Cultural Psychol 3:283–292.

Individuals low in social and personal power are more likely to agree with peace proposals, expect greater future conflict, and be pessimistic concerning the future.

3043. Laver AB: Precursors of psychology in ancient Egypt. J Hist Behav Sciences 8:181–195.

Some idea of ancient Egyptian psychology can be found in temple and tomb evidence on the mortuary cult; the heart as the seat of life, the brain, the name, the *ba,* the *ka,* the shadow, the mind and heart.

3044. Lefley HP: Modal personality in the Bahamas. J Cross-Cultural Psychol 3:135–148.

The modal personality of Bahamian adults is

characterized by passivity, hostility and acquiescence to authority, internalization of anger, lack of achievement orientation, emphasis on interpersonal relations and psychological equilibrium, and deemphasis of economics.

3045. Leiblich A, Ninio A, Kugelmass S: Effects of ethnic origin and parental SES on WPPSI performance of pre-school children in Israel. J Cross-Cultural Psychol 3:159–168.

Differences in level of mental ability can be found for Israeli groups of different origins, but no significant difference in pattern of mental ability is found.

3046. Leon CA: Psychiatry in Latin America. Br J Psychiatry 121:121–136.

Machismo nurtures violence. There is a vicious-circle relationship between lack of adequate health services and magical or folk practices of medicine.

3047. Lerner RM, Korn SJ: The development of body-build stereotypes in males. Child Dev 43:908–920.

At all age levels, people hold a predominantly favorable view of the mesomorph, a markedly unfavorable view of the endomorph, and a somewhat negative but still favorable view of the ectomorph.

3048. Long BH, Henderson EH, Gantcheff H, Kastersztein J: Self-other orientations of English and French adolescents in Europe and Canada. Int J Psychol 7:181–189.

Although the precise origins for differences in interpersonal orientations are unclear, cultural effects for Canadian and European adolescents are obtained.

3049. Looft WR, Rayman BB: Children's judgments of age in Sarawak. J Soc Psychol 86:181–186.

Older children make more accurate age estimates of human figure drawings than younger children, using fatness and strength of drawing as decision aids.

3050. Loudon JB: Social anthropology and psychiatry. Psychol Med 2:1–6.

Confused short-term exploration by psychiatrists and social anthropologists of each other's territory without an up-to-date "map" has been a major source of difficulty in the past. Concentration by members of each discipline on the central interests of the other is likely to be less frustrating and more fruitful in the long run.

3051. Lowe JD Jr, Hildman LK: EPI scores as a function of race. Br J Soc Clin Psychol 11:191–192.

Analysis of the results of the EPI for black and white Southern students suggests that the testers might establish local norms for performance. Extraversion scores are significantly lower for blacks and higher for whites.

3052. McGhee PE: Methodological and theoretical considerations for a cross-cultural investigation of children's humor. Int J Psychol 7:13–21.

Identifying the cultural cues that lead children in different countries to fantasy-assimilate an event rather than reality-assimilate, and a consideration of nonmotivational bases, are some problems in the assessment of children's humor.

3053. McIntire WG, Nass GD, Dryer AS: A cross-cultural comparison of adolescent perception of parental roles. J Marriage Fam 34:735–740.

In a comparison of samples from the United States, Ghana, and Israel, perception of parent functioning in instrumental and expressive areas supports neither the Parsons-Bales nor Breznitz-Kugelmass models of role differentiation.

3054. McKendry JM, McKendry MS, Guthrie GM: Inflated expectations and social reinforcement in the lowland Philippines. J Cross-Cultural Psychol 3:83–92.

Planned social change tends to produce modern value systems and general contentment along with greater emphasis on governmental obligation to continue to meet the people's needs.

3055. McManus M: Behavior on nonoutcome problems of U.S. and Caribbean Island preschool children. Int J Psychol 7:163–167.

Netherland West Indies preschoolers demonstrate problem-solving processes similar to U.S. preschoolers. Though they do not possess the concept of "middle-size," systematic response preferences along these lines are obtained.

3056. Manganyi N: Body image, boundary differentiation, and self-esteeming behavior in African paraplegics. J Pers Assess 36:45–49.

Hypothesized pathological body image and higher passive-submission dimension for paraplegics are unsubstantiated. Experiment and control groups are characterized by a field-dependent perceptual framework, indefinite body-image boundaries, and lack of self-steering behavior as a consequence of the cultural circumstance.

3057. Marshall JF: A conceptual framework for viewing responses to family planning programs. J Cross-Cultural Psychol 3:1–22.

Decisionmaking with respect to family planning in a North Indian village involves individual cognitive and cultural response determinants. The response processes involved may be explained by a synthesis of conflict and dissonance theory.

3058. Matchett W: Repeated hallucinatory experiences as a part of mourning process among Hopi Indian women. Psychiatry 35:185–194.

Intense grief and the hope of "bringing back the dead" may trigger visual hallucinations of deceased family members in Hopi women mourners.

3059. Mayovich MK: Stereotypes and racial images—white, black and yellow. Int J Soc Psychiatry 18:239–253.

Except among children, explicitly derogatory racial epithets are disappearing but are being replaced by more subtle ethnic humor.

3060. Meade RD: Future time perspectives of Americans and subcultures in India. J Cross-Cultural Psychol 3:93–100.

Kshatriya, Sikh, Parsee, and American groups having higher achievement needs tend to write stories with themes concerning the future; while Brahmins, Vasiyas, Sudras, and Muslims write stories with themes concerning the past.

3061. Mehta PH, Rohila PK, Sundberg ND, Tyler LE: Future time perspectives of adolescents in India and the United States. Cross-Cultural Psychol 3:293–302.

Although there is a marked similarity between Indian and American views of life planning time perspectives, content analysis shows the American students emphasize leisure and own life events while Indians emphasize others' life events.

3062. Mieman RJ, Guthrie GM: The effects of age and cultural familiarity on children's categorization responses. J Soc Psychol 86:299–308.

A nonverbal intelligence test shows differences in conceptualization and strategy by age and the influence of cultural familiarity in the Philippines.

3063. Miller AG, Thomas R: Cooperation and competition among Blackfoot Indian and urban Canadian children. Child Dev 43:1104–1110.

There is a marked tendency for Blackfoot children to cooperate with each other when it is adap-

tive to do so. They are better able to inhibit competitive responses than are non-Indian children. This behavior may be related to the Blackfoot traditions of sharing material wealth within the family and the sharing of child-rearing and housekeeping duties. The specific way that cultural factors find expression in cooperative behaviors is not known.

3064. Missakian EA: Effects of adult social experience on patterns of reproductive activity of socially deprived male Rhesus monkeys. J Pers Soc Psychol 21:131–134.

Socially deprived adult male rhesus monkeys modify their behavior in peer groups by increased social grooming, decreased aggression, and increased mounting activity.

3065. Mitchell RE: Husband-wife relations and family-planning practices in urban Hong Kong. J Marriage Fam 34:139–146.

The female's degree of influence in family decisionmaking and degree of spousal communication are independent of family income and wife's education in family-planning practices.

3066. Mitchell TR, Dossett DL, Fiedler FE, Triandis HC: Culture training: validation evidence for the culture assimilator. Int J Psychol 7:97–104.

The culture assimilator can effectively reduce some stress encountered in working with members of other cultures.

3067. Momeni DA: The difficulties of changing the age at marriage in Iran. J Marriage Fam 34:545–551.

Economic and educational variables are more salient factors in determining actual age at marriage than laws determining minimum age.

3068. Morrill R: Consultation or control? The cross-cultural advisor-advisee relationship. Psychiatry 35:264–280.

Interpersonal relationships, role, and status, as opposed to "strange customs," are the primary determinants in advisor-advisee relationships.

3069. Morris PE, Reid RL: Canadian and British ratings of the imagery values of words. Br J Psychol 63:163–164.

The imagery of words is similar in degree between Canadian and British samples, though the British give consistently lower value ratings.

3070. Moudgil R: Child rearing practices and Hindu personality formation. Int J Soc Psychiatry 18:127–131.

In *The Twice Born,* Carstair's interpretations seem to be more the projections of his own ideas than adequate interpretation of Hindu childhood fantasies. Hindu practices can be understood as adaptations to particular events, and no resort to mystical "psychodynamic" principles need be made.

3071. Moulton R: Contradictory pressures on women. Contemp Psychoanal 8:188–189.

The film *Devi* demonstrates some of the more universal conflicts of women. Isolation, plus being caught between deification and exploitation, lead to a schizophrenic break in the central character, Doya.

3072. Munroe RL, Munroe RH: Obedience among children in an East African society. J Cross-Cultural Psychol 3:395–400.

African societies are generally rated highest in compliance socialization. Overall obediance among the Kikuyu is very high; however, in contrast to previous findings, Kikuyu children do not disobey their mother more than another child's mother. Compliance emphasis may be related to child's participation in daily economic activities.

3073. Munroe RL, Munroe RH: Population density and affective relationships in three East African societies. J Soc Psychol 88:15–20.

Quantity of interactions or, more likely, competitive and balancing actions may account for greater negative affective expression among the high-density Logoli, in comparison to the Gusii and Kipsigis of Kenya.

3074. Myambo K: Shape constancy as influenced by culture, Western education, and age. J Cross-Cultural Psychol 3:221–232.

Uneducated Africans tend to respond to the true shape of the objects regardless of age. European subjects respond to the retinal image shape, while the educated Africans give intermediate responses.

3075. Ndeti K: Sociocultural aspects of tuberculosis defaultation: a case study. Soc Sci Med 6:397–412.

The major causes of the high defaultation rate of tuberculosis patients in Machakos district (Kenya) are lack of understanding of the program, belief in traditional herbistry, lack of understanding of the disease, reliance on witch doctors, fatalism, financial limitations, and circumstantial or natural limitations.

3076. Omari IM, Cook H: Differential cognitive cues in pictoral depth perception. J Cross-Cultural Psychol 3:321–325.

Ability to perceive depth differs significantly according to the use of a certain lexical item in instructions which may serve to direct attention to certain relational phenomenon.

3077. Orley JH, Liff JP: The effect of psychiatric education on attitudes to illness among the Ganda. Br J Psychiatry 121:137–141.

Changing attitudes toward illness among educated Ugandans may be measured by a Semantic Differential instrument.

3078. Orpen C: The cross-cultural validity of the Eysenck Personality Inventory: a test in Afrikaans-speaking South Africa. Br J Soc Clin Psychol 11:244–247.

Significant correlations between EPI measures and Afrikaans-speakers' self-ratings indicate the validity of the Afrikaans version of the EPI.

3079. Orpen C: The effect of race and similar attitudes on interpersonal attraction among white Rhodesians. J Soc Psychol 86:143–146.

Interpersonal attraction is based more on attitude similarity than upon race of the other person.

3080. Orpen C, Pors H: Race and belief: a test of Rokeach's theory in an authoritarian culture. Int J Psychol 7:53–56.

Tests of Afrikaaner children show that race is more salient than perceived value similarity upon degree of desired social distance and appraisal of similarity. These results are inconsistent with Rokeach's interpretation.

3081. Orpen C, Tsapogas G: Racial prejudice and authoritarianism: a test in white South Africa. Psychol Rep 30:441–442.

In a "prejudiced" society, prejudiced attitudes serve a utilitarian rather than an ego-defensive function for its members.

3082. Padan-Eisenstark D: Career women in Israel: their birth order and their sibling groups' sex composition. J Marriage Fam 34:552–556.

Sex composition of a woman's sibling group is unrelated to her career-group status. However, youngest daughters are significantly represented among the study population of high-status career women.

3083. Palmieri RG, Suarez Y: The future outlook of Puerto Rican Vietnam-era hospitalized psychiatric patients. J Clin Psychol 28:394–399.

Puerto Rican Vietnam-era hospitalized psychiatric patients rate their expectations of support and understanding from their families, their concern about playing a mature adult role, and becoming active in a religious organization as "high." They show uncertainty and ambivalence with regard to their general view of the future, possibility of relapse, community understanding, and expectancies of friendship and understanding from others.

3084. Parin P: A contribution of ethno-psychoanalytic investigation to the theory of aggression. Int J Psychoanal 53:251–258.

Contrasts between the Agni and Dogon show that the latter can organize without internalizing aggression. Comparative research shows the specific cultural stamp of childhood on adult aggression and points out the role of the human environment. Aggressive impulses need not be organized or internalized in the Western manner.

3085. Pecjak V: Affective symbolism of spatial forms in two cultures. Int J Psychol 7:257–266.

Zambian males utilize a single dimension in spatially situating stimulus concepts, while Yugoslavian subjects employ several spatial dimensions. Greater stereotyping and lesser density of responses occur among Zambian subjects.

3086. Philip AE: Cross-cultural stability of second-order factors in the 16 PF. Br J Soc Clin Psychol 11:276–283.

Cattell's claims for the cross-cultural stability of second-order factors of the 16 PF cannot be substantiated for all factors.

3087. Polednak AP: Dermatoglyphics of Negro schizophrenic males. Br J Psychiatry 120:397–398.

Finger and palm prints differ between Negro schizophrenics and controls. The consistency is impressive, but further studies are needed using more adequate controls (such as normal Negro males from the same neighborhood as the schizophrenics).

3088. Poveda T: A perspective on adolescent social relations. Psychiatry 35:32–47.

Adolescent problems may be rooted in their immediate peer group setting, in institutional crises in society, or both.

3089. Pratt L: Conjugal organization and health. J Marriage Fam 34:85–95.

The hypothesis that marriages characterized by shared power, flexibility of sex role, and high levels of companionship will have higher levels of health and health behavior is generally sustained.

3090. Prichard A, Bashaw WL, Anderson HE: A comparison of the structure of behavioral maturity between Japanese and American primary-grade children. J Soc Psychol 86:167–174.

The factor structure of behavioral maturity is similar for Japanese and American children.

3091. Prince R: Fundamental differences of psychoanalysis and faith healing. Int J Psychiatry 10:125–128.

Psychoanalysis aims at independence and insight while the goal of faith healing is dependence. Each prepares the patient for a different social world.

3092. Query WT, Query JM: Aggressive responses to the Holtzman Inkblot technique by Indian and white alcoholics. J Cross-Cultural Psychol 3:413–416.

No differences are found between Indian and white alcoholics' behavioral or projective test indexes, thus refuting common stereotypes of Indian alcoholic aggression. Fantasy substitutes for aggression and oral dependence are more characteristic among Indians.

3093. Ramon S: The impact of culture change on schizophrenia in Israel. J Cross-Cultural Psychol 3:373–382.

Israeli families of schizophrenic offspring from Yemen are higher on scores of cultural deviance and lower in communication defects than a comparable group from Poland. Defects in communication are conducive to cultural deviance among the Yemen group.

3094. Ramu GN: Geographic mobility, kinship and the family in South India. J Marriage Fam 34:147–152.

Geographic and occupational mobility has caused a breakdown in the extended localistic patrilineal kinship system. Expressive and instrumental kinship ties are maintained, in spite of spatial distance, as an adaption to the industrial setting.

3095. Rascovsky A, Rascovsky M: The prohibition of incest, filicide, and the sociocultural process. Int J Psychoanal 53:271–276.

Prohibition of incest was the earliest motive for filicide. Guilt and paranoia are fostered among offspring by parental threats of filicide and accusations of parracide.

3096. Raychaudhuri M: Some thorny issues in cross-cultural research on creativity: a rejoinder to Aronow's comment. J Pers Assess 36:304–306.

Given the educational circumstances in India, equating backgrounds is a difficult task. Nevertheless adequately matched samples are employed in a study of creativity, sex, and Rorschach responses.

3097. Razavieh AA, Hosseini AA: Family, peer, and academic orientation of Iranian adolescents. J Psychol 80:337–344.

Iranian adolescents are strongly oriented to parents, teachers, and education, without showing any evidence of a youth subculture.

3098. Reinhardt AM, Gray RM: Anomia, socioeconomic status, and mental disturbance. Community Mcnt Hcalth J 8:109 119.

Subjects' feelings of anomia maintain a significant relationship with psychiatric impairment within socioeconomic categories. The proportion of subjects reporting psychiatric symptomatology decreases with increasing status but the relative risk of such symptoms for highly anomic respondents (compared to nonanomic subjects within each socioeconomic category) is much higher for the highest status groups than for the lower groups.

3099. Robbins MC, Pelto PJ, DeWalt BR: Climate and behavior: a biocultural study. J Cross-Cultural Psychol 3:331–334.

Cross-cultural and cross-national tests of the hypothesis that amount of emotional expression covaries with climate and weather suggest some patterned relationships between the variables and the need for further research in biocultural anthropology.

3100. Rosen BC, LaRaia AL: Modernity in women: an index of social change in Brazil. J Marriage Fam 34:353–360.

Factor analysis of interview data provides two indexes of modernity for the industrial and nonindustrial milieu. Modernity is positively related to educational level, work experience, and voluntary association membership.

3101. Roth M: Human violence as viewed from the psychiatric clinic. Am J Psychiatry 128:1043–1056.

Biological and psychopathological inadequacies in an individual may result in frustrative-impulsive aggression or altruistic aggression. Psychiatrists must participate in a greater understanding of how to prevent destructuve aggression while preserving the uniqueness of the individual.

3102. Rudestam KE: Demographic factors in suicide in Sweden and the United States. Int J Soc Psychiatry 18:79–90.

Since Sweden and the United States have in common a democratic government, a high standard of living, a progressive morality, and an inheritance of the Protestant ethic, it is not surprising that a great many cultural similarities appear in data provided by close survivors of suicide victims in Stockholm and Los Angeles.

3103. Sarwer-Foner GJ: On human territoriality: a contribution to instinct theory. Can Psychiatr Assoc J Supp. 17:169–183.

Expressions of territoriality noted in patients add to our knowledge of human instincts and the manner in which they cathect the biological apparatus and are channelized onto an object by this apparatus.

3104. Schaffner B: The cultural background. Contemp Psychoanal 8:190–193.

The historical and cultural setting in which the events in the film *Devi* take place are important to understanding the film. Medical care in rural India was very primitive, and there was a strong popular belief in the healing powers of the goddess Kali. The father, by cultural standards, was obligated to lead the life of a hermit. His daughter-in-law's life is totally destroyed despite her humility, submission to "duty," and extreme sacrifice in the cause of her husband, her father-in-law, and her religion.

3104a. Schechner R: Incest and culture: A reflection on Claude Levi-Strauss. Psychoanal Rev 58: 563–572.

Levi-Strauss's theory of exchange and its basis in the incest taboo is compared and contrasted with the biological incest theories of Lindzey and Freud.

3105. Schecter DE: Portrayal of the life cycle. Contemp Psychoanal 8:185–187.

In *Devi*, a sense of inevitable tragedy emerges strikingly as the acting out of a socially powerful old man goes unchallenged. To maintain a leader's image of power and his belief system, a whole community must come to grief. There is a frightening similarity between this and the passive acceptance of belief systems in contemporary times.

3106. Schlossman HH: God the Father and His Sons. Am Imago 29:35–52.

The recurrent theme of brother pairs, in which the older is defeated while the younger supplants the former, represents the sacrifice of the elder son begat by a primitive god. Such a practice was part of the transitional matriarchal phase of social organization that gave way to patriarchal culture arising from population growth, wars, and the development of a warrior caste.

3107. Schmeidler G, Windholz G: A nonverbal indicator of attitudes: data from Thailand. J Cross-Cultural Psychol 3:383–394.

The nonverbal responses of Thai students to abstract concepts are more similar to those of their American counterparts than are responses to words describing social roles.

3108. Sechrest L, Fay TL, Zaidi SMH: Problems of translation in cross-cultural research. J Cross-Cultural Psychol 3:41–56.

Although the techniques of back-translation and decentering have much to recommend their use in cross-cultural research, the use of a carrier language may be particularly appropriate, especially in multicultural studies.

3109. Settlage CF: Cultural values and the superego in late adolescence. Psychoanal Study Child 27:74–97.

The nature of the relationship between the late adolescent and his society, between his superego and the values and traditions of his culture, hinges greatly on his earliest experiences of play in his relationship with his mother, the process of separation-individuation, and the attainment of objective constancy.

3110. Shapira A, Lomranz J: Cooperative and competitive behavior of rural Arab children in Israel. J Cross-Cultural Psychol 3:353–360.

Arab-Israeli boys from the same village Hamula (extended family) are less cooperative than a group of boys from mixed Hamulas, while girls from the same Hamula were more cooperative than girls from mixed Hamulas group. In general, this Arab culture resembles cooperative rather than competitive cultures.

3111. Sharp D, Cole M: Patterns of responding in the word associations of West African children. Child Dev 43:55–65.

The overall level of paradigmatic responding to verbs and adjectives by educated Kpelle people is quite low by European and U.S. standards. Paradigmatic responding increases both as a function of age and educational level. Education, however, is only one of the factors that increases age-related trends toward paradigmatic responding.

3112. Shaw ME, Iwawaki S: Attributions of responsibility by Japanese and Americans as a function of age. J Cross-Cultural Psychol 3:71–82.

Japanese youths attribute the same responsibility for negative and positive outcomes, while Americans attribute more responsibility for negative outcomes. Both attribute more responsibility for high intensity than low intensity outcomes. These findings may be considered in terms of cultural differences in values and reward patterns.

3113. Sheehan PW, Stewart SJ: A cross-cultural study of eidetic imagery among Australian aboriginal children. J Soc Psychol 87:179–188.

Eidetic imagery is strongest in the most tribally oriented group of aboriginal children. Memory imagery fails to consistently differentiate groups having differential contact with European society.

3114. Shore JH: Suicide and suicide attempts among American Indians of the Pacific Northwest. Int J Soc Psychiatry 18:91–96.

The West Coast and Plateau groups of Indians have a reported suicide rate of 28 per 100,000. The profile of the subject who completes suicide is a man in his thirties, single or separated, who hangs or shoots himself. Individuals who attempt suicide appear to come from a different population than those who complete the act. Self destructve attempts are a learned behavior pattern in certain Indian communities.

3115. Shore JH, Bopp JF, Waller TR, Dawes JW: A suicide prevention center on an Indian reservation. Am J Psychiatry 128:1086–1091.

Suicide prevention centers for American Indians reflect differing sociopolitical milieus, patient population characteristics, and community involvement.

3116. Shore JH, Van Fumetti B: Three alcohol programs for American Indians. Am J Psychiatry 128:1450–1454.

Tribally sponsored alcoholism rehabilitation programs stress community involvement in planning and operating the programs, court participation, and uniform standards of patient evaluation.

3117. Siann G: Measuring field-dependence in Zambia: a cross-cultural study. Int J Psychol 7: 87–96.

Zambian and non-Zambian comparison groups' performance on two embedded-figure tests, the Rod and Frame Test, and a verbal test reveals no evidence that African performance is superior to Western performance where proprioception is important. The former group does better on these tests than on tests where vision is important.

3118. Simons RC, Sarbadhikary D: Suicide attempters admitted to the University of Malaya Medical Center Psychiatric unit. Int J Soc Psychiatry 18:97–103.

Patients who had made a suicide attempt at some time in their lives could not be discriminated from others in such factors as age, ethnic group, religion, marital status, immigration, and occupational status. Suicide attempters are often female and English educated.

3119. Sinha D, Chaubey NP: Achievement motive and rural economic development. Int J Psychol 7: 267–272.

Although differences are not significant, younger subjects from highly developed villages show lower achievement motive scores than older subjects, while the younger generation from backward villages shows more motivation than their elders. In general, those subjects from more developed villages have higher scores than those from lesser villages.

3120. Sinha JBP, Yusuf SMA: Effects of locus of control on choice shift in a cross-cultural perspective. J Soc Psychol 88:177–183.

Individuals transfer decision control to the group. Competence may facilitate shifts by East Indian student groups toward more risky positions, while trust only facilitates unethical risky shift.

3121. Smith MC, Pearn MA: Conventional lecture versus discovery training methods in the preparation of immigrant bus drivers. J Cross-Cultural Psychol 3:407–412.

Asian and African immigrants to England perform better at one level of difficulty after conventional training, while nonimmigrants perform better after discovery training.

3122. Solnit AJ: Aggression: a view of theory building in psychoanalysis. J Am Psychoanal Assoc 20:435–450.

The postulation of the theory of aggression as an instinctual drive has been productive in illuminating vicissitudes of child development and behavior.

3123. Sommerland EA, Bellingham WP: Cooperation-competition: a comparison of Australian European and aboriginal school children. J Cross-Cultural Psychol 3:149–158.

Australian aboriginal children show more cooperative performance than European Australian children. An aboriginal group preparing for secondary education shows more competitive behavior than other aboriginal children. The role of kinship as a determinant could not be supported.

3124. Spencer DJ: Suicide in the Bahamas. Int J Soc Psychiatry 18:110–113.

Compared to many other parts of the world the suicide rate in the Bahamas is low, although it equals that recorded in other Caribbean countries and in Africa. Suicide has not increased with increasing urbanization and a change to a Euro-American type of culture.

3125. Staples R: The matricentric family system: a cross-cultural examination. J marriage Fam 34: 156–165.

Examples of matricentric family systems (Caribbean, Afro-American, and the Nayar) suggest some commonalities and variations and point up the necessity of clarifying the matricentric family concept.

3126. Staton RD: A comparison of Mexican and Mexican-American families. Fam Coordinator 21: 325–330.

From their Mexican heritage, Mexican-American families retain a masculine emphasis, obedience to authority, father dominance, separation of sex roles, and the importance of family. Deemphasis of these features should be expected with increasing acculturation.

3127. Suomi S, Harlow HF, McKinney WT: Monkey psychiatrists. Am J Psychiatry 128:927–932.

Initiation of social contact in a nonthreatening manner by young monkey "therapists" may successfully reverse the experimentally induced isolate behavior of other monkeys.

3128. Szalay LB, Lysne DA, Bryson JA: Designing and testing cogent communications. J Cross-Cultural Psychol 3:247–258.

The strength of associative linkages for American and Korean groups is directly informative to the degree that they are subjectively viewed as related.

3129. Tajfel H, Jahoda G, Nemeth C, Rim Y, Johnson NB: The devaluation by children of their own national and ethnic group: two case studies. Br J Soc Clin Psychol 11:235–243.

In situations that are not characterized by tension or clear ethnic distinctions, Scottish, English, and Israeli children are sentitive to social influences that lead to devaluation of own group in comparison with a dominant group.

3130. Tanaka Y: Values in the subjective culture: a social psychological view. J Cross-Cultural Psychol 3:57–70.

Although there are culturally unique subsystems of values, the presence of certain common essential values (both positive and negative) has implications for intercultural cooperation.

3131. Taylor DM, Simard LM: The role of bilingualism in cross-cultural communication. J Cross-Cultural Psychol 3:101–108.

Assessment of communicational efficiency among mixed and same ethnic dyads of French-Canadian and English-Canadian factory workers suggests that cross-cultural communication can be as efficient as within group communication.

3132. (Deleted)

3133. Teoh J: The changing psychopathology of amok. Psychiatry 35:345–351.

Once a conscious form of violent behavior, "running amok" has since become unconsciously motivated because of negative sanctions by society. The amok syndrome occurs in many cultures and is not as culture-bound as once thought.

3134. Thayer S, Alban L: A field experiment on the effect of political and cultural factors on the use of personal space. J Soc Psychol 88:267–272.

An experimenter wearing a flag button encountered smaller interaction distances in conservative Little Italy (in 1970) than did a wearer of a peace button, but no significant differences were obtained for the same experiment in Greenwich Village. A European cultural background of smaller social distance, which is facilitated by perceived compatibility, may account for the results in Little Italy.

3135. Thomas DL, Weigert AJ: Determining nonequivalent measurement in cross-cultural family research. J Marriage Fam 34:166–178.

Pretesting of instruments upon bilinguals and discarding items that produce nonequivalent measures are a necessary prerequisite to cross-cultural research.

3136. Tomeh AK: Birth order and dependence patterns of college students in Lebanon. J Marriage Fam 34:361–374.

Paternal authority is seen as most important for first borns with respect to academic/economic interests. The first-born girl's relatively high dependence upon family members theoretically indicates that the form is tradition oriented.

3137. Torrey E: What Western psychotherapists can learn from witch doctors. Am J Orthopsychiatry 42:69–76.

Important considerations common to both witch doctors and psychotherapists are naming an illness, the personal qualities of the therapist, the patients' expectations, and the techniques of therapy.

3138. Tseng MS: Attitudes toward the disabled— cross-cultural study. J Soc Psychol 87:311–312.

Adaptation, culture, locus of control, and anxiety interact to structure American Asian students' attitudes toward the disabled. Negative attitudes are associated with high levels of anxiety and external control.

3139. Uno Y, Koivumaki JH, Rosenthal R: Unintended experimenter behavior as evaluated by Japanese and American observers. J Soc Psychol 88:91–106.

Sex and cultural differences in interpretation along visual and auditory channels of experimenter behavior are obtained for Japanese and American samples.

3140. Vaglum P: Contrasting multi-generational attitudes toward psychosis in two Norwegian families. Fam Process 11:311–320.

The reactions of two families to schizophrenic daughters are the result of cultural, socioeconomic, and psychological backgrounds. These reactions parallel Levi-Strauss's division of social patterns for dealing with deviants: antropophage societies (keep and hide the deviant) and antropoemetric societies (expel and forget the deviant).

3141. Vetta A: Conservation in aboriginal children and "genetic hypothesis." Int J Psychol 7:247–255.

M. M. deLemos's earlier study on conservation failed to incorporate several variables and shows some errors in analysis. Dasen's recent replication revealed no genetic differences between full and part aboriginal children. The former study is not a confirmation of a race-intelligence genetic hypothesis. Conditions of inequality in European-aboriginal contact must be considered in interpreting performance or conservation tasks.

3142. Viljoen HG, Grober E: A comparison between the moral codes of the American, Korean, and a group of Afrikaans-speaking South African students. J Soc Psychol 86:147–150.

Differences between Americans and Afrikaans speakers, but not between Koreans and South Africans, indicate that moral codes are influenced by social structure and situational factors more than common values.

3143. Von Mering O: The diffuse health aberration syndrome: a bio-behavioral study of the perennial out-patient. Psychosomatics 13:293–303.

The "professional patient" and his analog, a "mature" health delivery structure with functions that tend to be guided by maintenance and support, repair, and reuse mechanism, rather than by growth and development, generation and production processes, develop a continuing relationship in which the patient has neither freedom from struggle nor the security to live in resignation or passivity. In this enantiomorphous behavior unit each participant operates as a feed-back control system or an energy exchange system.

3144. Weisz JR: East African medical attitudes. Soc Sci Med 6:323–333.

Medical traditions in East Africa are hundreds of years old and extremely tenacious, especially among the rural population but also among surprising numbers of the urban, the wealthy, and the well educated. Proposals to incorporate the witch doctor into modern practice are unwise.

3145. Werner EE: Infants around the world: cross-cultural studies of psychomotor development from birth to two years. J Cross-Cultural Psychol 3:111–134.

Traditional rural infants show greater motor acceleration in the first year, and a greater postweaning decline in adaptive and language development during the second year, than do Westernized urban infants on five continents.

3146. Westermeyer J: Chippewa and majority alcoholism in the Twin Cities: a comparison. J Nerv Ment Dis 155:322–327.

Differences exist between Chippewa and majority alcoholics in the Twin Cities (Minneapolis and St. Paul, Minnesota). These differences can be related to sociocultural variables rather than to intrinsic differences in the alcoholism syndrome as it occurs in these two groups.

3147. Westermeyer J: A comparison of amok and other homicide in Laos. Am J Psychiatry 129:703–707.

Social variables, such as separation from family and role crisis, are more important in the precipitation of amok behavior than are psychopathological causes.

3148. Westermeyer J: Options regarding alcohol use among the Chippewa. Am J Orthopsychiatry 42:398–403.

Patterns of drinking are not uniform among American Indians but vary along a spectrum ranging from complete abstinence to chronic alcoholism.

3149. Whitehurst RN: Some comparisons of conventional and counterculture families. Fam Coordinator 21:395–402.

Comparison of ideal types in eight activity areas (child rearing, religion, etc.) suggests that counterculture families may be superior in meeting needs.

3150. Whittaker JO, Whittaker SJ: A cross-cultural study of geocentrism. J Cross-Cultural Psychol 3:417–421.

American, Argentenian, Fijian, Indian, and New Zealand college students' world map drawings reflect geocentrism in that one's own country is disproportionately large and neighboring countries are generally included.

3151. Wober M: Culture and the concept of intelligence: a case in Uganda. J Cross-Cultural Psychol 3:327–328.

There is a clear tendency among educated Ugandans to reduce the traditional association between the concepts of ability and slowness, and toward the more Western ability-quickness association.

3152. Wober M, Musoke-Mutanda F: Patience, and gratification preferences among Ugandan school children. J Soc Psychol 87:141–142.

Sex and social-class differences are evident for delayed reward preferences, punishment-patience, and time estimations. Time estimation is not associated with gratification preferences for Ugandan children.

3153. Wohl J, Tapingkae A: Values of Thai university students. Int J Psychol 7:23–31.

Thai students emphasize practical and familial (responsibility, duty) values, show allegiance to traditional culture, and view education as the means to economic security.

3154. Yaukey D, Thorsen T: Differential female age at first marriage in six Latin American cities. J Marriage Fam 34:375–379.

Higher level of education generally corresponds with patterns of later ideal and real ages of first marriage. Consensual earlier marriage is associated with low education and rural birth.

3155. Yeh EK: The Chinese mind and human freedom. Int J Soc Psychiatry 18:132–136.

Chinese students' fantasies convey less spontaneity, less gregariousness, and less concern with peer acceptance than those of American students. The Chinese generally are more thoughtful and lacking in direction and optimism. It is the task of contemporary Chinese to integrate what they learn from Western democracy into a system that is compatible with traditional Chinese culture in order to establish true "freedom."

3156. Zahn MA, Ball JC: Factors related to cure of opiate addiction among Puerto Rican addicts. Int J Addict 7:237–246.

Cured subjects had fewer prior arrests, later age of drug use, and were living with spouses and employed.

3157. Za'rour GI: Superstitions among certain groups of Lebanese Arab students in Beirut. J Cross-Cultural Psychol 3:273–282.

Superstitiousness decreases with increasing level of education. Females and art students are more superstitious than males and science students.

3158. Ziegler M, King M, King JM, Ziegler SM: Tribal stereotypes among Ethiopian students. J Cross-Cultural Psychol 3:193–200.

Stereotyping of four ethnolinguistic groups by Ethiopian students reflects ingroup and outgroup positive and negative evaluations, individual differences, and trends toward modernization.

3159. Zigas V, Van Delden J, Rodrigue R: New Guinea: studies relating the medical and behavioral sciences. Soc Sci Med 6:681–695.

The juxtaposition of traditional New Guinea and Australian culture has produced many conflicts for

individuals that can lead to emotional stress and mental illness. The adjustment from one culture to the other can be a difficult and alienating one, without understanding and creative assistance from social agencies.

3160. Zung WWK: A cross-cultural survey of depressive symptomatology in normal adults. J Cross-Cultural Psychol 3:177–184.

Rank ordering of self-rated depression scores show Czechoslovakia to be highest, followed by Sweden, Germany, Spain, England, and the United States. Factor analysis indicates qualitative similarities across the cultures studied.

1973

3161. Ablon J: Reactions of Samoan burn patients and families to severe burns. Soc Sci Med 7:167–178.

Samoan survivors of a disastrous fire in California suffered much initial distress, but few experienced acute or lasting emotional problems. Specific Samoan cultural, social, and religious patterns mitigated psychiatric morbidity.

3162. Adams FM, Osgood CE: A cross-cultural study of the affective meanings of color. J Cross-Cultural Psychol 4:135–156.

The possibility of universal trends in the affective meaning of color is suggested by a multi-cultural study encompassing estimates of strength, activity, and goodness-badness of specific colors. Brightness of color is generally associated with positive evaluation and negative potency.

3163. Adinolfi AA, Watson RI, Klein RE: Aggressive reactions to frustration in urban Guatemalan children: the effects of sex and social class. J Pers Soc Psychol 25:227–233.

American and Guatemalan children respond similarly to the Rosenzweig Picture Frustration Study. For lower-class males, internalizing aggression leads to peer rejection while externalizing aggression leads to positive peer evaluation.

3164. Allen J: The Indian adolescent: psychosocial tasks of the Plains Indians of Western Oklahoma. Am J Orthopsychiatry 43:368–375.

The dilemma of acculturation without assimilation and resulting confusion of identity is the basis of symptomatology of Plains Indian adolescents.

3165. Amir Y, Bizman A, Rivner M: Effects of interethnic contact on friendship choices in the military. J Cross-Cultural Psychol 4:361–373.

No significant changes in friendship choices occur as a result of interethnic contact in the Israeli army, although in specific contact situations, soldiers of European origin chose more Middle Eastern friends.

3166. d'Anglejan A, Tucker GR: Communicating across cultures: an empirical investigation. J Cross-Cultural Psychol 4:121–130.

The ethnic background of French-English professional translators significantly influences their ability to communicate with monolingual groups. Cultural differences that underly surface linguistic codes may be an obstacle to effective communication.

3167. Arlow JA: Perspectives on aggression in human adaptation. Psychoanal Q 42:178–184.

Theories of aggression may be categorized into biological-instinctual, frustration, and social learning. Psychoanalysis furnishes data about human experience that no other method of investigation can offer.

3168. Barraclough BM: Differences between national suicide rates. Br J Psychiatry 122:95–96.

Rank orders of suicide rates of nations are independent of ascertainment procedures and therefore reflect real differences in the incidence of suicide.

3169. Bateson G: The cybernetics of "self": a theory of alcoholism. Psychiatry 34:1–18.

The theology of Alcoholics Anonymous coincides closely with an epistemology of cybernetics. The addicted alcoholic is operating, when sober, in terms of an epistemology that is conventional in Occidental culture but that is not acceptable to systems theory.

3170. Bergeron AP, Zanna MP: Group membership and belief similarity as determinants of interpersonal attraction in Peru. J Cross-Cultural Psychol 4:397–412.

Among Peruvian university students, belief similarity with other groups is a reliable determinant of interpersonal attraction, but group membership accounts for significantly more variance.

3171. Bergman RL: A school for medicine men. Am J Psychiatry 130:663–666.

A psychiatrist participates in a training program of a Navaho school for medicine men and describes Navaho curative ceremonies and rituals as well as the reactions of medicine men to his teachings.

3172. Bethlehem DW: Cooperation, competition and altruism among schoolchildren in Zambia. Int J Psychol 8:125–135.

Maximization of own and relative gain are the operant motives in gaming for white and African Zambian children in the urban setting. Absence of altruism and cooperation are evident. Stronger evidence relating cooperativeness and competitiveness to game behavior is necessary.

3173. Bieder RE: Kinship as a factor in migration. J Marriage Fam 35:429–439.

Kin ties contributed to initial settlement of a nineteenth-century frontier community, and subsequent increase in extended families and kinship network also retarded out-migration.

3174. Bloom JD: Migration and psychopathology of Eskimo women. Am J Psychiatry 130:446–449.

Eskimo women have higher rates of psychopathology and of migration than Eskimo men. The impetus for migration may come from dissatisfaction with a low status in Eskimo culture.

3175. Bornstein MH: Color vision and color naming: a psychophysiological hypothesis of cultural difference. Psychol Bull 80:257–285.

Physiological differences in visual processing may be related to semantic categorization. Cross-cultural comparisons of color-naming systems suggest a geographic pattern of color-naming confusion.

3176. Borsuch RL, Barnes ML: Stages of ethical reasoning and moral norms of Carib youths. J Cross-Cultural Psychol 4:283–301.

Observed stages of ethical development for town and village Carib boys appear to function independently of the youths' perceived moral norms. General age and residence differences in stages appear consistent with stage theory.

3177. Bowden E: Persisting and disappearing traits in the development of precivilized societies: a preliminary note. J Cross-Cultural Psychol 4:413–426.

Male-dominant and equidominant-female-dominant societies may be scaled and the number of declining and persisting traits after maximum development may be identified. Traits that constitute an index of sociocultural development and a marriage-pattern factor are defined.

3178. Brody EB: Psychiatric implications of industrialization and rapid social change. J Nerv Ment Dis 156:300–305.

The mental problems of developing nations caught up in a rapid process of modernization may be approached both from the point of view of prevalent symptom patterns and of the delivery of reparative and preventive services. Specific issues influencing the nature both of prevailing mental health problems and of service delivery include migration, literacy, local folk medicine, and the status of the family.

3179. Brown GA: An exploratory study of interaction amongst British and immigrant children. Br J Soc Clin Psychol 12:159–162.

Immigrant children are more aggressive with each other and are more likely to make body contact with British children. Differences in verbal contact point to a language barrier.

3180. Brown GW: The mental hospital as an institution. Soc Sci Med 7:407–424.

Mental hospitals go through periods of reform and decline. This tendency stems from aspects of social organization, as well as the beliefs of the medical profession concerned with these institutions.

3181. Brunetti PM: Health in ecological perspective. Acta Psychiatr Scand 49:393–404.

The problems of human health should be viewed in the context of the crisis of a society that, dictated by the laws of a faulty economic system rather than governed by the biological imperatives of the human condition, deteriorates the individual through deterioration of his life sphere.

3182. Burton-Bradley BG: Niuginian psychiatry and acculturation. Int J Soc Psychiatry 19:44–48.

Acculturation stress arising from such contributing factors as overurbanization, anomie, racial discrimination, class and intergenerational conflicts, and the effect of differential social and educational opportunities color the picture of psychiatric disease processes in New Guinea.

3183. Calogeras RC: "Emic" and "etic" research strategies for psychoanalysis. Bull Menninger Clin 37:598–614.

Emic statements of descriptions of behavior require one to enter the world of purpose, meaning, and attitude that are "regarded as appropriate by the actors themselves." Etic statements or descriptions of behavior depend upon "distinctions judged appropriate by the community of scientific observers." Ways that have evolved in anthropology of viewing research data have relevance for psychiatry.

3184. Calogeras RC: Levi-Strauss and Freud: their "structural" approaches to myths. Am Imago 30:57–79.

There is often a parallel between Levi-Strauss's and psychoanalytic structural approaches. Both Levi-Strauss and Freud were searching for the unconscious meaning but in different areas of the mind. Levi-Strauss's greatest divergence from the psychoanalytic approach lies in his insistence on the dialectic-Cartesian logic of mythical thinking.

3185. Carlson JS: Moral development in Lao children. Int J Psychol 8:25–35.

The development of the idea of justice closely fits the emic approximation. The bases of the development of subjective responsibility and justice may be less related to adult constraint and peer-group relations than is suggested by Piaget.

3186. Carment DW, Hodkin B: Coaction and competition in India and Canada. J Cross-Cultural Psychol 4:459–469.

Greater lack of effects of dyadic coaction on performance for Indian than Canadian students may be explained by adaptation to crowded environment and lack of concern for the performance of the partner.

3187. Carment DW, Paliwal TR: Correlates of birth control practices in India. J Cross-Cultural Psychol 4:111–119.

Scores of North Indian factory workers on an internal-external control scale show that those in favor of contraception are more internal than those against. More workers who made a sole decision on vasectomy tend to view the outcome as negative than those who made a joint-spouse decision. More Sikhs than Hindus support contraception.

3188. Carstairs GM: Psychiatric problems of developing countries. Br J Psychiatry 123:271–277.

In developing countries, patterns of morality and morbidity have been undergoing rapid change. To insure that the peoples of the developing countries receive the best possible psychiatric care, inappropriate carry-overs from Western medicine should be discontinued and real efforts made to understand the peculiarities of each culture.

3189. Caudill WA: The influence of social structure and culture on human behavior in modern Japan. J Nerv Ment Dis 157:240–257.

When studying the combined social and cultural effects of change and continuity in Japan, it would be useful to include more comparisons with other countries in the world than the United States, such as those of Southeast Asia and Europe.

3190. Caudill WA, Schooler C: Child behavior and child rearing in Japan and the United States: an interim report. J Nerv Ment Dis 157:323–338.

Caudill's longitudinal study and cross-cultural analyses of observations of the behavior of infants and their mothers were important steps forward in demonstrating the early and persistent effects of culture on personality.

3191. Chandra S: The effects of group pressure in perception: a cross-cultural conformity study in Fiji. Int J Psychol 8:37–39.

Fijian subjects, and Indian subjects in particular, conform more to group pressure than subjects in the United States, Brazil, Lebanon, Rhodesia, and Hong Kong tested in other studies. Such behavior is a reflection of an authoritarian society with group orientations. High rates of conformity among females may be related to their lower social status and independence.

3192. Chaney EM: Old and new feminists in Latin America: the case of Peru and Chile. J Marriage Fam 35:331–343.

New feminist activity appears unlikely since relations between the sexes lack competition due to mutual definitions of women's proper areas of activity.

3193. Chang SC, Kim K: Psychiatry in South Korea. Am J Psychiatry 130:667–669.

Shamanism, Buddhism, Confucianism, and folk medicine have had a preventive or even curative effect on Korean psychological distress. Western psychotherapy is applicable in principle in Korea, but with technical modifications. There has been a recent upsurge in the study of indigenous cultural traditions and their relevance to mental health.

3194. Chopra GS: Studies on psycho-clinical aspects of long-term marijuana use in 129 cases. Int J Addict 8:1015–1026.

Many physical and psychological effects of various preparations of cannabis can be observed in long-term users.

3195. Claridge GS, Chappa HJ: Psychotism: a study of its biological basis in normal subjects. Br J Soc Clin Psychol 12:175–186.

Psychotism is a normal personality dimension. Its biological basis is a particular kind of nervous typological organization that in the extreme form is manifest in psychotic disorders.

3196. Cohen LM: Women's entry into the professions in Colombia: selected characteristics. J Marriage Fam 35:322–330.

Women's participation in new educational and occupational roles is associated with strong support shown by family, teachers, or others.

3197. Conklin GJ: Emerging conjugal role patterns in a joint family system: correlates of social change in Dharwar, India. J Marriage Fam 35:742–748.

Urbanization and education result in an increase in conjugal role patterns with no decline in joint family households, supporting Goode's concept that education leads to conjugal family patterns prior to industrialization.

3198. Constantinople A: Masculinity-femininity: an exception to a famous dictum? Psychol Bull 80:389–407.

Current tests for M-F measurement in adults are inadequate.

3199. Cottrell AB: Cross-national marriage as an extension of an international life style: a study of Indian-Western couples. J Marriage Fam 35:739–741.

Indian-Western cross-national marriages are an extension of an established international life-style rather than other-cultural involvement.

3200. Cvetkovich GT, Lonner WJ: A transnational comparison of individual birth planning decision for hypothetical families. J Cross-Cultural Psychol 4:470–480.

Large similarities in abstract familial concepts across national samples from West Germany, the Netherlands, India, and United States suggest that such similarity may underlie cultural differences found in previous family research.

3201. Dawson JLM: Effects of ecology and subjective culture on individual traditional-modern attitude change, achievement motivation, and potential for economic development in the Japanese and Eskimo societies. Int J Psychol 8:215–225.

An ecological model of the interaction effect of ecological, socialization stratification, modern attitude change, achievement motivation, and economic development variables may be partially supported with Japanese and Eskimo data and seems to have some predictive power across subsistence societies.

3202. Dawson JLM, Young BM, Choi PPC: Developmental influences on geometric illusion susceptibility among Hong Kong Chinese children. J Cross-Cultural Psychol 4:49–74.

Among Hong Kong Chinese, illusion susceptibility decreases to age 12 and later increases to age 21, due to exposure to a sophisticated environment. Comparison with the United States and the Arunta supports the carpentered-world hypothesis and a relationship between horizontal-vertical susceptibility and desert-urban differences in perceptual inference. Differences in retinal pigmentation and the cross-sectional nature of the study may have influenced the results.

3203. Deregowski JB, Ellis HD, Shepherd JW: A cross-cultural study of recognition of pictures of faces and cups. Int J Psychol 8:269–274.

Within the context of examining the relationship between field independence and socialization and cultural values, a hypothesis on recognition of faces and cups by Africans and Europeans is tested but unconfirmed.

3204. Diaz-Guerrero R: Interpreting coping styles across nations from sex and social class differences. Int J Psychol 8:193–203.

Differences in coping style (active or passive) are related to age, sex, and social-class differences.

3205. Doi LT: Omote and ura: concepts derived from the Japanese 2-fold structure of consciousness. J Nerv Ment Dis 157:258–261.

The Japanese are driven toward the two-fold structure of consciousness represented by *omote* ("face") and *ura* ("mind") in their cultural heritage. Various types of psychopathology can be characterized in terms of *omote* and *ura*.

3206. Draguns JG: Comparisons of psychopathology across cultures: issues, findings, directions. J Cross-Cultural Psychol 4:9–47.

Cross-cultural studies of psychopathology gener-

ally favor the concept of cultural plasticity of psychopathology and suggest that this represents a caricature and exaggeration of culturally shared adaptive behavior patterns. In light of this issue, research on normal and abnormal subjects from several cultures is proposed.

3207. Duberman L: Step-kin relationships. J Marriage Fam 35:283–292.

Comparison of stepparent and stepsibling relationships and primary family relationships provides clues to the formation of reconstituted families, primary groups, and the process of socialization.

3208. Dunbar J, Brown M, Vuorinen S: Attitudes toward homosexuality among Brazilian and Canadian college students. J Soc Psychol 90:173–183.

Brazilians show more antihomosexual prejudice and greater tendency to so label a male if he exhibits a single feminine trait. Findings are consistent with W. Churchill's concept of the sex-negative culture.

3209. Eaves LJ: The structure of genotypic and environmental covariation for personality measurements: an analysis of the PEN. Br J Soc Clin Psychol 12:275–282.

Covariation between extraversion and neuroticism items may be explained by unitary action of environmental influences, but there is little evidence for psychoticism. Unitary genetic influences may account for N item covariation, and more than one genetic factor for E item covariation. There is no clear indication of unitary genotypic factors for P items.

3210. Edwards DJA: A cross-cultural study of social orientation and distance schemata by the method of doll placement. J Soc Psychol 89:165–173.

Instruction language, subject residence, degree of acculturation, sex composition of doll dyad, and acquaintance level attached to the dyad are variable aspects influencing doll placement by rural and urban Xhosa, Xhosa students, and white students.

3211. Eiduson B, Cohen J, Alexander J: Alternatives in child rearing in the 1970's. Am J Orthopsychiatry 43:720–731.

Countercultural child-rearing attitudes and practices, such as multiple caretaking, antisexist attitudes, heightened interest in social relationships, and generalized trust of adults, affect the psychological growth of the child.

3212. Elias MF, Samonds KW: Exploratory behavior of Cebus monkeys after having been reared in partial isolation. Child Dev 44:218–220.

Cebus monkeys reared in isolation exhibit characteristics similar to those of rhesus monkeys reared under equivalent conditions; namely, slight retardation of development, stereotyped behavior, decreased exploration, and the appearance of greater timidity.

3213. Engebretson D: Human territorial behavior: the role of interaction distance in therapeutic interventions. Am J Orthopsychiatry 43:108–116.

"Action language" reveals the individual's schemata for organizing interpersonal behavior. Socially dysfunctional behaviors of this type have implications for the therapeutic process.

3214. Fanibanda DK: Cultural influence on Hutt's adaptation of the Bender-Gestalt test: a pilot study. J Pers Assess 37:531–536.

Comparison of American and East Indian graduate student groups indicates some differences in performance.

3215. Favazza AR, Favazza BS: The Columbia University rebellion of 1968: a psycho-social commentary. J Oper Psychiatry 5:24–31.

An understanding of the intrapsychic motivations of leaders in the student rebellion contributes to an understanding of their declared motivations.

3216. Feder S: Clerambault in the ghetto. Int J Psychoanal Psychother 2:240–247.

A modern case of erotomania in a black ghetto woman suggests the relationship between the syndrome and paranoid psychosis.

3217. Feierabend RL, Feierabend IK, Sleet DA: Need achievement, coerciveness of government, and political unrest: a cross-national analysis. J Cross-Cultural Psychol 4:314–325.

Increases in need achievement over long periods of time are positively related to political unrest and coerciveness of regime and may indicate rapid rates of social and economic change.

3218. Ferraris Oliverio A: Children's evaluations of family roles: a cross-cultural comparison. Int J Psychol 8:153–158.

The Draw-A-Family Test results of Italian and Ivory Coast children clearly reflect the egocentric behavior of children and tendency to represent the father as distinct from the rest of the group. Con-

trasting role and family structure between monogamous and polygamous societies and the sex of the leading figure as reflected in these drawings permits further assessment of cultural patterns of family life.

3219. Fleiss JL, Gurland BJ, Simon R, Sharpe L: Cross-national study of diagnosis of the mental disorders: some demographic correlates of hospital diagnosis in New York and London. Int J Soc Psychiatry 19:180–186.

New York patients diagnosed as having an affective disorder differ only slightly in psychopathology from patients called schizophrenic, whereas London patients assigned to one of these clusters of diagnoses differ markedly from those assigned to the other. In neither New York nor London is there an association between diagnosis and social class.

3220. Foulks EF, Katz S: The mental health of Alaskan natives. Acta Psychiatr Scand 49:91–96.

Alcoholism is the major mental health problem among Alaskan native groups. Paranoid personality disorders are most frequently seen in Southeastern Indian groups, while depression is characteristic of the larger villages that are predominantly Eskimo. Mental disorder is significantly correlated with increases in population size, cash economy, and Westernization.

3221. Fox GL: Another look at the comparative resources model: assessing the balance of power in Turkish marriages. J Marriage Fam 35:718–730.

The contribution of wife's resources, such as educational background and economic skills, has a greater independent impact upon conjugal power than those of the husband.

3222. Fox GL: Some determinants of modernism among women in Ankara, Turkey. J Marriage Fam 35:520–529.

Type of community background, educational level, marriage age, and exposure to mass media systematically influence a woman's traditional-modernity orientation in the family-centered role of wife.

3223. Friedlander D: Family planning in Israel: irrationality and ignorance. J Marriage Fam 35:117–124.

Family size in Israel is small or declining, despite ignorance of family planning and efficient contraception. Family-planning programs are effective only when the socioeconomic context is taken into consideration.

3224. Gardner RC, Kirby DM, Arboleda A: Ethnic stereotypes: a cross-cultural replication of their unitary dimensionality. J Soc Psychol 91:189–195.

Factor analysis and stereotype differential rating of the concept "Chinese" by Filipino students indicate evaluative, stereotype, and social distance dimensions. Individual differences in stereotypy are independent of evaluative or social distance reactions to the group.

3225. Ghei SN: A cross-cultural comparison of the social desirability variable. J Cross-Cultural Psychol 4:493–500.

Ratings of socially desirable and undesirable personality statements are quite similar across linguistic groups in India and between Indian and U.S. subjects.

3226. Ghei SN: Female personality patterns in two cultures. Psychol Rep 33:759–762.

The modal qualities evident among female, American collegians are openness and spontaneity in expression of sexual impulse and a strong need for social activity. Asian Indian counterparts show qualities of achievement, endurance, and persistence.

3227. Gillis LS, Stone GL: A follow-up study of psychiatric disturbance in a Cape coloured community. Br J Psychiatry 123:279–283.

Reevaluation after several years of colored people in Cape Peninsula indicates that those previously adjudged free of psychiatric symptoms tend to remain well and about half of those previously adjudged psychiatrically disturbed were still so. Similar findings hold with regard to psychiatric impairment.

3228. Gobeil O: El susto: a descriptive analysis. Int J Soc Psychiatry 19:38–43.

"Susto," a Peruvian syndrome characterized by fear, soul loss, and earth "power," aids insecure people in reestablishing contact with society and permitting them to feel wanted and appreciated.

3229. Goetzl U: Mental illness and cultural beliefs in a Southern Italian immigrant family: a case report. Can Psychiatr Assoc J 18:219–222.

In a Southern Italian peasant society, beliefs in "streghe" and the "mal occhio" are well ingrained and commonplace. Their origin, in part, lies in an attempt to attribute to outside forces the painful reality of "la miseria." Therapists must recognize the profound effect upon the manifestation of mental disorders that culture can have.

3230. Goldschmid ML, Bentler PM, Debus RL, Rawlinson R, Kohnstamm D, Modgil S, Nicholls JG, Reykowski J, Strupczewska B, Warren N: A cross-cultural investigation of conservation. J Cross-Cultural Psychol 4:75–88.

Results indicate fairly consistent age trends in conservation development across Australia, Holland, New Zealand, Poland, and Ugandan cultures.

3231. Goodnow J, Friedman SL, Bernbaum M, Lehman EB: Direction and sequence in copying: the effect of learning to write in English and Hebrew. J Cross-Cultural Psychol 4:263–282.

Common developmental trends in the sequence of strokes displayed in copying geometric designs may be found for American and Israeli children. Generalization from letter patterns is nonlinear to age and experience.

3232. Gordon C, Gaitz CM, Scott J: Value priorities and leisure activites among middle aged and older Anglos. Dis Nerv Syst 34:13–26.

The conceptualization of the functions and characteristics of leisure is influenced by value systems. In examining data on the relationship among values, leisure activities, and mental health, investigators must pay careful attention to the ethnic, age, and sex contribution of the sample.

3233. Gransberg G: A note on delay of gratification among the Hopi. J Soc Psychol 91:151–152.

The high ability of Hopi children to delay gratification is consistent with other cross-cultural findings and the suggestion that children in horticultural societies are trained in agricultural responsibility.

3234. Gransberg G: The psychological integration of culture: a cross-cultural study of Hopi type initiation rites. J Soc Psychol 90:3–7.

Early Hopi child-rearing indulgence, followed by compliance training, leads to aggression and independence, which are counteracted by initiation rites featuring masks and whipping. The occurrence of this type of initiation rite to child rearing in other societies supports the premise of psychological integration of culture.

3235. Gray-Little B: The salience of negative information in impression formation among two Danish samples. J Cross-Cultural Psychol 4:193–206.

When presented with negative and positive descriptions of an unknown person, Danish subjects, like Americans, tend to show the disproportionate effect of negative information on the impression formed.

3236. Green R, Fuller M: Family doll play and female identity in pre-adolescent males. Am J Orthopsychiatry 43:123–127.

Doll-playing behavior of feminine boys correlates more closely with typical females than with typical males.

3237. Greenleaf E: "Senoi" dream groups. Psychother Theory Res Practice 10:218–222.

The Senoi culture of the Malay Peninsula is characterized by a remarkable lack of violence and a profound attention to the interplay between dreams and waking life. The Senoi share their dreams every morning, and group interpretations are made to successfully effect personal change and group cohesiveness.

3238. Grey A: Oedipus in Hindu dreams, Gandhi's life and Erikson's concepts. Contemp Psychoanal 9:327–355.

The dependency resolution process offers an alternative explanation of the Oedipus complex and may be applied to an understanding of Mohandas Gandhi's life.

3239. Gruenfeld L, Weissenberg P, Loh W: Achievement values, cognitive style and social class. Int J Psychol 8:41–49.

Controlling for social class has considerable importance in cross-cultural comparisons. Contrary to expectations, American students are more skeptical than Peruvians concerning their ability to achieve on the basis of merit rather than ascription. Small apparent national differences in optimism and cognitive style are mostly due to social-class differences.

3240. Hall AL, Bourne PG: Indigenous therapists in a Southern black urban community. Arch Gen Psychiatry 28:137–142.

Root doctors, faith healers, magic vendors, and neighborhood prophets, and trained community residents are functionally integrated into the health care resources of an urban black community.

3241. Hamburg DA: An evolutionary and developmental approach to human aggressiveness. Psychoanal Q 42:185–196.

Study of primates shows the aggressive behavior between man and man, man and animals, and human groups has been a prominent feature of human experiences for a very long time. The mechanisms of transmission at the biological level remain for future research to determine.

3242. Hammerschlag CA, Alderfer CP, Berg D: Indian education: a human systems analysis. Am J Psychiatry 130:1098–1102.

Off-reservation boarding schools should be converted into residential treatment facilities for seriously disturbed Indian children, and should be replaced by public schools having a greater community involvement.

3243. Handel A: Cognitive styles among adolescents in Israel. Int J Psychol 8:255–268.

Investigation into construct validity for the Embedded Figures Test and the Rod and Frame Test indicates a low degree of empirical equivalence between the two and therefore brings into question interpretations on the common variance with tests of ability.

3244. Handel A: The D 48 as a measure of general ability among adolescents in Israel. J Cross-Cultural Psychol 4:302–313.

Results of the use of the D 48 with four Israeli adolescent samples supports its cross-cultural suitability as a measure of general ability.

3245. Harding T: Psychosis in a rural West African community. Soc Psychiatry 8:198–203.

In Ibarapa district, severe psychosis is an important cause of incapacity. The existence of an established method of treatment for psychosis in the community and a firm belief in a supernatural cause of madness accounts for the hesitancy in seeking allopathic medical advice.

3246. Hartog J: Ninety-six Malay psychiatric patients: characteristics and preliminary epidemiology. Int J Soc Psychiatry 19:49–59.

The absence of parents and the stresses of urban life increase the manifestation of psychiatric symptoms and hospitalization for mental disorders among the Malays. More urban patients are anxious and depressed and have somatic symptoms than rural patients.

3247. Hassan R, Benjamin G: Ethnic out-marriage rates in Singapore: the influence of traditional sociocultural organization. J Marriage Fam 35:731–738.

Ethnicity, religion, and traditional ideals more strongly influence family organization than do class or education as demonstrated by variations in Malay, Indian, and Chinese interethnic marriages.

3248. Hays WC, Mindel CH: Extended kinship reactions in black and white families. J Marriage Fam 35:51–57.

Comparison of contact and aid patterns, number of resident kin, indicates that extended kinship is a more important, relevant structure for blacks than whites.

3249. Heron A, Dowel W: Weight conservation and matrix-solving ability in Papuan children. J Cross-Cultural Psychol 4:207–219.

Fifty percent of a sample of Papuan children with a median age of 13 years are classified as conservers by a nonverbal method. Matrix-solving ability is largely unrelated to conservation status.

3250. Hines GH: The persistence of Greek achievement motivation across time and culture. Int J Psychol 8:285–288.

Need for achievement persists across generational time and culture for Greek communities in diverse countries, to the extent that child-rearing practices are constant.

3251. Hollos M, Cowan PA: Social isolation and cognitive development: logical operations and role-taking abilities in three Norwegian social settings. Child Dev 44:630–641.

Language stimulation and schooling among Norwegian children in a farm community, a village, and a town do not seem to play a major role in the development of logical operations.

3252. Holmstrom EI: Changing sex roles in a developing country. J Marriage Fam 35:546–554.

Rural migrant wives in Turkey are more autonomous than their village peers. However, this autonomy is achieved at some psychic expense for those migrant wives who are most exposed to the urban situation.

3253. Holzner AS, Ding LK: White dragon pearls in Hong Kong: a study of young women drug addicts. Int J Addict 8:253–272.

Female heroin addicts have a background of poverty, weak family and social ties, unstable employment, and quasi-legal occupations. The drug subculture provides relief from the social problems of straight society.

3254. Hopkins B, Wober M: Games and sports: missing items in cross-cultural psychology. Int J Psychol 8:5–14.

Games and sports have qualities that lend themselves to employment in cross-cultural research on perception and cognition, social change, abstract abilities, and cooperation and conflict (through the application of game theory to games per se).

3255. Huang LC, Harris MB: Conformity in Chinese and Americans: a field experiment. J Cross-Cultural Psychol 4:427–434.

Chinese are generally more conforming than Americans. In both countries the occupational status of a behavioral model has more effect than does competence on conformity. High status-low competence models and low status-high competence models are more likely to be imitated than other models.

3256. Huffer V: Australian aborigine: transition in family grouping. Fam Process 12:303–316.

Missionary influence in the last half century has brought about a transition from polygyny to monogamy among the Lardil. Today there is a tendency for young women not to marry, but to incorporate their offspring into the parental household. The pattern that is developing is suggestive of potential matriarchal dominance.

3257. Jahasz P: Pathogenic factors eliciting neurosis in the inhabitants of a Hungarian village in the years following the formation of agricultural cooperatives. Int J Soc Psychiatry 19:173–179.

Economic consolidation and cultural indifference are two conflicting factors in the life of rural Hungarian peasants. As the closed community of the village loosens up, the responsibility the peasants feel toward each other diminishes. Marital conflicts, problems of the successive generations, and chronic alcoholism increase.

3258. Jaquette J: Women in revolutionary movements in Latin America. J Marriage Fam 35:344–354.

Feminist planks in revolutionary platforms may be linked to the participation of female guerrillas, but their relationship is modified by identification with the international left and its closeness to the peasants. Feminists' issues are not salient to peasant-oriented platforms.

3259. Jay J, Birney R: Research findings on the kibbutz adolescent: a response to Bettelheim. Am J Orthopsychiatry 43:347–354.

The hypothesis that kibbutz adolescents exhibit greater repression than others is disputed. There is little difference on most personality variables as measured by the Marlowe-Crowne Social Desirability Scale.

3260. Jensen B: Human reciprocity: an arctic exemplification. Am J Orthopsychiatry 43:447–458.

The study of Greenlandic Eskimos sheds light on a universal problem of how to create a variety of sociocultural patterns that meet the basic human need of close interpersonal relationships.

3261. Jones IV, Horne DJ DeL: Psychiatric disorders among aborigines of the Australian Western desert. Soc Sci Med 7:219–228.

A survey of 959 Australian Western Desert and Kimberely aborigines reveals a prevalence rate slightly lower than that found in Western communities. The absence of overt anxiety, homosexuality, and suicide may be related to indigenous cultural patterns.

3262. Joseph Ed: Aggression redefined—its adaptational aspects. Psychoanal Q 42:197–213.

The definition of aggression may be broadened to include all forceful behavior and activities that involve approaching, or going toward, an object.

3263. Kagan J, Klein RE, Haith MM, Morrison FJ: Memory and meaning in two cultures. Child Dev 44:221–223.

Recognition memory of American five- and eight-year-olds is superior to that of similar aged Guatemalan children. However, 11-year-olds in both cultures perform at an equally high level. The availability of an appropriate verbal label does not always enhance recognition memory of simple geometric forms.

3264. Kagitcibasi C: Psychological aspects of modernization in Turkey. J Cross-Cultural Psychol 4:157–174.

Traditional and modern personality types may be noted for Turkish high school students. The traditional type is associated with family control characteristic of immobile, low socioeconomic status, and rural homes.

3265. Kahn MW, Delk JL: Developing a community mental health clinic on an Indian reservation. Int J Soc Psychiatry 19:299–306.

The community psychology model appears to be an effective way of working with Papagos. Tribal approval and support is important in working with an ethnic-cultural minority group with considerable language and cultural differences.

3266. Kaplan RM, Goldman RD: Interracial perception among black, white and Mexican-American high school students. J Pers Soc Psychol 28:383–389.

Black students perceive whites and Mexican-Americans as different. Mexican-American students do not perceive a difference between themselves and the other groups. Black and Mexican-American students are more aware of each others' characteristics than of white students' characteristics.

3267. Katchadourian HA, Churchill CW: Components in prevalence of mental illness and social class in urban Lebanon. Soc Psychiatry 8:145–151.

A significant association exists between social class and the incidence of mental illness, with the upper class in urban Lebanon showing the highest rate. However, among the prevalence population, lower-class patients predominate. The relative role of other significant variables, such as religion, must be examined before extensive interpretations of social-class data can be made.

3268. Katchadourian HA, Churchill CW: Education and mental illness in urban Lebanon. Soc Psychiatry 8:152–161.

Educational level is significantly related to the prevalence and types of treated psychiatric illness. The least educated Lebanese have the highest utilization rates of psychiatric services.

3269. Kelly R: Mental illness in the Maori population of New Zealand. Acta Psychiatr Scand 49:722–734.

Acculturation stresses contribute to recent increases in mental illness observed among the Maori. Other factors that contribute to life stresses: the Maori are educationally disadvantaged, they represent a racial minority, and many have assumed migrant status.

3270. Khokhlov NE, Gonzalez AEJ: Cross-cultural comparison of cognitive consistency. Int J Psychol 8:137–145.

Significant differences exist in American and Greek subjects' responses to cognitive inconsistency, the balance effect being inoperative in the Greek sample. The assumption of a universally operative balancing effect model of cognitive consistency may be an artifact.

3271. Kinzer NS: Priests, machos and babies: or, Latin American women and the Manichaean heresy. J Marriage Fam 35:300–312.

Female unemployment and illiteracy are more salient factors explaining high birthrates than Roman Catholic opposition to contraceptives or the cultural ethos of machismo.

3272. Kinzie JD, Bolton JM: Psychiatry with the aborigines of West Malaysia. Am J Psychiatry 130: 769–773.

West Malaysian aborigine schizophrenics may be successfully treated in a hospital that emphasizes their own culture. Aborigine members of the hospital staff provide follow-up services in the villages of the jungle.

3273. Kinzie JD, Ryals J, Cottington F, McDermott JF: Cross-Cultural study of depressive symptoms in Hawaii. Int J Soc Psychiatry 19:19–24.

Among Japanese, Chinese, and Caucasian students at the University of Hawaii, Asian females have the highest prevalence of moderate to severe depression as measured by the Zung Self-Rating Depression Scale. Social class, religion, length of residency in Hawaii, position in family, and number of siblings are not related to depression. The Asian-American students' introverted, reserved, deferential, "turning toward self" life-style is exaggerated under stress to produce depressive symptoms.

3274. Kleinfeld JS: Effects of nonverbally communicated personal warmth on the intelligence test performance of Indian and Eskimo adolescents. J Soc Psychol 91:149–150.

While some students' scores remained the same and others' scores changed, the importance of non-verbal warmth is suggested by the study and may have shown greater effects if the examiner's race had been different.

3275. Korten FF: The stereotype as a cognitive construct. J Soc Psychol 90:29–39.

The function of the stereotype for American and Ethiopian students may be to permit reduction of environmental uncertainty through prediction.

3276. Krug SE, Kulhavy RW: Personality differences across regions in the United States. J Soc Psychol 91:73–79.

Samples from the Northeast, Southeast, Midwest, Western Mountain, Southwest, and West Coast of the United States, measured on the 16 PF, provide the factor structure of personality differences across geographic regions.

3277. Krupinski J, Stoller A, Wallace L: Psychiatric disorders in East European refugees now in Australia. Soc Sci Med 7:31–49.

Jewish refugees have low rates of schizophrenia and high upward mobility. The high rates of psychiatric disorders of Polish, Russian, and Ukranian refugees are proportionate to their experiences during World War II. Neither family support nor the degree of assimilation in Australia has a protective influence on the refugees studied.

3278. Kugelmass S, Lieblich I, Ben-Shakhar G: Information detection through differential GSRs in Bedouins of the Israeli desert. J Cross-Cultural Psychol 4:481–492.

Findings of higher skin conductance and low rates of GSR reactivity among Israeli Bedouins are confirmed among Abu Rhabiah Bedouins. Differential GSR reactivity among Jewish and Bedouin samples seems to be related to formal education.

3279. Kuromaru S: Changes in Japanese mother-child separation anxiety in Japan (1963–1972). J Nerv Ment Dis 157:339–345.

Familial and community changes in Japan are reflected in the increase of children who behave completely independent of their mothers, and of those who assume superficial independence forced by their mothers' anxiety at home. The proportion of separation anxieties intrinsic to two-year-old children, however, remains relatively stable despite drastic social change.

3280. Lammermeier PJ: The urban black family of the nineteenth century: a study of black family structure in the Ohio Valley, 1850–1880. J Marriage Fam 35:440–456.

The majority of nineteenth-century urban black families were patriarchal, two-parent nuclear households; however, during the 1870s, there was an increasing trend toward matriarchal extended families.

3281. Lamont J, Tyler C: Racial differences in rate of depression. J Clin Psychol 29:428–432.

On a measure of depression, racial groups score highest to lowest in the following order: Japanese-American, Mexican-American, Chinese-American, white, and black. The black has a ready-made villain (the white) to blame for misfortune. The Chinese culture does not emphasize control over children's behavior through internalized guilt, as is more likely in Japanese and perhaps Mexican cultures. White-American culture does not inculcate internalized guilt except possibly where Christian beliefs are adhered to strongly.

3282. Lane STM: Semantic differential scales for Portugese speakers in Brazil. Int J Psychol 8:147–152.

Specific studies into the opposition of adjectives in semantic differential scales and the theoretical meaning of the three universal dimensions are necessary. Psychological processes of the acquisition of meaning may be more complex than previously suggested.

3283. Langgulung H, Torrance EP: A cross-cultural study of children's conceptions of situational causality in India, Western Samoa, Mexico, and the United States. J Soc Psychol 89:175–183.

Sixth-grade children, advantaged children, and children in the United States and India are more causally oriented than fourth graders, disadvantaged children, and their Mexican and Western Samoan counterparts.

3284. Larsen KS, Arosalo U, Lineback S, Ommundsen R: New left ideology—a cross-national study. J Soc Psychol 90:321–322.

National characteristics may partly account for the differing factor structures for new left ideology between Japan, the United States, and Norway.

3285. Laszlo E: A systems philosophy of human values. Behav Sci 18:250–261.

Values are expressions of various states of adaptation of the individual to his biological and sociocultural environment. In a science of normative values, patterns of optimum physical and mental development would be defined.

3286. Lauer RH: The social readjustment scale and anxiety: a cross-cultural study. J Psychosom Res 17:171–174.

There is a strong relationship between measures of anxiety and the social readjustment rating scale among English and American subjects.

3287. Lebra TS: Compensative justice and moral investment among Japanese, Chinese, and Koreans. J Nerv Ment Dis 157:278–291.

Japanese, Koreans, and Chinese show striking differences between responses to sentence-completion tasks measuring individuals' moral values.

3288. LeCompte WF, LeCompte GK: Generational attribution in Turkish and American youth: a study of social norms involving the family. J Cross-Cultural Psychol 4:175–191.

Results of factor analysis support the notion that Turkish youths' attitude changes occur in the direction of more individualism despite paternal constraints, and suggest that not all social norms are affected by modernity pressures. The generation gap as perceived by youth appears to be a multivariate phenomenon.

3289. Leff JP: Culture and the differentiation of emotional states. Br J Psychiatry 123:299–306.

Developed countries show a greater differentiation of emotional states than developing countries. American Negro patients show significantly less emotional differentiation than white American patients.

3290. Leginski W, Izzett RR: Linguistic styles as indices for interpersonal distance. J Soc Psychol 91:291–304.

Although both influence estimates of interpersonal distance and involvement, linguistic style is more influential than interaction content.

3291. Lerner RM, Karson M: Racial stereotypes of early adolescent white children. Psychol Rep 32:381–382.

Lower-middle-class junior high school students in Detroit hold an unfavorable view of the black figure and a positive view of the white figure.

3292. Lester BM, Klein RE: The effect of stimulus familiarity on the conservation performance of rural Guatemalan children. J Soc Psychol 90:197–205.

Rural Guatemalan children show superior performance on conservation tasks using familiar materials and demonstrate improvement with second testing.

3293. Lester D: Fear of the dead in nonliterate societies. J Soc Psychol 90:329–330.

Findings of an association between fear of the dead, measured by extent of supernatural causes of illness in the society, and experience of love-oriented punishment technique, are not confirmed with data assessing fear of the dead in terms of funerary custom.

3294. Lidz RW, Lidz T, Burton-Bradley BG: Cargo cultism: a psychosocial study of Melanesian millenarianism. J Nerv Ment Dis 157:370–388.

Cargo cults are a way of regaining self-esteem by projecting blame on an outside group and/or promoting an intrapsychic reunification through relying on one's own ancestors and mores while eliminating foreign influences. Cultist thinking, with its profound ethnocentricity, poor boundary formation, and cognitive regression, contributes to our understanding of schizophrenic thinking.

3295. Liss JL, Welner A, Robins E, Richardson M: Psychiatric symptoms in white and black inpatients. Compr Psychiatry 14:475–481.

Greater association between symptoms and diagnosis is found in white patients discharged from inpatient services than in black patients. Differences in symptoms between black and white patients cannot be explained by a difference in frequency of psychiatric disorders.

3296. Lohr JM, Staats A: Attitude conditioning in Sino-Tibetan languages. J Pers Soc Psychol 26:196–200.

The language-conditioning effect on attitudes is significant among Cantonese, Japanese, and Korean speakers.

3297. MacArthur RS: Some ability patterns: Central Eskimos and Nsenga Africans. Int J Psychol 8:239–247.

Cognitive ability patterning for young Central Eskimos and Nsenga Zambians suggests that ecology and upbringing foster some differences in field independence and reasoning. The former show broad field independence of abilities with a cluster of abilities involving inductive reasoning from nonverbal stimuli; while the conformity upbringing of the latter shows a blurring of such a distinction.

3298. MacMurray J: Aggression, schizophrenic reactions and epilepsy: some transcultural correlations. Int J Soc Psychiatry 19:25–30.

The differential effects of urbanization act directly upon the incidence rates of schizophrenia and epilepsy. The amount of expressed aggression depends upon individual encounters, which in turn depend upon the relationship of the species to the environment.

3299. Madsen MC, Kagan S: Mother-directed achievement of children in two cultures. J Cross-Cultural Psychol 4:221–228.

In two experimental situations, Mexican mothers give more rewards for failure than do Los Angeles mothers, while Los Angeles mothers choose more difficult achievement goals for their children and do not lower the goal following failure, as do the Mexican mothers.

3300. Marcovitz E: Aggression in human adaptation. Psychoanal Q 42:226–233.

Aggression is a necessary mode of adaptation. Any attempt to eliminate aggression from either the human constitution or behavior is absurd.

3301. Marriott JAS: Family background and psychiatric disorders: experience with admissions to the University Hospital of the West Indies. Can Psychiatr Assoc J 18:209–214.

Despite cultural differences among the white, Chinese, and general Jamaican population in the West Indies, the pattern of hospital admissions is very similar to that of psychiatric units in more highly developed countries.

3302. Marsella AJ, Kinzie D, Gordon P: Ethnic variations in the expression of depression. J Cross-Cultural Psychol 4:435–458.

Japanese-American and Caucasian-American depression patterns are dominated by existential symptoms, while somatic symptoms are more characteristic of Chinese-Americans. Both Oriental groups manifest a cognitive symptom pattern. Symptoms may be related to extensions of self-conditioned socialization experiences.

3303. Martinez C: Community mental health and the Chicano movement. Am J Orthopsychiatry 43:595–601.

The Chicano movement overlaps with the community mental health movement. Mexican-Americans have been stereotyped in epidemiological studies.

3304. Masuda M, Hasegawa RS, Matsumoto G: The ethnic identity questionnaire: a comparison of three Japanese age groups in Tachikawa, Japan, Honolulu, and Seattle. J Cross-Cultural Psychol 4:229–244.

Quantification of ethnic identity shows an attenuation of cultural attitudes and beliefs in all three locations. The elderly in the three locations show agreement representative of a core that may be termed *Meiji Japaneseness.* In Seattle and Honolulu, age groups of the next generation are more similar than their Tachikawa counterparts.

3305. Meade RD, Barnard WA: Conformity and anticonformity among Americans and Chinese. J Soc Psychol 89:15–24.

Americans show greater anticonformity than do Chinese students, and, although Americans make greater shifts in opinion under group pressure, Chinese make more shifts overall.

3306. Meade RD, Brislin RW: Controls in cross-cultural experimentation. Int J Psychol 8:231–238.

Cross-cultural research in psychology requires the same controls that are maintained in other psychological research. Control problems at the loci of stimulus, subject, and reaction recording must be considered in this light.

3307. Meade RD, Singh L: Changes in social distance during warfare: a study of the India/Pakistan War of 1971. J Soc Psychol 90:325–326.

Although both Indian Hindus and Muslims increased their social distance for Pakistani Muslims, Hindus increased their social distance to Indian Muslims and Muslims decreased social distance toward each other.

3308. Meade RD, Singh L: Motives for child-bearing in American and in India. J Cross-Cultural Psychol 4:89–110.

Significant differences between sexes and cultural groups—American, upper-caste Hindus, and Indian Muslims—are found for desired number of children, sex ratios, ages, and naming of children by childless college students.

3309. Mechanic D: The contributions of sociology to psychiatry. Psychol Med 3:1–4.

As sociological research efforts develop on matters relevant to psychiatric practice, greater attention must be given to improved concepts and measurements of psychiatric disabilities; clearer specification of the factors intervening between social and environmental change and individual pathology; clearer separation between the factors causing illness, the process of seeking help, and factors affecting the course of illness and disability; and greater cooperation between the relevant behavioral disciplines.

3310. Meers DR: Psychoanalytic research and intellectual functioning of ghetto-reared, black children. Psychoanal Study Child 28:395–417.

Retardation of the ghetto child is a culture-specific expression of psychopathology.

3311. Meir EI, Sohlberg S, Barak A: A cross-cultural comparison of the structure of vocational interests. J Cross-Cultural Psychol 4:501–508.

Vocational interests in Western and non-Western (Jewish and Arab) cultures have a similar circular configuration as indicated by smallest space analysis.

3312. Michael ST: A social class dependent factor in questionnaire research. J Psychiatr Res 10:73–82.

Responses of low socioeconomic respondents to certain types of questions in the Midtown Manhattan Mental Health Study fit recent observations that language is an encoding of developmental social-class experiences and determines the mode of an individual's management of social problems.

3313. Miller AG: Integration and acculturation of cooperative behavior among Blackfoot Indian and non-Indian Canadian children. J Cross-Cultural Psychol 4:374–380.

Blackfoot and white children from integrated schools show an intermediate frequency of cooperative responses to children from Blackfoot or white schools.

3314. Miller RE, Levine JM, Mirsky IA: Effects of psychoactive drugs on nonverbal communication and group social behavior of monkeys. J Pers Soc Psychol 28:396–405.

Stimulants, tranquilizers, and hallucinogens have differential effects on nonverbal communication and group social behavior in rhesus monkeys.

3315. Miller RJ: Cross-cultural research in the perception of pictorial materials. Psychol Bull 80:135–150.

There are cross-cultural differences in the ways people respond to pictorial materials. This finding is important in preparing educational and stimulus materials cross-culturally.

3316. Miller SI, Schoenfeld L: Grief in the Navajo: psychodynamics and culture. Int J Soc Psychiatry 19:187–191.

The abnormal grief reaction prevalent among the Navaho is not different in kind from that seen in other peoples. It is, however, different in that the culture predisposes the individual to certain psychologic mechanisms leading to this reaction. The prohibition against mourning for longer than four days, the sanction against expression of anger, and the general fear of the dead all operate toward this end.

3317. Monahan TP: Marriage across racial lines in Indiana. J Marriage Fam 35:632–640.

Characteristics of interracial marriage, age, birthplace, residence, occupational level, are variable for each group (white, Negro, other) and no single pattern could be found for the whole.

3318. Moran LJ: Comparative growth of Japanese and North American cognitive dictionaries. Child Dev 44:862–865.

The child's early cognitive dictionary structure is an endogenous creation, not an imitation of the parents' dictionary structure. In children, whether Japanese or North American, an early endogenous principle for organizing lexical entries is "action upon referent." Culture predetermines the operative component of adult dictionary structures as well as the figurative component.

3319. Morgan RW: Migration as a factor in acceptance of medical care. Soc Sci Med 7:865–873.

Recent immigrants are as receptive or more receptive to modern medical practices and beliefs than are long-standing Logos residents. Innovated medical demonstration programs in a developing urban area should be aimed initially at migrants as a target group.

3320. Morrill RG: The dynamics of cultural change: the effect of cross cultural communication on small group behavior in Thailand. Soc Psychiatry 8:162–182.

Cultural change as measured by Thai medical student verbal assertiveness with American teachers is correlated with English language ability but is not related to socioeconomic variables, which are usually thought relevant.

3321. Morrison SD: Intermediate variables in the association between migration and mental illness. Int J Soc Psychiatry 19:60–65.

Help should be provided to migrants in areas that would allow the maximum maintenance of ethnic identity and the maximum time to learn the language and customs of the new environments. Community mental health clinics should be staffed by people as culturally similar to their catchment area as possible.

3322. Morsbach H: Aspects of nonverbal communication in Japan. J Nerv Ment Dis 157:262–277.

Students of Japanese language and culture should acquaint themselves with important aspects of nonverbal communication accompanying, supplementing, and/or replacing Japanese verbal communication.

3323. Moxley RL: Family solidarity and quality of life in an agricultural Peruvian community. J Marriage Fam 35:497–504.

The social solidarity of rural families, as measured by Guttman scale and nonscale measures, are strongly related to medical practices.

3324. Mumford E: Sociology and aggression. Psychoanal Q 42:234–238.

We must consider the reality of aggression and social conflict as necessary forces and move on to consideration of how to structure the goals and modalities of their expression in society, and with what consequence.

3325. Munroe RH, Munroe RL: Population density and movement in folktales. J Soc Psychol 91:339–340.

Folktales from Logoli society, which has a high population density relative to the Gusii and Kipsigis, show more psychological concern with freedom of physical mobility than the folktales of the latter two societies.

3326. Munroe RL, Munroe RH, Daniels RE: Relation of subsistence economy to conformity in three East African societies. J Soc Psychol 89:149–150.

Partial confirmation on the relationship between conformity socialization and subsistence is obtained between the herding Kipisigis and agricultural Gusii, but lack of significant difference with the Logoli is not explained.

3327. Munroe RL, Munroe RH, Nerlove SB: Male pregnancy symptoms and cross-sex identity: two replications. J Soc Psychol 89:147–148.

Additional data on the Luo and Bantu-speaking Gusii of Kenya provide some support for previous findings of a relationship between male pregnancy symptomatology and measures of sex identity.

3328. Mustafa G: Society in relation to mental health in Kenya. J Nerv Ment Dis 156:295–296.

Social changes incident to industrialization, detribalization, and urbanization, along with the increasing acceptance of Western medicine in Kenya, appear to be related to a progressively increasing rate of mental hospital admissions since 1950.

3329. Neki J: Guru-chela relationship: the possibility of a therapeutic paradigm. Am J Orthopsychiatry 43:755–766.

The guru-chela relationship in India aims at total life transformation and is based on a process of discipline in which the guru enables his disciple to attain the state of positive freedom.

3330. Neki JS: Psychiatry in South-East Asia. Br J Psychiatry 123:257–269.

The mental health problem of South-East Asian countries must be understood not only in the light of Western influences but also through Eastern explanations of unique native behavior patterns and their dynamics.

3331. Olsen GA: Sexual norms under the influence of altered cultural patterns in Greenland. Acta Psychiatr Scand 49:148–158.

Sexual behavior among unmarried people in Greenland today bears no relation to the original Eskimo norms, but, as a result of the increasing number of unmarried Danes in Greenlandic society, is in conformity with Danish sexual norms.

3332. Olsen NJ: Family structure and independence training in a Taiwanese village. J Marriage Fam 35:512–519.

Mothers in extended families of a Taiwanese village are not likely to train their children to be self-reliant.

3333. Orpen C: The Quick Test with coloreds in South Africa. Psychol Rep 32:897–898.

The Quick Test is a fairly valid indicator of intelligence for this group.

3334. Otsyula W: Native and Western healing: the dilemma of East African psychiatry. J Nerv Ment Dis 156:297–299.

In Kenya folk healing and religious-magical belief systems, especially those concerned with the influence of ancestral spirits, continue to provide the context of both Western medical practice and national development. This is possibly because modern medical facilities are so few and inadequate that people have not been able to rely upon them.

3335. Owoc PJ: On culture and conservation once again. Int J Psychol 8:249–254.

A firm definition of the salience of age and schooling to conservation should prove useful in isolating the proper setting for observing cognitive change in Nigeria.

3336. Ozturk O: Ritual circumcision and castration anxiety. Psychiatry 36:49–60.

Ritual circumcision is performed in Turkey without anesthesia during critical childhood stages. Through societal processes circumcision becomes an important ego need in the development of self-concept and identity.

3337. Page HW: Concepts of length and distance in a study of Zulu youths. J Soc Psychol 90:9–16.

Schooling and urban residence promote the development of Euclidean spatial concepts in some Zulu youths, while others tend to retain early topological concepts.

3338. Parens H: Aggression: a reconsideration. J Am Psychoanal Assoc 21:34–60.

The aggressive drive has an inherently nondestructive, egosyntonic current and a current that is inherently destructive.

3339. Pattison EM, Lapins NA, Doerr HA: Faith healing: a study of personality and function. J Nerv Ment Dis 157:397–409.

Within the framework of the assumptive world view in which faith-healing subjects live, their personality structures and magical belief systems are not abnormal but are part of a coping system that provides ego integration for the individual and social integration for the subculture.

3340. Premack D, Anglin B: On the possibilities of self-control in man and animals. J Abnorm Soc Psychol 81:137–151.

It should be possible to examine the socialization process and conditions and describe them so that self-control may be developed in an animal or enable us to show why an animal may be incapable of such process. The procedure by which an animal may develop one-organism control, or self-control, may illuminate this process.

3341. Redlich F: The anthropologist as observer: ethical aspects of clinical observations of behavior. J Nerv Ment Dis 157:313–319.

Caudill's concealed study which contributed to his book, *The Psychiatric Hospital as a Small Society,* would probably not be done today in light of an increasing concern about ethics. However, when Caudill undertook his study, he struggled with its problems and solved them honestly and courageously as best as he could.

3342. Reed FW, Udry Jr: Female work, fertility, and contraceptive use in a biracial sample. J Marriage Fam 35:585–596.

The relationship between female work and fertility is strong and basically the same for blacks and whites; however, no strongly conclusive findings can be made for a relationship between work participation and contraceptive use.

3343. Rin H, Schooler C, Caudill WA: Culture, social structure and psychopathology in Taiwan and Japan. J Nerv Ment Dis 157:296–312.

Factor analysis of the symptom patterns of hospitalized Taiwan-Chinese and Japanese mental patients reveal both cross-cultural differences and culturally specific symptom factors.

3344. Rollins JH: Reference identification of youth of differing ethnicity. J Pers Soc Psychol 26:222–231.

Among third-generation Italian, Polish, Portuguese, Irish, Jewish, French-Canadian, and Yankee students a significant correlation is found between ethnic involvement of members and degree of rejection of each group by members of other groups.

3345. Rosenberg GS, Anspach DF: Sibling solidarity in the working class. J Marriage Fam 35:108–113.

The thesis that sibling solidarity is a characteristic of American kinship has been overexaggerated for urban working-class groups. Sibling solidarity may vary throughout the life cycle and may be a source of support when the conjugal relationship dissolves.

3346. Ross JA: Influence of expert and peer upon Negro mothers of low socioeconomic status. J Soc Psychol 89:79–84.

Advice from an expert is more effective than peer opinion for Negro mothers seeking child-rearing guidance.

3347. Saiyadain MS: Effect of sexual level of education of F-score: a cross-cultural study. Psychol Rep 33:548.

American Indian students, irrespective of their years in school and sex, score significantly higher on F-score (authoritarianism) than their American counterparts.

3348. Salaff JW: The emerging conjugal relationship in the People's Republic of China. J Marriage Fam 35:705–717.

Mate selection and marital arrangements in China are now contracted more freely than in the past, but attitudes toward obligation to households and to parents are much slower to change.

3349. Saxena AP: Modernization: a typological approach. J Soc Psychol 90:17–27.

Village Indians high on individual and system variables of change display more modernity in scores measuring response to agricultural innovation than those individuals high on only one variable or low on both variables.

3350. Schoenfeld LS, Miller SI: The Navajo Indian: a descriptive study of the psychiatric population. Int J Soc Psychiatry 19:31–37.

The Navaho medicine man is the primary source of medical care for many Indians with organic illnesses. The lack of manic illness among the Navahos may be explained by a genetic mechanism, since intermarriage has been infrequent among Navahos who continue to live on the reservation. The lack of sexual deviations is difficult to explain.

3351. Schwab J, McGinnis N, Warheit G: Social psychiatric impairment: racial comparisons. Am J Psychiatry 130:183–187.

Rapid social change in the Southeast, as well as social and economic depreciation, help explain the differing impairment rates among adult whites and blacks.

3352. Sechrest L, Fay T, Zaidi H, Flores L: Attitudes toward mental disorder among college students in the United States, Pakistan, and the Philippines. J Cross-Cultural Psychol 4:342–360.

Pakistani and Filipino attitudes on mental illness are more similar, though the Pakistanis illustrate greater heterogeneity in attitudes.

3353. Sethi BB, Gupta SC: Sibling position in India: psychiatric and non-psychiatric patients. Am J Psychother 27:61–69.

In India the eldest or early born are psychiatrically affected to a significantly greater extent than the later born in both the psychiatric and nonpsychiatric patients. This finding can be understood in terms of Indian cultural attitudes toward children.

3354. Sethi BB, Nathawat SS, Gupta SC: Depression in India. J Soc Psychol 91:3–13.

Urbanism, industrialization, and social change contribute to depression; while the concomitants of rural living probably deter depression. Somatic and psychological manifestations are more frequent than guilt feelings.

3355. Shanas E: Family-kin networks and aging in cross-cultural perspective. J Marriage Fam 35:505–511.

Contrary to popular belief, the elderly find their primary psychological and social support in the family and kin networks in the United States as well as in Denmark, Britain, Yugoslavia, and Poland.

3356. Shapiro ET, Pinsker H: Shared ethnic scotoma. Am J Psychiatry 130:1338–1341.

A shared ethnicity between therapist and client, rather than helping the therapist better understand the client as many writers have indicated, may actually lead to "blind spots" that inhibit or prevent understanding.

3357. Sheehan PW: The variability of eidetic imagery among Australian aboriginal children. J Soc Psychol 91:29–36.

Variability of eidetic imagery across relatively unacculturated samples of Bamyili and Hooker Creek aboriginal children and the lower incidence of eidetic imagery among the more tribally oriented in Hooker Creek sample perpetuate the puzzle of eidetic imagery in cross-cultural research.

3358. Shenken LI: An application of ethology to aspects of human behavior. Br J Med Psychol 46:123–134.

Psychoanalytic theory can be allied with the ethological concept to the mutual advantage of both disciplines. The submissive factor of dominance-subordination needs to be given more attention.

3359. Shore J, Kinzie J, Hampson J, Pattison E: Psychiatric epidemiology of an Indian village. Psychiatry 36:70–81.

Study of a Pacific Northwest Coastal Indian village provides data supporting the contention that subjects experiencing social disorganization are more vulnerable to stress and the development of psychiatric morbidity such as alcoholism, neurotic symptoms, or peptic ulcers.

3360. Shore JH, Stone DL: Duodenal ulcer among Northwest Coastal Indian women. Am J Psychiatry 130:774–777.

An analysis of a psychiatric epidemiologic survey and follow-up study shows a high prevalence rate of duodenal ulcer among Indians of the coastal Pacific Northwest. The high rate found among the tribe, and particularly among the female members, is related to their current minority- and poverty-group acculturation stresses and to a matrilineal culture.

3361. Siegel RK: An ethnological search for self-administration of hallucinogens. Int J Addict 8:373–393.

Laboratory, anthropological, and sociological findings indicate that a wide variety of infrahuman species deliberately or accidentally self-administer hallucinogens. As with man, the primary ethologic effect is social isolation.

3362. Sieka FL, Jaques ME, Hartl RFP: Attitudinal factor patterns across three cultures: Denmark, Greece and the United States. Int J Soc Psychiatry 19:10–18.

In American, Greek, and Danish cultures, social deviates are less acceptable than physically and mentally disabled persons. When compared to mental and social deviates, nondisabled persons have more positive affect and feel less socially distant to physically disabled persons.

3363. Smart RC, Smart MS: New Zealand preadolescent's parent-peer orientation and parent perceptions compared with English and American. J Marriage Fam 35:142–148.

In New Zealand, 11 and 12 year olds score highest in mean score on a moral dilemma test. A parent-perception test indicates that boys and girls receive more socializing than their English and U.S. peers.

3364. Smith HE: The Thai family: nuclear or extended. J Marriage Fam 35:136–141.

The nuclear family is the ideal form and statistical normative form in Thai villages.

3365. Smith JH, Pao PN, Schweig NA: On the concept of aggression. Psychoanal Study Child 28:331–346.

Aggressive modes derive from a primitive "automatic" flight mechanism that is part of the primary mental endowment. Libidinal and aggressive drives are both derived from a primitively "blind" flight mechanism. Such a conceptualization accounts for convergent and divergent motivation more adequately than do concepts of instinctual fusion and defusion.

3366. Smith T: The susceptibility of Xhosa groups to a perspective illusion. J Soc Psychol 90:331–332.

The introduction of perspective set to Xhosa subjects influences illusion susceptibility in only the most acculturated group.

3367. Spiro ME: The Oedipus complex in Burma. J Nerv Ment Dis 157:389–395.

Myths, folkways, and residential patterns in Burma are dimensions of parent-child tension that comprise the basic elements of the Oedipus complex. Temptations and/or accusations of incest constitute one of the grounds for the avoidance of parent-child households.

3368. Srole L, Fischer AK: The social epidemiology of smoking behavior 1953 and 1970: the Midtown Manhattan study. Soc Sci Med 7:341–358.

Tobacco smoking is an item of behavior that is entangled in the most complicated social and psychological processes. Exploration into the etiologies of smoking behavior warrant high scientific status.

3369. Statt D: Flag choices of elite American and Canadian children. Psychol Rep 32:85–86.

Responses to the U.N., U.S., Russian, and Canadian flags are similar for both national samples. The choice patterns parallel the choices of nonelite children.

3370. Stein HF: Cultural specificity in patterns of mental illness and health: a Slovak-American case study. Fam Process 12:69–82.

The study of mental illness in its cultural context is exemplified with a Slovak-American case family with a schizophrenic member. Cultural relativism is an analytic tool that must be applied to field data.

3371. Stevens EP: The prospects for a women's liberation movement in Latin America. J Marriage Fam 35:313–321.

Comparison of Latin America's social and economic position with that of North American postindustrial societies' women's liberation movements suggests that a similar pattern will not take place in Latin America in the near future.

3372. Steward M, Steward D: The observation of Anglo-, Mexican-, and Chinese-American mothers teaching their young sons. Child Dev 44:329–337.

Interactional analysis of mothers teaching preschool-age children a sorting and motor skill game reveals that ethnicity is the simple best predictor of maternal teaching and of child response.

3373. Stewart VM: Tests of the "carpentered world" hypothesis by race and environment in America and Zambia. Int J Psychol 8:83–94.

Muller-Lyer and Sander Parallelogram tests of American Negroes and Zambian samples indicate that when environment is held constant and pigmentation varied, no differences in illusion susceptibility occur. When pigmentation is held constant and environment varied, a positive relationship between degree of carpenteredness and susceptibility is noted. Although no single factor accounts for illusion susceptibility, some support is obtained for the carpentered world hypothesis, and for females to be more susceptible than males.

3374. Stinnett N, Talley S, Walters J: Parent-child relationships of black and white high school students: a comparison. J Soc Psychol 91:349–350.

Although the black family is often more mother centered, black students seem to experience closer parent-child relationships than are inferred from indexes of family strength based solely on demographic variables.

3375. Strong B: Toward a history of the experiential family: sex and incest in the nineteenth century family. J Marriage Fam 35:457–466.

The experiential family of nineteenth-century America encouraged latent incestuous attachments between mothers and sons.

3376. Suomi SJ: Repetitive peer separation of young monkeys: effects of vertical chamber confinement during separations. J Abnorm Psychol 81:1–11.

Chamber-separated rhesus exhibit higher levels of self-directed activity than cage-separated monkeys, while both groups show more post test despair and maturational arrest than nonseparated monkeys.

3377. Suomi SJ: Surrogate rehabilitation of monkeys reared in total social isolation. J Child Psychol Psychiatry 14:71–77.

Limited reversals of deficits produced by six months of isolation rearing from birth can be obtained in monkey subjects via exposure to surrogates and fellow isolates. However, they fail to develop sophisticated social behaviors such as play.

3378. Suomi SJ, Eisele CD, Grady SA, Tripp RL: Social preferences of monkeys reared in an enriched laboratory social environment. Child Dev 44:451–460.

Rhesus monkeys reared in a nuclear family environment prefer their mothers to other adult females, their fathers to other adult males, their mothers to their fathers, but exhibit no preference among siblings and peers.

3379. Stratton J: Cops and drunks: police attitudes and actions dealing with Indian drunks. Int J Addict 8:613–622.

Police attitudes and actions toward Navaho public drunkenness suggest a need for a shift from the punitive role to one of prevention and rehabilitation.

3380. Szalay LB, Bryson JA: Measurement of psychocultural distance: a comparison of American blacks and whites. J Pers Soc Psychol 26:166–177.

The distance between American whites and blacks may be assessed by comparing the dimensions of dominance, affinity structure, and intergroup similarity of concepts. The overall distance is small, but there is some variation across social domains.

3381. Taylor DM, Bassili JN, Aboud FE: Dimensions of ethnic identity: an example from Quebec. J Soc Psychol 89:185–192.

Language and cultural background are more salient factors in ethnic identity than geographic region, for French and English Canadians.

3382. Thakur GP, Thakur M: Some Indian data on reliability estimates of Forms A and B of the EPI. J Pers Assess 37:372–374.

Generally high reliability demonstrates that the EPI may be used for personality measurement in India.

3383. Tidrick K: Skin shade and need for achievement in a multiracial society: Jamaica, West Indies. J Soc Psychol 89:25–33.

White bias in the society probably contributes to differing n Ach scores by light and dark subjects as measured by the TAT.

3384. Triandis HC: Subjective culture and economic development. Int J Psychol 8:163–180.

The view that there is a universal psychological state that can be labeled "modernity" and measured with appropriate questions is too simplistic a view of this complex phenomenon. Measures such as those associated with the measurement of subjective culture variables may prove useful in mapping modernity, its forms, and processes.

3385. Tulkin SR, Leiderman PH: Infancy in a cultural context: Caudill's contribution to comparative child development. J Nerv Ment Dis 157:320–322.

The sum of Caudill's work indicates that only a combination of detailed naturalistic observations, controlled studies, and empathic immersion can serve as a proper basis for comparison across cultures.

3386. Turnage TW, McGinnies E: A cross-cultural comparison of the effects of presentation mode and meaningfulness on short-term recall. Am J Psychol 86:369–380.

Chinese subjects learn faster with visual input, while American subjects learn faster with auditory input.

3387. Twaddle AC: Illness and deviance. Soc Sci Med 7:751–762.

Illness is at once biophysical, social, psychological, and cultural in nature. The deviance framework, while fruitful, is not adequate for a full sociological understanding of illness or illness behavior.

3388. Van Lawick-Goodall J: The behavior of chimpanzees in their natural habitat. Am J Psychiatry 130:1–12.

Although human primates are unique, chimpanzees have behavior patterns that resemble those of man such as dominance, adolescence, affectionate familial bonds, and a long period of dependence on mother.

3389. Vassiliou G, Vassiliou VG: Subjective culture and psychotherapy. Am J Psychother 27:42–51.

Subjective culture, defined as the way in which individuals perceive their social milieu, presents significant across-milieu variations. Social psychological research concerning subjective culture has developed reliable and valid instruments. It is now possible to apply psychotherapy to the issue of milieu specificity.

3390. Vassiliou VG, Vassiliou G: The implicative meaning of the Greek concept of Philotimo. J Cross-Cultural Psychol 4:326–341.

When an individual moves into a more complex milieu in Greece, role perceptions become more important and conduct ceases to be regulated by group norms. Philotimo, love of honor, is expressed so as to allow for individual interpretations in various contexts.

3391. Veevers J: The social meanings of parenthood. Psychiatry 36:291–310.

Parenthood, in dominant cultural definitions, may be a religious, moral obligation, a civic responsibility, natural behavior, and a condition that imparts meaningfulness to sex and marriage.

3392. Wagatsuma H: Ishiwara Shintaro's early novels and Japanese male psychology. J Nerv Ment Dis 157:358–369.

Conflicts between passivity and activity, symptomatic of phallic character, are well portrayed in Ishiwara's novels.

3393. Walton J: The bio-social evolution of the human mind. Int J Soc Psychiatry 19:136–142.

If genes or instincts determined human behavior, psychology itself would be almost pointless. Therapeutic activity, instead of focusing always on personality resolution, may sometimes be purposeful if directed toward changing the sociocultural environment.

3394. Watson RI: Investigation into deindividuation using a cross-cultural survey technique. J Pers Soc Psychol 25:342–345.

A significant positive relationship exists between deindividuation and aggressiveness in many different cultures.

3395. Waziri R: Symptomatology of depressive illness in Afghanistan. Am J Psychiatry 130:213–217.

Symptoms of depression have the same incidence in Afghanistan as in Western culture. Suicidal thoughts, attempts, or intentions are much less frequent in Afghan patients than in patients in the West.

3396. Weinstein EA: Symbolization and the Sapir-Whorf hypothesis. Contemp Psychoanal 9:133–135.

The central idea of the Sapir-Whorf hypothesis is that language is not simply a device for reporting experience but, to a significant degree, defines experience for its speakers. Although it is impossible to prove the hypothesis, it remains an example of creative thinking and is of the greatest relevance to psychoanalysis.

3397. Welner A, Liss JL, Robins E: Psychiatric symptoms in white and black inpatients: follow-up study. Compr Psychiatry 14:483–488.

Black patients have a significantly higher rate of delusions and hallucinations than whites. The difference in symptomatology, rather than in the psychiatric disorder, is characteristic more of the group. A structured interview is of particular importance as a diagnostic tool for black patients.

3398. Westermeyer J: Assasination in Laos. Arch Gen Psychiatry 28:740–743.

Some cases of assassination in Laos resemble American frontier vigilantism. Assassination incidents may be grouped according to criminal recidivism, dysocial behavior such as witchcraft, and abuse of power by officials.

3399. Westermeyer J: Grenade-amok in Laos: a psychosocial perspective. Int J Soc Psychiatry 19:251–260.

Culturally defined weapons are employed in amok outbursts. Generally it is the most destructive implement widely available. There may be more useful information in the political and economic milieus within which amok occurs than in the delusions and hallucinations of an incarcerated person who has run amok.

3400. Westermeyer J: On the epidemicity of amok violence. Arch Gen Psychiatry 28:873–879.

Amok has certain epidemic characteristics, may be ethnically transmitted, and is related to sociohistorical change factors. Amok does not tend to be found in women, since they are less susceptible than men to sociocultural flux.

3401. White KG, Juhhasz JB, Wilson PJ: Is man no more than this? Evaluative bias in interspecies comparison. J Hist Behav Sciences 9:203–212.

The concept of man as "animal plus" in relation to other species has markedly influenced comparative ethological studies. The continuity view, which has encouraged quantitative comparison between the behaviors of various species, has been plagued by an evaluative bias. Proper understanding necessitates the qualitative view—man is neither more nor less than any other animal.

3402. Whiting B, Edward CP: A cross-cultural analysis of sex differences in the behavior of children aged three through eleven. J Soc Psychol 91:171–188.

Universal sex differences in child behavior to 11 years may be well explained by socialization differences, though socialization pressures seem consistent across many cultures. The learning environment may be responsible for many characteristics thought to be innate.

3403. Williams JA Jr, Stockton R: Black family structures and functions: an empirical examination of some suggestions made by Billingsley. J Marriage Fam 35:39–50.

Some modification of Billingsley's typology of black family structures is necessary to expand its usefulness.

3404. Williams JE, Best DL, Wood FB, Filler JW: Changes in the connotations of racial concepts and color names: 1963–1970. Psychol Rep 33:983–996.

For Caucasian students the events of the black identity movement during 1963–1970 are associated with a greater tendency toward the equation of color-person and ethnic concepts, with no appreciable changes in the affective meanings of ethnic concepts themselves.

3405. Wilson GD: Projective aggression and social attitudes. Psychol Rep 32:1015–1018.

Styles of aggression and modes of response to frustration are partial determinants of individual differences in social attitudes and belief patterns.

3406. Wimberly H: Conjugal-role organization and social networks in Japan and England. J Marriage Fam 35:125–130.

The merits of Harris's thesis, that conjugal role segregation is attributable to the existence of mono sex groups, over that of Bott's (segregation degree varies with family's social network), may be considered in terms of comparative Japanese-English data.

3407. Wintrob RM: The influence of others: witchcraft and rootwork as explanations of behavior disturbances. J Nerv Ment Dis 156:318–326.

Witchcraft is very common in sub-Saharan Africans, and belief in it is also shared by urbanized people in America. Folk healers, rootworkers, and houngans comprise an alternative medical system consistent with the beliefs and practices of the people they serve. The wish of the patient or his family for treatment by such people should be neither ridiculed nor denied.

3408. Withycombe JS: Relationships of self-concept, social status, and self-perceived social status and racial differences of Paiute and white elementary school children. J Soc Psychol 91:337–338.

Self-concept and social status are related for Paiute children, but not self-concept and perceived social status, or perceived status and actual status. High self-concept may result in peer acceptable behavior, and popularity may be irrelevant in Paiute culture.

3409. Wittkower ED, Dubreuil G: Psychocultural stress in relation to mental illness. Soc Sci Med 7:691–704.

Cultural stress factors are related to mental illness. Psychiatrists and anthropologists should cooperate in the field of reduction of mental illness by social engineering.

3410. Wittkower ED, Weidman HH: Magical thought and the integration of psychoanalytic and anthropological theory. Contemp Psychoanal 9: 481–501.

Efforts to synthesize the theory of the unconscious in psychoanalysis and cognitive theory in anthropology may prove to be one of the most productive areas of inquiry in the next decade.

3411. Wober M: East African undergraduates' attitudes concerning the concept: intelligence. Br J Soc Clin Psychol 12:431–432.

Concepts of intelligence and quickness are not systematically related but may be separate constructs. The relationship in certain cultures between intelligence and nonquickness, plus nutritional and other factors, may account for lengthier time required for cognitive performance in these contexts.

3412. Wolff HH: Aggression in relation to health and illness. Br J Med Psychol 46:23–27.

Inappropriate handling of aggressiveness and self-assertiveness can result in not only psychological or social difficulties but in structural lesions. Such physical symptoms may coexist or alternate with psychiatric manifestations. Human aggression can be explained in terms of not only biological potential and frustrating stimuli but also psychological makeup, including inner and outer relationships.

3413. Wong M, Singer K: Abnormal homicide in Hong Kong. Br J Psychiatry 123:295–298.

The pattern of normal and abnormal homicide in Hong Kong resembles that in England, Wales, and Philadelphia in a large number of characteristics. The main difference is quantitative—the high prevalence of normal homicide victims in Hong Kong. Other differences include the sex of homicidal offenders and victims and the mode of inflicting death.

3414. Yamaguchi T, Yamaguchi A: Permissiveness and psychotherapy in Japan. J Nerv Ment Dis 157:292–295.

In Japan a psychotherapeutic approach in which the therapist is permissive of the patient's human imperfections is crucial. Because the therapist there is an authority figure and thus a father surrogate, his permissiveness may enable the patient to accept his own imperfections.

3415. Young L, Suomi S, Harlow H, McKinney W: Early stress and later response to separation in Rhesus monkeys. Am J Psychiatry 130:400–405.

Rhesus monkeys separated from mother and

confined in a vertical chamber at birth later respond to separation and reunion by displaying increased self-mouthing, self-clasping, huddling, and rocking. The data indirectly support previous studies showing a relationship between human psychopathology and the combination of early-life separation and recent separation.

3416. Zacalloni M: Subjective culture, self-concept and the social environment. Int J Psychol 8:183–192.

A multistage focused introspection method for exploring the self-concept of a cultural group may have some validity, but further work is indicated. A major variable in the subjective structuring of social environment for American and French radical students is political ideology.

3417. Zak I: Dimensions of Jewish-American identity. Psychol Rep 33:891–900.

Jewish and American identity has dual and orthogonal dimensions and does not form a bipolar continuum.

1974

3418. Abernethy V: Dominance and sexual behavior: a hypothesis. Am J Psychiatry 131:813–817.

Male dominance facilitates male-female copulatory behavior, while female dominance inhibits it.

3419. Adams BN: Doing survey research cross-culturally: some approaches and problems. J Marriage Fam 35:568–574.

The principal difficulties encountered in an Ugandan-Asian study of the elderly are communication and motivation. A study in African secondary schools encountered primary communication problems that were overcome by pretesting.

3420. Adams BN: The kin network and the adjustment of the Ugandan Asians. J Marriage Fam 36:190–195.

Presence of kin is an important motive for resettlement choice for one third of the respondents; for most, economic, educational, and other motives take precedence. For Ugandan-Asian males, kin network functions instrumentally; for females, kin provides an emotional defense mechanism.

3421. Albaugh BJ, Anderson PO: Peyote in the treatment of alcoholism among American Indians. Am J Psychiatry 134:1247–1250.

Indian alcoholics benefit from a treatment program that offers occupational and cultural therapy, including participation in the services of the Native American Church (peyote meetings).

3422. Bahr HM, Chadwick BA: Conservatism, racial intolerance and attitudes toward racial assimilation among whites and American Indians. J Soc Psychol 94:45–56.

Conservatism among Seattle Indians is comparable to that among whites and is generally correlated with support for Indian assimilation. White conservatives are more likely to give racially intolerant responses, but there is no such association among Indians.

3423. Baldwin JD, Baldwin JI: The dynamics of interpersonal spacing in monkeys and man. Am J Orthopsychiatry 44:790–806.

Both man and other primates divide space into patterns that reflect personality and social factors. Operant and Pavlovian conditioning are key determinants of spacing activities.

3424. Barnicot NA: Penrose's work and views in relation to anthropology. Br J Psychiatry 125:553–558.

Penrose emphasized that the study of the abnormal is only meaningful against the background of variation in the general population. He shared an interest in the causes of variation with genetically oriented anthropologists.

3425. Bash KW, Bash-Liechti JB: Studies on the epidemiology of neuropsychiatric disorders among the population of the city of Shiraz, Iran. Soc Psychiatry 9:163–171.

There is no significant difference in psychiatric morbidity between the city of Shiraz and a representative rural area. Total psychiatric morbidity is significantly greater among the poor.

3426. Beiser M, Burr WA, Collomb H, Ravel JL: Pobough Lang in Senegal. Soc Psychiatry 9:123–129.

Pobough Lang is a West African folk illness characterized by compulsive geophagia, pallor, weakness, edema, depression, anxiety, and social isolation. Some features of the illness are probably related to iron lack and other nutritional deficiencies. Other features are related to the ambiguous cultural definition of, and negative response to, the manifest behavior. The determinants of the cultural response are unclear.

3427. Benyoussef A, Cutler JL, Levine A, Mansourian P, Phan-Tan T, Baylet R, Collomb H, Diop S, Lacombe B, Ravel J, Vaugelade J, Diebold G: Health effects of rural-urban migration in developing countries—Senegal. Soc Sci Med 8:243–254.

Nonreligious and traditional practices remain importantly active among rural dwellers but are decreasingly significant among urban migrants in Dakar. While urban males trust both folk and modern therapy, urban females believe more in modern medicine.

3428. Beit-Hallahmi B, Paluszny M: Twinship in mythology and science: ambivalence, differentiation, and the magical bond. Compr Psychiatry 15: 345–353.

Fascination and ambivalence are common psychological elements in both mythological and scientific approaches to twinship. The Old Testament mythological tradition, which emphasized competition and individuation in twin pairs, and the Greek mythological tradition, which emphasized fusion and intimacy, are both reflected in modern approaches to the study of twinship.

3429. Bellak L, Antell M: An intercultural study of aggressive behavior on children's playgrounds. Am J Orthopsychiatry 44:503–511.

German adults are significantly more often aggressive toward German children, and German children toward other children, than are either the Italians or the Danes. Larger, more controlled studies are needed to confirm this observation, and great care needs to be taken in interpreting the significance of the observations.

3430. Berry JW, Annis RC: Acculturative stress: the role of ecology, culture and differentiation. J Cross-Cultural Psychol 5:382–406.

Greater discontinuity across Amerindian cultures is associated with greater acculturative stress, while at the individual level within communities psychological differentiation is negatively related to acculturative stress.

3431. Berry JW, Annis RC: Ecology, culture and psychological differentiation. Int J Psychol 9:173–193.

High field independence for hunting societies, and high differentiation in social and affective domains are evident for Cree, Carrier, and Tsimshian communities. The influence of socialization on differentiation and possible relationship between stratification and sex differences are suggested.

3432. Billig O, Burton-Bradley BG: Psychotic art in New Guinea: a cross-cultural study. J Nerv Ment Dis 159:40–62.

The regression evident in schizophrenic art points out the element of basic psychobiological factors in transcultural mental functioning. The influences of cultural socialization and enculturation on graphics become less important as regression to the primitive occurs and psychosis progresses.

3433. Bond MH, Shiraishi D: The effect of body lean and status of an interviewer on the non-verbal behavior of Japanese interviewees. Int J Psychol 9:117–128.

Females are more responsive to variables of body posture and status manipulation than are males.

3434. Bortner RW, Bohn CJ, Hultsch DF: A cross-cultural study of the effects of children on parental assessment of past, present and future. J Marriage Fam 36:370–378.

Differences by country, socioeconomic status, sex, and concern for children are obtained for three countries. The data suggest that males feel presence of children more necessary for their well-being than do females.

3435. Boyer LB, Boyer RM, Hippler AE: The Alaskan Athabaskan Potlatch ceremony. Int J Psychoanal Psychother 3:343–365.

Awareness of the social structure, the socialization aspects, and psychological dynamics of the potlatch ceremony may render psychotherapy among Athabaskans more effective.

3436. Brand ES, Ruiz RA, Padilla AM: Ethnic identification and preference. Psychol Bull 81:860–890.

The most consistent finding in ethnic research in the United States is preference by both white and black children for white experimental stimuli. It is moot whether these studies reflect minority preferences for white stimuli or mirror partial subject responses within biased designs.

3437. Brehmer B: A note on the cross-national differences in cognitive conflict found by Hammond et al. Int J Psychol 9: 51–56.

Subtle differences in experimental procedure account for observed differences in conflict reduction for Americans and Europeans by Hammond and his associates. Since there are no differences in cognitive capacity in this case, there are no differences in cognitive conflict.

3438. Brekke B, Williams JD: Conservation and reading achievement of second grade bilingual American Indian children. J Psychol 86:65–70.

Correlations between three measures of reading level and successful performance on conservation tasks are found for Zuni bilingual children.

3439. Brislin RW: The Ponzo Illusion: additional cues, age, orientation, and culture. J Cross-Cultural Psychol 5:139–161.

The ecological hypothesis that explains the Ponzo Illusion can be supported with data obtained from Guam and Pennsylvania.

3440. Brody EB: Psychocultural aspects of contraceptive behavior in Jamaica: individual fertility control in a developing country. J Nerv Ment Dis 159:108–119.

The family and household systems of Jamaica, exclusion from the cultural process of the dominant group, and a "culture of motherhood" contribute to psychocultural conflict for Jamaican women and resultant contraceptive behaviors.

3441. Bromberg W, Hutchison SH: Self-image of the American Indian: a preliminary study. Int J Soc Psychiatry 20:39–44.

Images in Indian drawings present a unity of social relatedness and a dependence on the body image to effectively communicate with others in the environment. Indians depend on an inner life as a guide for social reactions as witnessed by the high percentage of self-orientation in their drawings. There is less variation between individual Indian drawings than is found in a similar group of white drawings.

3442. Brown GA: A reply to Turner and Sevinc. Br J Soc Clin Psychol 13:217–218.

Suggestion for distinguishing the influence of sex from ethnicity on British-immigrant interactions is welcome; however, with respect to the question of observer bias, a positivistic stance on research involving person perception may be untenable.

3443. Bunton PL, Weissbach TA: Attitudes toward blackness of black preschool children attending community-controlled or public schools. J Soc Psychol 92:53–59.

Children exposed to problack education show greater identification with dolls of their own race than prior to exposure.

3444. Burke AW: Socio-cultural aspects of attempted suicide among women in Trinidad and Tobago. Br J Psychiatry 125:374–377.

East Indian females swallow domestic substances more often than Africans, though both groups give similar reasons for their actions. The attempted suicide rate is similar among all persons in each subcultural group, although East Indian attempters are older and Africans younger.

3445. Burton-Bradley BG: Social change and psychosomatic response in Papua, New Guinea. Psychother Psychosom 23:229–239.

Cultural forces produce symptom formation. The clinical spirit-possession syndrome is precipitated by the cosmic and sociopolitical views of the people. Delusional states are predominantly grandiose, the result of technological disparity between local and alien cultures.

3446. Butcher JN, Gur R: A Hebrew translation of the MMPI: an assessment of translation adequacy and preliminary validation. J Cross-Cultural Psychol 5:220–227.

The Hebrew translation of the MMPI performs in Israel as the MMPI does in the United States, as shown by group mean profiles for normal Israeli subjects.

3447. Carment DW: Indian and Canadian choice behavior in a maximizing difference game and in a game of chicken. Int J Psychol 9:213–221.

East Indians are less competitive in a risky chicken game, but their greater competitiveness in a maximizing game reflects the tendency to maximize gain. Differences in response conditions and strategy are also aspects of risk taking.

3448. Carment DW: Indian and Canadian choice behavior in a mixed motive game. Int J Psychol 9:303–316.

Females and East Indians are more competitive than males and Canadians in a maximization game. Knowledge of own score worked to reduce male competitiveness.

3449. Carment DW: Internal versus external control in India and Canada. Int J Psychol 9:45–50.

Specific components on an internal-external scale between two cultures may provide detailed data; whereas examination only of performance on the full scale may result in misleading conclusions.

3450. Carment DW: Risk-taking under conditions of chance and skill in Indians and Canadians. J Cross-Cultural Psychol 5:23–36.

Indians are more conservative in gambling situations and skill tasks than Canadians. Indian performance is similar to that of individuals showing low achievement, failure avoidance, and belief in external control of reinforcement.

3451. Carringer DC: Creative thinking abilities of Mexican youth: the relationship of bilingualism. J Cross-Cultural Psychol 5:492–504.

Some empirical evidence can be offered for the advantage conferred by bilingualism on creative abilities. Bilinguals have greater cognitive flexibility and can focus attention on idea, content, and meaning rather than words, form, and symbol.

3452. Chopra GS, Smith JW: Psychotic reactions following cannabis use in East Indians. Arch Gen Psychiatry 30:24–27.

Potency and dosage schedule of cannabis, and younger age, are related to the occurrence of a toxic psychosis. Delusions and hallucinations tend toward mythologic-religious themes among East Indians.

3453. Ciborowski T, Choy S: Nonstandard English and free recall: an exploratory study. J Cross-Cultural Psychol 5:271–281.

Hawaiian dialect speakers are bidialectal, showing verbal skills in standard English and Hawaiian Island dialects.

3454. Chang SC: Morita therapy. Am J Psychother 28:208–221.

Morita therapy may be discussed as a method of psychotherapy and as a formulation of a philosophy of life derived from the traditional culture of Japan.

3455. Chu SS: Some aspects of extended kinship in a Chinese community. J Marriage Fam 35:628–633.

Patterns of extended kinships persist in Taiwan despite modernization, and ideally follow a family type cycle from stem to nuclear to stem.

3456. Chun K, Campbell JB, Yoo JH: Extreme response style in cross-cultural research: a reminder. J Cross-Cultural Psychol 5:465–480.

The consequences of the extreme style phenomenon have been neglected in cross-cultural research and merit greater attention.

3457. Cohen SB, Sweet JA: The impact of marital disruption and remarriage on fertility. J Marriage Fam 36:87–96.

Given the complexity of the relationship between marital disruption and fertility, the fertility deficit, after controlling the factors of age, race, divorce, earlier marriage, and duration of marriage is about 0.1 children.

3458. Conklin GH: The extended family as an independent factor in social change: a case from India. J Marriage Fam 35:798–804.

Urbanization and education have not led to an increase in the proportion of sons' separating property prior to father's death but has permitted, contrary to the literature, an increase in the shared property among brothers in the joint family to meet economic developmental needs.

3459. Connor JW: Acculturation and changing need patterns in Japanese-American and Caucasian-American college students. J Soc Psychol 93: 293–294.

EPPS results on acculturation of Japanese-American students need patterns are subject to differing interpretations depending upon whether comparison is made with the 1952 normative group or with a contemporary Caucasian student group.

3460. Connor JW: Acculturation and family continuities in three generations of Japanese Americans. J Marriage Fam 36:159–168.

Though considerable acculturation has occurred, third-generation Japanese-Americans continue to place an emphasis on the ideal family and generate dependency needs, though less so than for the first and second generation.

3461. Conrad RD, Kahn MW: An epidemiological study of suicide and attempted suicide among the Papago Indians. Am J Psychiatry 131:69–72.

Papago suicide rates exceed the national rate but are not as high as that of other tribes. Young male alcoholics are the most common victims. Urban Papagos are at higher risk than their reservation counterparts.

3462. Danziger K: The acculturation of Italian immigrant girls in Canada. Int J Psychol 9:129–137.

Female socialization in the immigrant family follows conservative patterns with respect to decision-making and autonomy and may reflect an attempt to preserve traditional culture through the female role.

3463. David KH: Cross-cultural use of the Porteus Maze. J Soc Psychol 92:11–18.

Systematic future use of the maze in conjunction with environmental variables and performance measures is recommended, given past difficulties of equating cultural groups.

3464. Davison GR: Linguistic determinants of choice-reaction time among aborigines and white Australians. J Cross-Cultural Psychol 5:199–211.

Aboriginal adolescents record greater choice-reaction times on moiety division and color tasks. For the white Australian group, codability is slightly related to choice-reaction times.

3465. Dawson JLM, Young BM, Choi PPC: Developmental influences in pictorial depth perception among Hong Kong Chinese children. J Cross-Cultural Psychol 5:3–22.

Increase in three-dimensional pictorial perception among Hong Kong Chinese children occurs from ages 3 to 17 and is superior in males after age 8, possibly stemming from increased testosterone output interacting with environmental stimulus. The Chinese sample with harsher socialization shows lower scores than an Eskimo sample with more permissive socialization.

3466. Deregowski JB: Effects of symmetry upon reproduction of Kohs-type figures: an African study. Br J Psychol 65:93–102.

Zambizi subjects tend to build symmetric responses to both asymmetric and symmetric stimuli, but this tendency changes when the stimuli are altered so that their nature remains constant.

3467. Deregowski JB, Ellis HD: A cross-cultural study of recognition memory for faces. Int J Psychol 9:205–211.

European and black Africans tend to better recognize members of their own ethnic group than other ethnic groups. Response biases may provide clues to stereotyping behavior.

3468. Deregowski JB, Munro E: An analysis of "polyphasic pictorial perception." J Cross-Cultural Psychol 5:329–343.

The tendency to use background cues and figure arrangement to interpret pictured sequence of events is more common among Rhodesian and Zambian subjects than Canadian subjects.

3469. Destounis N: Aggression: culture and psychosomatic medicine. Psychother Psychosom 24:123–125.

The current technological revolution decreases man's capacity for adaptation due to inevitable physical, social, economic, cultural, and psycholog-

ical stresses, and leads to anxiety, aggression, violence, and psychosomatic disorders.

3470. Devereux EC, Shouval R, Bronfenbrenner U, Rodgers RR: Socialization practices of parents, teachers, and peers in Israel: the kibbutz versus the city. Child Dev 45:269–281.

Kibbutz and city parents are seen by preadolescents as equally supportive, but the latter are more salient as disciplinarians. Neither the peer group nor the metaplet are perceived as supportive figures, but both are salient as agents of discipline and approval.

3471. Diamond MJ, Bond MH: The acceptance of "Barnum" personality interpretations by Japanese, Japanese-American, and Caucasian-American college students. J Cross-Cultural Psychol 5:228–235.

Personality cliches are accepted as true by three groups of students. The high acceptance of Barnum personality statements across cultures indicates that more elaborate procedures may not be necessary.

3472. Dien DS: Parental Machiavellianism and children's cheating in Japan. J Cross-Cultural Psychol 5:259–270.

The Machiavellian individual is generally a skillful manipulator. The first or only children of low Mach mothers of simple nuclear families tend to cheat more than those of high Mach mothers. First or only children of high Mach parents of simple nuclear families show the least amount of cheating.

3473. DiMarco N: Stress and adaptation in cross-cultural transition. Psychol Rep 35:279–285.

Selecting Peace Corps trainees on their language and job-performance skills, along with their capacity to accept feelings of aggression, would increase the likelihood that they would move toward adaptation and change.

3474. Dizmang LH, Watson J, May PA, Bopp JF: Adolescent suicide at an Indian reservation. Am J Orthopsychiatry 44:43–49.

Those committing suicide are frequently cared for by more than one individual in their developing years, experience many more losses by desertion or divorce than do controls, are arrested more times the year prior to their suicide, are arrested at a significantly earlier age, and are more frequently sent to boarding school. These factors indicate the greater individual and familial disruption experienced by the suicidal youths.

3475. Dlugokinski E, Kramer L: A system of neglect: Indian boarding schools. Am J Psychiatry 131:670–673.

Boarding-school experiences accentuate rather than resolve problems for Indian children. Suggestions for their improvement include greater involvement of the students and recognition of tribal differences.

3476. Douglas FM: Prescientific psychiatry in the urban setting. Am J Psychiatry 131:279–282.

Some patients from a ghetto culture area in Los Angeles believe in ghosts and spirits and rely on indigenous practitioners.

3477. Druckman C, Ali A, Bagur JS: Determinants of stereotypy in three cultures. Int J Psychol 9:293–302.

Agreement between India, Argentina, and the United States on evaluative traits for friendly nations is consistent with previous findings. Familiarity and friendliness have culture-specific salience for ethnocentrism.

3478. Edney JJ: Human territoriality. Psychol Bull 81:959–975.

Theoretical work on human territoriality includes a small number of classificatory systems and conceptualizations, but no comprehensive theory.

3479. Ehrenkranz J, Bliss E, Sheard MH: Plasma testosterone: correlation with aggressive behavior and social dominance in man. Psychosom Med 36:469–475.

Socially dominant males have significantly higher testosterone levels than nonaggressive ones. The presence of more anxiety in the socially dominant males may help to explain the fact that they show more acceptable control for their aggressive behavior, even though it may still be felt as abrasive by others.

3480. Engberg LE: Household differentiation and integration as predictors of child welfare in a Ghanaian community. J Marriage Fam 36:389–399.

Integration and differentiation rather than individual measures are both important family dimensions in the consideration of welfare status. The level of woman's differentiation is the only strong predictor of family size.

3481. Erwin J, Flett M: Responses of Rhesus monkeys to reunion after long-term separation: cross-sexed pairings. Psychol Rep 35:171–174.

Mere exposure is not a sufficient condition for the formation of enduring heterosexual relationships between rhesus monkeys. Adult female-female bonds contribute more to group cohesion than does adult heterosexual affection.

3482. Ewing JA, Rouse BA, Pellizzari ED: Alcohol sensitivity and ethnic background. Am J Psychiatry 131:206–210.

The low rate of alcohol abuse and alcoholism among Orientals may have physiological rather than cultural origins.

3483. Fabrega H: Problems implicit in the cultural and social study of depression. Psychosom Med 36:377–398.

The fluid nature of depression, in particular the fact that the components of the disease mean different things to members of various social groups, creates special analytical difficulties that must be taken into account in evaluating empirical results.

3484. Favazza AR: A critical review of studies of national character: a psychiatric-anthopological interface. J Oper Psychiatry 6:3–30.

National character is no longer a valid scientific complex.

3485. Favazza AR: Oedipus interruptus: a psychiatric-anthropological interface. J Oper Psychiatry 5:37–51.

Anthropologists may interpret the psychiatric concept of the Oedipus complex too narrowly. Cultural differences do not negate the concept of the Oedipus concept.

3486. Feather NT, Hutton MA: Value systems of students in Papua New Guinea and Australia. Int J Psychol 9:91–104.

Value differences between students of two nations may be attributed to the saliency of security needs, traditions, and emergent nationality in Papua, New Guinea, as a developing country, in contrast to the affluent society of Australia.

3487. First-Dilic R: The life cycle of the Yugoslav peasant farm family. J Marriage Fam 36:819–826.

The structure of the peasant family changes across the process of life cycle stages. The farm wife gradually loses her dominance in the household, while retaining autonomy without decisionmaking power for the barnyard. The older the family the more autocratic division of labor and less democratic power structure.

3488. Frias CA: A transcultural survey of psychiatric opinion on schizophrenia. Compr Psychiatry 15:225–231.

Argentinian university psychiatrists are more psychoanalytic than the more eclectic Americans, yet most clinicians see schizophrenia as an illness with poor outcome.

3489. Gallimore R: Affiliation motivation and Hawaiian-American achievement. J Cross-Cultural Psychol 5:481–491.

Cultural variations in the motivational antecedents of achievement are supported by data from Hawaiian-Americans.

3490. Gallimore RL, Weiss LB, Finney R: Cultural differences in delay of gratification: a problem of behavior classification. J Pers Soc Psychol 30: 72–80.

The consumption of resources by Hawaiian and Japanese-American students may be interpreted in terms of the relationship between cultural values and resource usage.

3491. Gardiner HW: Human figure drawings as indicators of value development among Thai children. J Cross-Cultural Psychol 5:124–130.

Cultural values tend to be reflected in children's drawings. Thai children indicate a general preference for modern dress and Oriental smiling faces, although some sex differences may be noted.

3492. Garza-Guerrero AC: Culture-shock: its mourning and the vicissitudes of identity. J Am Psychoanal Assoc 22:408–429.

Mourning for the massive loss of loved objects —the abandoned culture—and its concomitant threats to the individual's identity constitute the common denominator of culture shock.

3493. Gerson M: The family in the kibbutz. J Child Psychol Psychiatry 15:47–57.

The family is the cornerstone of the kibbutz. Parent-child relations in the kibbutz are positive and there is less emotional dependence than in the traditional family situation. This seems to be related to the absence of economic dependence and the greater diffusion of object relations at a tender age.

3494. Giel R, Kitaw Y, Workneh F, Mesfin R: Ticket to heaven: psychiatric illness in a religious community in Ethiopia. Soc Sci Med 8:549–556.

Religious communities in the churchyards of the Coptic churches of Ethiopia, while tolerant of mar-

ginal people, are not plagued by large numbers of psychotics. Life in the communities to some extent prevents the development of institutionalization, which is often a secondary handicap of psychotics.

3495. Gluck JP, Sackett GP: Frustration and self-aggression in social isolate Rhesus monkeys. J Abnorm Psychol 83:331–334.

In baseline living conditions, male isolate rhesus monkeys demonstrate higher levels of self-aggression than female isolates. Frustration leads to transitory intensification of self-aggression.

3496. Gonzalez AEJ, Davis WM: Sex differences and cognitive consistency: a Greek and North American contrast. J Cross-Cultural Psychol 5: 301–311.

The tendency to achieve cognitive consistency is mediated by culture and sex variables that affect attitude saliency.

3497. Gonzales-Tamayo E: Dogmatism, self-acceptance, and acceptance of others among Spanish and American students. J Soc Psychol 94:15–25.

Spanish Catholic high school students are higher in dogmatism and lower in acceptance of others than American Catholic students. Differences according to sex, class, and father's educational background are also indications of the role of society in attitude differences.

3498. Gough HG, Quintard G: A French application of the CPI Social Maturity Index. J Cross-Cultural Psychol 5:247–252.

The CPI social maturity index is validated for the French, and evidence may be presented that the index is meaningful for female samples.

3499. Greenfield PM: Comparing dimensional categorization in natural and artificial concepts: a developmental study among the Zinacantecos of Mexico. J Soc Psychol 93:157–171.

The ability to apply verbal concepts in sorting increases with age for Zinacantecos, regardless of formal education. Simple familiarity with the sorting material (flowers as opposed to rods) has no positive effect on sorting behavior that seems to be influenced by the cultural relevance of the dimension to be employed or ability to generate attributes applicable to the classificatory array.

3500. Han EYH: Responses of Chinese university students to the Thematic Apperception Test. J Soc Psychol 92:315–316.

Taiwan Chinese subjects display long response time, tell lengthy stories, identify ghosts and teacher-student relationships predominantly, and show great sexual misidentification.

3501. Hartog J: A transcultural view of sibling rank and mental disorder. Acta Psychiatr Scand 50:33–49.

The transcultural approach based on populations with various birthrate patterns refutes the suggestion that sibling-rank effects are merely birthrate artifacts and points to an epidemiological approach to the question.

3502. Henderson S: Care-eliciting behavior in man. J Nerv Ment Dis 159:172–181.

Examination of the phylogeny and ontogeny of care-elicitation behavior in man and pathological care-eliciting syndromes contribute to an understanding of this aspect of attachment phenomena and indicate certain relationships between seemingly diverse psychiatric disorders.

3503. Hill D: Non-verbal behavior in mental illness. Br J Psychiatry 124:230–231.

The pathology of nonverbal behavior is most evident in severe chronic mental illness. Biologically determined mechanisms take over and determine patterns of behavior.

3504. Hines GH: Achievement motivation levels of immigrants in New Zealand. J Cross-Cultural Psychol 5:37–48.

British, Australian, and American immigrant entrepreneurs and educators do not differ in need for achievement from their homeland counterparts.

3505. Honess T, Kline P: The use of the EPI and the JEPI with a student population in Uganda. Br J Soc Clin Psychol 13:96–98.

Since the EPI and JEPI measure a common factor, the tests are valid in Uganda. Patterns for sex and age are similar to those in Britain, although comparison with the British norm should be tentative.

3506. Ho YF, Lee LY: Authoritarianism and attitude toward filial piety in Chinese teachers. J Soc Psychol 92:305–306.

Filial piety is associated with greater authoritarianism as measured by the F scale and a scale developed for the study in Hong Kong.

3507. Hsu J, Tseng W: Family relations in classic Chinese opera. Int J Soc Psychiatry 20:159–172.

The analysis of family relations, as presented in Chinese cultural products, operas, and children's stories, enables us to understand more about the psychodynamics and psychopathology of the Chinese patients and to offer more effective treatment. Although the structure of the Chinese family has changed in some ways to meet the needs of modernization and urbanization, it still preserves its traditional pattern in terms of functioning as described in classic Chinese opera.

3508. Hutchinson IW: The functional significance of conjugal communication in a transitional society. J Marriage Fam 36:580–587.

The nature of conjugal communication among Filipino couples, with respect to different issues (obligations, parent-child problems), reflects degrees of traditional-contemporary family norms and expectations.

3509. Ikemi Y, Ago Y, Nakagawa S, Mori S, Takahashi N, Suematsu H, Sugita M: Psychosomatic mechanism under social changes in Japan. Psychother Psychosom 23:240–250.

Drastic changes in the sociocultural background have exerted a serious influence upon the health of the Japanese. The impact of Westernization has brought out characteristic and weak points in the Japanese character and has influenced the incidence and course of such diseases as bronchial asthma.

3510. (Deleted)

3511. Irwin MH, Schafer GN, Feiden CP: Emic and unfamiliar category sorting of Mano farmers and U.S. undergraduates. J Cross-Cultural Psychol 5:407–423.

Levels of sorting performance are related to the use of an emically appropriate familiar task. Mano Liberian farmers perform better on rice-sorting tasks, and U.S. students perform better on card-sorting tasks.

3512. Jahoda G, Deregowski J, Sinha D: Topological and Euclidean spatial features noted by children. Int J Psychol 9:159–172.

Cultural and subcultural differences in Euclidean and unrelated spatial responses in selecting an odd form from a choice of three are noted, although topological responses are constant. Unrelated responses may more directly reflect spatial ability than Euclidean responses.

3513. Jahoda G, McGurk H: Pictorial depth perception in Scottish and Ghanaian children: a critique of some findings with the Hudson test. Int J Psychol 9:255–267.

Methodological-procedural differences and test limitations render cross-cultural comparison of Hudson task results inappropriate. A new test of three-dimensional perception, when compared to Hudson's, reduces the performance differences between Ghanaian and Scottish children.

3514. Jilek WG, Todd N: Witchdoctors succeed where doctors fail: psychotherapy among Coast Salish Indians. Can Psychiatr Assoc J 19:351–356.

Many Indian patients are likely to benefit more from involvement in native therapeutic activities than from exclusive contact with Western resources. In the Fraser Valley, treatment is combined with indigenous procedures in close cooperation with native therapists.

3515. Jilek-Aall L: Psychosocial aspects of drinking among Coast Salish Indians. Can Psychiatr Assoc J 19:357–361.

In order to solve his "core complex" the Indian has to find a solution to his conflict with the white man. Alcohol has turned out to deepen rather than resolve this conflict. Any assistance rendered by non-Indian agencies must rely on Indian initiative and on active involvement of the local Indian population.

3516. Johnson FA, Marsella AJ, Johnson CL: Social and psychological aspects of verbal behavior in Japanese-Americans. Am J Psychiatry 131:580–583.

Gender and status differences, nonverbal communication, and the emphasis on self-effacing behavior, all important elements of Meiji-era Japan brought by migrants to Hawaii, may be significant in their current social context.

3517. Johnson LB, Proskauer S: Hysterical psychosis in a prepubescent Navajo girl. J Am Acad Child Psychiatry 13:1–16.

A case history exemplifies the complex interaction of intrapsychic, familial, and cultural factors determining psychiatric symptom formation and resolution among the Western Navaho. Developmental and psychodynamic knowledge, tempered with due respect for cultural differences, provides a practical basis for child psychiatric work across cultural boundaries.

3518. Jones J, Shea J: Conservatism measure in Papua New Guinea. J Cross-Cultural Psychol 5:172–183.

A high nonlinear relationship between high conservatism and high divergent thinking may be partly accounted for by degree of European contact, social change, and religious homogeneity.

3519. Kagan S: Field dependence and conformity of rural Mexican and urban Anglo-American children. Child Dev 45:765–771.

There is a greater generalized tendency toward passivity and compliance among rural Mexican than urban Anglo-American children. Such tendencies may be related to child-rearing practices.

3520. Kapur RL, Kapur M, Carstairs GM: Indian Psychiatric Interview Schedule (IPIS). Soc Psychiatry 9:61–69.

The IPIS is a structured instrument for investigating psychopathology in an Indian setting. Because of their frequency in the Indian setting, somatic symptoms, sexual symptoms, possession states, and delusions of supernatural persecution are specially dwelt upon.

3521. Kapur RL, Kapur M, Carstairs GM: Indian Psychiatric Survey Schedule (IPSS). Soc Psychiatry 9:71–76.

The IPSS is a variation of a structured interview procedure with a multistage design, not all the stages being necessary for each respondent. A large proportion of the inquiry can be reliably conducted by nonpsychiatrists after a short training program.

3522. Karno M, Edgerton RB: Some folk beliefs about mental illness: a reconsideration. Int J Soc Psychiatry 20:292–296.

The folk notions of the Mexican-American and, to a lesser extent, the less urban Anglo-American may represent canny, accumulated observations rather than "mythology" and prejudice.

3523. Katchadourian H: A comparative study of mental illness among the Christians and Moslems of Lebanon. Int J Soc Psychiatry 20:56–67.

Christians significantly outnumber Moslems in the overall patient population. Moslem males have high rates of mania and drug addiction while Christian males display more paranoia. There is a preponderance of anxiety reactions among Christians, and depression among Moslems.

3524. Keats DM, Keats JA: The effect of language on concept acquisition in bilingual children. J Cross-Cultural Psychol 5:80–99.

Delayed post tests of three groups (two bilingual

and one monolingual) trained in the acquisition of conservation of weight in one language show that a logical concept can be acquired in either language with some generalization to other concepts. Some support is given to Piagetian notions of the independence of thought and language mode.

3525. Kim CS: The Yon'jul-hon or chain-string form of marriage arrangement in Korea. J Marriage Fam 36:575–579.

Korean matchmakers function to preserve the prescribed marriage rules (kinship) by incorporating all new female married villagers into the system and to manipulate the system of class endogamy.

3526. Kinzie JC, Teoh JI, Tan ES: Community psychiatry in Malaysia. Am J Psychiatry 131:573–577.

One must understand the concepts and value systems of a culture before assessing its openness to mental health consultation.

3527. Kiritz A, Moos RH: Physiological effects of social environments. Psychosom Med 36:96–114.

Social environmental factors have pronounced effects on human physiological processes. Social stimuli associated with the relationship dimensions of support, cohesion, and affiliation generally have positive effects.

3528. Klauss R, Bass BM: Group influence on individual behavior across cultures. J Cross-Cultural Psychol 5:236–246.

West German and Swiss managers are high in conformist patterns, while British and Austrian managers are lowest. Japanese managers reveal a complex pattern with anticonformist tendencies.

3529. Kleinfeld JS: Effects of nonverbal warmth on the learning of Eskimo and white students. J Soc Psychol 92:3–9.

Although there is some possibility that Eskimo children may be more sensitive to expression of warmth than white children, differences are not numerous or consistent. Warmth in teaching style does seem to have relevance for learning by students.

3530. Kline P, Mohan J: Cultural differences in item endorsements in a personality test—Ai3Q—in India, Ghana, and Great Britain. J Soc Psychol 94:137–138.

Different cultural factors, in terms of attitudes, events, and general milieu, can produce different item endorsements. Special tests with appropriate and equivalent items must be developed for cross-cultural research.

3531. Kojak G: The American community in Bangkok, Thailand: a model of social disintegration. Am J Psychiatry 131:1229–1233.

A socially disintegrated American community in Bangkok, Thailand, has a high prevalence of psychopathology. Observations confirm the effect of social integration on a population's mental health.

3532. Koomen W: A note on the authoritarian German family. J Marriage Fam 36:634–636.

Prior to World War II, parental control of young men was equally authoritarian in Germany and the United States. The only significant difference between the two countries was with respect to Germany's greater authoritarian attitudes toward rural-born women.

3533. Korten FF: The influence of culture and sex on the perception of persons. Int J Psychol 9:31–44.

Cultures may apply different perceptual categories to peoples. Ethiopians stress opinions, beliefs, and interactions over ability and knowledge, which are categories most used by American males.

3534. Kugelmass S, Lieblich A, Bossik D: Patterns of intellectual ability in Jewish and Arab children in Israel. J Cross-Cultural Psychol 5:184–198.

In contrast to urban Jewish subsamples, the pattern profiles for two rural Arab Israeli samples are distinctly different on the WPPSI.

3535. Kuo ECY: The family and bilingual socialization: a sociolinguistic study of a sample of Chinese children in the United States. J Soc Psychol 92:181–191.

Parental attitudes and behaviors regarding the two languages influence the relative bilingual proficiency of the Chinese-American preschooler.

3536. Laffal J, Monahan J, Richman P: Communication of meaning in glossolalia. J Soc Psychol 92:277–291.

Audience response to speaking in tongues is generally consistent with respect to meaning but does not necessarily parallel the speaker's intended meaning. Personal and affective content is generally attributed to such speech.

3537. Lambo TA: Psychotherapy in Africa. Psychother Psychosom 24:311–326.

The cultures of Africa recognize the different layers of the human psyche and, consequently, the existence of conscious and unconscious forces that determine human behavior. Methods of African psychotherapy vary from individual to group, from magio-religious rites to well-formulated quasi-mathematical procedures, from the use of hypnosis, trances, and suggestion to mystic invocations to the spirits.

3538. LaPorta EM: Aggression, error and truth. Int J Psychoanal 55:379–381.

The dialectic between internal and external reality and man's innate tendency to discover the truth is reflected in Brazilian cults of African origin.

3539. Lebra TS: The interactional perspective of suffering and curing in a Japanese cult. Int J Soc Psychiatry 20:281–286.

Japanese culture puts a high premium on the ability to play an expected role in a given social system rather than to be an independent actor. Susceptibility to the wishes of others, coupled with the capacity for role substitution, comprises a major ingredient of Japanese culture. The Salvation Cult mobilizes and intensifies underlying cultural values for therapeutic purposes.

3540. Leff JP: Transcultural influences on psychiatrists' rating of verbally expressed emotion. Br J Psychiatry 125:336–340.

Psychiatrists from developed centers agree with psychiatrists from developing centers in their perception of the degree of emotional differentiation shown by patients from developed centers. However, their ratings of patients from developing centers indicate a significant disagreement. Psychiatrists' assessments of developing centers are more likely to be accurate.

3541. Lefley HP: Social and familial correlates of self-esteem among American Indian children. Child Dev 45:829–833.

Although socialization practices do not differ, both mothers and children of the more socially intact Miccousukee tribe have significantly higher self-esteem than the more acculturated Seminoles. The antecedents of self-esteem should be sought not only in parental treatment, or in subgroup status alone, but in the functional interrelationships of familial, social, and cultural variables.

3542. Levine SV, Eastwood MR, Rae-Grant Q: Psychiatric service to Northern Indians: a university project. Can Psychiatr Assoc J 19:343–349.

High poverty and unemployment levels, tremendous school dropout rate, high suicide rate, violent effects of alcohol abuse among the Northern Cree and Ojibway Indians—are all indices of social and psychological misery and are causally related to emotional problems.

3543. Levinson D: The etiology of skid rows in the United States. Int J Psychiatry 20:25–33.

The Bowery men are never totally separated from the larger society and retain strong emotional ties to it. The men are extremely ambivalent about their place in the world. However, they apparently feel they must stay on skid row because they are unable to tolerate the stresses of everyday life in the outside world and have become acculturated into the Bowery subculture.

3544. Lewis TH: An Indian healer's preventive medicine procedure. Hosp Community Psychiatry 25:94–95.

The catch-the-stone ceremony, similar to "yuwipi sings," is an approach to the health problems of the isolated rural dweller and the very poor as practiced by the Teton Dakota Indians. Reservation dwellers frequently consult native practitioners because they prefer them, or in addition to public health clinics or physicians in nearby cities.

3545. Li AKF: Parental attitudes, test anxiety, and achievement motivation: a Hong Kong study. J Soc Psychol 93:3–11.

Parental attitudes of Hong Kong Chinese for achievement-oriented girls are characterized by dominance and limited communication in contrast to attitudes for achievement-oriented boys.

3546. Lifshitz M: Achievement motivation and coping behavior of normal and problematic preadolescent kibbutz children. J Pers Assess 38:138–143.

Achievement-motive score is highly related to the child's peer-group hierarchical status rather than ability to deal with undefined or chance situations. Normal girls score higher than normal boys or problematic children.

3547. McClintock CG: Development of social motives in Anglo-American and Mexican-American children. J Pers Soc Psychol 29:348–354.

Comparison of choice behavior in a maximizing difference game shows that competitive choice becomes more dominant with each grade level and over trial blocks. Anglo children sampled are more competitive than Mexican-American children.

3548. McGinnies E, Nordholm LA, Ward C, Bhanthumnavin DL: Sex and cultural differences in perceived locus of control among students in five countries. J Consult Clin Psychol 42:451–455.

Swedish students are most external, followed in order by those from Japan, Australia, New Zealand, and the United States. Females have higher belief in external control than males. Swedes and Japanese differ most from each other and from other cultures.

3549. Malpass RS, Symonds JD: Value preferences associated with social class, sex, and race. J Cross-Cultural Psychol 5:282–300.

Class, rather than race or sex, best differentiates groups for the value composites of good life, pleasant working conditions, balance and adjustment, and artistic creativity. Blacks show higher preference than whites for the religiousness value composite.

3550. Marsella AJ, Murray MD, Golden C: Ethnic variations in the phenomenology of emotions: shame. J Cross-Cultural Psychol 5:312–328.

Results on a semantic differential of emotions, including shame, point out differences between ethnic groups in the connotative meaning of shame for Japanese-Americans, Chinese-Americans, and Caucasian-Americans. Cultural differences in meaning have implications for ethnopsychiatry, diagnosis, and therapy.

3551. Marsella AJ, Quijano WY: A comparison of vividness of mental imagery across different sensory modalities in Filipinos and Caucasian-Americans. J Cross-Cultural Psychol 5:451–464.

Filipinos have greater vividness of imagery than Americans and differ in the rank order of scores for different sensory modalities. The results may be seen in terms of the impact of socialization on personality and linguistic mediation of imagery.

3552. Matovu HL: Changing community attitudes towards epilepsy in Uganda. Soc Sci Med 8:47–50.

Community attitudes toward epilepsy in Uganda are amenable to both lecture-discussion and written materials methods of change. Even in areas where literacy rates might be relatively low, written materials can still be used with some success. However, some attitudes and beliefs cannot be influenced by either method.

3553. Mayo JA: The significance of sociocultural variables in the psychiatric treatment of black outpatients. Compr Psychiatry 15:471–482.

Traditional methods of outpatient treatment will not be effective with many ghetto blacks unless some perceptual change on the part of white middle-class therapists occurs. Recognition of differential perceptions according to race will avoid inappropriate labeling of these perceptions as illness, thereby freeing therapist and patient to communicate freely.

3554. McIntire WG, Nass GD, Dreyer AS: Parental role perceptions of Ghanian and American adolescents. J Marriage Fam 36:185–189.

The general pattern of parental perception counters Parsons and Bales's theory of the universality of the instrumental-expressive sex-role division of labor.

3555. McKinney WT: Primate social isolation. Arch Gen Psychiatry 31:422–426.

The mechanisms producing severe behavior disorders through social isolation in the early life of rhesus monkeys are not fully understood but may be likened for heuristic purposes to human psychopathological states, in terms of clarifying the interaction between rearing conditions, neurobiological consequences, and subsequent social behaviors.

3556. Melikian LH, Diab LN: Stability and change in group affiliations of university students in the Arab Middle East. J Soc Psychol 93:13–21.

Group affiliations of Arab university students have been more stable than changing from the early fifties to seventies, although political affiliations have become increasingly important.

3557. Meyer-Bahlburg HFL, Boon DA, Sharma M, Edwards JA: Aggressiveness and testosterone measures in man. Psychosom Med 36:269–274.

It appears unlikely that a significant portion of the variance of aggression, as measured by questionnaires, can be accounted for by postpubertal androgen production.

3558. Miller PM: A note on sex differences on the semantic differential. Br J Soc Clin Psychol 13:33–36.

Higher means for women may be due to greater need for social approval rather than greater impulsivity.

3559. Minde KK: Study problems in Ugandan secondary school students: a controlled evaluation. Br J Psychiatry 125:131–137.

Problem students vary from their control peers on a number of background variables. Systemic relaxation of muscle groups improves 70 percent of students with "brain-fag," a syndrome characteristically African.

3560. Moore NC: Psychiatric illness and living in flats. Br J Psychiatry 125:500–507.

Flat dwelling does not cause an increase in psychiatric illness. The incidence of psychiatric illness among flat dwellers is the same on different floor levels and in different types of blocks (whether high, low, with balcony or staircase access).

3561. Moran LJ, Huang I: Note on cognitive dictionary structure of Chinese children. Psychol Rep 34:154.

The cognitive structure of Chinese children, like that of their Japanese and North American peers, is organized around the central principle of "action upon referent."

3562. Murase T, Johnson F: Naikan, Morita, and Western psychotherapy. Arch Gen Psychiatry 31:121–128.

Naikan therapy is similar to, but differs from, Morita therapy in terms of duration, meditation pattern, and orientation of introspection. The therapies are superior to one another only in a culturally relative sense, but both clearly contrast with Western psychotherapy.

3563. Murphy HBM: Differences between mental disorders of French Canadians and British Canadians. Can Psychiatr Assoc J 19:247–257.

Canadians of British origin differ from Canadians of French origin with respect to the symptomatology, frequency, course, and probably the treatability of mental disorder. Attention to maintaining social ties is more important for the French-Canadian patient than for the British-Canadian, who conversely requires more attention to be paid to his intrapsychic ties.

3564. Nash H: Judgment of the humanness/animality of mythological hybrid (part-human, part-animal) figures. J Soc Psychol 92:91–102.

Subjects show considerable consistency in judgments along a human-animal continuum of ancient Egyptian, Near Eastern, and Greek mythological figures; these judgments are related to extent of specific features and feelings aroused by the representation.

3565. Okaha A, Bishry Z, Kamel M, Hassan AH: Psychosocial study of stammering in Egyptian children. Br J Psychiatry 124:531–533.

Aggression, irritability, and shyness are more common in stammerers. Both psychological and physical factors may precipitate stammering.

3566. Parkin M: Suicide and culture in Fairbanks: a comparison of three cultural groups in a small city of interior Alaska. Psychiatry 37:60–67.

Suicidal behaviors among nonnatives are exaggerated by the selective movement of emotionally disturbed persons into the area, and compounded by employment, economic, and climatic conditions. Native suicidal behaviors seem increased by prejudicial devaluation and stresses in cultural transition to which Eskimos are more vulnerable than their Indian counterparts.

3567. Pastner C McC: Accommodations to Purdah: the female perspective. J Marriage Fam 36:408–414.

By examining the integration of sexual roles into total cultural systems, a similarity between the tactics used by Pakistani women to influence male decisionmaking and Western female stereotyped devices can be defined as variations on a similar theme. This holistic view permits analysis and comparisons of behavioral accommodations.

3568. Peck EC: The relationship of disease and other stress to second language. Int J Soc Psychiatry 20:128–133.

Stress may have an effect on self-expression in a second language. Accurate clinical assessments of bilingual patients must consider age at second language acquisition, attitude toward second language, and stress.

3569. Peskin H, Giora Z, Kaffman M: Birth order in child-psychiatric referrals and kibbutz family structure. J Marriage Fam 36:615–627.

Findings that kibbutz male first borns and urban female first borns are more likely to be referred for psychiatric help suggest the presence of differential stress and status for the two sexes in these environments.

3570. Peszke MA, Wintrob RM: Emergency commitment: A transcultural study. Am J Psychiatry 131:36–40.

Peer review of commitments at the state or county level and a reasonably uniform code of commitment standards may help balance civil rights with better patient treatment. Psychiatrists in six continents are involved with emergency involuntary hospitalization.

3571. Podmore D, Chaney D: Educational experience as an influence on "modern" and "traditional" attitudes: some evidence from Hong Kong. J Soc Psychol 94:139–140.

Responses to attitude statements indicate that young people with secondary or higher education, or Anglo-Chinese education, would be more modern than those without higher education or Chinese education only.

3572. Podmore D, Chaney D: Family norms in a rapidly industrializing society: Hong Kong. J Marriage Fam 36:400–407.

Responses from young people indicate that Western conjugal family norms regarding spouses, parents, and children coexist with traditional norms applied to older generations.

3573. Powell GE, Tutton SJ, Stewart RA: The differential stereotyping of similar physiques. Br J Soc Clin Psychol 13:421–424.

Superficially similar physiques (of the same general somatotype) are clearly differentiated in terms of stereotype. Two different physiques may not be rated differently by subjects as long as some quality is shared. A socioexpectation model of behavior-physique is more plausible than Sheldon's genetic relationship.

3574. Prachuabmoh V, Knodel J, Alers JO: Preference for sons, desire for additional children, and family planning in Thailand. J Marriage Fam 36: 601–614.

Although there is some preference for sons, Thai families desire to have offspring of both sexes. The number of children present in the family is a greater determinant of family planning than is the sex of the offspring.

3575. Pradhan PV, Shah LP: Ecology and psychiatry in Bombay—India. Int J Soc Psychiatry 20:302–310.

In Bombay and other developing countries, the processes of social integration or cohesion, and disintegration or disruption, seem to be in balance. No explosion of mental health problems has taken place as expected. Rather than accepting the consequences of industrialization uncritically and passively it is necessary to find out and reinforce the values and social, cultural, and ecological forces that need to be preserved along with technological advances.

3576. Price-Williams DR, LeVine RA: Left-right orientation among Hausa children: a methodological note. J Cross-Cultural Psychol 5:356–363.

Hand identification and doll tests among Nigerian Hausa children may test a less developed form of reversibility that is present in children. Minor variations in orientation assessment techniques may produce results that are substantially different, reflecting the need for replication and further research.

3577. Price-Williams DR, Ramirez M III: Ethnic differences in delay of gratification. J Soc Psychol 93:23–30.

Black and Mexican-American fourth graders are more inclined to choose immediate reward than are Anglo children. Mistrust of the investigator is clearly a factor in black children.

3578. Ramirez M, Castaneda A, Herold PL: The relationship of acculturation to cognitive style among Mexican Americans. J Cross-Cultural Psychol 5:424–433.

Mexican-American subjects from a traditional community are more field dependent than subjects from a traditional Anglo-influenced community, who are more field independent. Children and mothers from a dualistic community are intermediate.

3579. Ramirez M, Price-Williams DR: Cognitive styles of children of three ethnic groups in the United States. J Cross-Cultural Psychol 5:212–219.

Black and Mexican-American children and females are significantly more field dependent than Anglo children, confirming the suggestion that emphasis on group identity is related to field dependence.

3580. Ramu GN: Urban kinship ties in South India: a case study. J Marriage Fam 36:619–627.

In the urban setting, interaction is primarily with a small kindred. Father is not viewed as one of one's "significant" kin. Kin ties are likely to be based more upon ego-oriented choice, as the matrilineal tendencies in the urban setting illustrate.

3581. Reite M, Kaufman IC, Pauley JD, Stynes AJ: Depression in infant monkeys: physiological correlates. Psychosom Med 36:363–367.

Depressive disorders in man have frequently been linked to disturbances in diencephalic function, and certain physiological parameters affected in depressed monkey infants are ultimately under diencephalic regulation. These regulatory mechanisms are influenced by the social stress of maternal separation.

3582. Reitz HJ, Groff GK: Economic development and belief in locus of control among factory workers in four countries. J Cross-Cultural Psychol 5:344–355.

A locus of control scale shows that workers from developed countries (United States, Japan) are more internal on leadership and success, while workers from Oriental countries (Japan, Thailand) are more external in respect than workers from the United States and Mexico.

3583. Rendon M: Transcultural aspects of Puerto Rican mental illness in New York. Int J Soc Psychiatry 20:18–24.

Transculturation problems may account for the high incidence of mental illness among Puerto Ricans in New York. Belief in "Espiritismo" may lead to hysterical dissociative episodes that, because of the diagnostician's failure to understand cultural phenomena, have been diagnosed as schizophrenia.

3584. Rice AS, Ruiz RA, Padilla AM: Person perception, self-identity, and ethnic group preference in Anglo, black, and Chicano preschool and third-grade children. J Cross-Cultural Psychol 5:100–108.

At the preschool level, only Anglo subjects express a preference for their own ethnic group, while at the third-grade level only the Chicano subjects show strong preference for own ethnic group.

3585. Rodreigues A, Comrey AL: Personality structure in Brazil and the United States. J Soc Psychol 92:19–26.

Major factors of personality, as indicated from Comrey Personality Scale data in Rio de Janeiro, do not appear to be specific to a given culture.

3586. Ruppenthal GC, Harlow MK, Eisele CD, Harlow HF, Suomi SJ: Development of peer interactions of monkeys reared in a nuclear family environment. Child Dev 45:670–682.

Rhesus monkeys reared for the first three years of their life in a nuclear-family environment rapidly develop sophisticated patterns of social behavior and maintain levels of interactive play longer than do feral-raised monkeys.

3587. Rutter M, Yule W, Berger M, Yule B, Morton J, Bagley C: Children of West Indian immi-

grants: rates of behavioral deviance and of psychiatric disorder. J Child Psychol Psychiatry 15:241–262.

West Indian children in London manifest more behavioral difficulties at school but they do not differ from other children in terms of disorder shown at home, nor do they differ in terms of emotional disturbance in any setting.

3588. Ryback D: Child rearing and child care among the Sino-Thai population of Bangkok. J Soc Psychol 92:307–308.

Thai students believe that extensive mother-infant contact, casual weaning and toilet training, and discouragement of aggressive expression are aspects of Thai child rearing.

3589. Sachs DA: The WISC and the Mescalero Apache. J Soc Psychol 92:303–304.

Some age and sex differences on WISC subtests may be compared to standardized norms.

3590. Sampath HM: Prevalence of psychiatric disorder in a Southern Baffin Island Eskimo settlement. Can Psychiatr Assoc J 19:363–367.

Most of the major mental disorders do exist in contemporary Eskimo settlements with a relatively high prevelance. Etiological implications would appear to revolve around changes in the social organization that are the result of the modernization process now taking place in the Arctic.

3591. Sandju HS, Allen DE: Family planning in rural India: personal and community factors. J Marriage Fam 36:805–813.

Individual and family education are conducive to birth control. Within the community as a whole, informational communication and peer emulation are conducive to family planning.

3592. Scherer SE: Proxemic behavior of primary school children as a function of their socioeconomic class and subculture. J Pers Soc Psychol 29:800–805.

Although middle-class children show greater interaction distance than lower-class children, there is a lack of subcultural differences between black and white children.

3593. Schwartzman J: The individual, incest, and exogamy. Psychiatry 37:171–180.

An intense mother-child dyad is necessary for healthy development. The incest taboo and exogamy are important safeguards to insure proper distance and separation between parent and child.

3594. Scott WA: Cognitive correlates of maladjustment among college students in three cultures. J Consult Clin Psychol 42:184–195.

Personal maladjustment among Anglo-American, New Zealand, and Japanese students is associated with a tendency to employ affectively neutral, ambivalent, and inconsistent terms to describe self, acquaintances, and family.

3595. Shafi M: Short term psychotherapy in adult school phobia: a transcultural perspective. Int J Psychoanal Psychother 3:166–177.

Some students, both American and alien, show symptoms similar to childhood school phobia.

3596. Shapiro AH, Berlyne GM, Finberg J: The influence of heat upon intellectual test performance and cardiac activity of three groups in the Negev desert. Int J Psychol 9:281–292.

Mental test performance is unaffected by heat, although heart-rate increase and heart-rate patterns are found to differ for the groups. Ethnic membership and test familiarity appear more basic to test scores.

3597. (Deleted)

3598. Sinha D, Shukla P: Deprivation and development of skill for pictorial depth perception. J Cross-Cultural Psychol 5:434–450.

Familial deprivation has a retarding effect on pictorial depth perception for Indian orphans of 5 to 6½ years, but not for 3 to 4 year olds. The homogeneity and absence of stimulation of orphanage environment also continues to this phenomenon.

3599. Stein HF: "All in the Family" as a mirror of contemporary culture. Fam Process 13:279–316.

The Bunker household is paradigmatic of American culture, and as such can be analyzed in order to delineate the dynamics of American culture.

3600. Stewart VM: A cross-cultural test of the "carpentered world" hypothesis using the Ames Distorted Room Illusion. Int J Psychol 9:79–89.

American and Zambian performance with the Ames Illusion suggests some relationship between environmental factors and illusion susceptibility. Greater susceptibility for females on this illusion is inconsistent with previous findings of lesser susceptibility on Muller-Lyer and Sander Parallelogram illusions.

3601. Stoker DH, Meadow A: Cultural differences in child guidance clinic patients. Int J Soc Psychiatry 20:186–202.

There are significant and consistent differences in psychopathology between Mexican-American and Anglo-American children, which can be related to culturally determined aspects of family structure, family interaction, role conflicts, and personality structure.

3602. Stromberg J, Peyman H, Dowd JE: Migration and health: adaptation experiences of Iranian migrants to the city of Teheran. Soc Sci Med 8:309–323.

The Moslem religious affiliation of most Iranians and institutions such as the passenger house and the teahouse function in Teheran to ease the adaptive process of migrants from rural areas to the large diverse city. These adaptive institutions favor males more than females in their adjustment to urban life.

3603. Sutcliffe CR: The effects of differential exposure to modernization on the value orientations of Palestinians. J Soc Psychol 93:173–180.

The extent of the effect of differential exposure to modernization upon preferences in value orientations varies according to the variable employed as a marker of exposure and the measure of value orientation.

3604. Sween J, Clignet R: Type of marriage and residential choices in an African city. J Marriage Fam 36:780–793.

Ethnic and occupational determinants of individual goals condition the direction of behavioral contrasts between urban monogamy and polygyny, but specific means to these ends affect contrasts in residential choices. Within the process of urbanization the range of marriage and residential choices becomes broader, thus the association between these choices becomes more indeterminant.

3605. Tatara M: Problem of separation and dependency: some personality characteristics met in psychotherapy in Japan and some technical considerations. J Am Acad Psychoanal 2:231–241.

Japanese cultural values favor interdependence and reliance on others. The psychotherapist in Japan needs to accept the interdependent need of the patient and therapist as a basic pattern of Japanese culture.

3606. Taylor DM, Jaggi V: Ethnocentrism and causal attribution in a South Indian context. J Cross-Cultural Psychol 5:162–171.

Hindu subjects attribute socially desirable behavior of the ingroup to internal causes and undesirable behavior to external causes. The converse is the case for behavior of a Muslim outgroup as evaluated by Hindus.

3607. Taylor LJ, deLacey PR: Three dimensions of intellectual functioning in Australian aboriginal and disadvantaged European children. J Cross-Cultural Psychol 5:49–58.

Significant differences are indicated by tests between aboriginal and Australian European children's performance on the Peabody Picture Vocabulary Test. No differences are found between samples on tests of operational and divergent thinking.

3608. Thomas DR: Social distance in Fiji. J Soc Psychol 93:181–185.

Culturally shaped sex-role differences may account for the greater social distance shown by Fiji-Indian mothers to ethnic outgroups than by Fijian mothers.

3609. Todd JL, Shapira AL: U.S. and British self-disclosure, anxiety, empathy, and attitudes to psychotherapy. J Cross-Cultural Psychol 5:364–369.

U.S. subjects are more self-disclosing and more favorable toward psychotherapy than British subjects.

3610. Tomeh AK: Alienation: a cross-cultural analysis. J Soc Psychol 94:187–200.

Societal development influences the greater alienation found in traditional Middle Eastern society, although there is some similarity within cultures. American students with professional backgrounds show higher normlessness than Middle Eastern counterparts.

3611. Torrey EF, Torrey BB, Burton-Bradley BG: The epidemiology of schizophrenia in Papua New Guinea. Am J Psychiatry 131:567–573.

The combination of bias, referral habits of doctors, community tolerance, disease, accessibility to medical care, and migration is not an adequate explanation for the sharply different patterns of prevalence of schizophrenia in Papua. Concomitants to Western civilization, such as viruses, may be etiologic agents.

3612. Triandis HC, Weldon DE, Feldman JM: Level of abstraction of disagreements as a determinant of interpersonal perception. J Cross-Cultural Psychol 5:59–79.

Results of two experiments suggest that the higher the level of abstraction of a dyadic disagreement, the greater the damage of the disagreement to interpersonal perceptions.

3613. Turner C, Sevinc M: Interaction amongst British and immigrant children: a methodological note. Br J Soc Clin Psychol 13:215–216.

Incomplete evaluation of sex and observer bias as factors in British-immigrant interaction interpretations diminish the validity of Brown's conclusions.

3614. vanKeep PA, Kellerhals JM: The impact of socio-cultural factors on symptom formation: some results of a study on aging women in Switzerland. Psychother Psychosom 23:251–263.

Biology and culture partially overlap. The impact of aging and of the menopause, as measured by climacteric complaints and subjective adaptation to daily life, is more severe in women of the lower social classes.

3615. Waxler NE: Culture and mental illness: a social labeling perspective. J Nerv Ment Dis 159:379–395.

Observed differences in types, rates, and outcomes of mental disorders in Ceylon, Mauritius, and Western cultures may be due more to the impact of societal response (social labeling) and belief systems rather than to social causes or degrees of tolerance per se. Western belief in personal causation, rather than supernatural causation, of mental illness may lead to longer duration of illnesses.

3616. Von Eckardt UM: Cultural factors in heroin addiction in Puerto Rico. J Am Acad Psychoanal 2:129–137.

Puerto Rican heroin abuse is the result of an attempt to find a coping instrument by individuals trapped in a radical social transformation. Drug abuse, in fact, may not represent a psychiatric problem at all.

3617. Wagner DA: The development of short-term and incidental memory: a cross-cultural study. Child Dev 45:389–396.

Memory performance of urban-educated Yucatan children is similar to that of American middle-class children. Development of selective attention is independent of short-term memory development and is probably influenced by both school and certain cultural factors.

3618. Weakland JH: The "double-bind theory" by self-reflexive hindsight. Fam Process 13:269–278.

The double-bind theory should be viewed as a communication on communication, as observational, and as suggestive of future research, both practical and theoretical.

3619. Weiner S, Weaver L: Begging and social deviance on skid row. Q J Stud Alcohol 35:1307–1315.

Panhandling alcoholics' behavior is clearly more deviant than that of nonpanhandling alcoholics.

3620. Weller L, Natan O, Hazi O: Birth order and marital bliss in Israel. J Marriage Fam 36:794–797.

Marital adjustment is rated as high for a combination of first-born and later-born, or middle-born spouses; and characterized as low when both-spouses are only children or both-spouses are first-born.

3621. Wen C: Secular suicidal trend in postwar Japan and Taiwan. Int J Soc Psychiatry 20:8–17.

The spectacular suicidal rates manifested in Japanese and Taiwanese in the last two decades cannot be explained easily or solely on a single factor or hypothesis.

3622. Westermeyer J: Opium smoking in Laos: a survey of 40 addicts. Am J Psychiatry 131:165–170.

The histories, social milieu and competence, and demographic characteristics of 40 Laotian addicts and their families suggest that Laotian addiction may be an endemic rather than an epidemic phenomenon as in the United States.

3623. Westermeyer J, Hausman W: Cross-cultural consultation for mental health planning. Int J Soc Psychiatry 20:34–38.

In cross-cultural consulting for mental health planning, the consultant must know the target population well. He should be trained in behavioral sciences, social psychiatry, have had experience in supervision in consultation and have had prior cross-cultural experience.

3624. Williams TN: Childrearing practices of young mothers: what we know, how it matters, why it's so little. Am J Orthopsychiatry 44:70–75.

Children of single women who keep and rear their children often experience multiple caregivers. Because of the young age of many of these mothers they seem to share certain characteristics and attitudes that are reflected in their treatment and interaction with their children.

3625. Willie CV: The black family and social class. Am J Orthopsychiatry 44:50–60.

Blacks cannot be stereotyped as a homogeneous population. Middle-class blacks tend to be affluent conformists, working-class blacks respectable marginals who achieve upward mobility by their wits, and lower-class blacks exhibit a lack of commitment arising out of fears of trusting in an untrustworthy society.

3626. Wilson GD, Lee HS: Social attitude patterns in Korea. J Soc Psychol 94:27–30.

A general factor of conservatism and the results confirm the universality of social attitude patterns in association with demographic variables.

3627. Wintrob RM, Diamen S: The impact of culture change on Mistassini Cree youth. Can Psychiatr Assoc J 19:331–342.

The effects of cultural change on the sense of alienation and of commitment among Mistassini Cree youth are clearly evident. Identity conflict remains a dominant characteristic of Mistassini students, but the sense of inadequacy in the face of an alien and dominant culture has significantly decreased.

3628. Wittkower ED, Warnes H: Cultural aspects of psychotherapy. Am J Psychother 28:566–573.

Cross-cultural preferences in forms of psychotherapy depend on differences in etiologic views and on cultural and ideologic differences. Psychoanalysis has gained ground in the United States because of cultural emphasis on individualism, work therapy in the Soviet Union because of Marxist ideology, and autogenic training in Germany and Morita therapy in Japan because of culturally imposed rigid self-discipline in these two countries.

3629. Wittkower ED, Warnes H: Transcultural psychosomatics. Psychother Psychosom 23:1–12.

Race, life expectancy, diet, gastrointestinal and worm infection, as well as psychosocial stress and basic personality may account for the differences and inconsistencies in cross-cultural comparisons of the rates of psychosomatic disorders.

3630. Worchel S: Societal restrictiveness and the presence of outlets for the release of aggression. J Cross-Cultural Psychol 5:109–123.

Restrictive societies, those having unilineal kin groups and without sorcery, are more likely to have common warfare and games of physical skill as sanctioned outlets for aggression than non restrictive societies.

3631. Yamamoto J, Iga M: Japanese enterprise and American middle-class values. Am J Psychiatry 131:577–579.

Japanese immigrants have adapted and progressed in American middle-class culture because business and social institutions transplanted from Japan have fostered a positive group identity, and because the work and educational values of the Japanese samauri and merchant groups are similar to those of middle-class Americans.

3632. Young BBC, Kinzie JD: Psychiatric consultation to a Filipino community in Hawaii. Am J Psychiatry 131:563–566.

Leadership, community planning organizations, and a sense of community identity prevented the social disintegration of a predominantly Filipino village in Hawaii that underwent severe economic and social changes.

3633. Youniss J: Operational development in deaf Costa Rican subjects. Child Dev 45:212–216.

Costa Rican deaf people appear to advance normally in operational development. Coupling milieu and language differences has no substantial impact on manifestation of several Piagetian operations.

3634. Youniss J, Dean A: Judgment and imaging aspects of operations: a Piagetian study with Korean and Costa Rican children. Child Dev 45:1020–1031.

There are no milieu differences in judgment tasks of operations, but there are milieu differences in imaging problems.

Author Index

Subject Index